Entrepreneurship

Third Edition

William D. Bygrave
Babson College

Andrew Zacharakis
Babson College

WILEY

To Frederic C. Hamilton and John H. Muller, Jr., pioneers, entrepreneurs, and benefactors of Babson College.

Vice President & Executive Publisher	George Hoffman
Executive Editor	Lisé Johnson
Project Editor	Brian Baker
Editorial Assistant	Jacqueline Hughes
Associate Director of Marketing	Amy Scholz
Marketing Manager	Kelly Simmons
Photo Editor	Kathleen Pepper/Lisa Gee
Associate Production Manager	Joyce Poh
Senior Production Editor	Yee Lyn Song
Cover Designer	Kenji Ngieng
Cover Photo Credit	Georgette Douwma/Getty Images

This book was set in 10.5/12pt Adobe Garamond by Laserwords Private Limited, Chennai, India and printed and bound by Courier Kendallville. The cover was printed by Courier Kendallville.

This book is printed on acid free paper.

Founded in 1807, John Wiley & Sons, Inc. has been a valued source of knowledge and understanding for more than 200 years, helping people around the world meet their needs and fulfill their aspirations. Our company is built on a foundation of principles that include responsibility to the communities we serve and where we live and work. In 2008, we launched a Corporate Citizenship Initiative, a global effort to address the environmental, social, economic, and ethical challenges we face in our business. Among the issues we are addressing are carbon impact, paper specifications and procurement, ethical conduct within our business and among our vendors, and community and charitable support. For more information, please visit our Web site: www.wiley.com/go/citizenship.

Evaluation copies are provided to qualified academics and professionals for review purposes only, for use in their courses during the next academic year. These copies are licensed and may not be sold or transferred to a third party. Upon completion of the review period, please return the evaluation copy to Wiley. Return instructions and a free of charge return shipping label are available at www.wiley.com/go/returnlabel. Outside of the United States, please contact your local representative.

Library of Congress Cataloging-in-Publication Data

Bygrave, William D., 1937-
  Entrepreneurship / William Bygrave, Babson College, Andrew Zacharakis, Babson College. -- Third edition.
      pages cm
  Includes bibliographical references and index.
  ISBN 978-1-118-58289-3 (pbk.)
  1. New business enterprises. 2. Entrepreneurship. 3. Small business--Management. I. Zacharakis, Andrew. II. Title.
    HD62.5.B938 2014
    658.4'21–dc23
              2013033076

Printed in the United States of America
10 9 8 7 6 5 4 3 2

CONTENTS

vi | **Contents**

PREFACE

The green shoots of entrepreneurship give an economy its vitality. They give rise to new products and services, fresh applications for existing products and services, and new ways of doing business. Entrepreneurship stirs up the existing economic order and prunes out the dead wood. Established companies that fail to adapt to the changes cease to be competitive in the marketplace and go out of business.

Within the broadest definition, entrepreneurs are found throughout the world of business because any firm, big or small, must have its share of entrepreneurial drive if it is to survive and prosper. This textbook focuses on starting and growing independent new ventures. It is based on entrepreneurship courses taught at Babson College and at universities around the world.

One of the most common questions that entrepreneurship educators are asked is, Can entrepreneurship be taught? Our response is that anyone with a desire to become an entrepreneur will be more successful if he or she has taken a course on how to start and grow a new venture. About 30% of the students who have taken the new-venture course at Babson College since 1985 have gone on to start full-time businesses at some time in their careers. Many have started more than one.

While this textbook empowers would-be entrepreneurs to start and grow their new ventures, it's not only for them. Any student who reads this book will learn about the entrepreneurial process and the role of entrepreneurship in the economy. We believe that all business students, regardless of whether they start a new business, will benefit from learning about entrepreneurship. After all, entrepreneurship and small business create most of the jobs in the U.S. economy and account for almost half the GDP. They are ubiquitous, and so integral to the economy that almost every student will work in one way or another with entrepreneurs and small businesses after graduation. This textbook will stand students in good stead—not only for starting their own firms, but also for dealing with startups as investors, bankers, accountants, lawyers, customers, vendors, employees, landlords, and in any other capacity.

An entrepreneurial revolution has transformed the economy since the mid-1970s. Central to that revolution is information technology, especially personal computers and the Internet. Information technology has profoundly changed the way companies do business, none more so than startup companies. Today's students were born after the personal computer came into common use, and they came of age in the era of the Web. We believe they need an entrepreneurship text in which information technology is completely integrated all the way through.

This book combines concepts and cases to present the latest theory about entrepreneurship and relate actual experiences. The concepts cover what would-be entrepreneurs need to know to start and grow their businesses, and the cases illustrate how real entrepreneurs have gone out and done it. They cover all stages of the entrepreneurial process, from searching for an opportunity to shaping it into a commercially attractive product or service, launching the new venture, building it into a viable business, and eventually harvesting it.

Chapter 1 discusses the role of entrepreneurship in the U.S. economy and looks at the entrepreneurial competitiveness of nations throughout the world. Chapter 2 is an overview of the factors critical for starting a new enterprise and building it into a successful business.

Chapters 3 through 8 look in detail at what budding entrepreneurs need to do before they open their doors for business. The section starts with searching for opportunities and evaluating them. It explains how to build a workable business model and covers marketing, strategy, team building, financial projections, and business planning. At the end of this section students know how to write a business plan and how much startup capital they need to start their ventures.

The next section, Chapter 9 through 11, deals with financing businesses. Chapter 9 reviews the sources of financing for starting and growing businesses, both in the United States and worldwide. Chapter 10 discusses the nuts and bolts of raising money, particularly equity, to start and grow a business. Chapter 11 examines debt and other sources of financing.

Entrepreneurs need to understand the legal and tax issues associated with organizing a new business. They also need to know how to protect their intellectual capital. Chapters 12 explores these topics.

Anyone can start a new venture, but very few new businesses grow into substantial enterprises. Chapter 13 discusses what it takes to grow a business into a healthy company that provides financial rewards for the entrepreneur and good jobs for employees.

Finally, Chapter 14 looks at social entrepreneurship. Today, many students are looking at business ideas that may not only earn a profit, but also address a social concern.

Each chapter is accompanied by a case study of entrepreneurs in action. We chose the cases carefully, using these criteria:

- The entrepreneurs and their companies represent a spectrum of situations and industries that is as broad as we could make it.
- The judgment point in most cases occurs in the 21st century—some as recently as 2012 .
- All stages of the entrepreneurial process are covered, from pre-startup through harvest.
- Almost all the entrepreneurs in the cases are in their 20s and 30s; some are recent graduates.

There's no substitute for the experience gained from actually starting a business, but we believe that by completing the case studies in this book students will gain wisdom that would take years to pick up by trial and error as entrepreneurs starting and building businesses from scratch.

Each chapter ends with a unique Opportunity Journal. Here students can reflect on the lessons learned and think about how to apply them to their own entrepreneurial ventures or to managing their careers. Finally, a Web exercise builds upon key concepts covered in each chapter.

New to this Edition

The third edition has been thoroughly updated and enhanced throughout. Since the second edition, the United States and the world have seen increasing turmoil: the great recession; continuing wars in Iraq and Afghanistan; the Arab spring; a major oil spill in the Gulf of Mexico; earthquakes in Haiti and Chile; and an ongoing debate over climate change, just to name a few issues. To that end, we've noticed that more students than ever before are interested in not only creating great companies, but also addressing social issues. Thus, we've added a new Chapter 14 on Social Entrepreneurship, written by our colleagues Brad George and Candida Brush. Brad and Candy provide a typology of differing social entrepreneurial ventures, ranging from non-profits to for-profit businesses with a strong social mission. The chapter also provides metrics beyond the traditional financial measures to gauge the impact of the social venture.

We replaced several older cases. Vera Bradley steps through the process by which two women created an iconic brand, leveraging what they knew and were passionate about. Zumba looks at how three South American entrepreneurs created a new exercise craze. It explores the entrepreneurs as they try to determine the best business model for their venture. Eu Yang Sang looks at how a highly successful Singaporean company works to grow into new global markets; specifically China and the United States. The company has to consider how customers in these markets are different and also what kinds of channels might be appropriate to reach these customers. Zeo looks at how three college age founders build their team. They recruit and form a scientific advisory board; they seek and hire a CEO to help the company penetrate and build its market. Meta Carta details the capital raising process for a venture through good times and bad. It graphically illustrates the impact of dilution, especially during a down round. Tessera shows how a smaller entrepreneurial company can patent its technology, license it and protect its intellectual property from companies that would try to steal it. Finally, Year Up illustrates the creation of a social venture that works with underprivileged minority teens by providing them with mentors and internships. The company is trying to identify the best way to grow and reach more teens. With these changes, we are confident that the third edition of Entrepreneurship, not only continues our mission of empowering and enabling young entrepreneurs, but enhances it.

Teaching Supplements

Instructor's Manual

The Instructor's Manual has been designed to facilitate convenient lesson planning and includes the following:

- *Sample Syllabi.* Suggestions are given on dividing up the chapter material based on the frequency and duration of your class period.
- *General Chapter Outline.* The main headers provide a quick snapshot of all of the chapter content.
- *Case Teaching Notes.* Detailed teaching notes go into depth on the material covered in each chapter's accompanying case. They include discussion questions, classroom activities, and additional information on the businesses and entrepreneurs from the cases.

This comprehensive resource can be found on the Instructor Companion Site at www.wiley.com/college/bygrave

PowerPoint Slides

A robust set of PowerPoint slides gives you the ability to completely integrate your classroom lecture with a powerful visual statement of chapter material. The entire collection of roughly 150 slides is available for downloading from the Instructor and Student Companion Sites.

Test Bank

With 60 questions per chapter, the test bank consists of multiple choice, true/false, and short answer questions of varying difficulty. A computerized version of this test bank is also available on the Instructor Companion Site so that you can customize your quizzes and exams. Access these resources on the Instructor Companion Site.

Additional Cases

In addition to the 14 cases included in the book, additional cases, available on the book's companion site, give instructors more choices and give students more real-life examples. Cases available online include:

Adam Air
Andres Galindo
Ajay Bam
Alexander Norman and Toni Randolph-Norman
BladeLogic
ClearVue
College Coach
Matt Grant
Enox
CardSmith
Makers Mark
Vayusa (the *Ajay Bam* second case)
Beautiful Legs by Post
Living Patio Rooms
Malincho
Neverfail
Matt Coffin
Jon Hirschtick
SolidWorks (the *Jon Hirschtick* second case)
David Pearlman
StudentCity.Com
Nancy's Coffee
Earth Watch

Video Cases

Several videos accompany cases from the book, engaging students and giving them the opportunity to hear first-hand accounts from the entrepreneurs themselves. Available on the Instructor Companion Site, these videos are ideal lecture launchers and a great way to grab a class's attention. Ask your local Wiley representative for more information. Video cases include:

Alison Barnard
Jim Poss
College Coach
P'kolino
DayOne
Feed Resource Recovery

Acknowledgments

A comprehensive textbook on entrepreneurship covers a very wide range of disciplines that require specialized knowledge, so we invited leading experts to write some of the chapters.

◉ Entrepreneurial marketing is an emerging academic discipline; two of its leading experts are Abdul Ali at Babson College and Kathleen Seiders at Boston College, who wrote Chapter 6, "Entrepreneurial Marketing."

- Joel Shulman, Babson College, who specializes in entrepreneurial finance, contributed Chapter 11, "Debt and Other Forms of Financing."
- Legal, tax issues and Intellectual Property go hand in hand when setting up a new business; Richard Mandel, who is a Babson professor and a partner with the law firm Bowditch and Dewey that specializes in small business, wrote Chapter 12 along with Joseph Iandorio and Kirk Teska, who are patent attorneys in the firm that bears their names.
- Babson professors Donna Kelley and Edward Marram wrote Chapter 13, "Entrepreneurial Growth." Kelley is an expert on innovation, and Marram specializes in growing businesses.
- Professors Brad George and Candida Brush of Babson College wrote Chapter 14.

We thank all the contributing authors for their commitment and dedication to making this book as valuable as it can be for students.

We are forever indebted to everyone involved in the entrepreneurial process who has shared experience and wisdom with us. They include entrepreneurs from novices to old hands, informal investors, business angels, venture capitalists, bankers, lawyers, and landlords—indeed, anyone involved with entrepreneurs. We have learned so much from them. We're especially thankful for all the students and alumni we have worked with over the years. Their feedback has helped us shape what we teach and how we teach it.

We believe that entrepreneurs who successfully build businesses are inherently good coaches and teachers; they have to be if they are to develop and encourage employees. This generosity is borne out by their willingness to share their know-how with budding entrepreneurs. One important way in which entrepreneurs have done that is by allowing us to write cases about them and their companies, and then by coming to class when the cases are discussed. We make a video of each entrepreneur in a question-and-answer session with students immediately after the case is taught for the first time. Those videos, which are an integral part of the case study, are available to instructors using this textbook.

A huge "thank you" to the principals featured in the case studies in this book. They are Alberto Aghion, Alison Barnard, Barbara Baekgaard, Doug Brenhouse, Gerald Chertavian Tom DiStefano, Jason Donahue, Shane Eten, Richard Eu, Dan Hermann, Igor Khandros, Reg Mathelier, Patricia Miller, Joel Pedlikin, Alberto "Beto" Perez, Alberto Perlman, Jim Poss, Ben Rubin, J.B. Schneider, Eric Shashoua, Antonio Turco-Rivas, and Andrew Zenoff.

We thank all the case writers who researched and wrote the cases in this book and on its companion Web site. We'd also like to thank our student research assistants, who helped track down relevant examples in the popular press, acted as our first-draft readers, and worked hard on the instructional support materials. They are current and former Babson MBA students Alexey Amerikov, Rich Enos, Don Gourley, Sara Gragnolati, Mark Itkovitz, Mahmoud Mattan, Henry McGovern, Richard Raeke, Ge Song, and Brian Zinn.

It is a pleasure to be members of the Arthur M. Blank Center for Entrepreneurship at Babson College. Our Babson colleagues are an inspiration. They are pioneers of entrepreneurship education who are continually coming up with new ways of teaching. The Babson faculty comprises a marvelous mix of academics and what we call "pracademics"—practicing academics—who are entrepreneurs, venture capitalists, angel investors, lawyers, and others associated day-to-day with starting and running businesses. Candida Brush, chairperson of the entrepreneurship department and director of the Babson Arthur M. Blank Center for Entrepreneurship, has been highly supportive. We have benefited from discussions with Brian Abraham, Rob Adler, Abdul Ali, Matt Allen, Fred Alper, Lakshmi Balachandra, Craig Benson, Jean-Luc Boulnois, Dennis Ceru, Les Charm, Alan Cohen, Andrew Corbett, Caroline Daniels, Mary Gale, Brad George, Len Green, Patricia Greene, Mike Gordon, Howard Gross, Tim Habbershon, John Halal, Neal Harris, Bill Johnston, Donna Kelley, Julian Lange, Nan Langowitz, Bill LaPoint, Ray Marcinowski, Tim Marken, Ed Marram, Maria Minniti, Christopher Mirabile, Diane Mulcahy, Kevin Mulcahy, Kevin Mulvaney, Heidi Neck, Eric

Noyes, Ernie Parizeau, Elizabeth Riley, Angelo Santinelli, Joel Shulman, and Yasu Yamakawa, all of whom teach at Babson College. We'd also like to acknowledge three of our biggest supporters and mentors who passed away since the earlier editions were published, Glenn Kaplus, Jeffry Timmons, and Natalie Taylor. Their long-time influence and contributions to Babson College was invaluable. We miss them.

The Babson administration and staff have supported our efforts: The past president and provost, Leonard Schlesinger and Shahid Ansari, and current president and provost, Kerry Healey and Dennis Hanno motivated us with their enthusiasm for entrepreneurship education. Michael Fetters, formerly provost, encouraged us to write this book and gave us permission to include the cases in the book. Fritz Fleischmann, former dean of faculty, eased our labor by supporting sabbatical leaves for both of us. William Lawler, former associate dean of the graduate school, provided financial support for the writing of some of the cases; David Wylie edited some of them; and Valerie Duffy made sure that the case collection was up to date.

We are thankful for the financial support we received from the benefactors of the Frederic C. Hamilton Chair for Free Enterprise and the John H. Muller, Jr. Chair for Entrepreneurship.

We greatly appreciate all the help that we received from the staff at Wiley and its affiliates. Lisé Johnson, Executive Editor, and Brian Baker, Project Editor, were a continual source of inspiration and encouragement. Kathleen Pepper and Lisa Gee organized the selection of pictures. Kathy Whittier of Walsh & Associates, Inc. did a fine job of line editing our manuscript.

Many reviewers offered thoughtful suggestions that have improved this book. We are indebted to every one of them:

Richard Benedetto, *Merrimack College*
Lowell Busenitz, *University of Oklahoma*
Pat H. Dickson, *Georgia Institute of Technology*
Hung-bin Ding, *Loyola University*
William Gartner, *Clemson University*
Todd A. Finkle, *University of Akron*
Vance H. Fried, *Oklahoma State University*
Jeffrey June, *Miami University of Ohio*
Mark Lieberman, *USC Marshall School of Business*
Heidi Neck, *Babson College*
William R. Sandberg, *University of South Carolina*
P.K. Shukla, *Chapman University*

Finally, we are both indebted to our families, our patient and supportive wives, and our beautiful and talented children. Thank you for being so understanding when we were pushing hard to meet our deadlines.

Andy Freeberg/Getty Images

Tony Avelar/AFP/Getty Images

Bill Gates and Steve Jobs: Entrepreneurial leaders who drove the information technology revolution that transformed the way in which we live, work, and play.

THE POWER OF ENTREPRENEURSHIP

This is the entrepreneurial age. More than 500 million persons worldwide either were actively involved in trying to start a new venture or were owner-managers of a new business in 2012.[1]

More than 1,500 new businesses are born every hour of every working day in the United States. Entrepreneurs are driving a revolution that is transforming and renewing economies worldwide. Entrepreneurship is the essence of free enterprise because the birth of new businesses gives a market economy its vitality. New and emerging businesses create a very large proportion of the innovative products and services that transform the way we work and live, such as personal computers (PCs), computer software, the Internet and the World Wide Web (WWW or Web), social media, biotechnology drugs, overnight package deliveries, and big-box stores. They generate most new jobs; from 1993 through 2011, companies with 500 or fewer employees created 64% of all new jobs in the United States; that number increased slightly to 67% from mid-2009 through 2011 in the aftermath of the worst recession since the Great Depression of the 1930s.[2]

There has never been a better time to practice the art and science of entrepreneurship. But what is entrepreneurship? Early in the 20th century, Joseph Schumpeter, the Moravian-born economist writing in Vienna, gave us the modern definition of an entrepreneur: a person who destroys the existing economic order by introducing new products and services, by introducing new methods of production, by creating new forms of organization, or by exploiting new raw materials. According to Schumpeter, that person is most likely to accomplish this destruction by founding a new business but may also do it within an existing one.

Schumpeter explained how entrepreneurs had suddenly increased the standard of living of a few industrialized nations.[3] When the Industrial Revolution began in England around 1760, no nation had enjoyed a standard of living equal to that of Imperial Rome 2,000 years earlier. But from 1870 to 1979, for example, the standard of living of 16 nations jumped sevenfold on average.[4]

This chapter is written by William D. Bygrave.

Very few new businesses have the potential to initiate a Schumpeterian "gale" of creative destruction, as Apple Computer did in the computer industry. The vast majority enter existing markets. So, in this textbook, we adopt a broader definition of entrepreneurship than Schumpeter's. Ours encompasses everyone who starts a new business. Our entrepreneur is the person who perceives an opportunity and creates an organization to pursue it. And the entrepreneurial process includes all the functions, activities, and actions associated with perceiving opportunities and creating organizations to pursue them. Our entrepreneur's new business may, in a few rare instances, be the revolutionary sort that rearranges the global economic order, as Walmart, FedEx, Apple, Microsoft, Google, eBay, and Amazon.com have done and social networking companies such as Facebook and Twitter are now doing. But it is much more likely to be of the incremental kind that enters an existing market.

The Changing Economy

General Motors was founded in 1908 as a holding company for Buick. On December 31, 1955, General Motors became the first American corporation to make over $1 billion dollars in a year. At one point, it was the largest corporation in the United States in terms of its revenues as a percentage of gross domestic product (GDP). In 1979, its employment in the United States peaked at 600,000. In 2008, General Motors reported a loss of $30.9 billion and burned through $19.2 billion in cash. In a desperate attempt to save the company in February 2009, GM announced plans to reduce its total U.S. workforce from 96,537 people in 2008 to between 65,000 and 75,000 in 2012. By March 2009, GM, which had already received $13.4 billion of bailout money from the U.S. government, was asking for an additional $16.6 billion. The Obama administration forced GM's

CEO, Rick Wagoner, to resign; his replacement, Fritz Henderson, said that bankruptcy was a real possibility. It became a reality when GM filed for bankruptcy in June and emerged a shrunken company 40 days later. In 2012, its US workforce was 77,000.

Walmart was founded by Sam Walton in 1962. For the fiscal year ending on January 31, 2012, Walmart had record sales of $443.9 billion, record earnings of $15.8 billion, and free cash flow of $10.7 billion. Walmart is the world's largest corporation, with 2.2 million associates and 10,130 stores in 2012.

"We're all working together; that's the secret. And we'll lower the cost of living for everyone, not just in America, but we'll give the world an opportunity to see what it's like to save and have a better lifestyle, a better life for all. We're proud of what we've accomplished; we've just begun."

—Sam Walton (1918–1992)

In this chapter, we will look at the importance of entrepreneurship and small business to the United States and the global economies, describe the entrepreneurial revolution, present a conceptual model for the entrepreneurial sector of the economy, and use it to explain major factors in the revolution; finally, we will compare and contrast entrepreneurial activity among nations within the context of the conceptual model.

Entrepreneurship and Small Business in the United States

In 2010, there were 28 million or so U.S businesses, of which approximately 99.9% were small businesses.[5] In general, businesses with 500 or fewer employees are classified as small.[6] They account for half the private-sector workers and 42.9% of the private payroll, and they generate approximately half the non-farm private GDP. If the small-business sector of the

U.S. economy were a nation, its GDP would rank third in the world behind that of the U.S. medium- and big-business sector and the entire economy of China, ahead of Japan, and far ahead of Germany, the United Kingdom, France, and Italy.[7]

Not only are small businesses the engine for job creation, but also they are a powerful force for innovation. They hire 43% of all high-tech workers and produce approximately 16 times more patents per employee than large firms; those patents are twice as likely as large firm patents to be among the 1% most cited.[8] Their share of U.S. research and development (R&D) grew from 5.9% in 1984 to an estimated 20.7% in 2003, with the dollar value growing from $4.4 billion in 1984 to an estimated $40.1 billion in 2003—a ninefold increase.[9]

Half of the 28 million small businesses are part-time undertakings and half are full-time. Approximately 5.8 million small businesses are employer companies with one or more employees in addition to the self-employed owner.[10] About two-thirds of the full-time businesses are unincorporated and one-third are incorporated. Self-employment is more prevalent among men than women, whites, and Asians; and in construction, services, and agriculture industries.[11]

At any one time, approximately 7 million *nascent entrepreneurs* in the United States are trying to create a new business; they have conceived an idea for a new venture and have taken at least one step toward implementing their idea. Many of them abandon their ventures during the gestation period and never actually open their businesses; nonetheless, each year at least 3 million new ventures are born, of which about 75% start from scratch. Most of the others are purchases of existing businesses.[12] Two in every three businesses are started in the owner's home. Most remain tiny because they are part-time businesses, but around 600,000 have at least one full-time employee.

Survival rates for new businesses were the focus of several different studies.[14] One of the most thorough was done at the U.S. Census Bureau by Alfred Nucci, who calculated the 10-year survival rates of business establishments.[15] He found that 81% survive for at least one year, 65% for two years, 40% for five years, and 25% for 10 years. The survival rate for independent startups was slightly lower. For example, the one-year rate was 79% instead of 81%. The chance of survival increased with age and size. Survival rates also varied somewhat with industry but not as strongly as with age and size.

Of course, survival does not necessarily spell success. In general, the median income of small business owners is almost the same as that of wage and salary earners. However, the income distribution is much broader for small business owners, which means that they are more likely to have significantly less income or significantly more income than wage and salaried workers.[16] But small business owners are also building equity in their companies as well as taking income from them, so it is possible that small business owners are better off overall than their wage-earning cohorts. However, a study of business owners disposing of their businesses through sale, closure, passing it on, and other methods found that comparatively few saw their standard of living changed by their business. Only 17% reported that their business had raised their standard of living, while 6% reported the opposite.[17]

Looking back at the new business formation index, we can see that it was stable through the 1950s and most of the 1960s; there was virtually no growth. By 1970, net new business formation was growing, and the growth continued through the 1970s and 1980s and into the 1990s.[18] No one noticed the change at the time. One of the first documented references to what was taking place was a December 1976 article in *The Economist* called "The Coming Entrepreneurial Revolution."[19] In this article, Norman Macrae argued that the era of big business was drawing

A survey by ACNielsen International Research in July 2005 found the following:[13]

- 58% of Americans say they've dreamed of starting a business and becoming their own boss.

- The most common reason for wanting to start a business is to increase one's personal income (66% of respondents), followed by increased independence (63%).

- The primary barriers to starting a business are insufficient financial resources (cited by 49% of respondents) and satisfaction with their current situation (29%).

to an end and that future increases in employment would come mainly from either smaller firms or small units of big firms. In 1978, David Birch published his book *Job Creation in America: How Our Smallest Companies Put the Most People to Work*.[20] The title says it all. It captures the important finding from Birch's comprehensive study of business establishments.

No issue gets the attention of politicians more than job creation. Birch's findings and the stream of research that ensued forever changed the attitude of policymakers toward small business.[21] Until then, most of their focus had been on big business. After all, in 1953 Charles Erwin Wilson, then GM president, is reported to have said during the hearings before the Senate Armed Services Committee, "What's good for General Motors is good for the country." At the time, GM was one of the largest employers in the world—only Soviet state industries employed more people.[22]

Entrepreneurial Revolution

On November 1, 1999, Chevron, Goodyear Tire & Rubber Company, Sears Roebuck, and Union Carbide were removed from the Dow Jones Industrial Average (DJIA) and replaced by Intel, Microsoft, Home Depot, and SBC Communications. Intel and Microsoft became the first two companies traded on the NASDAQ exchange to be listed in the DJIA.

This event symbolized what is now called the *entrepreneurship revolution* that transformed the U.S. economy in the last quarter of the 20th century. Intel and Microsoft are the two major entrepreneurial driving forces in the information technology revolution that has fundamentally changed the way in which we live, work, and play. SBC (formerly Southwestern Bell Corporation) was one of the original "Baby Bells" formed after the U.S. Department of Justice antitrust action resulted in the breakup of AT&T. It is an excellent example of how breaking up a monopoly leads to entrepreneurial opportunities. And Home Depot exemplifies the big-box stores that have transformed much of the retail industry.

Intel was founded in Silicon Valley by Gordon Moore and Robert Noyce and funded by Arthur Rock, the legendary venture capitalist. Gordon Moore, the inventor of Moore's Law,[23] and Robert Noyce, one of the two inventors of the integrated circuit,[24] had been at the birth of Silicon Valley with William Shockley, the co-inventor of the transistor, when Shockley Semiconductor Laboratory was founded in Mountain View in 1956. They left Shockley in 1957 to found Fairchild Semiconductor, which in 1961 introduced the first commercial integrated circuit. In 1968, they left Fairchild to start Intel.

Ted Hoff, employee number 12 at Intel, invented the microprocessor in 1968. In 1971, Intel launched the first commercial microprocessor, heralding a new era in integrated electronics. Then, in 1974, it launched the first general-purpose microprocessor, the Intel 8080, which was the brain of the first personal computer,[25] the Altair 8800—a $439 hobbyist's kit—announced by MITS (Micro Instrumentation and Telemetry Systems of Albuquerque) on the front cover of the January 1, 1975, edition of *Popular Electronics*.

> *"When I was 19, I caught sight of the future and based my career on what I saw. I turned out to have been right."*
>
> — Bill Gates

According to personal computer folklore, Paul Allen, then working at the minicomputer division of Honeywell in Massachusetts, hurried to his childhood friend and fellow computer enthusiast, Bill Gates, who was a Harvard sophomore, and waving *Popular Electronics* with a mock-up of the Altair 8800 on its front cover, exclaimed, "This is it! It's about to begin!" Within a month or so, Gates had a version of BASIC to run on the Altair. He and Allen joined together in an informal partnership called Micro-Soft and moved to Albuquerque.

Microsoft grew steadily by developing software for personal computers. By 1979, it had moved to Bellevue, Washington, near Seattle, where Gates and Allen had grown up. It then had revenue of more than $2 million and 28 employees. It got its big break in 1980–1981 when, building on the core of a product acquired from Seattle Computer Products, Microsoft introduced MS-DOS for IBM's first PC. Fourteen years later, when Microsoft released Windows 95 in 1995, it sold 4 million copies in four days. Its success helped to move the personal computer into 250 million homes, businesses, and schools worldwide. In the early 1990s, Microsoft committed itself to adding Internet capabilities to its products. When Microsoft joined the DJIA in 1999, there were more than 200 million Internet users, up from 3 million just five years earlier.

SBC came about in 1984 because of the breakup of AT&T. SBC's growth has come mainly through acquisitions, so we are not making the case that SBC itself is especially entrepreneurial. However, the breakup of AT&T did unleash a wave of entrepreneurship that produced the explosive growth of the telecommunications industry in the last 20 years. According to a recent survey, the top five innovations since 1980 are the Internet, cell phones, personal computers, fiber optics, and email.[26] No doubt about it, the phenomenal growth of wireless communications and the Internet would not have happened if AT&T had been allowed to keep its pre-1983 stranglehold on the telecom industry. (AT&T floundered after it was broken up. In 2004, it was dropped from the DJIA, and in 2005, it was acquired by SBC, which then adopted AT&T, Inc., as its corporate name; as a result, AT&T's legendary "T" ticker symbol on the New York Stock Exchange returned to the DJIA.)

Home Depot was founded in 1979 by Bernie Marcus and Arthur Blank. The chain of hardware and do-it-yourself (DIY) stores holds the record for the fastest time for a retailer to pass the $30 billion, $40 billion, $50 billion, $60 billion, and $70 billion annual revenue milestones. It is the second largest retailer in the United States, surpassed only by Walmart. And it almost set the record for the fastest time from starting up to joining the DJIA when it was only 20 years old. By comparison, Walmart was 35 years old when it displaced F. W. Woolworth in the DJIA. Along with Walmart, Home Depot has set the pace for the retail industry in the last two decades. Together, the two account for more than 2% percent of the nation's GDP and 1.7 million jobs.

Bernard Marcus and Arthur Blank, founders of Home Depot

At the turn of the 20th century, about 50% of U.S. workers were employed in agriculture and domestic service. Less than 100 years later, the number was about 4%. Much of this transformation came about because innovations, many of them introduced by entrepreneurs, made agriculture a shining example of increasing productivity, and labor-saving products such as the vacuum cleaner, gas and electric ranges, washing machines and clothes dryers, dishwashers, automobiles, lawnmowers, floor polishers, processed foods, microwave ovens, and services increased the productivity of household labor. The proportion of the workforce in manufacturing grew from 19% in 1900 to 27% in 1950, thereby providing alternative employment opportunities for farm laborers and domestic workers.

By 2005, only 17% of U.S. jobs were in the goods-producing sector and 83% were in the service-providing sector; the proportion of knowledge-based jobs was estimated to be more than 50%. The DJIA reflects the changing face of the U.S. economy: In 1896, the 12 companies that made up the DJIA reflected the dominance of agriculture and basic commodities; in 1928—the first time the DJIA comprised 30 companies—the members reflected the importance of manufacturing, retailing, and the emerging radio industry; and in 2012, the shift is toward knowledge-based, communications industries, and financial services.

DJIA Companies		
1896	**1928**	**2012**
American Cotton Oil	Allied Can	3M
American Sugar	Allied Chemical	Alcoa
American Tobacco	American Smelting & Refining	American Express
Chicago Gas	American Sugar	AT&T
Distilling & Cattle Feeding	American Tobacco	Bank of America
General Electric	Atlantic Refining	Boeing
Laclede Gas Light	Bethlehem Steel	Caterpillar
National Lead	Chrysler	Chevron Corporation
North American	General Electric	Cisco Systems
Tennessee Coal, Iron & Railroad	General Motors	Coca-Cola
U.S. Leather	General Railway	DuPont
U.S. Rubber	Goodrich	ExxonMobil
	International Harvester	General Electric
	International Nickel	Hewlett-Packard
	Mack Trucks	The Home Depot
	Nash Motors	Intel
	North American	IBM
	Paramount Publix	Johnson & Johnson
	Postum	JPMorgan Chase
	Radio Corporation	UnitedHealth Group
	Sears, Roebuck	McDonald's
	Standard Oil (NJ)	Merck
	Texas Corporation	Microsoft
	Texas Gulf Sulphur	Pfizer
	Union Carbide	Procter & Gamble
	U.S. Steel	Travelers
	Victor Talking Machines	United Technologies Corporation
	Westinghouse	Verizon
	Woolworth	Walmart
	Wright	Walt Disney

Of course, only a few of the entrepreneurial giants ever get into the DJIA, which is composed of only 30 of the most widely held stocks. The following are some of the other legendary entrepreneurs and their companies that played important roles in the entrepreneurship revolution of the last 30 years.

Perhaps one of the most revolutionary entrepreneurial ideas outside of high-tech industries was Fred Smith's notion to deliver packages overnight anywhere in the United States. Smith identified a need for shippers to have a system designed specifically for airfreight that could accommodate time-sensitive shipments such as medicines, computer parts, and electronics in a term paper that he wrote as a Yale undergraduate. Smith's professor did not think much of the idea and gave it a C. After tours of duty in Vietnam, Smith founded his company, Federal Express (FedEx) in 1971, and it began operating in 1973 out of Memphis International Airport. In the mid-1970s, Federal Express had taken a leading role in lobbying for air cargo deregulation, which finally came in 1977. These changes allowed Federal Express to use larger aircraft and spurred the company's rapid growth. Today FedEx has the world's largest all-cargo air fleet, including McDonnell-Douglass MD-11s and Airbus A-300s and A-310s.[27]

In 1971, when Southwest Airlines began operations, *interstate* airline travel was highly regulated by the federal government, which had set up the Civil Aeronautics Board (CAB) in 1938 to regulate all domestic air transport as a public utility, setting fares, routes, and schedules. The CAB was required to ensure that the airlines had a reasonable rate of return. Most of the major airlines, whose profits were virtually guaranteed, favored the system.

Not surprisingly, competition was stifled, and almost no new airlines attempted to enter the market. However, *intrastate* passenger travel was not regulated by the CAB, so Southwest, following the pioneering path of Pacific Southwest Airline's (PSA's) service within California, initiated passenger service within Texas. The success of PSA and Southwest in providing cheap airline travel within California and Texas provided powerful ammunition for the deregulation of *interstate* travel, which came about in 1981 as a consequence of the Airline Deregulation Act of 1978.[28] Since deregulation, more than 100 startup airlines have inaugurated interstate scheduled passenger service with jet aircraft.[29] Herb Kelleher, the charismatic co-founder of Southwest Airlines, is often credited with triggering airline deregulation by persevering with his legal battle to get Southwest airborne in the face of fierce legal opposition from Braniff, Trans-Texas, and Continental Airlines. Two of those airlines took their legal battle all the way to the U.S. Supreme Court, which ruled in Southwest's favor at the end of 1970.[30]

Robert Swanson was 27 when he hit upon the idea that a company could be formed to commercialize biotechnology. At that time, he knew almost nothing about the field. By reading the scientific literature, Swanson identified the leading biotechnology scientists and contacted them. "Everybody said I was too early—it would take 10 years to turn out the first microorganism from a human hormone or maybe 20 years to have a commercial product—everybody except Herb Boyer."[31] Swanson was referring to Professor Herbert Boyer at the University of California at San Francisco, co-inventor of the patents that, according to some observers, now form the basis of the biotechnology industry. When Swanson and Boyer met in early 1976, they almost immediately agreed to become partners in an endeavor to explore the commercial possibilities of recombinant DNA. Boyer named their venture Genentech, an acronym for genetic engineering technology. Just seven months later, Genentech announced its first success, a genetically engineered human brain hormone, somatosin. According to Swanson, they accomplished 10 years of development in seven months. Most observers say it was Swanson's entrepreneurial vision that brought about the founding of the biotech industry. By 2012, there were about 1,850 U.S. biotech companies with combined revenues of more than $87 billion.[32] At almost the same time that Swanson was starting Genentech in southern San Francisco, not many miles away Steve Jobs and Stephen Wozniak were starting Apple Computer in Silicon Valley. Their computer, the Apple I in kit form, was an instant hit with hobbyists. The Byte Shop—the first full-time computer store anywhere in the world, which opened in Silicon Valley in December 1975—ordered 25 of them in June 1976. The owner of The Byte Shop asked Jobs to put the Apple I computer board in a case because his customers were asking for complete units, not just kits. When they did so, both Apple and The Byte Shop had a hot product on their hands. The Byte Shop grew to a chain of 75 stores. "Without intending to do so, Wozniak and Jobs had launched the microcomputer by responding to consumer demand."[33]

Genentech's initial public offering (IPO) in October 1980, followed by Apple's IPO only two months later, signaled that something magical was stirring in the biotech and personal computer industries. It triggered a wave of venture capital investment and IPOs in both industries.

A tipping point in the infant personal computer industry was the introduction of the VisiCalc spreadsheet. Dan Bricklin conceived it when he was sitting in an MBA class at Harvard in 1978, daydreaming about how he could make it easier to do repetitive calculations. Bricklin designed the prototype software to run on an Apple II. Together with Bob Frankston, he formed a company, Software Arts, to develop the VisiCalc spreadsheet. When they introduced their first version in May 1979, it turbocharged the sale of Apple computers. Subsequently, sales of IBM PCs were rocketed into the stratosphere by Mitch Kapor's Lotus 1-2-3 worksheet.

The late 1970s and the early 1980s were miraculous years for entrepreneurial ventures in the computer industry. Miniaturization of hard-disk drives, a vital component in the information technology revolution, was pioneered by Al Shugart, first at Shugart Associates, then at Seagate Technology. Dick Eagan and Roger Marino started EMC Corporation in 1979, initially selling computer furniture, and with the seed money from that, they launched into selling Intel-compatible memory. From that beginning, Eagan and Marino built EMC into a company that during the 1990s achieved the highest single-decade performance of any listed stock in the history of the New York Stock Exchange. Today it is the dominant company in the data storage industry.

Robert Metcalfe, the inventor of Ethernet, founded 3Com in 1979 to manufacture computer network products. 3Com built its business around Ethernet plug-in cards for personal computers. Today Ethernet is so widely used that it is usually built into most PC motherboards.

Michael Dell, while still a student at the University of Texas, Austin, in 1984, began selling IBM-compatible computers built from stock components that he marketed directly to customers. By concentrating on direct sales of customized products, Dell became the largest manufacturer of personal computers in the world, and Michael Dell was CEO longer than any other executive in the PC hardware industry.

Entrepreneurs were at the conception and birth of new products and services that have transformed the global economy in the last 35 years. However, what is turning out to be the biggest of them all began in 1989 when Tim (now Sir Timothy) Berners-Lee conceived the World Wide Web. We are in the midst of a revolution that is changing our lives more profoundly and faster than anyone could have imagined before the Web became operational in 1992. No major new product has been adopted as quickly by such a large percentage of the U.S. population as the Web.

Time for New Technologies to Penetrate 25% of U.S. Population	
Household electricity (1873)	46 years
Telephone (1875)	35 years
Automobile (1885)	55 years
Airplane travel (1903)	54 years
Radio (1906)	22 years
Television (1925)	26 years
VCR (1952)	34 years
PC (1975)	15 years
Mobile Phone (1983)	13 years
World Wide Web (1992)	5 years

Source: The Wall Street Journal, June 1997; http://en.wikipedia.org/wiki/Advanced_Mobile_Phone_Service; www.netbanker.com/2000/04/internet_usage_web_users_world.html.

Web: Three Revolutions Converge

In 1989, when Tim Berners-Lee wrote a proposal to develop software that resulted in the World Wide Web, he was not the first to conceive the idea. As far back as 1945, Vannevar Bush proposed a "memex" machine with which users could create information "trails" linking related text and illustrations and store the trails for future reference.[34]

As it turned out, he was 50 years ahead of the technologies that were needed to implement his idea. After all, the first digital computer was then only a couple of years old. Fifteen years later Ted Nelson, inspired by Bush's "memex," was the first person to develop the modern version of hypertext. He wrote—prophetically, as it turned out—in 1960 that "the future of humanity is at the interactive computer screen....the new writing and movies will be interactive and interlinked....we need a world-wide network to deliver it....[35]

But Nelson, too, was far ahead of the technology. In 1962, there were fewer than 10,000 computers in the world. They cost hundreds of thousands of dollars, they were primitive machines with only a few thousand bytes of magnetic core memory, and programming them was complicated and tedious. AT&T had a monopoly over the phone lines that were used for data communication. And the ARPANET, which was the forerunner of the Internet, had not yet been conceived.[36]

Berners-Lee was a 25-year-old physics graduate of Oxford University working as a consultant at CERN, the European Particle Physics Laboratory in Geneva, Switzerland, in 1980 when he wrote his own private program for storing information using the random associations the brain makes. His Enquire program, which was never published, formed the conceptual basis for his future development of the Web.[37] In 1980, the technology existed for implementing Berners-Lee's concept, but the power of the technology was low, and the installed base of computers was tiny compared to what it would be 10 years later. By 1989, when he revived his idea, three revolutions were ready for it. They were in *digital technology, information technology (IT)*, and *entrepreneurship*. The semiconductor revolution enabled the digital revolution, which in turn enabled the IT revolution. By 1992, when the Web was released by CERN, the Internet had 1 million hosts, computers were 1,000 million times faster, and network bandwidth was 20 million times greater than 20 years earlier. The entrepreneurship revolution meant that there was an army of entrepreneurs and would-be entrepreneurs, especially in the United States, with the vision and capacity to seize the commercial opportunities presented by the Web. In February 1993, the National Center for Supercomputing Applications (NCSA) released the first alpha version of Marc Andreessen's Mosaic. By December 1994, the Web was growing at approximately 1% a day—with a doubling period of less than 10 weeks.[38] In the next 10 years, Internet usage exploded.* By 2009, users numbered 1.7 billion, which was about 25% of the entire population of the world.

Entrepreneurship Revolution Strikes Gold

Marc Andreessen moved to Silicon Valley in 1994, teamed up with veteran IT entrepreneur Jim Clark, and incorporated Mosaic Communications (later renamed Netscape Communications). Clark put $6 million of his own money into Mosaic, and venture capitalists added another $6 million.[39] Their intent was to create a browser that would surpass the original Mosaic. It was a classic Silicon Valley startup with programmers working 18-hour days, seven days a week, sometimes even working 48 hours at one stretch just coding. In October 1994, the Netscape browser was posted as a download on the Internet. In no time at all, it was the browser of choice for the majority of Web users; in December 1994, Netscape Communications began shipping Netscape Navigator, which started to produce income.

Netscape Navigator was an instant success, gaining 75% of the browser market within four months of its introduction. Netscape Communications was only 16 months old when it went public in August 1995. Its IPO was one of the most spectacular in history and made Jim Clark the first Internet billionaire. According to an article in *Fortune*, "It was the spark that touched off the Internet boom."[40]

A gold rush was under way. "Netscape mesmerized investors and captured America's imagination. More than any other company, it set the technological, social, and financial tone of the Internet age."[41] A generation of would-be entrepreneurs was inspired by Netscape's success. What's more, corporate executives from established businesses wanted to emulate Jim Barksdale, the former president of McCaw Communications, who joined Netscape's board in October 1994, became CEO in January 1995, and made a huge fortune in just eight months. Investors—both angels and venture capitalists—hustled to invest in Internet-related startups. It seemed as if everyone was panning for Internet gold, not only in Silicon Valley but also throughout the United States—and a couple of years later throughout the rest of the world.

---

* The Internet and the World Wide Web (now usually called the Web) are two separate but related entities. However, most people use the terms interchangeably. The Internet is a vast network of networks, a networking infrastructure. The Web is a way of accessing information over the Internet. It is an information-sharing model that is built on top of the Internet.

WORLD INTERNET USAGE AND POPULATION STATISTICS

	Population (2011 estimate)	Internet Users Dec. 31, 2000	Internet Users Dec. 31, 2011	Penetration (% Population)	Growth 2000-2011
Africa	1,037,524,058	4,514,400	139,875,242	14%	2988%
Asia	3,879,740,877	114,304,000	1,016,799,076	26%	790%
Europe	816,426,346	105,096,093	500,723,686	61%	376%
Middle East	216,258,843	3,284,800	77,020,995	36%	2245%
North America	347,394,870	108,096,800	273,067,546	79%	153%
Latin America/Caribbean	597,283,165	18,068,919	235,819,740	40%	1205%
Oceania/Australia	35,426,995	7,620,480	23,927,457	68%	214%
WORLD TOTAL	6,930,055,154	360,985,492	2,267,233,742	33%	528%

Source: internetworldstats.com http://www.internetworldstats.com/stats.htm

Netscape is a superb example of American venture capital at its best, accelerating the commercialization of innovations especially at the start of revolutionary new industries driven by technology. Venture capital was in at the start of the semiconductor and the minicomputer industries in the late 1950s and early 1960s and the biotech and personal computer industries in the late 1970s, and now it was eager to invest in what promised to be the biggest revolution of them all, the Internet and the Web.

Venture capital is not invested exclusively in technology companies. It was in at the beginning of the overnight package delivery industry with its investment in Federal Express, at the start of major big-box retailers such as Home Depot and Staples, and at the creation of new airlines including JetBlue. No wonder Jiro Tokuyama, then dean of the Nomura School of Advanced Management in Japan and a highly influential economist, stated that entrepreneurial firms and venture capital are the great advantages that Americans have.[42] Since the early 1970s, approximately $500 billion of venture capital have backed 32,000 U.S. companies. In 2010, those venture-backed companies employed more than 12 million people, or 11% of the private-sector employment, and generated revenues of $3.1 trillion, or 21% of the U.S. GDP.[43]

The Web presented numerous opportunities that were soon being exploited by entrepreneurs. It created a huge demand for more and more capacity on the Internet, which in turn presented opportunities for hardware and software entrepreneurs. They were fortunate to find venture capitalists eager to invest in their startups. The period from 1996 through 2000 was a golden era for classic[44] venture capitalists and the entrepreneurial companies they invested in. It was golden both metaphorically and literally, as more and more venture capitalists and entrepreneurs seemed to have acquired the Midas touch. Some of the financial gains from venture-capital-backed companies were indeed of mythological proportions. For instance, Benchmark Capital's investment of $5 million in eBay multiplied 1,500-fold in just two years.[46] True, Benchmark's investment in eBay set the all-time record for Silicon Valley, but there were plenty of instances when investments increased at least a hundredfold and in some cases a thousandfold. With investments such as those, overall returns on U.S. classic venture capital soared, with the one-year return peaking at 143% at the end of the third quarter in 2000, compared with average annual returns in the mid-teens prior to the golden era.

During a 1999 news conference at the World Economic Forum in Davos, Switzerland, reporters pestered Bill Gates again and again with variations of the same question: "These Internet stocks, they're a bubble?" An irritated Bill Gates finally confronted the reporters: "Look, you bozos, of course they're a bubble, but you're all missing the point. This bubble is attracting so much new capital to the Internet industry; it is going to drive innovation faster and faster."[45]

But the gold rush came to an end in 2000. The Internet bubble burst. Many companies failed, others were forced into fire-sale mergers, investors were hammered, many jobs were lost, and doom and gloom were pervasive. There was much hand-wringing about the incredible wastefulness of the U.S. method of financing new industries. However, by August 9, 2005—the tenth anniversary of Netscape's IPO—some companies founded during the gold rush were thriving. The market capitalization of just four of them—Google, eBay, Yahoo, and Amazon.com—was about $200 billion, which handily exceeded all the venture capital invested in all the Internet-related companies through 2000; what's more, it even topped the combined amount raised from venture capital and IPOs. Granted, there were many more losers than winners, but five years after the bust, it was clear that U.S. society as a whole had already benefited mightily and the best was yet to come—but not for everyone. As Schumpeter observed, revolutionary entrepreneurship creates new products, services, and business methods that undermine and sometimes destroy old ones.

Creative Destruction

The Web is blowing gales of creative destruction through many old industries, none more so than that of print newspapers, whose publishers were slow to recognize their business models were endangered—perhaps fatally—by the Web. Some long-established U.S. newspapers, such as the *Rocky Mountain News* and the *Tucson Citizen*, have shut down completely; others have drastically reduced their operations; and a few, including the *Christian Science Monitor* and the *Seattle-Post Intelligencer*, now publish only on the Web and no longer produce print editions. *Newsweek's* final print edition was published on December 31, 2012, ending almost 80 years in print. Several prominent newspaper chains, including the Tribune Company, the Minneapolis Star Tribune, Philadelphia Newspapers, and the Sun-Times Media Group, have filed for bankruptcy. The 2009 demise of *Editor and Publisher*, the 125-year-old trade magazine for the newspaper industry, seemed to symbolize the plight of the industry.

Newspapers had not only withstood potential competition from the introduction of other forms of news broadcasting, such as radio in the 1920s and 1930s, television in the 1950s, and 24-hour cable news channels in the 1980s and 1990s, but also actually prospered more and more, so why should they have foreseen in the early1990s the havoc that the fledgling Web was about to wreak on their industry? What most print publishers did not foresee was that the Web would undermine the two basic sources of newspaper revenues, advertising and paid circulation; annual ad revenue, for example, plunged from its peak of more than $60 billion in 2000 to $20 billion in 2012.[47] The underlying cause is the changes in society brought about by the Internet, which was used by about 80% of the U.S. population in 2012 compared with less than 3% in 1993.[48] Web portals such as Yahoo, social networking services such as Twitter, and individual bloggers give readers instant access to breaking news stories and often break news ahead of the old media; Google and other search engines make it easy to find stories from anywhere in the world at lightning speed; and perhaps best of all, it is free. For advertisers, the allure of the Web over print newspapers and magazines is that it allows them to target ads to individuals—every Web user is now a market segment of just one individual—and it provides much better metrics for tracking the effectiveness of ads.

The Internet has devastated the print media's business model, and publishers are groping for a new one. Some think it will be a hybrid of print and the Web; others believe that print will continue to lose ground to the Web and more papers will publish only Web editions. And what else in this age of government bailouts? Some in Congress have even proposed a "Newspaper Revitalization Act" to help ailing newspapers.[49]

Causes of the Entrepreneurial Revolution

The United States has always been a nation of entrepreneurs. But why has it become more and more entrepreneurial since the end of the 1960s—creating what is now called the entrepreneurial revolution?

First, we need to step back and look at the U.S. economy in the decades before the 1970s. The Great Depression, which followed the stock market collapse of October 1929, had an enormous effect on society. By 1932, when Franklin Roosevelt was elected president, over 13 million Americans had lost their jobs, and the gross national product had fallen 31%. The Roosevelt administration implemented many policies to try to bring the nation out of the Depression, but it was not until World War II that the nation once again started to become prosperous. The end of the war in 1945 heralded an era of economic growth and opportunity. But the memories left by the Depression meant that workers preferred secure jobs with good wages and benefits that medium and big companies offered. And big business was booming.

The late 1940s and the 1950s and 1960s were the era of the corporate employee. They were immortalized by William Whyte in *The Organization Man*,[50] in which he "argued in 1956 that American business life had abandoned the old virtues of self-reliance and entrepreneurship in favor of a bureaucratic 'social ethic' of loyalty, security and 'belongingness.' With the rise of the postwar corporation, American individualism had disappeared from the mainstream of middle-class life."[51] The key to a successful career was this: "Be loyal to the company and the company will be loyal to you." Whyte's writing assumed the change was permanent and it favored the large corporation.

Big American businesses were seen as the way of the future, not just in the United States but worldwide. John Kenneth Galbraith's seminal book *The New Industrial State*[52] and Jean-Jacques Servan-Schreiber's *Le Défi Américain* (The American Challenge)[53] both "became the bible to advocates of industrial policies"[54] supporting big business. Both books were instant best sellers. *Le Défi Américain* sold 600,000 copies in France alone and was translated into 15 languages. Galbraith wrote in 1967, "By all but the pathologically romantic, it is now recognized that this is not the age of the small man." He believed that the best economic size for corporations was "very, very large."

The works of Whyte, Galbraith, and Servan-Schreiber were required reading in universities through the 1970s. Schumpeter's work was hardly ever mentioned,[55] and when it was, it was his book *Capitalism, Socialism, and Democracy*, published in 1942,[56] in which he was very pessimistic that capitalism would survive. Unlike Karl Marx, who believed the proletariat would bring about the downfall of capitalism, Schumpeter reasoned that the very success of free enterprise would create a class of elites who would favor central control of the economy and thereby curb free enterprise. His first book, *The Theory of Economic Development*,[57] originally published in German in 1911, in which he endorsed entrepreneurship, was hardly ever mentioned. What's more, in the 1970s there was an abundance of university courses dealing with Karl Marx and almost none dealing with entrepreneurship. It's not surprising that the world was first alerted to the entrepreneurial revolution by a journalist, Norman Macrae, rather than by an academic scholar. About a decade later, researchers confirmed retrospectively that entrepreneurial activity had indeed been on the increase in the United States in the 1970s.[58]

Entrepreneurship did not disappear in the 1930s, 1940s, 1950s, and 1960s; it simply did not grow very much. What brought about the change in the economy that stirred up entrepreneurship around 1970? To try to understand what changes were taking place, we need to look at the social, cultural, and political context of an economy. A framework for this perspective is presented in Figure 1.1, the Global Entrepreneurship Monitor (GEM) model for the economy.[59]

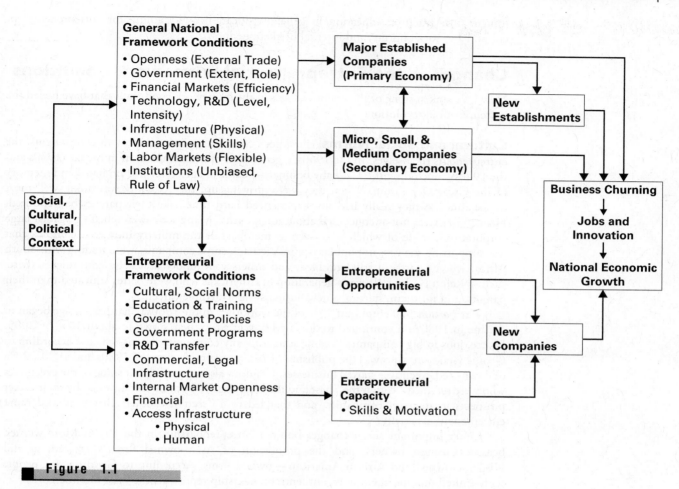

Figure 1.1

GEM model of economic growth

The central argument[60] of the GEM model is that national economic growth is a function of two sets of interrelated activities: those associated with established firms and those related directly to the entrepreneurial process. Activity among established firms explains only part of the story behind variations in economic growth. The entrepreneurial process may also account for a significant proportion of the differences in economic prosperity among countries and among regions within countries.

When looking at the nature of the relationship between entrepreneurship and economic growth, it is important to distinguish between entrepreneurial opportunities and entrepreneurial capacity. What drives entrepreneurial activity is that people perceive opportunities and have the skills and motivation to exploit them. The outcome is the creation of new firms and, inevitably, the destruction of inefficient or outmoded existing firms. Schumpeter's process of creative destruction is captured in the model by business churning. Despite its negative connotation, creative destruction actually has a positive impact on economic growth—declining businesses are phased out as startups maneuver their way into the market. These dynamic transactions occur within a particular context, which the GEM model calls *entrepreneurial framework conditions* and which includes factors such as availability of finance, government policies and programs designed to support startups, R&D transfer, physical and human infrastructure, education in general, education and training for entrepreneurship, cultural and social norms, and internal market openness.

Changes in the Entrepreneurial Framework Conditions

Now let's look at some of the major changes in the framework conditions that have fueled the entrepreneurial revolution.

Cultural and Social Norms. First, let's consider the most important components, the entrepreneurs themselves. In the 1960s, a generation of Americans born in the late 1930s and the 1940s—including the first baby boomers—came of age. They had no first-hand memory of the Great Depression. When they were growing up, the economy was doing well most of the time, so they really had not experienced hard times like their parents had endured. Hence, they were not as concerned about job security. Many were even rebelling against large corporations, some of which were seen as members of the military-industrial complex that was supporting the very unpopular war in Vietnam; some companies were trading with South Africa, where apartheid still prevailed; and others were under attack by consumer activists such as Ralph Nader.[61] It was a generation of Americans who were better educated than their parents, and for them, starting a new business was a credible career.

The *Fortune* 500 employed 20% of the workforce in the 1960s. That percentage began to decline in 1980 and continued to do so every year since then, down to about 10% by 2005. Hence, jobs in big companies became scarcer. Many companies downsized, and according to George Gendron, who was the publisher of *Inc.* magazine during the 1980s and 1990s, 20% of downsized executives started businesses. Gendron also suggested that some of the executives who were retained—often the "best and the brightest"—became disillusioned by their career prospects in stagnant companies, and that led to a "second exodus" that produced more entrepreneurial activity.[62]

Other important social changes boosted entrepreneurship in the 1990s. More women became business owners, and the proportion of Asian-owned firms increased, as did Hispanic-owned and African American—owned firms. According to Gendron, for people with limited options in employment, entrepreneurship represents the "last meritocracy."

Government. The 1970s were the decade when Washington bailed out Penn Central Railroad, Lockheed, and Chrysler. Washington seemed more concerned with big business than with small. But it did recognize the need to pay attention to startups with high potential, especially the ones funded by venture capitalists. There had been a burst of venture-capital-backed startups in the last half of the 1960s. But in the early 1970s, venture capital dried up to a trickle. Looking back from the perspective of 2012, when $26.7 billion of new money flowing into the venture capital industry seems routine, it is scarcely believable that only $10 million of new money was committed in 1975. Congress took urgent steps in 1978 to stimulate the venture capital industry, including reducing the capital gains tax and easing the ERISA prudent man rule, which had inhibited pension funds from investing in venture capital funds. The pension floodgates opened, and the inflow of venture capital increased to $4.9 billion by 1987. Likewise, venture capital invested in portfolio companies increased from a low of $250 million in 1975 to $3.9 billion in 1987—a 16-fold increase.[63]

The government asserted its role of ensuring *market openness* by minimizing anticompetitive behavior. We've already mentioned that legislation toward the end of the 1970s deregulated the airfreight and airline passenger industries. That was followed in the early 1980s by the U.S. Justice Department's move to break up AT&T's monopoly.

The government deserves immense credit for its funding of R&D in government, universities, and corporations, both directly and indirectly through purchases of products.

Its support was vital in the development of the computer, communications, biotech, and many other industries.

Washington activated the Small Business Innovation Research (SBIR) program in 1983 to ensure that small businesses shared some of the federal R&D dollars for new technology-based developments. In 2009, around 5,800 awards, totaling $2.2 billion, went to small businesses as a result of the SBIR program. In general, funds awarded under the SBIR program go to develop new technologies that are high risk and high reward. Some might say it is pre-venture capital money. From that viewpoint, $2 billion is a significant amount when compared with $1.7 billion that venture capitalists invested in 350 seed-stage companies in 2009. A total of $30 billion has been awarded over the 28 years of the SBIR program through 2010.[64] Symantec, Qualcomm, DaVinci, and iRobot received R&D funding from this program.

R&D Transfer. Commercial development of intellectual property resulting from federally funded research is a major benefit to the U.S. economy. It was given a major boost by the passage of the Bayh-Dole Act, implemented in 1980. The primary intent of that law was to foster the growth of technology-based small businesses by allowing them to own the patents that arose from federally sponsored research. Under Bayh-Dole, universities were allowed to grant exclusive licenses—a feature that was regarded as crucial if small businesses were to commercialize high technologies that were inherently risky propositions.[65]

Before 1980, U.S. universities were granted about 300 patents a year. In 2003, they applied for about 10,000. In 1980, 25 to 30 universities had offices for technology transfer. Today, more than 1,200 do.[66] *The Economist* hailed Bayh-Dole as "the most inspired piece of legislation to be enacted in America over the past half-century." *The Economist* estimated that Bayh-Dole had created 2,000 new companies and 260,000 new jobs and had contributed $40 billion annually to the U.S. economy.[67] That assessment was made almost 10 years ago, and more progress has been made since then.[68]

The government itself has technology transfer offices at most of its research laboratories[69] and many large companies have licensing offices. IBM, for example, which annually spends about $6 billion on R&D, was granted 6,478 patents in 2012. It generates about $1 billion annually from licensing intellectual property, which comprises both patents and copyrights.

Fruits of Federally Funded R&D

The success of Bayh-Dole goes far beyond the efforts of Bob Dole and Birch Bayh. This legislation combined the ingenuity and innovation from our university laboratories with the entrepreneurial skills of America's small businesses. Most importantly, this combination created the incentive necessary for private investment to invest in bringing new ideas to the marketplace. The delicate balance of ingenuity, entrepreneurship, and incentive upon which the success of Bayh-Dole has depended must not be disrupted.

A few of the products that have been produced in the last six years include

- Taxol, the most important cancer drug in 15 years, according to the National Cancer Institution.
- DNA sequencer, the basis of the entire Human Genome Project.
- StormVision, which airport traffic and safety managers use to predict the motion of storms.
- Prostate-specific antigen test, now a routine component of cancer screening.
- V-Chip, which allows families to control access to television programming.

Statement of Senator Birch Bayh to the National Institutes of Health, May 25, 2004.

Physical Infrastructure. The biggest change in entrepreneurship in the last 10 years is due to the Web, the great equalizer. Small businesses now have at their fingertips a tool so powerful that it is leveling the playing field. Big businesses no longer enjoy as many scale economies as they did before the Internet. Information that could have been gathered only by a multitude of market researchers can now be found with a search engine and a couple of clicks of a mouse. Entrepreneurs don't have to spend a fortune to reach customers with print, radio, and television advertising; they can target their potential customers anywhere in the world via the Web. When they want to find a vendor, the Web is there to help them—as it is when they are seeking employees, bankers, and investors. Furthermore, the cost of communications of all kinds (except snail mail) has plummeted since AT&T was broken up. A long-distance telephone call that cost 40 cents a minute in 1980 now can be made for as little as 1 cent. And if these entrepreneurs need to travel by air, they can shop the Web to find the cheapest ticket, automobile rental, and hotel room.

The worldwide distribution of goods and services is now open to everyone. Just consider what eBay has already done to change the entrepreneurial landscape. According to a 2005 study by ACNielsen International Research, 724,000 Americans report that selling on eBay is their primary or secondary source of income.[70] An American entrepreneur can sell merchandise to a customer anywhere in the world; PayPal (founded in 1998 and now part of eBay) can ensure that the entrepreneur receives payment speedily and securely online; the merchandise can be delivered to the buyer within a day or so via FedEx; and buyer and seller can track the shipment online at each step of its journey.

Outsourcing services and goods makes companies more efficient and effective. Entrepreneurs can now focus on their company's core competency and let vendors take care of noncore items such as payroll, Web hosting, telemarketing, manufacturing, and distribution. There are even companies that will help entrepreneurs find outsource partners. Outsourcing enables small businesses to act like big ones, and some small companies are even called *virtual companies* because they outsource so much of their work.

For some entrepreneurs, business incubators combine many of the advantages of outsourcing. Incubators provide not only physical space but also shared services. Many incubators also provide ready access to human infrastructure. In 1980, there were only 12 business incubators in the United States; over the period between 1985 and 1995, the number of U.S. incubators grew 15-fold, from 40 to nearly 600[71]—and by 2006, there were some 1,115 incubators.[72] The National Business Incubation Association (NBIA) estimated that in 2005 alone, North American incubators assisted more than 27,000 startup companies that provided full-time employment for more than 100,000 workers and generated annual revenue of more than $17 billion.[73]

Thomas Samson/Gamma-Rapho/Getty Images

Jack Dorsey, founder and chairman of Twitter at a conference in Paris in December 2009.

Human Infrastructure. Access to human infrastructure is as important as access to physical infrastructure—maybe more so. The human infrastructure for entrepreneurs grew rapidly in the last 20 years or so, and gaining access to it has never been easier. Thirty years ago, starting a new venture was a lonely pursuit, fraught with pitfalls that would have been avoided by someone with prior entrepreneurial experience. Today numerous entrepreneurship experts gladly help people who are starting or growing companies. There are support networks, both informal and formal, of professionals who know a lot about the entrepreneurial process. Just search the Web for "entrepreneur AND assistance AND *your town*," and you might be astonished by the number of hits.

Education, Training, and Professionalization. Entrepreneurship education and training is now readily available, part of the professionalization of entrepreneurship that has taken place over the last 20 years.[74] According to Gendron, a body of knowledge and skills has developed over the last 20 years to enhance the chances of entrepreneurial success. A good illustration is the widely dispensed advice that would-be entrepreneurs should write a business plan before they launch their new ventures. The world of entrepreneurship is awash with information about business plans. The field has come a long way since the pioneers of entrepreneurship training put writing a business plan at the core of their programs in the 1970s.[75]

When Babson College and the University of Texas started their internal business plan competitions in 1985, only a few schools had entrepreneurship courses. Now more than 60% of four-year colleges and universities have at least one entrepreneurship course, and many have entrepreneurship centers. Today entrepreneurship training courses are readily available to all sectors of the population.

The Accidental Entrepreneur

Like many other scientists and engineers who have ended up founding companies, I didn't leave Caltech as an entrepreneur. I had no training in business; after my sophomore year of college I didn't take any courses outside of chemistry, math, and physics. My career as an entrepreneur happened quite by accident.

There is such a thing as a natural-born entrepreneur.... But the accidental entrepreneur like me has to fall into the opportunity or be pushed into it. Most of what I learned as an entrepreneur was by trial and error, but I think a lot of this really could have been learned more efficiently.

— *Gordon Moore (co-founder of Fairchild Semiconductor in 1957 and Intel in 1968).*[76]

Financial. Raising money for a new business is seldom easy, but the process of raising startup and expansion capital has become more efficient in the last 20 years or so. In 1982, for instance, an economist at the National Science Foundation stated that venture capital was shrouded in empirical secrecy and an aura of beliefs.[77] The same held true for angel investing. In contrast, today there is an abundance of help. The amount of venture capital under management has grown from $3.7 billion in 1980 to $199 billion in 2012.[78] We do not have reliable numbers for business angel investors, but we do know that informal investors—everyone from parents to external business angels—now invest more than $100 billion annually in startup and baby businesses. Furthermore, informal investors are ubiquitous. Five percent of American adults report that they "invested" in someone else's venture in the last three years.[79] It is impossible to claim that the availability of financing has driven the entrepreneurial revolution, but it does appear that sufficient financing has been available to fuel it.

Churning and Economic Growth

Technological change, deregulation, competition, and globalization presented countless opportunities, which American entrepreneurs seized and commercialized. It caused a lot of *churning*, or Schumpeter's creative destruction. But 11 new businesses with employees were started for every 10 that died over the decade 1990–2000.[80] It is this churning that gives the economy its vitality. Only a society that willingly adapts to change can have a dynamic economy.

Entrepreneurial competition, according to Schumpeter, "strikes not at the margins of the profits . . . of the existing firms but at their foundations and very lives." Established companies that stick with their old ways of doing business self-destruct as their customers turn to new competitors with better business models.

We can find examples of churning in every industry that is not a monopoly or a regulated oligopoly. Who can recall VisiCalc or for that matter Lotus 1-2-3? At the height of their fame they were two of the most widely used software packages for PCs. Today Excel is the spreadsheet of choice. In one week alone in May 1982, when Digital Equipment Corporation (DEC) introduced its ill-fated Rainbow PC, four other companies introduced PCs.[81] At the peak of the PC industry frenzy in the early 1980s, more than 200 companies either had introduced PCs or were planning to do so. Only a handful of PC manufacturers exists today. DEC, which in 1982 was the second largest computer manufacturer in the world, was eventually bought by Compaq, which in turn merged with Hewlett-Packard. In 2004, IBM sold its PC division to Lenovo, a company founded in 1984 by a group of academics at the government-backed Chinese Academy of Sciences in Beijing.

Not only did the advent of the PC churn up the entire computer industry, but also it virtually wiped out the typewriter industry. And it changed the way office work is organized. Secretaries had to learn computer skills or they were out of work.

And who knows what the future holds for the PC itself? In February 2013, one of the giants of the PC industry, Dell Inc., is likely to be bought out by a group of investors headed by Michael Dell, its founder; Dell is hoping to revive the company whose sales are dropping as laptop PCs face increasing competition from tablet computers, such as the iPad, and smartphones. Indeed, in 2013 Schumpeterian disruptions abound throughout the information technology space: The PC industry is being upset by mobile, and servers and data storage are being challenged by the cloud.

More examples of churning: Southwest Airlines is now the most successful U.S. airline; two of its giant rivals in 1971 no longer exist, and the third, Continental, has been bankrupt twice, in 1983 and 1990. United Airlines, US Airways, Hawaiian Airlines, ATA Airlines (also known as American Trans Air), Delta, Northwest, Aloha Airlines, and American Airlines have all been in Chapter 11 bankruptcy, and only a handful of the 100 or so passenger airlines started up since deregulation are still around. Who goes to a travel agent to get a regular airline ticket or book a hotel room today? Where is the fax machine headed? Likewise video stores and CD retailers? Why are newspapers laying off workers? Who is buying a film camera? And even entrepreneurship academics had to watch out. Donald Trump, building on his TV success with *The Apprentice*, started Trump University in 2005 to teach—what else?—entrepreneurship; but so far success has eluded Trump in the education field.

"The power of Walmart is such, it's reversed a 100-year history in which the manufacturer was powerful and the retailer was sort of the vassal. . . . It turned that around entirely."
— Nelson Lichtenstein, University of California, Santa Barbara

Granted, churning causes a lot of disruption—and nowhere more than in the lives of those who lose their jobs as a result. But overall, society is the beneficiary. Entrepreneurship produces new products and services, it increases productivity, it generates employment, and in some cases, it keeps inflation in check. Economists estimate that Walmart alone knocked 20%—perhaps as much as 25%—off the rate of inflation in the 1990s.[82] According to Alfred Kahn, the father of airline deregulation, airline passengers are now saving $20 billion a year.[83] And with Skype™ and the Internet, you can "talk to anyone, anywhere in the world for free. Forever."[84]

Next we will look at how other nations as well as the United States are faring with entrepreneurship.

Global Entrepreneurship Monitor

The Global Entrepreneurship Monitor (GEM) was conceived in 1997* to study the economic impact and the determinants of national-level entrepreneurial activity. GEM is the largest coordinated research effort ever undertaken to study population-level entrepreneurial activity. Since its inception, a total of 99 economies accounting for approximately 95% of the world's GDP and 85% of its population have participated in GEM's annual study. Because of its worldwide reach and rigorous scientific method, GEM has become the world's most influential and authoritative source of empirical data and expertise on the entrepreneurial potential of nations.[85]

The main objectives of GEM are to gather data that measure the entrepreneurial activity of nations and other data related to entrepreneurial activity; to examine what national characteristics are related to levels of entrepreneurial activity; and to explain how differences in entrepreneurial activity are related to different levels of economic growth among nations. GEM distinguishes between two types of entrepreneurial activity:[86]

- *Nascent entrepreneurs* are individuals who are actively trying to start a new business but who have not yet done so.
- *Baby business managers* are owner-managers of a new business that is no more than 42 months old.

There are three main measures of entrepreneurial activity:

- TEA (total entrepreneurial activity) is the percentage of the adult population that is either nascent entrepreneurs or baby businesses owner-managers or both. It measures the overall entrepreneurial activity of a nation.
- TEA (opportunity) is the percentage of the adult population that is trying to start or has started a baby business to exploit a perceived opportunity. They are classified as improvement-driven opportunity motivated if they additionally seek to improve their income or independence through entrepreneurship.
- TEA (necessity) is the percentage of the adult population that is trying to start or has started a baby business because all other options for work are either absent or unsatisfactory.

Principal Findings from GEM

In 2012, more than 198,000 people in 69 economies participated in the annual GEM study, collectively representing all regions of the world and a broad range of economic development levels.** The World Economic Forum's (WEF) *Global Competitiveness Report* identifies three phases of economic development based on GDP per capita and the share of exports comprising primary goods. According to the WEF classification, the *factor-driven* phase is dominated by

---

* GEM in itself is an example of not-for-profit (social) entrepreneurship. It was conceived in 1997 by Babson College and London Business School professors. It was prototyped with bootstrap funding and volunteers and was officially launched in 1998 with research teams from 10 nations and supported with funding raised by each team from national sponsors. By 2009, it had evolved into an international consortium of more than 200 researchers from more than 60 nations, with a combined annual budget of about $4 million. It produces annual global reports on the overall state of entrepreneurship in those nations, country-specific reports, and reports on special topics such as female entrepreneurship, financing, and job creation. More than 100 global and regional reports can be read and downloaded at www.gemconsortium.org.

** Some of the text in the following sections was excerpted from the *GEM 2012 Global Report* http://www.gemconsortium .org/docs/download/2645

subsistence agriculture and extraction businesses, with a heavy reliance on (unskilled) labor and natural resources. The focus of development efforts tends toward building a sufficient foundation of basic requirements. In the *efficiency-driven* phase, an economy has become more competitive with further development accompanied by industrialization and an increased reliance on economies of scale, with capital-intensive large organizations more dominant. This phase is generally accompanied by improved (and improving) basic requirements, and attention is then directed toward developing the efficiency enhancers. As development advances into the *innovation-driven* phase, businesses are more knowledge-intensive, and the service sector expands.

Activity

Total Entrepreneurial Activity (TEA) is a key indicator of GEM. It measures the percentage of adults (aged 18–64) in an economy who are nascent and new entrepreneurs. In economies with low GDP per capita, TEA rates tend to be high, with a correspondingly higher proportion of necessity-motivated entrepreneurship. Conversely, high GDP economies show lower levels of entrepreneurship, but a higher proportion of those with opportunity-motivations. To at least some extent then, development levels are associated with particular patterns in the level and type of entrepreneurial activity.

The highest average TEA rates (Table 1.1) were found in sub-Saharan Africa and Latin America/Caribbean. Zambia (41%) and Ecuador (27%) reported the highest rates in these regions. The Asia Pacific/South Asia region showed a mix of TEA levels with Thailand (19%) and China (13%) recording the highest rates.

While TEA rates were typically higher than established business rates in factor-driven economies, the gap narrows in the innovation-driven economies, with some showing more established business owners than entrepreneurs. For example, Greece, Spain, Switzerland, Ireland, and Finland in the EU and Japan, Republic of Korea, and Taiwan in Asia show at least one-third more established business owners than entrepreneurs. When viewed geographically, non-EU and Middle East and North Africa (MENA) regions have low rates of both TEA and established business ownership while Sub-Saharan Africa has high rates of both, although TEA rates are much higher—twice as high on average compared with established business ownership.

Differences across regions can also be seen in the reasons for business discontinuance. For example, financing was identified as the key issue in business discontinuance in sub-Saharan Africa, but was less an issue in Asia. In the United States and the European Union, individuals cited other jobs or business opportunities more often than those in other regions as a reason for business discontinuance—these are generally considered more positive causes.

Necessity- and Opportunity-Driven Entrepreneurs

GEM defines necessity-driven entrepreneurs as those who are pushed into starting businesses because they have no other work options and need a source of income. Opportunity-motivated entrepreneurs, on the other hand, are those entering this activity primarily to pursue an opportunity. The latter are further distinguished as improvement-driven opportunity motivated if they additionally seek to improve their income or independence through entrepreneurship.

Necessity-driven motives tend to be highest in the factor-driven economies. With greater economic development levels, the proportion of entrepreneurs with necessity motives generally declines, while improvement-driven opportunity increasingly accounts for a great proportion of motives. Geographic differences exist, however, even at the same economic development level. For instance, the Latin America/Caribbean region, generally containing efficiency-driven economies, reported twice as many entrepreneurs with improvement–driven opportunity

| TABLE 1.1 | Entrepreneurial Activity in the 69 GEM Countries in 2012, by Geographic Region |

(Rate in columns 3-6 is the percent of adults 18-64 engaged in the specified activity.)

Country	Economy Classification F=factor, E=efficiency, I=Innovation	Nascent entrepreneurship rate	New business ownership rate	Early-stage entrepreneurial activity (TEA) rate	Established business ownership rate	Discontinuation of businesses rate	Necessity-driven (% of TEA)	Improvement-driven opportunity (% of TEA)
LATIN AMERICA & CARRIBEAN								
Argentina	E	12	7	19	10	5	35	47
Barbados	E	10	7	17	12	3	12	63
Brazil	E	4	11	15	15	5	30	59
Chile	E	15	8	23	8	5	17	69
Colombia	E	14	7	20	7	7	12	48
Costa Rica	E	10	5	15	3	3	20	48
Ecuador	E	17	12	27	19	8	36	30
El Salvador	E	8	8	15	9	8	35	39
Mexico	E	8	4	12	5	4	13	52
Panama	E	7	3	9	2	2	19	57
Peru	E	15	6	20	5	7	23	53
Trinidad & Tobago	E	9	7	15	7	5	15	60
Uruguay	E	1	5	15	5	5	18	40
Average		11	7	17	8	5	22	51
MIDDLE EAST & NORTH AFRICA								
Algeria	F	2	7	9	3	7	30	47
Egypt	F	3	5	8	4	5	34	23
Iran	F	4	6	11	10	5	42	36
Israel	I	3	3	7	4	4	19	46
Palestine	F	6	4	10	3	8	42	27
Tunisia	E	2	2	5	4	4	35	42
Average		4	5	8	5	6	34	37
SUB-SAHARAN AFRICA								
Angola	F	15	19	32	9	26	24	38
Botswana	F	17	12	28	6	16	33	48
Ethiopia	F	6	9	15	10	3	20	69
Ghana	F	15	23	37	38	16	28	51
Malawi	F	18	20	36	11	29	42	43
Namibia	E	11	7	18	3	12	37	37
Nigeria	F	22	14	35	16	8	35	53
South Africa	E	4	3	7	2	5	32	40
Uganda	F	10	28	36	31	26	46	42
Zambia	F	27	15	41	4	20	32	46
Average		15	15	28	13	16	33	47

Continued

TABLE 1.1 *(Continued)*

ASIA PACIFIC & SOUTH ASIA								
China	E	5	7	13	12	4	37	39
Japan	I	2	2	4	6	1	21	66
Republic of Korea	I	3	4	7	10	3	35	46
Malaysia	E	3	4	7	7	2	13	61
Pakistan	F	8	3	12	4	3	53	24
Singapore	I	8	4	12	3	4	15	54
Taiwan	I	3	4	8	10	6	18	43
Thailand	E	9	11	19	30	3	17	67
Average		5	5	10	10	3	26	50
EUROPEAN UNION								
Austria	I	7	3	10	8	4	11	38
Belgium	I	3	2	5	5	2	18	62
Denmark	I	3	2	5	3	1	8	71
Estonia	E	9	5	14	7	4	18	49
Finland	I	3	3	6	8	2	17	60
France	I	4	2	5	3	2	18	59
Germany	I	4	2	5	5	2	22	51
Greece	I	4	3	7	12	4	30	32
Hungary	E	6	4	9	8	4	31	35
Ireland	I	4	2	6	8	2	28	41
Italy	I	2	2	4	3	2	16	22
Latvia	E	9	5	13	8	3	25	46
Lithuania	E	3	4	7	8	2	25	51
Netherlands	I	4	6	10	9	2	8	66
Poland	E	5	5	9	6	4	41	30
Portugal	I	4	4	8	6	3	18	53
Romania	E	6	4	9	4	4	24	38
Slovakia	I	7	4	10	6	5	36	43
Slovenia	I	3	3	5	6	2	7	64
Spain	I	3	2	6	9	2	26	33
Sweden	I	5	2	6	5	2	7	49
UK	I	5	4	9	6	2	18	43
Average		5	3	8	7	3	21	47
NON-EUROPEAN UNION								
Bosnia and Herzegovina	E	5	3	8	6	7	58	20
Croatia	E	6	2	8	3	4	34	36
Macedonia	E	4	3	7	7	4	52	29
Norway	I	4	3	7	6	1	7	70
Russia	E	3	2	4	2	1	36	31
Switzerland	I	3	3	6	8	2	18	57
Turkey	E	7	5	12	9	5	31	55
Average		4	3	7	6	4	34	43
UNITED STATES								
USA	I	9	4	13	9	4	21	59

Source: *GEM 2012 Global Report*. http://www.gemconsortium.org/docs/download/2645

motives than those with necessity motivations. In contrast, the non-EU region, also with mainly efficiency-driven economies, reported almost equal levels of either motive.

Age Distribution

Economies in all geographic regions showed bell-shaped age distributions with the highest entrepreneurship rates generally occurring among 25- to 34-year-olds (Figure 1.2). High participation levels also occurred in the next oldest age group: 35–44 years. Together, these two age categories made up close to 50% or more of all entrepreneurs. In Chile, Republic of Korea, Singapore, Netherlands, UK, and the United States, the 35- to 44-year-olds had the highest level of participation in entrepreneurship among the age groups.

Entrepreneurship was prevalent among youth in the non-EU economies, where half of the entrepreneurs were between 18–34 years of age. China was also distinct in having a high proportion of young entrepreneurs, with 57% between 18 and 34 years of age, and less than one-quarter falling into the older age groups (45–64 years). In certain economies, there was a flattening out of the bell-shaped curve, where similar participation levels were reported across all or most of the age ranges. Examples of this pattern include Palestine, Japan, Pakistan, Hungary, and Bosnia/Herzegovina.

Gender Differences

GEM findings have consistently reported greater involvement in entrepreneurship among men than women in most economies. The ratio of male to female participation in early-stage entrepreneurial activity varied considerably across the sample (Figure 1.3). Participation among men and women was almost equal in most sub-Sahara Africa economies, while men were 2.8

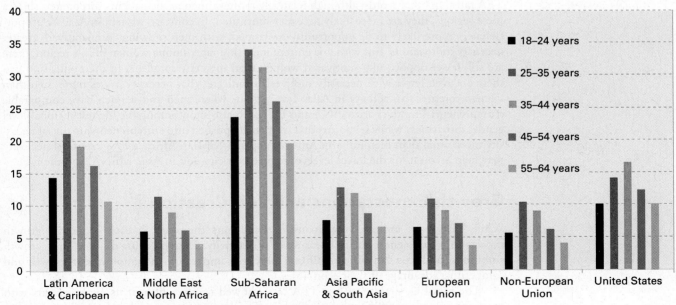

Source: GEM 2012 Global Report. http://www.gemconsortium.org/docs/download/2645

Figure 1.2

TEA by Age for Geographic Regions

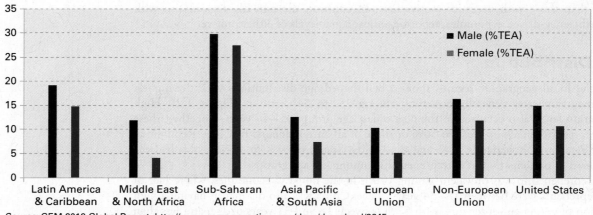

Source: GEM 2012 Global Report. http://www.gemconsortium.org/docs/download/2645

Figure 1.3

TEA by Gender for Geographic Regions

times more likely than women to start a business in the MENA region. In Egypt, Palestine, and Republic of Korea, less than one-fifth of all entrepreneurs were women. More notably, only 5% of the entrepreneurs in Pakistan were women. The only economies where female TEA rates were higher than male were in Ecuador and Panama in Latin America, Ghana and Nigeria in sub-Saharan Africa, and Thailand in Asia.

An analysis of opportunity and necessity motives shows that men in Latin America and sub-Saharan Africa are more likely opportunity-motivated, while women have higher necessity motives. This is interesting, given that these regions have fewer differences between the sexes in TEA rates. In other words, although relatively more women participate in entrepreneurship in these regions, they are more likely necessity-motivated. In contrast, women in Asia are proportionately more likely to be opportunity-motivated, with men showing comparatively greater necessity motivations. But with low entrepreneurship rates among women in this region, there are still fewer opportunity-motivated women than men entrepreneurs in the population; yet there are even fewer with necessity motives. It indicates that necessity drives more men than women to enter this activity in Asia. Two regions where men and women have comparable entrepreneurial motives are MENA and EU; both also show among the highest regional-level gender disparities. While it appears that women are pushed into entrepreneurship out of necessity more often than men in Latin America and sub-Saharan Africa, a lower sense of necessity may help account for the lower levels of female participation in Asia, MENA, and the EU.

Growth Expectations and Job Creation

While TEA rates indicate how many entrepreneurs there are in each economy, growth expectations represent a quality measure of this activity. Entrepreneurs differ in their growth ambitions, and this can have significant potential impact on the employment growth and competitive advantage of their economies.

The non-EU, despite its low TEA rate, showed nearly a fifth of its entrepreneurs with projected growth of 20 or more employees. The United States exhibited a high proportion of 20+ growth projections in addition to the highest TEA rate among the innovation-driven economies, demonstrating both the prevalence of entrepreneurship and its impact on the U.S. economy. Turkey, Latvia, Singapore, China, and Colombia also displayed both high TEA and high proportions of 20+ growth entrepreneurs relative to other economies in their regions.

We now look at the prevalence of high-growth expectations among both nascent entrepreneurs and owner-managers of baby businesses, as identified in GEM's Adult Population Surveys from the years 2004 to 2009.[87]

The GEM method enables the categorization of early-stage startup attempts according to their growth expectations. GEM asks all identified early-stage entrepreneurs how many employees they expect to have (other than the owners themselves) within five years' time. Out of every 10 early-stage entrepreneurs, seven expected some job creation. However, expectations of high growth are rare among nascent and new entrepreneurs. Only 14% of all those involved in startup attempts expected to create 20 or more jobs, while 44% expected to create five or more jobs.

High-growth entrepreneurs, also known as "gazelles," receive heightened attention from policymakers because their firms contribute a disproportionate share of all new jobs created by new firms.[88, 89] Figure 1.4 shows the prevalence rates of high-expectation entrepreneurial activity (HEA) in the working-age population.

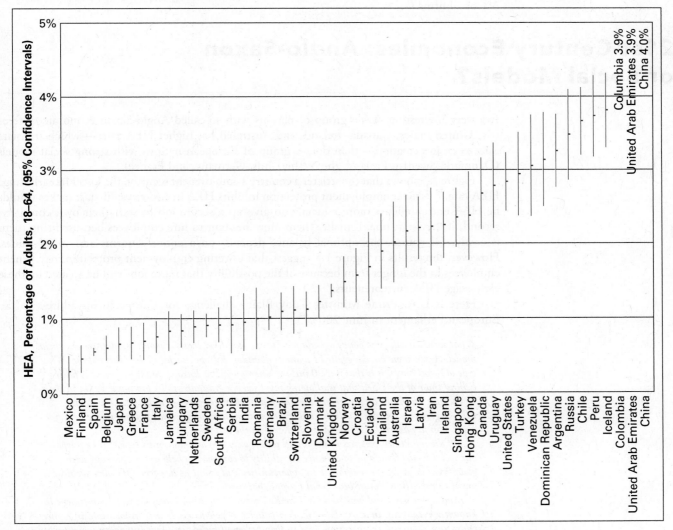

Source: GEM Adult Population Survey, 2004–2009.

Figure 1.4

Early-Stage HEA rates in 2004– 2009

Among high-income countries, the United Arab Emirates, Iceland, the United States, Canada, Singapore, Ireland, and Australia had the highest levels of HEA over the 2004–2009 period. The HEA rate for these countries is well over 1%. The lowest levels of HEA, at under 0.5%, occur in Spain, Belgium, Japan, and France. HEA rates can vary even among broadly similar high-income countries. Among the large European Union economies, the United Kingdom and Germany exhibit higher HEA rates than do France and Spain. In the Benelux countries, the Netherlands' rate is higher than Belgium's. In Scandinavia, Iceland was at the top on this measure, while Finland was at the bottom and Sweden, Denmark, and Norway were in the middle.

Although GEM data are for expected job creation, they are consistent with empirical studies of actual job creation. For instance, one study found that 4% of new firms in the United Kingdom created 50% of all jobs created by all new firms.[90] And another study reported that more than 70% of the employment growth in the United States came from only 3% of all firms.[91]

21st-Century Economies: Anglo-Saxon or Social Models?

It is very interesting that a group of nations with so-called Anglo-Saxon economic systems (the United States, Canada, Ireland, and Australia) has higher HEA rates—which translate into more job creation—than does a group of European nations with strong social models (Denmark, Sweden, Finland, the Netherlands, Germany, and France).

Figure 1.5 shows that the stricter a country's employment security, the lower its early-stage HEA rate.[92] Stricter employment protection inhibits HEA in two ways: First, it makes would-be HEA entrepreneurs more reluctant to give up a secure job to start their own company; second, if they start one, it makes them more hesitant to hire employees because firing them is costly. Of course, the optimal balance depends on a nation's norms and social values. However, the results in Figure 1.5 suggest that lowering employment protection may benefit employees in the longer term because of the possibility that more jobs will be created by these early-stage HEA entrepreneurs.

Here is U.K. Prime Minister Tony Blair's challenge for Europe in his address to the European Parliament in June 2005:[93]

> *What would a different policy agenda for Europe look like? First, it would modernize our social model. Again some have suggested I want to abandon Europe's social model. But tell me: What type of social model is it that has 20 million unemployed in Europe, productivity rates falling behind those of the USA; that is allowing more science graduates to be produced by India than by Europe; and that, on any relative index of a modern economy—skills, R&D, patents, IT—is going down, not up. India will expand its biotechnology sector fivefold in the next five years. China has trebled its spending on R&D in the last five.*
>
> *Of the top 20 universities in the world today, only two are now in Europe.[94] The purpose of our social model should be to enhance our ability to compete, to help our people cope with globalization, to let them embrace its opportunities and avoid its dangers. Of course we need a social Europe. But it must be a social Europe that works.*
>
> *And we've been told how to do it. The Kok report[95] in 2004 shows the way. Investment in knowledge, in skills, in active labor market policies, in science parks and innovation, in higher education, in urban regeneration, and in help for small businesses. This is modern social policy, not regulation and job protection that may save some jobs for a time at the expense of many jobs in the future.*

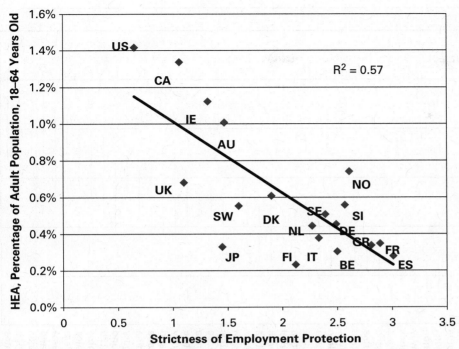

Source: GEM Adult Population Survey, 2004–2009; Office of Economic Cooperation and Development, Employment Strictness Data, 2004.

Figure 1.5

Strictness of employment protection and early-stage HEA rates in 2004– 2009

Early in 2006, Dominique de Villepin, France's prime minister, proposed legislation aimed at cutting chronic youth unemployment by easing rigid labor laws that make it very difficult to fire employees. Students rose up all over France to protest the proposed changes and shut down classes at half of France's 84 state-run universities in the biggest student uprising since 1968 (when student riots forced the De Gaulle government to hold an election). The students' attitude in 2006 was summed up by these comments:[96]

> Elodie, 21, a sociology student, said: "The issues are different from those our parents were protesting about. We are marching for the right to proper jobs."
> Romain, 20, a communications student, said: "We don't want the Anglo-Saxon economic model here."

One survey discovered that the top career goal of three-quarters of young French people was to be a civil servant.[97] This is in stark contrast to the United States, where the majority of young people want to be an entrepreneur at some time during their career.[98] But it does not follow that young people in France and other European countries with social models are more likely than their U.S. counterparts to become engaged in entrepreneurial activities with a social goal. On the contrary, when GEM made its first comprehensive study of social entrepreneurship in 2009, European nations had a lower level of early-stage social entrepreneurial activity (SEA) than did the United States (see Figure 1.6).

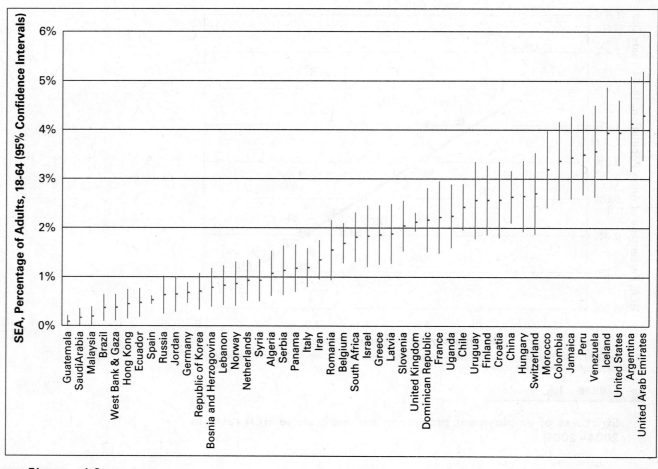

Figure 1.6

Early-Stage SEA Rates by Country, 2009

CONCLUSION

Entrepreneurial activity in the United States now accounts for much of the nation's prosperity and its competitiveness in the global economy. The disappearance of "old" jobs, particularly in mature manufacturing industries, and their replacement by "new" jobs, especially in service and knowledge-based industries, is disconcerting to workers whose jobs are threatened. But society has to accept *churning*—the creation of new enterprises and the destruction of obsolete ones—because it gives the U.S. economy its vitality.

The entrepreneurial framework includes factors such as availability of finance, government policies and programs designed to support startups, R&D transfer, physical and human infrastructure, general education, specific education and training for entrepreneurship, social and cultural norms, and internal market openness. All of these factors combined determine the degree of entrepreneurial activity in a nation, or for that matter in a region within a nation. Among large innovation-driven economies, the United States sets the entrepreneurial benchmark. What's more, the so-called Anglo-Saxon economic systems seem to engender more entrepreneurial activity than systems dominated by the social model, which is the prevalent system in much of continental Europe. The question remains: How do both Anglo-Saxon and social economies find an entrepreneurial path that leads them out of the economic crisis?

In this chapter, we have looked at the importance of entrepreneurship to national economies. In the following chapters, we will look at the specifics of how entrepreneurs start and grow their new ventures.

YOUR OPPORTUNITY JOURNAL

We are excited that you are exploring an entrepreneurial journey, one that may lead you to launch a business while in college, after graduation, or at some future point in your life. We know that all great entrepreneurs are avid readers and thinkers, and as such, we encourage you to capture some of your thoughts as you read this book. These thoughts may focus on a new venture that you are interested in creating, or they may focus more on your entrepreneurial career plan. In either event, we will close each chapter with space for you to reflect on what it means to you and your potential venture.

Reflection Point	Your Thoughts...
1. What world-changing industries or opportunities do you see developing over the next five to 10 years?	
2. What innovations or new technologies will drive these world-changing opportunities?	
3. Which regions of the world have the greatest potential for developing these opportunities? Which are you most interested in?	
4. What skills do you need to develop to take advantage of these opportunities?	

WEB EXERCISE

What do you think will be the next major innovation (like, e.g., the Internet) that changes the way we live, work, and play? Search the Web to identify trends, statistics, and other evidence to support your insight. (*Hint*: Venture capitalists in the United States have a knack for spotting emergent industries.)

NOTES

[1] Estimate based on GEM Adult Population Surveys. www.gemconsortium.org.

[2] Small Business Administration. *Frequently Asked Questions*. www.sba.gov/advo.

[3] Schumpeter, J. A. *The Theory of Economic Development*. Cambridge, MA: Harvard University Press. 1934. (This book was originally published in German in 1911.)

[4] Maddison, A. *Phases of Capitalist Development.* New York: Oxford University Press. 1989. Baumol, W. J. Entrepreneurship and a Century of Growth. *Journal of Business Venturing*, 1(2): 141–145. 1986.

[5] SBA Office of Advocacy. *Frequently Asked Questions.* September 2009. www.sba.govg/advo.

[6] For the Small Business Administration definitions of *small business* refer to www.sba.gov/gopher/Financial-Assistance/Defin/defi4.txt.

[7] This is based on GDPs and actual currency exchange rates in 2012.

[8] Small Business Administration. *Frequently Asked Questions.* http://web.sba.gov/faqs/faqindex.cfm?areaID = 24.

[9] www.nvca.org/pdf/VentureImpact2004.pdf based on the data from National Science Foundation (NSF), *R&D in Industry: 1991–2000*, Tables A3 and A4; NSF, *Preliminary Release, 2001 and 2002*, Tables A3 and A4; NSF, *Infobrief: U.S. R&D Projected to Have Grown Marginally in 2003*.

[10] *The Shape of Small Business.* www.nfib.com/object/PolicyGuide2.html.

[11] Steven H. Hipple. Self-employment in the United States. *Monthly Labor Review*, September 2010, p. 17.

[12] It is impossible to establish a precise upper limit because many new ventures are abandoned very soon after they are started and never get entered into any data set that tracks startups.

[13] www.forbes.com/businesswire/feeds/businesswire/2005/07/21/businesswire20050721005296r1.html.

[14] Kirchhoff, Bruce A. *Entrepreneurship and Dynamic Capitalism.* Westport, CT: Praeger. 1994.

[15] Nucci, A. The Demography of Business Closings. *Small Business Economics*, 12: 25–39. 1999.

[16] *The Shape of Small Business.* www.nfib.com/object/PolicyGuide2.html.

[17] Dennis, W. J., Jr.,, and Fernald, L. W., Jr., The Chances of Financial Success (and Loss) from Small Business Ownership. *Entrepreneurship Theory and Practice*, 1: 75–83. 2002.

[18] *The Shape of Small Business.* www.nfib.com/object/PolicyGuide2.html. The net business formation index was discontinued in 1995 when one of its two components was no longer available.

[19] Macrae, N. The Coming Entrepreneurial Revolution. *The Economist. December* 15, 1976.

[20] Birch, David L. *Job Creation in America: How Our Smallest Companies Put the Most People to Work.* New York: Free Press. 1978.

[21] For example: Acs, Z. *The New American Evolution.* Washington, DC: U.S. Small Business Administration, Office of Economic Research. June 1998. Kirchhoff, Bruce A. *Entrepreneurship and Dynamic Capitalism.* Westport, CT: Praeger. 1994.

[22] At one point, General Motors was the largest corporation ever to exist in the United States in terms of its revenues as a percentage of GDP. In 1953, Charles Erwin Wilson, then GM's president, was named by President Eisenhower as secretary of defense. When he was asked, during the hearings before the Senate Armed Services Committee, if as secretary of defense he could make a decision adverse to the interests of General Motors, Wilson answered affirmatively but added that he could not conceive of such a situation "because for years I thought what was good for the country was good for General Motors and vice versa." Later this statement was often garbled when quoted, suggesting that Wilson had said simply, "What's good for General Motors is good for the country." At the time, GM was one of the largest employers in the world—only Soviet state industries employed more people. http://en.wikipedia.org/wiki/Charles_Erwin_Wilson.

[23] "The observation made in 1965 by Gordon Moore, co-founder of Intel, that the number of transistors per square inch on integrated circuits had doubled every year

since the integrated circuit was invented. Moore predicted that this trend would continue for the foreseeable future. In subsequent years, the pace slowed down a bit, but density has doubled approximately every 18 months, and this is the current definition of Moore's Law. Most experts, including Moore himself, expect Moore's Law to hold for at least another two decades." *Source* www.webopedia.com/TERM/M/Moores_Law.html.

[24] Working independently and unaware of each other's activity, Jack Kilby at Texas Instruments and Robert Noyce at Fairchild Semiconductor Corporation invented almost identical integrated circuits at the same time. "In 1959 both parties applied for patents. Jack Kilby and Texas Instruments received U.S. patent #3,138,743 for miniaturized electronic circuits. Robert Noyce and the Fairchild Semiconductor Corporation received U.S. patent #2,981,877 for a silicon-based integrated circuit. The two companies wisely decided to cross license their technologies after several years of legal battles, creating a global market now worth about $1 trillion a year." *Source* http://inventors.about.com/library/weekly/aa080498.htm.

[25] The first personal computers were actually called microcomputers. The phrase "personal computer" was common currency before 1981 and was used as early as 1972 to characterize Xerox PARC's Alto. However, due to the success of the IBM PC, what had been a generic term came to mean specifically a microcomputer compatible with IBM's specification. *Source* http://en.wikipedia.org/wiki/Ibm 5150.

[26] The top 25 in descending order are the Internet, cell phone, personal computer, fiber optics, email, commercialized GPS, portable computers, memory storage disks, consumer-level digital cameras, radio frequency ID tags, MEMS, DNA fingerprinting, air bags, ATMs, advanced batteries, hybrid cars, OLEDs, display panels, HDTVs, space shuttles, nanotechnology, flash memory, voice mail, modern hearing aids, and short-range high-frequency radio. *Source* www.cnn.com/

2005/TECH/01/03/cnn25.top25.innovations.

[27] www.fedex.com/us/about/today/history.

[28] http://en.wikipedia.org/wiki/Airline_De regulation_Act.

[29] Jordan, W. A. *Airline Entry Following U.S. Deregulation: The Definitive List of Startup Passenger Airlines, 1979–2003.* www.trforum.org/forum/getpaper.php?id = 22&PHPSESSID = 119446d6d13ce93d 6c6aea3df05010ce.

[30] www.tsha.utexas.edu/handbook/online/articles/SS/eps1_print.html.

[31] Bygrave, W. D., and Timmons, J. A. *Venture Capital at the Crossroads.* Boston: Harvard Business School Press. 1992.

[32] Biotechnology in the USA: Market Research Report. NAICS NN001. August 2012. www.ibisworld.com/industry/default.aspx?indid=2001

[33] Rogers, E. M., and Larsen, J. K. *Silicon Valley Fever: Growth of High-Technology Culture.* New York: Basic Books. 1984.

[34] Bush, Vannevar. As We May Think. *The Atlantic Monthly.* July 1945.

[35] Nelson, Ted. The Story So Far. *Ted Nelson Newsletter*, No. 3. October 1994.

[36] www.computerhistory.org/exhibits/internet_history/Internet_history_80s.html.

[37] *Tim Berners-Lee, Inventor of the World Wide Web, Knighted by Her Majesty Queen Elizabeth II.* www.w3.org/2004/07/tim bl_knighted.

[38] *New Scientist Magazine.* December 17, 1994.

[39] www.smartcomputing.com/editorial/dictionary/detail.asp?DicID = 17855.

[40] Lashinsky, Adam. Remembering Netscape: The Birth of the Web. www.fortune.com/fortune/print/0,15935,1081456,00.html.

[41] Ibid.

[42] Gevirtz, D. *The Entrepreneurs: Innovation in American Business.* New York: Penguin Books. 1985. p. 30.

[43] *Impact: The Economic Importance of Venture Capital-Backed Companies to the U.S.*

Economy. National Venture Capital Association. 2010.

44 Classic venture capital is money invested privately in seed, startup, expansion, and late-stage companies. The term *classic* is used to distinguish it from money invested privately in acquisitions, buyouts, mergers, and reorganizations.

45 www.forbes.com/2001/02/06/0207VC .html.

46 Friedman, T. L. *The World Is Flat.* New York, NY: Farrar, Straus and Giroux. 2005.

47 Fitzgerald, Mark. How Did Newspapers Get in This Pickle? *Editor & Publisher. March* 18, 2009. www.editorandpublisher .com/eandp/columns/newspaperbeat_dis play.jsp?vnu_content_id = 1003952561. And www.techdirt.com/articles/201209 16/14454920395/newspaper-ad-revenue -fell-off-quite-cliff-now-par-with-1950- revenue.shtml

48 World Bank, *World Development Indicators.* www.google.com/search?hl = en& source = hp&q = Internet + users + united + states&aq = 2&oq = Internet + users + &aqi = g10.

49 http://thehill.com/blogs/blog-briefing- room/news/59523-obama-open-to- newspaper-bailout-bill.

50 Whyte, W. *The Organization Man.* New York: Simon & Schuster. 1956.

51 Postrel, V. How Has "The Organization Man" changed? *The New York Times. January* 17, 1999.

52 Galbraith, J. K. *The New Industrial State.* Boston: Houghton Mifflin. 1967.

53 Servan-Schreiber, J. J. *The American Challenge.* New York: Scribner. 1968.

54 Macrae, Norman. *We're All Entrepreneurial Now-17 April 1982.* www. normanmacrae.com/intrapre-neur.html.

55 For example, a mid-1980s study by Calvin Kent of the content of popular principles of economics "revealed that entrepreneurship was either neglected, improperly presented, or only partially covered." Kent, C. A., and Rushing, F. W. Coverage of Entrepreneurship in Principles of Economics Textbooks: An Update. *Journal of Economics Education* 20, 184–189. Spring 1999.

56 Schumpeter, J. A. *Capitalism, Socialism, and Democracy.* Third edition. New York: Harper Torchbooks. 1950. (Originally published in 1942).

57 Schumpeter, J. A. *The Theory of Economic Development.* Cambridge, MA: Harvard University Press. 1934. Reprinted edition, Cambridge, MA: Harvard University Press, 1949.

58 Blau, D. M. A Time-Series Analysis of Self-Employment in the United States. *Journal of Political Economy,* 95: 445–467. 1987. Evans, D., and Leighton, L. S. The Determinants of Changes in U.S. Self-Employment. *Small Business Economics,* 1(2): 111–120. 1987.

59 Acs, Z. J., Arenius, P., Hay, M., and Minniti, M. *The Global Entrepreneurship Monitor: 2004 Executive Report.* www.gemconsortium.org.

60 This is excerpted from Reynolds, P. D., Hay, M., Bygrave, W. D., Camp, S. M., and Autio, E. *Global Entrepreneurship Monitor: 2000 Executive Report.* www.gemconsortium.org.

61 Ralph Nader's best-selling book *Unsafe at Any Speed: The Designed-In Dangers of the American Automobile,* published in 1965, claimed that automobile manufacturers were ignoring safety features, like seat belts, and were reluctant to spend money on improving safety.

62 *George Gendron on the State of Entrepreneurship.* December 2002. www. pioneerentrepreneurs.net/bigidea_gen dron.php.

63 Bygrave, W. D., and Timmons, J. A. *Venture Capital at the Crossroads.* Boston: Harvard Business School Press. 1992.

64 Statement of Edsel M. Brown Jr. Assistant Director Office of Technology U.S. Small Business Administration Before the House Committee on Small Business United States House of Representatives April 22, 2009.

www.house.gov/smbiz/hearings/hearing-4-22-09-technology-economic-recovery/Brown.pdf.

65 Nelson, L. The Rise of Intellectual Property Protection in the American University. *Science*, 279 (5356): 1460–1461. 1998. www.sciencemag.org/cgi/content/full/279/5356/1460.

66 Morris. D. Who Gets the Fruits of Public R&D? *Minneapolis Star Tribune*. November 28, 2004. www.ilsr.org/columns/2004/112804.html.

67 Innovation's Golden Goose. *The Economist*. December 12, 2002.

68 Statement of Senator Birch Bayh to the National Institutes of Health. May 25, 2004. http://ott.od.nih.gov/Meeting/Senator-Birch-Bayh.pdf.

69 www.nal.usda.gov/ttic/guide.htm.

70 Singletary, M. How to Get the Most Bang from eBay. *Maine Sunday Telegram*. August 7, 2005.

71 Wiggins, J., and Gibson, D. V. Overview of US Incubators and the Case of the Austin Technology Incubator. *International Journal of Entrepreneurship and Innovation Management*. 3(1/2): 56–66. 2003. www.ic2.org/publications/Incubator%20Paper%20with%20Joel.pdf.

72 National Business Incubation Association, *Business Incubation Frequently Asked Questions*. www.nbia.org/resource_library/faq/index.php#3.

73 Ibid.

74 *George Gendron on the State of Entrepreneurship*. December 2002. www.pioneerentrepreneurs.net/bigidea_gendron.php.

75 Lange, J., Mollov, A., Pearlmuttter, M., Singh, S., and Bygrave, W. *Pre-Startup Formal Business Plans and Post-Startup Performance: A Study of 116 New Ventures*. Presented at the Babson Kauffman Entrepreneurship Research Conference, Babson College. June 2005.

76 Moore, G. E. The Accidental Entrepreneur. Originally published in *Engineering & Science* (California Institute of Technology), 57(4): 23–30. Summer 1994. http://nobelprize.org/physics/articles/moore.

77 Boylan, M. *What We Know and Don't Know About Venture Capital*. American Economic Association Meeting, December 28, 1981, and National Economist Club, January 19, 1982.

78 *National Venture Capital Association Yearbook, 2013*.

79 Bygrave, W. D. *Global Entrepreneur-ship Monitor*: 2004 *Financing Report* (with Steve Hunt). www.gemconsortium.org.

80 www.sba.gov/advo/research/dyn_b_d8902.pdf.

81 Rifkin, G., and Harrar, G. *The Ultimate Entrepreneur: The Story of Ken Olsen and Digital Equipment Corporation*. Chicago, IL: Contemporary Books. 1998.

82 Lichtenstein, N. Is Walmart Good for America? *PBS Frontline*. June 9, 2004. www.pbs.org/wgbh/pages/frontline/shows/walmart/interviews/lichtenstein.html.

83 www.news.cornell.edu/stories/April05/HEC.05.cover.html.

84 www.skype.com.

85 Autio, E. *Global Entrepreneurship Monitor: GEM-Mazars Special Report on High-Expectation Entrepreneurship*. 2005. www.gemconsortium.org.

86 Excerpted from GEM global reports and special reports. www.gemconsortium.org.

87 This section contains excerpts from Bosma, N., and Levie, J. *Global Entrepreneurship Monitor: 2009 Executive Report*. www.gemconsortium.org.

88 Storey, D. *Understanding the Small Business Sector*. London: Routledge. 1994.

89 Birch, D. *Who Is Creating Jobs?* Cambridge, MA: Cognetics. 1995.

90 Storey, D. *Understanding the Small Business Sector*. London: Routledge. 1994.

91 Birch, D. *Who Is Creating Jobs?* Cambridge, MA: Cognetics. 1995.

[92] The same relationship has also been found in regression analyses, controlling for individual-level and regional-level determinants of high-expectation entrepreneurship. See Bosma, N., and Levie, J. *Global Entrepreneurship Monitor: 2009 Executive Report.* www.gemconsortium.org.

[93] Address to the EU Parliament by Prime Minister Blair. June 23, 2005. http://news.bbc.co.uk/1/hi/uk_politics/4122288.stm.

[94] The brains business. *The Economist,* September 8, 2005. www.economist.com/surveys/displaystory.cfm?story_id = 4339960

[95] Kok, Wim. *Facing the Challenge: The Lisbon Strategy for Growth and Employment.* Report from the High Level Group chaired by Wim Kok. November 2004. http://europa.eu.int/growthandjobs/pdf/kok_report_en.pdf.

[96] Randall, Colin. Students March in Paris as the Unrest Spreads. March 15, 2006. www.telegraph.co.uk/news/worldnews/europe/france/1513073/students-march-in-paris-as-the-unvest-spreads.html.

[97] Harriss, J. A. Celebrating 70 Years of Socialism. *The American Spectator,* 39(3): 53. April 2006.

[98] Several studies have been done on the interests that young people have in entrepreneurship. For example, in their book *The E Generation: Prepared for the Entrepreneurial Economy,* Marilyn Kourilsky and William Walstad (Kendall/Hunt Publishing, Dubuque, Iowa, 2000) explain that youth are overwhelmingly interested in entrepreneurship. In fact, they found that 6 out of 10 young people aspire to start a business of their own. The Gallup Organization, in conjunction with the Kauffman Foundation, conducted the first national poll on entrepreneurship. What they found was that 70% of students polled wanted to start their own business. www.entre-ed.org/testimony.htm.

America rules   **1**
The world's top universities*

1	Harvard University	America
2	Stanford University	America
3	University of Cambridge	Britain
4	University of California (*Berkeley*)	America
5	Massachusetts Institute of Technology	America
6	California Institute of Technology	America
7	Princeton University	America
8	University of Oxford	Britain
9	Columbia University	America
10	University of Chicago	America
11	Yale University	America
12	Cornell University	America
13	University of California (*San Diego*)	America
14	Tokyo University	Japan
15	University of Pennsylvania	America
16	University of California (*Los Angeles*)	America
17	University of California (*San Francisco*)	America
18	University of Wisconsin (*Madison*)	America
19	University of Michigan (*Ann Arbor*)	America
20	University of Washington (*Seattle*)	America

* Ranked by a mixture of indicators of academic and research performance, including Nobel prizes and articles in respected publications

Source: Jiao Tong University, Shanghai.

Alison Barnard

Having spent her Saturday morning redesigning window displays, folding inventory, and following up with a supplier who seemed disinclined to take back an entire shipment she felt was unacceptable, Alison Barnard, 27, was finally settled at her desk in the corner—fully intending to make some progress on her growing management task list. Chief among those neglected missions was getting up to speed on her software system for monitoring sales and inventory.

In-jean-ius, her upscale "jeans and t-shirt" boutique in Boston's North End, was attracting professional and wealthy women from Maine to Rhode Island. As one of many satisfied customers wrote, "Alison has an uncanny ability to match up the right person with the perfect pair of jeans. If you have ever gone 'jean shopping' you know that that is not an easy thing to do! Experience In-jean-ius for yourself. You won't shop for jeans anywhere else again."

March 2006. Alison looked up from her work with a weary smile.

> *Open just over six months, and actuals are tracking nearly twice my projections....*

As it had from the very beginning, running her hit venture continued to consume nearly every waking hour. The creative, high-energy founder was far less concerned with burning out than with having the day-to-day concerns usurp her ability to plan and manage for growth. And with only one full-time employee—not yet fully trained—Alison couldn't expect much relief anytime soon.

Her attention was suddenly drawn to an exchange between her salesperson and a well-dressed, middle-aged woman who was favoring a sleek pair of low rises. From where she sat, Alison could see that the woman was built for something a bit less daring. When the associate began fishing for the correct size in that style, Alison left her desk (and her task list) to steer the sale toward a more conservative brand that would ultimately prove to offer the best fit. Another satisfied customer....

Alison Barnard: Shopper

Like many rural-suburban American teens, young Alison Barnard had been an avid shopper. But there was something more. The daughter of a serial entrepreneur and an enterprising mother, she had developed an eye for opportunity and value-add that she ceaselessly trained on the business of creating a unique upscale shopping experience: trends, service, selection, presentation, decor. Despite her keen interest in retailing, she headed off for college with a more conservative career track in mind:

> *I really thought I wanted to be in brand management, marketing, or retail consulting. I figured that someday I would have a store but thought it might be something I'd do when I retired, like you kind of hung out in your store.*
>
> *But I had all of these ideas. I like clothing, I like the shopping experience, and I like dealing with people. One idea was to have an all-black store because black apparel is such a staple for any woman's wardrobe.*

In May 2002, Alison received her undergraduate degree in business from the University of Richmond. Back in the Boston area, her first job was with a dot-com startup. She left there for an interesting opportunity with another high-potential venture. While the work environment there was most definitely not for her, that "mistake" would have a major impact on her career trajectory.

Catalysts

Hired as part of the seminar development team at a medical device company in Cambridge, Massachusetts, Alison quickly discovered that her talents weren't exactly appreciated:

> *They were part of this old boy network that really looked down on females. They told me, for example, that I needed to cover on Thursdays for the receptionist when she went to lunch. Swell. I hated that place, and I immediately began interviewing for something better.*
>
> *At one point, I went on a job interview, and since my boss approved of higher education, I told her I had gone to Babson College to investigate their MBA program. When I checked into it in order to support my little lie, I found out that Babson had a one-year program that looked really interesting; you're there, you're focused and doing it, and then you're out.*

Alison began the One-Year MBA at Babson in the spring of 2003. Since she was still brainstorming retail store concepts with anyone who would engage, her mom's hairdresser suggested that as a next step she ought to get some floor time in the real world. That summer Alison started work as a part-timer at an upscale boutique near Boston. Although she still had no immediate plans to develop a new venture, her MBA studies melded well with her exposure to retailing:

> *I quickly realized that my first concept about an all-black store was a bad idea. Women buy black, but they don't shop for it. They'll even go into a store and say they want anything but black—because they have too much black in their wardrobe. But then in the end, they'll buy something black.*
>
> *At the time, I was really getting into jeans myself. At Babson, I wore jeans and a t-shirt every day. My first pair was Sevens, one of the early entrants into what I would call the premium denim revolution. Jeans are no longer just weekend wear; they are worn in the workplace and for going out. Premium denim has become a fashion staple, and women now have an average of about eight pairs of jeans in their wardrobe.*
>
> *So an all-jeans store became sort of my fun idea—something I thought would be just another idea that would be passed by. Still, my concept was interesting enough to attract a team in class to do the business plan.*

Realizations

Nothing Alison and her team members discovered in their research surprised her in the least (see Exhibit 1.1). When asked what pain point she expected her store to relieve, she didn't hesitate a moment:

> *Women's point of pain is themselves. The reality is that every female hates herself in some sort of way. And if she doesn't like something about her body, jeans can bring out the worst qualities. But they can also make you look great if they fit right.*
>
> *There are some decent stores in the area that sell premium jeans (see Exhibit 1.2), but they all forget to mention the fact that fit is by far a woman's number one concern when searching for jeans. Women are not brand loyal; they are fit loyal.*

When she graduated in the spring of 2004, Alison was offered an opportunity to learn even more:

> *The woman who was managing the boutique was going on maternity leave starting in the fall. The partners knew I wanted to open a store someday and they said that they would train me and help me out until she returned in the spring of 2005.*

EXHIBIT 1.1	Research Findings

What Women Want: Survey Results

We conducted primary research through a survey of 90 women in the Boston area to find out their jean-buying habits, including number of jeans owned, where they purchase their jeans, brands they are loyal to, and what they would like to see in a jean store. The complete results can be found in Exhibit 1.2.

The survey conducted to extract the jean-purchasing behaviors of 90 females aged 21–35 reveals the following:

- Women are willing to spend money for jeans

  - 28% $25-$50
  - 16% $51–$75
  - 14% $76–$85
  - 17% $86-$100
  - 16% $101–$130
  - 9% $130+

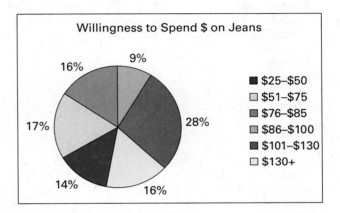

- Fit matters and influences where and which brands women purchase

  - 86.7% of woman said their one reason for shopping at certain stores was that these stores carried jeans that fit them
  - Brand preference is based on fit

- 82% of women say they are not loyal to one brand of jean. Woman need more....

  - More selection → 49.4% want more options
  - More information → so many jean brands and styles and so little time
  - More help → make the process less time consuming, less of a hassle

In addition, open-ended questions regarding what they dislike about the jean-buying process and what they would like to see in a new jean store environment revealed the following:

- Overall, women dislike the jean-buying process, even though they enjoy buying a new pair of jeans.

- Disorganization of the store and inconsistency of jean sizes by brands made woman want to see more sales help, which was lacking in the stores they currently frequent for jean buying.

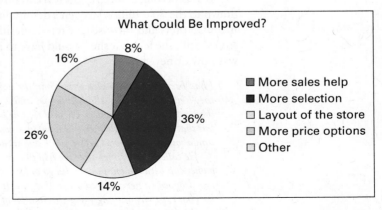

EXHIBIT 1.2	Premium Jean Stores in Eastern Massachusetts					
Store	Private Label	Trendy Jean Brands	Jean Expertise	Knowledgeable Customer Service	Welcome Atmosphere	Large Selection of Brands
Jean Therapy		X	X	X		
The National Jean Co.		X		X		X
Banana Republic	X					
Express	X					
Riccardi		X				X
Diesel	X		X	X		
Intermix		X			X	
Gap	X					
Mudo		X	X	X		
Lucky Brand	X					
Jasmine Sola*		X			X	X
Jeans Addiction		X		X		X

*Luciano Manganella, who founded this upscale boutique in Harvard Square in 1970, four years after emigrating from Italy, sold Jasmine Sola in the summer of 2005 to the nearly national 500-store New York & Co. This move, Manganella said, was the only way he could expand beyond his present 15 stores to an expected 25 stores—all on the East Coast—by the end of 2006. The undisclosed amount of the sale was estimated to be in excess of $20 million.

Alison accepted their offer. She soon discovered, however, that they would be delivering far less than they promised:

> *I never got anything we had agreed to, including health insurance or training of any kind. I did learn how to handle receivables, pricing, dating, and ordering, but I figured out that stuff on my own by examining the invoices and checking in the orders.*

It wasn't long before Alison was certain that she could run a shop of her own. She was still drawn to the $6.3 billion women's denim market, a highly fragmented space with hundreds of manufacturers and inconsistent retail offerings, from boutiques, chain stores, and department stores. Still, she felt that she "would have to jump on it right away before anyone else did"—it was now or never:

> *I had been keeping my idea secret from the store owners because I didn't trust them at all. Sure, they liked me, but they also had money and resources. That summer, I was attending a fashion show with one of the owners. He said that he had always wanted to open a jeans and t-shirt store but that his business partner—a woman—wasn't interested in the concept. At that point, I told him about my idea, and before you know it, we were talking about going into business together.*
>
> *He called a few times after the trip to talk it over. We never touched on details like money or ownership breakdown, but we did go to look at a spot in Wellesley [Massachusetts]. But then he just dropped it; never talked about it again. It was as if we had never had a conversation about it! That's the sort of thing you get from a lot of people in this industry.*
>
> *But how was I going to do it alone? Where was I going to get the money?*

Commitments

Based on her projections (see Exhibit 1.3), Alison expected her retail store would have first-year sales of just over $375,000. She had also calculated that startup costs, including build-out

EXHIBIT 1.3	Five-Year Projections, Income Statement				
Sales	**Year 1**	**Year 2**	**Year 3**	**Year 4**	**Year 5**
Jeans					
Unit Sales	1,635	1,962	2,315	2,547	2,801
Average Price	135	142	149	156	164
	220,725	278,604	344,935	397,332	459,364
Tops					
Unit Sales	2,453	3,434	4,120	4,862	5,737
Average Price	54	40	42	45	48
	132,462	137,360	173,040	218,790	275,376
Accessories					
Unit Sales	550	633	791	988	1,235
Average Price	45	45	50	50	55
	24,750	28,485	39,550	49,400	67,925
Total Sales	**377,937**	**444,449**	**557,525**	**665,522**	**802,665**
Cost of Sales					
Jeans	94,912	119,589	148,171	171,137	197,663
Tops	58,860	61,803	79,108	97,237	126,313
Accessories	11,550	13,283	12,452	15,565	19,457
Total Cost of Sales	165,322	194,675	239,731	283,939	343,433
Sales Expenses					
Credit Card Commissions	10,222	12,000	14,737	17,482	21,186
Discounts & Promos	2,759	3,476	4,307	4,975	5,746
Returns	14,031	16,470	20,228	23,995	29,078
Damage & Theft	12,026	14,117	17,338	20,567	24,924
Total Sales Expenses	39,038	46,063	56,610	67,019	80,934
Gross Margin	**173,577**	**203,711**	**261,184**	**314,564**	**378,298**
Buying Expenses Incl Travel	2,400	3,600	4,000	4,200	4,400
Administration					
Rent	17,500	31,200	32,400	33,600	34,800
Staff Salaries & Benefits	24,960	31,200	33,600	33,600	33,600
Staff Payroll Taxes	7,488	9,360	10,080	10,080	10,080
Management Salaries	51,996	52,800	55,000	60,000	65,000
Management Payroll Taxes	15,439	15,840	15,840	15,840	15,840
Health Insurance	3,000	3,000	3,000	3,000	3,000
Interest	900	1,200	1,040	880	720
Communications & Media	3,300	3,300	3,300	3,300	3,300
Professional Fees	4,308	4,308	4,308	4,308	4,308
Depreciation	12,266	13,381	13,381	13,381	13,381
Insurance	2,880	2,880	2,880	2,880	2,880
Utilities (Electric & Gas)	4,200	4,200	4,200	4,200	4,200
	148,237	172,669	179,029	185,069	191,109
Total Expenses	**150,637**	**176,269**	**183,029**	**189,269**	**195,509**
Pretax Profit	22,940	27,442	78,155	125,295	182,789
Net Profit	**14,844**	**17,425**	**47,914**	**76,265**	**110,825**

(Continued)

EXHIBIT 1.3 (Continued)					
Sales	**Year 1**	**Year 2**	**Year 3**	**Year 4**	**Year 5**
Beginning Cash	125,000	19,077	47,883	125,561	235,571
Inflows					
Sales	377,937	444,449	557,525	665,522	802,665
Depreciations	12,233	13,381	13,381	13,381	13,381
Outflows					
Cost of Sales	(165,322)	(194,675)	(239,731)	(283,939)	(343,333)
Sales Expenses	(39,038)	(46,063)	(56,610)	(67,018)	(80,934)
Marketing Expenses	(2,400)	(3,600)	(4,000)	(4,200)	(4,400)
Admin. Expenses	(148,237)	(172,669)	(179,029)	(185,069)	(191,109)
Note Payment	(20)	(2,000)	(2,000)	(2,000)	(2,000)
Taxes	(8,096)	(10,017)	(30,798)	(49,030)	(71,964)
Pre-opening & Build-Out	(58,000)				
Opening Inventory	(75,000)				
Increase in A/P			18,940	22,364	26,990
Net (Outflow) Inflow	(105,923)	28,806	77,678	110,010	149,296
Ending Cash Balance	19,077	47,883	125,561	235,571	384,867

and inventory, would be in the range of $125,000. She was confident that she could attract investors, but first she wanted to secure a location that would be acceptable to what she was sure would be her toughest constituency:

> Fashion denim manufacturers are represented by showrooms in New York City and in LA [Los Angeles]. They are very committed to their brands—and very particular about whom they will sell to. To avoid saturation, they won't sell to a store that is too close to another client, and they will even shut off an established shop that locates a new store too close to another buyer. Territory protection is a great asset for existing stores, but it makes it very hard to find locations that have the right customer traffic and are not in conflict with existing vendors.

Alison's boyfriend, Bryan, was active in the Boston real estate market. On weekends, Alison often accompanied him as he made the rounds to various properties he was managing. One icy morning in early 2005, Alison fell for a corner location in the North End:

> This place was a bit removed from the busiest section of Hanover Street, but the outside was SO nice; all dark wood, newly redone. I had Bryan call the number because as a real estate agent, I knew they would take him seriously. He set up a meeting with the landlord—a top neurosurgeon who owned the building as an investment. He had already denied seven previous proposals, but said he liked mine a lot.

Soon, they were talking hard numbers:

> I learned a lot in negotiating with him because he had a huge ego—just like a lot of good surgeons do. I had to figure out how to make him feel he was still getting something out of it. He was also getting stuck on little details. For example, he wanted to control my window displays and be able to go to arbitration over it.

And the space may have been beautiful on the outside, but the inside was unbelievably awful. It was scary. It needed new floors, new ceilings, new walls, and a new heating system.

In late February, Alison signed a three-year lease that included a few months of free rent—she now had until September. All along, her father had felt strongly that she should have lined up the capital first:

My dad was saying, "What are you thinking?" He totally disagreed with what I was doing, but I told him I'd find the money. He loaned me the deposit on the location, and he called up my uncle, who is an accountant. The three of us sat down and came up with an investment offering.

Finding the Money

Before she went the equity route, Alison wanted to investigate other avenues. The news was not good:

My dad referred me to some people he knew at Boston Private Bank—very conservative. Talks went fine until they became insistent that, if they were going to do anything, they would have to have a guarantor for the loan—a co-signer. Well, I wasn't going to do that; I wanted this to be my responsibility.

I tried to get an SBA loan through a small bank on the North Shore, but I had no collateral, and I was paying off student loans. They said no way because, even though the SBA would be backing it, a bad loan would give them a worse rating through the SBA. I looked into grants, but the process was too long. I also tried to get startup funding through the Hatchery Program at Babson. They said no as well; that really surprised me.

With the clock ticking on her lease, Alison went ahead with the investor plan she had crafted with her closest advisors:

We were not going to give people the option of deciding how much money they could invest. Instead, we said this is the deal: There are six slots of $25,000 each, and your options are full equity, debt/equity, or full debt.[1]

I sent an e-mail to all my contacts saying that this is where I am and that I was looking for investors. A lot of people responded to me; I was shocked.

A former classmate at Babson (who had started a men's skin-care line) e-mailed to say that he was very upset with me because he thought I was giving up way too much equity. But I didn't look at it that way at all. It was a different business model; he was going to the masses, and I was very local.

Her father was in for one share; all equity. He uncle let her choose, so she set him up as a debt/equity investor. She had a Babson woman (who had always liked her idea) in for all equity and a private investor in Denver for all debt. The final two shares were to be all equity:

A guy I used to work with told me he wanted to do $50,000, but he wanted to do it for 15% equity instead of 12.5%. I quickly said no. I had deals in place with other people; those are the terms. He said that's fine, he'd still like to do it.

Armed with a bit of cash and some solid commitments, Alison charged forward to make her vision a bricks-and-mortar reality.

---

[1] The valuation for the offer was based on her Year One sales projections. Each $25,000 investment would be worth 6.25% in equity. Debt/equity investors could choose either 10,000/15,000 debt/equity ratio or 15,000/10,000 debt/equity ratio. The all-debt interest rate was originally 10%, but when a wealthy investor from Denver offered an all-debt loan at 8%, the terms were adjusted to maintain parity.

Building Momentum (and Shelving)

Having initially envisioned a space in the range of 1,800 square feet, Alison found the 600 square foot shell to be a significant creative challenge—so much so that she hired an expert:

I needed to accommodate a starting inventory of around 600 pairs of jeans and a selection of tops (see Exhibit 1.4). My biggest concern was we had to have wide enough aisles to walk around.

EXHIBIT 1.4	Opening Inventory: Brand Selection
Denim Vendors	**T-Shirt/Tops Vendors**
ABS	ABS
AG	C & C California
Bella Dahl	Central Park West
Big Star	Custo
Blu Jeanious	Ella Moss
Cambio	Hale Bob
Chip and Pepper	Jakes
Christopher Blue	James Perse
Citizens of Humanity	Juicy Couture
Habitual	Lilla P.
Hudson	Michael Stars
IT Jeans	Mimi & Coco
James Jeans	Muchacha
Juicy Couture	Notice
Kasil	Rebecca Beeson
Notify	Splendid
Paper Denim & Cloth	Susana Monaco
Parasuco	Three Dots
Red Engine	Troo
Rock & Republic	Velvet
Sacred Blue	
Saddelite	
Salt Works	
Seven for All Mankind	
Tacto	
True Religion	
Tylerskye	
Womyn	
Yanuk	

I thought I could do it myself, but against my better judgment, I hired an interior designer. I worked with him and came up with a compact shelving system that started almost at the floor and went up only as high as I could reach. I am 5'5"?, and that is about the average. If someone was shorter, I could get it for them. I really wanted my store to feel very comfortable and warm—like you're in a good friend's closet. But the designer never quite got the need to maximize the space.

She added with a smile that she had been able to attract effective talent to the task of building out her vision:

> Bryan built all of the shelving with his father, an engineer. I showed them my drawings, gave them the measurements, and they did it. He actually project managed the build-out, and we did a lot of the work together. I saved so much money because of him. We painted it ourselves, and did other little things here and there. The contractors knew him well, and since he gives them so much business, they were willing to cut us breaks here and there. I went around and found furniture pieces for practical use that would make it feel more homey, like an armoire, a big dining room table, and a couple of benches. The furniture is all white, so the store has a shabby-chic feeling to it.

To monitor her sales and margins, Alison invested in a high-end software inventory system. The trouble was that the salesperson had yet to train her, and he wasn't returning her calls. But that challenge would have to wait; it was time to buy.

Learning Curves

With investors in place and the build-out moving along, Alison flew to Los Angeles and New York to haggle (and sashay) for "permission" to play:

> I had a list of brands that I wanted, based on my experience at the boutique. I was very concerned about fit and consistency. I was constantly looking at other girls' butts, so I knew that there was a core group of "in fashion" trendy jeans that I needed to have and that people liked. I also had to have some Mom jeans: higher-waisted, not young, but still sophisticated and nice looking.
>
> From there, it was about attending big trade shows in New York to touch the material and examine the styles. That doesn't tell you much about fit, and unfortunately you can't try on the floor samples.
>
> Buying is always stressful. There are times when my head is pounding and everything looks the same. The sellers are really snobby, and I had to dress totally trendified so they could look me up and down and say, "Okay, you can buy from us." Great, thanks. If I'm a good business-person, does the way I'm dressed matter at all? No, of course not; but that's what it's like.
>
> Although I had a pretty good idea of what I needed for my opening inventory, I did make some mistakes. I also bought some jeans that I would not have normally, but I couldn't get some of the brands that I wanted to start with—they wouldn't sell to a new store.

The denim reps that did sell to her demanded full payment up front. Using bank cards secured with her mother's credit, Alison pulled together a $75,000 inventory of jeans, tops, and accessories like trendy shoes and jewelry. That's when she was given a bit of a scare:

> A month before I opened, my last investor calls to say he's going to knock his investment down because he didn't want to be an aggressive shareholder. I panicked; I was in the final phases of my build-out, I had done all my buying, and here he was telling me I was going to be $25,000 short!

Despite her angst, Alison decided to sit tight. Things were moving along nicely, and it wasn't long before she realized that she'd be able to open her store without the additional capital.

In-jean-ius

A week before her opening in July 2005, Alison hired a friend of a friend as her first employee. Her mom was there to help out, along with her 17-year-old sister. The plan was to be open from around lunchtime to just past dinnertime, six days a week, and stay open a bit later on Sundays. Alison explained that it was soon evident that the location required a flexible approach:

> *The North End is interesting because in the summer they have a variety of feasts and festivals. I was often staying open until nearly midnight. I was working all the time—anything that would make a sale. I immediately surpassed my business plan estimates, and it kept building.*

As a new retailer in town, she attracted a few of the usual suspects who thought they might be able to take advantage of the young proprietor. They thought wrong:

> *The area is safe, but like any city neighborhood, it has its share of drug addicts. The first week I was open, two junkies came in. The guy was distracting me while the girl was stealing. I knew what was going on, but I didn't see her take anything. The general idea is that unless you see them do it, you can't do anything.*
>
> *When they left, a girl walks in and says, "Excuse me, those two just walked out with a pair of jeans." Well, I am not a very tough person—I grew up in the suburbs—and I don't know what I was thinking or what came over me, but I ran after them. I took the jeans out of the guy's hand and the bag off of her shoulder. I told her that I knew she had jewelry of mine, and I found it in there. I walked away from them to call the police. They ran away and my neighbors got in their car to go find them. They took my younger sister with them because she knew what they looked like.*
>
> *They found them and brought them back to the store so I could positively ID them. They were arrested and taken away. From then on, everyone in the North End thought hey, she's tough—and the druggies, who all talk, stayed away.*

Soon after that, Alison was in hot pursuit again:

> *I chased another girl down the street, and when I wouldn't let her get in her car, she tried to punch me. Bryan tells me all the time I have to stop doing that; someday I could get hurt.*
>
> *Of course, I tell my employees not to do anything like that; just call the police. But I take it so personally; that's mine, you're stealing from me! How can you do that? Don't you know I'm a new business?*

Over the next few months, Alison's total loss to theft was a single pair of shoes and a pair of earrings. The other good news was that sales continued to track far ahead of her estimates. In the first six months, the store had generated a net income of $20,307 on sales of $294,061. Alison explained that, although word of mouth was an important factor in her early success, attracting the imagination of the local press had been key:

> *I'm not the only one who has had this idea, and other trendy jeans stores have definitely gotten their share of press, but people are really taking to my message: "You're going to get help, and we're going to work with you to find jeans that fit. We have jeans for everybody." Nobody else is saying that this is all about fit, and that's the message that I relay in every piece of PR that I send out. And they keep coming to talk to me.*

While the young entrepreneur was thrilled with how things were going, she was ready to start spending less time on the sales floor and more time with strategic and management challenges. Easier said than done.

Fold or Finance?

Since the local press always seemed to focus on *her* skills and *her* story, Alison wondered how that might impact her ability to replicate her concept:

> *How do you grow when the store is about you? People come here because they like dealing with me. How do I duplicate myself? That's not to say that someone can't do what I'm doing and do it well, but employees are never going to treat people exactly the way you do. I have a lot of learning to do in terms of managing my employees, delegating, and sharing my knowledge.*

One of her many priorities was to develop a training manual that, in addition to describing the particular fit characteristics of various brands, would clearly articulate her vision for customer service. She thought of contacting the Ritz-Carlton in Boston—to her mind a master of customer service—to see if they might let her review their training materials. Until she did have some documentation in place though, she'd have to communicate her philosophy on the fly:

> *I sort of torture my employees when they're hired. They have to come in and spend a few hours trying on everything in the store—like a restaurant that requires their servers to try everything on the menu so they can talk about it.*
>
> *I am also pretty strict about keeping the store neat and organized. I think that is so important in a small space like this. Whenever I come into the store, I can immediately see items that are unfolded or out of place.*
>
> *My office is a desk in the corner, so I'm right there to offer help or teach them the little tricks I've learned. I also try to stay at my desk and let them take care of whoever comes in, but I can't just keep quiet if they are not saying the right thing. I always have to get my two cents in.*

Now that she had a full-time employee nearly up to speed and a sharp former classmate from Babson working on weekends as a fun job, Alison had begun to carve out some time each week to recharge:

> *I have had to give up spending much time with Bryan, and that has been a huge problem. My taking Sundays has become so important because we get to spend time together. Despite the fact that he is also an entrepreneur, he has had a really big struggle with the idea that he is number two to this business. That's been hard and it's something we're working on.*

Her other challenging relationship was with the numbers:

> *Nailing down the actuals is a big issue for me, and I am in the process of doing that. I'm not bad with financials, but they are a bit intimidating; I am really just much more into customer service and marketing. There are so many other things that I could be doing to bring in sales, so I'd rather do those things first.*
>
> *It's true; I would rather have my store neat and folded than work on my financials. That is always my first priority. If the store looks good, then I can do other things. The problem is that I am constantly rearranging the store, and that is my way of being creative: putting different things together, doing the windows over every week.*
>
> *My uncle does my accounting, and I am paying close enough attention to know I'm doing much better than my projections, but I need to focus on it more. And I need to find a training course for that inventory software so I can run those reports and coordinate things the right way.*

Down by One

It had been one of the best-selling days to date. Alison closed her shop at 8:30 that night and returned to her desk with the absurd idea that she might have some energy left for paperwork. It wasn't just that she was tired; she now had a brand-new challenge on her plate: That day her one full-time employee had given her two-week notice.

Preparation Questions

1. Is this business scalable? Discuss the limitations and challenges.
2. What tasks and goals should Alison be focusing on at this stage of her venture?
3. Discuss the signing of a lease prior to having the money. What was the risk?
4. Discuss her fundraising and valuation. If you were an equity investor, what return expectations would you have?
5. If women are coming to Alison's store from all over, how important is location? Discuss the implications for growth.

cpb/cnb/Finalpixx/NewsCom

Facebook Founder and CEO Mark Zuckerberg leaves his Palo Alto, CA office.

THE ENTREPRENEURIAL PROCESS

An **entrepreneur** is someone who perceives an opportunity and creates an organization to pursue it. The **entrepreneurial process** includes all the functions, activities, and actions that are part of perceiving opportunities and creating organizations to pursue them. But is the birth of a new enterprise just happenstance and its subsequent success or failure a chance process? Or can the art and science of entrepreneurship be taught? Clearly, professors and their students believe that it can be taught and learned because entrepreneurship is one of the fastest growing new fields of study in American higher education. A study by the Kauffman Foundation found that 61% of U.S. colleges and universities have at least one course in entrepreneurship.[1] It is possible to study entrepreneurship in certificate, associate's, bachelor's, master's, and PhD programs.

That transformation in higher education—itself a wonderful example of entrepreneurial change—has come about because a whole body of knowledge about entrepreneurship has developed during the past two decades or so. The process of creating a new business is well understood. Yes, entrepreneurship can be taught. No one is guaranteed to become a Bill Gates or a Donna Karan, any more than a physics professor can guarantee to produce an Albert Einstein or a tennis coach can guarantee a Serena Williams. But students with the aptitude to start a business can become better entrepreneurs.

> An entrepreneur is someone who perceives an opportunity and creates an organization to pursue it.

> The entrepreneurial process includes all the functions, activities, and actions that are part of perceiving opportunities and creating organizations to pursue them.

This chapter is written by William D. Bygrave.

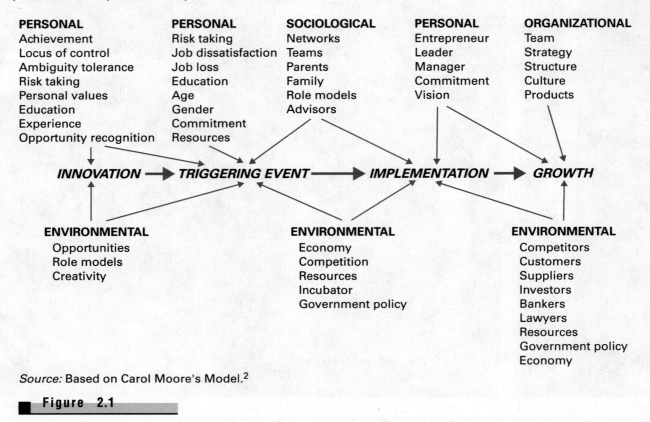

PERSONAL
Achievement
Locus of control
Ambiguity tolerance
Risk taking
Personal values
Education
Experience
Opportunity recognition

PERSONAL
Risk taking
Job dissatisfaction
Job loss
Education
Age
Gender
Commitment
Resources

SOCIOLOGICAL
Networks
Teams
Parents
Family
Role models
Advisors

PERSONAL
Entrepreneur
Leader
Manager
Commitment
Vision

ORGANIZATIONAL
Team
Strategy
Structure
Culture
Products

INNOVATION → **TRIGGERING EVENT** → **IMPLEMENTATION** → **GROWTH**

ENVIRONMENTAL
Opportunities
Role models
Creativity

ENVIRONMENTAL
Economy
Competition
Resources
Incubator
Government policy

ENVIRONMENTAL
Competitors
Customers
Suppliers
Investors
Bankers
Lawyers
Resources
Government policy
Economy

Source: Based on Carol Moore's Model.[2]

■ Figure 2.1

A model of the entrepreneurial process

Critical Factors for Starting a New Enterprise

We will begin by examining the entrepreneurial process (see Figure 2.1). These are the factors—personal, sociological, organizational, and environmental—that give birth to a new enterprise and influence how it develops from an idea to a viable enterprise. A person gets an idea for a new business through either a deliberate search or a chance encounter. Whether he or she decides to pursue that idea depends on factors such as alternative career prospects, family, friends, role models, the state of the economy, and the availability of resources.

Origins of Home Depot

Bernie Marcus was president of the now-defunct Handy Dan home improvement chain, based in California, when he and Arthur Blank were abruptly fired by new management. That day and the months that followed were the most pivotal period in his career, he says. "I was 49 years old at the time and I was pretty devastated by being fired. Still, I think it's a question of believing in yourself. Soon after, we [Blank and Marcus] started to realize that this was our opportunity to start over," says Marcus.

Marcus and Blank then happened upon a 120,000-square-foot store called Homeco, operating in Long Beach, California. The two instantly realized that the concept—an oversized store packed with merchandise tagged with low prices—had a magical quality. They wanted to buy the business, but it was essentially bankrupt. Marcus and Blank talked Homeco owner Pat Farah into joining them in Atlanta, and the trio, along with Ron Brill, began sketching the blueprint for Home Depot.[3]

There is almost always a *triggering event* that gives birth to a new organization. Perhaps the entrepreneur has no better career prospects. For example, Melanie Stevens was a high school dropout who, after working a number of minor jobs, had run out of career options. She decided that making canvas bags in her own tiny business was better than earning low wages working for someone else. Within a few years, she had built a chain of retail stores throughout Canada.

Sometimes the person has been passed over for a promotion or even laid off or fired. Howard Rose had been laid off four times as a result of mergers and consolidations in the pharmaceutical industry, and he had had enough of it. So he started his own drug packaging business, Waverly Pharmaceutical. Tim Waterstone founded Waterstone's bookstores after he was fired by W. H. Smith. Ann Gloag quit her nursing job and used her bus-driver father's $40,000 severance pay to set up Stagecoach bus company with her brother, exploiting legislation deregulating the United Kingdom's bus industry. Jordan Rubin was debilitated by Crohn's disease when he invented a diet supplement that restored his health; he founded a company, Garden of Life, to sell that diet. Noreen Kenny was working for a semiconductor company and could not find a supplier to do precision mechanical work, so she launched her own company, Evolve Manufacturing Technologies, to fill that void. The Baby Einstein Company was started by Julie Aigner-Clark when she discovered that there were no age-appropriate products available to help her share her love of art, classical music, language, and poetry with her newborn daughter. Jim Poss, while walking down a Boston street, observed a trash vehicle idling at a pick up point, blocking traffic, with smoke pouring out of its exhaust, while litter was still prevalent on the street. Poss was struck by the thought that there had to be a better way; it led to his invention of the Big Belly solar-powered trash compactor.

For some people, entrepreneurship is a deliberate career choice. Sandra Kurtzig was a software engineer with General Electric who wanted to start a family and work at home. She started ASK Computer Systems Inc., which became a $400 million-a-year business.

Where do would-be entrepreneurs get their ideas? More often than not it is through their present line of employment or experience. A study of the *Inc.* 500—"America's [500] fastest growing companies"—found that 57% of the founders got the idea for their new venture in the industry they worked in, and an additional 23% got it in a related industry. Hence, 80% of all new high-potential businesses are founded in industries that are the same as, or closely related to, the one in which the entrepreneur has previous experience. That is not surprising because it is in their present employment that entrepreneurs will get most of their viable business ideas. Some habitual entrepreneurs do it over and over again in the same industry. Joey Crugnale, himself an *Inc.* 500 Hall of Famer and an *Inc.* Entrepreneur of the Year, became a partner in Steve's Ice Cream in his early 20s. He eventually took over Steve's Ice Cream and created a national franchise of some 26 units—and a new food niche, gourmet ice creams. In 1982, Crugnale started Bertucci's, where gourmet pizza was cooked in wood-fired brick ovens, and built it into a nationwide chain of 90 restaurants. Then he founded Naked Restaurants as an incubator to launch his innovative dining concepts. The first one, the Naked Fish, opened in 1999 and brought his wood-fired grill approach to a new niche: fresh fish and meats with a touch of Cubanismo.

Others start businesses over and over again in related industries. In 1981, James Clark, then a Stanford University computer science professor, founded Silicon Graphics, a computer manufacturer with 1996 sales of $3 billion. In April 1994, he teamed up with Marc

Andreessen to found Netscape Communications. Within 12 months, its browser software, Navigator, dominated the Internet's World Wide Web (WWW or Web). When Netscape went public in August 1995, Clark became the first Internet billionaire. Then in June 1996, Clark launched another company, Healtheon (subsequently merged with WebMD), to enable doctors, insurers, and patients to exchange data and do business over the Internet with software incorporating Netscape's Navigator.

Much rarer is the serial entrepreneur such as Wayne Huizenga, who ventures into unrelated industries: first in garbage disposal with Waste Management, next in entertainment with Blockbuster Video, then in automobile sales with AutoNation. Along the way, he was the original owner of the Florida Marlins baseball team, which won the World Series in 1997.

What factors influence someone to embark on an entrepreneurial career? Like most human behavior, entrepreneurial traits are shaped by *personal attributes* and *environment*.

A. Personal Attributes

In the entrepreneurial 1980s, there was a spate of magazine and newspaper articles that were entitled "Do you have the right stuff to be an entrepreneur?" or words to that effect. The articles described the most important characteristics of entrepreneurs and, more often than not, included a self-evaluation exercise to enable readers to determine if they had the right stuff. Those articles were based on flimsy behavioral research into the differences between entrepreneurs and nonentrepreneurs. The basis for those exercises was the belief, first developed by David McClelland in his book *The Achieving Society*, that entrepreneurs had *a higher need for achievement* than nonentrepreneurs and that they were moderate risk takers. One engineer almost abandoned his entrepreneurial ambitions after completing one of those exercises. He asked his professor at the start of an MBA entrepreneurship course if he should take the class because he had scored very low on an entrepreneurship test in a magazine. He took the course, however, and wrote an award-winning plan for a business that was a success from the very beginning.

There is no neat set of behavioral attributes that allows us to separate entrepreneurs from nonentrepreneurs. A person who rises to the top of any occupation, whether an entrepreneur or an administrator, is an achiever. Granted, any would-be entrepreneur must have a need to achieve, but so must anyone else with ambitions to be successful.

It does appear that entrepreneurs have a *higher internal locus of control* than nonentrepreneurs, which means that they have a stronger desire to be in control of their own fate.[4] This has been confirmed by many surveys in which entrepreneurs said independence was a very important reason for starting their businesses. The main reasons they gave were independence, financial success, self-realization, recognition, innovation, and roles (to continue a family tradition, to follow the example of an admired person, to be respected by friends). Men rated financial success and innovation higher than women did. Interestingly, the reasons that nascent entrepreneurs gave for starting a business were similar to the reasons given by nonentrepreneurs for choosing jobs.[5]

The most important characteristics of successful entrepreneurs are shown in Figure 2.2.

B. Environmental Factors

Perhaps as important as personal attributes are the external influences on a would-be entrepreneur. It's no accident that some parts of the world are more entrepreneurial than others. The most famous region of high-tech entrepreneurship is Silicon Valley. Because everyone in Silicon Valley knows someone who has made it big as an entrepreneur, role models abound. This situation produces what Stanford University sociologist Everett Rogers called "Silicon Valley fever."[6] It seems as if everyone in the valley catches that bug sooner or later and wants to start a business. To facilitate the process, there are venture capitalists

Dream	Entrepreneurs have a vision of what the future could be like for them and their businesses. And, more important, they have the ability to implement their dreams.
Decisiveness	They don't procrastinate. They make decisions swiftly. Their swiftness is a key factor in their success.
Doers	Once they decide on a course of action, they implement it as quickly as possible.
Determination	They implement their ventures with total commitment. They seldom give up, even when confronted by obstacles that seem insurmountable.
Dedication	They are totally dedicated to their businesses, sometimes at considerable cost to their relationships with friends and families. They work tirelessly. Twelve-hour days and seven-day workweeks are not uncommon when an entrepreneur is striving to get a business off the ground.
Devotion	Entrepreneurs love what they do. It is that love that sustains them when the going gets tough. And it is love of their product or service that makes them so effective at selling it.
Details	It is said that the devil resides in the details. That is never more true than in starting and growing a business. The entrepreneur must be on top of the critical details.
Destiny	They want to be in charge of their own destiny rather than dependent on an employer.
Dollars	Getting rich is not the prime motivator of entrepreneurs. Money is more a measure of success. Entrepreneurs assume that if they are successful they will be rewarded.
Distribute	Entrepreneurs distribute the ownership of their businesses with key employees who are critical to the success of the business.

Figure 2.2

The 10 Ds—The most important characteristics of a successful entrepreneur

who understand how to select and nurture high-tech entrepreneurs, bankers who specialize in lending to them, lawyers who understand the importance of intellectual property and how to protect it, landlords who are experienced in renting real estate to fledgling companies, suppliers who are willing to sell goods on credit to companies with no credit history, and even politicians who are supportive.

Knowing successful entrepreneurs at work or in your personal life makes becoming one yourself seem much more achievable. Indeed, if a close relative is an entrepreneur, you are more likely to want to become an entrepreneur yourself, especially if that relative is your mother or father. At Babson College, more than half of the undergraduates studying entrepreneurship come from families that own businesses, and half of the *Inc.* 500 entrepreneurs in 2012 had a parent who was an entrepreneur.[7] But you don't have to be from a business-owning family to become an entrepreneur. Bill Gates, for example, was following the family tradition of becoming a lawyer when he dropped out of Harvard and founded Microsoft. He was in the fledgling microcomputer industry, which was being built by entrepreneurs, so he had plenty of role models among his friends and acquaintances. The United States has an abundance of high-tech entrepreneurs who are household names. One of them, Meg Whitman (eBay and Hewlett-Packard), is so well known that she was the gubernatorial candidate preferred by 41% of California voters in 2012 . Some universities are hotbeds of entrepreneurship. For example, Massachusetts Institute of Technology (MIT) has produced numerous entrepreneurs among its faculty and alums. Companies with an MIT connection transformed the Massachusetts economy from one based on decaying shoe and textile industries into one based on high technology.

According to [a 2009 MIT] study, "Entrepreneurial Impact: The Role of MIT," which analyzes the economic effect of MIT alumni–founded companies and its entrepreneurial ecosystem, if the active companies founded by MIT graduates formed an independent nation, their revenues would make that nation at least the 17th-largest economy in the world . . .

The overall MIT entrepreneurial environment, consisting of multiple education, research and social network institutions, contributes to this outstanding and growing entrepreneurial output. Highlights of the findings include:

An estimated 6,900 MIT alumni companies with worldwide sales of approximately $164 billion are located in Massachusetts alone and represent 26 percent of the sales of all Massachusetts companies.

4,100 MIT alumni–founded firms are based in California, and generate an estimated $134 billion in worldwide sales.

States currently benefiting most from jobs created by MIT alumni companies are Massachusetts (estimated at just under one million jobs), California (estimated at 526,000 jobs), New York (estimated at 231,000 jobs), Texas (estimated at 184,000) and Virginia (estimated at 136,000).[8]

It is not only in high tech that we see role models. Consider these examples:

- It has been estimated that half of all the convenience stores in New York City are owned by Koreans.
- It was the visibility of successful role models that spread catfish farming in the Mississippi Delta as a more profitable alternative to cotton.
- Portland, Oregon, has 40 microbreweries within its city boundaries, which according to the Oregon Brewers Guild is more than any other city in the world.
- Hay-on-Wye—a tiny town in Wales with 1,500 inhabitants—has 39 secondhand bookstores. It claims to be the "largest used and antiquarian bookshop in the world." It all began in 1961 when Richard Booth, an Oxford graduate, opened his first bookstore.

African Americans make up 12% of the U.S. population but owned only 4% of the nation's businesses in 1997.[9] One of the major reasons for that low number is the lack of entrepreneurial role models. A similar problem exists among Native Americans. Fortunately, this situation is rapidly improving. Between the 1992 and 1997 censuses, the number of minority-owned businesses grew more than four times as fast as U.S. firms overall, increasing from 2.1 million to about 2.8 million firms.[10] According to the 2007 census, Hispanics/Latinos owned 8.5% of the nation's businesses, African Americans owned 7.0%, Asian Americans owned 5.9%, and American Indians and Alaskan Natives owned 1.1%.[11]

⚘ Other Sociological Factors

Besides role models, entrepreneurs are influenced by other sociological factors. *Family responsibilities* play an important role in the decision to start a company. It is a relatively easy career decision to start a business when you are 25 years old, single, and without many personal assets and dependents. It is a much harder decision when you are 45 and married, with teenage children preparing to go to college, a hefty mortgage, car payments, and a secure, well-paying job. A survey of European high-potential entrepreneurs, for instance, found that on average they had 50% of their net worth at risk because it was tied up in their businesses. And at 45+, if you fail as an entrepreneur, it will not be easy to rebuild a career working for another company. But despite the risks, plenty of 45-year-olds are taking the plunge; in fact, the median age of the CEOs of the 500 fastest-growing small companies, the *Inc.* 500, in 2009 was 41,[12] and the median age of their companies was six years.[13]

Another factor that determines the age at which entrepreneurs start businesses is the trade-off between the *experience* that comes with age and the *optimism* and *energy* of youth.

As you grow older you gain experience, but sometimes when you have been in an industry a long time, you know so many pitfalls that you are pessimistic about the chance of succeeding if you decide to go out on your own. Someone who has just enough experience to feel confident as a manager is more likely to feel optimistic about an entrepreneurial career The best performing businesses owned by Babson alumni, for example, were started when the entrepreneurs had 10 years management experience after graduation. Perhaps the ideal combination is a beginner's mind with the experience of an industry veteran. A beginner's mind looks at situations from a new perspective, with a can-do spirit.

Twenty-seven-year-old Robert Swanson was a complete novice at biotechnology but was convinced that it had great commercial potential. His enthusiasm combined with Professor Herbert Boyer's unsurpassed knowledge about the use of recombinant DNA to produce human protein. The two just assumed that Boyer's laboratory bench work could be scaled up to industrial levels. Looking back, Boyer said, "I think we were so naïve, we never thought it couldn't be done." Together they succeeded and started a new industry.

Marc Andreessen had a beginner's mind in 1993 when, as a student and part-time assistant at the National Center for Supercomputing Applications at the University of Illinois, he developed the Mosaic browser and produced a vision for the Internet that until then had eluded many computer industry veterans, including Bill Gates. When Andreessen's youthful creativity was joined with James Clark's entrepreneurial wisdom, earned over a dozen years as founder and chairman of Silicon Graphics, it turned out to be an awesome combination. Their company, Netscape, distributed 38 million copies of Navigator in just two years, making it the most successful new software introduction ever.

We cannot specify how much managerial expertise it takes to become a skilled entrepreneur. But we do know that venture capitalists recognize that neophyte high-tech entrepreneurs, especially very young ones, do not have enough experience, so they often recruit seasoned entrepreneurial managers to guide them. An example is Google, where Eric Schmidt was hired as CEO to guide Page and Brin.[14] Then after 10 years at the helm, Schmidt announced he would step aside to allow Page to take over the reins as CEO in 2011.

Before leaving secure, well-paying, satisfying jobs, would-be entrepreneurs should make a *careful estimate of how much sales revenue* their new businesses must generate before they will be able to match the income they presently earn. It usually comes as quite a shock when they realize that, if they are opening a retail establishment, they will need annual sales revenue of at least $750,000 to pay themselves a salary of $70,000 plus fringe benefits such as healthcare coverage, retirement pension benefits, and long-term disability insurance. Seven hundred and fifty thousand dollars a year is about $15,000 per week, or about $2,500 per day, or about $250 per hour, or about $4 per minute if they are open 6 days a week, 10 hours a day. Also, they will be working much longer hours and bearing much more responsibility if they become self-employed. A sure way to test the strength of a marriage is to start a company that is the sole means of support for your family. For example, 22.5% of the CEOs of the *Inc.* 500 got divorced while growing their businesses. On a brighter note, 59.2% got married, and 18.3% of divorced CEOs remarried.[15]

When they actually start a business, entrepreneurs need a host of *contacts*, including customers, suppliers, investors, bankers, accountants, and lawyers. So it is important to understand where to find help before embarking on a new venture. A network of friends and business associates can be of immeasurable help in building the contacts an entrepreneur will need. They can also provide human contact, which is important because opening a business can be a lonely experience for anyone who has worked in an organization with many fellow employees.

Fortunately, today there are more organizations than ever before to help fledgling entrepreneurs. Often that help is free or costs very little. The Small Business Administration (SBA) has Small Business Development Centers in every state, it funds Small Business Institutes, and its Service Core of Retired Executives provides free assistance to entrepreneurs. Many colleges and universities also provide help. Some are particularly good at writing business plans, usually at no charge to the entrepreneur. There are hundreds of incubators in the United States where fledgling businesses can rent space, usually at a very reasonable price, and spread some of their overhead by sharing facilities such as copying machines, secretarial help, answering services, and so on. Incubators are often associated with universities, which provide free or inexpensive counseling. There are numerous associations where entrepreneurs can meet and exchange ideas.

Evaluating Opportunities for New Businesses

Let's assume you believe that you have found a great opportunity for starting a new business. How should you evaluate its prospects? Or, perhaps more importantly, how will an independent person such as a potential investor or a banker rate your chances of success? The odds of succeeding appear to be stacked against you because, according to small business folklore, only 1 business in 10 will ever reach its 10th birthday. This doesn't mean that 90% of the estimated 3 million businesses that are started every year go bankrupt.[16] We know that even in a severe recession, the number of businesses filing for bankruptcy in the United States has never surpassed 100,000 in any year. In an average year, the number is about 35,000. Even in 2008, when small businesses were hit hard by a severe recession, the number of bankruptcies was fewer than 45,000.[17] So what happens to the vast majority of the ones that do not survive 10 years? Most just fade away: They are started as part-time pursuits and are never intended to become full-time businesses. Some are sold. Others are liquidated. Only 700,000 of the 3 million are legally registered as corporations or partnerships—a sure sign that many of the remaining 2.3 million never intended to grow because, in general, an entrepreneur will go to the bother and expense of registering a new venture as a separate legal entity only if it is expected to become a full-time business with employees. Hence, the odds that your new business will survive may not be as long as they first appeared to be. If you intend to start a full-time, incorporated business, the odds that the business will survive at least eight years with you as the owner are better than one in four, and the odds of its surviving at least eight years with a new owner are another one in four. So the eight-year survival rate for incorporated startups is about 50%.[18]

But survival may not spell success. Too many entrepreneurs find that they can neither earn a satisfactory living in their businesses nor get out of them easily because they have too much of their personal assets tied up in them. The happiest day in an entrepreneur's life is the day doors are opened for business. For unsuccessful entrepreneurs, an even happier day may be the day the business is sold—especially if most personal assets remain intact. What George Bernard Shaw said about a love affair is also apt for a business: Any fool can start one, but it takes a genius to end one successfully.

How can you stack the odds in your favor so that your new business is a success? Professional investors, such as venture capitalists, have a talent for picking winners. True, they also pick losers, but a startup company funded by venture capital has, on average, a four-in-five chance of surviving five years—better odds than for the population of startup companies as a whole. Very few businesses—perhaps no more than one in a thousand—will ever be suitable candidates for investments from professional venture capitalists. But would-be entrepreneurs can learn a lot by following the evaluation process used by professional investors.

There are three crucial components for a successful new business: the opportunity, the entrepreneur (and the management team, if it's a high-potential venture), and the resources needed to start the company and make it grow. These are shown schematically in Figure 2.3 in the basic Timmons framework. At the center of the framework is a business plan, the result of integrating the three basic ingredients into a complete strategic plan for the new business.

The parts must fit together well. It's no good having a first-rate idea for a new business if you have a second-rate management team. Nor are ideas and management any good without the appropriate resources.

The crucial driving force of any new venture is the lead entrepreneur and the funding management team. Georges Doriot, the founder of modern venture capital, used to say something like this: "Always consider investing in a grade-A man with a grade-B idea. Never invest in a grade-B man with a grade-A idea." He knew what he was talking about. Over the years he invested in about 150 companies, including Digital Equipment Corporation (DEC), and watched over them as they struggled to grow. But Doriot made his statement about business in the 1950s and 1960s. During that period, there were far fewer startups; U.S. firms dominated the marketplace, markets were growing quickly, there was almost no competition from overseas, and most entrepreneurs were male. Today, in the global marketplace, with ever-shortening product life cycles and low growth or even no growth for some of the world's leading industrial nations, *the crucial ingredients for entrepreneurial success are a superb entrepreneur with a first-rate management team and an excellent market opportunity.*

It's often said that entrepreneurship is largely a matter of luck. That's not so. We do not say that becoming a great quarterback, a great scientist, or a great musician is a matter of luck. There is no more luck in becoming successful at entrepreneurship than in becoming successful at anything else. In entrepreneurship, it is a question of recognizing a good opportunity when you see one and having the skills to convert that opportunity into a thriving business. To do that, you must be prepared. So in entrepreneurship, as in any other profession, *luck is where preparation and opportunity meet.*

In 1982, when Rod Canion proposed to start Compaq to make personal computers, there were already formidable established competitors, including IBM and Apple, and literally hundreds of companies were considering entering the market or had already done so. Despite the competition, Ben Rosen of the venture capital firm Sevin Rosen Management Company invested in Compaq. Started initially to make transportable PCs, Compaq quickly added a complete range of high-performance PCs and grew so fast that it soon broke Apple's record for the fastest time from founding to listing on the *Fortune* 500.

What did Ben Rosen see in the Compaq proposal that made it stand out from all the other personal computer startups? The difference was Rod Canion and his team. Rod Canion had earned a reputation as an excellent manager at Texas Instruments. Furthermore, the market for personal computers topped $5 billion and was growing at a torrid pace. So Rosen had found a superb team with a product targeted at an undeveloped niche, transportable PCs, in a large market that was growing explosively. By 1994, Compaq was the leading PC manufacturer with 13% of the market.

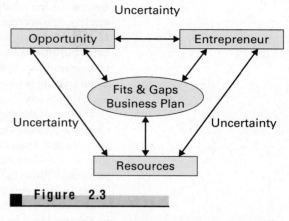

Figure 2.3

Three driving forces (Based on Jeffry Timmons' framework)[19]

> The crucial ingredients for entrepreneurial success are a superb entrepreneur with a first-rate management team and an excellent market opportunity.

> In entrepreneurship, as in any other profession, luck is where preparation and opportunity meet.

A. The Opportunity

Perhaps the biggest misconception about an idea for a new business is that it must be unique. Too many would-be entrepreneurs are almost obsessed with finding a unique idea. Then, when they believe they have it, they are haunted by the thought that someone is just waiting to steal it from them. So they become super-secretive, reluctant to discuss it with anyone who doesn't sign a nondisclosure agreement. That makes it almost impossible to evaluate the idea, and many counselors who provide free advice to entrepreneurs refuse to sign nondisclosure agreements. Generally speaking, these super-secret, unique ideas are big letdowns when the entrepreneurs reveal them. Some notable recent examples were "drive-through pizza by the slice," "a combination toothbrush and toothpaste gadget," and "a Mexican restaurant in

Boston." One computer programmer said he had a fantastic new piece of software for managing hairdressing salons. He was completely floored when he found that less than a month previously another entrepreneur had demonstrated a software package for exactly the same purpose. Another entrepreneur had an idea for fluoride-impregnated dental floss. Not three months later, the identical product turned out to be available in Boots—Britain's largest chain of drug stores and a major pharmaceutical manufacturer.

Almost any idea a would-be entrepreneur might have will also have occurred to others. In fact, some of the most revolutionary thoughts in the history of humankind occurred to more than one person almost simultaneously. Newton and Leibnitz independently invented calculus within a few years of each other; Darwin was almost preempted by Wallace in publishing his theory of evolution; Poincaré almost formulated a valid theory of special relativity about the same time Einstein did; and the integrated circuit was invented in 1959, first by Jack Kilby at Texas Instruments and then independently by Robert Noyce at Fairchild a few months later. And as we read in Chapter 1, Berners-Lee was not the first person to introduce the concept of hypertext. Nor was Google the first company to introduce a Web search engine.

> The idea in itself is not what is important. In entrepreneurship, ideas really are a dime a dozen. Developing the idea, implementing it, and building a successful business are the important things.

So the idea in itself is not what is important. In entrepreneurship, ideas really are a dime a dozen. Developing the idea, implementing it, and building a successful business are the important things. Alexander Fleming discovered penicillin by chance but never developed it as a useful drug. About 10 years later Ernst Chain and Howard Florey unearthed Fleming's mold and immediately saw its potential. They soon were treating patients in England with it, and before the end of World War II, penicillin was saving countless lives. It was a most dramatic pharmaceutical advance and heralded a revolution in that industry.

> Would-be entrepreneurs who are unable to name a customer are not ready to start a business. They have found an idea but have not yet identified a market need.

According to the late Stanford Professor Rajeev Motwani, who mentored Sergey Brin and Larry Page, "At some point these guys said, we want to do a company. Everybody said you must be out of your minds. There are like 37 search engines out there and what are you guys going to do? And how are you going to raise money, how will you build a company, and these two guys said, we'll just do it and they went off and did it. And then they took over the world."[20]

The Customer

Many would-be entrepreneurs fail to think carefully enough about who makes up the market for their product or service. They should have a very specific answer to this question: "Can you give me the names of prospective customers?" If they have a consumer product—let's say it's a new shampoo—they should be able to name the buyers at different chains of drug stores in their area. If they are unable to name several customers immediately, they simply have an idea, not a market. There is no market unless customers have a real need for the product—a proven need rather than a hypothetical need in the mind of a would-be entrepreneur. A few rare cases may be revolutionary new products with markets waiting to be formed, but most entrepreneurial ideas are for existing products with improved performance, price, distribution, quality, or service. Simply put, customers must perceive that the new business will be giving them better value for their money than existing businesses.

The Timing

Time plays a crucial role in many potential opportunities. In some emerging industries, there is a definite window of opportunity that opens only once. For instance, about 35 years ago, when videocassette recorders (VCRs) were first coming into household use in the United States, there was a need for video stores in convenient locations where viewers could pick up movies on the way home from work. Lots of video retail stores opened up on main streets and in shopping centers. They were usually run by independent store owners. Then the distribution of videos changed. National chains of video stores emerged. Supermarket and drug store chains entered the market. Then the technology changed, and VCR cassettes were replaced by digital video discs (DVDs), which are much less bulky. You can get DVDs via postal mail, download them via the Internet, or pick them up at vending machines and conventional video stores. Today the window of opportunity for starting an independent video store is closed.

In other markets—high-quality restaurants, for example—there is a steady demand that does not change much from year to year, so the window of opportunity is always open. Nevertheless, timing can still be important because, when the economy turns down, those kinds of restaurants are usually hit harder than lower-quality ones; thus, the time to open one is during a recovering or booming economy.

If the window of opportunity appears to be very brief, it may be that the idea is a consumer fad that will quickly pass away. It takes a very skilled entrepreneur indeed to make money out of a fad. When Lucy's Have a Heart Canvas of Faneuil Hall Marketplace in Boston introduced shoelaces with hearts on them, they flew off the shelves. Children and teenagers could not get enough of them for their sneakers. The store ordered more and more of them. Then demand suddenly dropped precipitously. The store and the manufacturer were left holding huge inventories that could not be sold. As a result, the store almost went under.

Slimming Fad Fades Fast, Inventories Balloon

The late Dr. Robert C. Atkins built a business around the low-carbohydrate, high-protein diet that bears his name. The 1992 and 1999 editions of his book *Dr. Atkins' New Diet Revolution* sold more than 10 million copies worldwide. The book is among of the top 50 best-selling books ever published and was on *The New York Times* best-seller list for five years. Atkins' company, Atkins Nutritionals, Inc., expanded into 250 food products (nutrition bars, shakes, bake mixes, breads) and nearly 100 nutritional supplements (antioxidants, essential oils) in more than 30,000 outlets. Sales ramped up rapidly at the beginning of the 2000s. Demand was boosted in 2003 by a widely publicized article in the May edition of the influential *New England Journal of Medicine*, reporting that subjects on a low-carb, high-protein diet not only lost weight but also—and perhaps more importantly—had an increase in good cholesterol levels and a decrease in triglycerides, which was contrary to expectations. In October 2003, Goldman Sachs & Company and Boston-based Parthenon Capital LLC bought a majority stake in the firm for an estimated $700 million.

At the peak of the low-carb "get-thin-quick" craze in January 2004, 9.1% of the U.S. population claimed to be on the diet. There were 16 national distributors of low-carb products. National supermarkets introduced low-carb products. Food manufacturers rushed to promote low-carbohydrate products. The diet was so popular that it was partially blamed for the bankruptcy of Interstate Bakeries, the producer of Twinkies and Wonderbread. Then the fad faded fast. By 2005, only 2.2% of Americans were on low-carb diets. The fall was so precipitous that manufacturers were caught with bloated inventories. Surplus low-carb products were being shipped to Appalachian food banks. For the year ended 2004, Atkins Nutritionals lost $341 million. In August 2005, it filed for Chapter 11 with liabilities of $325 million The number of its products was slimmed down to 40 from more than 300 at the peak of the low-carb fad; the company was bought by Roark Capital in 2010.

Most entrepreneurs should avoid fads or any window of opportunity they believe will be open for a very brief time because it inevitably means they will rush to open their business, sometimes before they have time to gather the resources they will need. That can lead to costly mistakes.

The Entrepreneur and the Management Team

Regardless of how right the opportunity may seem to be, it will not become a successful business unless it is developed by a person with strong entrepreneurial and management skills. What are the important skills?

First and foremost, entrepreneurs should have experience in the same industry or a similar one. Starting a business is a very demanding undertaking indeed. It is no time for on-the-job training. If would-be entrepreneurs do not have the right experience, they should either get it before starting their new venture or find partners who have it.

Some investors say the ideal entrepreneur is one who has a track record as a successful entrepreneur in the same industry and who can attract a seasoned team. Half the CEOs of the *Inc.* 500 high-growth small companies had started at least one other business before they founded their present firms. When Joey Crugnale acquired his first ice cream shop in 1977, he already had almost 10 years in the food service industry. By 1991, when Bertucci's brick-oven pizzeria went public, he and his management team had a total of more than 100 years' experience in the food industry. They had built Bertucci's into a rapidly growing chain with sales of $30 million and net income of $2 million.

Without relevant experience, the odds are stacked against the neophyte in any industry. An electronics engineer thought he had a great idea for a chain of fast-food stores. When asked if he had ever worked in a fast-food restaurant, he replied, "Work in one? I wouldn't even eat in one. I can't stand fast food!" Clearly, he would have been as miscast as a fast-food entrepreneur as Crugnale would have been as an electronics engineer.

True, there are entrepreneurs who have succeeded spectacularly with no prior industry experience. Jeff Bezos of Amazon.com, Anita Roddick of The Body Shop, Ely Callaway of Callaway Golf, and Richard Branson of Virgin Airlines are four notable examples. But they are the exceptions.

Second to industry know-how is *management experience*, preferably with responsibility for budgets or, better yet, accountability for profit and loss. It is even better if a would-be entrepreneur has a record of increasing sales and profits. Of course, we are talking about the *ideal* entrepreneur. Very few people measure up to the ideal. That does not mean they should not start a new venture. But it does mean they should be realistic about the size of the business they should start. Eighteen years ago, two 19-year-old students wanted to start a travel agency business in Boston. When asked what they knew about the industry, one replied, "I live in California. I love to travel." The other was silent. Neither of them had worked in the travel industry, nor had anyone in either of their families. They were advised to get experience. One joined a training program for airline ticket agents; the other took a course for travel agents. They became friends with the owner of a local Uniglobe travel agency who helped them with advice. Six months after they first had the idea, they opened a part-time campus travel agency. In the first six months, they had about $100,000 of revenue and made $6,000 of profit but were unable to pay themselves any salary. In that way, they acquired experience at no expense and at low risk. Upon graduation, one of them, Mario Ricciardelli, made it his full-time job and continued building the business and gaining experience at the same time. In 2012, after many bumps in the road, the business—now named Studentcity.com—is one of the largest student travel businesses in the world.

Resources

It's hard to believe that Olsen and Anderson started DEC with only $70,000 of startup capital and built a company that at its peak ranked in the top 25 of the *Fortune* 500 companies. "The nice thing about $70,000 is that there are so few of them, you can watch every one," Olsen said. And watch them he did. Olsen and Anderson moved into a 100-year-old building that had been a 19th-century woolen mill. They furnished it with secondhand furniture, purchased tools from the Sears catalog, and built much of their own equipment as cheaply as possible. They sold $94,000 worth of goods in their first year and made a profit at the same time—a very rare feat indeed for a high-tech startup.

Successful entrepreneurs are frugal with their scarce resources. They keep overheads low, productivity high, and ownership of capital assets to a minimum. By so doing, they minimize the amount of capital they need to start their business and make it grow.

> Entrepreneurial frugality requires
>
> ■ Low overhead,
> ■ High productivity, and
> ■ Minimal ownership of capital assets.

Determining Resource Needs and Acquiring Resources

In order to determine the amount of capital that a company needs to get started, an entrepreneur should first assess what resources are crucial for the company's success in the marketplace. Some resources are more critical than others. What does the company expect to do better than any of its competitors? That is where it should put a disproportionate share of its very scarce resources. If the company is making a new high-tech product, technological know-how will be vital, and the most important resource will be engineers and the designs they produce. Therefore, the company must concentrate on recruiting and keeping excellent engineers and on safeguarding the intellectual property they produce, such as engineering designs and patents. If the company is doing retail selling, the critical factor will most likely be location. Choosing the wrong initial location for a retail store just because the rent is cheap can be a fatal mistake because it's unlikely there will be enough resources to relocate.

When Southwest Airlines started up in 1971, its strategy was to provide frequent, on-time service at a competitive price between Dallas, Houston, Austin, and San Antonio. To meet its objectives, Southwest needed planes that it could operate reliably at a low cost. It was able to purchase four brand-new Boeing 737s—very efficient planes for shorter routes—for only $4 million each because the recession had hit the airlines particularly hard and Boeing had an inventory of unsold 737s. From the outset, Southwest provided good, reliable service and had one of the lowest costs per mile in the industry.

Items that are not critical should be obtained as thriftily as possible. The founder of Burlington Coat Factory, Monroe Milstein, likes to tell the story of how he obtained estimates for gutting the building he had just leased for his second store. His lowest bid was several thousand dollars. One day he was at the building when a sudden thunderstorm sent a crew of laborers working at a nearby site to his building for shelter from the rain. Milstein asked the crew's foreman what they would charge for knocking down the internal structures that needed to be removed. The foreman said, "Five." Milstein asked, "Five what?" The foreman replied, "Cases of beer."

A complete set of resources includes everything the business will need, but a business does not have to do all of its work in-house with its own employees. It is often more effective to subcontract the work. That way it doesn't need to own or lease its own manufacturing plant and equipment or to worry about recruiting and training production workers. Often, it can keep overhead lower by using outside firms to do work such as payroll, accounting, advertising, mailing promotions, janitorial services, and so on.

Even startup companies can get amazingly good terms from outside suppliers. An entrepreneur should try to understand the potential suppliers' marginal costs. *Marginal cost* is the cost of producing one extra unit beyond what is presently produced. The marginal cost of the laborers who gutted Milstein's building while sheltering from the rain was virtually zero. They were being paid by another firm, and they didn't have to buy materials or tools.

A small electronics company was acquired by a much larger competitor. The large company took over the manufacturing of the small company's products. Production costs

Google founders Larry Page and Sergey Brin bought a terabyte of disks at bargain prices and built their own computer housings in Larry's dorm room, which became Google's first data center. Unable to interest the major portal players of the day, Larry and Sergey decided to make a go of it on their own. All they needed was a little cash to move out of the dorm—and to pay off the credit cards they had maxed out buying a terabyte of memory. So they wrote up a business plan, put their PhD plans on hold, and went looking for an angel investor. Their first visit was with a friend of a faculty member.

Andy Bechtolsheim, one of the founders of Sun Microsystems, was used to taking the long view. One look at their demo and he knew Google had potential—a lot of potential. But although his interest had been piqued, he was pressed for time. As Sergey tells it, "We met him very early one morning on the porch of a Stanford faculty member's home in Palo Alto. We gave him a quick demo. He had to run off somewhere, so he said, 'Instead of us discussing all the details, why don't I just write you a check?' It was made out to Google Inc. and was for $100,000."

The investment created a small dilemma. Since there was no legal entity known as "Google Inc.," there was no way to deposit the check. It sat in Larry's desk drawer for a couple of weeks while he and Sergey scrambled to set up a corporation and locate other funders among family, friends, and acquaintances. Ultimately, they brought in a total initial investment of almost $1 million.

On September 7, 1998, more than two years after they began work on their search engine, Google Inc., opened its door in Menlo Park, California. The door came with a remote control, as it was attached to the garage of a friend who sublet space to the new corporation's staff of three. The office offered several big advantages, including a washer and dryer and a hot tub. It also provided a parking space for the first employee hired by the new company: Craig Silverstein, now Google's director of technology.

Excerpted from *Google History*.[21]

Jb Reed/Bloomberg/Getty Images

Google founders Sergey Brin (L) and Larry Page (R) smile prior to a news conference during the opening of the Frankfurt bookfair on October 7, 2004, in Frankfurt, Germany

shot up. An analysis revealed that much of the increase was due to a rise in the cost of purchased components. In one instance, the large company was paying 50% more than the small company had been paying for the same item. It turned out that the supplier had priced the item for the small company on the basis of marginal costs and for the large company on the basis of total costs.

Smart entrepreneurs find ways of controlling critical resources without owning them. A startup business never has enough money, so it must be resourceful. It should not buy what it can lease. Except when the economy is red hot, there is almost always an excess of capacity of office and industrial space. Sometimes a landlord will be willing to offer a special deal to attract even a small startup company into a building. Such deals may include reduced rent, deferral of rent payments for a period of time, and building improvements made at low or even no cost. In some high-tech regions, landlords will exchange rent for equity in a high-potential startup.

When equipment is in excess supply, new businesses can lease it on very favorable terms. A young database company was negotiating a lease with IBM for a new minicomputer when its chief engineer discovered that a leasing company had identical secondhand units standing idle in its warehouse. The young company was able to lease one of the idle units for one-third of IBM's price. About 18 months later, the database company ran out of cash. Nevertheless, it was able to persuade the leasing company to defer payments because by then there were even more minicomputers standing idle in the warehouse, and it made little economic sense to repossess one and add it to the idle stock.

A. Startup Capital

You've developed your idea, you've carefully assessed what resources you will need to open your business and make it grow, you've pulled all your strategies together into a business plan, and now you know how much startup capital you need to get you to the point where your business will generate a positive cash flow. How are you going to raise that startup capital?

There are two types of startup capital: **debt** and **equity**. Simply put, with debt, you don't have to give up any ownership of the business, but you have to pay current interest and eventually repay the principal you borrow; with equity, you have to give up some of the ownership to get it, but you may never have to repay it or even pay a dividend. So you must choose between paying interest and giving up some of the ownership.

In practice, your choice usually depends on how much of each type of capital you can raise. Most startup entrepreneurs do not have much flexibility in their choice of financing. If it is a very risky business without any assets, it will be impossible to get any bank debt without putting up some collateral other than the business's assets—and most likely that collateral will be personal assets. Even if entrepreneurs are willing to guarantee the whole loan with their personal assets, the bank will expect entrepreneurs to put some equity into the business, probably equal to 25% of the amount of the loan. If your personal assets are less than the amount of the loan, the bank might recommend an SBA-guaranteed loan, in which case you would have to put in more equity.

The vast majority of entrepreneurs start their businesses by leveraging their own savings and labor. Consider how Apple, one of the most spectacular startups of all time, was funded. Steve Jobs and Stephen Wozniak had been friends since their school days in Silicon Valley. Wozniak was an authentic computer nerd. He had tinkered with computers from childhood, and he built a computer that won first prize in a science fair. His SAT math score was a perfect 800, but after stints at the University of Colorado, De Anza College, and Berkeley, he dropped out of school and went to work for Hewlett-Packard. His partner, Jobs, had an even briefer encounter with higher education: After one semester at Reed College, he left to look for a swami in India. When he and Wozniak began working on their microcomputer, Jobs was employed at Atari, the leading video game company.

Apple soon outgrew its manufacturing facility in the garage of Jobs' parents' house. Their company, financed initially with $1,300 raised by selling Jobs' Volkswagen and Wozniak's calculator, needed capital for expansion. They looked to their employers for help. Wozniak proposed to his supervisor that Hewlett-Packard produce what later became the Apple II. Perhaps not surprisingly, Hewlett-Packard declined. After all, Wozniak had no formal qualification in computer design; indeed, he did not even have a college degree. At Atari, Jobs tried to convince founder Nolan Bushnell to manufacture Apples. He too was rejected.

However, on the suggestion of Bushnell and Regis McKenna, a Silicon Valley marketing ace, the two partners contacted Don Valentine, a venture capitalist, in the fall of 1976. In those days, Jobs' appearance was a holdover from his swami days; he definitely did not project the image of Doriot's grade-A man, even by Silicon Valley's casual standards. Valentine did not invest. But he did put them in touch with Armas Markkula, Jr., who had recently retired from Intel a wealthy man. Markkula saw the potential in Apple, and he knew how to raise money. He personally invested $91,000, secured a line of credit from Bank of America, put together a business plan, and raised $600,000 of venture capital.

"[Mike Markkula] emphasized that you should never start a company with the goal of getting rich. Your goal should be making something you believe in and making a company that will last." Steve Jobs.[22]

In 2000, Steve Jobs said, "I was very lucky to have grown up in this industry. I did everything coming up—shipping, supply chain, sweeping floors, buying chips, you name it. I put computers together with my own hands. As the industry grew up, I kept on doing it."[23]

"In November 2009, Steve Jobs was voted CEO of the decade by *Fortune*. In the first decade of the 21st century, he reordered three industries: music with the iPod, movies with Pixar, and mobile phones with the iPhone. And back in the 1970s he shook up the computer industry with the Apple. Reordering one market as Henry Ford did with automobiles, Fred Smith with package delivery, Conrad Hilton with hotels, and Jeff Bezos with book retailing is an extraordinary achievement for any one lifetime; reordering four as Steve Jobs did before he was 55 is a gigantic feat."[24] But he was not yet done: A year or so before he died in 2011, he made that five industries when he introduced the iPad, the first tablet computer, which was an instant success; within a couple of years it was severely eroding the sales of PCs. According to Steve Jobs, "The reason that Apple can come out with products like the iPad is that we've always tried to be at the intersection of technology and liberal arts."[25] Some marketing gurus even claim that Steve Jobs's tally of five should really be six because his Apple store concept is a major innovation in retailing.

The Apple II was formally introduced in April 1977. Sales took off almost at once. Apple's sales grew rapidly to $2.5 million in 1977 and $15 million in 1978. In 1978, Dan Bricklin, a Harvard business student and former programmer at DEC, introduced the first electronic spreadsheet, VisiCalc, designed for the Apple II. In minutes, it could do tasks that had previously taken days. The microcomputer now had the power to liberate managers from the data guardians in the computer departments. According to one source, "Armed with VisiCalc, the Apple II's sales took off, and the personal computer industry was created." Apple's sales jumped to $70 million in 1979 and $117 million in 1980.

Steve Jobs and his legacy at the launch of the iPad in 2010

©AP/Wide World Photos

In 1980, Apple sold some of its stock to the public with an initial public offering (IPO) and raised more than $80 million. The paper value of their Apple stock made instant millionaires of Jobs ($165 million), Markkula ($154 million), Wozniak ($88 million), and Mike Scott ($62 million), who together owned 40% of Apple. Arthur Rock's venture capital investment of $57,000 in 1978 was suddenly worth $14 million, an astronomical compound return of more than 500% per year, or 17% per month.

By 1982, Apple IIs were selling at the rate of more than 33,000 units a month. With 1982 sales of $583 million, Apple hit the *Fortune* 500 list. It was a record. At five years of age, it was at that time the youngest company ever to join that exclusive list.

Success as spectacular as Apple's has never been equaled. Nonetheless, its financing is a typical example of how successful high-tech companies are funded. First, the entrepreneurs develop a prototype with personal savings and **sweat equity**, or ownership earned in lieu of wages. Then a wealthy investor—sometimes called an *informal investor* or *business angel*, who knows something about the entrepreneurs, or the industry, or both—invests some personal money in return for equity. When the company is selling product, it may be able to get a bank line of credit secured by its inventory and accounts receivable. If the company is growing quickly in a large market, it may be able to raise capital from a formal venture capital firm in return for equity. Further expansion capital may come from venture capital firms or from a public stock offering.

The vast majority of new firms will never be candidates for formal venture capital or a public stock offering. Nevertheless, they will have to find some equity capital. In most cases, after they have exhausted their personal savings, entrepreneurs will turn to family, friends, and acquaintances (see Figure 2.4). It can be a scary business. Entrepreneurs often find themselves with all their personal net worth tied up in the same business that provides all their income. That is double jeopardy because, if their businesses fail, they lose both their savings and their means of support. Risk of that sort can be justified only if the profit potential is high enough to yield a commensurate rate of return.

Would-be entrepreneurs sometimes tell me that they did not start their ventures because they could not raise sufficient money to get started. More often than not, they were unrealistic about the amount of money that they could reasonably have expected to raise for their startup businesses. I tell them that many of the best companies started with very little capital. For example, 50% of companies on the 2008 list of *Inc.* 500 companies were started with less than $25,000; 87% of all the companies on the list were funded with money from the entrepreneurs, 19% with money from family and friends, 17% with bank loans, and only 3% with venture capital,[26] which is by far the rarest source of seed-stage investment. It is estimated that at most only 1 in 10,000 of all new ventures in the United States has venture capital in hand at the outset and only 1 in 1,000 gets venture capital at any stage of its life.

	All Nations	U.S.
Close family member	40%	44%
Other relative	11%	6%
Work colleague	10%	9%
Friend/Neighbor	28%	28%
Stranger	9%	7%
Other	2%	6%
	100%	100%

Source: Global Entrepreneurship Monitor.[27]

Figure 2.4

Relationship of investor to entrepreneur

IV Profit Potential

The level of profit that is reasonable depends on the type of business. On average, U.S. companies make about 5% net income. Hence, on one dollar of revenue, the average company makes a five-cent profit after paying all expenses and taxes. A company that consistently makes 10% is doing very well, and one that makes 15% is truly exceptional. Approximately 50% of the *Inc.* 500 companies make 5% or less; 13% of them make 16% or more. Profit margins in a wide variety of industries for companies both large and small are published by Robert Morris Associates, so entrepreneurs can compare their forecasts with the actual performance of similar-sized companies in the same industry.

Any business must make enough profit to recompense its investors (in most cases that is the entrepreneur) for their investment. This must be the profit after all normal business expenses have been accounted for, including a fair salary for the entrepreneur and any family members who are working in the business. A common error in assessing the profitability of a new venture is to ignore the owner's salary. Suppose someone leaves a secure job paying $70,000 per year plus fringe benefits and invests $100,000 of personal savings to start a new venture. That person should expect to take a $70,000 salary plus fringe benefits out of the new business. Perhaps in the first year or two, when the business is being built, it may not be possible to pay $70,000 in actual cash; in that case, the pay that is not actually received should be treated as deferred compensation to be paid in the future. In addition to an adequate salary, the entrepreneur must earn a reasonable return on the $100,000 investment. A professional investor putting money into a new, risky business would expect to earn an annual rate of return of at least 40%, which would be $40,000 annually on a $100,000 investment. That return may come as a capital gain when the business is sold, or as a dividend, or as a combination of the two. But remember that $100,000 compounding annually at 40% grows to almost $2.9 million in 10 years. When such large capital gains are needed to produce acceptable returns, big capital investments held for a long time do not make any sense unless very substantial value can be created, as occasionally happens in the case of high-flying companies, especially high-tech ones. In most cases, instead of a capital gain, the investor's return will be a dividend, which must be paid out of the cash flow from the business.

The cash flow that a business generates is not to be confused with profit. It is possible, indeed very likely, that a rapidly growing business will have a negative cash flow from operations in its early years even though it may be profitable. That may happen because the business may not be able to generate enough cash flow internally to sustain its ever-growing needs for working capital and the purchase of long-term assets such as plant and equipment. Hence, it will have to borrow or raise new equity capital. So it is very important that a high-potential business intending to grow rapidly make careful cash-flow projections so as to predict its needs for future outside investments. Future equity investments will dilute the percentage of ownership of the founders, and if the dilution becomes excessive, there may be little reward remaining for the entrepreneurs.

Biotechnology companies are examples of this problem: They have a seemingly insatiable need for cash infusions to sustain their research and development (R&D) costs in their early years. Their negative cash flow, or *burn rate*, sometimes runs at $1 million per month. A biotechnology company can easily burn up $50 million before it generates a meaningful profit, let alone a positive cash flow. The expected future capital gain from a public stock offering or sale to a large pharmaceutical company has to run into hundreds of millions of dollars, maybe into the billion-dollar range, for investors to realize an annual return of 50% or higher, which is what they expect to earn on money invested in a seed-stage biotechnology company. Not surprisingly, to finance their ventures biotechnology entrepreneurs as a group have to give up most of the ownership. A study of venture-capital-backed biotechnology companies found that after they had gone public, the entrepreneurs and management were left with less than 18% of the equity, compared with 32% for a comparable group of computer software companies.[28]

> For entrepreneurs, happiness is a positive cash flow.

We've said that most businesses will never have the potential to go public. Nor will the owners ever intend to sell their businesses and thereby realize a capital gain. In that case, how can those owners get a satisfactory return on the money they have invested in their businesses? The two ingredients that determine return on investment are (1) the amount invested and (2) the annual amount earned on that investment. Entrepreneurs should invest as little as possible to start their businesses and make sure that their firms will be able to pay them a "dividend" big enough to yield an appropriate annual rate of return. For income tax purposes, that "dividend" may be in the form of a salary, bonus, or fringe benefits rather than an actual dividend paid out

Awash with Cash

Apple is an awesome money machine. Apple's stash of cash kept piling up so that by 2012 its cash and short-term investments stood at $114.2 billion. It was enough money to give each household in the United States $1,026, or put another way, it was enough to purchase an iPad for every American more than 5 years old.

In 2012, Apple generated $4.6 billion of cash flow from operations every month—almost $7,429 per second on the basis of a five-day working week, eight hours per day. No wonder Apple, with a market capitalization of more than $620 billion, was the most valuable company in history. www.apple.com/pr/library/2012/07/24Apple-Reports-Third-Quarter-Results.html

of retained earnings. Of course, the company must be generating cash from its own operations before that dividend can be paid. For entrepreneurs, happiness is a positive cash flow. And the day a company begins to generate **free cash**—that is, more cash than needed to sustain operations and purchase assets to keep the company on its growth trajectory—is a very happy day in the life of a successful entrepreneur.

Ingredients for a Successful New Business

The great day has arrived. You found an idea, wrote a business plan, and gathered your resources. Now you are opening the doors of your new business for the first time, and the really hard work is about to begin. What are the factors that distinguish winning entrepreneurial businesses from the also-rans? Rosabeth Kanter prescribed Four Fs for a successful business,[29] a list that has been expanded into the Nine Fs for entrepreneurial success (see Figure 2.5).

First and foremost, the founding entrepreneur is the most important factor. Next comes the market. This is the "era of the other," in which, as Regis McKenna observed, the fastest-growing companies in an industry will be in a segment labeled "others" in a market-share pie chart. By and large, they will be newer entrepreneurial firms rather than large firms with household names; hence, specialization is the key. A successful business should focus on niche markets.

The rate of change in business gets ever faster. The advanced industrial economies are knowledge based. Product life cycles are getting shorter. Technological innovation progresses at a relentless pace. Government rules and regulations keep changing. Communications and travel around the globe keep getting easier and cheaper. And consumers are better informed about their choices. To survive, let alone succeed, a company has to be quick and nimble. It must be fast and flexible. It cannot allow inertia to build up. Look at retailing: The historical giants such as Kmart are on the ropes, while nimble competitors dance around them. Four of the biggest retailing successes are Les Wexner's The Limited, the late Sam Walton's Walmart, Bernie Marcus and Arthur Blank's Home Depot, and Anita Roddick's The Body Shop. Entrepreneurs such as these know that they can keep inertia low by keeping the layers of management as few as possible. Tom Peters, an authority on business strategy, liked to point out that Walmart had three layers of management, whereas Sears had 10 a few years back

Founders	Every startup company must have a first-class entrepreneur.
Focused	Entrepreneurial companies focus on niche markets. They specialize.
Fast	They make decisions quickly and implement them swiftly.
Flexible	They keep an open mind. They respond to change.
Forever-innovating	They are tireless innovators.
Flat	Entrepreneurial organizations have as few layers of management as possible.
Frugal	By keeping overhead low and productivity high, entrepreneurial companies keep costs down.
Friendly	Entrepreneurial companies are friendly to their customers, suppliers, and employees.
Fun	It's fun to be associated with an entrepreneurial company.

■ Figure 2.5

The Nine Fs for entrepreneurial success

when Walmart displaced Sears as the nation's top chain of department stores. "A company with three layers of management can't lose against a company with ten. You could try, but you couldn't do it!" says Peters. So keep your organization flat. It will facilitate quick decisions and flexibility and will keep overhead low.

Small entrepreneurial firms are great innovators. Big firms are relying increasingly on strategic partnerships with entrepreneurial firms in order to get access to desirable R&D. The trend is well under way. Hoffmann-La Roche, hurting for new blockbuster prescription drugs, purchased a majority interest in Genentech and bought the highly regarded biotechnology called PCR (polymerase chain reaction) from Cetus for $300 million. Eli Lilly purchased Hybritech. In the 1980s, IBM spent $9 billion a year on research and development, but even that astronomical amount of money could not sustain Big Blue's commercial leadership. As its market share was remorselessly eaten away by thousands of upstarts, IBM entered into strategic agreements with Apple, Borland, Go, Lotus, Intel, Metaphor, Microsoft, Novell, Stratus, Thinking Machines, and other entrepreneurial firms for the purpose of gaining computer technologies.

When it comes to productivity, the best entrepreneurial companies leave the giant corporations behind in the dust. According to 2012 computer industry statistics, Dell's revenue per employee was $549,000 and Microsoft's was $788,000, while Hewlett-Packard's was $363,000 and IBM's was $250,000. Of course, Dell subcontracts more of its manufacturing, but this does not explain all the difference. Whether you hope to build a big company or a small one, the message is the same: Strive tirelessly to keep productivity high.

But no matter what you do, you probably won't be able to attain much success unless you have happy customers, happy workers, and happy suppliers. That means you must have a friendly company. It means that everyone must be friendly, especially anyone who deals with customers. "The most fun six-month period I've had since the start of Microsoft" is how Bill Gates described his astonishing accomplishment in reinventing his 20-year-old company to meet the threat posed by Internet upstarts in the mid-1990s. In not much more than six months of Herculean effort, Microsoft had developed an impressive array of new products to match those of Netscape. Having fun is one of the keys to keeping a company entrepreneurial. If Microsoft's product developers had not been having fun, they would not have put in 12-hour days and sometimes overnighters to catch up with the Netscape. And big as it is, Microsoft still has the entrepreneurial spirit. In June 2009, Microsoft introduced its Bing search engine to compete with Google's; four months after its introduction, Bing had already captured almost 10% of the lucrative search and advertising market.[30] By December 2012, that share had increased to 16.3% and Google's appeared to have plateaued at 66.7%.

Most new companies have the Nine Fs at the outset. Those that become successful and grow pay attention to keeping them and nurturing them. The key to sustaining success is to remain an entrepreneurial gazelle and never turn into a lumbering elephant and finally a dinosaur, doomed to extinction.

When it introduced the first personal computer (PC) in 1981, IBM stood astride the computer industry like a big blue giant. Two suppliers of its personal computer division were Intel and Microsoft. Compared with IBM, Intel was small and Microsoft was a midget. By 2002, Intel's revenue was $26.8 billion and Microsoft's was $28.4 billion. Between 1998 and 2002, Microsoft's revenue increased 86%, while IBM's stood still. In 2002, IBM — the company that invented the PC — had only 6% of the worldwide market for PCs. In December 2004, IBM announced that it was selling its PC division to Lenovo, the leading Chinese manufacturer of PCs. By then it was Microsoft's Windows operating system and Intel's microprocessors — the so-called WINTEL — that were shaping the future of information technology. And in 2013, Microsoft's Windows is threatened by Google's Android, which has become the operating system of choice of handheld devices except those made by Apple.

It is easy to start a business in the United States; anyone can do it. What distinguishes successful entrepreneurs from less successful ones is the ability to spot an opportunity for a high-potential venture and then to develop it into a thriving business. As the business grows, the successful entrepreneur is able to attract key management team members, to motivate employees, to find more and more customers and keep them coming back, and to build increasingly sophisticated relationships with financiers.

CONCLUSION ☐

YOUR OPPORTUNITY JOURNAL ☐

Reflection Point	**Your Thoughts. . .**
1. What life events might trigger your entrepreneurial career?	
2. What ideas do you have for a new business?	
a. What ideas can you draw from your past work experience?	
b. What ideas can you draw from your family's work experience?	
3. Which of your personal attributes will most help you succeed as an entrepreneur?	
4. Which attributes do you think you need to further develop?	
5. Who are your entrepreneurial role models? Can you foster any of them into mentors?	
6. Is your idea an opportunity? Explain.	
7. Is the timing right to launch your venture?	
8. What are some cost-effective ways for you to get started?	

NOTES ☐

[1] According to the 2002 Kauffman study, 1,992 two- and four-year colleges and universities offered at least one course in entrepreneurship, up from about 300 in the 1984–1985 academic year. http://money.cnn.com/magazines/fsb/fsb-archive/2006/03/01/8370301/index.htm.

[2] Moore, Carol. "Understanding Entrepreneurial Behavior." In J. A. Pearce II, and R. B. Robinson, Jr., eds., *Academy of Management Best Paper Proceedings*. Forty-sixth Annual Meeting of the Academy of Management, Chicago, 1986.

[3] www.stores.org/archives/jan99cover.asp.

[4] Brockhuas, R. Risk-Taking Propensity of Entrepreneurs. *Academy of Management Journal*, 23: 509–520. 1980.

5 Carter, N. M., Gartner, W. B., Shaver, K. G., and Gatewood, E. J. The Career Reasons for Nascent Entrepreneurs. *Journal of Business Venturing*, 19: 13–39. 2003.

6 Rogers, E. M., and Larsen, J. K. *Silicon Valley Fever: Growth of High-Technology Culture*. New York: Basic Books. 1984.

7 *Inc.* 500. September 2012.

8 Excerpted from http://web.mit.edu/newsoffice/2009/kauffman-study-0217.html.

9 www.census.gov/Press-Release/www/2001/cb01-54.html.

10 www.census.gov/Press-Release/www/2001/cb01-115.html.

11 www.census.gov/Press-Release/www/releases/archives/cb05_108_table.xls.

12 *Inc.* 500. September 2009.

13 *Inc.* 500. 25(12): 2004. *Inc.* 500 CEO Survey 2004. www.inc.com/multimedia/slideshows/content/crunchingnumbers_pagen_3.html.

14 It is also an excellent example of what venture capitalists call value-added.

15 *Inc.* 500. 22(15). 2000.

16 For more information on startups and failures, refer to William Dennis, *The Shape of Small Business*. NFIB Foundation. www.nfib.com/object/PolicyGuide2.html.

17 www.sba.gov/advo/research/rs204tot.pdf.

18 Detailed information on survival rates can be found in: Boden, R. J., Jr., *Analysis of Business Dissolution by Demographic Category of Business Ownership*. 2000. www.sba.gov/advo/research/rs204tot.pdf. Kirchhoff, Bruce A., and Phillips, Bruce D. *Innovation and Growth Among New Firms in the U.S. Economy*. Frontiers of Entrepreneurship Research, Babson College, Wellesley, MA. 1989. pp. 173–188. Kirchhoff, Bruce A. *Entrepreneurship and Dynamic Capitalism*. Westport, CT: Praeger. 1994. Phillips, Bruce D., and Kirchhoff, Bruce A. Formation, Growth, and Survival: Small Firm Dynamics in the U.S. Economy. *Small Business Economics*, 1: 65–74. 1989.

19 Timmons, Jeffry A. *New Venture Creation*. Homewood, IL: Richard D. Irwin. 2001.

20 Obituary: Professor Rajeev Motwani. June 9, 2009. www.telegraph.co.uk/news/obituaries/technology-obituaries/5487846/Professor-Rajeev-Motwani.html.

21 www.google.com/corporate/history.html.

22 Isaacson, Walter. *Steve Jobs*. New York, NY: Simon and Schuster, 2011. P. 78.

23 *Business Week*. February 6, 2006. p. 66.

24 www.telegraph.co.uk/technology/apple/6513511/Steve-Jobs-voted-CEO-of-the-decade.html.

25 Isaacson, Walter. *Steve Jobs*. New York, NY: Simon and Schuster, 2011. P. 494.

26 *Inc.* September 2008.

27 The information in Figure 2.4 was extracted from the Global Entrepreneurship Monitor data set. www.gemconsortium.org.

28 Bygrave, William D., and Timmons, Jeffry A. *Venture Capital at the Crossroads*. Boston, MA: Harvard Business School Press. 1992.

29 Kanter, Rosabeth Moss. *Change Masters: Innovation and Entrepreneurship in the American Corporation*. New York: Simon & Schuster. 1985.

30 AFP. November 17, 2009. www.google.com/hostednews/afp/article/ALeqM5iFIa_CCCc6QwmkYkicyfMLE_oGiQ.

Vera Bradley

Fort Wayne, Indiana Barbara Baekgaard and Pat Miller sat at a small table covered with many swatches of brightly colored fabrics being considered for the next product launch. The cottage industry business they had founded several years earlier had taken on a life of its own. From humble beginnings in the basement of Barb's home, they had proven both the feasibility and value of the market for attractive ladies' handbags and luggage. But as sales grew, so did issues with production capacity and quality to name a few. The two pondered the future. What financial resources and human resources would they need to scale up to the next level? How would growth affect the friendly, fun culture they had worked so hard to create?

Origins

Barbara Baekgaard was wrist deep in wallpaper glue one day in 1981 when the doorbell rang. Who could it be? She had only recently moved into her new home in the Wildwood Park neighborhood of Fort Wayne, Indiana. At the door were Patricia (Pat) Miller and her 5-year-old son, Jay. Pat had stopped in to welcome Barb and her family to the neighborhood. As Pat recalls:

> I was the welcoming committee of one, and Barb answered the door. If you know anything about Barb, you'll know that she was redecorating—taking wall paper down and putting her own stamp on the house. She asked me if I knew how to hang wallpaper, and I said, no, and she asked, 'How would you like to learn?' That was the beginning of our first business, Up Your Wall, a wallpaper-hanging business.
>
> We were good partners because she remembered every joke she's ever heard, and I was a good audience. She also liked to hang wallpaper around windows and doors, the more complicated stuff, while I enjoyed doing the straight walls.

The two women became fast friends and business partners, hanging wallpaper by day and raising their families by night. Up Your Wall, however, would be superseded within a year by another, more promising venture.

In March of 1982, the partners made a trip to Florida to celebrate the birthday of Barb's father. While waiting for a connecting flight in Atlanta's Hartsfield-Jackson Airport, they noticed that many passengers were carrying Land's End duffle bags and other utilitarian garment bags and luggage. Barb describes their observation:

> While we were waiting for our plane, I looked around and realized that we weren't the only women with unattractive luggage. In fact, I didn't see one woman in the entire airport carrying anything that would be considered attractive. I knew that there was a look out there that was cute and trendy, but I didn't own any of it, probably because it was too expensive and not functional.

In fact, both Laura Ashley, known for its floral printed fabrics, and Pierre Deux, maker of French country-style handbags and accessories, targeted the high-end of the market with attractive products. Pat recalls that their Florida trip included a visit to a Pierre Deux retail store: "We loved that . . . it was part of our inspiration. There was nothing like that in this country." However, neither of these potential competitors produced a duffle bag suitable for weekend or air travel. Barb and Pat discussed their luggage dilemma on the trip back to Fort

Wayne. "We liked the shapes of the bags we saw," recalls Barb, "but not their appearance." The women wondered if they could make attractive but functional bags for everyday use and travel at a price that would appeal to a broader audience.

The day after returning to Fort Wayne, Barb and Pat visited Joann Fabrics, a retail chain of fabric stores, where they purchased material with various patterns, stripes, and colors. They mixed and matched these in an effort to create a distinctive quilted cotton look of their own.

Once they had the designs they liked and cut out patterns, the team hired a woman who had done clothing alteration for their other home-based venture, running clothing trunk shows.[1] She was paid for sewing the prototype bags Barb and Pat had designed. These initial prototypes included a duffle bag suitable for weekend travel, a smaller bag they called the "sport," and a purse. There was enough fabric to make a dozen, which they hoped to sell at an upcoming trunk show. Says Pat:

> We needed to do some market research and wanted to be certain that it was unbiased. We couldn't let friends who came to the trunk show know that we had developed these products—they might buy them simply because they were our friends. So, we had to come up with a brand name that didn't have either my name or Barb's name in it. We decided to use Barb's mother's name, Vera Bradley. My mother's name was Wilma Polito. That name didn't have a prayer of sticking as a brand, so we settled on Vera Bradley Designs.

The day of the trunk show was plagued by inclement weather, but attendance was high and the show was a success. All twelve of the prototype bags sold, and customers were asking for more.

Because the trunk sale attendees were generally middle-aged and older women, the two entrepreneurs looked for another segment in which to test the appeal of their products. Barbara had two daughters in college at the time, one at Michigan State and the other at Marymount College in New York, so they decided to extend their informal market research to college campuses. Barbara sent several bags to each daughter and asked them to find out what their friends thought of them. The response from both campuses was extremely enthusiastic.

With affirmation that their bags were potential winners, the ladies set out to purchase more material and commission the sewing of more bags. Each borrowed $250 from her husband, and with cash in hand they set off once again to Joann Fabrics.

The Founders

Barbara Baekgaard had attended Marymount College in New York and Barat College in Lake Forest, Illinois, where she studied sociology. Her father was in the gift candle business and he often took Barb to gift shows and other industry events. Her mother, after whom the company is named, had several small cottage businesses of her own. Barbara credits her mother for her work ethic, as well as her eye for design. "What I knew about business at that time I learned from them," she says. "Things like finance were not even in the realm of my knowledge, but I was doing what I knew best—design."

Barb's parents had bequeathed her other important traits: energy and unflappable optimism. "There are people who think they can, and people who think they can't. I'm the think you can type," she says. "I am shocked when things don't go right for me. Just shocked." Her

---

[1] A "trunk show" is a special sale in which a vendor or designer presents merchandise directly to consumers in a home or other unique venue.

fondest aphorisms reflect a deeply ingrained optimism: "Often wrong, but never in doubt." "Good is the enemy of great—never settle for good."

Like Barbara, Pat Miller had family members who influenced and shaped her attitudes toward business and customers. As a young girl she often worked in her grandfather's grocery store. "I learned a lot about business from working in that store—inventory control, bookkeeping, marketing, running the cash register, and dealing with customers," she says. "I was always in the store and did a little of everything. And I knew that [in the future] I wanted to be connected with business." She followed through on her intentions, earning a BS in business education from Indiana University, and then teaching business to high school students for six years.

The Early Years

With the success of their prototypes among trunk show attendees and college students, the founders knew that they were onto something of value. But would their bags appeal to a broader audience in a retail setting? The annual Chicago Gift Show, a major buyers-meet-sellers event, was coming up on the calendar in September 1982. It seemed a good place to test their products.

Barbara had attended various gift shows with her father, on behalf of his candle business. The Chicago Gift Show highlighted gift wares and home furnishings and was primarily attended by individuals who either owned or sold to gift shops and notions stores. Because handbags and luggage were not generally thought of as gifts, companies in that industry did not exhibit at the Chicago event, but favored other venues and trade shows where women's apparel accessories were typically featured. The founders, however, decided to try their luck in Chicago, thereby avoiding more competitive venues where standing out from the crowd would be a struggle. Says Barb:

> I remember calling to rent booth space. They told me that they didn't have our category of
> product at the show and didn't know where to put us. When we showed up we found our space
> in the bowels of McCormick Place, where the show is held. But we took it in stride and set up a
> wonderful display of our products, with flowers and pretty fabrics.

During an evening reception for the event's hundreds of vendors, Barb chanced to meet Will Little, who ran the show. The two got along very well, and Little asked to see her booth. After getting a look at how nicely the two newcomers had decorated their exhibit, and its unfavorable location, Little took it upon himself to have their booth moved to a more strategically placed space.

The show was a success for the two women, who sold over $10,000 in product. It was then that they realized two things: They had something potentially big on their hands, and they needed to purchase much more fabric and outsource the sewing in order to tap that potential. But where would they get the cash?

Initial Financing

Their question was soon answered—and from an unanticipated source. Shortly after the Chicago Gift Show, Barb and her husband made a trip to nearby Michigan to visit one of his former work colleagues. Still bubbling over from her Gift Show success, Barb explained her new business venture to their host, who listened with interest. Later in the evening, the gentleman asked her to step into his home office, where he presented her with a check for $2,500 dollars. "I almost fell over," Barbara recalls. "He said, 'I love your enthusiasm. If you are successful, consider this a loan; if not, it's a gift.'"

A bank relationship soon followed. Back in Fort Wayne the two founders paid a visit to Franklin Bank, where they hoped to obtain a $2,000, 90-day loan for fabric purchasing. They walked in with sample products in hand and asked to see someone about a loan. The receptionist introduced them to a loan officer who listened with their plans with what both later described as undisguised condescension. "And where are you going to sell those bags?" he asked with a bemused chuckle. After a few more questions about the business, the loan officer unenthusiastically described the bank's terms and produced the proper documents, which Barb and Pat signed.

As they left the bank, Barb turned to Pat and asked what she thought about their experience with the loan officer. Pat was blunt and brief: "He didn't get it at all." With that, the two made an about face, marched back into the bank, and demanded that they be assigned to another banker—someone who understood and believed in their business. The bank introduced them to Robert Marshall, who would be their banker and friend for many years to come. Marshall took a strong interest in the venture and would often drop in on their workplace to see how things were progressing and to offer business advice. When Marshall went to work for another bank, the Vera Bradley account followed him.

Neither partner had knowledge or experience in financing. Recognizing this weakness, they turned for help to the local office of SCORE (Service Corps of Retired Executives)[2] and requested someone with financial expertise. SCORE introduced them to volunteer George Cook, a retired financial executive. His skills nicely complement those of the two entrepreneurs.

One of Cook's first initiatives was to show Barb and Pat how to analyze their cost of goods to ensure that they priced items in a way that would produce a healthy gross margin. He went on to study their production, distribution, and associated sales and marketing costs to understand what it would take to make a profit. Cook emphasized the importance of understanding costs and minimizing expenses in order to make the most of the venture's limited capital. Under his guidance, the company established sound bookkeeping and inventory procedures and produced monthly financial statements and inventory reports in order to control the business.

In the years that followed, the business would need more capital in order to finance its growing sales. That need would be met first by a cash infusion from the founders who mortgaged their homes to raise capital, and by a bank line of credit.

Production

Production at the company's "cottage industry" level involved cutting fabric into patterns, followed by sewing the cut pieces into finished products—both labor-intensive activities. Recognizing that their core skills were in design and sales, the partners decided to outsource sewing to people in the community who did it well. Barb was a good sewer but, as she said, "I shouldn't be in the basement sewing. I should be out selling."

Working out of Barb's basement, the founders cut fabric, sometimes with the help of their children. All the materials needed to produce a bag—including zippers, thread, labels, and instructions—were then packaged into individual kits that freelance sewers would pick up and later return as finished goods for inspection. Outsourcing of manufacturing continued.

---

[2] SCORE (Service Corps of Retired Executives) is a free and confidential small business mentoring services staffed by retired executives.

as revenues grew. "Our future was sales and design," Barb asserted many years latter. "We wouldn't have been good at manufacturing."

By 1986 the business had grown to the point that Vera Bradley needed more space. The next year it constructed a building with more than enough space for its current requirements, leasing out what it didn't need.

Brand Image

From the beginning, Vera Bradley bags had a distinctive look: vibrant colors, unusual patterns, and clever designs. "I've always thought that design was the engine that pulled our train," Pat likes to say. She and Barb wanted their products to stand out and be identifiable as Vera Bradley, even when their labels were not visible. With that in mind, every newly introduced product had a unique design or pattern feature, yet maintained the Vera Bradley "look." This distinctiveness reinforced the brand image and kept current customers coming back for more. However, every change represented a risk of being stuck with unsalable merchandise.

The founders' concern with the "look" of their products extended to the public's perceptions of Vera Bradley, the company. In their view, it was important for the business to look professional and larger than it actually was in those early days. They did not want customers or suppliers to think of Vera Bradley as a basement operation. With that in mind, Barbara instructed her children not to answer the phone during business hours. Meanwhile, Pat, with help from Barbara's daughter, Joanie, designed a striking and professional-looking letterhead and business cards. Joanie also lent her artistic skills the first company catalog (Exhibit 2.1). Product shipments used new boxes rather than reused boxes and packing material. According to Barb:

> We didn't want people to know that we were working out of the basement. You have to look as though you are a strong, successful business. So everything sent out had to look as though we were in the most beautiful corporate setting around, and doing well.

Sales

The 1982 Chicago Gift Show gave the company some exposure to the distribution channel. Developing relationships and creating a network of repeat customers within that channel would require much more work. As with other functions of the nascent enterprise, the two founders began with a do-it-yourself approach. Whenever either of them was out and about they would look for local gift shops, walk in, introduce themselves and the company, show samples, and ask for an order. They also recruited friends and family as independent sales representatives: Barb's mother, sisters, college friends, friends of friends—they turned to people whom they knew and liked and asked if they would represent the company's products in their geographic areas. The first of these reps was Barb's college roommate, a resident of upscale Arlington, Virginia. She enlisted in 1983.

Sales representatives were responsible for developing a customer base of primarily gift stores in their geographic areas. Reps would take orders, but would not be paid commissions until sold items were paid for. The reasoning behind this compensation strategy originated in Barb's earlier gift trade experience. Many shop owners, she knew, were slow to pay. If reps were paid only *after* receivables were collected, they would naturally avoid store owners of dubious creditworthiness. That strategy also benefited cash flow at a time when cash was scarce.

EXHIBIT 2.1 **From the first company catalog, circa 1985**

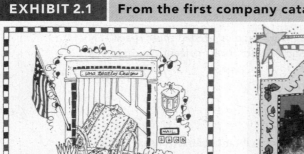

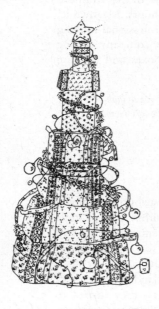

Source: The Company with permission.

In a matter of months, Vera Bradley had many independent representatives taking orders from gift shops in several states. Each rep had a direct or indirect relationship with one or both founders. And as their numbers grew, so did revenue: from a mere $11,000 dollars in 1982 to $503,000 dollars in 1985, to $4.8 million in 1990 (Exhibit 2.2). And the business community took notice. In 1985, Barb and Pat received the national "Entrepreneur of the Year Award" from Ernst & Young, LLC (see Exhibit 2.3).

EXHIBIT 2.2	Early revenues and expenses ($000s)		
	Fiscal Yr 1982 4 months	Fiscal Yr 1985 12 months	Fiscal Yr 1990 12 months
Sales	11	503	4,757
Cost of Goods	7	289	2,311
Gross Profit	4	214	2,446
Selling/Admin Expenses	2	178	2,142
Income before other Inc/(Exp)	2	35	
Interest income			23
Miscellaneous			5
Interest expense		(7)	(46)
State tax expense			
Other income/(Expense)		(7)	(19)
Income before distribution	2	28	285

Source: The Company with permission.

EXHIBIT 2.3	Barb and Pat's advice to entrepreneurs

Concentrate on what you do best.
Don't be satisfied with the status quo—innovate and practice continuous improvement.
Choose the right people to work with: vendors, bankers, and employees.
Networking is important; it's important when people like you and you like them.
Don't be afraid to take risks.
Take one day at a time.
Follow your passion and have fun!

Downs and Ups

In the beginning, Barbara and Pat did everything but the sewing themselves—even selling. They brought in employees only as they needed them. The founders recognized from day one of their association how their aptitudes and interests overlapped in some areas and complemented in others. They made the most of this as they divided their labors in managing their growing enterprise. As COO Jill Nichols, who joined the company as controller in 1989, observed their roles in those earlier years, "Barb focused on design—the creative side—and sales, while Pat was more concerned with operations. Pat's more oriented to processes, and Barb is more into the creative side."

Like every enterprise, Vera Bradley experienced a number of setbacks and made its share of mistakes. Barb and Pat's natural optimism, however, led them to work through these stumbles without discouragement. In one case, Pat mistakenly placed an order for hundreds of 20-inch bag zippers when their design called for a 12-inch item. Rather than fight with the supplier over an exchange—and possibly lose credibility as a buyer—the two women decided to turn lemons into lemonade: They created a new bag design with a 20-inch zipper. In another case, Barb placed an ad in a direct mail catalog for a particular bag made from an off-the-shelf fabric. That fabric was then ordered from the manufacturer in anticipation ad-generated sales. "Sorry, that fabric has been discontinued," the manufacturer replied. Since it was too late to pull the ad, Barb and Pat bit the bullet and ordered 2,000 yards of a special printing of the fabric in question, enough for some 650 bags. This special order was costly, but the customers were happy.

In some cases, the entrepreneurs caught lucky breaks and made the most of them. One of these has become a favorite tale of the founders, and a part of company lore. While exhibiting at a New York City gift show in 1989, a woman approached the company's booth just as the hall was closing. She asked Pat if Vera Bradley would consider doing a special collection. Pat suggested that they discuss it further. The unidentified woman said, "I'll give you a call," and then disappeared into the crowd exiting the building. Moments later, Pat kicked herself for not getting the woman's card. "Who knew if she would ever call us?"

Not long thereafter, the woman phoned the company and asked if Pat and Barb would be in New York anytime soon. As it happened, both founders were heading to New York for yet another gift show, so the woman suggested that they have lunch at Tavern on the Green. Located in New York City's Central Park, Tavern of the Green was a popular tourist stop, and the second largest grossing restaurant in the country!

And so they met for lunch. After dining, the conversation turned to business. Barb and Pat assumed that their hostess was interested in products she had seen at the gift show, and were prepared to discuss an order, at which point Pat excused herself to go to the ladies room. When Pat returned, she found that their hostess had gone off momentarily to assist with a busload of tourists that had just pulled up. Barb leaned over and whispered her latest intelligence: The woman did not run the gift shop; she owned the entire place and wanted them to design a special collection of bags for Tavern on the Green! Their next meeting took place in the restaurateur's apartment at the Dakota on Central Park West, where the three began designing the collection. The eventual release of the Tavern on the Green pattern gave a boost and credibility to the Vera Bradley brand.

Sourcing a Key Input

Fabric was the key raw material of the business. As sales accelerated, the founders realized that purchasing fabric at retail prices would impair profitability. Retail fabric was generally priced at four and one-half times wholesale. They needed to establish relationships with fabric wholesalers, but had not yet realized that their purchase volumes were still too small to interest wholesale textile suppliers. Pat noticed that some of the bolts of cloth they were using were imprinted with their manufacturers' names and address. She created a list of these and sent letters to each one requesting a meeting. To her surprise, none responded.

One of the manufacturers, VIP, was located in New York City, not far from the college where Barb's daughter was enrolled. So, Pat suggested that Barb drop in on that company the next time she visited the campus, which she did. Without invitation, Barb showed up in VIP's lobby and introduced herself. Mistaking Barbara for a representative of the much larger company with a name similar to Vera, the receptionist whisked her off to meet the company's Vice President of Sales, Leo Driscoll. As the two talked shop, Leo realized that they weren't speaking the same language. Barb didn't appear to understand the standard terms of the trade.

He asked me at one point how many pieces I wanted and I responded, 'As many as you can sell me.' To me, a piece was a two foot swatch; [to people in the trade] a piece was 25 yards. Then he asked, 'Who are you with again?' and I said, 'Vera Bradley.' His next comment was, 'How did you get in here?'

Leo wasn't interested in taking on a small customer like Vera Bradley, but he was amused and impressed by his guest's affirmative attitude. The two hit it off so well that he accepted her order for 500 yards of fabric—VIP's rock-bottom minimum order quantity.

Barbara attributes her success in this and similar encounters to advice received from her father many years earlier: "First, sell yourself, then your company, and then your product." In the years that followed, Leo Driscoll became a friend and mentor to Vera Bradley, and his company was rewarded with larger and larger orders.

Culture

Barbara and Pat knew from the start that company culture would play a large role in their success and their own personal satisfaction. Because they thought of the company as a family, they hired family members, relatives, friends, and friends of friends who seemed to fit in with the Vera Bradley family—people whom Pat and Barb would enjoy spending time with: "nice people" who felt as passionate about the products as they did. "We focus less on the bottom line than on our culture, giving back [to the community], and having fun," Barb says.

If you walk around this office, you'll see that people are laughing and having fun. Everyone is on even terms here. You never say, 'She works for me.' Instead, we work together. I'm insulted when someone says, 'Barb is my boss.' We're in this together. [For example], I had six of the girls over for dinner at my house last night. We had all been working late.

Growth and Challenges

By 1990, Vera Bradley bags were catching on in many parts of the country, and each semiannual new product launch was more successful than the previous one. The founders were happy with their progress and the fact that they were creating jobs in and around Fort Wayne. But they were barely beyond the level of a cottage business, and a number of hurdles stood between them and the larger enterprise they both envisioned:

- The business had outgrown the current system of farming out manufacturing to independent sewers who showed up in increasing numbers at Barb's basement door. And the quality of their work was disturbingly variable.

- Gift stores were their "bread and butter," but these represented a small segment of the venues where women shopped.

- Despite initial market testing success with college-age girls, the bulk of sales was going to 30- to 60-year-old women. Would it be possible to address a younger demographic without losing these committed customers?

- Vera Bradley had to design its products around the off-the-shelf fabrics offered by VIP and other wholesalers—mixing and matching existing patterns to produce uniquely styled bags. Manufacturers needed a 9,000-yard order before they would print a special pattern, but the company's production had not yet reached that level. This was putting a constraint on Vera Bradley's number one capability: design.

Never short on confidence, Pat and Barb pondered each of these issues.

Discussion Questions

1. Describe the personal attitudes of the two entrepreneurs and their approach to challenges and opportunities.

2. What resources were critical to getting the company off the ground?

3. Comment on the market research and the level of analysis and planning employed by Barb and Pat.

4. What is your opinion of the company's sales and distribution strategy? Its production strategy? Can you cite feasible alternatives to these, given Vera Bradley's resources?

5. What appear to be the critical brand-building factors in this industry? Are the founders focused and executing on the right things?

6. Will Vera Bradley's initial focus on middle-aged and older women lock it out of expansion to a younger demographic market?

7. Describe the network of helpers and stakeholders enlisted by the two founders and how that network helped the company.

8. Is Barb and Pat's focus on company culture advisable during this early stage of company development and growth? Comment on the sustainability of that culture if and when the company experiences major growth.

©AP/Wide World Photos

Steve Ells and Chipotle

OPPORTUNITY RECOGNITION, SHAPING, AND RESHAPING

Entrepreneurship is all about opportunity. Would-be entrepreneurs often have one of two things on their minds: "How do I come up with a good business idea?" and "Is this idea big enough to make a successful business?" This chapter focuses on evaluating ideas and assessing whether they are indeed good opportunities. While an idea is necessary to entrepreneurship, it isn't sufficient. To have a successful entrepreneurial endeavor, your idea needs to be an opportunity.

Belief in your idea is a great thing. But first step back and ask a more important question: "Is this idea an *attractive* opportunity?" Moving from an idea to a viable opportunity is an iterative process. Entrepreneurs need to conduct a series of tests—what we refer to as **market tests**—to identify interesting ideas and then see whether they are viable opportunities. Each test is an escalation of commitment, an important step to successfully launching the venture. So the process of recognizing, shaping, and reshaping an opportunity combines thought and action to take the idea from formulation to execution. Both are critical as you embark on your entrepreneurial adventure. In this chapter, we will lay out the process from the very beginning—the idea—and move through opportunity shaping and reshaping.

This chapter is written by Andrew Zacharakis.

From Glimmer to Action: How Do I Come Up with a Good Idea?

We said in the preceding chapter that most successful ideas are driven by the entrepreneur's personal experience. Entrepreneurs gain exposure to their fields through their jobs and use this experience to identify possible opportunities for a new venture. Considering that many students have limited work experience, you may not have the knowledge base to generate a new idea. So how, then, does a student find a worthy idea?

Start by looking inside yourself and deciding what you really enjoy. What gives you energy? What can you be passionate about for the many years it will take to start and grow a successful company? For those who lack this professional experience or who find they haven't enjoyed their professional life to date, it takes effort to find the answers to these questions.

Finding Your Passion

Think long-term. What are your goals for your degree, and where would you like to be five years and 10 years down the road? Most students have difficulty envisioning the future. They know they want an exciting job with lots of potential (and, of course, above-average pay), but they haven't really thought about their careers in detail. Students often have a general idea of which industries and types of jobs are interesting to them (say, "something in finance"), but they lack a clear sense of what type of company they want to work for after college (culture, customers, and so forth). After all, school is a time of self-discovery, and this self-discovery is critical for both undergraduates and MBAs. In fact, many people enroll in MBA programs with the express goal of switching careers or industries and use the graduate program as a stepping-stone toward a field they are more passionate about. It can thus pay dividends to spend time thinking beyond the next exam, semester, or year.

Launching an entrepreneurial venture takes a tremendous amount of time and energy, and you will have difficulty sustaining that level of energy if you aren't passionate about the business. How do you go about finding your passion? There are two primary ways. First, think deeply about all the things that give you joy. What do you do in your spare time? What are your hobbies? What types of newspaper and magazine articles or Internet blogs do you read? The reality of our capitalistic society is that all those things you enjoy likely have ancillary businesses around them. Some are obvious. Many students have a passion for investment finance. They have been tracking stocks for a number of years and trade them for their personal portfolio. There are many viable businesses associated with personal finance, ranging from directly trading stocks to providing analysis of the industry through a blog, for instance.

Other passions may not have as many clear-cut examples of ancillary businesses. You may have a passion for hiking. On the surface, hiking seems like a free endeavor, yet there are numerous ancillary businesses that support this activity, ranging from designing, manufacturing, and distributing hiking gear and clothing to providing specialty tours for the extreme hiker. Take World Class Teams,[1] for example. This company was founded by Robyn Benincasa, a former triathlete and adventure racer. After winning the Eco-Challenge, she decided to turn her passion for adventure and the outdoors into a business. Today World Class Teams provides team building and experiential education programs to all kinds of clients. Or take one of the best-known examples in this industry—Yvon Chouinard. One of the pioneers of mountaineering and rock climbing, Chouinard turned his knack for creating useful climbing tools into a small business that served most of his friends in the California climbing community. Today his company, Patagonia, is a world leader in outdoor sporting clothes and equipment and continues to pioneer as a model for socially responsible businesses.

The world is full of examples of enterprising individuals who turned their passions into a lifetime of fulfilling work. After your initial search of "self," you may still have a fuzzy sense of what you're passionate about. To help refine your self-analysis, talk to people in your sphere of influence.

While it is often difficult for people to be introspective about what they love, your strengths may be clearer to those who know you well. The first place to start is your family. They have watched you grow and have seen what you excel at and enjoy. Ask your parents what they see as your greatest strengths. What weaknesses do they think you are blind to? What activities over the years have given you the greatest joy? Just keep in mind that, while your parents and other family members clearly know you best, their perspective may be somewhat biased. Michael Dell of Dell Computers originally enrolled in premed courses while in college to please his father, who was an orthodontist.[2] He would hide his computers in his roommate's bathtub while his parents came to visit.[3] In your search, also go outside your family and ask your friends, teachers, and former work associates (even if the latter group is limited to your old manager at McDonald's). How do they perceive you? The insight others provide is usually surprising. We all have blind spots that prevent us from seeing ourselves in a clear light. Seeking the opinions of others can help us overcome those blind spots and better understand our true passions.

During your search of "self," you may realize that you are passionate about something but haven't yet developed the skill set to successfully translate that passion into a viable business. For example, you may fall in love with a new restaurant idea—say, fast-casual Thai—but never have worked in a restaurant. Opening a restaurant is a worthy goal, but many students don't want to put in the effort to learn about the business. Instead of going to work as a waiter in a restaurant upon graduation, they will take a corporate job with a life insurance company. They rationalize that the pay is better and this will give them the nest egg needed to launch their restaurant. While we don't want to downplay the importance of cash flow, if you or others on your team haven't earned some deep experience in the operations of a restaurant, you will burn through your nest egg quickly and likely fail. Instead of taking the bigger paycheck, go work at a restaurant. You'll learn what customers like and how to deliver it cost effectively, while also earning a bit of money. More importantly, you will have an "apprenticeship" at a successfully run restaurant and will learn many of the major areas that you need to watch out for when the time comes to launch your own restaurant. This apprenticeship won't make you rich in the short term, but it will provide a platform for greater personal wealth and fulfillment in the long run. If you truly want to be an entrepreneur, you will need to make countless sacrifices. One of the first may be bypassing a higher-paying job for the opportunity to roll up your sleeves and gain hands-on experience in your field of choice. Just remember that the knowledge you gain will be far more valuable than the salary you give up.

Chipotle Startup Story

After gradating from the Culinary Institute of America, Steve Ells moved to San Francisco, where he worked for Stars, a high-end restaurant. The inspiration for Chipotle came from the efficient economic model and fresh ingredients used by small Mexican "taquerias" or taco shops in the Mission District of San Francisco. In 1993, with the idea of using authentic Mexican ingredients with a twist and a $85,000 loan from his parents, Ells opened his first Chipotle in a converted Dolly Madison ice cream shop in Denver, near the University of Denver campus.[4]

Three months after opening its doors, Chipotle received an "A" rating from the *Rocky Mountain News*, and customers flocked to the tiny location, leading Ells to add two new Chipotle locations in 1995.[5] Leveraging the growing popularity of fast-casual restaurants and creating a mission of *Food with Integrity*, Ells has been able to grow Chipotle into a nationwide chain.[6] On January 26, 2006, Chipotle went public raising over

$173M. In its first day as a public company, the stock rose 100%, resulting in the best U.S.-based IPO in six years.[7]

In 2011, Chipotle had revenues of $2.27B, net income of $215M and employed 30,940 people in 1,316 locations across the US, Canada, England and France.[8] Chipotle stock has risen over 500% from 2006–2011, far outperforming any competitors in the restaurant sector and the market as a whole.

Once you identify your passions, you have a strong base to start to identify ideas for business opportunities. Today's business environment is intensely competitive, and simple replication (another computer company) is often a recipe for failure. You will need to work on developing ideas that are unique and have something in them that can be a source of sustainable competitive advantage. This process is the focus of the next section, and it will help you understand how to take a basic idea and turn it into a great opportunity.

Idea Multiplication

All great ideas start with a seed of an idea. The trick is moving from that seed to something that is robust, exciting, and powerful. Doing so requires input from others, such as your fellow co-founders, trusted mentors, friends, and family. Spend as much time as possible brainstorming your idea with this group. These informal conversations help you think through the idea and flesh it out. You will learn more about some of the shortcomings or challenges of the business idea, and you will also gain new insights on how it might grow beyond that first product or service.

John Harding/Time Life Pictures/Getty Images

David Kelly, the Stanford engineering professor who founded IDEO, an innovative design firm

We offer one caution, however: Avoid becoming a "cocktail-party entrepreneur." This is the individual who always talks of becoming an entrepreneur or brags of the ideas he or she thought of that others turned into exciting, profitable ventures. In other words, a cocktail-party entrepreneur is all talk and no action. Anybody can be a cocktail-party entrepreneur because it doesn't require any effort or commitment, just a few people who are willing to listen. To become a true entrepreneur requires effort beyond that first conversation. It requires continual escalation of commitment.

We have found a few useful processes that help move you beyond the simple initial idea. The first is called **idea multiplication** and is best exemplified by IDEO, the idea think tank responsible for many of the product innovations we take for granted. For instance, that thick, grippable toothbrush you use every morning was developed by IDEO, as was the design of your computer monitor and any number of other products you use every day. Figure 3.1 highlights the top IDEO innovations over the years. IDEO, founded by Stanford engineering professor David Kelley, is hired by leading corporations worldwide to develop and design new products. We can learn a lot by observing its process.[9] There are four basic steps: (1) Gather stimuli, (2) multiply stimuli, (3) create customer concepts, and (4) optimize practicality. Let's talk about each.

Gather Stimuli. All good ideas start with the customer. Most often, entrepreneurs come across ideas by noting that there is some product or service they would like but can't find. This is your first interaction with a customer—yourself. To validate this idea, you need to go further by gathering stimuli.[10] IDEO does this through a process called *customer anthropology*, in which the IDEO team goes out and observes customers in action in their natural environment and identifies their pain points.[11] For example, in an ABC *Nightline* segment about IDEO, the team went to a grocery store to better understand how customers shop and, more specifically, how they use

Product	Year	Description
Computer mouse	1981	A computer mouse for navigating a computer desktop.
Compass	1982	The precursor to the modern day laptop.
Ford car audio system	1989	Audio system design for Ford automobiles.
Aerobie football	1992	Foam football with fins to stabilize the ball in air.
4000 & 7000 series LAN extender	1995	Cisco router series for controlling traffic on local-area computer networks.
Nike V12 sunglasses	1996	Breakthrough in style and functionality in sunglasses design.
ForeRunner	1997	Portable electronic heart defibrillator.
Yeoman XP-1	1997	GPS system for map plotting.
Humalog/humulin insulin pen	1998	Redesigned insulin pen injector for diabetes patients.
Leap	2000	Scientifically designed desk chair for enhanced comfort and back support.
i-Zone	2000	Disposable instant camera intended for children's market.
Apollo booster	2001	Redesign of children's car seats for Evenflo.
MoneyMaker Deep Lift Pump	2003	Human-powered irrigation pump for use in impoverished regions.
Windows home computing concept	2005	Computer interface linking personal entertainment and home computing units.
Shimano coasting bicycle	2006	Comfortable and low-maintenance bicycle to attract casual cyclists.
"Keep the Change" Service for Bank of America	2006	The service rounds up purchases made with a Bank of America debit card to the nearest dollar and transfers the difference from individuals' checking accounts into their savings accounts
Eli Lilly Kwikpen™	2007	Discreet, prefilled insulin device to help patients deliver their insulin.
Ethos water bottle	2007	Designed to convey the mission of providing clean water to Third World children.
Wee Generation diaper bag	2008	Eco-friendly diaper bag that is functional and durable.
Healthy Choice Fresh Mixers for Conagra	2008	Innovative packaging configuration is comprised of a strainer, bowl, and sauce container. The unique design delivers a fresher, more flavorful product.
Tendril Vision Home Energy-Management Solution	2009	A revolutionary digital display that promotes household energy savings
Peek Smartphone alternative	2009	Simple and cost-conscious mobile device to access email.
Node Chair for Steel Case	2010	A reconfigurable seat/desk combo that complements the way students learn—and the tools they use.
Designing the Ideal Home for "Wounded Warriors" for Clark Reality Capital	2011	Making housing truly accessible for disabled U.S. military veterans and their families

■ Figure 3.1

IDEO Innovations over the Years[12]

a shopping basket. The team's mission was to observe, ask questions, and record information. They did not ask leading questions in hopes that the customer would validate a preconceived notion of what that shopping cart should be. Instead, the questions were open ended.

Beware the leading question. As an entrepreneur who is excited about your concept, you may find it all too easy to ask, "Wouldn't your life be better if you had concept X?" or "Don't you think my product/service idea is better than what exists?" While this might be a direct way to validate your idea, it requires that people answer honestly and understand exactly what they need. Most people like to be nice, and they want to be supportive of new ideas—until they actually have to pay money for them. Also, many times people can't envision your product/service until it actually exists, so their feedback may be biased.

During the "gathering stimuli" phase, act as if you were Charles Darwin observing finches on the Galapagos Islands—just *observe*. Ideally, you'll gather stimuli as a team so that you have multiple interpretations of what you have learned.

Multiply Stimuli. The next phase in the IDEO process is to multiply stimuli. Here, the team members report back on their findings and then start brainstorming on the concept and how to improve upon the solution. One of our colleagues shared with us the trick of comedy improv for facilitating this process. A group of actors (usually three to four) poses a situation to the audience and then lets the audience shout out the next situation or reply that one actor is to give to another. From these audience suggestions, the actors build a hilarious skit. The key to success is to always say, "Yes, and . . . ." Doing so allows the skit to build upon itself and create a seamless and comical whole. Likewise, multiplying stimuli requires the team to take the input of others and build upon it. Be a bit wild-eyed in this process. Let all ideas, no matter how far-fetched, be heard and built upon because, even if you don't incorporate them into the final concept, they might lead to new insights that are ultimately important to the product's competitive advantage.

Remember that "Yes, and . . . ." means that you build upon the input of your colleagues. All too often in a group setting it is easy to say, "That won't work because . . . ." These kinds of devil's advocate debates, while important in the later phases of business development, can prematurely kill off creative extensions in this early phase. Also beware of "Yes, but . . . ." statements, which are really just another way of saying, "Your idea won't work and here's why . . . ." The key to this phase of development is to generate as many diverse ideas as possible.

As you go through this multiplication stage, *brain-writing* is a useful technique to avoid prematurely squashing interesting extensions. The process is like brainstorming, but the focus is on written rather than verbal communication. The biggest shortcoming of brainstorming is that it opens up the opportunity for the most vocal or opinionated members of the group to dominate the conversation and idea-generation process. In contrast, brain-writing ensures that everyone has a chance to contribute ideas. To start, the team identifies a number of core alternative variations to the central idea (if you have a disparate team, as you might for an entrepreneurship class, use each member's favored idea). Put the core ideas onto separate flip-chart sheets and attach them to the wall. Then the team and trusted friends, or classmates, go around and add "Yes, and . . . ." enhancements to each idea. Keep circulating among the flip-chart sheets until everyone has had an opportunity to think about and add to each idea. At the end of that cycle, you'll have several interesting enhancements to consider. Instead of publicly discussing the ideas, have everybody vote on the three to five they like best by placing different-colored sticky notes on the sheets. In essence, this is another "market test" in which your team and other interested parties are gauging the viability of the idea.[13]

Create Customer Concepts. Once you've narrowed the field to the idea and features you think have the most potential, the next step is to create customer concepts. In other words, build a simple mock-up of what the product will look like. This helps the team visualize the final product and see which features/attributes are appealing, which are detrimental, and which are nice to have but not necessary. Keep in mind that this mock-up doesn't need to be functional; it is just a tool to solidify what everybody is visualizing and to help the team think through how the product should be modified.

When your team is developing a service, your mock-up won't necessarily be a physical representation but rather some kind of abstract modeling of what you hope to achieve. For example, the initial mock-up for a restaurant is often just a menu. Entrepreneurs who want to take the research process even further will often test the product or service in a low-cost way. This process allows for rapid-fire prototyping of ideas, and it also provides the luxury of failing early and often before making substantial investments in a bricks-and-mortar establishment.

Rapid-Fire Prototyping

Kevin Plank, walk-on Maryland football player, found himself being slowed down by his 100% cotton under-shirts. "I was short and slow—I was looking for every second I could spare," he says. "Even if it was rain-ing outside, the sweat-soaked cottons gave me that slowed-down lethargic feeling."[14]

With a mission to develop a T-shirt using moisture-wicking fabric for athletic performance, Plank exper-imented with synthetic fabrics at a local tailor shop outside College Park, MD. Spending only $500, he ran through seven prototypes before deciding on the one he wanted to use. He asked his former teammates to try his prototypes, "My first goal was getting athletes to believe in the fact that they needed an alternative to a basic cotton T-shirt. The way you do that is with a great product, but you also do it with influencers."[15] As Plank's friends moved on to play in the NFL, he would send them T-shirts, requesting that they pass them out to other players in their locker rooms. People started to take notice of the brand when the front-page of USA Today featured Oakland Raiders quarterback Jeff George wearing an Under Armour mock turtle-neck. Soon after, Under Armour apparel was featured in two popular football movies, Any Given Sunday and The Replacements. Gaining considerable media atten-tion and positive reviews from players, word began to spread and orders began to increase.

In November 2005, Under Amour raised $157 mil-lion in its IPO, offering 12.1 million shares at $13/share.[16] Since its IPO, it has grown revenues 27.9% annually, reaching over $1.4B in 2011 and stock prices have increased from $13 to $50.[17] Under Armour now sponsors nine collegiate sports programs and some of the world's most famous athletes across multiple sports, including Tom Brady, Cam Newton, Bryce Harper, Ryan Howard, and Michael Phelps.[18]

Optimize Practicality. Quite often at this stage people "overdevelop" the product and incorporate every bell and whistle that the team has come up with during the brainstorming process. This is fine—the next and last step is to optimize practicality, when the team will identify those features that are unnecessary, impractical, or simply too expensive.

This is the phase in which it is important to play devil's advocate. As the IDEO developers state, it is a time for the "grown-ups" to decide which features are the most important to optimize. If the previous steps have gone well, the team has learned a tremendous amount about what the customer may want, and that means they have a deeper understanding of the features/attributes that create the greatest value for the customer. Referring to the Jim Poss case[19] presented at the end of this chapter, Jim and his team found that the most important attributes of his solar-powered trash receptacles were (1) durability—the bins were in public places, and rough treatment or vandalism was a real threat; (2) size—the receptacle couldn't be overly large, or it wouldn't fit in the public places intended, and the bags couldn't weigh too much when filled; and (3) price—the higher up-front purchase cost had to be offset by the reduced trips to collect trash so the receptacle would pay for itself within a year. Understanding these basic parameters helped Jim's team refine its original design. For durability, they found that sheet metal was a cost-effective casing, that a Lexan plastic cover on the solar panel prevented vandalism and accidental chipping, and so forth. They went through a similar process to determine the right size. These steps helped them to design a product that the customer would want at a price the customer was willing to pay.

The entire idea-generation process is iterative. At each of the four steps we've presented, you learn, adjust, and refine. You start to understand the critical criteria that customers use in their purchasing decision and the pain points in building your product or delivering your service. This process allows you to identify and refine your idea with relatively little cost, compared to the costs you'd incur if you immediately opened your doors for business with what you believed to be the most important attributes. Nonetheless, up to this point you still don't know whether your idea, which is now very robust and well thought out, is a viable opportunity.

Is Your Idea an Opportunity?

While the idea-generation process helps you shape your idea so that it is clearer and more robust, it is only part of the process. The difference between venture success and failure is a function of whether your idea is truly an opportunity. Before quitting your job and investing your own resources (as well as those of your family and friends), spend some time studying the viability of your idea. There are five major areas you need to fully understand prior to your launch: (1) customers, (2) competitors, (3) suppliers and vendors, (4) the government, and (5) the broader global environment (see Figure 3.2). We'll discuss each of these areas in turn.

The Customer

Who is your customer? This broad question, the first you must answer, can be problematic. For instance, you might be tempted to think, if you're hoping to open a restaurant, that anyone who would want to eat in a restaurant is your customer: in other words, just about everyone

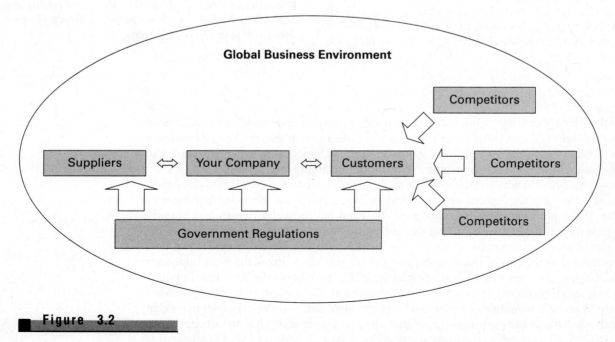

■ **Figure 3.2**

The opportunity space

in the world except for the few hundred hermits spread out across the country. But you need to narrow down your customer base so that you can optimize the features most important to your customer. So a better question is, "Who is your *core* customer?" Understanding who your primary customer lets you better direct your efforts and resources to reach that customer. You can further refine your definition.

Starting with your initial definition, break your customers down into three categories: (1) core customer group or primary target audience (PTA), (2) secondary target audience (STA), and (3) tertiary target audience (TTA). Most of your attention should focus on the PTA. These are the customers you believe are most likely to buy at a price that preserves your margins and with a frequency that reaches your target revenues. Let's consider our fast-casual Thai restaurant example. The sector is growing, even during an economic downturn, as consumers seek less-expensive food that does not sacrifice quality. Fast-casual restaurants usually have larger footprints (more square feet) than fast-food restaurants and food-court outlets. Thus, you want a customer willing to pay a bit more than a fast-food customer for perceived higher quality. A wise location might be a destination mall with tenants like Barnes & Noble, Pottery Barn, and other stores that attract middle-income and higher-income shoppers. Your PTA, in this situation, might be soccer moms (30 to 45 years old, with household incomes ranging from $50,000 to $150,000). These women tend to shop, watch what they eat, and enjoy ethnic food.

During the investigation stage, you would focus your attention on better understanding your PTA. How often do they shop? How often do they eat out? What meals are they more likely to eat outside the home? What other activities do they participate in besides shopping and dining out? What you are collecting is information about things like income and ethnicity (demographics), and about personality traits and values (psychographics).[20] Both categories help you design and market your product or service. During the launch phase, you would design the decor in a manner that most appeals to the PTA. You would create a menu that addresses their dietary concerns and appeals to their palette. During operations, you would market toward your PTA and train your employees to interact with them in an appropriate and effective manner. Note that the efforts across the three stages of your venture (investigation, launch, and operations) are different than they would be if you were launching a fast-food restaurant or a fancy sit-down French restaurant because your target audience is different.

While you should focus most of your attention on your PTA, the STA group also deserves attention. The PTA may be your most frequent, loyal customers, but to increase your revenues, you'll want to bring in some of your STA as well. In the restaurant example, your STA may be men with similar demographics as your PTA, older couples who are active and near retirement age, and younger yuppie post-college working professionals (see the box entitled "Fast-Casual Demographics"). These groups are likely to find your restaurant appealing but may not attend with the same frequency (possibly more on weekends or during the dinner hour versus lunch). Your STA may also be part of your growth strategy. For instance, after you get past your first two to three restaurants, you may choose to expand your menu or your location profile (urban centers, for instance). Understanding which STA is the most lucrative helps you make better growth decisions.

Fast-Casual Demographics

The most often cited reason for the growth in the fast-casual segment is the generation of consumers who grew up on fast food and won't eat it anymore. Add the aging baby boomers who are looking for healthier alternatives and who can afford to pay a little more for better quality. The price of a meal in a moderately priced restaurant has dropped; it's now only 25% more than the price of a meal purchased in a grocery store and prepared at home. . . making dining out an economically viable alternative. Other fast-casual demos:

- The 18–34 age group is most likely to opt for fast-casual and makes up 37% of the traffic at such outlets.

- A newly emerging segment of fast-casual consumers is married, dual-income couples with no kids (known as "DINKs"). These "DINKs" range in age from 35 to 54, and 38% own a home worth $100,000 to $199,000. They make up 28% of the customer base.

- 15% of fast-casual customers were under 18.

- Casual dining is too slow for kids . . . parents don't want to eat fast food.

- Fast-casual restaurants offer teens on dates a destination their parents are comfortable with that does not serve alcohol.

- Casual dining companies are responding to the fast-casual trend by aggressively marketing takeout business.

- Casual dining has now become an event . . . not a spur-of-the-moment dining decision.

- The number of fast-casual dining units has grown from 11,013 in 2007 to 13,643 in 2011.

- Annual traffic at Fast Casual restaurants has also increased from 4% to as much as 11% from 2007 to 2011. Conversely, traffic has been on the decline for fast food, casual dining, and midscale establishments from 2009–2011.

- In 2011 fast-casual restaurants accounted for $27 billion in annual sales.

- In 2011 the fast-casual segment represented 14% of all quick-service restaurant sales, compared to 5% percent 10 years ago. Moving forward, sales are forecasted to compound 8% annually over the next five years, according to Technomic.

Excerpted from E-Business Trends (Food and Beverage). August 21, 2002. www.army.mil/cfsc/documents/business/trends/_E-TRENDS-8-21-02.doc. Updated with facts from Webinar: Fast-Casual Restaurant Trends Forecast 2009. www.fastcasual.com/specialpub.php?i=97&s=4; and Minnick, Fred. Knowing Your Customer. *Fast Casual Magazine.* May 30, 2006. www.fastcasual.com/article.php?id=5120&na=1&prc=43

www.fastcasual.com/article/190159/NPD-Fast-Casual-only-growth-segment-during-down-economy

2012 Fast Casual Top 100 Movers and Shakers: The top restaurant chains, people, trends and technologies shaping the fast casual segment.

http://global.networldalliance.com/downloads/white_papers/fc_top100_042012_v7.pdf

Finally, your TTA requires a little attention. During the investigation and launch stage, you shouldn't spend much time on the TTA. However, once you begin operating, a TTA may emerge that has more potential than you originally realized. Keeping your eyes and ears open during operations helps you adjust and refine your opportunity to better capture the most lucrative customers. In our Thai restaurant example, you might find that soccer moms aren't your PTA but that some unforeseen group emerges, such as university students. If you segment your customer groups throughout the three stages as we have outlined, you'll be better prepared to adapt your business model if some of your preconceptions turn out to be incorrect.

We've said that it's important to understand your audience's demographics and psychographics. Part of your investigation phase should include creating customer profiles. Figure 3.3 provides a sampling of the types of demographics and psychographics that might be used in describing your customer.

Trends. Customers aren't static groups that remain the same over time. They evolve; they change; they move from one profile to another. In order to best capture customers, you need to spot trends that are currently influencing their buying behavior and that might influence it in the future. When considering trends, look at broader macro trends and then funnel down to a more narrow focus on how those trends affect your customer groups. Trends might also occur within customer groups that don't affect the broader population.

Demographics	Psychographics
Age	Social group (white collar, blue collar, etc.)
Gender	Lifestyle (mainstream, sexual orientation,
Household income	materialistic, active, athletic, etc.)
Family size/family life cycle	Personality traits (worriers, Type A's, shy,
Occupation	extroverted, etc.)
Education level	Values (liberal, conservative, open minded,
Religion	traditional, etc.)
Ethnicity/heritage	
Nationality	
Social class	
Marital status	

■ **Figure 3.3**

Common demographic/psychographic categories

One of the most influential trends in the macro environment within the United States over the last 50 years has been the life cycle of the baby boom generation. Born between 1946 and 1964, the country's 77.6 million baby boomers are usually married (69.4%), well educated (college graduation rates hit 19.1% at the end of the boomer generation, compared to just 6% for prior generations), and active (46% of boomers exercise regularly).[21] What links them as a generation is the experience of growing up in post–World War II America, a time of tremendous growth and change in this nation's history. Since they represent such a large percentage of the U.S. population, it is no wonder that they have created numerous new categories of products and services. For example, in the 1950s, the disposable diaper industry emerged and then exploded to the point where today it has $4 billion in sales. In the late 1950s and through the 1960s, the rapidly growing population created a need for large numbers of new schools, which in turn led to a building frenzy. (Now you know why so many schools were named after former President John F. Kennedy.) In the late 1960s and the 1970s, the rock-and-roll industry exploded. Then in the 1980s, as these baby boomers became parents, a new car category was created (the minivan), which saved Chrysler from bankruptcy. In the 1990s, the boomers were in their prime working years, and new investment categories emerged to help them plan for their retirement and their children's college educations. Today, as the boomers age, we see growth in pharmaceuticals and other industries related to the more mature segment. According to one market research firm, "boomers are expected to change America's concepts of aging, just as they have about every previous life stage they have passed through."[22] How does this macro trend influence your idea?

Numerous macro trends affect the potential demand for your product or service. Trends create new product/service categories, or emerging markets, that can be especially fruitful places to find strong entrepreneurial opportunities. The convergence of multiple trends enhances the power of an opportunity like the Internet boom. First, the personal computer (PC) was common in the workplace, and as a result, many Americans grew comfortable using it. That led to a proliferation of PCs in the home, especially for children and teenagers who used it for school, work, and video games. While the Internet had been available for decades, the development by Tim Berners-Lee of the World Wide Web (WWW or Web) system of hyperlinks connecting remote computers, followed by the development of the Mosaic Web browser (the precursor to Netscape and Explorer) and the proliferation of Internet service providers like Prodigy and AOL, created huge opportunities for commerce online. From the very first domain name—symbolics.com—assigned in 1985, the Web has evolved into an integral component of the modern economy. Even though many dot-coms failed, others, like eBay and Amazon, have established themselves as profitable household names. That many of these successful businesses have become multi-*billion*-dollar companies in less than a decade speaks to the incredible power of convergent trends.

Trends also occur in smaller market segments and may be just as powerful as macro trends; in fact, they may be precursors to larger macro trends. For example, according to Packaged Facts, a market research consultancy, the market for religious products (including blockbuster movies, pop music, clothing, books, and even games and toys) will reach $6 billion in annual sales by 2013, up from the $5.6 billion sold in 2004.[23] Indeed, major companies are capitalizing on this market. At the end of 2005, Starbucks announced it would be featuring a quotation on its coffee cups from Rick Warren, pastor and best-selling author of *The Purpose-Driven Life*, which includes the line "You were made by God and for God, and until you understand that, life will never make sense."[24] While the quote is just one of many that the company featured on its coffee cups, you can rest assured that the decision to include it was a calculated move to make the company's products more appealing to the growing Christian market.

Another important trend is the changing demographics of the U.S. population. According to the US Census Bureau, the projected Hispanic population of the United States will reach 133 million by 2050. According to this projection, Hispanics will constitute 30% of the nation's population.

With the incredible growth in both size and purchasing power of this untapped market, it's no wonder that companies are scrambling to serve emerging opportunities. The past decade has seen a proliferation of media outlets targeting the Spanish-speaking U.S. population, and since some pundits believe the Hispanic population could emerge as the next middle class, it's likely more and more companies will find ways to capture this enormous demographic.

Trends often foretell emerging markets and suggest when the window of opportunity for an industry is about to open. Figure 3.4 lists some influential trends over the last 50 years. However, it is the underlying convergence of trends that helps us measure the power of our ideas and whether they are truly opportunities.

Trend	Impact
Baby boom generation	Pampers, rock 'n' roll, television, minivans, real estate, McMansions, etc.
Personal computing	Internet, electronic publishing, spreadsheets, electronic communication
Obesity	Drain on healthcare system, growth of diet industry, changes in food industry, health clubs, home gyms
Dual-income households	Childcare, home services—landscaping, housecleaning, prepared foods
Smart phones	Apps, location based couponing, NFC (near field communication) and mobile payments, Ecommerce retailers moving to mobile, voice-activated commands.
High-speed Internet	Cloud computing, streaming media, free online education—Khan Academy, edX.org (free online courses from Harvard, MIT, Cal Berkeley, and University of Texas)
Touch computing	Tablet computers and eReaders—iPad, Blackberry Playbook, Window's Surface, Amazon Kindle Fire, Samsung Galaxy, Motorola Xoom. Touch-based operating systems—Windows 8 and Mac OS X Lion.
Social media	Widespread popularity of Facebook, Twitter, Linkedin, Pinterest, Google+. "Frictionless sharing" through social media apps like Spotify, Social Reader, and Gilt.

Figure 3.4

Important trends over the last 50 years

How Big Is the Market? Trends suggest increasing market demand. Thus, one of the questions that distinguish ideas from opportunities asks whether there is sufficient market demand to generate the level of revenues necessary to make this an exciting career option. As we pointed out in Chapter 2, an entrepreneur typically needs the new venture to generate a minimum of $750,000 per year in revenue to meet market rates on his or her forgone salary of $70,000 plus benefits. While this level might make a nice "mom and pop" store, many students are interested in creating something bigger. The larger your goals, the more important your market-demand forecasts. To accurately gauge your demand, start at the larger macro market and funnel demand down to your segment and your geographic location. Granted, as you expand, you'll likely move beyond your segment and your geographic origins, but the most critical years for any venture are its first two. You need to be certain that you can survive the startup, and that means you need to be confident of your base demand.

Let's go back to our Thai fast-casual restaurant example to begin to understand how large our market demand might be. Figure 3.5 steps through the demand forecast. It is best to start with the overall market size—in this case, the size of the entire restaurant industry in the United States. Next, segment the industry into relevant categories. We are interested in both the relative size of the fast-casual segment and the size of the ethnic segment. It would be ideal to find the size of the fast-casual-ethnic (or better yet, Thai) segment, but as you narrow down to your opportunity, there is likely to be less information because you may be riding new trends that suggest future demand that has yet to materialize. Finally, during your initial launch, you'll likely have some geographic focus. Extrapolate your overall market data to capture your geographic market. In this case, we took the population of the towns within a five-mile drive along the major thoroughfare on which our restaurant would be located and multiplied that

Restaurant Industry Sales Projections in 2012 — **$632 Billion**
Size of Market Segments
  Eating Places — **$419.2 Billion**
  Quick service restaurants including fast-casual — **$174 Billion**
  Fast-casual restaurants — **$24.3 Billion**
  Retail, vending, recreation, mobile — **$61.2 Billion**
  Managed services — **$44.4 Billion**
  Lodging place restaurants — **$31.4 Billion**
  Bars and taverns — **$18.9 Billion**
  Other — **$56.7 Billion**
Market share for ethnic restaurants — **$210.7 Billion**[25]
Market share by state

Massachusetts
  Overall Restaurant Sales — **$12.6 Billion**
  Ethnic — **$4.2 Billion**

Natick (we are opening in Natick shopping district)
  Massachusetts population. 6.59M
  Natick population. 33K
  Framingham population. 68K
  Wellesley population. 28K

Natick, Framingham, Wellesley population is 2% of total Massachusetts population
Natick, Framingham, Wellesley ethnic restaurant sales — **$82 Million**
Soccer moms (women between 30 and 45). . . . . .14K — **$8.9 Million**
  or 11% of Natick, Framingham, and Wellesley population

Figure 3.5

Market size for Thai fast-casual restaurant

percentage of the state population by the total spent in the state (Massachusetts). Basically, for this last step, you should try to assess the number of soccer moms in your geographic reach. The U.S. Census makes this very easy, as it breaks out demographics by town. Thus, it appears that there are roughly 14,000 soccer moms in this target market.

Market Size Today and into the Future. While it is important to size your market today, you'll also need to know how big it will be in the future. If you are taking advantage of trends, your market is likely growing. Attractive opportunities open up in growing markets because there is more demand than supply, and a new firm doesn't need to compete on price. In the early years, when the firm is going through a rapid learning curve, operational expenses will be proportionately higher than in later years, when the firm has established efficient procedures and systems. Furthermore, market growth means that your competitors are seeking all the new customers entering the market rather than trying to steal customers away from you.

Projecting growth is notoriously difficult, but you can make some educated guesses by looking at trends and determining overall market size as described earlier. Then make some estimates of what type of market penetration you might be able to achieve and how long it will take you to get there. If all else fails, the easiest thing to do is to verify past growth. As trend analysis tells us, past growth is usually correlated with future growth, which means you can make reasonable estimates based on historical numbers. The **S-curve** is a powerful concept that highlights the diffusion of product acceptance over time.[26] When a product or innovation is first introduced, few people are aware of it. Typically, the firm has to educate consumers about why they need this product and the value it offers. Hence, the firm concentrates its effort on early adopters. It is expensive to develop the right concept and educate the consumer, but the firm can offset this cost somewhat by charging a high price.

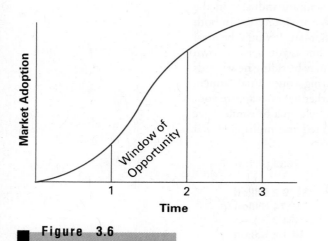

■ **Figure 3.6**

S-curve

As customers react to the concept, the company and other new entrants learn and modify the original product to better meet customer needs. At a certain point (designated as point 1 in Figure 3.6), customer awareness and demand exceed supply, and the market enters a fast-growth phase. During this time (the time between points 2 and 3 in Figure 3.6), a dominant design emerges, and new competitors enter to capture the "emerging market." Typically, demand exceeds supply during this phase, meaning that competitors are primarily concerned with capturing new customers entering the market. After point 3, market demand and supply equalize, putting price pressure on the companies as they fight to capture market share from each other. Finally, innovations push the product toward obsolescence, and overall demand declines.

Frequency and Price. Market size and growth are important, but we also need to think about how often our average customer buys our product or service and how much he or she is willing to pay. Ideally, our product or service would have perfectly inelastic demand: The customer would pay any price to have it. For a product with elastic demand, the quantity demanded will go down if the price goes up, and vice versa. Inelasticity results in the opposite—whether prices increase or decrease, the demand for the product stays stable. Consider front row seats for your favorite baseball team or theater production. Nearly everyone would like to sit in the front row, but most of us can't or don't because the price is too high. However, if the price were lowered by a certain amount, we might be more than happy to buy the tickets. This is an example of elastic demand: As price decreases, demand for that product increases.

In contrast, consider gasoline. People who rely on a car to get to work have little choice but to pay the prices charged at the pump. If prices go down, they are unlikely to buy more gas, and if prices go up, they will still need to buy enough gas to get to work and run errands. While not perfectly inelastic, the demand for gasoline is relatively inelastic. In reality, there will almost always be elasticity in customer demand, and our price will be a function of that elasticity. We need to determine the optimal price that encourages regular purchases, accounts for the value inherent in our product, and allows us to earn an attractive margin on the sale. These three variables are highly correlated, and an imbalance would hurt the profitability and even the viability of the firm.

In a classic mistake, some entrepreneurs use a penetration-pricing strategy. They reason that in order to pull customers from existing alternatives, the firm needs to price lower than the competition. Then, once the product is able to gain acceptance and market share, the company can raise prices to increase gross margins and better reflect underlying value. There are a number of flaws in this logic. First, as we've noted, attractive ventures are often launched in emerging markets where demand exceeds supply. This means that price is relatively inelastic. Consumers want the product and are willing to pay a premium for it. Second, many new products are designed to be better than existing alternatives. These products offer greater value than competitive products, and the price should reflect this greater value, especially since it usually costs more to add the features that led to it. Third, price sends a signal to the customer. If a product with greater value is priced lower than or the same as competing products, customers will interpret that signal to mean it isn't as good, despite claims that it has greater value.

Fourth, even if customers flock to the low-priced product, this rapid increase in demand can sometimes cause serious problems for a startup. Demand at that price may exceed your ability to supply, resulting in stock-outs. Consumers are notoriously fickle and are just as likely to go to a competitor as wait for your backlog to catch up.[27] Finally, these same customers may resist when you try to recapture value by raising prices in the future. They will have developed an internal sense of the value of your product, and they may take this opportunity to try other alternatives. The last thing you want is a business built around customers who are always searching for the lowest price. These will be the first people to leave you when a competitor finds a way to offer a lower price.

The Internet boom and bust saw many poor pricing decisions. Internet firms entered the market at very low price points. Take kozmo.com, for example. Many thought the company's revolutionary approach to delivering things like groceries and videos would change the way people shopped, but in the end, the value proposition was too good to be true. The company was delivering goods at a cost higher than it was charging. The total ticket for a simple order of a few sodas, a bag of chips, and a candy bar might be only $7, but kozmo.com was paying as much as $10 to the person who had to find those items and then deliver them. The venture-capital-backed company burned through almost all its cash before it finally recognized the flaw of its pricing logic, but by then, it was too late.[28]

In 2005, Amp'd Mobile, an edgy mobile phone service geared to 18- to 35-year-olds, was created as the first integrated mobile entertainment company for young people and early adopters. Sales exploded by 70% in the first quarter of 2007 to about 175,000 customers after running ads on MTV Networks emphasizing the carrier's mobile music and video services.[29] With the average revenue per subscriber being over $100, collecting payments from the youth proved to be a challenge. By May, the number of nonpaying customers reached 80,000, nearly half of Amp'd's customer base. On June 1, 2007 Amp'd Mobile filed for Chapter 11 bankruptcy protection. According to the bankruptcy filing, "The debtor began to find a host of credit and collections problems (that) contributed ultimately to a liquidity crisis."[30]

The argument many unsuccessful Internet entrepreneurs made at the time was that the "number of eyeballs" looking at a site was more important than profitability, which firms figured would come later as they developed a critical mass of customers. These firms reasoned that they could charge lower prices than brick-and-mortar outlets (traditional stores that the customer had to physically visit) because they didn't have the overhead costs of renting or buying so many store locations. Furthermore, Internet companies could serve a larger volume of customers via a single Web site than a chain of stores could serve in thousands of physical locations. For the most part, these strategies failed due to a number of reasons.

First, the Internet firms continued reducing prices to the point where they weren't generating a positive gross margin. The continued decrease in price was a function of competition. New online firms that were basically identical started to appear. For instance, a competitive online pet product marketplace and a difficult financing environment led to the demise of pets.com and petopia.com. Pets.com stock had fallen from over $11 per share in February 2000 to $0.19 per share in November 2000, resulting in liquidation. Similarly, petopia.com was struggling with only $8.8 million in sales in 1999 and $48 million in losses. Only a month after pets.com shutdown, strategic partner, Petco, acquired petopia.com. Traditional retailers responded by adding Web sites as an additional channel of distribution. Toys "R" Us was able to enter and secure new customers at one-tenth the cost of Toys.com due to higher name recognition.

Finding the right price to charge is difficult. It requires understanding your cost structure. You cannot price under your cost of goods sold (COGS) for an extended period of time unless you have lots of financing (and are certain that access to financing will continue into the future). Thus, your minimum price should be above your COGS. Some firms look at their cost to produce a unit of the product and then add a set percentage on top of that cost to arrive at the price. This is called **cost-plus pricing**, and the problem is that it may set your price lower or higher than the underlying value of your product or service. For example, if you price at 40% above marginal cost, that may result in your product being a great value (software usually has gross margins of 70% or better) or drastically overpriced (groceries often have gross margins in the 20% range).

A better approach is to assess market prices for competing products. For instance, consider GMAT test-preparation courses that help students strengthen their business school applications. At the time of this writing, a quick scan of Kaplan and Princeton Review reveals that prices for their classroom GMAT programs are both $1,599. Given the similarities of the content, structure, and results of these programs, it is no surprise that their prices are comparable. Over the years, Kaplan and Princeton Review have gained deep insight into what parents will pay. For an entrepreneur entering this marketplace, Kaplan and Princeton Review provide a starting point in deciding what price can be charged. The entrepreneur would adjust his or her price based on the perceived difference in value of the offering.

Many entrepreneurs claim that they have no direct competition so it is impossible to determine how much customers might pay. In such cases, which are very rare, it is essential to understand how customers are currently meeting the need that you propose to fill. Assess how much it costs them to fulfill this need and then determine a price that reflects the new process plus a premium for the added value your product delivers.

Margins. For new ventures, research suggests that gross margins of 40% are a good benchmark that distinguishes more attractive from less attractive opportunities. It is important to have higher gross margins early in the venture's life because operating costs during the early years are disproportionately high due to learning curve effects. For instance, no matter how experienced they are in the industry, your team will incur costs as you train yourselves and new hires. Over time, the team will become more efficient, and the associated costs of operations will reach a stability point. Another reason for keeping margins high is that the new venture will incur costs prior to generating sales associated with those costs. For instance, well before you are able to generate any leads or sales, you will need to hire salespeople and invest time and money training them. Even if you are a sole proprietorship, you will incur costs associated with selling your product or service before you receive any cash associated with the sale. For instance, you may have travel expenses like airline tickets or gasoline for your car and infrastructure expenses like a new computer and office furniture. This lag between spending and earning creates a strain on cash flows, whether you are a one-person shop or a growing enterprise, and if your margins are thin to begin with, it will be harder to attract the investment needed to launch.

It typically takes three to five years for a firm to reach stability and for operating costs to stabilize. At this point, strong firms hope to achieve net income as a percentage of sales of 10% or better. If the net income margin is lower, it will be hard to generate internal cash for growth or to attract outside investors, to say nothing about generating returns for the founding team.

The exceptions to this rule are businesses that can generate high volumes. During the 1980s and 1990s, many new ventures sought to replicate the Walmart concept. Staples, Office Max, Home Depot, and Lowe's are good examples. Gross margins on these businesses range from 10% to 33% and net income margins from 1.8% to 6.5%. However, the stores do such enormous volumes that they are still able to generate huge profits. For example, in the 12-month period ending on January 31, 2013, Walmart projects operating income of $27.8 *billion*, which is more in profits than the vast majority of all U.S. companies had in sales, and it was able to do so because it generated $469 billion in sales during the same period. Walmart's gross profit margin of 24.8% is small by most measures, but its sales and profit numbers are clear indicators that its business strategy is working.

The performance of these big companies suggests another kind of industry structure that can be very attractive—fragmented industries. Prior to the launch of Staples and Home Depot, people filled their office supply and hardware needs through "mom and pop" companies. These small enterprises served small geographic regions and rarely expanded beyond them. The big-box stores entered these markets and offered similar goods at much lower prices against which "mom and pop" firms couldn't compete.

While entering a fragmented industry and attempting to consolidate it, as big-box stores do, can create huge opportunities, the financial and time investments required are substantial. For instance, Arthur Blank and Bernard Marcus founded Home Depot in 1978 in the Atlanta area. While its individual stores had enormous sales and profit potential, the company needed significant up-front capital for the initial building costs and inventory, and it raised venture capital, followed by $7.2 million from its 1981 public offering (which translates to $17.5 million in 2011 dollars). Almost 10 years later, Thomas Stemberg founded Staples and followed a nearly identical path in office supplies. Here, again, the startup costs were enormous, and the company relied heavily on its founders' experience in retailing. Staples raised $33.83 million in venture capital before it went public in April 1989, raising $51.3 million.[31] The bottom line is that such opportunities are rarer than in emerging markets, and they require a team with extensive industry experience and access to venture capital or other large institutional financing resources.

Reaching the Customer. Reaching the customer can be very difficult, even for the most experienced entrepreneur. Take the example of the founder of Gourmet Stew.[32] After completing her MBA, she spent many years with one of the top three food producers in the country, where she gained a deeper understanding about the industry. In the 1980s, she joined a small food startup company that developed a new drink concept that became widely

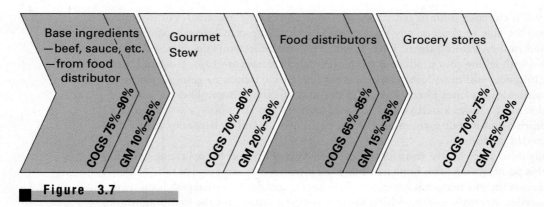

■ **Figure 3.7**

Value chain of Gourmet Stew

successful and was ultimately acquired by Kraft Foods. Still a young woman, she cashed out and started her own venture, Gourmet Stew. Its first product was beef stew in a jar, like Ragú spaghetti sauce. The product tasted better than competitors like Hormel Stew (in a can). Despite her extensive entrepreneurial and industry experience and even though her product tasted better, the entrepreneur couldn't overcome one obstacle: how to reach the customer.

Stew in a jar is usually distributed in grocery stores, but this is a very difficult market to enter on a large scale. The industry is consolidated and mature, with only 19 chains throughout the entire country. Large product and food companies like Procter & Gamble and General Mills control much of the available shelf space, due to their power and ability to pay the required slotting fees.[33] Grocery stores also have an incentive to deal with fewer rather than more suppliers because it improves their internal efficiency.

Given that, companies that sell only a few products, such as Gourmet Stew, have a more difficult time accessing large chain stores. And even though smaller chains may find a unique product like Gourmet Stew appealing, it costs one-product companies more to distribute through these channels, since they have to deal with multiple vendors instead of sealing a few large distribution agreements. Alternatively, Gourmet Stew could work with a large food brokerage company, but that would mean giving a portion of its margins to the brokerage. With all these options, the economics of distribution make it almost impossible to generate a decent margin on this type of company.

One of the most overlooked keys to entrepreneurial success is distribution. How *do* you reach the customer? While Gourmet Stew might have been able to reach the customer through alternative distribution channels like the Internet, these are likely to generate lower sales volume and higher marketing expenses because you have to educate the customer not only about what your product is but also about where to find it.

It is important to understand the entire value chain for the industry you are competing in. You need to lay out the distribution of your product from raw materials all the way to the end consumer. Figure 3.7 captures the value chain for Gourmet Stew.[34] From the figure, you can see the respective gross margins of the players—note that their net income margins would be much lower if based on their operating costs. The higher gross margins of the grocery stores indicate their relative power. Consider whether there is a variation on your business idea that would allow you to enter the portion of the value chain where greater margins are available. In sum, you must understand the entire value chain in order to determine where opportunities to make a profit might exist.

While Gourmet Stew wasn't successful at gaining distribution, the box featuring Stacy's Pita Chips shows how a small food company can slowly gain distribution and build momentum to the point where it achieves a successful harvest for the entrepreneurs.

Stacy's Pita Chips Gaining Widespread Distribution

Stacy's Pita Chips didn't start out as a snack food maker. Instead, Stacy Madison, a social worker by training, and Mark Andrus, a psychologist, wanted to open a restaurant. Their first venture was a small food cart that sold pita bread wraps in downtown Boston. They were instantly successful and soon had long lines of hungry customers waiting for their freshly made wraps. Some of these potential customers tired of waiting in line and would give up before placing an order. To minimize the number of lost customers, Stacy and Mark started serving seasoned pita chips, baked from the bread they had left at the end of each day. The pita chips were a hit. In addition to great roll-up sandwiches, customers had a delicious incentive while they waited in line. Eventually, the couple was running two businesses and had to make a choice. They chose the pita chips, figuring they'd be able to gain national growth more rapidly. A new venture was born.

Even though Stacy and Mark had a great product, the question was, "How could they reach the end consumer en masse?" Most people buy chips in the grocery store, but getting space in the snack aisle is nearly impossible. Large distributors sell to grocery stores, and they are interested only in products that their buyers (the grocery stores) want. Recognizing this problem, Stacy decided that there was another way into this channel; Stacy's would place its chips in the natural food aisle and the in-store delis.

Stacy and Mark attended trade shows and made direct contact with grocery stores, sold them on their product, and secured trial placements in the stores. Stacy supplied display racks for her chips to each store and worked hard to increase consumer awareness by giving sample chips to shoppers. Without a distributor, Stacy's Pita Chips often shipped their product via UPS, but once they secured 10 or more stores in a particular geographic region, they went to the stores and asked who distributed snacks to them. The stores often contacted the distributors on Stacy's behalf, asking them to handle the product for them. Stacy noted, "Having customers that the distributor sold to gave us leverage. They wanted to carry our products because we created customer demand for them." Once Stacy's had a few large distributors in line, the company gained momentum, and other stores and distributors wanted to carry the product. In 2005, Stacy's hit $60 million* in sales, and Frito-Lay, the largest snack food maker in the world, finalized the acquisition of the company in January 2006.

Compiled from a personal interview with Stacy Madison, March 22, 2006.
*Frito-Lay Is Extending Its Healthy Snack Offerings with the Acquisition of Stacy's Pita Chips, Randolph, Mass., for an Undisclosed Sum. *Brandweek* 46.43: 5(1). Nov. 28, 2005.

The Competition

Would-be entrepreneurs often say, "I have a great idea, and the best part is there's NO COMPETITION." If that were true, then as long as you have a customer, you have a license to print money. However, most nascent entrepreneurs turn out to be defining their competition too narrowly. For example, an overly optimistic entrepreneur might suggest that Gourmet Stew has no competition because there are no other companies producing stew in a jar. That doesn't account for Hormel canned stew (direct competition). It doesn't account for the multitude of frozen pizzas and other prepared foods that customers can bring home from the grocery store (more direct competition). It ignores the customers' options of preparing their own secret recipe for stew (indirect competition) or going out to eat (substitute). In other words, Gourmet Stew's competition isn't just stew in a jar; it is all the other businesses competing for a share of the consumer's stomach. Entrepreneurs ignore these competitors and substitutes at their peril.

To fully identify the competition, start with the customer. How is the customer currently fulfilling the need or want you intend to fill? You must identify direct competitors, indirect competitors, and substitutes. The number and strength of your competitors mirror the market structure. In a mature market, the industry is likely consolidated, and the power of existing competitors is likely strong. From the Gourmet Stew example, the industry is highly consolidated. Ten major prepared-food companies—Tyson Foods Inc., Nestle S.A., Kraft Foods Inc., JBS USA, Dean Foods Co., General Mills Inc., Smithfield Foods Inc., Mars Inc., Kellogg Co., and ConAgra Foods Inc. —control 45% of the market.[35] Entering this market is difficult, as we saw earlier, because the major competitors control the primary channel of distribution.

Even if you successfully enter the market, the strength of your competitors enables them to retaliate. Competitors, because of their economies of scale and scope, can lower prices to a point that makes it difficult for new ventures to compete. They can spend more on their advertising campaign and other marketing expenditures and increase their visibility due to greater resource reserves or easier access to capital. The good news is that many times strong competitors won't bother with new startups because they're so small that they aren't noticeable or because they don't feel threatened in either the short or the medium term. However, entrepreneurs should plan for contingencies just in case the larger competitors retaliate earlier than expected.

When markets are emerging, like the market for video game consoles, fewer products compete for customers primarily because the demand exceeds the supply. The main struggle within these markets is trying to find and own the dominant design that will become the customer favorite. A recent example of convergence toward a dominant design is the smartphone industry. In the early years, there were a multitude of potential operating systems that used different network providers and different phone manufacturers. In 1993, IBM and Bell South partnered to create the world's first smartphone. Dubbed Simon, the smartphone featured a touchscreen, predictive text, and apps like maps, stock prices, and a camera that could be used by plugging in software cards into the phone. From 1996–2000, Nokia and Ericsson entered the smartphone market with a number of unique phones running on the Symbian Operating System. From 2001–2003, Palm and Microsoft both introduced a line of phones running on their own operating systems, Palm OS and Microsoft Windows Mobile. From 2003–2006, Blackberry dominated the smartphone market with the introduction of the first smartphone optimized for wireless email use. In 2007, Apple changed the smartphone game with its release of the first generation iPhone. In 2008, Taiwanese smartphone manufacturer HTC unveiled the first smartphone powered by Google's Android OS.[36,37]

According to the research firm IDC, Google's Android is the world's most popular smartphone OS. In 2012, Android accounted for over 104 million units sold and 68% of the smartphone OS market share. Apple's iOS took 17% market share while Symbian, Research in Motion, Linux and Microsoft accounted for a collective 16% market share.[38]

Figure 3.8 shows some of the competing mobile operating systems and their market shares over the past five years. Note that in 2007 the Symbian OS controlled 64% of the marketplace, Windows Mobile had 12%, Blackberry 10%, and Linux 10%. Symbian became the dominant operating system primarily because it was included in the most popular smartphones at the time, the Nokia smartphones. With the instant popularity of the open source Android OS in 2008, smartphone manufacturers converged toward the Android OS, existing smartphone manufacturers and new manufacturers alike adopted the Android platform. This example highlights the evolution of most marketplaces. Once a dominant design is in place, the market moves rapidly to maturity.

Emerging markets are characterized by "stealth" competitors. Entrepreneurs often believe their idea is so unique that they will have a significant lead over would-be competitors. But just as your venture will operate "under the radar" as it designs its products, builds its infrastructure, and tests the product with a few early beta customers, so will a number of other new ventures likely be at similar stages of development. While it is relatively easy to conduct due diligence on identifiable competition, it is extremely difficult to learn about competition that isn't yet in the marketplace. Thus, it is imperative for new ventures to scan the environment to identify and learn about stealth competition.

Year	Android (Google)	Blackberry (RIM)	iOS (Apple)	Linux	Palm/WebOS (Palm/HP)	Symbian (Nokia)	Windows Mobile (Microsoft)	Bada (Samsung)	Other
2007	0%	10%	3%	10%	1%	64%	12%	0%	0%
2008	0%	17%	8%	8%	2%	53%	12%	0%	0%
2009	4%	20%	15%	5%	1%	47%	9%	0%	0%
2010	24%	17%	16%	0%	0%	39%	4%	0%	0%
2011	46%	11%	19%	0%	0%	20%	2%	0%	3%
2012-Q1	56%	7%	23%	0%	0%	9%	2%	3%	1%
2012-Q2	68%	5%	17%	2%	0%	4%	4%	0%	0%

■ Figure 3.8

Smartphone operating systems move toward a dominant design[39-43]

There are several sources of intelligence you can tap. It is probable that your competition is using inputs, and thus suppliers, similar to what you are. As you interview your potential suppliers, make sure to query them about similar companies with whom they are working. While the suppliers may not divulge this information, more often than not they don't see it as a conflict of interest to do so. Outside professional equity capital can also help you determine competitors. Angels and venture capitalists see many deals and have knowledge about how an industry is developing even if they haven't funded one of your stealth competitors. Again, you can talk to professional investors about who they see as strong emerging competitors. Furthermore, a number of widely available databases track and identify companies that receive equity financing. PricewaterhouseCoopers publishes MoneyTree,[44] which allows you to screen new investments by industry, region, and venture capitalists making the investment. VentureWire is one of many daily e-mail newsletters published by Dow Jones that tracks current deals—and the best part is that VentureWire Alert is free.[45] The smart entrepreneur will diligently monitor his or her industry and use these resources, as well as many others, to avoid being surprised by unforeseen competition. An excellent source of industry gossip is trade shows.

While your direct competition is most relevant to your success, you also should spend some time understanding why your target customer is interested in your indirect competitors and substitutes. As you increase your knowledge of the total marketplace, you will start to understand the key success factors (KSFs) that distinguish those firms that win and those that lose. KSFs are the attributes that influence where the customer spends money. If we think once again about Gourmet Stew, customers base their food purchasing decisions on a number of factors, including taste, price, convenience (time to prepare and serve), availability (the distribution channel issue discussed earlier), and healthy attributes of the food, among other factors. As you gather data on these factors, constructing a competitive profile matrix to identify the relative strength of each will help you decide how to position your venture in the marketplace (see Figure 3.9). Gauge how well your competitors are doing by tracking their revenues, gross margins, net income margins, and net profits. Note that we don't yet know what the figures are for Gourmet Stew because it has yet to hit the marketplace. Likewise, "homemade stew" in the figure is the creation of the consumer, who buys all the ingredients separately at the grocery store.

As you examine the competitive profile matrix, you understand the competitors' strategy and which customers they are targeting. Hormel, for example, is targeting price-sensitive, convenience-minded consumers. Typical customers might include males living on their own, college students, or others who don't have the time or desire to cook but are living on a budget. Homemade stew, on the other hand, falls in the domain of persons who enjoy cooking and have more time. Stay-at-home parents may have the time to shop for all the ingredients and to cook the stew from scratch, or weekend gourmets might like to have something special for guests or family. Gourmet Stew might appeal to families where both parents work outside the

	Gourmet Stew	Hormel	Homemade	DiGiorno Pizza
Taste	Good	Fair	Excellent	Fair
Price	High $3.50	Medium $1.89	Low	Very high $6.50
Convenience	High	High	Low	High
Availability	Low	High	High	High
Healthy	Medium	Low	High	Medium
Revenues		<$135 million*		$500 million*
Gross Margins		23.7%*		34.9%*
Net Income Margins		16.5%*		
Net Profit		$22.3 million*		loss*

*Financial figures for Hormel and DiGiorno are for the whole company, not just the product.

■ **Figure 3.9**

Competitive profile matrix

home. They want quality food but don't have the time to cook it from scratch and are not as sensitive to prices. Last, DiGiorno pizza (a higher-quality pizza) is targeting families who want something in the freezer for those nights that they just don't have time to cook. While there are many more competitors than we have highlighted in the matrix, it is often best to pick representative competitors rather than to highlight every potential company. The matrix is a tool to help you understand the competitive landscape by drilling down deep on a few key competitors. Although you'll want to be aware of every potential competitor and substitute, focusing on a few in depth will help you devise a successful strategy.

From this information, you can start to get the broad guidelines of the competitors' strategies—Hormel is pursuing a low-cost strategy—and of what might be an appropriate strategy for Gourmet Stew. It might pursue a differentiation strategy of better quality at a higher price. Moreover, considering the difficulties of entering the distribution channels, it might focus on a niche strategy. Maybe Gourmet Stew could access health-oriented grocery stores like Whole Foods. Understanding the marketplace helps you formulate a strategy that can help you succeed.

Suppliers and Vendors

Understanding the customers and competition is critical to determining whether your idea is indeed an opportunity, but other factors also need consideration. Referring back to the value chain we created for Gourmet Stew (see Figure 3.7), you'll notice that suppliers are providing commodity goods such as beef, vegetables, and other food products. These types of vendors usually have limited power, which means that more of the ultimate gross margin in the chain goes to Gourmet Stew. A sudden rise in the market price of beef, however, could have a negative impact on your margins even though your power over suppliers is strong. A diversified offering that includes vegetarian stew, for example, can guard against such problems.

In other instances, your suppliers can have tremendous power, and that will directly affect your margins. For example, Microsoft, as the dominant operating system and core software provider, and Intel, as the dominant microprocessor supplier, have considerable power over PC manufacturers. Microsoft has gross margins of 74% and Intel has gross margins of 63%[46, 47] whereas average gross margins for PC manufacturers are between 9% and 40%.[48, 49] Putting aside the strong competition in the mature PC market for a moment, the fact that suppliers have so much power lessens the opportunity potential for entrepreneurs entering the PC market—unless they find an innovation to supplant the Microsoft operating system or the Intel chip.

The Government

For the most part, the U.S. government is supportive of entrepreneurship. Taxes are lower than in most nations in the world, the time required to register a new business is shorter, and the level of regulations is generally lower. However, in certain industries, government regulation and involvement are significantly higher, such as in pharmaceuticals and medical devices. For example, consider a startup company that produces a stent that more quickly and effectively removes kidney stones. In order to bring this product to market, you would have to guide your product through Food and Drug Administration (FDA) approval. The approval process is often lengthy, taking on average 12 years and over $350 million to get a new drug from the laboratory onto the pharmacy shelf.[50] During this time, the startup company is incurring costs with no revenue to offset the negative cash flow, increasing the time to break even, and also increasing the amount of money at risk if the venture fails. While the upfront time and expense are entry barriers that reduce potential future competition, your company benefits only if the product proves successful in gaining both FDA approval and adoption by doctors. Thus, as an entrepreneur, you need to be aware of government requirements and their impact on your business. If the requirements are stringent, such as getting FDA approval, and the potential margins you can earn are relatively low, it is probably not a good opportunity. In the case above, the stents command a very high margin, so the company can more than recoup its investment if it successfully navigates FDA approval and secures wide doctor adoption.

The Global Environment

As the world marketplace becomes global, your opportunity is increasingly strengthened by looking overseas. What international customers fit within your PTA, STA, and TTA? How easy is it to reach them? When might you go international? On the flip side, you also need to be aware of your international competitors. Have they entered your market yet? When might they? It is increasingly common for entrepreneurial firms to use an outsourcing strategy, which means that you may need to evaluate international vendors and their relative power. In Chapter 4, we go into much greater detail on global strategies, but for now, let's see whether the global environment makes your idea a stronger or weaker opportunity.

The Opportunity Checklist

Figure 3.10 summarizes the concepts we have covered in this chapter. Use it to evaluate your idea to see whether it is a strong opportunity or to evaluate several ideas simultaneously to see which one has the greatest promise. While your opportunity would ideally fit entirely in the middle column under "Better Opportunities," there will be some aspects where it is weak. Examine the weak aspects and see how you can modify your business model to strengthen them. In the end, of course, the goal is to be strong in more areas than you are weak.

"I Don't Have an Opportunity"

After doing a thorough analysis, some entrepreneurs conclude that the marketplace isn't as large or accessible or that the competition is much greater than they expected, and they quickly reach the conclusion that they should abandon their dreams. But in fact, if you analyze every aspect of the business and if you do your assessment completely, you'll always find a reason for the business to fail. There is no perfect business. There will be areas of weakness in any business model, and it is human nature to amplify those weaknesses until they seem insurmountable.

Customer	Better Opportunities	Weaker Opportunities
Identifiable	Clear "core" customer	Several possible customer groups
Demographics	Clearly defined and focused	Fuzzy definition and unfocused
Psychographics	Clearly defined and focused	Fuzzy definition and unfocused
Trends		
Macro market	Multiple and converging	Few and disparate
Target market	Multiple and converging	Few and disparate
Window of opportunity	Opening	Closing
Market structure	Emerging/fragmented	Mature/decline
Market size		
How many	Core customer group is large	Small core customer group and few secondary target groups
Demand	Greater than supply	Less than supply
Market growth		
Rate	20% or greater	Less than 20%
Price/Frequency/Value		
Price	Gross Margin > 40%	Gross Margin < 40%
Frequency	Often and repeated	One time
Value	Fully reflected in price	Penetration pricing
Operating expenses	Low and variable	Large and fixed
Net Income Margin	>10%	<10%
Volume	Very high	Moderate
Distribution		
Where are you in the value chain?	High margin, high power	Low margin, low power
Competition		
Market structure	Emerging	Mature
Number of direct competitors	Few	Many
Number of indirect competitors	Few	Many
Number of substitutes	Few	Many
Stealth competitors	Unlikely	Likely
Strength of Competitors	Weak	Strong
Key success factors		
Relative position	Strong	Weak
Vendors		
Relative power	Weak	Strong
Gross margins they control in the value chain	Low	High
Government		
Regulation	Low	High
Taxes	Low	High
Global environment		
Customers	Interested and accessible	Not interested or accessible
Competition	Nonexistent or weak	Existing and strong
Vendors	Eager	Unavailable

Figure   3.10

Opportunity checklist

Step back, take a second look, and ask yourself two questions: First, how can you modify your business model so that it isn't as weak in those aspects? Second, what can go right as you launch your business?

The entrepreneurial process is one of continuous adjustment. Many times entrepreneurs stick stubbornly to an idea as it was originally conceived. After a thorough customer and competitive analysis, you need to find ways to modify the business concept so that it better matches the needs of your customer and so that it has advantages over your competitors. The more you learn about the opportunities that exist for your product, the more you must refine your business plan. For instance, as you open your doors and customers come in and provide feedback, you'll find more ways to improve your business model. If you ignore feedback and remain stuck to your initial concept as you originally visualized it (and possibly as you wrote it in your plan), you are more likely to fail. The business planning process is ongoing, and you'll learn more about your opportunity at every step along the way. Therefore, to prematurely abandon your concept after some negative feedback from your analysis is a mistake unless the negatives far outweigh the positives in Figure 3.10.

It is also natural to assume the worst possible outcomes, fixating on the weak aspects of the business model and failing to recognize what can go right. For example, Ruth Owades, who founded Calyx & Corolla (a direct flower-delivery service from the growers to your home), persisted in launching a mail-order catalog called *Gardener's Eden* for unique gardening tools even though the initial analysis suggested it would be difficult to break even in the first year.[51] While Owades envisioned her business as seasonal—customers would order gardening supplies during the spring planting season—she found that she had two seasons: People also used the catalog during the Christmas season for gifts. She found, too, that the amount people would spend per order was higher than expected, making the dynamics of the business much more robust than she initially imagined.

Your pre-launch analysis is just a starting point. You need to understand the variables in your business model, how they might be greater or less than you initially imagine, and what that might mean for your business. In the next chapter, we will define and examine business models—how you make money and what it costs to generate revenues.

> "Analysis and criticism are of no interest to me unless they are a path to constructive, action-bent thinking. Critical type intelligence is boring and destructive and only satisfactory to those who indulge in it. Most new projects—I can even say every one of them—can be analyzed to destruction."
>
> — *Georges Doriot,*
> *Founder of the modern venture*
> *capital industry*

CONCLUSION

All opportunities start with an idea. We find the ideas that most often lead to successful businesses have two key characteristics. First, they are something that the entrepreneur is truly passionate about. Second, the idea is a strong opportunity as measured on the opportunity checklist. To be sure of having a strong opportunity, entrepreneurs need a deep understanding of their customers, preferably knowing the customers by name. Better opportunities will have lots of customers currently (market size) with the potential for even more customers in the future (market is growing). Furthermore, these customers will buy the product frequently and pay a premium price for it (strong margins). Thus, entrepreneurs need to be students of the marketplace. What trends are converging, and how do these shape customer demand today and into the future?

Savvy entrepreneurs also recognize that competitors, both direct and indirect, are vying for the customers' attention. Understanding competitive dynamics helps entrepreneurs shape their opportunities to reach the customer better than the competition can. As this chapter points out, the entrepreneurial environment is holistic and fluid. In addition to their customers and competitors, entrepreneurs need to understand how they source their raw materials (suppliers) and what government regulation means to their business. If all these elements—customers, competitors, suppliers and government—are favorable, the entrepreneur has identified a strong opportunity. The next step is successfully launching and implementing your vision.

YOUR OPPORTUNITY JOURNAL

Reflection Point	Your Thoughts...
1. What do you really enjoy doing? What is your passion? Can your passion be a platform for a viable opportunity?	
2. What do your friends and family envision you doing? What strengths and weaknesses do they observe? How do their insights help lead you to an opportunity that is right for you?	
3. What ideas do you have for a new business? How can you multiply the stimuli around these ideas to enhance them and identify attractive opportunities?	
4. Put several of your ideas through the opportunity checklist in Figure 3.10. Which ideas seem to have the highest potential?	
5. How can you shape, reshape, and refine your opportunities so that they have a greater chance to succeed and thrive?	
6. Identify some early, low-cost market tests that you can use to refine your opportunity. Create a schedule of escalating market tests to iterate to the strongest opportunity.	

WEB EXERCISE

Subscribe to the free listserve VentureAlert (http://www.dowjones.com/privateequityventure capital/product-vw.asp). Track the stories on a daily basis. Which companies are receiving venture capital? What trends does this flow of money suggest? How might these trends converge to create new opportunities?

NOTES

1 www.worldclassteams.com/welcome.htm.

2 www.fastcompany.com/magazine/44/dell.html.

3 Boyett, Joseph, and Jimmie Boyett. The Guru Guide to Entrepreneurship: A Concise Guide to the Best Ideas from the World's Top Entrepreneurs. New York: Wiley, 2001, p. 258.

4 www.chipotle.com/en-US/chipotle_story/chipotle_story.aspx

5 money.cnn.com/2010/10/06/small business/chipotle_started.fortune/index.htm

6 http://blogs.laweekly.com/squidink/ 2010/06/fast_food_using_slow_ food.php

7 http://articles.marketwatch.com/2006-01-26/news/30706373_1_chipotle-ipo-steve-ells-chipotle-shares

8 http://sec.gov/Archives/edgar/data/ 1058090/000119312512052969/ d280751d10k.htm

9 See the ABC *Nightline* segment "The Deep Dive" aired on July 13, 1999.

10 The four-step process outlined in this chapter—gather stimuli, multiply stimuli, create customer concepts, and optimize practicality—comes from a process outlined by Doug Hall. See Hall, D. *Jump Start Your Brain, 2.0*. Cincinnati, OH: Clerisy Press. 2008.

11 *Pain points* are those aspects of a current product or service that are suboptimal or ineffective from the customer's point of view. Improving on these factors or coming up with an entirely new product or service that eliminates these points of pain can be a source of competitive advantage.

12 Compiled from IDEO Web site at http://ideo.com/portfolio and from Edmondson, Amy C. "Phase Zero: Introducing New Services at IDEO." Boston: Harvard Business School Publishing. December 14, 2005, p. 13.

13 For those of you who are interested in learning more about brain-writing, visit www.mycoted.com/Brainwriting

14 http://sportsillustrated.cnn.com/2009/ more/04/09/under.armour/index.html

15 http://sportsillustrated.cnn.com/2009/ more/04/09/under.armour/index.html

16 http://articles.marketwatch.com/2005-11-18/news/30769699_1_armour-s-ipo-trading-debut-stock-market-debut

17 Under Armour 2011 Annual Report http://files.shareholder.com/downloads/ UARM/1887461670x0x553892/ 7bb998c7-0789-453b-8245-f11ec4419 fe7/2011_FINAL_Annual_Report.pdf

18 www.underarmour.jobs/our-history.asp

19 Bygrave, W., and Hedberg, C. *Jim Poss* (case). Wellesley, MA: Babson College. 2004.

20 Psychographic information categorizes customers based on their personality and psychological traits, lifestyles, values, and social group membership. It helps you understand what motivates customers to act in the ways they do and is important because members of a specific demographic category can have dramatically different psychographic profiles. Marketing strictly based on demographic information will be ineffective because it ignores these differences. Our use of soccer moms captures both the demographic and the psychographic attributes of a broad customer profile.

21 *The U.S. Baby Boomer Market: From the Beatles to Botox*. Third edition. Rockville, MD: Packaged Facts. November 2002, pp. 8–10.

22 Ibid., p. 7.

23 *The Religious Publishing and Products Market in the U.S.* Sixth edition. Rockville, MD: Packaged Facts. August 2008, p. 2.

24 Grossman, Cathy Lynn. Starbucks Stirs Things Up with a God Quote on Cups. *USA Today*. October 19, 2005. www.usatoday.com/life/2005-10-19-starbucks-quote_x.htm.

25 Fullservice Steams Ahead. *Restaurants USA*. October 2001. http://national restaurantassociation.org/tools/magazi nes/rusa/magArchive/year/article/?Arti cleID=671. This article estimates that ethnic food accounts for one-third of total restaurant sales, so we multiplied the total industry size by one-third.

26 Brown, R. Managing the "S" Curves of Innovation. *Journal of Consumer Marketing*, 9(1): 61–72. 1992.

27 *Backlog* is the sales that have been made but not fulfilled due to lack of inventory to finalize the sale.

28 Slaton, Joyce. *Webvan, Kozmo—RIP. Money Lessons We've Learned from the Last Mile Failures*. July 21, 2001. http://

articles.sfgate.com/2001-07-12/technology/17606161_1_webvan-kozmo-delivery/2.

29 www.cellular-news.com/story/23071.php

30 www.businessweek.com/stories/2007-06-05/ampd-mobile-runs-out-of-juicebusinessweek-business-news-stock-market-and-financial-advice

31 VentureXpert.

32 The names of the company and the entrepreneur are disguised.

33 Slotting fees are fees that supermarket chains charge suppliers for providing shelf space in their stores.

34 Information for this value chain was gathered from financial data on sample industry companies found at http://biz.yahoo.com/ic/340.html and linked pages.

35 General rankings for food sales found at http://biz.yahoo.com/ic/profile/340_1349.html; www.foodprocessing.com/top100/index.html

36 www.bitrebels.com/technology/the-evolution-of-smartphones-infographic/

37 www.businessweek.com/articles/2012-06-29/before-iphone-and-android-came-simon-the-first-smartphone#p1

38 http://finance.yahoo.com/news/world wide-market-share-smartphones-220747882--finance.html

39 www.gartner.com/it/page.jsp?id=910112

40 www.gartner.com/it/page.jsp?id=1306513

41 www.gartner.com/it/page.jsp?id=1543014

42 www.gartner.com/it/page.jsp?id=2017015

43 http://finance.yahoo.com/news/world wide-market-share-smartphones-220747882--finance.html

44 https://www.pwcmoneytree.com/MTPublic/ns/index.jsp

45 https://www.fis.dowjones.com/CustomPub/Subscribe.aspx?pi=VCA

46 http://ycharts.com/companies/MSFT/gross_profit_margin

47 http://ycharts.com/companies/INTC/gross_profit_margin

48 http://ycharts.com/companies/AAPL/gross_profit_margin

49 www.taipeitimes.com/News/biz/archives/2012/02/17/2003525647

50 www.drugs.com/fda-approval-process.html

51 Stevenson, H., Von Werssowetz, R., and Kent, R. *Ruth Owades*. Case 383051, Cambridge, MA: Harvard Business School Publishing. 1982.

Jim Poss

On his way through Logan Airport, Jim Poss stopped at a newsstand to flip through the June 2004 *National Geographic* cover story that declared "The End of Cheap Oil." Inside was a two-page spread of an American family sitting among a vast array of household possessions that were derived, at least in part, from petroleum-based products: laptops, cell phones, clothing, footwear, sports equipment, cookware, and containers of all shapes and sizes. Without oil, the world will be a very different place. Jim shook his head.

> *. . . and here we are burning this finite, imported, irreplaceable resource to power three-ton suburban gas-guzzlers with "these colors don't run" bumper stickers!*

Jim's enterprise, Seahorse Power Company (SPC), was an engineering startup that encouraged the adoption of environmentally friendly methods of power generation by designing products that were cheaper and more efficient than 20th-century technologies. Jim was sure that his first product, a patent-pending solar-powered trash compactor, could make a real difference.

> *In the United States alone, 180,000 garbage trucks consume over a billion gallons of diesel fuel a year.*

By compacting trash on-site and off-grid, the mailbox-sized "BigBelly" could cut pick-ups by 400%. The prototype—designed on the fly at a cost of $10,000—had been sold to Vail Ski Resorts in Colorado for $5,500. The green technology had been working as promised since February, saving the resort lots of time and money on round-trips to a remote lodge accessible only by snow machine.

Jim viewed the $4,500 loss on the sale as an extremely worthwhile marketing and proof-of-concept expense. Now that they were taking the business to the next level with a run of 20 machines, Jim and his SPC team had to find a way to reduce component costs and increase production efficiencies.

Jim returned the magazine to the rack and made his way to the New York Shuttle gate. An investor group in New York City had called another meeting, and Jim felt that it was time for him to start asking the hard questions about the deal they were proposing. These investors in socially responsible businesses had to be given a choice: Either write him the check they had been promising—and let him run SPC the way he saw fit—or decline to invest altogether so he could concentrate on locating other sources of funding to close this $250,000 seed round. So far, all Jim had received from this group were voices of concern and requests for better terms—it was time to do the deal or move on.

Green Roots

As a kid, Jim Poss was always playing with motors, batteries, and electronics. He especially enjoyed fashioning new gadgets from components he had amassed by dismantling all manner

Carl Hedberg prepared this case under the supervision of Professor William Bygrave, Babson College, as a basis for class discussion rather than to illustrate either effective or ineffective handling of an administrative situation. Funding provided by the F. W. Olin Graduate School of Business and a gift from the class of 2003. Copyright © by Babson College 2004.

of appliances and electronic devices. He also spent a lot of time out of doors cross-country skiing with his father. Jim said that by his senior year in high school, he knew where he was headed:

> *I had read* Silent Spring[1] *and that got me thinking about the damage we are doing to the earth. And once I started learning about the severity of our problems—that was it. By the end of my first semester at Duke University, I had taken enough environmental science to see that helping businesses to go green was going to be a huge growth industry.*

Jim felt that the best way to get businesses to invest in superior energy systems was to make it profitable for them to do so. In order to prepare himself for this path, Jim set up a double major in Environmental Science and Policy and Geology—with a minor degree in engineering. He graduated in 1996 and found work as a hydrologist, analyzing soil and rock samples for a company that engineered stable parking lots for shopping malls. He didn't stay long:

> *That certainly wasn't my higher calling. I poked around, and within six months I found a fun job redesigning the production capabilities at a small electronics firm. Soon after that, I started working for this company called Solectria; that was right up my alley.*

As a sales engineer at Solectria—a Massachusetts-based designer and manufacturer of sustainable transportation and energy solutions—Jim helped clients configure electric drive systems for a wide range of vehicles. He loved the work and developed an expertise in using spreadsheets to calculate the most efficient layout of motors, controllers, power converters, and other hardware. By 1999, though, he decided that it was once again time to move on:

> *Solectria had a great group of people, but my boss was a micro-manager and I wasn't going to be able to grow. I found an interesting job in San Francisco as a production manager for a boat manufacturing company—coordinating the flow of parts from seven or eight subcontractors. When the [Internet] bubble burst, the boat company wasn't able to raise capital to expand. My work soon became relatively mundane, so I left.*

This time, though, Jim decided to head back to school:

> *I had now worked for a bunch of different businesses and I had seen some things done well but a lot of things done wrong. I knew that I could run a good company—something in renewable energy, and maybe something with gadgets. I still had a lot to learn, so I applied to the MBA program at Babson College. I figured that I could use the second-year EIT[2] module to incubate something.*

---

[1] *Silent Spring*, written in 1962 by Rachel Carson, exposed the hazards of the pesticide DDT, eloquently questioned humanity's faith in technological progress, and helped set the stage for the environmental movement. Appearing on a CBS documentary shortly before her death from breast cancer in 1964, the author remarked, "Man's attitude toward nature is today critically important simply because we have now acquired a fateful power to alter and destroy nature. But man is a part of nature, and his war against nature is inevitably a war against himself. . . [We are] challenged as mankind has never been challenged before to prove our maturity and our mastery, not of nature, but of ourselves."

[2] The Entrepreneurship Intensity Track (EIT) was a compressed and highly focused entrepreneurship curriculum for graduate students at Babson College. The program provided a select group of MBAs who intended to become full-time entrepreneurs as soon as they graduated with the necessary skills to take their new venture ideas through the critical stages of exploration, investigation, and refinement, so they could launch their businesses during the spring of their second year.

Opportunity Exploration

Between his first and second years at Babson, Jim applied for a summer internship through the Kauffman Program. He sent a proposal to the Spire Corporation—a publicly traded manufacturer of highly engineered solar electric equipment—about investigating the market and feasibility of solar-powered trash compactors. Jim had copied his idea to someone he knew on the board, and the same week that the HR department informed him that there were no openings, he got a call from the president of the company:

> Roger Little had talked with the board member I knew and said that while they weren't interested in having me write a case study on some solar whatever-it-was, he said they'd like me to write some business plans for Spire—based on their existing opportunities and existing operations. I said sure, I'll take it.

That summer, Jim worked with the executive team to complete three business plans. When they asked him to stay on, Jim agreed to work 15 hours per week—on top of his full-time MBA classes. He mentioned that every month or so he would bring up his idea for a solar-powered trash compactor with the Spire executives, but their answer was always the same:

> I was trying to get them to invest in my idea or partner with me in some way, and these guys kept saying, "It'll never work." So I just kept working on them. I did the calculations to show them that with solar we could do ten compactions a day and have plenty [of electric charge] on reserve for a run of cloudy weather. Finally, they just said that they don't get into end-user applications.

Early in his second year, Jim attended a product design fair featuring young engineers from Babson's new sister school, the Franklin W. Olin School of Engineering. He connected with Jeff Satwicz, an engineering student with extensive experience in remote vehicle testing for the Department of Defense. When Jim got involved with a project that required engineering capabilities, he knew who to call:

> I went up the hill to Olin to ask Jeff if he'd like to help design a folding grill for tailgating—he said sure. It's funny, the two schools are always talking about working together like that, but it doesn't happen until the students sit in the Café together and exchange ideas. That's how it works; the faculty wasn't involved—and they didn't really need to be.

Although Jim didn't stay with the grill team, the project had forged a link with an engineer with a penchant for entrepreneurship. Now certain of his trajectory, Jim incorporated the Seahorse Power Company (SPC)—a nod to his ultimate aspiration of developing power systems that could harness the enormous energy of ocean waves and currents.

Understanding that sea-powered generators were a long way off, Jim began to investigate ways to serve well-capitalized ventures that were developing alternative-energy solutions. One idea was to lease abandoned oil wells in California for the purpose of collecting and selling deep-well data to geothermal energy businesses that were prospecting in the area. When Jim sought feedback, he found that even people who liked his concept invariably pointed him in a different direction:

> Everybody kept telling me that wind was where it's at—and they were right; it's the fastest growing energy source in the world. All the venture capitalists are looking at wind power. I realized, though, that if I was going to make wind plants, I'd have to raise two to five hundred

million dollars—with no industry experience. Impossible. So instead, I started looking at what these [wind-plant ventures] needed.

The DAQ Buoy

Jim discovered that The Cape Wind Project, a company working to build a wind farm on Nantucket Sound, had erected a $2.5 million, 200-foot monitoring tower to collect wind and weather data in the targeted area. Jim felt that there was a better way:

> *Meteorological testing is a critical first step for these wind businesses. I thought, whoa, they've just spent a lot of money to construct a static tower that probably won't accurately portray the wind activity in that 25-square-mile area. And without good data, it's going to be really hard for them to get funding.*

> My idea was to deploy data buoys that could be moved around a site to capture a full range of data points. I spent about six months writing a business plan on my data acquisition buoy—the DAQ. I figured that to get to the prototype stage I'd need between $5 and $10 million. This would be a pretty sophisticated piece of equipment, and a lot of people worried that if a storm came up and did what storms typically do to buoys, we'd be all done. I was having a hard time getting much traction with investors.

Finding the Waste

Even while he was casting about for a big-concept opportunity, Jim had never lost sight of his solar compactor idea. With the spring semester upon him, he decided to see if that business would work as an EIT endeavor. Although he was sure that such a device would be feasible—even easy—to produce, he didn't start to get excited about the project until he took a closer look at the industry:

> *I did an independent study to examine the trash industry. I was about a week into that when I looked at the market size and realized that I had been messing around with expensive, sophisticated business models that didn't offer close to the payback as this compactor would.*
>
> *U.S. companies spent $12 billion on trash receptacles in 2000, and $1.2 billion on compaction equipment in 2001. The average trash truck gets less than three miles to the gallon and costs over $100 an hour to operate. There are lots of off-grid sites[3] that have high trash volumes—resorts, amusement parks, and beaches—and many are getting multiple pick-ups a day. That's a tremendous waste of labor and energy resources.*

Joining him in the EIT module was first-year MBA candidate Alexander Perera. Alex had an undergraduate degree in Environmental Science from Boston University, as well as industry experience in renewable energy use and energy-efficiency measures. The pair reasoned that if a solar compactor could offer significant savings as a trash collection device, then the market could extend beyond the off-grid adopters to include retail and food establishments, city sidewalks, and hotels (see Exhibit 3.1).

---

[3] Sites without electrical power.

EXHIBIT 3.1 **Target Customers**

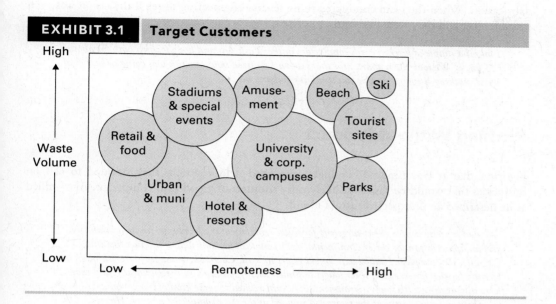

Gearing Up

By the time the spring semester drew to a close, they had a clear sense of the market and the nature of the opportunity—in addition to seed funding of $22,500: $10,000 from Jim's savings, and $12,500 through the Hatchery Program at Babson College. Since solar power was widely perceived as a more expensive, more complex, and less-efficient energy source than grid-power, it was not surprising to discover that the competition—dumpster and compaction equipment manufacturers—had never introduced a system like this. Nevertheless, Jim and Alex were certain that if they could devise a reliable, solar-powered compactor that could offer end users significant cost savings, established industry players could be counted on to aggressively seek to replicate or acquire that technology.

Understanding that patent protections were often only as good as the legal minds that drafted them, Jim had sought out the best. The challenge was that most of the talented patent attorneys he met with were far outside his meager budget. In May 2003, Jim got a break when he presented his idea at an investor forum:

> I won $1,500 in patent services from Brown and Rudnick.[4] That might not have taken me too far, but they have a very entrepreneurial mindset. They gave me a flat rate for the patent—which is not something many firms will do. I paid the $7,800 upfront, we filed a provisional patent in June, and they agreed to work with me as I continued to develop and modify the machine.

Jim's efforts had again attracted the interest of Olin engineer Jeff Satwicz, who in turn brought in Bret Richmond, a fellow student with experience in product design, welding, and

---

[4] Brown Rudnick Berlack Israels, LLP, Boston, Massachusetts.

fabrication. When the team conducted some reverse-engineering to see if the vision was even feasible, Jim said they were pleasantly surprised:

> *I found a couple of kitchen trash compactors in the Want Ads and bought them both for about 125 bucks. We took them apart, and that's when I realized how easy this was going to be. . . of course, nothing is ever as easy as you think it's going to be.*

Pitching Without Product

Figuring that it was time to conduct some hard field research, they decided to call on businesses that would be the most likely early adopters of an off-grid compactor. Alex smiled as he described an unexpected turn of events:

> *We had a pretty simple client-targeting formula: remoteness, trash volume, financial stability, and an appreciation for the environmental cachet that could come with a product like this. Literally, the first place I called was the ski resort in Vail, Colorado. Some eco-terrorists had recently burned down one of their lodges to protest their expansion on the mountain, and they were also dealing with four environmental lawsuits related to some kind of noncompliance.*
>
> *This guy Luke Cartin at the resort just jumped at the solar compactor concept. He said, "Oh, this is cool. We have a lodge at Blue Sky Basin that is an hour and a half round trip on a snow cat. We pick up the trash out there three or four times a week; sometimes every day. We could really use a product like that. . . ." That's when you put the phone to your chest and think, Oh my gosh . . .*

Jim added that after a couple of conference calls, they were suddenly in business without a product:

> *I explained that we were students and that we had not actually built one of these things yet (sort of). Luke asked me to work up a quote for three machines. They had been very open about their costs for trash pick-up, and I figured that they'd be willing to pay six grand apiece. I also had a rough idea that our cost of materials would fall somewhat less than that.*
>
> *Luke called back and said that they didn't have the budget for three, but they'd take one. I was actually really happy about that because I knew by then that making just one of these was going to be a real challenge.*

In September, SPC received a purchase order from Vail Ski Resorts. When Jim called the company to work out a payment plan with 25% upfront, Luke surprised them again:

> *He said, "We'll just send you a check for the full amount, minus shipping, and you get the machine here by Christmas." That was great, but now we were in real trouble because we had to figure out how to build this thing quickly, from scratch—and on a tight budget.*

Learning by Doing

The team set out to design the system and develop the engineering plans for the machine that SPC had now trademarked as the "BigBelly Solar-Powered Trash Compactor." Although his

Olin team was not yet versant with computer-aided design (CAD) software, Jim saw that as an opportunity:

> These guys were doing engineering diagrams on paper with pens and pencils—but now we were going to need professional stuff. I said that we could all learn CAD together, and if they made mistakes, great, that's fine; we'd work through it.

Concurrent to this effort was the task of crunching the numbers to design a machine that would work as promised. As they began to source out the internal components, they searched for a design, fabrication, and manufacturing subcontractor that could produce the steel cabinet on a tight schedule. Although the team had explained that SPC would be overseeing the entire process from design to assembly, quotes for the first box still ranged from $80,000 to $400,000. Jim noted that SPC had an even bigger problem to deal with:

> On top of the price, the lead times that they were giving me were not going to cut it; I had to get this thing to Colorado for the ski season!
> So, we decided to build it ourselves. I went to a local fabricator trade show, and discovered that although they all have internal engineering groups, some were willing to take a loss on the research and development side in order to get the manufacturing contract.
> We chose Boston Engineering since they are very interested in developing a relationship with Olin engineers. They gave me a hard quote of $2,400 for the engineering assistance and $2,400 for the cabinet. By this time, we had sourced all the components we needed, and we began working with their engineer to size everything up. Bob Treiber, the president, was great. He made us do the work ourselves out at his facility in Hudson (Massachusetts), but he also mentored us, and his firm did a ton of work pro bono.

Fulfillment and Feedback

As the Christmas season deadline came and went, the days grew longer. By late January 2004, Jim was working through both of the shifts they had set up: from four in the morning to nearly eleven at night. In February, they fired up the device, tested it for three hours, and shipped it off to Colorado (see Exhibit 3.2). Jim met the device at their shipping dock, helped unwrap it, met the staff, and put a few finishing touches on the machine. Although it worked, even at zero degree temperatures, it had never been tested in the field. Jim left after a few days, and for two weeks, he endured a deafening silence.

Jim wrestled with how he could check in with SPC's first customer without betraying his acute inventor's angst about whether the machine was still working, and if it was, what Vail thought about it. Finally, when he could stand it no longer, he placed the call under the guise of soliciting satisfied-customer feedback. The news from Vail nearly stopped his heart:

> They said that they had dropped the machine off a forklift and it fell on its face. Oh man, I thought; if it had fallen on its back, that would have been okay, but this was bad—real bad. And then Luke tells me that it was a bit scratched—but it worked fine. He told me how happy they were that we had made it so robust. When I asked how heavy the bags were that they were pulling out of the thing, he said, "I don't know; we haven't emptied it yet." I was astounded.

As it turned out, the Vail crew discovered that the single collection bag was indeed too heavy—a two-bin system would be more user-friendly. The resort also suggested that the inside cart be on wheels, that the access door be in the back, and that there be some sort of wireless notification when the compactor was full.

| EXHIBIT 3.2 | The BigBelly Arrives in Vail |

a.

b.

As the SPC team got to work incorporating these ideas into their next generation of "SunPack" compactors, they were also engineering a second product that they hoped would expand their market reach to include manufacturers of standard compaction dumpsters. The "SunPack Hippo" would be a solar generator designed to replace the 220-volt AC-power units that were used to run industrial compactors. The waste-hauling industry had estimated that among commercial customers that would benefit from compaction, between 5% and 20% were dissuaded from adopting such systems because of the setup cost of electrical wiring. SPC planned to market the system through manufacturing and/or distribution partnerships.

Protecting the Property

While the interstate shipment of the BigBelly had given SPC a legal claim to the name and the technology, Jim made sure to keep his able patent attorneys apprised of new developments and modifications. SPC had applied for a provisional patent in June 2003, and it had one year to broaden and strengthen those protections prior to the formal filing. As that date approached, the attorneys worked to craft a document that protected the inventors from infringement, without being so broad that it could be successfully challenged in court.

The SPC patents covered as many aspects of Sun Pack products as possible, including energy storage, battery charging, energy-draw cycle time, sensor controls, and wireless communication. The filling also specified other off-grid power sources for trash compaction, such as foot pedals, windmills, and waterwheels.

Even without these intellectual property protections, though, Jim felt that they had a good head start in an industry segment that SPC had created. Now they had to prove the business model.

The Next Generation

While the first machine had cost far more to build than the selling price, the unit had proven the concept and had been a conduit for useful feedback. A production run of 20 machines, however, would have to demonstrate that the business opportunity was as robust as the prototype appeared to be. That would mean cutting the cost of materials by more than 75% to around $2,500 per unit. SPC estimated that although the delivered price of $5,000 was far more expensive than the cost of a traditional trash receptacle, the system could pay for itself by trimming the ongoing cost of collection (see Exhibit 3.3).

EXHIBIT 3.3 **Customer Economics**

Remote Locations (e.g., Ski Resorts)

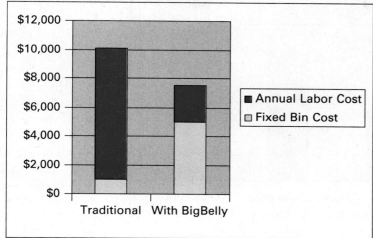

Urban Locations

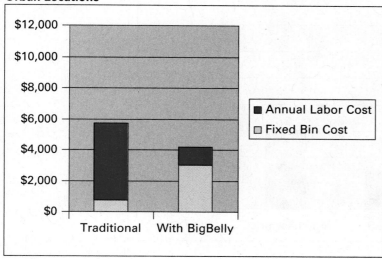

The team had determined that developing a lease option for the BigBelly would alleviate new-buyer jitters by having SPC retain the risk of machine ownership—a move that could increase margins by 10%. Over the next five years, SPC expected to expand its potential customer pool by reducing the selling price to around $3,000—along with a corresponding drop in materials costs (see Exhibit 3.4).

 **EXHIBIT 3.4** **BigBelly Economics**

Near Term

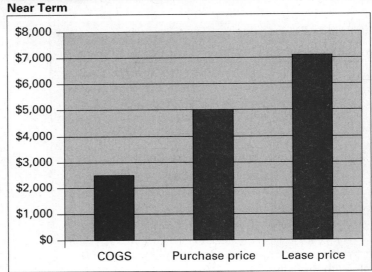

In Five Years

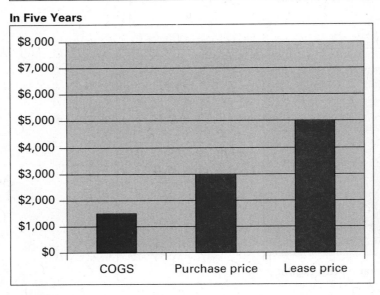

EXHIBIT 3.5 **BigBelly CAD Schematic**

a.

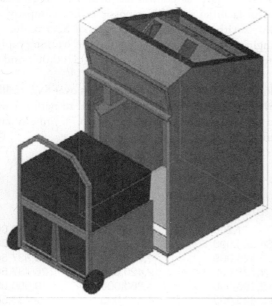

b.

With steel prices escalating, the SPC team designed their new machines with 30% fewer steel parts. They also cut the size of the solar panel and the two-week battery storage capacity in half and replaced the expensive screw system of compaction with a simpler, cheaper, and more efficient sprocket-and-chain mechanism (see Exhibit 3.5).

In order to offer an effective service response capability, the team tried to restrict its selling efforts to the New England area, although "a sale was a sale." One concern that kept cropping up was that this unique device would be a tempting target for vandals.

Team members explained that the solar panel on top was protected by a replaceable sheet of Lexan,[5] that all mechanical parts were entirely out of reach, and that the unit had already proven to be quite solid. The general feeling, Jim noted, was that if the machine could be messed with, people would find a way:

> One state park ranger was worried that it would get tossed into the lake, so I assured him that the units would be very heavy. He said, "So they'll sink really fast. . . "

Jim added that the overall response had been very favorable—so much so that once again, there was a real need for speed:

> We have pre-sold nearly half of our next run to places like Acadia National Park in Maine, Six Flags amusement park in Massachusetts, Harbor Lights in Boston, beaches on Nantucket, and to Harvard University. Fifty percent down-payment deposits should be coming in soon, but that won't cover what we'll need to get this done.

---

[5] A clear, high-impact-strength plastic used in many security applications.

Projections and Funding

During this "early commercialization period," Jim was committed to moderating investor risk by leveraging on-campus and contractor facilities as much as possible. The company was hoping to close on an A-round of $250,000 with a pre-money valuation of $2.5 million by early summer to pay for cost-reduction engineering, sales and marketing, and working capital. The following year the company expected to raise a B-round of between $700,000 and $1 million.

SPC was projecting a positive cash flow in 2006 on total revenues of just over $4.7 million (see Exhibit 3.6). The team members felt that, if their products continued to perform well, their market penetration estimates would be highly achievable (see Exhibit 3.7). Jim estimated that by 2008, SPC would become an attractive merger or acquisition candidate.

EXHIBIT 3.6 SPC Financial Projections	2004	2005	2006	2007	2008
BigBelly Unit	50	300	1,200	3,600	9,000
Sales	$225,000	$1,200,000	$4,200,000	$10,800,000	$22,500,000
BigBelly Revenues	0	120,000	525,000	1,620,000	3,937,500
Hippo Royalty Revenues	225,000	1,320,000	4,725,000	12,420,000	26,437,500
Total Income	146,250	660,000	2,100,000	4,860,000	9,000,000
COGS	78,750	660,000	2,625,000	7,560,000	17,437,500
Gross Income	400,000	1,600,000	2,600,000	5,000,000	11,000,000
SG&A	($321,250)	($940,000)	$25,000	$2,560,000	$6,437,500
EBIT					

EXHIBIT 3.7 Market Size and Penetration					
Top-Down	**2004**	**2005**	**2006**	**2007**	**2008**
SunPack Market* (Billion)	$1.0	$1.0	$1.0	$1.0	$1.0
SunPack % Penetration	0.0%	0.1%	0.5%	1.2%	2.6%
Bottom-Up					
Total Potential Customers**	30, 000	30,000	30,000	30,000	30,000
Potential Units/Customer	20	20	20	20	20
Total Potential Units	600,000	600,000	600,000	600,000	600,000
Cumulative Units Sold	50	350	1,550	5,150	14,150
Cumulative % Penetration	0.0%	0.1%	0.3%	0.9%	2.4%

*Assume a $600,000,000 BigBelly market (5% of $12 billion worth of waste receptacles sold to target segments), plus a $400,000,000 power unit market ($1.2 billion worth of compacting dumpsters sold/$12,000 average price × $4,000 per power unit).

**Assume 400 resorts, 600 amusement parks, 2,000 university campuses, 5,000 commercial campuses, 2,200 hotels, 4,000 municipalities, 57 national parks, 2,500 state parks and forests, 3,700 RV parks and campgrounds, and 17,000 fast-food and retail outlets.

In January 2004, as Jim began work on drafting an SBIR[6] grant proposal, his parents helped out by investing $12,500 in the venture. That same month, while attending a wind energy conference sponsored by Brown and Rudnick, Jim overheard an investor saying that he was interested in putting a recent entrepreneurial windfall to work in socially responsible ventures. Jim decided it was worth a try:

I gave him my three-minute spiel on the compactor. He said that it sounded interesting, but that he was into wind power—after all, this was a wind-power conference. "Well then," I said, "have I got a business plan for you!"

That afternoon Jim sent the investor the most recent version of the data acquisition buoy business plan. That led to a three-hour meeting where the investor ended up explaining to Jim why the DAQ was such a good idea. Jim said that the investor also understood how difficult it would be to get the venture fully funded:

[The investor] said, "Well, I sure wish you were doing the Data Acquisition Buoy, but I can also see why you're not." I assured him that my passion was, of course, off-shore wind, and that it was something I was planning to do in the future. So he agreed to invest $12,500 in the compactor—but only because he wanted to keep his foot in the door for what SPC was going to do later on.

In February, after the folks at Vail had come back with their favorable review, Jim called on his former internship boss at the Spire Corporation. Roger Little was impressed with Jim's progress, and his company was in for $25,000. In April, the team earned top honors in the 2004 Douglass Foundation Graduate Business Plan Competition at Babson College. The prize—$20,000 cash plus $40,000 worth of services—came with a good deal of favorable press as well. The cash, which Jim distributed evenly among the team members, was their first monetary compensation since they had begun working on the project.

Although SPC could now begin to move ahead on the construction of the next 20 cabinets, Jim was still focused on the search for a rather uncommon breed of investor:

This is not a venture capital deal, and selling this idea to angels can be a challenge because many are not sophisticated enough to understand what we are doing. I had one group, for example, saying that this wouldn't work because most trash receptacles are located in alleys—out of the sun.

Here we have a practical, common-sense business, but since it is a new technology, many investors are unsure of how to value it. How scalable is it? Will our patent filings hold up? Who will fix them when they break?

Earlier that spring Jim had presented his case in Boston to a gathering of angels interested in socially responsible enterprises. Of the six presenters that day, SPC was the only one offering products that were designed to lower direct costs. During the networking session that followed, Jim said that one group in particular seemed eager to move ahead:

They liked that Spire had invested, and they seemed satisfied with our projections. When I told them that we had a $25,000 minimum, they said not to worry—they were interested in putting in $50K now, and $200K later. In fact, they started talking about setting up funding milestones so that they could be our primary backers as we grew. They wanted me to stop fundraising, focus on the business, and depend on them for all my near-term financing needs.

---

[6] The Small Business Innovation Research (SBIR) program is a source of government grant funding driven by 10 federal departments and agencies that allocated a portion of their research and development capital for awards to innovative small businesses in the United States.

At this point I felt like I needed to play hardball with these guys; show them where the line was. My answer was that I wasn't at all comfortable with that, and that I would be comfortable when I had $200K in the bank—my bank. They backed off that idea, and by the end of the meeting, they agreed to put in the $50,000; but first they said they had to do some more due diligence.

Momentum

By May 2004, the Seahorse Power Company had a total of six team members.[7] All SPC workers had been given an equity stake in exchange for their part-time services. The investor group expressed deep concern with this arrangement, saying that the team could walk away when the going got tough—and maybe right when SPC needed them most. Jim explained that it wasn't a negotiable point:

They wanted my people to have "skin in the game" because they might get cold feet and choose to get regular jobs. I told them that SPC workers are putting in 20 hours a week for free when they could be out charging consulting rates of $200 an hour. They have plenty of skin in this game, and I'm not going to ask them for cash. Besides, if we could put up the cash, we wouldn't need investors, right?

As Jim settled into his seat for the flight to New York, he thought some more about the investors' other primary contention—his pre-money valuation was high by a million:

These investors—who still haven't given us a dime—are saying they can give me as much early-stage capital as SPC would need, but at a pre-money of $1.5 million, and dependent on us hitting our milestones. With an immediate funding gap of about $50,000, it's tempting to move forward with these guys so we can fill current orders on time and maintain our momentum. On the other hand, I have already raised some money on the higher valuation, and maybe we can find the rest before the need becomes really critical.

Preparation Questions

1. Apply the Timmons entrepreneurship framework (entrepreneur-opportunity-resources) to analyze this case.
2. Discuss Jim Poss' fundraising strategies. What other options might be considered for raising the funds SPC needs? Is this a good investment?
3. Discuss the growth strategy. What additional market(s) should Poss pursue?

---

[7] Three of the most recent equity partners were Richard Kennelly, a former Director at Conservation Law Foundation where he concentrated on electric utility deregulation, renewable energy, energy efficiency, air quality, and global warming; Kevin Dutt, an MBA in Operations Management and Quantitative Methods from Boston University with extensive work experience in improving manufacturing and operational practices in a range of companies; and Steve Delaney, an MBA from The Tuck School at Dartmouth College with a successful track record in fund-raising, business development, market strategy, finance, and operations.

Blake Mycoskie of TOMS shoes.

CHAPTER 4

UNDERSTANDING YOUR BUSINESS MODEL AND DEVELOPING YOUR STRATEGY

Once you've identified your opportunity, the next step is to devise a strategy to pursue that opportunity. While you're probably familiar with the basic strategy categories from previous coursework—differentiation, low cost, niche—many would-be entrepreneurs fail to grasp the intricacies of devising and implementing their strategy. All strategies are driven by the company's business model. Therefore, before you state that your firm is going to use a differentiation strategy or a niche strategy, you need to understand exactly what your business model is.

The Business Model

Every firm's business model consists of two components: a revenue model and a cost model. The **revenue model** breaks down all the sources of revenue that your business will generate. For instance, if you own a restaurant, your basic revenue model will separate food and beverage

This chapter is written by Andrew Zacharakis.

into two main sources of revenue. You can take that further and break down the revenue model by meals (breakfast, lunch, and dinner), categories of food (Italian, American, etc.), or even food item (pizzas, hamburgers, etc.). The more detailed your categories, the more information you can glean about how certain aspects of your business are performing.

The **cost model** identifies how you are spending your resources to make money. It includes your cost of goods sold (COGS) and your operating expenses. Basically, the business model is represented by your company's income statement. Understanding the business model enables entrepreneurs to make decisions that lead to greater revenue for lower costs.

Many of the world-changing businesses that have formed over the last 10 years have struggled to find a viable business model. For example, it took Twitter, a social networking and micro-blogging service founded in March 2006, several years to generate revenue. In 2009, Twitter CEO Evan Williams noted, "We will make money, and I can't say exactly how because . . . .we can't predict how the businesses we're in will work." Also, "We think Twitter will make money. I think it will take some time to figure it out."[1] After building a huge user base, Twitter monetized advertiser tweets that end up on search engines. When consumers choose to follow the "tweeting company," Twitter is paid. In 2012, Twitter generated almost $130 million in ad revenue.[2]

The Revenue Model

All businesses must generate revenue if they are to survive. Even nonprofit organizations need revenue, whether from donations or a combination of donations, government grants, and income generated from sales of a product or service. Without this revenue, nonprofits would be unable to achieve their missions. Breaking down the revenue sources into categories helps an entrepreneur understand how the firm can increase each.

Different revenue categories often require variations on the firm's central strategy to achieve the highest possible outcomes. For instance, Amazon.com's revenue model consists of a number of categories according to the products it sells online. On its Web site, customers can find everything from books and music to toys, computers, and electronics. In addition, the company breaks out sales by geographic region (see Figure 4.1). While Amazon markets its site heavily, spending close to $1.6 billion annually to draw customers to it, Amazon varies its strategy based on the product categories. For example, Amazon initially touted itself as "The Earth's Biggest Bookstore," which meant it had to carry (or have access to) more titles than its competitors. In 2012, Amazon's business model stands as a centralized variant of the "long-tail" business model in which it sells less of more. In statistics, a probability distribution can be described as having a "long tail" when the greater share of its population is contained under its tail than it would in a normal distribution. Amazon seeks to sell a little bit of everything, and a lot of just a few things. This model allows it to remain the online retailer of choice to the increasingly unique wants and desires of a highly individualized market. The strengths of Amazon's business model lay its unprecedented customer reach (anyone with an Internet connection), and its huge selections of products. However, this model has tradeoffs. Amazon's margins are slim, and getting slimmer. From 2007 to 2010, Amazon's profit margin was 3.4%, on average. In 2011, it was 1.3%. In comparison, eBay's profit margins at the end of 2011 were 27.7%, and Google's were 25.7%.[3] In a multi-year effort to improve its margins, Amazon has morphed into a "marketplace" where other companies are able to pay Amazon to sell their goods on Amazon's Web site, and store and ship through Amazon's warehouses and fulfillment systems. Amazon has also added new revenue sources such as Web services to serve software developers and those who require high-end server performance via on-demand data storage and computing capacity. This expansion allows other companies to leverage economies of scope in line with Amazon's core strengths and theoretically allows Amazon to develop new revenue streams that more closely resembled the profit margins of eBay and Google.

	2006	2007	2008	2009	2010	2011
Total Revenue	**$10.711**	**$14.835**	**$19.166**	**$24.509**	**$34.204**	**$48.077**
Media	7.067	9.242	11.084	$12.774	$14.888	$17.779
Electronics	3.361	5.210	7.540	$11.082	$18.363	$28.712
Other	.283	.383	.542	$653	$953	$1.586
North America	**$5.869**	**$8.095**	**$10.228**	**$12.828**	**$18.707**	**$26.705**
Media	3.582	4.630	5.350	$5.964	$6.881	$7.959
Electronics	2.024	3.139	4.430	$6.314	$10.998	$17.315
Other	.263	.326	.448	550	828	$1.431
International	**$4.842**	**$6.740**	**$8.938**	**$11.681**	**$15.497**	**$21.372**
Media	3.485	4.612	5.734	$6.810	$8.007	$9.820
Electronics	1.337	2.071	3.110	$4.768	$7.365	$11.397
Other	.020	.057	.094	103	125	$155
Cost of Revenue	**$8.255**	**$11.482**	**$14.896**	**$18.978**	**$26.561**	**$37.288**
Gross Profit	**$2.456**	**$3.353**	**$4.270**	**$5.531**	**$7.643**	**$10.789**
Operating Expenses						
Fulfillment	.913	1.253	1.597	2.052	2.898	4.576
Marketing	.259	.336	.469	.680	1.029	1.630
Technology & Content	.608	.715	.882	1.240	1.734	2,909
General & Administrative	.176	.200	.229	.328	.470	.658
Other Operating Expenses	.010	.009	−.024	.102	.106	.154
Stock-Based Compensation Exp.	.101	.185	.275	−.341	−.424	−.557
Total Operating Expenses	**$2.067**	**$2.698**	**$3.428**	**$4.061**	**$5.813**	**$9.370**
Operating Income	**$.389**	**$.655**	**$.842**	**$1.129**	**$1.406**	**$.862**

Source: Amazon.com Annual Report. US$ in millions

Figure 4.1

Amazon.com's business model

Different revenue categories for a firm are influenced by "drivers" that are directly correlated with the level of revenues the company earns. Using Amazon again, we see that the number of customers buying products from the site has the greatest influence on the revenues generated, especially electronics. Digging deeper, we find that other drivers influence revenue as well. For instance, it isn't just how many customers buy but also how much they spend per purchase and how often they buy (once a year, six times a year, etc.). The picture is still incomplete because not every person who visits Amazon will buy. Some people visit Amazon to comparison shop, while others use it to research products, which they then buy from another retailer.. Thus, other revenue drivers include the percentage of visitors to the site who make a purchase and the number of times those customers will visit before actually completing a transaction.

While consumer awareness of the Amazon brand influences all the drivers, Amazon can pursue any number of tactics to move the drivers in its favor. For example, advertising enhances Amazon's overall brand image. In addition, Amazon uses tactics such as bundling to increase the average order size (people who buy this product often also buy the following products). Many other tactics, such as co-branding with strategic partners and offering affiliates a percentage of sales for referrals, help to increase the number of visits to the site as well as the number of times a year that people visit.

All these drivers influence the revenues that Amazon achieves. Entrepreneurs who understand the central drivers and how to influence them can formulate strategies to achieve their goals. If you don't fully understand your revenue drivers, you won't achieve the greatest success.

Amazon's "long-tail" model, although recent, is well established. Yet, there are a number of other innovative models that entrepreneurs might want to consider. Three such models are the "Freemium," "One-for-one," and the "Ad-supported" model.

In a Freemium business model one or more customer segments constantly benefits from a free offer financed by another paying segment. Well-known examples include Skype and Google Drive. In both cases Skype and Google offer free services to all, supported by the revenue generated providing premium services to paying customers for Internet telecommunications and online storage, respectively. However, how can this work?

An excellent resource on business models is *Business Model Generation*, by Osterwalder, Pigneur, and Clark. They note that economists have long known that the demand generated for something that is free is multiple times greater than the demand generated for even a very low price. The Freemium business model works in today's digital age because the COGS to deliver these services is a lot less than it used to be. In fact, the COGS for free digital services can be viewed as a marketing expense because it generates customer awareness, facilitates faster product iteration through customer feedback, and helps develop brand recognition. Freemium business models often subsidize free offerings through advertising. For example, Gmail users get free email but face a barrage of advertments. Last, there is the bait-and-switch variant of Freemium, exemplified by the razor industry.[4] Customers often receive a free razor in the mail, but then have to buy expensive razors going forward.

For those who like to combine shopping with support for a worthy cause there is the "one-for-one" business model. First introduced by TOMS shoes in 2006, one customer segment (in this case, shoe buyers in developed countries) makes a purchase at a price that essentially reflects a doubling of COGS. Then that same product is provided to another customer segment free (in TOMS case, a child in the developing world). This is a potentially powerful business model, particularly for social entrepreneurs because it combines two psychological rewards for buyers, which can substantially increase their willingness to pay a premium for the product.[5]

Finally, an ad-supported model is basically an expansion of the double-sided platform model exemplified by broadcast radio/television, newspapers, and most recently Google's search engine. In this business model, customers trade permission and attention for services. An innovative example of this new variant is a Finnish telecommunications company called BLYK, a "free" ad-supported mobile phone network that offers text messages and customer-to-customer calls. In 2012, BLYK transformed from being a mobile phone company to a company that partners with other mobile phone companies in the Netherlands (Vodaphone), India (Aircel), and the UK (Orange). It focuses on a younger demographic (ages 16-29), presumably because they may be naturally more attracted to BLYK's value proposition. Users signed up to the network received advertising messages on their mobile phones, and in return are given a monthly 1000 free Blyk-to-Blyk calls and 1000 free texts to any networks. The launch advertisers include Beachmasters, Universal Pictures, McDonald's, Pearle, and Electronic Arts. Demonstrating the potential of its business model, in 2012, BLYK reached over 4 million opt-in subscribers. [6]

The Cost Model

Typically, a firm needs to spend money to influence the revenue drivers. Thus, entrepreneurs also need to understand the cost model, which includes two primary categories: COGS and operating costs. Referring to Figure 4.1, we can identify the cost model for Amazon. COGS represent those costs directly associated with the revenue source. For a product company, COGS generally includes the raw materials and direct labor needed to make the product. For a retailer like Amazon, COGS is the cost of purchasing the products from various manufacturers that Amazon then sells.[7]

Some products have a very small COGS. For example, once developed, software is very cheap to produce. COGS may include only the cost of buying and burning a CD, packaging it, and shipping it to a retailer or customer.[8] COGS may be even lower if the software can be downloaded from the Web. For service firms, COGS is mostly composed of the direct labor involved in delivering the service. For instance, at a consulting firm, COGS would be the salary costs of the consultants working on the project, and at a tutoring company, COGS would be the hourly wages paid to the tutors for every hour worked.

As with revenues, we categorize COGS by product categories. For Amazon, strong control would suggest that it break out COGS for books, toys, electronics, and so on and directly tie each COGS to the revenue generated by that product category. However, in its publicly available financials, Amazon doesn't break out COGS. We suspect its internal reporting is more detailed, but since business is highly competitive, companies usually reveal as little detail as they can in public reports. Those internal details help entrepreneurs understand which products have strong gross margins and which products don't.

By understanding how sales drive COGS, entrepreneurs can achieve higher margins as well as increase revenues. For example, e-books read on the Kindle, iPad, or other devices have revolutionized Amazon.com's business model. Electronic delivery is another way to capture revenue, and it significantly reduces cost. The book doesn't have to be packaged and shipped. If a book is not in stock or is out of print, Amazon.com can now deliver it electronically, whereas in the past, it would have to either forgo the order or buy a minimum quantity of the book from the publisher, which would greatly increase COGS. Technology is allowing Amazon.com's business model to change toward an on-demand revenue and cost model that provides greater flexibility.

Many firms outsource production to more efficient producers in order to increase gross margins. P'kolino, a playroom furniture company founded by Antonio Turco-Rivas and JB Schneider, outsources production of its lower-end items to China. Moving production offshore can greatly reduce the manufacturing costs and thereby increase gross margins, but there may be other trade-offs to consider. To start, what other costs will P'kolino incur from outsourcing? Transportation costs will be much higher from China, and travel costs will increase, as P'kolino founders periodically visit the production sites to monitor quality and manage relationships. Do the savings from less expensive overseas manufacturing offset these increased transportation and travel costs? The answer is usually yes, given the high cost of manufacturing in the United States, but there are yet more factors to consider. Lead times for overseas outsourcing will have to be longer. If P'kolino is slow in moving its designs to the manufacturer, it may miss the critical holiday selling season. If the company has some proprietary components, outsourcing may cause manufacturing details to leak and seriously damage the firm's competitive advantage.

Along with influencing gross margins, outsourcing can powerfully reduce the up-front fixed costs the firm would incur if it produced its products itself. New ventures require more time to break even due to high up-front fixed costs. Outsourcing production means the firm is moving from fixed expenses to variable expenses because it is paying the subcontractor based on the number of units it produces.

TOMS Shoes turned to offshoring production to support sudden growth. Blake Mycoskie started TOMS in 2006 after he witnessed the level of poverty among villagers in Argentina. The villagers could not even afford to put shoes on their feet. Mycoskie purchased 200 pairs of local shoes and came back to Los Angeles with a mission. He asked local retail stores to purchase a pair of shoes, and with the proceeds from that sale, he would give a pair of shoes to a child in need. Eventually, a few local boutiques agreed to sell Mycoskie's shoes. Then the *Los Angeles Times* caught word of TOMS and ran an article about it. That weekend $88,000 in orders came in (equal to about 2,000 pairs, at $44/pr.). Mycoskie only had 140 pairs of shoes on hand. Mycoskie quickly hired numerous interns to call customers and persuade them to wait eight weeks to have their shoes delivered. Mycoskie quickly boarded a plane back to Argentina where he arranged for 40,000 pairs of shoes to be manufactured. Within a few weeks, Mycoskie sold and shipped every pair in that first batch. [9] Worldwide over 500 retailers have collaborated with Mycoskie to sell over 2,000,000 pairs of shoes (for an estimated $88 million in revenue), with an equal number of shoes having been given away to a child in need.

Avoiding the huge up-front costs of building a factory decreases the time to break even. However, as we noted earlier, firms do not want to outsource their competitive advantage. Outsourcing production rarely jeopardizes firms' competitive advantage because their advantage usually isn't in the production process. Nonetheless, entrepreneurs must remain careful.

Operating costs provide the other main component of the cost model. Referring to Figure 4.1, we find that Amazon incurs large marketing expenses (17.4% of operating costs in 2011) to ensure that its brand continues to be at the forefront of consumers' minds. Rapid delivery is also important for the company's strategy. Fulfillment costs accounted for 49% of operating costs in 2011. By examining Amazon's cost model, we get a sense of the key elements of its strategy: brand recognition through marketing, world-class Web technologies and content (ensuring that customers have a pleasant experience when they visit the site), and quick delivery through high-tech fulfillment operations.

To create a viable business model, Amazon must develop and sustain clear competitive advantages. For instance, the company spends a considerable amount of money marketing the brand. This is essential for an Internet company that has little or no brick-and-mortar retail presence. In addition, we see that the company's cost of sales is 77% of revenues, which suggests that Amazon is pursuing a high-volume, low-cost strategy. This is related to the high marketing costs already mentioned because generating high volume takes significant marketing and advertising investments. The Kindle and other forms of electronic delivery that cut printing and fulfillment costs may lower the cost of sales if Amazon, rather than the publisher, is able to capture these savings.

We also see that Amazon's competitive advantage stems from keeping an enormous selection of products available at competitive prices. At the time of Amazon's founding, the average book superstore carried 150,000 titles in stock. Amazon started with 1 million titles. Again, the strategies are interdependent. By having a far greater selection than local stores, the company increases the likelihood of customer purchases and also increases the chances that a customer purchasing a unique title will purchase another book he or she has been meaning to buy. This availability strategy enables Amazon to meet the needs of customers who want their purchases quickly, but it leads to high inventory and fulfillment expenses. All these expenses lead to lower net income margins, but this is offset in turn by high volumes. Consider Walmart—it may average net margins in the low single digits, 3.7% in 2011, but when it is achieving those margins on *hundreds of billions* of dollars in revenue, $419 billion for 2011, the end result is billions of dollars of profit. Amazon pursued a similar strategy, and it was an expensive one. The company needed significant up-front capital while establishing itself. Prior to going public in May 1997, Amazon raised $10.6 million from private equity sources. Although it raised $54 million in public offerings, it still needed to raise an additional $1.25 billion in 1999 by selling convertible bonds to institutional investors such as investment banks and insurance companies.[10] Amazon didn't become profitable until 2003.[11]

Once entrepreneurs understand their basic business model, they can build a strategy to compete and win in the marketplace. The strategy and business model are interrelated: Entrepreneurs can have a broad sense of what overall strategy they want to pursue, but until they have a full understanding of their business model, it is difficult to move on to tactics to implement that strategy.

The First-Mover Myth

Beware entrepreneurs who claim they have a "first-mover advantage." This claim is part and parcel of the "we don't have any competition" claim discussed in the previous chapter. Most entrepreneurs who make these claims don't truly understand the nature of their business and what a first-mover advantage really is. Remember Netscape? Remember the Rio Player? Remember. . . the iPhone? All were lauded as first movers, yet all were usurped by followers. Netscape, later surpassed by Internet Explorer, and then by 2012, Google Chrome reigned as the supreme browser coupled with the Google search engine. Then along came the iPod, iTunes, iPad, and Dropbox. Even the vaunted iPhone can already hear Android's footsteps. Of these first movers, none have been able to consolidate their gains into long-term market dominance. This is because simply being first has little long-term advantage unless you can create the eco-system that sustains your initial success. Let us look at Google again. Is Google innovative? Google launches a new product nearly weekly; however, it always seems that you have seen or heard of each product somewhere before. Google Drive is essentially a twist on Dropbox. Google Play is a twist on the iTunes store. Google Tablet is a twist on the iPad, and Google+ is a lot like Facebook. Is Google just copying the first-movers and current leaders? Is it simply trying to make up for a lack of innovation? No, Google is very innovative. However, Google excels at eco-system innovation, not product innovation. Dropbox has no ecosystem connected to it once launched. Google created Google Drive to give the users of Gmail, Google+, and Google Docs a seamless experience inside a single eco-system that connects both your contacts, files, and friends all in one place. Thus, being first in of itself is not enough.

Even if you are first and gain a substantial customer base, you may not succeed with a first-mover advantage. Jonathan Abrams, founder of Friendster, the first online social network, took his Web site live in March 2003 and six months later garnered 3 million users.[12] In August 2003, MySpace emerged, and by the end of 2004, its site had 22 million monthly users compared to Friendster's 1 million. By 2011, Friendster ceded the U.S. market to Facebook, but still has a strong presence in Southeast Asia. Today, Facebook, launched in February 2004 by Mark Zuckerberg, dominates the social networking business with 1.0 billion users compared to Twitter's 500 million.[13]

These examples illustrate several key aspects about capturing a first-mover advantage.

- You have to be first (or very early) into the market.
- You need to capture a large percentage of the market quickly (which means fast growth).
- You need to create switching costs so the customer will stick with you (even in today's Internet world, where searching for competing brands is easy and low cost).

Gaining a first-mover advantage isn't impossible, but it is very difficult and expensive. For instance, it is fair to say that Amazon successfully executed a first-mover advantage, although technically it wasn't the first online bookseller. Amazon went from a startup company out of Seattle in July 1995 to a global firm with sales of $48 billion in 2011. It introduced Internet retailing to many customers and educated them on the benefits.

However, a first-mover advantage is expensive because firms have to quickly capture a large part of the available market. As we have discussed, Amazon raised over $1 billion to build its infrastructure (technology and fulfillment) and reach new customers. At the time of Amazon's initial public offering, company officials said, "Amazon will invest heavily in promotion and marketing, site development, and technology and operating infrastructure development. In addition, Amazon intends to offer attractive discounts that will reduce its already slim gross margins."[14] The company's formula for success depended on its ability to extend its brand position, provide customers with outstanding value and a superior shopping experience, and achieve sufficient sales volume to realize economies of scale.

The stage of the marketplace also contributes to the high costs of a first-mover advantage. Referring back the industry S-curve in Figure 3.6, you will see that a new market emerges slowly. Rather than investing marketing dollars to educate customers on why their product is better, in a new market companies find themselves educating customers on why they need the product in the first place. This can take a lot of time and money, and it is a unique challenge of emerging markets.

There is an added danger to being a first mover: You may get it wrong. The history of business is littered with first movers supplanted by offerings that better met the customer's needs. Figure 4.2 lists some first movers and the firms that eventually gained dominance in those markets.

Figure 4.2 and the success of Google and others tell us that being first does not by itself lead to success. For a first mover, a winning strategy is complemented by other components that lead to a sustainable, bundled competitive advantage, such as the Google ecosystem. eBay's initial success combined being first to the market with installing a strong seller base. All the mini-stores on eBay use the platform because of its ubiquitous name. These sellers knew they would have strong customer traffic because of the eBay brand. However, Amazon seems to have hacked away at that competitive advantage with its own marketplace. Tracing Amazon's history shows how the company continues to evolve a sustainable competitive advantage. Breaking out from simply being an online bookseller, Amazon made a heavy bet on brand awareness led firms such as Toys "R" Us to partner with it, further enhancing Amazon's own brand. Amazon coupled this strategy with a rapid fulfillment infrastructure that allows the company to gain a cost advantage on efficiently delivering products to customers on a timely basis. Amazon then set its sights squarely on eBay when it leveraged economies of scope to allow anyone to sell through its marketplace, which allowed it to surge past eBay in terms of annual customer traffic (14% vs. 8.8% of all ecommerce traffic in 2012). Amazon then moved to lock in customers with attractive annual flat-fee shipping offer that a less centralized marketplace such as eBay could be challenged to match.

Industry	First Mover	Current Leader
Social Networking	Friendster	Facebook
Video Games	Atari	Nintendo
Web Browser	Mosaic	Google Chrome
Internet Search Engine	Excite	Google
Word-Processing Software	WordStar	Microsoft Word
Personal Computer	Altair	Lenovo
Email	Juno	Google Gmail
Diet Soda	No-Cal	Diet Coke
Presentation Software	Harvard Graphics	Microsoft PowerPoint
Online Bookseller	Book Stacks Unlimited	Amazon
ATM Machines	Docutel	Diebold

■ **Figure 4.2**

Supplanting the first-mover advantage

Considering the high costs, it is nearly impossible to achieve a first-mover advantage without significant outside financing, most often venture capital financing. Less than 0.1% of all firms receive venture capital. Since most firms aren't attractive to venture capitalists or other large sources of capital, the first-mover advantage is often too expensive a strategy to pursue. Relax. As we have tried to illustrate, the first-mover advantage often fails anyway. Most successful firms win not because they have some inherent, large competitive advantage but because they execute better than the competition. These firms are flexible and adapt to the customer so that they continue to add value long after the initial launch.

Winning is more about implementing your strategy than about formulating some grand strategy that nobody has ever thought of before. Don't get us wrong—you absolutely need a well-thought-out strategy—but in the end, execution of that strategy will determine your success or failure.

Formulating a Winning Strategy

Winning strategies include some combination of the following attributes: better, cheaper, and faster. Your business needs to create some value for which people are willing to pay. P'kolino, the children's playroom furniture and toy company mentioned earlier, is pursuing customers with better design. The company expects parents and grandparents to pay more for a unique product that encourages creative play.

Super Delicious Chips: Food Should Taste Good

In 2006, Pete Lescoe founded Food Should Taste Good with the goal of making a unique new snack with great taste, healthy ingredients, and sophisticated flavor—those qualities that he is most passionate about in food. His company makes chips with all natural ingredients baked right into the chip rather than adhering to the industry standard of spraying on flavored seasoning. Food Should Taste Good products compete in the natural and organic salty snacks segment—whose sales have grown at a double-digit pace for the last two years, outpacing growth in the wider salty snacks segment.

Today, Food Should Taste Good is one of the largest natural snack brands in the United States. It makes natural tortilla chips in a variety of differentiated flavors such as Sweet Potato, Lime, Olive, Chocolate, Multigrain, and Jalapeno. Food Should Taste Good's product line-up includes kettle-cooked sweet potato chips and other natural snacks. All of Food Should Taste Good's chips are gluten free, cholesterol free, and have zero grams trans-fats. They are also certified Kosher, and many varieties are certified vegan.

In February 2012, General Mills recognized the advantage that Food Should Taste Good had built and acquired the company to be part of its Small Planet Foods division for natural and organic products. Lescoe will continue with the business as creative director.[15]

Pete Lescoe, founder of FoodShouldTasteGood, Inc., is pursuing a better product strategy. We would expect to see their competitive advantages reflected in the business models of both these firms. P'kolino should achieve high gross margins because parents—and more specifically, financially well-off parents—are willing to pay a premium for well-designed children's furniture and toys. Its margins may be offset somewhat by the distribution channels the firm uses. If, for example, it uses Pottery Barn, the prestigious and powerful retailer may appropriate more of those gross margins. While P'kolino might be able to retain stronger gross margins by selling directly to parents, it would incur higher operating costs such as marketing and fulfillment infrastructure costs. Entrepreneurs can capture the trade-offs between different approaches by examining their relative impacts on the net income margin. Food Should Taste Good's production process is more efficient. Spray-on flavors are a headache because the process gums up equipment, which then requires lots of cleaning and downtime after each production run. In contrast, flavoring via "inclusion" of ingredients is cleaner, faster, and cheaper.

We can summarize P'kolino's competitive advantage as better designs and Food Should Taste Good's as better taste. Other companies may have a branding advantage or just execute better than the competition. Whatever the company's competitive advantages, it needs to take steps to protect them. There are numerous paths for doing so. If you have a unique product that includes significant intellectual property, you may file for patent protection or choose to maintain trade secrets. (Chapter 13 covers intellectual property issues in greater detail.)

The People Are What Matters

Students often think that their company needs to have an explicit, identifiable, and patentable competitive advantage. However, more often than not, your competitive advantage will be complemented by the tacit knowledge held by the people within your company. Southwest Airlines, for example, has consistently been one of the most profitable airlines, a result partially due to its direct route strategy (rather than the hub-and-spoke system of the old-line airlines). Southwest employees also work more efficiently than their counterparts at traditional airlines. Existing airlines have tried and failed to imitate their friendly customer interactions and motivation to get airplanes quickly serviced and back into the air. In other words, Southwest's competitive advantage is inherent in the tacit knowledge of its employees. The most difficult aspects of a firm's strategy to imitate are the people and the execution of the strategy. From the very beginning of your company's life, you need to create a culture that is conducive to fostering the human elements of your business.

Probably the most important thing founders do is to create the organization's culture. While the original culture will evolve, companies tend to be replications of what they were in the past, so it is critical that you get the culture right at the beginning. You need to create an atmosphere that encourages people to bond to the company. Yes, your people believe in the mission; yes, they believe in the product; but more importantly, the members of your team need to believe in each other and want to continue to be part of the organization. Let's break building and maintaining a culture into three main categories: values, selection, and structure.

Values. As the founder, you need to identify what values you want to drive your organization. Values are beliefs shared by all members. For example, JetBlue based its organization building on five core values:[16]

- ◉ Safety
- ◉ Caring
- ◉ Integrity
- ◉ Fun
- ◉ Passion

Values communicate what kind of work environment founders want to create and what guidelines they use in hiring future employees. For JetBlue, safety is a central value, and without question, this is a critical value for the airline industry. The other values communicate that JetBlue treats its employees the way it expects its employees to treat the customers. The values put into place at the company's founding will flow through to formulating and implementing the strategy. More importantly, values create the foundation on which your company will grow.

Selection. It's important to hire the right person the first time. Communicating the values you've identified to new team members goes a long way toward making sure there is a fit between the employee and the company. Every new person added to the company will reinforce the values you've put in place, thereby helping to sustain the company's culture. JetBlue focuses on its five core values when interviewing job candidates and structures its interview questions around these values.[17]

In 1971, when Herb Kelleher founded what is now America's largest domestic air carrier, Southwest Airlines, he was driven to increase the mobility of the common citizen. He sought to do this by offering low-cost fares, and trimmed costs and services to do so. He knew that underpinning this no-frills approach had to be an enjoyable customer experience. A critical early decision was the hiring of his flight attendant staff that would become the face of Southwest to its customers. Southwest decided to outfit its flight attendants is hot pants and go-go boots (again, this was the 1970s). The only applicants for the job, considering the uniforms, came from the ranks of cheerleading squads and marching band majorettes. Then a funny thing happened. Southwest thought it had hired flight attendants with one key attribute, a figure that was a good fit for the uniform, but quickly realized they had hired people with a much more important attribute, a natural enthusiasm. The cheerleaders were all about spreading enthusiasm, about cheering people on, and convincing the common citizen that they "can win." The cheerleaders were such a perfect fit, Southwest Airlines began only to recruit cheerleaders.[18]

The lesson for an entrepreneur here is simple: You must clearly determine what critical qualities you need in an employee, where you are going to look for it, and how you are going to recognize and measure it.

Structure. The structure of a new venture changes as it matures. Early on, it is very informal as the founders and a few early hires do a wide variety of tasks. There are several things to keep in mind as you build your early organization. First, you need to hire people who can "wear many hats"—who can work on a prototype, contact vendors, create budgets, and talk to customers as the need arises. It can often be a mistake to hire a corporate lifer who is used to working in one functional area and having expensive administrative support. Such employees, while talented, may not operate well in the informal startup environment.

Second, as team-building expert Elizabeth Riley[19] says, "over-hire." That is, find team members and early-stage employees who are overqualified for the tasks they will initially be doing. While you might save some money by hiring someone else with fewer skills, as a young and resource-constrained new venture, you won't have the time and money to help that person learn on the job.

Finally, you need to create a flexible organizational structure. While you may have an organizational chart, reporting and communications need to be free to flow throughout the organization. That means that any employee during this startup phase can freely talk to any other. This loose structure facilitates learning about your business model, about processes that do and don't work, about customers' needs, and so forth. It fosters and promotes flexibility. The universal truth about strategy formulation and business planning as a whole is that it needs to change and adjust during implementation based on your customers' reactions. If you build a flexible organization, you will be in a better position to adjust your strategy. As the organization matures, the structure will necessarily become more formalized. While it is easy to be informal with 5, 10, or even 20 employees, it is inefficient when you have 150.

In sum, an organization's culture starts at its founding and determines your strategy—and ultimately your success—for the life of the organization. Take time to think about what kind of culture you want and create a plan to make sure it is implemented.

Entry Strategy

Successful launches are iterative. Southwest Airlines didn't start with a nationwide route plan but instead serviced routes between Dallas, Houston, and San Antonio. After this initial market test in Texas, the company adjusted its processes, improved upon its customer interactions, and then added more routes. Over time, the carrier has continued to add routes and today flies to 97 cities in 41 states nationwide.[20] Since its inception, Southwest has flown one type of airplane—the Boeing 737—which helps streamline its operation. In addition, the company has focused on using less-congested airports and flying point-to-point rather than using the hub-and-spoke system of traditional airlines. Each new route proved the Southwest business model and created an opportunity to reevaluate and improve the product. Raising millions in advance of a national route structure and then launching nationwide from day one would have surely led to failure for Southwest, considering the high startup costs of creating an airline. By advancing step by step, the company learned a lot of lessons that it otherwise would have missed. Likewise, you should devise an entry strategy for your firm that allows you to test your concept in the market at a relatively low cost.

Benchmarking. Before you raise a dime of outside capital, first learn from others. Benchmark competitors and learn "best practices" from firms that operate inside and outside your industry of interest. Create a simple matrix that identifies the firm and its strategy, core customers, sources of competitive advantage, basic revenue model (including margins), and major cost categories—and any other elements that you think might be useful. JetBlue followed much of Southwest's formula during its startup phase. Its founder and former CEO, David Neeleman, worked for six months as an executive vice president at Southwest Airlines before he was fired. At JetBlue, Neeleman placed a high priority on creating a cooperative company culture and hiring the right people to fit that model. Initially, JetBlue flew only one type of jet. The flight attendants help clean up the plane for quicker turnarounds at the gate.[21]

The Serial Entrepreneur: Can Lightning Strike Twice?

What happens when an entrepreneur is forced from the company he founded? If you're a serial entrepreneur like David Neeleman, you start another airline. On Valentine's Day in 2007, an ice storm blanketed the East Coast. JetBlue had to cancel 1,700 flights and stranded 130,000 passengers. That exposed poor operations and communication. Most airlines responded by canceling flights prior to the storm and sending passengers home, but JetBlue thought the weather would break and it would be able to fly. Instead, the storm hit with a fury, and there were stories of JetBlue passengers confined to their planes for as long as five hours as they waited on the tarmac for the weather to break. Neeleman was publically apologetic, even creating a YouTube clip to apologize directly to his customers.

JetBlue created a Customer Bill of Rights, which highlighted how they would treat customers affected by future storms. But it wasn't enough. In May 2007, Neeleman was fired as CEO from JetBlue—the company he founded in 2000.

But Neeleman wasn't down for long. In December 2008, Brazilian-born Neeleman launched Azul Airlines, based in Brazil, after securing $200 million from investors—many of them the same investors who previously backed JetBlue. Azul—Portuguese for blue—is trying to replicate JetBlue's low-cost airline success in an emerging economy where flying is almost 50% more per mile than in the United States. Today, Azul Brazilian Airlines is the third largest airline in Brazil, with 10% market share. It has served over 19 million passengers and it has been recognized as the best low-cost airline in Latin America by Skytrax. It looks like lightning can strike twice.[22]

	JetBlue	Southwest	United	American	FedEx
Strategy	Low cost	Low cost	Geographic coverage (national and international)	Geographic coverage	International, overnight package delivery
Core Customer	Leisure traveler	Leisure traveler	Business and leisure	Business and leisure	Business
Competitive Advantage	Cost structure (non-union, no hubs, smaller airports)	Cost structure (no hubs, smaller airports)	Size of fleet, geographic coverage	Size of fleet, geographic coverage	Size of fleet, geographic coverage, entry barriers
Revenue Model	Airfare, freight	Airfare, freight	Airfare, freight	Airfare, freight	Package
Cost Model	Labor, fuel, aircraft, landing fees, and infrastructure	Same	Same plus higher costs associated with "hub" system	Same plus higher costs associated with "hub" system	Same plus higher costs associated with "hub" system
Other	Investment in IT, customer focus, employee focus, hands-on CEO	Standardized aircraft, customer and employee focus, hands-on CEO			Investment in IT, employee focus, hands-on CEO

■ **Figure 4.3**

Benchmarking comparison for JetBlue

Figure 4.3 compares JetBlue during its launch phase to some of its competition. It highlights a gap in the marketplace where JetBlue could enter (geographic opening for a low-cost carrier out of New York) as well as the ways different firms are competing. You can see that a low-cost, point-to-point system focusing on leisure travel makes sense, and it appears that JetBlue should pursue this strategy. Gathering this initial information puts you in a position to do an initial, ideally low-cost, market test.

We included Federal Express (FedEx) in the matrix because entrepreneurs should look outside their immediate industry and identify "best practice" companies there. From FedEx, JetBlue can learn the power of a state-of-the-art information technology infrastructure as well as lessons on creating an effective corporate culture.

Initial Market Test. You can devise your initial market test once you have a strong understanding of the competition. For JetBlue, the initial market test entailed operating one route and then expanding routes based on what it had learned. If you are planning to open a restaurant and believe you will compete based on unique recipes and cuisine, preparing your menu for family and friends would be a simple, low-cost test. Do they like the food? What other items might they like to see on the menu? Note that you can do this test without spending any money on an actual location. Next you might see about catering one or two events. Here, you can test whether people will pay for your cuisine and further refine your menu. The next step might be to offer your food on a mall cart that sells smaller items in common areas at shopping malls. Are people drawn to your cart? Do they buy? This test helps you determine location. What kind of traffic patterns does the business need? Which demographic group is most drawn to the cuisine? Based upon your learning during this market test, you might be ready to open your first restaurant. Figure 4.4 illustrates a market test schedule. Developing this schedule not only guides your learning but also helps you understand when, how, and how much it will cost to achieve the next milestone.

The concept of escalating market tests is powerful. While you can visualize and plan for your business in great detail over a long period of time, you never truly learn whether it is a viable business until you make a sale. Too many entrepreneurs make the mistake of spending $1 million or more to open up that first restaurant only to find that customers don't like the basic concept. Adapting your concept at that point is more costly than it would have been if you had completed some earlier market tests. If you adapt your menu and cuisine at every step in Figure 4.4, you'll be much closer to a winning concept when you open your first restaurant.

It is important to remember that successful new-venture creation is an iterative process. Regardless of how large your company grows, you will continually adapt your business based on what you learn at each market test. At a company like Microsoft, for instance, new software products go through an alpha test, during which the company uses the software internally.

Market Test	What You Expect to Learn	Timing
Prepare dinner for family and friends	Do they like the menu? What else would they add? When would they eat this food? How often?	2–3 events over the next month.
Try to sell a catering event	Can you actually sell the concept? Can you prepare larger quantities in an efficient manner? How does preparing large quantities impact taste?	1–2 events one month after the initial test.
Rent a mall cart	What kind of people (demographics) are attracted to your concept? When do they buy (lunch, dinner)? How much do they buy? How often do they buy? What kind of traffic patterns seem to be most conducive to the business?	Operate for 1–2 months. Do this by month 3 of business.
Open first restaurant	What preparation processes are most effective? What kind of staffing do you need? What hours of operation capture the largest percentage of customers?	6 months after launch.
Open second restaurant	Can the processes be replicated? Do the same types of customers come into this location? What attributes seem to define the best location?	Open 1 year after first restaurant.
Open restaurants 3–5	Can you replicate processes? What processes need to be established at the central level to oversee all the restaurants?	Open in years 2–5.
Franchise the concept	Are potential franchisees interested in your concept? Are your processes sound so that a franchisee can replicate your company-owned restaurants?	Franchise in years 5–8.

Figure 4.4

Market test schedule

After the software is debugged, it goes to a beta site. In beta, a handful of customers use the product and report back problems as well as additional functions that they would like to see. Based upon the feedback, the company might continue with more beta tests. Once they feel that the product is close to their goal, managers release it to the larger market. As any company that has been through a product recall can attest, prematurely releasing a product is an incredibly expensive proposition. The costs include the possibility of having to distribute replacements for defective units, the opportunity costs of disgruntled customers who choose not to buy from you again, and the broader costs of damage to your reputation in the market as customers spread the word that your product is inferior. A controlled launch plan will help you manage the process and avoid these potentially debilitating costs.

Creating a Platform. Figure 4.4 shows the concept of creating a platform on which to grow your business. Opening the first restaurant is the platform, whereas opening successive restaurants is a growth strategy. For many entrepreneurs, opening one restaurant may be the end goal, but others will have larger aspirations. Frank Day grew his restaurant empire to include 144 casual dining restaurants: 44 brewery restaurants (Rock Bottom Restaurant and Brewery, Walnut Brewery, ChopHouse, and Sing Sing) and 100 Old Chicagos. Day is a role model for creating a hugely successful business. He "got into the game" by opening one restaurant he used for experience and learning. In order to differentiate his Old Chicago in Boulder, Colorado, Day began offering a selection of 110 beers. As he expanded the chain to new locations, Day allowed the restaurants to reflect their local communities and focused on the ambience. Day then replicated his highly successful business model and grew the business into multi-million-dollar chains, with estimated revenues for the private company of over $381.7 million in 2009.[23] In 2010, Centerbridge Capital Partners merged it with Biersch Brewery Restaurant Group, into what is now CraftWorks Restaurants and Breweries. Frank Day moved from CEO to chairman and now presides over the combined operations of some 200 restaurants comprised of 60 units of Old Chicago Pizza and Taproom, 37 units of Rock Bottom Restaurant & Brewery, and 32 units of the Gordon Biersch Brewery Restaurant Group. Additionally, CraftWorks owns numerous "specialty concept" restaurants consisting of 12 units of The Chophouse, 4 units of the Big River Grill & Brewing Works, 2 units of Sing Sing Dueling Pianos, and one unit each of the Blue Water Grille, A1A Ale Works, Ragtime Tavern Seafood & Grill, Seven Bridges Grille & Brewery, and the Walnut Brewery.[24]

This strategy works across industries and marketplaces. P'kolino, for example, entered the children's furniture and toy market with a few designs. As the owners started selling their products and learned what aspects customers liked and didn't like, they continued to add designs. Over time, they have entered different segments by offering different levels of quality. This type of learning reduces your up-front costs and exposes you to new opportunities that you might not otherwise perceive because you are interacting with customers. Finally, if the worst case should occur and you fail, you will lose less than if you boldly jumped in with multiple restaurants or products all at once.

Opening that first restaurant or selling your first product is your entry into the marketplace. You'll need to have an overriding entry strategy as we discussed earlier—perhaps differentiation. You'll also need to have marketing, operating, and financial plans in place to help achieve your strategy. Much of this is covered in other courses you've taken, and we will explore business planning in depth in Chapters 7 and 8 as well. The key for your entry strategy is to find a pathway into the industry and a way of surviving the first two to three years when most businesses are operating with a negative cash flow. Starting in year three, you need to envision how you will not only grow your firm but also thrive.

Growth Strategy

The first two to three years of any new venture are about survival. The firm has to prove that its customers are interested in its offerings, refine its operations, and increase its visibility.

After the first couple of years, many firms will seek growth. In Figure 4.4, we see growth as a function of adding more company-owned restaurants and then ultimately franchising the concept. Managing growth is difficult, and Chapter 14 goes into greater detail on these issues. Our goal here is to think about strategies for growth—what works, when it works, and why it works. Although experience suggests that the first few years of a new venture should focus on testing the market and refining your business model, it is never too early to start thinking about how you will grow. We will explore several common growth strategies.

Franchising. As shown in the example in Figure 4.4, franchising is a strong growth strategy if you have a replicable business model. Most often franchising is used with retail concepts, such as McDonald's or Mail Boxes Etc. We can summarize the keys to success with franchising as follows:

- ◉ Replicability—The business model is well established and proven. As the franchisor, you have worked out the processes of opening and operating a business unit (which is captured in the Franchising Disclosure Document and details the operations, quality controls, policies, procedures, and financial aspects of the business).

- ◉ Control—The brand is the lifeblood of your business. A poor franchisee can damage your brand, so you need to have monitoring systems in place. Control is also important to ensure that the franchisee is accurately reporting revenues because this controls the revenue you'll receive from your franchising royalty.

Franchising leads to two types of growth. First, it speeds growth as it brings in new capital to fund that growth. Specifically, the franchisees fund new unit development. Subway is the classic example. In fact, many critics argue that Subway takes advantage of its franchisees (see Box). Subway's growth was phenomenal. Starting with three company stores in 1965, it grew to 134 by 1979 and has exploded to more than 37,976 franchises today. Subway is ubiquitous in the United States and operates in 99 other countries [25] around the world. It has focused on achieving long-term growth and expanding in countries with high population density, available disposable income, and political and economic stability.[26] Figure 4.5 shows the top 10 franchise operations in the world,[27] current revenue, number of units, and sales per store.

Second, franchising adds new revenues—the royalty fee and the franchising fee. Franchisees owe the franchisor a royalty ranging from 2% to 12.5% on every dollar earned.[34] For this royalty, the franchisor promises to support the franchisee. Often the fee will include

#	Chain	U.S. Total Franchise Sales	U.S. Franchise Units	Sales per Store
1	McDonald's	$34.2 billion	14,098	$2,425,876
2	Subway	$11.4 billion	24,722	$461,128
3	Starbucks	$9.75 billion	10,787	$903,866
4	Wendy's	$8.5 billion	5,876	$1,446,562
5	Burger King	$8.4 billion	7,231	$1,161,665
6	Taco Bell	$6.8 billion	5,674	$1,198,449
7	Dunkin Donuts	$5.92 billion	7,015	$843,906
8	Pizza Hut	$5.4 billion	7,595	$710,994
9	KFC	$4.5 billion	4,793	$938,869
10	Chick-Fil-A	$4.05 billion	1,600	$2,531,250

Source: Technomic/Restaurant Finance, compiled by Blue MauMau 2011

■ **Figure 4.5**

Top 10 franchisors

The Dark Side of Franchising: Does Subway Take Advantage of Its Franchisees?

Although franchising is an excellent growth strategy for the franchisor, as well as a means for individual franchisees to start their own tried-and-true business, franchising is not without its problems. For example, many critics and franchisees feel that Subway is not a good partner. In 1998, Dean Sagar, the staff economist of the U.S. House of Representatives' Small Business Committee, said, "Subway is the biggest problem in franchising and emerges as one of the key examples of every abuse you can think of."[28]

Today Subway has over 37,976 restaurants,[29] but that rapid growth has caused some dissension. Many franchisees believe that Subway has violated their agreements by allowing new franchisees to open close to existing restaurants, thereby cannibalizing sales. "In many markets Subway has overbuilt," says International Association of Independent Subway Franchisees (IAISF) Executive Director Leslee Scott. "There are guys who were doing $8,000 a week three or four years ago who today are doing $4,500."[30]

Although most Subway franchisees are happy and profitable, the franchise business model is ripe for conflict. "The franchising business is, at its core, antagonistic," says Tom Schmidt, an attorney who is suing the Houston-based Marble Slab Creamery ice cream chain on behalf of nine Marble Slab franchisees. Schmidt continues, "Franchisees must also play by strict rules, and those rules are constantly changing according to the parent company's whims."[31] Thus, franchisees and franchisors need to be aware of and prepare for likely conflict.

For example, Subway changed how its multi-million-dollar advertising budget is controlled. Jim Hansen, CEO of the North American Association of Subway Franchisees (NAASF), says, "The new franchisee agreement 'threatens' control franchisees have over the advertising funds.";[32] So the NAASF, an independent group representing about 67% of all Subway franchisees, along with the Subway Franchisee Advertising Fund Trust, filed lawsuits seeking to bar Subway from instituting these new terms. The groups claimed that, "if left intact, the agreement would give Subway the power to redirect franchisee advertising contributions to a separate entity at any time."[33]

royalties the franchisees must pay for advertising, but sometimes this charge is a separate fee. The franchisor pools the advertising royalties and spends it on behalf of the franchisees for regional and national TV, radio, newspaper, magazine, and Internet ads.

The franchisees also pay a fee to secure the rights to the franchise. This ranges from $25,000 for a relatively undeveloped brand to $45,000 for a McDonald's. Moreover, McDonald's requires a downpayment that must come from non-borrowed personal resources, exclusive of a personal residence. The initial downpayment is 40%[35] of the total cost of a new restaurant, which ranges between $959,450 and $2,110,700, plus McDonald's requires the franchisee to have an additional $750,000 in non-borrowed personal resources after the down payment.[36] For the most part, these fees cover the overhead for managing and monitoring the system, but they are also a source of growth capital.

Some franchisors bring in additional revenue by selling supplies to their franchisees. In fact, the franchising business model can be so lucrative that William Ackman, whose Pershing Square Capital Management once owned a 4.9% stake in McDonald's, challenged the firm to spin off all its company-owned stores, which, according to his analysis, dragged down the firm's profit. After two years of pressure, Ackman ultimately failed to get the change he wanted and sold all of his shares in McDonald's at the end of 2007.[37] However, it is necessary to have company-owned stores in the launch and early years, while the entrepreneur tests and refines the basic operations and market acceptance of the concept. Successful company-owned stores also allow the franchisor to charge larger franchise fees.

Expanding Your Product Mix. Many companies start with one product, but as they gain traction in the marketplace, they recognize new opportunities to add to their product mix. Building your product mix should increase your revenue at a rate greater than the associated costs. In other words, you should be able to spread your existing costs across a larger product base. You might use the same vendor to provide raw materials or to produce your product. That would increase your power to secure better terms when negotiating. You also might leverage your existing distribution channels. By selling more products through these channels, you increase your negotiating power.

The key is to leverage your firm's experience as you become more familiar with your core customers and your own operations. Whole Foods, for example, has included lifestyle departments at its stores in Austin and Los Angeles, selling all-natural housewares and clothing. "The development and incorporation of Whole Foods Market Lifestyle reflects the company's founding values into other aspects of life," said Marci Frumkin, a Whole Foods regional marketing director. "The new lifestyle store is another example of how Whole Foods leads by example. . . educating consumers about organic food, natural products and ethical business practices."[38] Like Whole Foods, you should search for ways to extend your product mix that leverage your existing production or customer relationships.

Adding products is a means to grow, but it is not risk free. Eighty percent of new products are failures.[39] The risk is that the company will incur development expenses, the market may not accept the new product, and the unsuccessful product line could reflect unfavorably on the reputation of the existing products. You need a coherent strategy to minimize the risks of new products. Start with your firm's competitive advantage. What do you do better than anybody else? For P'kolino, that advantage is innovative designs. Adding designs increases P'kolino's power by giving it more visibility with its distributors, such as Babies 'R' Us. P'kolino also decreases its cost of direct distribution by selling a wider range of products on its Web site and by having enough products in a catalog to try a direct-mail strategy. Furthermore, this strategy gives the company more leverage with its vendors. More products ideally result in a larger production volume, which suggests that P'kolino can negotiate better terms.

iRobot was a Massachusetts-based startup focused on building robots on specification for government agencies and industry until it created the Roomba. This innovative self-propelled and self-controlled vacuum cleaner helped iRobot move into the lucrative consumer products market. Rather than partnering with another firm and selling the technology, iRobot decided it could manufacture the Roomba overseas. Although it still builds robots for military and industrial use, iRobot began to focus on branching into other consumer products.[40] Today iRobot is a public company generating over $427 million in sales with several new product innovations such as floor-vacuuming robots (Roomba: over 6 million sold), floor-washing robots (Scooba), shop-sweeping robots (Dirt Dog), pool-cleaning robots (Verro), gutter-cleaning robots (Looj), and programmable robots. iRobot has also sold 3,000 PackBot tactical military robots deployed in support of explosive hazards detection missions in Afghanistan and Iraq.

A product growth strategy identifies synergies within the firm and then leverages those synergies in conjunction with the company's customer knowledge. While sound management imagines what the firm will pursue for product growth during the launch phase, in reality many new opportunities will appear only once you have started selling your first product and gained firsthand market intelligence.

Geographic Expansion. Expanding geographically is another common growth strategy. This natural growth is based on the underlying assumption that customers should like your product or service elsewhere if they like it in the location where you founded the company. All the larger retail companies in existence today had roots in one geographic region before they grew outward. Walmart started in Arkansas, while McDonald's was originally located in Bakersfield, California.

You can plan geographic expansion systematically, or it can happen haphazardly. Oftentimes potential customers will come across your product through the media or the Internet and want it. Founded in Milwaukee in 1844, Pabst Blue Ribbon (PBR) is a beer that is most commonly associated with America's blue-collar Midwest, or hipsters who want to (ironically) appear blue-collar. Which is why anyone could be forgiven for not foreseeing that, in 2010, PBR responded to sudden strong demand in China with exports that are bottled, and seductively marketed like champagne, and priced at $44 per bottle. [41] While opportunistic growth can be a smart move, entrepreneurs benefit from developing and following a coherent strategy.

When planning geographic expansion, you'll want to weigh a number of factors:

- Customers—First and foremost, are the customers in the new location similar to those in areas with existing operations? Your initial strategy is predicated on delivering a product or service that satisfies the needs or wants of a core customer group. For your initial expansion, you want to leverage the knowledge you've gained from serving customers in your initial location. For example, College Coach,[42] a college advisory service, targets well-to-do parents through two primary channels: First, the company sets up retail stores in affluent suburbs, and second, it partners with large *Fortune* 500 companies such as IBM to provide human resource benefits. College Coach was founded and based in Newton, Massachusetts, an affluent suburb of Boston. Its initial expansion efforts were to the suburbs of New York City and Chicago. The rationale behind these locations was the prevalence of well-to-do parents who are focused on getting their children into Ivy League schools and other top universities across the country. Thus, College Coach seeks geographic regions characterized by affluent pockets where a high percentage of kids apply to top-tier universities.

- Vendors—Can you continue to use the same vendors? If not, what costs will you incur to establish new relationships? Remember, the greater your volume, the stronger your negotiating position. If you can continue with the same vendors, you will have greater bargaining power, but that power becomes diluted if you add vendors.

- Distribution—Can you use the same distribution channels? As with vendors, you can increase your leverage and reduce your marginal costs by moving more volume through existing distribution channels.

These factors should guide your decision making as you formulate your growth strategy. If you look at the geographic expansion of retail operations, you'll note that they strive for a critical mass within a region before moving to another region. For example, Dunkin' Donuts is highly concentrated in the northeastern United States. There are approximately 169 Dunkin' Donuts outlets within a five-mile radius of Boston: one outlet for every 3,500 residents. Customers in the Boston area know the company well, and its core customers view stopping at Dunkin' Donuts for their morning coffee as integral to their morning routine. Not only does this high concentration keep the brand at the forefront of the customer's mind, but also it gives Dunkin' Donuts considerable operating efficiencies. The key is balancing your company's saturation point—the point when new expansion within the region cannibalizes existing operations—against its opportunities to expand to new regions.

Today with the Internet, it is easier than ever to expand across many regions simultaneously. Potential customers find out about your product and then contact you about buying the product or representing your company in a new region. Before accepting these offers, make sure you understand the trade-offs. First, most sales and even unsolicited orders require time and effort on your part. This is time and effort that is diverted from establishing your company in its existing regions. Second, your company may not have the infrastructure in place to support the buyer after the sale. Third, consider any additional costs for transporting the product to the customer. While unsolicited orders can be attractive, make sure you understand the hidden costs (mostly in time and effort) that you incur as you fill them.

International Growth. International growth is a special case of geographic expansion. In today's global economy, new entrepreneurial firms often should consider expansion at their inception. Advances in logistics, technology, and manufacturing have allowed smaller and younger firms to compete globally. Firms that look globally from the outset often have tightly managed organizations, innovative products, and strong networks for marketing. They also have more-aggressive growth strategies, use more distribution channels, and have more experienced management teams. They don't simply export but instead choose foreign direct investment in the countries in which they seek to operate. With their global reach, they can introduce innovative products to new markets, giving them an advantage over startups that operate only in the domestic sphere. They also may operate in industries that are globally integrated from the start.[43]

The U.S. Commerce Department's Exporter Database (EDB) reveals that in 2010 the total number of U.S. firms exporting goods stood at 293,100[44]—up approximately 20% from the 245,945 firms that exported in 2006. In another study, Rodney Shrader and colleagues[45] estimate that one-third of all small manufacturing firms derive at least 10% of their revenues from foreign sources. Unfortunately for a new venture, going global increases risk and costs money. Pat Dickson[46] provides a model that illustrates when and how entrepreneurial ventures go global (see Figure 4.6)

Dickson notes that there are three types of global entrepreneurial firms. Those in the first category, *gradual globals*, enter international markets in stages in order to reduce their risk. During their initial expansion, gradual globals will enter countries similar to their domestic market and use processes that require lower costs and commitment, such as exporting. Over time, they will enter more, and increasingly dissimilar, countries. Gradual globals will also expand their entry modes, moving from exporting to foreign direct investment, for example. The second category of entrepreneurial firms is *born global*. These firms plan to enter international markets right from their outset. Those in the final category, *born-again globals*, have been operating only domestically, but some triggering event, such as an unsolicited order from abroad, causes them to move rapidly into new international markets. Although there is a

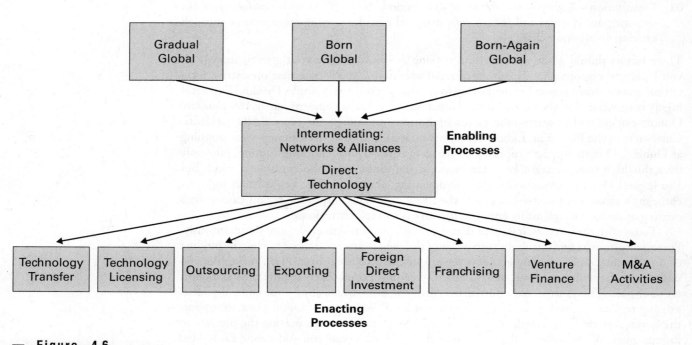

Figure 4.6

The entrepreneurial firm's international expansion process

lot of debate about which type of firm is most likely to succeed globally, entrepreneurs need to think about international business from day one.

Dickson suggests that entrepreneurs pursue enabling strategies, given that new ventures are resource constrained. For instance, they can use intermediaries to reduce needed resources or use low-cost methods, such as the Internet, that enable them to make contact with potential international partners. In many cases, entrepreneurs can tap their existing networks, such as employees, investors, vendors, or customers, to facilitate international entry. One of your vendors, for instance, may have distribution capabilities in another country that you can use on a variable-cost basis. You might also pursue alliances with other companies. The Internet enables entrepreneurs to directly access international markets in a low-cost manner. You can market to firms worldwide by simply putting up a Web site. You can proactively manage relationships overseas by using the Internet and email. TOMS shoes leverages the strong appeal of its one-for-one business philanthropic business model to attract many high-profile designers, such as Ferragamo, to produce new designs for its shoes. These designs, produced in high-end design houses of Europe and America, are then sent via the Web to TOMS production facilities in China, Ethiopia, Argentina, and Brazil.[47] Companies are adapting to a growing trend called telepresence systems. Telepresence refers to a set of technologies that allow persons to feel as if they are physically present at a location other than their true location.[48] Whatever enablers you use, it is easier today to enter global markets than ever before. Dickson's model moves from enabling to enacting processes. There are eight primary means to expand globally.

- Technology transfer (joint venture)—When firms choose to enter the global market, they may need to decide whether to sell their technology or produce it abroad themselves. Producing technology overseas can involve significant risk and investment. On the other hand, having a partner firm in the target country or region produce and distribute your product can reduce your entry costs. The costs of technology development and production often lead young firms to build alliances and joint partnerships and to focus on niche markets.[49] However, there is a risk you'll lose control of the technology because the partner firm will gain insight into how you produce the product.

- Technology licensing—Perhaps the most common means to enter a foreign market is to secure an agent to represent the company abroad. Here, the entrepreneur may decide that he or she is better off letting a foreign company produce and sell the product, perhaps rebranded under its own name, and taking a royalty as compensation. Licensing reduces risk from an operational perspective. While this is an excellent means of generating revenue and conserving resources, it also is a lost opportunity to extend your own brand into new markets.

- Outsourcing—Outsourcing allows businesses to handle key attributes of their products while handing over the responsibility for development and manufacturing to a subcontractor. The outsourced production may be sent back to the company's home country for sale. It is often the first logical step as a firm seeks to expand globally. This is basically the strategy that P'kolino is considering, and the primary reason to look at global outsourcing is cost savings.

- Exporting—The cheapest and easiest way to enter new markets is to sell from your headquarters. However, as always there are trade-offs. First, it is harder to establish a critical mass in the country if you don't have anyone on the ground, and as mentioned earlier, you may incur additional costs in after-sales support. Your customers also may have difficulty contacting you or providing information about the market and their needs. You incur the transportation costs and risks of getting your products through the target country's customs. A second alternative is to hire a sales representative in the target country. The advantages are that sales representatives have deep knowledge of the country and presumably a strong network they can leverage in selling the product. However, agency theory suggests there are risks to consider.[50] First, it is difficult for you to confirm that agents are as skilled as they might claim (which is referred to as *adverse selection*). Second, it is difficult to ensure that the agent is honoring the contract (which is referred to as *moral hazard*).

- Foreign direct investment (FDI)—Under this strategy, companies set up a physical presence in the countries of interest, whether that is a sales office, retail outlets, production facilities, or something else. The startup retains control of the assets and facilities, an issue that can prove expensive. The primary means of FDI are acquiring foreign assets and building and expanding current facilities overseas. FDI is usually beyond the means of most early-stage companies. French clothing line Chloé tested the Chinese market by exporting the product first through retail stores. Then, once it learned that Chinese customers liked the product, it started to establish its own retail outlets in Beijing and then Shanghai. Today Asia accounts for over 50% of sales of this high-end fashion house, with 70[51] locations in the Asia Pacific.[52] It plans to branch out slowly from those locations.[53] Similarly, Jeff Bernstein started Emerge Logistics[54] by using China's bureaucratic red tape and the unwillingness of American companies to invest in Chinese facilities to his advantage. Bernstein's logistics company has 14 customers such as Harley-Davidson, Mercedes-Benz, and Siemans. For example, Mercedes-Benz needed to ensure effective, reliable after-market parts support for luxury vehicles sold in China. Emerge provided a warehousing facility, customs clearance management, and local delivery to dealers and distributors throughout China.[55]

- Franchising—Some see franchising as a low-risk method of entering a foreign market because it allows the firm to license an operational system. Yet there can be difficulties in monitoring the international franchisee and ensuring that it protects the company's brand (moral hazard). Until recently, the Chinese as a whole had a dim view of franchises.[56] The biggest foreign retailer in China, Carrefour, rapidly closed many of its franchised stores in 2012, which were organized into a loose structure. Franchise owners' profits depended upon supplier-paid entrance fees and sales commissions to protect their profit margins. Carrefour attempted to pass price increases onto the consumer. Those attempts were stopped by the Chinese government in November 2012 after seeing a 62% year-over-year inflation in food prices.

- Venture financing—According to Dickson, venture capital is both an enabling and an enacting mechanism. What he means is that the available capital and expertise provided by venture capitalists may enable a firm to go international using any of the previously mentioned means to enter a market. However, research suggests that venture capital often leads to mergers and acquisitions with foreign companies.

- Merger and acquisition (M&A)—For some businesses, buying an overseas firm may be the most efficient manner to enter a foreign market. You gain an instant presence in the country with an established infrastructure. M&As also allow an entrepreneurial company to grow and expand quickly. Some research shows that firms that use acquisitions for expansion have a higher survival rate than do those that choose a startup.[57] The capital required means that the firm must secure venture capital or go public; thus, this method is beyond the means of most early-stage entrepreneurs.

As the world becomes increasingly connected, entrepreneurs need to look beyond their home borders to see whether they can expand on their initial opportunity. While it is more difficult to enter and operate in a country that you are not familiar with, technology and increasing trade are reducing the knowledge gap. As research points out, more and more entrepreneurs are becoming global early in their companies' lives. As an entrepreneur, you need to be aware of your options, and the Dickson model provides a solid framework for understanding them.

CONCLUSION

This chapter moves beyond opportunity recognition to implementation. Once you understand your business model, it is time to think about how you will enter the marketplace and grow your firm. During entry, you are proving that your business model is viable and profitable. Are customers buying your product at the prices you need to be profitable? As you learn more about your customer and business, you'll modify your original vision. Entry into the marketplace provides a platform to identify new opportunities and to reshape your business so that it is best positioned to grow and thrive. Thus, it's wise to think about your growth strategy from the very beginning. Today that growth is more likely than ever to mean you'll consider international expansion.

YOUR OPPORTUNITY JOURNAL

Reflection Point	Your Thoughts...
1. Describe your business model. What are your primary sources of revenue? What are your revenue drivers? Your COGS? Your operating expenses?	
2. What is your overall strategy? Why does this strategy help you sell to customers? What tactics can you employ to increase your revenues?	
3. What is your entry strategy? How does this create a platform for your business to grow?	
4. What is your growth strategy? How big do you want your firm to be? How long might it take for it to get there?	

WEB EXERCISE

Pull the income sheets from three companies in the industry that you are interested in entering. Try to find companies that are pursuing different strategies. Examine their business models and see if you can identify the drivers that they are influencing to achieve their strategy. What lessons can you learn for your own venture? What new elements can you incorporate into your business model? How do you tie these elements to your strategy?

NOTES

1. Needleman, Rafe. Twitter Still Has No Business Model, and That's OK. *CNET News*. March 27, 2009. http://news.cnet.com/8301-17939_109-10205736-2.html.

2. www.twitter.com

3. Osterwalder, Alexander, Yves Pigneur, and Tim Clark. *Business Model Generation: A Handbook for Visionaries, Game Changers, and Challengers*. Hoboken, NJ: Wiley, 2010, pp. 214–215. Print.

4. Ibid., pp. 89–90.

5. www.toms.com

6. www.blyk.com

7. The actual accounting definition of COGS is the inventory at the beginning of the period, plus the cost of inventory purchased during the period, minus the inventory remaining at the end of the period.

8. Many software firms amortize research and development and include it in COGS.

9. www.toms.com

10. Mitchell, Dan. Amazon Raises Big Money with Debt Offering. *CNET News*. January 28, 1999. www.cnet.com.

11. Happy e-birthdays; Internet Businesses. *The Economist*, 376(8436): 62. July 23, 2005.

12. A Cautionary Tale. *Fast Company*. December 19, 2007. www.fastcompany.com/magazine/115/open_features-hacker-dropout-ceo-cautionary-tale.html.

13. http://newsroom.fb.com/Key-Facts; http://techcrunch.com/2012/07/31/twitter-may-have-500m-users-but-only-170m-are-active-75-on-twitters-own-clients

14. Millot, J. Amazon.com Expects to Generate $34 Million from IPO. *Publishers Weekly New York*, 244(13): 11. March 31, 1997.

15. www.generalmills.com/Media/NewsReleases/Library/2012/February/food_taste_good_2_29.aspx

16. Gittell, J., and O'Reilly, C. *JetBlue Airways: Starting from Scratch*. Case 9–801–354. Cambridge, MA: Harvard Business School Publishing. 2001.

17. Ibid.

18. Sinek, Simon. *Start with Why*. New York: Penguin Books Ltd. 2009

19. Elizabeth Riley is a successful entrepreneur who started Mazza and Riley, Inc., an internationally recognized executive search firm. She has spent much of her career placing people in venture-backed companies.

20. www.southwest.com/html/about-southwest/history/fact-sheet.html

21. Salter, C. And Now the Hard Part. Fast Company, 82: 66. May 1, 2004.

22. Mount, Ian. JetBlue Founder's Revenge: A New Airline. CNNMoney.com. March 20, 2009. http://money.cnn.com/2009/03/19/smallbusiness/jetblue_founder_flies_again.fsb; Baily, Jeff. JetBlue's C.E.O. Is 'Mortified' After Fliers Are Stranded. *The New York Times*. February 19, 2007. www.nytimes.com/2007/02/19/business/19jetblue.html?_r = 1&oref = slogin.

23. www.coloradodaily.com/cu-boulder/ci_16662654#axzz2ANRASvSP

24. www.craftworksrestaurants.com/index.htm

25. www.subway.com/subwayroot/exploreourworld.aspx

26. Duecy, E. Global Growth, Urban Sites Speed Subway Along Track Toward Overtaking McDonald's. *Nation's Restaurant News*, 39(6): 4. February 7, 2005.

27. http://finance.yahoo.com/news/the-most-popular-fast-food-restaurants-in-america.html

28. Behar, Richard. Why Subway Is the Biggest Problem in Franchising. *Fortune*, 137:126. March 16, 1998.

29. www.subway.com/subwayroot/exploreourworld.aspx

30 Goff, L. Encroachment Complaints Hasten Litigation, *Unity. Franchise Times*, 2(4): 3–4. 1996.

31 McCuan, J. Six Things to Consider before You Buy a Franchise. Smartmoney.com, April 5, 2005. www.smsmallbiz.com/bestpractices/Six_Things_to_Consider_Before_You_Buy_a_Franchise.html.

32 Johannes, Amy. Franchisees Sue Subway over $400 Million Ad Fund. *Promo*. July 20, 2006. http://promomagazine.com/retail/subway_sued_ad_funds_072006.

33 MacMillan, Douglas. Franchise Owners Go to Court. *BusinessWeek Online*. January 29, 2007. www.businessweek.com.

34 http://money.cnn.com/2004/04/29/pf/howmuchfranchise.

35 www.aboutmcdonalds.com/mcd/franchising/us_franchising/aquiring_a_franchise/new_restaurants.html

36 *Purchasing Your Franchise*. http://about mcdonalds.com.

37 Burritt, Chris, and Burton, Katherine. Bill Ackman Sells McDonald's Stake After Stock Surges (Update 4). *Bloomberg News*. December 5, 2007. www.bloomberg.com/apps/news?pid=20601103&sid=aZ6kcnn5qqUo&refer=us.

38 Desjardins, Doug. Whole Foods Goes Hollywood with Lifestyle Store. *DSN Retailing Today. November* 7, 2005.

39 Shanahan, L. Designated Shopper. *Brandweek*, 40(1): 38. January 4, 1999.

40 Buchanan, Leigh. Death to Cool. *Inc.*, 25(7): 82–88. July 2003.

41 http://newsfeed.time.com/2010/07/21/pabst-blue-ribbon-is-classy-and-expensive-in-china/

42 www.getintocollege.com.

43 McDougall, Patricia P., Oviatt, Benjamin M., and Shrader, Rodney C. A Comparison of International and Domestic New Ventures. *Journal of International Entrepreneurship*. 1, No. 1 (2003): 59–82.

44 www.census.gov/foreign-trade/Press-Release/edb/2010/edbrel.pdf

45 Shrader, Rodney C., Oviatt, Benjamin M., and McDougall, Patricia P. How New Ventures Exploit Trade-Offs Among International Risk Factors: Lessons for the Accelerated Internationalization of the 21st Century. *Academy of Management Journal*, 43(6): 1227–1247. 2000.

46 Dickson, P. Going Global. In A. Zacharakis and S. Spinelli, eds., *Entrepreneurship*. Volume 2. Geenwich, CT: Praeger. 2006, pp. 155–177.

47 http://traffichoss.com/ferragamo-custom-designer-toms-shoes

48 What Is TelePresence? March 28, 2007. www.kolabora.com/news/2007/03/28/what_is_telepresence.htm.

49 Eden, L., Levitas, E., and Martinez, R. J. The Production, Transfer and Spillover of Technology: Comparing Large and Small Multinationals as Technology Producers. *Small Business Economics*, 9(1): 53–66. 1997.

50 Zacharakis, A. L. Entrepreneurial Entry into Foreign Markets: A Transaction Cost Perspective. *Entrepreneurship: Theory and Practice*, 21(3): 23–39. 1997.

51 www.chloe.com/#/boutiques/Asia-Pacific-4/en

52 Fenton, Susan. HK Designer Sees Upside in "Made in China" Label. *Reuters. September* 17, 2008. http://uk.reuters.com/article/stageNews/idUKHKG6544920080917.

53 Movius, L. Chloé Launches in China. *WWD*, 190(137): December 29, 2005. www.movius,us/articles/index.html.

54 www.emergelogistics.com/index.htm

55 Flannery, Russell. *Red Tape. Forbes*, 171(5): 97–100. March 3, 2003.

56 A&W Closes Its Eight Restaurants in China. *Associated Press*. February 3, 2004. http://thestar.com.my/news/story.asp?file=/2004/2/3/latest/15819AWcloses&sec=latest.

57 Vermeulen, Freek, and Barkema, Harry. Learning Through Acquisitions. *Academy of Management Journal*, 44(3): 457–476. 2001.

CASE   # Zumba Fitness

Alberto Perlman walked out of the old warehouse that served as the offices of Zumba Fitness and into the hot Miami sun. He had just finished meeting with his two partners and the company that they had started with such a bang four years earlier seemed on the ropes. The agreement they had with the marketing company that produced and promoted their exercise videos had broken down, and despite selling millions of dollars' worth of videotapes featuring their unique Latin-based exercise routine called Zumba, the company had not been able to provide enough profitability for it to do more than scrape by. One of his partners, Alberto Aghion, was even looking at starting a medical billing company. With only about $14,000 left in the bank, they needed to figure out how to either make this business profitable or start looking for other opportunities.

Childhood Friends

The Salesman: Alberto Perlman

Alberto Perlman was born and raised in Bogota, Colombia, where his family was very involved in business and entrepreneurship. His great-grandfather had immigrated to Bogota from Jerusalem in the pursuit of business opportunities. Starting out by selling textiles door-to-door, his grandfather gradually built the second largest retail store in the country. It was clear that growing up in this environment had a great influence on Alberto.

From the beginning, Perlman seemed destined for business. When he was 6 years old, his father bought him a digital watch with a game on it. The enterprising young Perlman proceeded to loan it to a classmate on weekends in exchange for 750 pesos (approximately $10). When his parents found out, they apologized to the boy's mother and made him return all the money, but a budding entrepreneur was born.

In high school, Perlman noticed a vacant lot near the school that was being occupied by a number of homeless people. At his school, like many others, it was cool to have a car and drive to school. However, Perlman realized that many of the students couldn't drive their cars because they could not find a place to park. He approached the people living in the lot and offered a deal. He would pay them if they would let students park there and keep an eye on the cars. He then charged his classmates 90,000 pesos (about $45 at that time) each month to park. This venture, too, was short-lived.

> *Unfortunately, the people found out what I was charging and they started going direct. So, I figured out that being a middle man is not a good deal.*

Despite these early setbacks, it was apparent to everyone that he was destined to be an entrepreneur.

This case was written by Professor Bradley George as a basis for class discussion rather than to illustrate either effective or ineffective handling of an administrative situation. Funding was provided by the Teaching Innovation Fund at Babson College.

I always knew I was going to do business, but I was a bit rebellious as a teenager and I told my mom I was going to study philosophy. My mom said, "I would never tell any of my kids this, but YOU. . . I'm telling you. You were born to do business. I would never force any of my kids to do anything, but I'm forcing you to do business. So go find a business school."

After graduating from high school, Perlman went backpacking through Europe with his childhood friend, Alberto Aghion, who would figure prominently in a number of his subsequent business ventures. Following the trip, Perlman enrolled in Babson College, a business school located outside of Boston, MA, known for its Entrepreneurship program.

While his official studies were in finance and MIS, Perlman continued his entrepreneurial ways in the U.S. He was fascinated with the Internet and in 1995–1996, while studying at Babson, he got together with two other students and started a Web design company called Cyber Spider Designs.

We went up and down Newbury Street trying to sell Web sites at a time when nobody had Web sites. We did the Web site for Boston Proper Real Estate. We did a flower site. It was all right. It paid the bills, but nobody was paying good money for that at the time.

It was also at Babson that Perlman made an impression on Professor Prichett, who ended up indirectly playing a key role in the founding of Zumba Fitness. Professor Prichett was impressed with his calculus student and introduced Perlman to his son, who worked at a New York consulting firm called the Mitchell Madison Group and who subsequently offered Perlman a job with the firm.

One of the first projects Perlman was given was working on direct response television advertising[1] for the First USA division of Bank One. While on this project, he spent considerable time analyzing the business model and operation of successful infomercial companies. Reflecting on his grandfather's retail business and his own experience as a middle man in his short-lived parking venture, he fell in love with the idea of direct marketing to consumers via television.

I always saw how difficult it was for suppliers to get their products into the stores. The infomercial industry was fascinating because you didn't have to go through a store. You didn't have to go to a big supplier like Walmart. You did it on your own merit. You bought media, created the commercial and it's your product.

By this time Alberto's father was working at a nearby private equity firm, and he was meeting with a Chilean newspaper company that was interested in developing an Internet strategy. Knowing his son's knowledge of the latest technologies, he asked if Alberto would be willing to talk with them. After meeting with them and helping them with their strategy, he realized that his expertise in emerging Internet technologies coupled with his background and connections in Latin American markets provided a unique opportunity for him to once again set out on his own. So, after ten months, he left his job with the Mitchel Madison Group to pursue Internet opportunities in Latin America.

Initially, Perlman, together with his brother and another friend, focused on building an Internet events company in which they would put on conferences for companies, entrepreneurs, and investors who were interested in Internet businesses in Latin America. This provided a way for him to both make money and make connections for future business opportunities.

---

[1] Direct response television (DRTV) is television advertising that asks consumers to respond directly to the company, typically by either visiting a Web site or calling a toll-free number. DRTV can be either short form (a commercial that is two minutes in length or less) or long form (any commercial that is longer than two minutes with a common form being the 30-minute infomercial).

We started calling companies like IBM and said, "Hey! Do you want to sponsor an event? It's called Latin Venture. We'll have all the entrepreneurs from Latin America there." And they said, of course. . . how much? Twenty-five thousand dollars. Done. So we sold, and that's when things were going like crazy and we made a couple hundred thousand dollars at our first event.

After the success of the Latin Venture event, Perlman used the money he had made to start an Internet incubator in which he raised money to invest in launching technology companies in Latin America. He was able to raise about $8 million, which they used to eventually fund nine different companies. It was also at this time that he convinced his long-time friend Alberto Aghion to turn down a job offer with Merrill Lynch and join him in one of the incubator's companies.

The Problem Solver: Alberto Aghion

Alberto Aghion grew up with Perlman in Bogota. They attended the same schools, had the same group of friends, and started becoming close friends in their early teens. When Perlman left for Babson following their European adventure together, Aghion decided to continue travelling and eventually ended up at the Hebrew University in Jerusalem, where he took courses in history, studying the Arab-Israeli conflict, and working odd jobs to make ends meet.

I had some crazy experiences. I went hiking in Africa. I hiked Kilimanjaro. I mean, I had a really interesting year. When you're 18 years old, you have no real responsibilities and it was an adventure in life. I'm really glad I took that year to do that because if I hadn't done that at that age, at that stage in my life, I couldn't have done that.

After spending a little more than a year abroad, Aghion returned to Colombia ready for a new challenge. He was always interested in looking at ways to solve problems of all kinds. He excelled in math and physics in high school, so as soon as he returned, he applied to study Industrial Engineering at the Universidad Javeriana in Bogota with the belief that an engineering education would give him a good foundation in problem-solving techniques that he could apply to a number of different situations. However, he soon found out that he did not enjoy the teaching philosophy at the school. As with many engineering programs, there seemed to be a focus on filtering out students early in the program. In addition, it was difficult adjusting to life back at home after more than a year on his own. He felt out of place and restless in Bogota, so he talked to his friend Perlman, who was in his second year at Babson. Perlman seemed to be happy in Boston, so Aghion decided to visit him and look into opportunities in the United States.

I went to a few colleges. I mean I checked out Northwestern. Boston College. A few interesting schools. And on the way back, I stopped in Miami and I saw the palm trees, the ocean. So, I also went to UM and FIU and I checked out those schools and actually I decided, you know what, I think I like Miami better. I'm not a cold weather fan.

He was accepted at both the University of Miami and Florida International University (FIU), but FIU was less expensive and they agreed to transfer his credits both from Bogota as well as from Israel, allowing him to graduate a year sooner, so he chose FIU where he majored in finance and international business.

I wanted to be an entrepreneur. I wanted to do different things. But I had no idea what I wanted to study. Also, I guess I got a little burned out at the university in Colombia. I mean,

I like problem solving. I guess maybe if I would have gone to a different school and had a different experience with engineering, I might have stayed with that career. But, because I didn't enjoy that methodology in Colombia, I said, you know what, this is not for me. And at the end of the day, I just wanted to do business. I had picked engineering because I was good at physics and calculus and problem solving, not necessarily because I wanted to be an engineer.

Aghion excelled in the new environment, getting straight A's for the first two years and graduating with a job offer from Merrill Lynch. He was considering this offer when he got a phone call from Perlman.

I spoke with Perlman, he was launching this whole incubator. Really exciting. Internet boom. All this interesting stuff. And he tells me, "Why the hell are you going to go work for a boring bank? Come work with me." So I said OK.

One of the first ventures Perlman and his partners invested in was FonBox, which was a service for providing a virtual office anywhere in Latin America. Aghion was asked to help develop FonBox, and he did a significant amount of work helping them develop the infrastructure for the business. They eventually sold it to J2 Communications for a loss.

By March 2001, they were working on nine different businesses when the Internet bubble burst. Most of their companies were early-stage companies in their first or second round of funding, and the capital for additional investments in Internet firms quickly dried up. With no funding available, a lack of new businesses to invest in, and $4M of the original investor's money remaining, they decided to continue to work with the firms they had invested in on the chance that one of them would be successful. They could then return what was left of the money to their investors rather than risk the remaining funds and the relationships with the investors they had worked so hard to establish.

The Third Alberto

Alberto "Beto" Perez grew up in Cali, Colombia, as the son of a young, single, working mother. Always an energetic child, he loved to perform. He would take his mother's hairbrush and use it like a microphone as he would sing and dance. In the same way that Perlman seemed destined for a career as an entrepreneur, Beto seemed born to dance. As his mother recalls,

When he was seven, I took Beto to see the movie Grease. *The next day, he was out on the street teaching John Travolta's dance moves to kids who were much bigger than he was.*

Growing up in Cali in the 1980s was difficult. Drugs and violence were common on the streets. Beto saw this firsthand when his mother got into an abusive relationship with a drug addict. When he was 14, his mother was hit by a stray bullet, and he had to work multiple jobs to help support the two of them. Despite these hardships, dance was a constant presence in his life.

As a teenager in the 1980s, I was always sneaking out to nightclubs to dance, and my mom was trying to keep me at home, safe.

When Beto was 16 his mother took a job in Miami, but he wanted to stay in Cali to pursue a career in dance. They would keep in touch via telephone and letters, but it would be a long, hard 10 years before they would see each other again.

During this time, Beto continued to try to make it as a dancer. When he was 17, he couldn't afford rent so he slept in the ice cream shop where he worked. He thought he finally had his big breakthrough when he was chosen to represent Colombia at a Latin dance competition in Miami. However, after spending his entire savings on costumes, his U.S. visa request was denied and he was unable to compete.

Because he couldn't afford to attend a dance academy, he worked as a courier in the morning and taught private dance lessons in the evening. The owner of the gym where Beto prepared his dance routines offered him an opportunity to teach a children's class in the summer. Because he was so popular, he was invited to teach more classes. A modeling agent gave him his first job as a choreographer and he gained national attention after winning a lambada competition at the age of 19. Eventually, he saved enough money to attend and graduate from the Maria Sanford Brazilian Dance Academy with a degree in choreography.

While dance was his passion, it was a series of fortuitous events that led to the creation of what is now known as Zumba. One evening a local gym owner telephoned Beto and asked if he could substitute for one of her aerobics instructors who had been injured. Although Beto had never taught aerobics, he needed the money so he accepted the job. He immediately went to a book store and bought a copy of Jane Fonda's *Workout Book* and tried to copy the moves in the book coupled with some of his own dance steps. The class went well, and soon Beto was regularly teaching aerobics classes as well as dance. Then fortune struck again. As Beto recalls,

> *At one of those sessions, I forgot to bring the music, and all I had were salsa and merengue tapes in my backpack. So I improvised, and that was the beginning of Zumba.*

Beto called his new style of aerobics "Rumbacize" as a tribute to the Latin influences behind many of the moves. As Beto's popularity increased, he found himself traveling to Bogota to do television commercials. Eventually, he moved there and began teaching at one of the top gyms in the city where one of his early students was Alberto Perlman's mother.

> *In 1994 Mrs. Perlman was taking my class in Bogota and announced, "This is the best class in the world!" I'll never forget that.*

In addition to his Rumbacize classes, he was gaining attention for his dancing and choreography. He was hired by Sony Music to work with some of their singers, and he helped with the choreography for singer-songwriter Shakira's breakthrough album, "Pies Descalzos." During this time, he began traveling more outside of Colombia and fell in love with the idea of moving to Miami, so he decided to sell everything and move to the United States. However, his lack of English skills made the transition difficult, and he had a hard time finding work.

> *I love Miami, and I knew this is where I wanted to live. At first it was not easy. No one knew who I was, I did not speak English and I ran out money. I even slept on the street one time.*

His big break came one afternoon when one of the gym managers decided to see what Beto could do, so she gave him an impromptu audition. It was the middle of the afternoon and she told Beto to teach a class to one student. Herself.

> *It was 3 p.m., and the gym was empty. Soon a passerby wandered in to watch, then two, three, four. After 20 minutes I had about 15 people. They thought it was a new class and wanted to sign up.*

The manager was impressed and offered Beto a job teaching Saturday mornings. Beto's passion, energy, charisma, and lively exercise programs became increasingly popular, and he soon found himself teaching classes of up to 160 students at gyms throughout the Miami area. Investors were approaching him about opening up his own gym.

The Birth of Zumba Fitness

Following the end of Perlman's incubator venture, Perlman and Aghion found themselves trying to decide what to do with their lives. Reflecting back on his brief time with the Mitchel Madison Group, Perlman was drawn back to the idea of an infomercial-based company. Perlman approached Aghion, who was considering going back into the finance world. Aghion was interested so they began brainstorming potential ideas. As Aghion recalls,

I still don't have a family. I still don't have anything. I want to take a risk. Things are happening and I was really interested in the infomercial industry. I thought that it was a good opportunity. And I remember talking to Perlman and saying, why don't we do an infomercial or something? If we make it, we could make a lot of money. And then we can figure something else out.

During this time, Perlman's family had moved to Miami, and his mother was once again taking Beto's classes. One day his mother suggested that he meet Beto. "Beto has something special," she told him. So Perlman arranged to meet Beto at a Starbucks to learn more. Beto's energy and passion were contagious and Perlman could envision his aerobics routines and personality as a great combination for his infomercial concept. Following their meeting, he immediately called his friend Aghion to see what he thought about the idea.

I remember my stomach saying, I LOVE IT. Ricky Martin was singing "Living La Vida Loca" at the Grammy's. Latin music is crossing over in the U.S. Tae Bo. Fitness. Beto. It clicked in my head immediately.

As Perlman recalls:

It was a gut decision. We were two out-of-work businessmen with no contacts in the fitness industry and a dancer who couldn't speak a word of English, and here we were deciding to launch a fitness business together. But we knew if we could capture the excitement of his class on video, people would go crazy for the music and the moves.

With little money between them, they decided to create their own video, which they would then use to as a marketing vehicle for launching the business. They spent the night laying down boards on the beach and the next morning made a video of Beto teaching a class. They then renamed the program "Zumba", which rhymed with "rumba," meaning "party" and Zumba Fitness was born.

Fitness Industry Business Models[2]

The fitness industry consists of a wide range of activities that people engage in for exercise. In general, most forms of exercise have experienced a decline in participation in recent years in the United States (Table C4.1). Notable exceptions are Pilates and yoga, which have seen dramatic increases in participation. Aerobics, while popular in the 1980s and 1990s, has seen a decline in participation since 1998 while other forms of exercising to music have remained relatively steady.

Companies in this industry have used a variety of approaches to enter and compete in this industry. Due to the fact that many of these forms of exercise can be done individually

---

[2]It should be noted that gyms and fitness clubs account for a major portion of the revenue in the fitness industry. However, these businesses do not specialize in a single form of exercise but rather differentiate themselves on the variety of offerings available. They require a physical location, equipment, and instructors, and members typically have access to most classes and equipment in exchange for a monthly membership fee.

TABLE C4.1						
Fitness Activity	**1998**	**2000**	**2004**	**2005**	**1 yr change (%)**	**Change from 1998 (%)**
Aerobics (High Impact)	7460	5581	5521	5004	−9.36425	−32.9223
Aerobics (Low Impact)	12774	9752	8493	9071	6.805605	−28.9886
Aerobics (Step)	10784	8963	8257	7062	−14.4726	−34.5141
Aerobics (Net)	21017	17326	15767	15811	0.279064	−24.7704
Other Exercise to Music	13846	12337	16365	14428	−11.8362	4.20338
Aquatic Exercise	6685	6367	5812	6237	7.312457	−6.70157
Calisthenics	30982	27790	25562	24854	−2.76974	−19.7792
Cardio Kick Boxing	n.a.	7163	4773	4163	−12.7802	n.a.
Fitness Bicycling	13556	11435	10210	10211	0.009794	−24.6754
Fitness Walking	36395	36207	40299	36348	−9.80421	−0.12914
Running/Jogging	34962	33680	37310	37810	1.340123	8.145987
Fitness Swimming	15258	14060	15636	14553	−6.92632	−4.62053
Pilates Training	n.a.	1739	10541	10355	−1.76454	n.a.
Stretching	35114	36408	40799	42266	3.595676	20.36794
Yoga/Tai Chi	5708	7400	12414	14656	18.06025	156.7624

or in groups, companies can target instructors or participants as their primary customers. Revenue models can range from unit sales models to franchising models, each with their own implications. Below are some of the approaches firms in this industry have used.

Franchise Model

Developed in 1969 by Judi Sheppard Missett, Jazzercise, Inc. is the world's leading franchiser of dance and fitness classes with over 5,000 franchises worldwide.[3] After creating the program, demand for her classes eventually exceeded her ability to single-handedly teach all her students, and she began training some of her early students to become teachers. These instructors agreed to pay a start-up fee and 30% of their gross revenues to Missett in exchange for the permission to use the Jazzercise brand.

In 1979, Jazzercise formally incorporated and in 1983 it formalized its franchise relationship with its certified instructors. Jazzercise instructors would pay a $500 franchise fee and, as with the early instructors, a royalty fee of 30% of gross revenues. In 1988, the company reduced the royalty fee to 20% paid monthly. In exchange for this, the company would provide corporate support to the franchisees in the form of marketing materials, national advertising on radio and TV, choreography, choreography notes, and business advice. The company maintains strict control over the brand and the routines, with instructors agreeing to only use corporate-developed choreography.

Instructor Training Model

First developed by circus performer and boxer Joseph Pilates while in an English internment camp in World War I, Pilates has become an increasingly popular form of exercise. Joseph

---

[3] Gale Group.

was said to be inspired by the ancient Greek ideal of man perfected in development of body, mind, and spirit and incorporated elements of Eastern philosophies into his exercise routines, which he called "contrology."[4] He expresses this holistic approach in his book, *Return to Life Through Contrology*, when he writes,

> *Contrology develops the body uniformly, corrects wrong postures, restores physical vitality, invigorates the mind, and elevates the spirit.*

After moving to New York City in 1925, Pilates established a studio where he continued to teach his form of exercise until his death in 1967. During and after this time, a number of his students opened their own studios (with Joseph's permission), teaching classical Pilates. Eventually, some of his original students developed their own unique methods, such as the Fletcher Method (Richard Fletcher) and the Gentry Method (Eve Gentry). Today there are a number of different businesses focused on Pilates in various forms, but each uses essentially the same business model.

Unlike Jazzercise, companies such as Balanced Body Pilates and Pilates Institute of America do not offer franchises, but rather generate revenue from individual instructor training and certification. This is similar to a unit sales revenue model, with the "unit" being the instructor. Certification costs generally run between $3000 and $7000, with specialty certifications adding additional costs for the instructor. Once an instructor is certified, he or she is not required to pay any additional amounts to the company. Instructors can then teach individual or group classes once certified. Some of these firms generate additional revenue through the sales of equipment that is used in special forms of Pilates.

Due to the various forms of Pilates' certification available, a major cost for these firms is brand management and differentiation. The company provides the instructors with training materials and runs training classes that result in certification, so other costs typically include facilities for training, instructors, and training materials.

Exercise Video Model

Another popular business model in this industry is a unit sales model through the production and sales of exercise videos and DVDs. While the revenue model is fairly straightforward, the cost structure can be more complicated. In this type of model, consumer awareness and distribution are critical. Distribution can be accomplished through direct sales via the Internet, sales through retail channels, and/or direct sales through infomercials. In each of these cases, creating brand awareness through marketing is a critical success factor. If infomercials are used, then the costs of producing and airing the infomercial needs to be considered. In the case of retail sales, potential slotting fees and gaining access to retail outlets can constitute a significant cost. For exercise programs that utilize music, companies also need to consider music licensing costs.[5]

---

[4] Ogle, Marguerite. "Joseph Pilates: Founder of the Pilates Method of Exercise," Ask.com

[5] There are two different types of music licenses that need to be considered for each song when producing a video or DVD. A mechanical license allows you to make multiple copies of the recording. This fee is used to pay royalties to the owner of the song's copyright. If you are pairing music with video or other media, this requires a synchronization license. In this case, the synchronization license replaces the mechanical license. If you are using an artist's actual recording, then a master license is required, which is paid to the owner of the master recording, typically the record label. If you hire someone to record a cover version of a song, the master license is no longer needed.

Zumba Fitness - The Early Years

Following their initial idea to establish an infomercial-based business, Perlman and Aghion built a Web site, and Perlman began going to the gyms in Miami marketing the video. Beto was teaching classes at Crunch South Beach at the time, and his boss, Donna Cyrus, introduced them to the founder of Crunch gyms. The founder was interested in their new fitness program and subsequently introduced them to a representative from a large firm that produced infomercials for various fitness products.

Perlman flew out to meet with them and show them the video. The company was impressed, and they entered into an agreement where the company would produce and air the infomercials and pay Zumba Fitness a royalty for each of the videos they sold. Within six months, they had sold hundreds of thousands of copies of the videos. Despite its popularity, the videos were barely making enough to cover the production costs for the infomercials, so Zumba Fitness was asked to forgo its royalty so that they could spend the money on marketing the videos via retail outlets. They agreed, but as a result of some miscommunication, the firm failed to get all of the necessary licenses for one of the songs. As a result, the company had to discontinue selling the videos. Following lengthy legal discussions, Zumba Fitness eventually bought back the rights to its fitness program in 2003 and started over on its own, this time using its own music.

After remaking the videos, Perlman, Aghion, and Beto continued selling a handful of videos online each day, packaging them themselves and driving them to the post office. Eventually, they partnered with a Colombian firm to produce an infomercial for the Latin American market. This went well for a while, but piracy became a big issue and sales dropped off. From there they tried to expand into the U.S. Hispanic market and met with some success. It was also during this time that they got another important break.

> So we were in Aghion's garage, which was our office, and we get a call from this lady saying she was from Kellogg's. We thought it was a scam, of course. She says that she wants to meet with us. She is from the ad agency for Kellogg's in Miami. She tells us that the CEO's wife bought the tapes off our infomercial and she loves them. And he had an idea that he could use Zumba as part of a health and fitness campaign. So we started talking and it ended up being a great deal over four years. That was totally the amount of money that we needed to survive from 2003–2006.

The company had also begun receiving calls from fitness instructors who had purchased the Zumba tapes and wanted to teach classes. So in 2003 Zumba Fitness held its first instructor training session. To their surprise, more than 150 people flew to Miami to learn first-hand from Beto. They continued to hold the training sessions every few months and this, coupled with the money from Kellogg's and the video sales, kept them afloat. Despite this, they still felt like they were not tapping the full potential of the business and money was getting tight.

At the Crossroads

Perlman thought about their predicament. On one hand, there was no doubt about the passion of the Zumba enthusiasts. Once people tried it, they fell in love with it. When they began offering the instructor training, they were amazed to see the same instructors come back again and again, even though they had already been trained. They even began setting up their own cameras and recorders at Beto's classes to capture the new moves and the music. On the other hand, they weren't making much money with their current model and their cash flow was unpredictable. Perlman's thoughts strayed back to the medical billing company Aghion had mentioned. This is ridiculous, he thought. We're not going to let this go. We have to do something. All these instructors keep coming back to Miami, and they are just in love with Zumba. We HAVE to be able to come up with something to make this work.

Assignment:

1. What business models could Zumba use?
2. Develop a revenue and cost model diagram for each of the options.
3. Which of these models would you recommend that they implement and why?
4. What are the key revenue and cost drivers for your recommended model?
5. What do you feel are the key aspects to implementing this model?

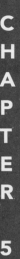

Porter Gifford/Hulton Archive/Getty Images

Nantucket Nectars manufacturing and bottling plant.

ENTREPRENEURIAL MARKETING

Marketing is at the heart of an organization because its task is to identify and serve customers' needs. In essence, marketing spans the boundaries between a company and its customers. It is marketing that delivers a company's products and services to customers and marketing that takes information about those products and services, as well as about the company itself, to the market. In addition, it is marketing's role to bring information about the customers back to the company. Although many people relate the term *marketing* to advertising and promotion, the scope of marketing is much broader. The American Marketing Association defines marketing as:

> *An organizational function and a set of processes for creating, communicating, and delivering value to customers and for managing customer relationships in ways that benefit the organization and its stakeholders.*[1]

Successful entrepreneurs select and optimize the marketing tools that best fit their unique challenges. Marketing practices vary depending on the type of company and the products and services it sells. Marketers of consumer products, such as carbonated soft drinks, use different tools than marketers of business-to-business products, such as network software. Companies

---

This chapter is written by Abdul Ali and Kathleen Seiders.

in the services sector, such as banks, market differently from companies that sell durable goods, such as automobile manufacturers.

Why Marketing Is Critical for Entrepreneurs

Marketing is a vital process for entrepreneurs because no venture can become established and grow without a customer market. The process of acquiring and retaining customers is at the core of marketing. Entrepreneurs must create the offer (design the product and set the price), take the offer to the market (through distribution), and, at the same time, tell the market about the offer (communications). These activities define the famous **Four Ps** of marketing: product, price, place (distribution), and promotion (communication).

Entrepreneurs often are faced with designing the entire "marketing system"—from product and price to distribution and communication. Because it is difficult and expensive to bring new products and services to market—especially difficult for new companies—they need to be more resourceful in their marketing. Many entrepreneurs rely on creativity rather than cash to achieve a compelling image in a noisy marketplace.

An important part of gaining the market's acceptance is building brand awareness, which, depending on the stage of the venture, may be weak or even nonexistent. Entrepreneurs must differentiate their company's product or service so its distinctiveness and value are clear to the customer. This is the job of marketing.

Marketing also plays a central role in a venture's early growth stages when changes to the original business model may be necessary. Companies focused on growth must be able to switch marketing gears quickly and attract new and different customer segments.

Entrepreneurs Face Unique Marketing Challenges

Entrepreneurial marketing is different from marketing done by established companies for a number of reasons. First, entrepreneurial companies typically have limited resources—financial as well as managerial. Just as they rarely have enough money to support marketing activities, they also rarely have proven marketing expertise within the company. Most entrepreneurs do not have the option of hiring experienced marketing managers. Time—as well as money and marketing talent—is also often in short supply. Whereas larger corporations can spend hundreds of thousands or even millions on conducting extensive marketing research, testing their strategies, and carefully designing marketing campaigns, new ventures find creative and less costly means to validate their ideas and reach customers.

Most entrepreneurs face daunting challenges. Their companies have little or no market share and a confined geographic market presence. As a result, they enjoy few economies of scale; for example, it is difficult for small companies to save money on "media buys" because their range of advertising is so limited. Entrepreneurs usually are restricted in their access to distributors—both wholesalers and retailers. On the customer side, entrepreneurs struggle with low brand awareness and customer loyalty, both of which must be carefully cultivated.

Not only is market information limited, but also decision making can be muddled by strong personal biases and beliefs. Early-stage companies often stumble in their marketing because of a product focus that is excessively narrow. Companies frequently assume that their products will be embraced by enthusiastic consumers when, in reality, consumer inertia prevents most new products from being accepted at all. Research has shown that common marketing-related dangers for entrepreneurs include overestimating demand, underestimating competitor response, and making uninformed distribution decisions.

Entrepreneurs market to multiple audiences: investors, customers, employees, and business partners. Because none of these bonds is well established for early-stage companies, entrepreneurs must be both customer oriented and relationship oriented. A customer orientation requires understanding the market and where it is going. A relationship orientation is needed to create structural and emotional ties with all stakeholders. *Thus, marketing helps entrepreneurs acquire resources by selling their ideas to potential investors and partners. It also allows entrepreneurs to leverage scarce resources through innovative business approaches.*

In this chapter, we consider entrepreneurial marketing in depth. Building upon the opportunity-defining and -refining discussion in Chapter 3, we provide direction on market research—that is, collecting information useful in making marketing and strategy decisions. Next we focus on implementing marketing strategies that make the most of these opportunities. We also look at how certain marketing skills serve to support a new company's growth.

Acquiring Market Information

An entrepreneur needs to do research to identify and assess an opportunity. Intuition, personal expertise, and passion can take you only so far. Some studies show that good pre-venture market analysis could reduce venture failure rates by as much as 60%.[2] But many entrepreneurs tend to ignore negative market information because of a strong commitment to their idea. Whereas Chapter 2 defined what an opportunity is and Chapter 3 presented a checklist for assessing how attractive your opportunity might be, this chapter provides a drill-down on how you collect data to validate your initial impressions of the opportunity.

We define **marketing research** as the collection and analysis of any reliable information that improves managerial decisions. Questions that marketing research can answer include the following: What product attributes are important to customers? How is customers' willingness to buy influenced by product design, pricing, and communications? Where do customers buy this kind of product? How is the market likely to change in the future?

There are two basic types of market data: **secondary data**, which marketers gather from already published sources like an industry association study or census reports, and **primary data**, which marketers collect specifically for a particular purpose through focus groups, surveys, or experiments. You can find a great deal of market information in secondary resources. Secondary research requires less time and money than primary research, and it should be your first avenue. Entrepreneurs sometimes use databases at college libraries to collect baseline information about product and geographic markets (Figure 7.5 in Chapter 7 lists some common databases).

Some types of primary data are easy to collect, for instance, with personal interviews or focus groups, but keep in mind the limitations of such data, such as observer bias and lack of statistical significance (because the samples are small). To ensure that they obtain high-quality data, some entrepreneurs hire marketing research firms to perform research studies. Lower-cost alternatives do exist: For example, a business school professor might assign the company's project to a student research team. In choosing a research approach, balance your quality and time constraints with the possible cost savings.

The appendix at the end of this chapter provides a list of possible questions to address in a customer research interview. You can structure such an interview as a one-on-one interaction or as a focus group. In focus groups, a discussion leader encourages five to 10 people to express their views about the company's products or services. The focus group has distinct stages, and you will need to ask specific questions to get good-quality information from the group participants. Figure 5.1 displays these stages and provides some example questions to use when conducting a focus group.

Stage	Examples of Effective Questions
Introduction	▣ Think of the last time you purchased Product X. What prompted or triggered this activity?
	▣ How often do you use X?
Rapport Building	▣ What are some of the reasons for so many products in this industry?
In-Depth Investigation	▣ Here is a new idea about this market. In what ways is this idea different from what you see in the marketplace?
	▣ What features are missing from this new product?
	▣ What would you need to know about this idea in order to accept it?
Closure	▣ Is this focus group discussion what you expected?

Figure 5.1

Focus group

Market Research for Revolutionary New Products?

Henry Ford is reputed to have said that if he had asked potential customers for his yet-to-be introduced automobile what they wanted, they would have replied, "a faster horse." Market research may be valuable for existing products and incremental improvements to them, but what is its value for revolutionary new products? By definition, a revolutionary new product has no SIC classification, so it is virtually impossible to gather meaningful data from secondary sources. And what use are the opinions of primary sources who are unfamiliar with the product because it is different from anything they have ever used? Steve Jobs (along with other Apple executives) had no faith in market research for the radically new products that he introduced. Here is what he had to say on that subject:

"Some people say 'give the customers what they want.' But that is not my approach. Our job is to figure out what they're going to want before they do."[3]

When asked, "Should [Apple] do some market research to see what customers wanted?" [Jobs] replied, "No, because customers don't know what they want until we've shown them."[4]

On the day he unveiled the Macintosh, a reporter from *Popular Science* asked Jobs what kind of market research he had done. Jobs responded by scoffing, "Did Alexander Graham Bell do any market research before he invented the telephone?"[5]

Jonathan Ive, Apple's senior vice president of industrial design, who gave Apple products their sleek, minimalist form, says that Apple has a good reason for not doing focus groups: "They just ensure that you don't offend anyone, and produce bland inoffensive products."[6]

Customer acceptance of an entrepreneur's idea is proof that the opportunity is worth pursuing. Entrepreneurs must understand the customer decision-making process and how to influence the customer's choice. Such customer understanding enables entrepreneurs to develop the right products at the right prices (create and capture value) and then market these products to the right customers in the right place (communicate and deliver value). Further, such knowledge of customers' behavior at each stage of the decision-making process helps entrepreneurs to be effective and efficient with their communication strategy to reach the target customers. Figure 5.2 provides an illustration of the role that marketing tools play in the customer choice process.

Marketing Strategy for Entrepreneurs

A company's marketing strategy must closely align with its resources and capabilities. Entrepreneurial companies with limited resources have little room for strategic mistakes. Segmentation, targeting, and positioning are key marketing dimensions that set the strategic framework. We begin this section by discussing these three activities and their role in marketing strategy. Then we examine the widely studied marketing elements known as the marketing mix: product, price, distribution (place), and communications (promotion).

Segmentation, Targeting, and Positioning

Segmentation and *targeting* are the processes marketers use to identify the "right" customers for their company's products and services. In Chapter 3, we talked about the segment your opportunity would initially target, what we call the primary target audience or PTA. As we move beyond opportunity recognition into implementation of a marketing strategy, we need to revisit our initial conceptions and refine what that PTA segment really means. A **segment** is a group of customers defined by certain common bases or characteristics that may be demographic, psychographic (commonly called *lifestyle characteristics*), or behavioral. Demographic characteristics include age, education, gender, and income; lifestyle characteristics include descriptors like active, individualistic, risk taking, and time pressured. Behavioral characteristics include consumer traits such as brand loyalty and willingness to adopt new products.

Marketers identify the most relevant bases for segmentation and then develop segment profiles. It's common to define a segment using a combination of demographic and lifestyle characteristics: for example, high-income, sophisticated baby boomers. Marketers also segment customers based on where they live (geography), how often they use a product (usage rates), and what they value in a product (product attribute preferences).

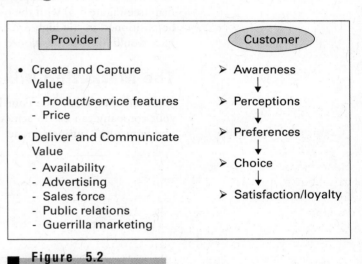

Figure 5.2

Understanding the customer choice process

Targeting compares the defined segments and then selects the most attractive one, which becomes the PTA. Target market definition is essential because it guides your company's *customer selection* strategy. The attractiveness of a segment is related to its size, growth rate, and profit potential. Your targeting decisions should also reflect your company's specific capabilities and longer-term goals. Accurate targeting is important for entrepreneurs; however, it is not always clear which customer segment(s) represents the best target market, and finding out may require some research and some trial and error. As we noted in Chapter 3, it is wise to identify secondary target audiences (STAs) in case the PTA doesn't meet expectations. Nevertheless, identifying the appropriate target market early on is critical because pursuing multiple targets or waiting for one to emerge is an expensive strategy.

To illustrate segmentation and targeting, let's look at the example of Nantucket Nectars, the beverage company founded by marketing-savvy entrepreneurs Tom Scott and Tom First. Relevant segment characteristics for this company are age, individualism, and health consciousness. In Nantucket Nectars' early days, its primary target market was young, active, health-oriented consumers who enjoyed breaking with conformity by choosing a noncarbonated soft drink alternative. As Nantucket Nectars gained public awareness, this gave the company power to move beyond its PTA to its STAs and ultimately the broader, nationwide drink market. Scott and First started the company with an initial investment of $9,000 and a production run of 1,400 cases. In 1997, they sold a majority stake in the business to Ocean Spray for $70 million. Cadbury bought the firm from Ocean Spray in 2002. At the time, Nantucket Nectars had estimated revenues of $80 million.[7] In 2008, Cadbury demerged its beverage business from its confectionary business, creating Dr. Pepper Snapple Group.

While segmentation and targeting profile a company's customers, **positioning** relates to competitors and to customers' *perceptions* of your product. Positioning usually describes a company's offering relative to certain product attributes—the ones customers care about most. Such attributes often include price, quality, and convenience, all of which can be scaled from high to low. For example, if brands of single-serve beverages were shown on a positioning map (see Figure 5.3) with the two dimensions of *price* and *quality*, Nantucket Nectars would be positioned in the high-price, high-quality (upper-right) quadrant, whereas a store-brand juice would likely be positioned in a low-price, low-quality (lower-left) quadrant.

The Marketing Mix

The marketing mix—the Four Ps of product, price, place, and promotion—is a set of tools your company can use to achieve its marketing goals. In fact, the marketing mix is so basic to a company's business model that *marketing* strategy often defines company or corporate

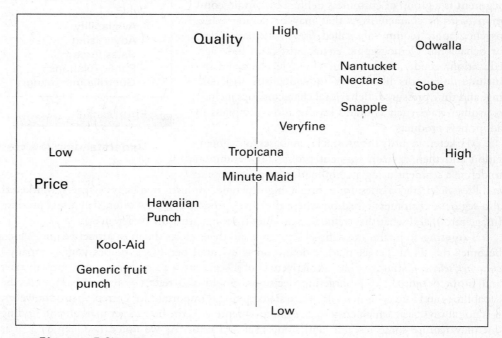

Figure 5.3

Nantucket Nectars' position map

strategy. In this section, we discuss the individual elements of the marketing mix, shown in Figure 5.4. Our focus is on the particular challenges entrepreneurial marketers face.

Product Strategy. We can divide product strategy into the **core product** and the **augmented product**. The core product is the essential good or service, while the augmented product is the set of attributes peripherally related to it. For example, Apple manufactures and markets its iPod, the core product, but it also provides iTunes for downloading music and product troubleshooting as augmented services.

Another way to look at the product variable part of the marketing mix is in terms of goods and services (the word *product* here can refer to either a service or a good). Whereas beverages and computers are obviously tangible goods, supermarkets, Internet service providers, and banks are services *and* offer service products, such as food shopping, Internet access, and debit accounts. The line between products and services has been eroding for some time. Furthermore, we live in a service economy, and a large part of the gross national product and new job creation are tied to services.

In your product strategy, you'll pay attention to the strength of the *value proposition* you are offering customers and make sure your products are clearly *differentiated*. You'll also be guided by the *product life cycle* in crafting your strategy and by *product diffusion theory* in assessing how fast consumers will adopt your products. Finally, from the beginning, you should be obsessively focused on *quality*.

Many entrepreneurs establish companies based on a new product or product line. When developing any new product, your company must ensure that it is truly addressing an "unmet consumer need"—that there is a real **customer value proposition (CVP). Customer value** is the difference between total customer benefits and total customer costs, which are both monetary and nonmonetary. A product attribute is not a benefit until consumers buy into the advantage.

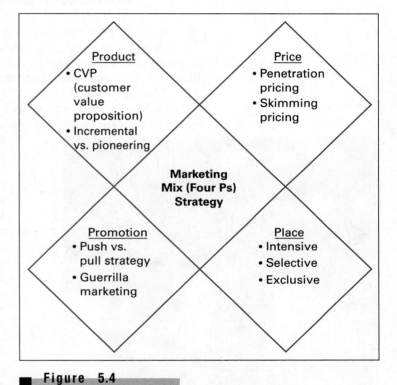

Figure 5.4

Marketing mix strategy for an entrepreneur

Identifying a CVP, also known as a *positioning statement*, is an essential step in the marketing of a product or service regardless of your industry. Any positioning statement has four elements: (1) target group and need, (2) brand, (3) concept, and (4) point of difference. The formula is straightforward. Entrepreneurs need to know which attributes customers consider important and how customers rate the company's products—and competing products—on each attribute. Figure 5.5 shows how you can identify the product/service attributes you'll consider when designing your offerings.

Product differentiation is important for initial product success as well as for longer-term brand building. In its early days, Maker's Mark, a sixth-generation, family-run Kentucky bourbon producer, leveraged the product-related attributes that make its bourbon unique (for example, wheat instead of rye, six-year fermentation, and small-batch production) to build a distinctive image for the brand. For decades, the company has been able to rely on these product differences to reinforce its quality position.

A venerable framework for understanding product strategy is the **product life cycle**. The stages of the product life cycle are **introduction, growth, maturity, and decline**. Product

		Perceived Performance	
		"Poor"	"Good"
Attribute	High	Improve	Maintain
Importance	Low	Monitor	De-emphasize

Source: Adapted from John A. Martilla and John C. James.[8]

Figure 5.5

Importance-performance analysis

life-cycle analysis can help you recognize how marketing requirements differ at each stage of a company's growth. During the introduction stage, marketers must educate the customer and secure distribution. During the growth stage, they must cultivate customer loyalty and build the brand. Differentiation is important during the maturity stage, and marketing efficiency is critical during the decline stage.

In a business environment with intense global competition and fast-paced technology, entrepreneurs must continue to develop new products in order to maintain a profitable market position, even after creating a winning new venture. New product development is critical for market longevity. Entrepreneurship combined with innovation equals success. Naturally, entrepreneurs need to understand new product opportunities and the new product development process if they are to ensure their venture's survival.

Because new products have varying levels of *newness* to both the company and the marketplace, entrepreneurs must make different kinds of *risk-return* trade-offs. At one extreme, pioneering or radical innovation represents a technological breakthrough or "new-to-the-world" product. Although pioneering products may be risky investments, they can produce handsome returns. At the other extreme, entrepreneurs may develop *incremental* products, which are modifications of existing products, or *product line extensions*. Incremental products are less risky to develop but typically produce a more modest return. Regardless of the type of new products you develop, bringing products to market quickly—by mastering the new product development process—is critical for gaining a competitive advantage.

If you introduce highly innovative products, be particularly attentive to consumer adoption behavior. Consumer willingness to adopt a new product is a major factor in the realm of technology products. The **product diffusion curve** (see Figure 5.6) captures adoption behavior graphically, showing customer segments called innovators, early adopters, early majority, late majority, and laggards. A number of factors affect the *rate of diffusion*, or how fast customers adopt a new product. If a product represents risk or is complex or is not completely compatible with existing products, then the market usually will adopt it at a fairly slow rate.

© Walter Bibikow/Corbis

Maker's Mark whiskey

Incremental Improvement versus Radical Innovation

In September 2010, 58.7 million Americans had smartphones and 37% of them were BlackBerrys. From that peak, U.S. sales of BlackBerrys slowed down while sales of Apple iPhones accelerated. By April 2011, more Americans were using iPhones than BlackBerrys; and by January 2013, only 5.9% of 129.4 installed smartphones in the United States were BlackBerrys compared with 37.8% iPhones and 52.3% with Android operating systems, of which the leader was Samsung.

BlackBerry was trapped in the viciously short smartphone life cycle and strived to compete by incrementally improving its outdated Java-based operating system, while companies such as Apple and Samsung introduced innovative smartphones with newer and better operating systems. At the end of January 2013, the BlackBerry 10 based on the new QNX operating system was launched, but most observers believed it was too late for BlackBerry to recapture very much of its lost market share.

Entrepreneurs sometimes err in being overly product focused, concentrating on the product as they conceive it rather than as customers may want it. One way to offset the danger of this mindset is to involve the customer in the design process. Custom Research, a Baldrige National Quality Award–winning marketing research firm, performs a comprehensive survey of each of its clients prior to beginning a project. This allows the company to learn exactly what the client expects and hopes to gain from its investment. The practice of studying the customer upfront not only results in better service quality but also enables you to deliver a highly customized product.

Finally, perhaps the most important product attribute for entrepreneurs is quality, which serves as a powerful differentiator and is needed to gain the recommendation of customers. Positive word-of-mouth recommendations are essential because most customers are not yet familiar with the company. Entrepreneurial companies with a quality orientation also find it easier to engage in internal marketing: Employees are more enthusiastic about and proud to be selling high-quality products than products of mediocre quality.

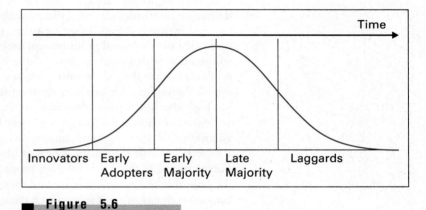

Figure 5.6

Product diffusion curve

Pricing Strategy. Developing an optimal pricing strategy is a daunting challenge for even the most sophisticated entrepreneurial company. Figure 5.7 shows various price-setting options.

Entrepreneurs incur many costs in starting a venture. Some are *fixed costs*, which do not change with the volume of production (such as facilities, equipment, and salaries), and some are *variable costs*, which do change with the volume of production (such as raw materials, hourly labor, and sales commissions). The price of a product/service must be higher than its variable cost (point A in Figure 5.7), or you will sustain losses with the sale of each additional unit. To operate successfully, an entrepreneurial venture must not only recover both fixed costs (point B) and variable costs (point A) but also make a reasonable profit (point C). The crash of many early dot-com businesses illustrates this simple financial logic, as a number of

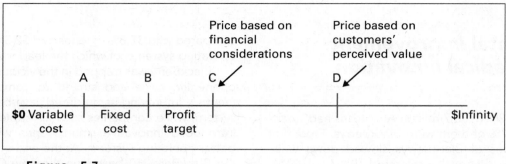

Figure 5.7

Pricing decision for an entrepreneur

these companies followed a "get-big-fast" strategy by aggressively selling their products below cost. Online grocery businesses such as Webvan fell into this trap: The expense of filling and delivering each order exceeded the profitability of the sale.

Many entrepreneurs, in setting prices, use a *cost-based method*, marking up a product based on its cost plus a desired profit margin (point C in Figure 5.7). Another method, often used in conjunction with a markup, is matching competitors' prices. A common problem with these methods is that they allow entrepreneurs to price too low, thereby "leaving money on the table." Pricing too low can hurt the long-term profitability of the venture. Of course, pricing too high also has a serious downside, as it can create a purchase barrier and limit sales.

So what choices does an entrepreneur have in identifying the most appropriate price? An alternative to cost-based and competitive pricing is *perceived value pricing* (point D), which is especially viable for pricing a new or innovative product or service. Entrepreneurs also can pursue strategies that trade off high profit margins for high sales, or vice versa. Determining the full value of a product/service and then using effective communications to convince target customers to pay for that value are challenging tasks even for an established company.

If possible, approach perceived value pricing with pre-market price testing, estimating the number of units customers will purchase at different price points. Two well-known pricing strategies, which represent opposite ends of the pricing spectrum, are price skimming and penetration pricing. **Price skimming** sets high margins; you can expect to gain limited market share because your prices will be relatively high. **Penetration pricing** aims to gain high market share with lower margins and relatively lower prices. For entrepreneurs with a product that brings something new to the marketplace, a skimming strategy is usually best. Unless your channels of distribution are very well established, a penetration strategy, generally reserved for mature products, is hard to implement.

We can represent price in a variety of ways. There are basic **price points** (also called *price levels*) for products, which are standardized or fixed, and there are **price promotions**—a tool by which marketers can achieve specific goals, such as introducing a product to a new customer market. Price promotions are short-term and use regular price levels as a base to discount from; they provide a way to offer customers good deals. Price promotions let you increase sales, reward distributors, gain awareness for a new product, and clear excess inventory. Periodically, Nantucket Nectars coordinates a price promotion with its retailers, who offer its 16-ounce juices (such as Peach Nectar) with an advertised, 25%-off price. This type of promotion typically doubles sales on the products, benefiting both the manufacturer and the retailers.

Price promotions often are necessary to maintain good relationships with distributors: Both wholesalers and retailers must offer price promotions in order to stay competitive. In business-to-business markets, companies often reward their business customers with volume discounts applied to the ongoing purchase of particular goods and services. Promotions are an important tool for entrepreneurs, too, who often use them to gain an initial position in the marketplace. At its earliest stage, Nantucket Nectars used *trade promotions* to motivate retailers to make the initial "buys" of their products and *customer promotions* to motivate the retailers' customers to try the products.

A common pricing strategy is **price discrimination**: charging different prices to different customer segments. Examples of this practice are highly varied and include the lower prices charged to shoppers using store loyalty cards and the differing price structures used to charge airline passengers. *Couponing* is a widely used form of price discrimination that rewards customers who care about receiving a discount but does not reward those who don't care enough to put forth the extra effort to redeem the coupon.

Pricing is important to entrepreneurs not just because it affects revenue and profit but also because it plays a role in how consumers perceive a product's position in the market. Price serves as a quality cue to consumers, especially when they have had limited experience with the product. The *economic perspective* views consumers as rational actors who buy when the perceived benefits of a product exceed its price. Those who study consumer behavior, however, understand that consumers' *willingness to pay* is not totally rational but is affected by a variety of psychological factors.

Entrepreneurs can use some marketplace wisdom relative to pricing. First, the selling effort for a product must match its price. Price skimming, for example, must be accompanied by a sophisticated, effective selling process. It is easier to lower than raise prices because customers are resistant to price increases. The more established the differentiation and/or quality of a product or service, the more price insensitive the consumer—if he or she values the perceived benefits. Customers also are less price sensitive when products and services are bundled into a single offer because this makes prices more difficult to compare. A good entrepreneur will be aware of both the pricing practices of competing companies and the pricing-related purchase behavior of consumers.

Distribution Strategy (Place). Distribution presents special challenges for entrepreneurs because channels of distribution often are difficult to set up initially. Figure 5.8 shows the structure of traditional distribution channels for consumer and business-to-business marketing. While established businesses may introduce new products, price points, and communications strategies, they usually rely on existing channels of distribution. For example, Crest, a Procter & Gamble brand, may introduce a new type of electric toothbrush with a distinctive price position and an innovative advertising campaign, but it will use its existing network of wholesalers and retailers to actually distribute the product. Entrepreneurs usually don't have this luxury.

Finding the right channel can be far less difficult than breaking into the right channel. Entrepreneurs who want to market food products, for instance, face enormous barriers when they try to get their products on supermarket shelves, as the Gourmet Stew case in Chapter 3 illustrated. Most supermarkets are national chains that charge large slotting fees. Even when brokers and distributors accept new products into their lines, they may be unwilling to dedicate much effort to selling them when the products are unknown.

Distribution can be problematic for entrepreneurial service companies as well as for those that manufacture goods. Distribution decisions for a service company often are location decisions because many services require that service providers interact directly with customers. Effective distribution is the availability and accessibility of a service to its target customers. As early-stage service companies grow, new locations often are the most important means of attracting new customers and increasing sales.

Starbucks is an international services-sector company with thousands of stores; nevertheless, the service is sold locally, and one location may be more or less successful than another. If a Starbucks location is unsuccessful, the company can cancel its lease and open an

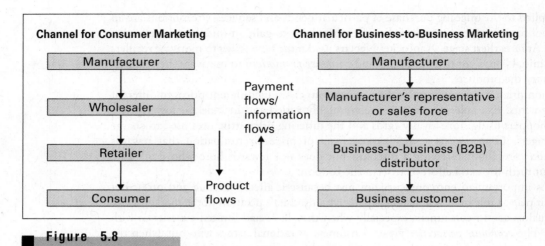

Channel for Consumer Marketing

Manufacturer

↓

Wholesaler

↓

Retailer

↓

Consumer

Payment flows/ information flows

↓ ↑

Product flows

Channel for Business-to-Business Marketing

Manufacturer

↓

Manufacturer's representative or sales force

↓

Business-to-business (B2B) distributor

↓

Business customer

Figure 5.8

Traditional distribution channels

alternative location in that neighborhood or focus on locations in other neighborhoods. But if an entrepreneur makes a bad location decision for his first or second or even third location, the financial loss can paralyze the company.

There is a great deal of *interdependency* in a distribution channel: Each channel member has a particular function to perform, and each relies on the others. Entrepreneurs especially are inclined to rely on other companies to fulfill certain distribution tasks. Many companies were able to enter the Internet retailing sector quickly because they could outsource *fulfillment*—warehousing, packing, and delivering the order—to another company, allowing them to maintain *virtual* companies with low fixed costs. In business-to-business channels, entrepreneurs often outsource their selling efforts to sales brokers who work for a marketing firm rather than investing the time and money to build their own sales force. There are disadvantages to this kind of outsourcing, though: Quality is hard to control, the information flow between you and your customer is interrupted, and longer-term cost economies are harder to achieve.

Sometimes channel partners don't do what you want or expect them to do. When Nantucket Nectars' co-founders became frustrated with their distributor's slow progress in getting the brand established, they took over distribution themselves. The company lost millions of dollars trying to change its distribution model, and it went back to contracting with distributors after it found more capable partners. Although distribution mistakes such as those made by Nantucket Nectars extract a price, they also teach early-stage companies what their capabilities are.

Distribution channel strategy includes three types of **channel coverage**: intensive, selective, and exclusive. The appropriate strategy depends on the type of product or service that you will sell. **Intensive** coverage works for consumer goods and other fast-moving products. The carbonated soft drink category is one of the most intensively distributed: Products are sold in supermarkets, drugstores, convenience stores, restaurants, vending machines, sporting event concessions, and fast-food outlets. **Selective** distribution brings the product to specific distributors, often limiting selection geographically by establishing a dealer network. Kate Spade sells her handbags and other fashion accessories to high-end, luxury department stores, as well as Kate Spade specialty stores, but not to mainstream retailers or mass merchandisers. Selective distribution can protect dealers and retailers from competition, while helping manufacturers maintain prices by thwarting price competition. The third coverage strategy,

exclusive distribution, is often used for luxury products. For some time, Neiman Marcus had exclusive rights to distribute the Hermès line of fashion accessories.

Channel partnerships (or *relationships*) have important implications for entrepreneurs. Often the channel member with the most power will prevail; for this reason, **channel power** is an important concept in distribution strategy. While channel partnerships can speed a young company's growth, preserve resources, and transfer risk, entrepreneurs must be careful not to sacrifice their direct relationship with customers. Most important, entrepreneurs must carefully manage their relationships with channel partners and monitor them over time.

Another widely applied concept, **channel conflict**, refers to situations where differing objectives and turf overlap, leading to true disharmony in the channel. Channel conflict was a high-profile phenomenon in the early days of the Internet, when many startup companies were using the strategy of **disintermediation**—cutting intermediaries out of traditional distribution channels by selling directly to customers. Amazon.com, the online bookseller, created conflict between book publishers and distributors and traditional book retailers. Because Amazon could buy in volume and avoid the high occupancy costs retailers pay, it could offer an enormous assortment at deeply discounted prices. Amazon's volume allowed it to negotiate low prices from publishers and wholesalers, who in turn alienated their other customers, the traditional book retailers in the channel.

Entrepreneurs succeed with their distribution strategies when they have a strong understanding of channel economics. Giro, the bicycle helmet company that outfitted both Greg LeMonde and Lance Armstrong—famous American winners of the Tour de France and in Armstrong's case subsequently discredited for using performance-enhancing drugs—gained initial access to the retail channel by offering high margins and selective distribution to preferred bike shops. This allowed the company to maintain its premium prices and establish loyalty among experts and cycling enthusiasts.

Current practice reflects a focus on multichannel distribution, which gives a company the ability to reach multiple segments, gain marketing synergies, provide flexibility for customers, save on customer acquisition costs, and build a robust database of purchase information. J.Crew, for instance, has been successful diversifying its store-based business to include strong catalog and online channels. But a multichannel strategy adds operating complexity and demands more resources, so entrepreneurs are best to approach these opportunities cautiously and be careful that their timing is in line with their capabilities and resources. For example, TiVo's strategy to push its innovative product through both specialty stores like Fry's and consumer-electronics superstores like Best Buy created problems for the successful launch of its product. TiVo should have used the specialty store channel exclusively in the beginning rather than both channels. Specialty stores are not willing to provide time and service to develop the market for an innovative product when they have to compete on price with consumer-electronics superstores.

Research shows that many of the most serious obstacles to entrepreneurial success are related to distribution. Specifically, entrepreneurs tend to be overly dependent on channel partners and short on understanding channel behavior in their industry. It is critical that entrepreneurs take the time to learn about distribution and make fact-based decisions about channel design and channel partnerships to overcome these threats to good distribution strategy.

Marketing Communications Strategy (Promotion).

Marketing communications convey messages to the market—messages about the company's products and services as well as about the company itself. The marketing communications element of the marketing mix is a mix within a mix: The **communications mix** is defined as *advertising, sales promotion, public relations, personal selling*, and *direct marketing* (sometimes included with advertising). The marketing communications mix and some of its key elements are shown in Figure 5.9.

The components of the communications mix, like those of the marketing mix, are often referred to as *tools*, and the use of these tools by marketers differs substantially across business and industry contexts. To illustrate, consumer product companies' communications are often aimed at mass markets and include advertising and sales promotions, whereas business-to-business companies use more customized, interactive tools, such as personal selling by a sales force. Of course, the communications a marketer uses are closely aligned with the specific type of product the company is attempting to sell as well as with the company's marketing objectives.

It is common marketing wisdom to use a variety of tools in marketing any product or service. Because of this focus on multiple methods and the need to integrate and coordinate these methods, we often call the process **integrated marketing communications**. A range of factors—including cost, timing, and target market—determines the selection of a company's key communications tools. The question you must answer is, "What is the most effective way to communicate with my customers and influence their actions?" And the sooner you can answer this, the better.

Two communications strategies are *push* and *pull*. A **push** strategy aims to push a product through the channel using tools such as trade promotions, trade shows, and personal selling to distributors or other channel members. A **pull** strategy's goal, on the other hand, is to create end-user demand and rely on that demand to pull the product through the channel. Pull strategies, which are directly targeted to end users, include advertising and consumer sales promotions, such as in-store specials. These strategies also are relevant for service companies. Fidelity Investments, for example, can push its mutual funds through brokers or advertise them directly to investors, who, the company hopes, will then request them.

Marketing communications is a broad and sophisticated field. Many of the most visible tools are primarily accessible to large companies with deep marketing budgets and in-house marketing talent. This is usually the case for large, national television and print advertising and high-penetration direct mail campaigns. Probably the greatest breadth of tools exists

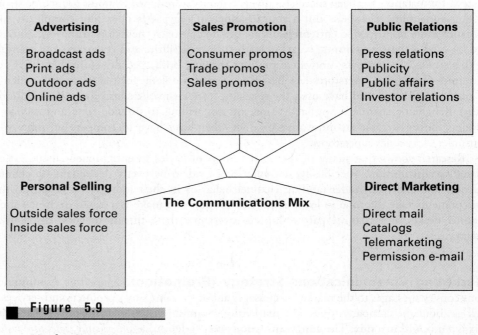

■ Figure 5.9

Marketing communications

within the domain of advertising, which includes everything from billboards to Web sites to local newspapers to Super Bowl commercials. There also are various direct marketing tools, including catalogs, direct mail and e-mail, telemarketing, and infomercials (vehicles for direct selling).

What *advertising* choices are available to an entrepreneur? Anything that is appropriate, affordable, and measurable, or at least possible to evaluate. Entrepreneurs can use traditional major media by focusing on scaled-back options, such as regional editions of national magazines, locally broadcast commercials on cable television stations, and local newspapers and radio stations. The disadvantage is that it's almost impossible to achieve advertising economies of scale. But you can efficiently conduct tightly targeted campaigns with a focus on cost control.

In addition to regionalized or localized major media, you have a number of minor media options. These include classified ads, the yellow pages and online information services, brochures, flyers, online bulletin boards, local canvassing (for business-to-business), and educational seminars or demonstrations. As mentioned above, most marketing experts support using multiple methods in combination, in part because different methods have particular strengths and weaknesses. But even though the media are varied, the message and the brand image you want to communicate should be strictly consistent. Two terms that are frequently mentioned in relation to advertising objectives are *reach* and *frequency*. **Reach** is the percentage of a company's target market that is exposed to an ad campaign within a specific period of time. **Frequency** is the number of times a member of your target market is exposed during that time period.

When selecting media, entrepreneurs match their communications goals to media capabilities. Radio is more targeted and intimate than other advertising media; it allows flexibility but requires repetition for the message to get through. Television has a large reach and is good for demonstrating product benefits but is usually expensive and entails substantial production costs. Many magazines with a long shelf life are well targeted (consider how many times a magazine may be read in a doctor's waiting room).

Newspapers are good for geographical targeting and promotional advertising but have a very short shelf life. Infomercials, which we may also consider a direct marketing tool, have production costs and a short life span but are persuasive and good for telling the product story. Online advertising allows companies to reach a specific and often desirable customer market. Figure 5.10 presents brief guidelines for the strategic use of advertising media.

Even entrepreneurs often go to marketing experts for advice about how to execute campaigns and how to frame an effective message. While some early-stage companies use established advertising agencies, others contract with freelance marketing professionals, many of whom have experience in the entrepreneurial domain. You'll want to learn the basics of advertising, public relations, and marketing research in order to be able to select and evaluate agencies or individuals you bring in to assist your company with its early-stage marketing.

The three primary types of **sales promotion** are *consumer promotions, trade promotions*, and *sales force promotions*. **Consumer promotions** are deals offered directly to consumers to support a pull strategy. **Trade promotions** are deals offered to a company's trade or channel partners—such as distributors or retailers—to support a traditional push strategy. **Sales force promotions** motivate and reward the company's own sales force or its distributors' sales forces.

There are two basic types of sales promotions: price and nonprice. We discussed price promotions earlier in the section on pricing strategy. *Consumer* price promotions include coupons, rebates, and loyalty rewards; *trade* price promotions include discounts, allowances, buyback guarantees, and slotting fees. Types of *consumer* nonprice promotions include product sampling, advertising specialties (such as t-shirts with a brand logo), contests, and sweepstakes. *Trade* nonprice promotions include trade shows and sales contests.

Advertising Medium	Key Factors for Entrepreneurs to Consider
Brochures and flyers	▣ Allow creative flexibility and focused message ▣ Production quantity and distribution must be well planned
Direct mail and e-mail	▣ Permits precise targeting and encourages direct response ▣ Results are measurable and can guide future campaigns
Infomercials	▣ Effective for telling a story and communicating or endorsing product benefits ▣ Costly to produce but measurable and good for collecting data
Internet communications	▣ A variety of options, such as banner ads and permission e-mail marketing ▣ Superior for collecting data and measuring responses
Magazines	▣ Can easily be targeted, are involving for readers, and have a long shelf life ▣ Offer budget flexibility but involve a long lead time
Newsletters	▣ Good creative opportunities and maximum control ▣ Cost factors (time and money) should be carefully considered
Newspapers	▣ Best medium for advertising promotions and reaching a geographically based or local market ▣ Shelf life is fairly short and ads are usually not carefully read
Outdoor	▣ Can have strong visual impact and repeat exposure; this medium is believed to offer a high return on investment ▣ Targeting is difficult because ads are location-bound
Radio	▣ Good potential for creativity and connecting with the audience; message can be easily varied ▣ Excellent for targeting but ads must be repeated to be effective
Telemarketing	▣ Interactive communication with one-on-one selling capabilities ▣ A direct response method that has faced increased regulation because it is seen by many to be intrusive
Television	▣ High media and production costs but superior reach; most effective way to present and demonstrate a product ▣ Commonly used for brand building
Yellow pages	▣ An important local medium used as a basic reference by consumers; necessary for credibility ▣ Low cost, but standardized format limits creativity

Figure 5.10

Strategic use of advertising media

The effects of sales promotions differ from the effects of advertising. In general, sales promotions produce more immediate, sales-driven results, whereas advertising produces a more long-term, brand-building result. Sales promotions have become increasingly popular with companies in the last couple of decades.

Many entrepreneurs derive great value from using **public relations (PR)** as a strategic communications tool. PR has two major dimensions: *publicity* and *corporate communications*.

When Google founder Larry Page introduced Google Pack at the 2006 Consumer Electronics Show, that was a corporate communication designed to move users away from competitor, Microsoft. When Google joined the O3b (other 3 billion) consortium—a group of companies that support World Wide Web (WWW or Web) access for Africa—it did so to gain positive publicity. Bill Samuels, Jr., the CEO of Maker's Mark Bourbon, used a personal connection and an elaborate plan to gain major-league publicity:

> Dave Garino covered the Kentucky area for The Wall Street Journal. Bill Jr. discovered that he and Dave had a mutual friend, Sam Walker, with whom Dave had gone to journalism school. Bill Jr. knew Dave was going to be in town covering an unrelated story and decided to try a unique approach to persuade him to do a story on Maker's Mark. Bill Jr. staged an event at the distillery and awarded exclusive rights to cover the show to a local news station. He found out which hotel Dave Garino was staying in and had Sam Walker arrange to meet Dave for cocktails in the hotel's bar. Next, Bill Jr. convinced the bartender to turn all the televisions above the bar to the local station that was covering the distillery show. When Dave saw the news footage, he asked Sam what Maker's Mark was and why, if there was so much interest in this distillery, had he never heard of it. When Sam replied that it was the local favorite and offered to introduce him to Bill Jr., he accepted. Subsequently, Dave and Bill Jr. spent three days developing a story that was published on the front page of The Wall Street Journal in August of 1980.
>
> Bill Jr. recalled: "From that one story we received about 50,000 letters inquiring about our product. The phone lines didn't stop ringing for weeks. We had one salesman at the time and we were trying to figure how to best capitalize from all this publicity."

And the rest, as they say, is history.[9]

Maker's Mark Waters Down Image, but Boosts Brand Recognition

In February 2013, Maker's Mark announced that it would be diluting the strength of its bourbon from 45% to 42% by volume and thereby increasing its output, which had fallen short of consumer demand. The announcement outraged some loyal drinkers, who immediately vented their anger via social media; reports of their protests soon spread to conventional media. One week later Bill Samuels, Jr., Maker's Mark Founder and Chairman Emeritus, and Rob Samuels, COO, in a Tweet headed "You spoke, we listened" handsomely apologized to their customers for their misstep and reversed their decision by stating that they would make it "just like we've made it since the very beginning."

According to BrandIndex data, Maker's Mark attention score shot up from 8 on February 9 before the dilution announcement to 24 by February 27, indicating that 24% of the population aged 21 and over had heard something good or bad about the brand in the last two weeks. The three-fold increase caused a few skeptics to question whether Maker's Mark's initial announcement was a deliberate marketing move to boost its name recognition rather than a public relations blunder. That was unlikely as it damaged Maker's Mark image. Also the last thing that Maker's Mark needed before it could increase production capacity was more demand that would result from increasing brand recognition. More likely it was following the lead of Tennessee whiskey icon, Jack Daniel's, which diluted its strength from 43% to 40% in 2004 with little adverse reaction from drinkers.

The Samuels swift and effective response is a good illustration of how to handle a public relations disaster in the Internet age when bad news and rumors go viral at lightning speed on the Web.

It is often argued that publicity is an entrepreneur's best friend, more valuable than millions of dollars of advertising. The reason is that PR is perceived as more credible and more objective; a reporter's words are more believable than those of an advertising agency. Also, the argument goes, PR is free! This, of course, is not true—it takes a significant amount of time and effort, sometimes money, and always the ability to leverage connections to generate good PR. If this were not the case, there would not be so many public relations firms charging high fees and battling for the media's attention. Savvy entrepreneurs with fledgling companies are good at managing their own PR. For example, they send out press releases announcing new products, key executive hires, and other significant company events to newspapers, trade magazines, and online media outlets.

For companies operating in a business-to-business environment or those that need to sell into an established distribution channel, *personal selling* is a core component of the communications mix. Although some companies separate sales and marketing, a company's sales force is often its primary marketing tool. Establishing and managing a sales force requires decisions related to sales force size, training, organization, compensation, and selling approaches.

A sales force is often considered to be a company's most valuable asset. Maintaining a strong sales force is an expensive proposition, though, and startup companies often face a difficult decision: whether to absorb the expense and sell directly or hire manufacturers' representatives (*reps*, sometimes called *brokers*) to sell the company's products (along with those of other companies) on commission. Reps are advantageous in that they have existing relationships with customers, but a company has more control—and a closer relationship with its customers—if it invests in its own sales force. A sales force may be organized geographically, by product line, by customer size, or by customer segment or industry. Compensation is usually some mix of base salary and commission, and incentives may be linked to gaining new customers, exceeding sales quotas, or increasing profitability. Current marketing practice places a high value on selecting and retaining customers based on their profit potential to the company. The sales force typically should have access to effective selling materials, credible technical data, and sales automation software that will ensure an effective and efficient selling process.

Personal selling is an important activity for entrepreneurs on an informal, personal level—through professional networking. Leveraging personal and industry connections is a key success factor, especially in the startup or early growth stage of the venture. But this is a time-consuming and often laborious process, which is often neglected and rarely fully optimized. Giro's founder, Jim Gentes, personally attended top triathlons and other high-profile races across the country, demonstrating his helmets and giving them to the best cyclists. He was ahead of his time in understanding the value of endorsements from world-class athletes.

Entrepreneurs can implement *direct marketing* campaigns to be broad based or to be local or limited in scope. Direct marketing methods include direct mail, catalogs, telemarketing, infomercials, and permission email (where consumers "opt-in" to receive messages). The effectiveness of direct media is easy to measure, and these media are ideal for building a database that can be used for future marketing and analysis. Direct marketing is an important tool for communicating with new or existing customers, whom you can target for mailings that range from thank-you notes to announcements of future promotions.

With the increased use of technology and databases in marketing, and the growth of the Internet channel, the practice of "one-to-one" marketing has become pervasive. This type of marketing is interactive and has qualities similar to personal selling: Your company can address a customer on an individual level, factoring in that customer's previous purchasing behavior and other kinds of information, and then respond accordingly. It is the use of databases that allows marketers to personalize communications and design customer-specific messages.

Customer Relationship Management (CRM) systems are designed to help companies compile and manage data about their customers. While CRM systems are usually large scale and expensive, an astute entrepreneur can set up a more fundamental system to capture and use customer data to facilitate relationship building. Part of this process is capturing the right metrics—for example, *cost of customer acquisition* or *average lifetime value of a customer*—and knowing how to act on them.

Guerrilla Marketing

Guerrilla marketing is marketing activities that are nontraditional, grassroots, and captivating—that gain consumers' attention and build awareness of the company. Guerrilla marketing is often linked to "creating a buzz" or generating a lot of word-of-mouth in the marketplace. The terms *buzz, viral,* and *word-of-mouth marketing* aren't interchangeable. According to the Word of Mouth Marketing Association (WOMMA), the three concepts are defined as in the accompanying box.[10]

Entrepreneurs may use all of these nontraditional promotion campaigns to get people's attention, especially younger generations who may not pay attention to TV campaigns and print media. Guerrilla marketing is also attractive to entrepreneurs because often they have to work with a limited or nonexistent promotion budget and traditional media are very expensive. Unfortunately for entrepreneurs, such nontraditional promotional methods are getting the attention of big marketers, who want to break through the clutter of existing media. BzzAgent, a Boston-based word-of-mouth marketing agency, has more than 500,000 agents who will try clients' products and then talk about them with their friends, relatives, and acquaintances over the duration of the campaign. It has worked with companies like Anheuser-Busch, General Mills, and Volkswagen. Procter & Gamble's (P&G's) four-year-old Tremor division has a panel of 200,000 teenagers and 350,000 moms who are asked to talk with friends about new products or concepts that P&G sends them. Some experts suggest that traditional marketers underused public relations or used it only as an afterthought, thus opening the door for creative guerrilla marketers.

It is easier to define what guerrilla marketing *does* than what it *is*. Guerrilla marketing is heard above the noise in the marketplace and makes a unique impact: It makes people talk about the product and the company, effectively making them "missionaries" for the brand. It creates drama and interest and positive *affect*, or emotion—all pretty amazing results. But in fact, truly good guerrilla marketing is as difficult as—and maybe more so than—good traditional marketing. Because lots of companies are trying to do it, it's harder to break free of the pack.

Think of guerrilla marketing as guerrilla *tactics* that you can apply to various media or elements of the communications mix rather than as entirely different communications tools. You can use guerrilla tactics in advertising (riveting posters in subways) and in personal selling (creative canvassing at a trade show), but you'll most likely use them as a form of PR—as tactics that garner visibility and positive publicity. The president of Maker's Mark practiced guerrilla marketing when he inspired *The Wall Street Journal*'s reporter to learn about and write the story of his bourbon. Nantucket Nectars' Tom and Tom were

TYPES OF GUERRILLA MARKETING

- ▣ Word-of-mouth marketing: Giving people a reason to talk about your products and services and making it easier for that conversation to take place.

- ▣ Buzz marketing: Using high-profile entertainment or news to get people to talk about your brand.

- ▣ Viral marketing: Creating entertaining or informative messages that are designed to be passed along in an exponential fashion, often electronically or by email.

ISSUES IN GUERRILLA MARKETING

- ▣ Identify challenges and develop creative solutions.

- ▣ Find the "inherent drama" in your offerings and translate that into a meaningful benefit.

- ▣ Get people's attention and get a "foot in the door" (generating the first sale).

- ▣ Create "buzz" once you get in the door (word-of-mouth marketing).

relentless guerrilla marketers, dressing up like grapes and making a stir on the Cape Cod highway on Memorial Day weekend as thousands of motorists were stuck in traffic and sending purple vans to outdoor concerts to distribute free juice before it became a common practice.

Much of what we now call *event marketing* is in the realm of guerrilla marketing because it is experiential, interactive, and lighthearted. But as we noted earlier, guerrilla tactics are becoming more and more difficult for entrepreneurs to execute because every corporate marketing executive is trying to succeed at guerrilla marketing, too, and has a much larger budget to employ. Sony Ericsson Mobile executed a guerrilla marketing campaign in New York City in which trained actors and actresses pretended to be tourists and asked passersby to snap a picture with the company's new mobile phone/digital camera product. Deceptive? Yes, but too commonplace a tactic to truly be controversial. Not every guerrilla campaign escapes controversy. In 2007, Cartoon Network's Adult Swim launched a guerrilla marketing campaign to promote the show *Aqua Teen Hunger Force*. The campaign used battery-powered electronic light boards of a middle-finger waving moon man hidden in various areas around 10 cities. People in Boston mistook the packages for bombs, and the police responded. Turner Broadcasting, the owner of Cartoon Network, was forced to pay $2 million to the city of Boston not only to cover the costs of police and bomb squad but also as a show of goodwill.[11]

An elaborate guerrilla marketing campaign in Toronto, designed to promote an HBO comedy series, featured street teams with TV-equipped backpacks to show pedestrians 30-second promotional clips, chalk drawings promoting the series at major intersections, and ads in the bathrooms of major media agencies that showcased giant quotes from reviews of the show. The attempt by large corporations and advertising agencies to set the standard for guerrilla marketing makes these tactics less accessible to small companies. Still, as long as entrepreneurs are sparked by creativity, guerrilla successes can still be possible, even though they require a continuous stream of ideas and energy.

In conclusion, entrepreneurs who create successful marketing strategies must have a clear vision of their goal. They also must understand how one strategic element affects another because, if the marketing mix elements of product, price, distribution, and communications are not perfectly compatible—if the mix is not internally logical—the strategy will not work. Even a good beginning strategy is not enough, however, because the marketplace is dynamic. Entrepreneurial companies, more so than mature businesses, must constantly reevaluate their strategy and how it is affecting growth.

Marketing Skills for Managing Growth

It is beyond the scope of this chapter to offer a comprehensive discussion of the next step: the marketing processes and capabilities a young company needs in order to pursue strong growth. However, two key areas for you to focus on are *understanding and listening to the customer* and *building a visible and enduring brand*.

Understanding and Listening to the Customer

Although intuition-based decision making can work well initially for some entrepreneurs, intuition has its limitations. Entrepreneurs must be in constant touch with their customers as they grow their companies. When a company decides to introduce its second product or open a new location, for example, it needs to be able to determine whether that product or location will be welcomed in the marketplace. Entrepreneurs with a successful first product or location often overestimate demand for the second, sometimes because their confidence encourages them to overrely on their own intuition.

Entrepreneurs must obtain information that will allow them to understand consumer buying behavior and customer expectations related to product design, pricing, and distribution. They also need information about the best way to communicate with customers and influence their actions. Finally, they need information about the *effectiveness* of their own marketing activities so they can continue to refine them. Marketers build relationships in part by using information to customize the marketing mix. Good entrepreneurial marketers do whatever it takes to build relationships with customers.

Entrepreneurs following a high-growth strategy need to continuously find new customer segments to support that growth. Bill Samuels, Jr., recognized that for Maker's Mark to grow significantly, the company would have to reach a new segment—drinkers of other types of alcohol—because the bourbon connoisseur market was near saturation. Rather than relying on his own intuition, Samuels studied the consumer market to understand where he would find his new customers and how he would attract them.

There are a number of ways to listen to customers; some require formal research, and others use informal systems for soliciting information and scanning the market environment. Leonard Berry cites a portfolio of methods that entrepreneurs can use to build a *listening system*.[12] These include:

- *Transactional surveys* to measure customer satisfaction with the company
- *New and lost customer surveys* to see why customers choose or leave the firm
- *Focus group interviews* to gain information on specific topics
- *Customer advisory panels* to get periodic feedback and advice from customers
- *Customer service reviews* to have periodic one-on-one assessments
- *Customer complaint/comment capture* to track and address customer complaints
- *Total market surveys* to assess the total market—customers and noncustomers

Building the Brand

All entrepreneurs face the need for **brand building**, which is the dual task of building brand awareness and building brand equity. **Brand awareness** is the customer's ability to recognize and recall the brand when provided a cue. Marketing practices that create brand awareness also help shape **brand image**, which is the way customers perceive the brand. **Brand equity** is the effect of brand awareness and brand image on customer response to the brand. It is brand equity, for example, that spurs consumers to pay a premium price for a brand—a price that exceeds the value of the product's tangible attributes.

Brand equity can be positive or negative. Positive brand equity is the degree of marketing advantage a brand would hold over an unnamed competitor. Negative brand equity is the disadvantage linked to a specific brand. Brand building is closely linked to a company's communications strategy. While brand awareness is created through sheer exposure to a brand—through advertising or publicity—brand image is shaped by how a company projects its identity through its products, communications, and employees. The customer's actual experience with the brand also has a strong effect on brand image.

Maker's Mark used its communications strategy, implemented through humorous, distinctive print advertising in sophisticated national magazines like *Forbes* and *Business Week*, to create a brand image that would help establish a high-end market for bourbon where none had existed in the past. The company created a likable, genuine brand personality for its bourbon. Because many of the advertisements were in the form of an open letter from Bill Samuels, Jr., to his customers, Samuels was able to represent and personalize the brand.

CONCLUSION

Marketing is often described as a delicate balance of art and science. Certainly developing the expertise to be a master marketer is difficult, especially for entrepreneurs who are constantly pulled in a thousand directions. Nevertheless, the task remains: to have customer knowledge and PR mastery and to recognize effective advertising as well as effective experiential promotion. Entrepreneurial marketers must, first and foremost, be able to sell: sell their ideas, their products, their passion, their company's long-term potential. And they must learn the skill of knowing where the market is going, now and into the future.

Early-stage companies often find it necessary to scale up or change focus. In these scenarios, competition can be a potent driver of marketing decisions, whether you are staying under the radar screen of giant companies or buying time against a clone invasion. But successful entrepreneurs will have a strong, focused marketing strategy—a consistent strategy—and therefore will not easily be thrown off course.

YOUR OPPORTUNITY JOURNAL

Reflection Point	Your Thoughts...
1. How do you learn about your customer?	
2. What secondary sources can you use?	
3. What primary data will you collect?	
4. How do you segment your market? Who's your PTA? Who are your STAs?	
5. How will you price your product?	
6. How will you distribute your product?	
7. What channels are available? Which channels are best? When will you add new channels?	
8. What is your marketing communications strategy? What mix of advertising, PR, personal selling, and direct marketing is most effective?	
9. What guerrilla tactics can you use to create a buzz? How will you get your product's buzz to be heard above the noise?	
10. Articulate what you would like your brand to be. How will you build it during launch? During growth?	

Scan the Web and identify the Internet marketing techniques of two to three companies. Start with the company's home page. What functionality does the page contain (just information, online selling interface, etc.)? Evaluate the home page's communications effectiveness. Next go to a search engine such as Google. What key search terms bring this company up on the first two or three pages? Does the company use paid Internet advertising? Affiliate programs? Are there any other unique aspects about the company's Internet strategy? How does what you've learned inform your Web strategy?

WEB EXERCISE

Appendix: Customer Interview

To whom should we ask the questions?
What possible information would we ask about?
Should the questions be open ended or structured?
How should the questions be sequenced?

General Outline: It Needs to Be Tailored to Meet Your Research Needs

1. Opening discussion (introduction and warm-up):

   Briefly describe research purpose, introduce self, ensure confidentiality of response, and state expected duration of the interview session.

   Opening statement: Think of the last time you purchased or used such a product. What prompted or triggered this activity? What specific activities did you perform to get the product or service? What was the outcome of your shopping experience?

2. Current practice:

   How do you currently purchase or use a product/service of interest? How did you go about deciding on what to buy? How frequently do you buy/use this product/service? How much do you buy/use each time? Where do you buy?

3. Familiarity/awareness about product/service:

   What other products/services/stores have you considered before deciding on the final product/service you bought?

4. Important attributes: If you were shopping for such a product, what would you look for? What is important? What characteristic(s) are important to you?

5. Perception of respondents:

   How would you compare different products/services? How well do you think of the product/service you bought compared with those of its competitors with respect to these attributes?

6. Overall satisfaction with or liking of the product/service: Ask satisfaction level and preference ranking among competitive products.

7. Product demo/introduction/description:

Purpose: Get reactions to the product concept and elicit a response that may identify additional decision drivers.

What do you like about this idea? What do you dislike? Does listening to this idea suggest some factors that you would consider important and that we have not discussed so far? Does it change the importance you attach to different factors before choosing a product or service?

Purpose: Determine the purchase intent of new product or service.

What will be the level of interest or willingness of respondents to buy or use this new product/service? At what price?

We would like to know how likely it is that you would buy such a product or service.

- ☐ Would definitely buy
- ☐ Would probably buy
- ☐ Might or might not buy
- ☐ Would probably not buy
- ☐ Would definitely not buy

We would like to know now how much you would be willing to pay for such a product or service:

- ☐ Would definitely pay $_____.

Please note that comparable products are priced at $_____. Now how much would you be willing to pay for such a product or service?

- ☐ Would definitely pay $_____.

8. Media habit:

How do you find out about a product or service?

What media do you read, listen to, or watch?

9. Demographic information:

Personal information should be asked at the end of the interview.

Age, income, occupation, gender, education, etc.

Size of the firm (revenue, total full-time staff, research and development staff), resources, experience, skills, etc.

10. Wrap-up:

Any final comments or ideas?

NOTES

1 American Marketing Association. 2004. www.marketingpower.com/content212 57.php.

2 Lodish, Leonard M., Morgan, Howard Lee, and Kallianpur, Amy. *Entrepreneurial*

Marketing. Hoboken, NJ: Wiley, 2001, p. xi.

3 Isaacson, Walter. 2011. *Steve Jobs*. New York: Simon and Schuster, p. 567.

4 Ibid., p. 143.

5 Ibid., p. 170.

6 www.macworld.com/article/1141509/jon athan_ive_london.html

7 Cadbury Does Yet Another Deal. *Beverage Digest*. Volume 41, Issue 1 May 2002.

8 Adapted from John A. Martilla and John C. James. Importance-Performance Analysis. *Journal of Marketing*, www.beverage-digest.com/editorial/020329 .php: 77–79. January 1977.

9 Seiders, Kathleen (1999), "Maker's Mark Bourbon" (case study and teaching note), Arthur M. Blank Center for Entrepreneurial Studies, Babson College.

10 Taylor, Catherine P. Psst! How Do You Measure Buzz? *AdWeek*, October 24, 2005.

11 Turner, Contractor to Pay $2M in Boston Bomb Scare. February 5, 2007. www.cnn .com/2007/US/02/05/boston.turner/ index.html.

12 Berry, Leonard L. *Discovering the Soul of Service*. New York, NY: Free Press. 1999. pp. 100–101.

CASE

Eu Yan Sang International, Ltd.

Singapore, 2009. Richard Eu was pleased with the progress of Eu Yan Sang (EYS), the 129-year-old company he served as Group CEO. Revenues had been growing by 10 to 20% annually since 2000, to S$208 million[*] for the fiscal year ending 30 June 2008, and each of the three major markets in which the company operated—Singapore, Hong Kong, and Malaysia—had contributed to that expansion.

As the leading retailer of traditional Chinese medicine (TCM) outside mainland China, the company owned more than 144 attractive retail stores, 21 TCM health clinics, and was experimenting with health spas in both Singapore and Kuala Lumpur, Malaysia.

Equally important, EYS had established indisputable quality leadership in its field. At a time when many herbal products and dietary supplements were found to be contaminated or subject of dosage variations, EYS's customers could be certain of quality, consistency, and safety. The power of its brand had been recognized in many ratings surveys, and, in 2008, the *Guangzhou Daily* included the company among its "Top 10 Favorite Brands" for the fourth consecutive year.

Mr. Eu could not, however, rest on the company's current success. His board wanted more growth. However, 10 to 20% annual growth would be difficult if not impossible to deliver within the confines of the company's core markets. The total populations of Hong Kong, Singapore, and Malaysia were approximately 38.6 million—7 million, 4.6 million, and 27 million respectively. EYS had to break into larger markets to achieve its growth goals. Although a foothold has been made in the Taiwan market (population 26 million), China and the United States were seen as likely targets. The company was already shipping products to both countries and had a small retail presence in China, but it had not yet developed strategic plans for exploiting either.

Expansion into China and the United States raised a number of questions. What customer, distribution, and regulatory challenges would have to be overcome in each country? Which of the company's product and marketing strengths, if any, would be applicable to those new markets? Should one market have priority over the other, or should they be attacked simultaneously? These were among the many questions that Richard Eu and his colleagues pondered.

The Company

Company founder Eu Kong left his home in southern China's Guangdong region in the 1870s to work in a small Malaysian tin mining town of Gopeng. Conditions there for laborers were dangerous and unhealthy, and many depended on opium to make their lives bearable. Eu Kong decided to use his knowledge of traditional Chinese remedies to improve the health of these miners. To that end he opened his first Chinese medicine shop in Gopeng in 1879, naming it "Yan Sang." In the Cantonese dialect, *Yan* means humane or kind,

[*]At the time this case was written, one Singapore dollar (S$) equaled 0.70 U.S. dollars (US$).

Richard Luecke, research assistant, prepared this case under the supervision of Professors Abdul Ali and Leslie Charm, Babson College, as a basis for class discussion rather than to illustrate either effective or ineffective handling of an administrative situation.

while *Sang* connotes birth, life, or livelihood. The company's current motto—"Caring for Mankind"--derives from this name.[1]

In 1890, Eu Kong passed the business on to his eldest son, Eu Tong Sen, who was active in both tin and rubber production. Eu Tong Sen expanded the TCM business in Malaysia and the surrounding region. Today, Eu Yan Sang is the leading provider of high-quality traditional Chinese medicine outside of China and was the first TCM company listed on the Singapore Exchange. Group CEO Richard Eu, who joined the business in 1989 after a successful career in merchant and investment banking, represents the fourth generation of family leadership. Today the company markets over 1,000 Chinese herbs and, under the Eu Yan Sang brand, 280 proprietary Chinese medicines. Beginning in 2007 it became the exclusive worldwide distributor for the Wisconsin (USA) Ginseng Cooperative, producer of what many believe to be the world's finest ginseng.

As described in company literature, EYS's vision is "To be a global consumer healthcare company with a focus in Traditional Chinese Medicine and Integrative Healthcare." Its stated mission is "To care for mankind by helping our consumers realized good life-long health."

Products

Traditional Chinese remedies have for centuries been sold in herb, root, leaf, and powdered form. Many of these take hours to prepare properly for use. Currently, the company offers over 280 product types, from raw herbs to manufactured remedies. In catering to the modern, convenience-oriented market, EYS had developed manufacturing methods for producing and packaging these remedies (and new ones) in ready-to-consume tablets, jellies, tea drinks, and elixirs. Exhibit 5.1 lists the company's best selling products and their revenues.

EXHIBIT 5.1	Key Eu Yan Sang Products	
		2008 Sales (S$millions)
Bo Ying Compound	Infant health	19.6
Bottled Bird's Nest	General health maintenance	19.5
Bak Foong Pills	Women's health	14.1
Lingzhi Cracked Spores Capsules	Immunity improvement	8.8
Essence of Chicken	General health maintenance	6.1
Total		68.1

In FY2008, these five leading products accounted for 33% of all company revenues. Eu Yan Sang's strategy is to diversify its product and revenue mix by launching nine to 12 new products each year. Typically, only two or three of these new products can be described as radically new. The rest are product line extensions: for example, Essence of Chicken enhanced with ginseng.

Revenue goals for these newly launched products are not specified in advance, and each is given a long time to prove itself in the market. Launches are not accompanied by major promotions, in part because of governmental restrictions on the advertising of health-related products. Instead, newly launched products are integrated into the product mix on store shelves. Store personnel highlight these new items by means of special displays and explain their health benefits to visiting customers. These efforts aim to generate word-of-mouth product awareness.

---

[1] Company Web site.

Products are packaged in a variety of quantities, depending on their intended uses. For example, Bottled Birds Nest represents 25 different SKUs. It is sold in individual 150 ml bottles, six-packs, and so forth. Prices range between S$40 and S$200 for these different quantities. Package quantities are also determined by whether the ingredients are in liquid or capsule form.

Traditional Chinese Medicine

The philosophy underlying traditional Chinese medicine (TCM) derives from the same bases that contributed to Taoism. That philosophy reflects the belief that the human body is composed of interlinking systems. Health is seen as dependent on balance within those systems. As described the University of Minnesota: "Traditional Chinese medicine focuses on achieving health and well-being through the *cultivation of harmony* within our lives. Harmony brings health, well-being, and sustainability. Disharmony leads to illness, disease, and collapse."[2]

TCM includes a number of practices originating in China, including diagnosis and treatments such as herbal medicine, dietary therapy, acupuncture, cupping, massage therapy, relaxation and meditation therapy, and physical exercises such as T'ai Chi Ch'uan.

Next to dietary therapy, herbal medicine of the type supplied by Eu Yan Sang is the most widely used mode of TCM treatment. Herbal medicine, usually formulated from two or more substances, is used both for the treatment and prevention of illness. There are thousands of traditional herbal formulas; TCM practitioners modify them to suit the subtle nuances of a patient's condition or state of health. Many are made in tea or soup form, or added to other foods.

Manufacturing

The company's products are processed and packaged in two Good Manufacturing Practice (GMP)–certified plants: one located in Hong Kong, and the other in Malaysia. The newly built, 130,000 square foot, state-of-the-art plant in Yuen Long, Hong Kong, was a S$21 million investment. That plant also houses facilities used for academic research and herbalist training.

RGtimeline/iStockphoto

2 "What Is Traditional Chinese Medicine?" University of Minnesota, Center for Spirituality and Healing, http://takingcharge.csh.umn.edu/therapies/tcm/what <accessed 5-19-2008.

Quality Assurance from Farm Fields to Consumers

Responding to worldwide concern over the quality and safety of food products originating in Asia, the company has taken major steps toward developing the highest product quality standards. In 2007, it began testing its herbs—an industry first. Using advanced analytical techniques, it obtained chromatographic "fingerprints" of over 500 essential TCM herbs. These fingerprints make it possible to eliminate the mistaken use of visually similar but biochemically different ingredients, a problem in the industry.

In March 2008, it announced the world's first program for certification of TCM herbs produced through the company's "good agronomic practices" (GAP) (Exhibit 5.2). The program extends through every step of the product cycle, from growing, to formulation and packaging, to shipping, to retailing. The aim is to ensure that high standards for safety and quality are maintained at *all* stages of the cycle. A proprietary software platform—iGates—was built to track all ingredients and all products through every step of the cycle (Exhibit 5.3). Agrifood Technologies of Singapore acts as a third-part observer in verifying quality compliance. "This is a giant step toward the future of TCM," according to a company press release:

> We believe that the EYSGAP-Herbs Certification will help to promote the global acceptance and trust of TCM products....As an industry leader, we are creating one recognizable quality standard specifically for TCM herbs. It adopts a scientific approach and uses advanced scientific methods of measurement and accuracy to ensure safety and traceability throughout the whole process. This is a world first and sets the path for how the TCM industry will operate in the future.[3]

EXHIBIT 5.2	EYSGAP Herb Certiæcation

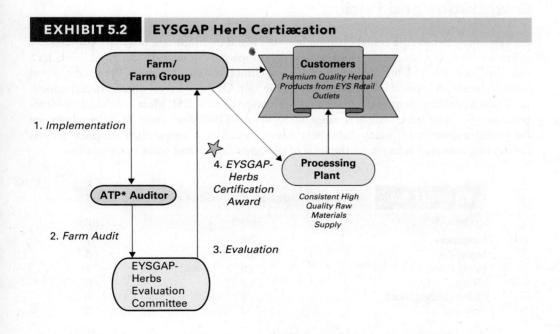

---

[3] Company press release, 31 March 2008. "Eu Yan Sang and Agrifood Technologies Launch of Eu Yan Sang Good Agronomic Practices for Herbs (EYSGAP-Herbs) Certification Scheme."

EXHIBIT 5.3 The iGATES integrated GAP-TCM System

Ensuring good quality raw
materials with full traceability
and food safety for herbs at
and from source

1. Good Herbal Production

Ensuring Accurate
Laboratory Testing
Results withChemical
& Genomic Profiling

**iGATES
[EYS-GAP
Certification
Scheme]**

**4. Good Distribution
Practice (GDP)**

Enabling traceability
of transported
finished goods

**2. Good Laboratory
Practice (GLP)**

3. Good Manufacturing Practice (GMP)

Assuring quality during
the manufacturing
process

Lingzhi was the first herb to obtain official certification under this quality regimen. The company's popular Wisconsin American Ginseng was the second.

Distribution and Pricing

Eu Yan Sang products are available throughout the world in drugstores, hospitals, convenience stores, health food stores, health clubs, and on the company's e-commerce site. In addition, EYS owns and operates 154 branded retail stores and clinics in Asia; the latter offer products and consultation with licensed TCM doctors (Exhibit 5.4). Of these several distribution channels, retail stores produce the majority of company revenues (Exhibit 5.5). Most individual customer purchases in these stores fall in a range of S$50 to S$100. And since TCM products are for health maintenance, many customers return monthly to renew their supplies. EYS is conducting customer research on the issue of customer loyalty and purchase frequency.

EXHIBIT 5.4	Retail Outlets and Clinics (as of late 2009)	
Country	Retail	Clinics
Singapore	38	17
Malaysia	64	3
Hong Kong	46	1
Macau	2	0
China (Guangzhou)	2	0
Taiwan	2	0

Source: Eu Yan Sang International, Ltd.

EXHIBIT 5.5	Revenue by distribution channel, FY2008, in S$ millions	
	Revenues	Change, 2007–2008
Retail	161.0	+16%
Wholesale	33.0	+17%
Clinics	13.7	+ 9%

Essentially all of the company's revenues come from three key geographic areas: Hong Kong, Singapore, and Malaysia (Exhibit 5.6).

EXHIBIT 5.6	Revenues by Key Geographic Region, FY2008, in S$ millions
Hong Kong	93.4
Singapore	60.2
Malaysia	49.2
All others	5.7

Source: Eu Yan Sang International, Ltd.

Owning to the higher quality of its ingredients and processing, EYS herbs and manufactured products have brand power and command a price premium over those offered by competitors. This price premium gives the company a gross margin of about 60%. Ironically, Chinese companies offer little competition for traditional Chinese medicine outside the borders of mainland China, with the result that EYS's competitors in its core markets are other Asian producers. Each of these competitors, however, confines its activities to a single country. Thus, for example, Hockhua is a retailing competitor in Singapore, but has no presence outside that country. It is simply a retailer and has no branded products of its own.

Marketing

EYS's marketing functions are handled by a lean corporate staff and small teams operating within each of three core geographically focused groups: Singapore, Hong Kong, and Malaysia. The corporate staff consists of a handful of people: Joanna Wong, Vice President of Brand Management and Corporate Communications, and her direct reports; a media relations specialist; and a brand manager. They routinely collaborate with the company's small product development team, particularly on matters relating to package design. At EYS, all packaging must conform with the brand image. The geographically focused marketing teams are also small, with two to three people (although the Malaysia team has four to six); each team handles advertising and promotion within its region and is accountable for sales results.

Marketing budgets vary year-to-year but are roughly 6% of annual sales (about S$12 million) and are allocated in roughly equal measures to corporate marketing and to each of the three core region teams. Corporate's focus tends to be on brand issues whereas the regional teams tend to concentrate on product promotion. The name "Eu Yan Sang" is the corporate name, the retail name, and the name that goes onto each product.

According to VP Joanna Wong, who joined the company in 2000 after a career as an independent advertising and promotion (A&P) consultant, EYS's A&P spending is opportunistically determined: "Marketing allocations to advertising and promotion are not determined by a strict formula, but by whatever is judged best for each product." She attributes the success of EYS's marketing campaigns to this flexible approach, which makes use of television, print media, "buy one, get one free" product promotions, and so forth. Television, however, tends to receive the larger share. Within that medium, the company makes frequent use of 30-minute health programs that highlight the benefits of particular EYS products.

Perhaps because of Joanna Wong's background in public relations, and the company's emphasis on marketing efficiency, television and print media promotion is supplemented with extensive publicity, which it generates internally and through an outside consultant. Publicity gives the company and its products low-cost exposure.

China

From its Singapore headquarters, Eu Yan Sang's leadership cannot ignore the revenue potential of its giant neighbor to the north. With that country's rising economic prosperity and population of 1.3 billion, vendors in almost every industry have been looking for ways to do business in China. For EYS, whose existence is based on traditional Chinese medicine, a Chinese presence seems natural. TCM is so much a part of mainland China's food and health culture that marketing efforts there, it believes, should encounter a receptive audience. But breaking into China will not be easy. As Richard Eu puts it, "In China, everything is difficult." Prominent among these difficulties is a paucity of market data on which to make business decisions. According to EYS management, the size of the Chinese TCM market as measured by purchasers, total sales, and every other important parameter is unknown. Even the numbers offered by trade associations are deemed unreliable.

The Regulation Hurdle

For health products manufactured outside China, the regulatory hurdle is challenging. Herbal and other TCM products sourced outside China must deal with the same registration process faced by pharmaceutical manufacturers. Applicants must also demonstrate that their products are *better* than equivalent domestically produced products. The registration process itself can take up to two and one-half years and cost millions. Once registered, these foreign-made products are subject to re-registration every few years; re-registration, however, takes only six months and is far less costly. In order to enter the country, EYS's products must go through this slow and expensive registration process.

As of mid-2009, two EYS products had been approved by the regulatory authority: Bo Yung Compound and Bak Foong Pills. Owing to their higher quality, these products sell at prices four to six times higher than those of equivalent Chinese products. "Our Bak Foong pills," says CEO Eu, "include 24 ingredients processed in a unique way. We use none of the short-cuts taken by state-run Chinese competitors." A bottle of EYS's Bak Foong pills, enough for three to four doses, generally retails for S$8 versus S$2.25 for a competing product.

Competition

EYS faces many domestic competitors within mainland China. Most are small, have no brand power, and offer products of unverified quality. However, larger vendors exist; chief among them are:

- Beijing's Tong Ren Tang Group, China's oldest (1669) and largest TCM producer. Its brand is well-known in China. Tong Ren Tang operates a chain of drugstores in China and has a system of worldwide distribution. According to the Economist Intelligence Unit, the company accounted in 2004 for an estimated 30% of Chinese herbal product sold in the UK (total 2004 UK market equals S$405 million). In October 2007, Tong Ren Tang and Greater China Corporation, a U.S. company, announced a partnership under the name Tong Ren Tang Wellness Corporation. According to a company press release, its goal is to "develop spa-like wellness centers that will provide treatments and products based upon China's famous Tong Ren Tang herbal medicines." In addition to a full line of herbal health products, these centers will offer customers acupuncture, massage, acupressure, Tuina, Tai-Chi, and other treatments.

- Sanjiu Medical and Pharmaceutical Company. One of China's largest pharmaceutical manufacturers, Sanjiu has many plantations around China where it raises herbs in conformance with government approved Good Agricultural Practices (GAP). The company has experienced several setbacks in investor confidence, beginning in 2001, when the China Securities Regulatory Commission found evidence of widespread misappropriation of assets. In 2005 it announced the sale of its chain of drug stores, and in 2007 the company was restructured through an investment by a major Chinese conglomerate.

Because of a current lack of transparencies in the Chinese business culture, the revenues and profitability of these and other competitors are undetermined. And, as noted earlier, the size of the Chinese TCM market is not specified with reliable statistics. Even data provided by TCM trade associations is suspect.

Options for Entering the Chinese Market

In 2009 two of EYS's flagship products were being sold through Chinese hospitals, some drugstores, one shopping mall store, and two retail counters. Other products, mostly fine herbs, were being imported as health foods, thus bypassing the regulatory process. Together, however, sales through these channels accounted for less than 4% of company revenues. To achieve meaningful market penetration, the company has concluded that it must pursue the retail channel.

How best to enter the retail channel is an unanswered question. The company's brand enjoys limited awareness in China, and the high price of EYS products means that it must target a relatively small but affluent segment of Chinese society. By its estimates, only 20 million (2%) of the 1,300 million Chinese fit EYS's target demographic profile: affluent individuals 35 years of age or older. The company has considered several market entry strategies:

- *Direct, door-to-door selling.* EYS had some discussions with Mary Kay China, which sells door-to-door in that country, but regulation has made door-to-store selling risky. The company also worries that its quality brand might be tarnished by door-to-door sales.

- *Corporate gift sales.* The gift-giving tradition is strong in China, both among individuals and corporations. Selling gift baskets of assorted EYS products through prestigious corporations would enhance the quality image of the brand and result in multi-product sales. This channel would require the hiring and training of corporate sales personnel in cities or regions populated by corporate headquarters.

- ▣ *Stand-alone stores.* EYS has extensive experience operating its own retail stores in Singapore, Hong Kong, and Malaysia. This option, however, would require high capital expenditures and an infrastructure of EYS personnel. The company worries that it lacks the brand visibility in China to support EYS branded stores. To test the feasibility, one store was opened in a Guangzhou shopping mall in 2009.

- ▣ *Stores within stores.* Following the model of cosmetic sales in the United States and elsewhere, the company envisions arrangements whereby it will have EYS sales counters, staffed by its own employees, located in upscale department stores in major Chinese cities. It estimates that 1,000 such counters would be capable of annually generating a total of S$21 million in five years. Two such counters were opened in 2009.

- ▣ *Stocking in leading retail stores.* Placement in leading retail stores seems an easy way to get a foot in the door, and as of spring 2008 EYS products were being carried by several leading retailers in China, including Watsons and Parkson.

- ▣ *Integrated health centers.* The company has experienced success in owning and operating integrated health centers in Malaysia and Singapore, and a new facility opened in Hong Kong in 2009. These centers are staffed by certified TCM doctors, who consult with patients, and by retail sales personnel who fill prescriptions and conduct transactions for other EYS products. The company acknowledges the difficulty of translating this business model to China, where it would have to compete with free Chinese medical service offered by the state. Also, recruiting certified doctors would be difficult since most TCM doctors pursue life-long careers with the national health service.

In July 2008 the company hired an individual to assess the challenge of entering China; it continued through the year to ponder the potential of each entry option.

Products

Because of the time and cost of product registrations in China, EYS anticipates that only a small number of products would be registered and introduced in the initial stage of any expansion strategy into China. One of these products would likely be Bottled Birds Nest, one of the company's highest revenue-producers. "Bottled Birds Nest is a much appreciated delicacy in China," says Joanna Wong, "but it is tedious to prepare in the traditional way. Our pre-prepared bottled version would give us a convenience advantage over local competitors."

Manufactured health supplements would also be considered for registration and introduction in China. Although competition is substantial within this product area, EYS's experience is that customers within China do not trust the safety and quality of domestically manufactured versions.

Pricing

EYS branded products are generally sold at premium prices in all markets where the company does business. That price premium is supported by empirical and customer-perceived measures of product quality. Further, EYS maintains price equity across markets. The company anticipates following the same pricing strategy in the China market.

Promotion

Will EYS promote its brand or its individual products? The company believes that it will have to do both upon entry into China, with decisions based on market conditions at the time. Because market entry would be limited initially to a small number of locations, local television, billboards, and public relations would be the favored avenues of promotion, with costs anticipated to be 10–11% of sales revenues during the early years (in contrast to the company's current 6% of revenues for promotion/advertising spending).

The United States

> For us, S$30 million to S$70 million within five years would represent a successful market entry. Anything less than S$7 million would be a failure. *CEO Richard Eu*

To EYS, the U.S. market also appears to hold great revenue potential. TCM is a practice that very few U.S. consumers embrace, and awareness of the EYS brand is nonexistent at the broad consumer level. Nevertheless, the number of individuals who fit the company's demographic profile—35 or older, affluent, health conscious—is much larger in the United States than in China. Also, there are fewer regulatory barriers to overcome.

EYS products are already selling in small volumes the United States, mostly through retail stores located in the country's many "Chinatowns." Those products are handled through two independent distributors: one on the east coast and one on the west coast. Current revenues from these U.S. distribution arrangements are described as "negligible" by the company.

The U.S. Market

Within the United States, TCM is a small category within the "dietary supplement" industry, which in 2007 was estimated to have annual sales of S$33,230 million (US$23,260 million) and projected growth of 6% each year through 2014, according to the *Nutrition Business Journal's* annual report.[4] Of that amount, approximately S$5,900 million was spent on herbals and botanicals. Chinese medical professionals are quick to point out that their treatments are completely different from dietary supplement herbs. As the American Chinese Medicine Association puts it, "ACMA treatments are professional medicine rather than dietary supplement herbs."[5] However, for regulatory purpose in the United States, they fall into the same category.

As defined by the Dietary Supplement Health and Education Act of 1994 (DSHEA), a dietary supplement is a product (other than tobacco) that is intended to supplement the diet; contains one or more dietary ingredients (including vitamins; minerals; herbs or other botanicals; amino acids; and other substances) or their constituents; is intended to be taken by mouth as a pill, capsule, tablet, or liquid; and is labeled on the front panel as being a dietary supplement.

The Food and Drug Administration (FDA), the U.S. governmental agency charged with regulating dietary supplements, indicates that there are more than 30,000 dietary supplement products on the market. These include (by the FDA's definition): vitamins, minerals, botanicals (i.e., herbals), sports nutrition supplements, weight management products, and specialty supplements. The most rapid growth is in botanicals such as echinacea (for colds and to improve immune system response), gingko biloba (for memory), ginseng (for male sexual

---

[4] As described in General Nutrition Corporation's 10K filing, 19 March 2009, 2.

[5] www.americanchinesemedicineassociation.org/Frequently_asked_questions.htm

performance),[6] garlic (for colds), and St. John's Wort (for depression), with sales of more than S$29 million each.

Estimates vary as to the number of Americans using dietary supplements. The Office of Dietary Supplements (part of the National Institute for Health) put the figure at 52% of the population in 2004 (with men at 47% and women at 56%) The Natural Products Association (NAP), a trade group, estimated in 2006 that 70% of the population used supplements. The NAP describes these consumers as being typically well-educated, both in general and about the products they're buying. The reasons for which they take supplements vary. A scientific study involving 2,500 Americans conducted in 2002 gave the reasons cited in Exhibit 5.7.

EXHIBIT 5.7	**Why Americans Take Dietary Supplements**
Herbals/Supplements	% of Responses
Health/good for you	16
Arthritis	7
Memory improvement	6
Energy	5
Immune booster	5
Joint	4
Supplement diet	4
Sleep aid	3
Prostate	3
Don't know/no reason specified	2
All others	45

Source: Kaufman DW, Kelly JP, Rosenberg L, et al. Recent patterns of medication use in the ambulatory adult population of the United States: the Slone survey. *Journal of the American Medical Association.* 2002; 287(3): 337-344.

Dietary supplements, per the *Nutrition Business Journal*, are distributed within the United States through many channels: retail health food stores such as GNC and New Chapter, mass-market stores such as CostCo and Trader Joe's (many of which have their own brands), mail order, multilevel marketing, and the Internet. One small California drug store chain, Pharmaca, uses a business model that integrates Western prescription medicines, health foods, and dietary supplements. Each of its stores has as small section dedicated to TCM products.

Expectations for future growth in the U.S. health food/dietary supplements industry are based on several demographic, healthcare, and lifestyle trends:

- *An increased focus on healthy living.* A study reported by *Nutrition Business Journal* found that 85% of Americans were engaged to some degree in health and wellness, up from 70% just a few years earlier.

- *Population aging.* According to the U.S. Census Bureau, the number of Americans 65 and older will increase by 56% between 2000 and 2020.

- *An increasing focus on fitness.* Spending by Americans on health clubs and exercise equipment continues to grow. Actual fitness in America, as measured by body mass (obesity), is bimodal, with the educated and affluent (EYS's target) being more fit and

---

[6] See http://thomasjmoore.com/pages/dietary_part2.html.

fitness conscious, and the less educated and less affluent being less fit and tending toward obesity.

Product Regulation

Generally, dietary supplement manufacturers do not need to register their products with regulators nor obtain approval before producing or selling their products in the United States. In the United States, the federal government regulates dietary supplements through the Food and Drug Administration (FDA). The enabling legislation is the Dietary Supplement Health and Education Act of 1994 (DSHEA). The FDA regulates supplements *as foods* rather than as drugs. It does not require purveyors of dietary supplement to prove the safety of their products in people, as it does with pharmaceuticals. Nor must a manufacturer prove the effectiveness of its product.

While a manufacturer may not make unverified claims of effectiveness, it can say that its product addresses a nutrient deficiency, or supports health in some way: e.g., "Supports prostate health," or "Omega-3 for heart health." If the manufacturer makes a claim, that claim must be followed by the statement "This statement has not been evaluated by the Food and Drug Administration. This product is not intended to diagnose, treat, cure, or prevent any disease."

Competition in the U.S Market

The U.S. TCM market, such as it is, has no dominant competitors. There are no established brands (including EYS), nor is there a regime of quality assurance. Dietary supplements in the United States have, in fact, often been found to be of poor quality, and TCM are equally suspect. For example, an NCCAM-funded study of ginseng products found that most contained less than half the amount of ginseng listed on their labels, and some contained contaminants. A similar study by the California Department of Health Services reported that 32% of the Asian patent medicines it tested contained pharmaceuticals or heavy metals not listed on the label.

Contamination and variability in the potency and quantities of active ingredients in dietary supplements has led the FDA to establish rules that require manufacturing, packaging, and labeling practices to ensure that a dietary supplement contains what it is labeled to contain and is not contaminated with harmful or undesirable substances.

TCM and American Consumers

Within urban China and neighboring regions such as Hong Kong and Singapore, TCM and Western medicine enjoy a collaborative relationship. Consumers see value in both. They use TCM to *maintain* health, but when health is imperiled—by a broken leg, for example—they are not reluctant to seek out Western medical procedures. The situation is much different in the West, where many if not most medical practitioners view TCM with skepticism—as unscientific, untested folk medicine. That skepticism in the medical community is slowly waning, and many medical schools now include classes on "alternative medicine" (including TCM) in their curricula. Empirical tests are also being conducted to assess the therapeutic efficacy of various herbs, acupuncture, and so forth. Western medicine is beginning to accept some of these practices as complementary or as alternative approaches to health and healing. Eu Yan Sang in encouraging these tests through participation with the Mayo Clinic.

As reported by the Harvard Medical School, the popularity of complementary and integrative medicine in the United States has increased dramatically in recent years. Other studies have documented that 42% of adults in the U.S. (82 million) routinely use complementary medical therapies to treat their most common medical conditions. In 1997, Americans made an estimated 629 million office visits to complementary therapy providers and spent an estimated S$38,300 million (US$27 billion) out-of-pocket on complementary care.[7]

Even though this segment of the population may be attracted to traditional Chinese medicine and its health benefits, EYS managers face two nagging questions:

1. Are U.S. consumers willing to pay for TCM products?
2. Given recent revelations about contaminated Chinese product imports, will American consumers be able to differentiate between those and EYS's high-quality products?

Chinese- and Asian-Americans: A Natural Constituency?

The company recognizes that it cannot expect broad market success in the United States without a substantial investment in consumer education about the benefits of TCM and how to practice it. However, the diverse U.S. population contains a large and growing segment of citizens and immigrants who are already familiar with and potentially friendly to TCM.

Roughly 3.6 million American are Chinese immigrants or of Chinese descent—1.2% of the total population. Their numbers are highly concentrated in some states and communities, making access to them through the retail channel practical. For example, the following large cities have Chinese American populations greater than 3%:

- San Francisco, California: 19.6% (152,620)
- Honolulu, Hawaii: 10.7% (39,600)
- Oakland, California: 8.0% (31,834)
- San Jose, California: 5.7% (51,109)
- Sacramento, California: 4.8% (19,425)
- New York, New York: 4.5% (361,531)
- Plano, Texas: 4.3% (10,750)
- Seattle, Washington: 3.4% (19,415)
- Boston, Massachusetts: 3.3% (19,638)

Many smaller communities *within* metro areas have Chinese American populations well over 20%. In California alone, these include:

- Monterey Park, California: 41.2% (24,758)
- San Marino, California: 40.6% (5,260)
- Arcadia, California: 34.0% (18,041)
- San Gabriel, California: 33.6% (13,376)
- East San Gabriel, California: 28.2% (4,096)
- Alhambra, California: 33.1% (28,437)
- Rosemead, California: 29.3% (15,678)

---

[7] News Release, Harvard Medical School Office of Public Affairs, Boston, Massachusetts, USA, July 11, 2000.

- ◉ Rowland Heights, California: 29.0% (14,057)
- ◉ Hacienda Heights, California: 22.4% (11,921)

Similar concentrations are found in other metro areas. Many of these same towns and cities are home to other Asian Americans. For instance, the city of Honolulu is about 11% Chinese American but 55% Asian American. Those concentrations are useful indicators of where the company's products would most likely enjoy initial success.

An undetermined percentage of the U.S. Chinese and Asian American population practices TCM to some degree. These people are described by the American Chinese Medicine Association as well-educated, open-minded, knowledgeable, aware of the side effects of pharmaceuticals, and believers in natural medicine.[8]

Options for U.S. Market Entry

The company is considering a number of entry points to the U.S. market, although none have been researched or planned in detail. These entry options include:

- ◉ *A chain of company-owned stores.* These stores would be patterned on the successful model used by EYS in Hong Kong, Singapore, and Malaysia, but modified for the U.S. market. CEO Richard Eu describes this model as the closest to his ideal. "I envision a GNC-style chain, perhaps integrated with Western health foods and supplements."

General Nutrition Centers, Inc. (GNC): An Industry Leader

GNC operates the world's largest nutrition retail store network. In 2009 it had:

- ◉ 2,614 company-owned stores in the United States and Puerto Rico
- ◉ 161 company-owned stores in Canada
- ◉ 954 domestic franchised stores
- ◉ 1,190 international franchised stores in 449 markets
- ◉ 1,712 GNC "store-within-a-store" under its strategic alliance with Rite Aid, a major U.S. drugstore chain

GNC's U.S. revenues from retail operations in FY2008 were US$1,219 million, or S$1,731 million. Slightly over 40% of those revenues came from the sale of vitamins, minerals, and health supplements, which include herbals.

Source: GNC 10K filing, 14 March 2009

- ◉ *Stores within stores.* Operate a special TCM section stocked with EYS products within high quality Western-style health food stores such as GNC or Pharmaca.
- ◉ *Distribute through upper-tier food stores.* The company cites the successful model provided by New Chapter, a Vermont producer of premium health supplements. That company's products are distributed. through quality-oriented retailers such as Whole Foods and Trader Joe's.

---

[8] "Frequently Asked Questions," American Chinese Medicine Association, www.americanchinesemedicineassociation.org/Frequently_asked_questions.htm (accessed 23 May 2007).

- *Expand current strategy of selling through "Chinatown" stores.* The company is current selling to stores that cater to Asian Americans through two distributors—one on each coast of the United States. It supports those sales with some TV and print advertising. Promotion decisions, however are controlled by the distributors.
- *Clinical services.* Company-owned clinics would offer acupuncture, or an "integrated model" of Western medicine and TCM. The company has substantial experience in managing and marketing this integrated model of TCM-based health service in Asia and Australia.

Products, Pricing, and Promotion

Since each of the market entry options is still in the thinking stage, issues such as pricing, positioning, distribution arrangements, promotion, brand-building, etc., remain largely unexplored. However, the company is inclined to follow the same premium pricing regime used in Asian markets. And because of the high cost anticipated in educating mainstream U.S. consumers on the benefits of TCM and EYS products, low-cost public relations would most likely be preferred over traditional advertising media.

Which Way Forward?

As a high-quality producer with a solid distribution base and brand recognition in its home territories, Eu Yan Sang is in a position that many product companies must surely envy. But it cannot rest on its past accomplishments. Management finds itself facing many strategic questions:

- Can it successfully leverage its current strengths to the untested markets of China and the United States?
- Given its limited resources, how should EYS prioritize its growth initiatives?
- What product, branding, pricing, and promotional strategies will make it successful in these very different markets?

U.S. Women's gymnastics celebrating its gold medal during the 2012 Olympics.

BUILDING THE FOUNDING TEAM

Despite the glowing tributes to superstar entrepreneurs that we all read about in the popular press, entrepreneurship is a team sport. Even Bill Gates, one of the richest men in the world, did not start Microsoft by himself. Instead, he and Paul Allen led a hardy team of bright young engineers to the semi-desert of Albuquerque in 1975 to develop the original microcomputer software, BASIC. The group included four programmers, a project manager, a production manager, a lead mathematician, a technical writer, and a bookkeeper. Despite their incredible intelligence and drive, Gates and Allen recognized that the company would never reach its potential with just the two of them.

Today, from its humble beginnings, Microsoft has become the leading software company in the world, with sales of almost $74 billion and 94,000 employees worldwide as of 2012.[1] Indeed, we could look at all the top companies in the world today and identify the team behind the lead entrepreneur, but the point is the same: Successfully launching a business requires support. Even if you are launching a small business, you'll quickly find that your potential to grow beyond a self-employment business requires a team, whether it's your spouse for moral support or a trusted advisor who mentors you through the growing pains you'll inevitably encounter. This chapter will look at the issues entrepreneurs face as they build their initial team and lead this group through the challenging launch process.

This chapter is written by Andrew Zacharakis.

Power of the Team

Teams provide multiple benefits. First and foremost, a team enables the entrepreneur to do more than he or she could accomplish alone. No matter how strong the entrepreneur, how many hours she puts into the business, or how many days a week she is willing to work, at some point a team becomes necessary to increase the capacity of the business. Babson College and the London Business School have been studying the impact of entrepreneurship on economies around the globe since 1999. One consistent finding is that businesses with growth aspirations plan on employing more than 20 people within the next five years.[2]

The size of your organization is also directly correlated to the amount of revenue your business can derive. For example, if you are launching a retailing business, your average sales per person will range from $50,600 per employee for a restaurant or bar to $468,800 per employee for a new car dealer.[3] So if you hope to grow a million-dollar business, you'll need to build up an organization capable of generating that kind of revenue. For a restaurant, that means you'll need 20-plus employees. Keep in mind that these figures are revenue and not profits. Thus, if you want $100,000 or more in profits each year, you'll likely need a much larger business. For a full-service restaurant, that has generated an annual average net income margin of 2.7%[4] before taxes over the last five years, you'd need sales of $3.7 million per year to pull out $100,000 in profits. Understanding these relationships going into your business will help you set goals and objectives for growing your company.

For growth, it's important to add employees who generate revenue. Too often, firms add support staff. While such employees can improve the effectiveness of the people they work for, their impact on revenue is often not large enough to pay for their salary, especially for the early-stage entrepreneurial company. Instead, hire a salesperson who will directly lead to new revenue. In the early years, it is critical to be focused on revenue-generating employees.

The power of the team extends beyond adding sales. Solo entrepreneurs suffer from a number of shortcomings, including a limited perspective, little moral support, and a small network. Research finds that teams have a higher chance of success due to an increased skill set,[5] an improved capacity for innovation,[6] and a higher social level of support,[7] among other factors.

Entrepreneurs benefit by hearing and evaluating suggestions from others about how to better define and shape their business concept. No matter how brilliant your idea is, it can be better. Solo entrepreneurs often fail to get feedback on their idea that could help them better match customer needs and thereby increase product demand. Remember, initially your concept is based upon your own perception of a customer need. Just because you are enthralled with the idea doesn't mean that it will generate widespread demand. Your team provides a good initial sounding board for ways to improve your idea. Granted, you can solicit this feedback from people outside your founding team (and you should), but you're likely to find that team members will provide more detailed suggestions because your success directly affects their own well-being. Moreover, your team members can help you evaluate the feedback you receive from outsiders. As we discussed in Chapter 3, your idea will continue to evolve during the entire entrepreneurial process, from pre-launch all the way through rapid growth. Getting different perspectives on the opportunity will help you come up with a more robust product or service.

Starting a business is hard work. You'll face a roller coaster of emotion as you achieve important milestones (your first sale) and hit unexpected pitfalls (your first unhappy customer). Unfortunately, most new ventures encounter far more pitfalls than milestones in the launch phase. It is all too easy to fold up and find regular employment when you hit a particularly tough problem. Having a team around you provides moral support. You're all in this together. You have a shared responsibility to work hard on each other's behalf because, if the business fails, it is not only you who needs to find alternative employment or opportunities but the rest of the team as well. Furthermore, a team means there are people you can confide in and share your frustrations with because they are facing them as well. The sympathetic ear enables you to let off steam and then refocus your attention on the problem at hand. Finally, it is more fun and rewarding to share the successes with a group of people who have been working toward the same goals. The power of a team is its shared vision of success.

Business is all about relationships. You need to establish relationships with suppliers, distributors, customers, investors, bankers, lawyers, accountants, and countless others. While well-networked individuals make better entrepreneurs, a team dramatically multiplies the size of even a good network. If you build your team wisely, you will gain access to a broader range of contacts that can help your business. This is often most evident in the fundraising phase. Early on, you will likely need to raise equity capital, and the bigger your team, the more contacts you have as you embark on finding that investment. At the very least, your team is a great source for co-investment. In the 2003 edition of the *Inc.* magazine list of the 500 fastest-growing firms, 17% of the entrepreneurs reported that co-founders were a source of seed financing. Even if the co-founders don't invest directly, they can tap their own friends and family for startup capital, as was the case at 10% of the companies on the 2003 *Inc.* listing.[8] Thus, the power of the team greatly enhances your network, which is the lifeblood of any business.

A team also rounds out the skill set needed to launch a business. Most lead entrepreneurs have a vision of the initial product, and many even have the skills necessary to build a prototype—as when a software engineer identifies a new video game opportunity. But it is almost impossible for one individual to possess all the skills necessary in the launch phase. For instance, a person with strong technical skills may lack the business know-how required to successfully introduce a new product to market, or a business guru may see a product need but lack the technical skill to build it. Even a business superstar is unlikely to possess all the business skills needed for long-term success. For example, a financial expert likely will need team members with marketing, sales, operations, and production experience, among others. The key is to understand your own strengths and weaknesses. Know what you know, and more importantly, know what you *don't* know. Once you have a strong sense of who you are, you can create a strategy to construct a powerful team. As you start to build up your team, identify the critical skills for success. Create job descriptions and a time line of when you need these people. Then work through your network to find the right candidates.

Where Do You Fit?

Just because the business is your idea doesn't mean you must be the CEO. Every entrepreneur needs to take a hard look at himself or herself and decide how to best contribute to the venture's success. Rob Kalin, founder and original CEO of Etsy.com, is a case in point. He took his concept of an online open craft fair that gave sellers personal storefronts to Union Square Ventures in November 2006. After raising $1M in Series A funding, Kalin began to scale Etsy by focusing on handmade and vintage items, as well as art and photography.[9] In November 2007, buyers spent $4.3 million by purchasing over 300,000 items for sale on the marketplace.[10] Etsy's rapid growth created the need for management with senior experience in large organizations. In 2008, Etsy hired Former NPR executive Maria Thomas as COO and Kalin quickly promoted her to CEO. Thomas grew Etsy into a profitable company and increased revenues sevenfold within two years.[11] In 2009, Thomas stepped down as CEO and returned the seat to Ex-CEO Rob Kalin. Was Kalin the right person to lead Etsy all along? The future would prove otherwise. In July 2011 Etsy's Board of Directors asked Chad Dickerson the company's CTO to take over the role of CEO.[12] Before joining Etsy, Dickerson served as Senior Director of Yahoo's in house startup incubator, Brickhouse & Advanced products team. Although Kalin's innovative nature nurtured and led the company's first few years of growth, Etsy's Board of Directors and investors felt the company's potential could best be reached by an experienced executive like Dickerson.

Granted, creating a new venture requires most people to develop new skills on the job, but you'll be encountering a plethora of new challenges in the launch process, and you need to understand your personal limits. Stubbornly keeping the CEO job could limit the potential of your venture and may even lead to its premature demise. So the question is, "How do you gauge what you already know and what you can comfortably grow into as your business evolves?"

The first thing to do is to update your resume. This document best captures your skill set to date. The key to revising and reviewing your resume is to do an *honest* and complete assessment of your demonstrated skills. This is not the time to exaggerate your accomplishments because the only person you're fooling is yourself. You need to understand how your skill set will help you achieve success.

A second thing to keep in mind as you update your resume is, "What do you really like to do and what do you dislike?" Too many product people fail as CEO because they don't like to sell. These entrepreneurs want to design a product—and then redesign it over and over until it is perfect. While there is definitely a place for this type of founder within a new venture, it's not in the CEO role, which is about selling your company to customers, investors, and vendors.

Even if you're still a student and have limited work experience, building your resume will help you examine what you have achieved. Do you see patterns in your resume that suggest some underlying strengths? Can you leverage these strengths as you try to launch a startup? Even if you are relatively young, recognize that many young entrepreneurs built companies large and small starting from their strengths. Mark Zuckerberg, for example, started the social-networking site Facebook in 2004 as a sophomore college student at Harvard University. He launched the company on his strengths: a passion for technology and computer programming, which was self-taught. He also started with some partners who added to and complemented his strengths. Co-founder and former Vice President of Engineering Dustin Moskovitz was his roommate at Harvard. Former Facebook Chief Technology Officer Adam D'Angelo was Zuckerberg's friend in high school, where they wrote software for the MP3 player Winamp that learned your personal music listening habits and then automatically created a custom playlist to meet your tastes. Other co-founders Chris Hughes and Eduardo Saverin helped in the early years to promote Facebook.[13] Although all were young, together they brought an understanding of technology and how young people like to connect and communicate with each other. As of October 2012, Facebook had over 1 billion members.[14]

Likewise, Babson MBA Pete Lescoe created Food Should Taste Good, Inc., in 2006 with the goal of making a unique new snack with great taste, real ingredients, and sophisticated flavor. Lescoe started from humble beginnings by creating multigrain and jalapeño chips in his tiny apartment kitchen in Waltham, MA. After months of revising recipes, calling stores and handing out samples, Lescoe finally made his first sale to a grocery store. Soon after, Food Should Taste Good won the Best New Product award at the Natural Products East Expo.[15] Sales began to grow and Lescoe started to create new innovative chip flavors such as olive, chocolate, sweet potato, and cinnamon. Focusing on the growing health concerns in the United States, Lescoe ensured that all chip varieties were gluten free, cholesterol free, and had zero grams trans fats. Plus, many varieties are certified vegan. Food Should Taste Good started to become a household name after being featured magazines like *Better Homes and Gardens*, *Good Housekeeping*, *Shape*, and *Women's Health*.[16] The brand's increased popularity did not go unnoticed; in February 2012 General Mills acquired Food Tastes Good for an undisclosed amount.[17] Lescoe's strengths lay in his ability to bootstrap the business, his persistent never-give-up sales attitude, and his ability to continually innovate new products that stay true to his vision.

Zuckerberg and Lescoe both started modestly and grew their businesses incrementally (at least in the beginning), which allowed them to develop their own skills in line with the growth of the business. Yet each of them had a key strength he could leverage in the early days, a platform from which he could launch his business. As you examine your resume, what key strength pops out at you? Is that strength a strong platform from which you can develop the skills necessary to be the company's CEO, or might you be better off taking another role, such as Rob Kalin did, and bring in a more seasoned leader? Can you sell, or are you better suited to another role? You can't build a successful team until you understand your strengths and the best place for you in the company today at its launch and in the future as it progresses through various stages of growth.

While most people are pretty good at identifying their own strengths, they often have trouble understanding their weaknesses. Peter Drucker, the management guru who published over 30 books and received the 2002 Presidential Medal of Freedom, suggested that we can all improve our own self-awareness by conducting feedback analysis.[18] His methodology is simple: Every time you make a major decision or take a significant action, record what you expect to happen. For instance, as you decide to take an entrepreneurship class, write down what you expect to learn and what grade you believe you will earn. Several months later, after an outcome has occurred, compare it to what you originally recorded. Are your expectations and your actual results similar? What's different, and why is it different? Drucker's exercise focuses you on performance and results so you can identify your strengths and work to improve them. Although this exercise and others can help you understand your own strengths, many times people who know you are better judges of you than you are.

Talk to those people in your sphere of influence, people who know you well and whom you respect. Talk to your parents, friends, bosses, employers, coaches, professors, and others who can gauge your capabilities. Ask them, "What do you see me doing? What are my strengths and how can these attributes translate into launching a successful venture? What areas do you think I need to work on, and how should I go about it?" It is also important to ask them about your weaknesses: "What characteristics might impede my success? How can I work to rectify them?" Understanding your weaknesses will help you devise a plan to overcome them, whether that be through self-improvement or by hiring the right people to compensate for your weaknesses.

When it comes to self-awareness, there are two types of people. First, there are those who are overly conscious of their own weaknesses; they are their own worst critics. This group may be reluctant to pursue a venture because they fear their own shortcomings will lead to failure. In contrast, the second group seems oblivious to their own weaknesses. While this group may be more likely to launch a business, they are also more likely to fail once they do so because they won't seek help or even recognize that they need help. It is important to strike the right balance between these two extremes. The key to doing so is to develop deep self-awareness.

In addition to self-reflection and feedback from friends and family, there is a wide array of psychological and personality tests available. Some classic examples are the Myers-Briggs Personality Type Indicator, the California Personality Inventory, and the Personal Interests, Attitudes and Values (PIAV) profile. These tests, which vary widely in cost, are designed to help individuals understand things like their underlying interests, motivations, and communication styles. They can provide valuable insights, but there are several important caveats to keep in mind when using them. First, always remember that no test, no matter how carefully designed and applied, can accurately predict an individual's likelihood for success in an entrepreneurial endeavor. Few things in life are as dynamic and unpredictable as an entrepreneurial environment, and for this reason, expect these tests only to give you a deeper understanding of your own strengths and weaknesses. Second, should you decide to take advantage of these resources, industry newsletter *HRfocus* strongly recommends that you have a trained professional administer and interpret the test for you and that you insist upon a test that has been statistically validated. This is a field with little regulation, and as a result, it is essential that you use assessments that have a proven track record.[19]

Finally, keep in mind that no single personality or demeanor is best suited for entrepreneurship. In fact, a study by *Inc.* magazine found that many of the most common assumptions about entrepreneurs were misleading or wholly inaccurate. For instance, a classic label applied to entrepreneurs is that of risk taker. In reality, the study found that CEOs of the *Inc.*

500 companies varied widely in their levels of risk tolerance. What many had in common, however, was an ability to work well under highly stressful conditions.[20] The lesson here is that entrepreneurs come in all shapes and sizes, and you need to be careful about letting common myths about entrepreneurs dissuade you from starting a business. Tests can't tell you whether you will be successful, but they can provide you with insights that you can use to help ensure your success.

The key thing to remember is that entrepreneurship is hard work. You will not become a millionaire overnight—or in five years. As Walter Kuemmerle notes, entrepreneurship requires patience.[21] As the Internet boom and bust taught us, it can be a mistake to grow too big too fast. It is cheaper to test the business model when a company is small and then shift strategies quickly to better adapt the model to the market reality.[22] This will take years, not months. So you need to ask yourself whether you have the patience to be an entrepreneur—this can be harder for the young and brash.

Once you understand who you are and what skill set you bring to the venture, the next step is to identify what other skills are necessary to successfully launch the business. Create a staffing plan that not only identifies key roles but also tells you when you need to fill those roles. Figure 6.1 provides an example, but staffing plans vary based on the type of company, stage of development, type of industry, and so on. Early on, you likely need only one or two other team members. At this stage, each team member needs to understand that early-stage companies are flat and nonhierarchical. It is more important to know what needs to be done than to worry about who should do it. Nonetheless, the roles for these members should be complementary, and each co-founder should also participate extensively in shaping the vision of the business. An ideal combination might have team members coming from different disciplines such as science and business. Or if they are in the same major field of study, they might have different functional specialties, such as finance and marketing or biology and microbiology. The co-founders will work together on the overall direction of the business, but it is also wise for them to identify and divide primary responsibilities. Many co-founders make the mistake of working on every task and decision together, which often leads to frustration and inefficiency. While everyone's input is valuable, consensus is often a deterrent to success. Someone needs to be in charge.

The sample staffing plan in Figure 6.1 is a working document that grows and evolves as the founding team achieves milestones and moves on to new tasks. The value in creating the staffing plan is that it helps you to anticipate where the company is going and to plan for those needs. Note that not all the positions are currently filled. It is wise in the launch stage to conserve resources, especially cash. Thus, the founders may take on some of the future roles as their skills permit. If, for example, the team needs a strong finance person with previous experience raising equity capital, it makes sense to start identifying that person early on but to delay bringing him or her onto the team until needed (which might be when the company raises a significant round of financing from angels or through a private placement). While we have found the staffing plan highlighted in Figure 6.1 to be useful, the Management Function Analysis Worksheet[23] is another useful staffing planning device.

Role	Primary Duties	Person Filling Role	When Needed
Product Development	Develop prototype	Lead entrepreneur	Now
Market Development	Customer research Channel development	Founder	Now
Finance	Raise outside capital	To be determined	Next month
Production	Identify manufacturing partners	To be determined	Three months from now

Figure 6.1

Staffing plan

How to Build a Powerful Team

Your staffing plan is the first step in building a powerful team. Your next challenge is to identify the individuals to fill the gaps. How do you identify the best candidates? The simple answer is to tap your personal network and the network of your advisors, but you'll want to go outside that network to broaden the pool of quality candidates. Work with your professors to make contacts with alumni. Search your college's alumni database to find people in the right industry and with the right kind of position. More often than not, alumni are willing to speak with current students. Even if the alumnus isn't willing or able to join your team, she may be able to recommend someone from her network. You should also check with your investors, accountant, lawyer, or other people affiliated with your efforts (if you have these people lined up already). Oftentimes, entrepreneurs will hire a lawyer or accountant earlier than they might need that individual just to tap into his or her network. Moreover, many law firms are willing to work for promising new ventures pro bono, at reduced rates, or for deferred compensation. Thus, it may make sense to hire your lawyer early in your launch process. The key to your success is continually building your network. This will help you meet challenges beyond filling out your team.

A natural place to find co-founders and other team members is your family and friends. A look at the *Inc.* 500 shows that 58% of entrepreneurs teamed up with a business associate, 22% with a personal friend, and 20% with their spouse or other family members.[24] Just remember that working with a close friend or family member can be a double-edged sword. On the plus side, you know these people well, so you have a strong sense of their work ethic and personal chemistry. This was definitely the case for Gilt Groupe co-founders, Alexandra Wilkis Wilson and Alexis Maybank. The two met in an undergrad Portuguese class while attending Harvard then decided to go to Harvard Business School together. After B-School, Wilkis Wilson started a career in luxury goods managing leather goods sales and planning for Louis Vuitton then overseeing operations of 15 BVLGARI North American stores.[25] May-

Alexandra Wilkis Wilson and Alexis Maybank, co-founders of Gilt Groupe

bank started her career as one of the early employees at eBay. After launching and running eBay Canada, she helped found eBay motors then moved on to General Manager and business Development Director for AOL's ecommerce businesses.[26] Living in New York, the friends shared a love for high fashion and sample sales. The two reconnected at a HBS mixer for new students and they found that their skills complemented each other's very well and their relationship added a level of trust that can only be found between friends. After securing Double Click co-founders Kevin P. Ryan and Dwight Merriman as early team members, they started Gilt Groupe—an online flash sale Web site featuring today's top designer labels. Gilt Groupe became wildly popular after being featured on the daytime talk show *The View* and in May 2011 was valued at $1 billion after it raised $138 million from investors, including Goldman Sachs Group and Softbank Group.[27] In April 2012, the duo released a book titled

By Invitation Only: How We Built Gilt and Changed the Way Millions Shop documenting their story to inspire entrepreneurship, especially in women.[28]

Another good source is working with family members. It can be difficult, because you are mixing a professional relationship with an already existing personal/familial relationship. John Earle, the founder of the $3.8-million apparel company Johnny Cupcakes has found a happy medium with his CFO/mom, "Momma Cupcakes." Lorraine Earle, a former office manager at a big Boston law firm, encouraged and bankrolled her son's business venture. In the early days of Johnny Cupcakes, she took on bookkeeping duties while John was the creative CEO. As the orders came piling in from the Internet, Lorraine's house became overrun with boxes of shirts.[30] With Johnny Cupcakes literally taking over her life at home, Lorraine decided to quit her job and become CFO of her son's company. First on her agenda was to locate a warehouse. As polar opposites, they operate under a system of checks and balances. Lorraine explains their business relationship, "He doesn't care about the money. He doesn't care about the bottom line. So I have to be extra diligent. I have to say "no" more than when he was a kid."[31] Similar dynamics occur when you hire friends. You need to relate to your friends in a different manner—a more professional manner—and this can stress the friendship. Recognizing the consequences of this new dynamic is the first step toward managing it, but there is more that you can do.

Before entering into a team relationship with family or friends (or anyone, for that matter), lay out as much as possible the previous accomplishments, industry profile, and years of experience that person has and the roles and responsibilities that person will fill in your organization going forward. Define decision and reporting responsibilities. We are not saying you need to have a highly formalized structure at an early stage of your venture's development, but you do need to clearly state expectations, tasks, and objectives. We have seen more teams self-destruct because of personal conflicts than because of lack of funding.

Although the circumstances surrounding the fallout between Facebook co-founders Mark Zuckerberg and Eduardo Saverin remain mysterious, Zuckerberg forced Saverin from the company. Saverin then sued Zuckerberg and Facebook.[32] The moral of the story is that founder conflict occurs and can escalate to the point of endangering the company. Setting expectations and responsibilities in advance of engaging in a relationship can help to mitigate damaging conflict.

It is not at all uncommon for friends to dive into starting a business before they have really considered how it could affect their relationship. An excellent example unfolds in the movie Startup.com. This outstanding documentary follows two close friends through the rise and fall of their company during the Internet boom and provides a dramatic example of how working together can affect the relationship of two lifelong friends. Although Kaleil Tuzman had to make the difficult and painful decision to fire his friend and co-founder, Tom Herman, the two were ultimately able to piece their friendship back together. This is just one example of the difficulties you may face. Again, the key is to have clear expectations of each other and understand that pitfalls will test your friendship.

Once you have identified the right co-founders or team members, there is still the hurdle of opportunity costs. The best candidates often are already employed in good jobs, frequently in the industry where you will be competing. That means at some point they will need to leave a well-paying job to join your venture, and most new businesses can't afford to pay market rates during the cash-strapped startup phase. In addition, there is much greater risk that a new business will fail, which compounds the personal opportunity costs that co-founders and early team members face. As the lead entrepreneur, you need to convince potential candidates that the job itself is intrinsically rewarding and growth oriented (team members get to do something they like and be part of creating something new and exciting) and that in the long run the financial payoff will be much greater. A young company offers potential team members opportunities to grow into higher management positions (and therefore higher deferred tax–advantaged pay) than might be possible at their current company and to have some ownership in the new venture (through either options or founder stock). These are both powerful tools for convincing talented candidates to take a risk with your company.

The more successful the targeted candidate, the harder it will be for you to successfully make these arguments; yet our research indicates that many people are willing and eager to jump into the entrepreneurial fray for the right opportunity. Make sure to present your best case. Sell candidates on the vision and back that up by showing them what you've accomplished to date, such as building and testing a prototype or securing outside financing.

Bootstrapping: Building the Team Based on Stage-of-Venture Life

Building your team requires resources, which are scarce in most nascent ventures. Co-founders must often live off their savings or their spouse's income during the early days, as it may be impossible to draw a salary. Recognizing that difficulty, you are likely to find that it is better to bootstrap your team build-out rather than putting everyone in place from day one. It's common for founders of smaller companies to stay at their current jobs and work on the business part-time at night and on weekends. Many companies are able to successfully develop prototypes or raise the first round of outside investment while the founders are still at their current job (although you should not continue working for a firm that you'll directly compete with).

Be careful, though, not to commingle activities. When you're at your current job, your attention should be focused on those duties that help your employer succeed. You should *not* use your employer's resources, like computers and copiers, without explicit permission. You should *not* expropriate intellectual property from your current employer to use in your new venture. And you most certainly should *not* solicit your employer's customers while you are still taking a paycheck from that employer. If you handle your startup well, you will often find that your current employer is supportive, especially if the business isn't directly competing with your proposed venture. Thus, you should notify your employer of your intentions as soon as possible.

Another means of earning a salary during the early days is to take a part-time job. While this may mean working as a waiter or for a temp agency, entrepreneurs will often consult in a related field until their main product or service is ready to go to market.

As a lead entrepreneur, you need to prepare for a diminished personal cash flow during the early years of your business, as you will often have to defer drawing a salary. Continuing to work for your current employer, building up a savings war chest, and delaying purchases of new cars or a house all contribute to sustaining you during the beginning. While painful, this frugality is often a small trade-off to pursue your dream, and if you are successful, you will likely receive a future payoff that will be well worth the initial risk and sacrifice.

Perhaps the most common means to protect your personal cash flow is to continue working in a full-time job during the early phases. The weekend and nighttime entrepreneur is common, but at some point you have to quit and work on your dream full time. For example, Ruthie Davis, founder of DAVIS by Ruthie Davis, an ultra-modern footwear company, continued to consult for Tommy Hilfiger where she had been Vice President of Marketing and Design for Women's Footwear. Ruthie's phenomenal success in launching "Tommy Girl Shoes" garnered the attention and support of the entrepreneur and founder Tommy Hilfiger. When Ruthie decided to launch her own firm, Tommy Hilfiger asked her to remain as a consultant for six months. This consulting agreement allowed Ruthie to maintain a salary, contacts and focus on building her brand.*

The trade-offs of this approach are clear. While you do maintain your personal income, every waking hour is devoted to either your regular job or your new venture. This dual-job strategy usually works only during the planning stages of your new venture—you can write a

---

* Presentation during 7th Annual Babson Forum on Entrepreneurship and Innovation, Babson College, Wellesley, MA. October 2, 2008.

business plan, build a prototype, and start to make some key vendor and customer contacts, but you likely can't launch the business while working full-time elsewhere.

In addition to the time constraints, there are other issues to consider. If you are being paid, that means your time and effort should go toward your current job. Make sure to work on the startup on your own time. There is also the potential for a lawsuit if your new business uses intellectual property developed on the company's time. Once you leave your full-time job, your previous company may feel like a jilted lover. Working to maintain a relationship with your former company is difficult—but not impossible. Follow the example of Ruthie Davis. She not only informed Tommy Hilfiger but also got his blessing to work on her business while continuing to consult for his. The risk of informing your current company, of course, is that you might be immediately terminated, but for the long term, it is better to be straight with those affected by your decision.

When you're bringing on team members, many of the same principles apply. Examine your staffing plan to assess when you need that individual on a part-time basis and when you need her on a full-time basis. If the person is critical to building your product, you'll need her sooner. If she will be your primary salesperson, you won't need her until you go to market. Accurately timing when different people join the team conserves company cash and helps the new hire manage her own personal finances. There are trade-offs, however. First, you need to plan ahead. It often takes four months or more to identify and hire key employees. Second, it is easy for a part-time worker to become disengaged from the startup. If your team member is still at his current job, that will likely take priority over your venture, especially if some special projects come up. Third, people who are already working on the startup full-time may resent that the other person isn't as heavily involved in the sweat and tears that characterize the venture. They may feel this person is getting a free ride. As the lead entrepreneur, you need to manage these perceptions and work to keep the part-time and future team members fully apprised of what is happening. Finally, until a person signs up, she is at greater risk of either changing her mind about joining the venture or walking away for another new opportunity. Understanding these risks will help you manage them and still preserve your cash flow. One way to handle these situations is to develop a compensation plan that excites your current and future team members.

Compensation

As resource constrained as new ventures are, you are likely hard-pressed to think about compensation for you and your team. At some point, however, you'll need to pay yourself and others in your organization. The more powerful your team members, the more compensation they will expect, whether that is in salary or in equity (but usually a combination). So how does a startup company determine what to pay its employees? How does it choose among wages, salary, bonuses, equity, or some combination of these options? The answers to these questions depend not only on the nature of your company but also on the nature of your team and employees.

Equity

There are several good reasons why most new ventures distribute equity to at least some of their employees. First, new companies often can't pay market rates for salary and wages. Equity can induce people to work for below-market rates with the expectation that at some point in the future they will be handsomely rewarded. As Lalitha Swart of Silicon Valley Bank put it, "People don't leave large corporations and take on risk without knowing there is an upside in stock."[33] Second, including some equity in the compensation package aligns the employee's interests with those of the company. Basically, the employees become owners, and their stock or options increase in value as the company prospers. Finally, the sense of ownership boosts morale, as employees perceive that everybody is in this together. This added camaraderie helps the team to stick together during the inevitable rough times in the early-launch phase. Of course, distributing equity throughout an organization isn't costless. It dilutes the founders' and investors' equity. You need to understand the trade-offs among motivating employees, conserving cash flow, and preserving your own equity. Understanding the trade-offs helps you develop a compensation plan.

There are two basic ways of distributing equity: founder shares and an option pool. As the name implies, **founder shares** are equity earned by founders of the company at the time it is officially established or when the first outside equity capital is invested (usually when it is first incorporated, although the shares may vest over time). Founder shares are most often given with no or minimal investment (maybe one cent per share) and are an acknowledgment of the "sweat equity" that the founders have invested in turning their idea into a company or of the track record and value of the founders. There are several considerations to keep in mind when granting founder shares. First, remember that granting shares to new parties dilutes your personal ownership, but this dilution is more than offset if you are granting shares to valuable co-founders who can help the company grow. For example, if you are opening a French restaurant and you have front-room experience as a maître d', it makes sense to co-found the restaurant with an accomplished French chef who can design and run the kitchen. It makes less sense to award founder shares to waiters, dishwashers, busboys, and other staff who are more transient and less central to the restaurant's competitive advantage. Founder shares should be reserved for those team members who are essential to turning the idea into reality.

How many people should get founder shares? It's a serious question. We advise entrepreneurs to keep this group small, usually no more than three people. Again, keep in mind the principle of preserving your equity by avoiding dilution. Once the founding team gets to be five or more, dilution can dramatically affect the capital appreciation that each founder receives, especially if the company needs to raise outside equity. Investors like to see founders with a significant stake in the company because "having skin in the game" focuses entrepreneurs on growing the company's future value rather than on maximizing current salaries. If, after a few rounds of outside investment, each of the founders has only 1% to 5% of the equity, they may start to recognize that no matter how big the company becomes, the long-term gain won't be sufficient to compensate them for all the hard work of getting the company to that point. Therefore, the founders might be more inclined to leave the new venture for greener pastures, and disruption in the leadership team is very difficult for emerging ventures to survive. The smaller the group of people who receive founder shares, the smaller this dilution problem. This is not to say that other team members should be precluded from equity participation, just that founder shares are not the best way to distribute equity to employees. Options are a better choice, and we'll touch on that topic shortly.

A third consideration regarding founder shares is how to divide them between the founders. Many first-time entrepreneurs fall into the trap of evenly dividing the shares among the founders. So if you have four founders, you might give each person 25% of the founder shares. A number of problems can arise from equal distribution. First and foremost, if each founder has an equal share, it can be hard to make important decisions because the group will want to have consensus. Even if one founder has been designated CEO, the others may perceive that their input needs to be given full consideration. At a minimum, this situation slows the decision-making process, but it can sometimes lead to disaster as the team stalls and becomes incapable of taking action. Another factor is that ambitious people tend to benchmark themselves against their peers. This means that a CEO will benchmark her compensation against that of other CEOs. If the founder shares are equally distributed, it is only a matter of time before the CEO recognizes that she is doing as much work as her peers but has less potential upside. This discrepancy acts as a disincentive to maintaining the level of commitment required by startups.

While there are no hard-and-fast rules for splitting founder stock, keep in mind these guiding principles centering on past contribution and expected future contribution. First, acknowledge the time and value of past contributions.[34] The entrepreneur who initiated the idea, started doing the leg work, and enticed co-founders to join deserves consideration for all of these efforts and also for her expected contribution going forward—maybe as much as 50% if the founder also continues in a major role as CEO or some other high-level manager. Second, the founder who is CEO should have most of the equity, often as much as 50% of the founder shares. Next, the founder who brings in the intellectual capital—say, a patent or invention—should have 20% to 30% of the founder shares. As you can see, it is difficult to put hard-and-fast rules on founder shares, because founders may assume multiple roles.

While these principles can guide the distribution, the final split comes down to a negotiation. Detail each founder's past and expected future contributions and the role he will assume in the organization and then divide the founders' stock accordingly. It can be useful to engage a lawyer with experience in this area. The lawyer can help you benchmark against other companies and offer outside validation that each founder is getting her due share.

Since you will want to minimize the distribution of founder shares, another way to reward other employees and future hires is through an option pool. An **option pool** is equity set aside for future distribution. Options basically give the holder the right to buy a share in the company at a below-market rate. The option price is often determined by the market price of the stock on the day the employee is hired (or in the case of a private company, the price at the last round of financing).

The principles we discussed about founder shares apply to options as well. An option pool will dilute the founders' equity—but to a much lower degree than broadening the number of people who receive founder shares. Granting options also helps align the employees' interests with those of the founders by making the employees partial owners of the company. Additionally, to exercise their options recipients must pay for the shares, which brings money into the company (although the amount is usually too small to be considered as a source of growth capital). During the Internet boom, companies liberally granted options. Unfortunately, as the boom turned to bust, many employees found their options "under water," meaning that the exercise price was greater than the current market price for the share. If options lose their value, they cease to be an incentive and retention tool. When this happens, employees are more likely to leave to seek new opportunities. However, if a company is growing, the value of the options should continue to grow, which increases the incentive and value for the employees.

Since granting options can mean giving up a significant piece of the organization, it is essential that owners know how to use these motivational tools effectively. The worst-case scenario is one in which the entrepreneur gives up equity in the company and receives little or none of the value that equity is supposed to create. Many rank-and-file employees have difficulty understanding exactly how they contribute to the value of the organization. Communicating with employees about the importance of their roles, and training everyone about how they can increase shareholder value, is essential.

According to the Beyster Institute, a nonprofit organization dedicated to improving the use of employee ownership, entrepreneurs can take several key steps to ensure that options improve organizational performance. First, employees need to fully understand the stock ownership program and how they will participate in it. Related to this point, employees should have a solid understanding of how the company is performing. Second, the staff must know how to measure company success and receive training on how to achieve it through their individual roles. Third, as we have mentioned, one of the great benefits of offering options is that it makes employees owners of the company and therefore encourages them to think like owners. However, the key here is that owners are typically more motivated to find solutions to problems or to develop innovations. An entrepreneur who offers options and doesn't harness or listen to this highly motivated workforce is failing to capitalize on the greatest benefit of offering ownership. Fourth, a stock ownership plan should offer employees a true opportunity to earn a financial reward. This potential for financial windfall is the key to stock-ownership plans.[35]

Once the company decides it wants to use options to motivate and reward employees, the question becomes how many options to issue and to whom. Research suggests that issuing options generates increased overall company value through gains in employee productivity and that this increased value offsets the dilution effect.[36] It is common for many technology firms to put aside 15% to 20% of their equity for employee options after a major investment round. From that pool, the company can decide to distribute options to all or just key employees. Don't make the mistake of distributing all the options to existing employees, but anticipate how many new hires you'll make over the coming years. Then you can come up with a distribution plan based on employee level. Higher-level employees—say, vice presidents and other upper-management employees—will get more options than lower-level employees. Keep in mind that you'll vest shares over an employee's tenure.

Although options are the most commonly used form of equity compensation, Financial Accounting Standards Board (FASB) regulations put into place in 2006 make them more expensive for both private and public companies. Specifically, companies must list options at fair-value as an expense on their income sheet rather than just as a footnote to their financials[37]. While it appears that the FASB rule hasn't dampened the use of options, there are other similar means to reward employees, including restricted stock, stock appreciation rights, and phantom stock.[38] **Restricted stock** is actual shares, rather than the option to buy shares, that are vested over time. The upside is that the expense is the current share price rather than the expected exercise price of an option. The downside is that the recipient gets the stock regardless of company performance, whereas employees exercise options only when the company's stock price increases. **Stock appreciation rights** accrue to employees only if the stock price increases (similar to options). Their advantage over options is that they tend to be lower cost to the company. Finally, **phantom stock** isn't really issued equity but a cash bonus paid to employees if the stock price appreciates over a set period of time. Phantom stocks are expensed over the vesting period, but they have the benefit of lowering dilution. The downside is that you'll need cash once the phantom stocks are exercised, and for a resource-constrained startup, cash is at a premium.

One of the main reasons to award options, founder stock, or one of the hybrids just mentioned is to keep key employees with the firm. However, what happens if you decide that someone needs to be fired due to poor performance, nonperformance, or any variety of other reasons? If it is a co-founder, that person likely has a sizable chunk of equity and any voting rights associated with it. That may mean the person can interfere with the operations of the business. An important means to protect you from an employee or co-founder who doesn't pan out as expected is to create a vesting schedule. **Vesting** basically means that people earn their shares or options over time, usually over four or more years. For example, if a co-founder is entitled to 25% of the company's shares, you may vest those shares in equal chunks over four years. That way if the person leaves or is fired in the first year, he walks away with only a quarter of the shares he would have been entitled to if he stayed. This maintains the unvested shares for distribution to future hires.

You can also structure an employment contract to permit the company to repurchase the employee's shares at cost, or some other predetermined rate, when she leaves or is dismissed from the company. You may negotiate a right of first refusal that gives the company or other existing shareholders the right to buy the equity of an ex-employee at the prevailing market rate. It is important for your employment agreement to state that the employee is an at-will employee, regardless of her ownership position in the company, in case you would need to fire that employee in the future. Failure to take this step can open your company up to the possibility of a minority shareholder lawsuit. To avoid lawsuits, you should define *fired for cause*, touching on what the company considers to be fraud, negligence, nonperformance, and so forth. Lawsuits aside, having a right of first refusal or the option to repurchase shares when the employee leaves preserves all the shares for redistribution among the remaining founders and employees. To avoid the time and energy of litigation, companies usually buy out fired co-founders after they reach a settlement.

The Dilution Effect: An Example

This hypothetical example shows what happens to an entrepreneur as her firm achieves various milestones/benchmarks of a successful launch and moves on to a harvest/liquidity event. To demonstrate dilution, assume valuations at different rounds (valuation is covered in detail in Chapter 10). The following are some typical milestones that a successful venture might reach.

Milestone Events

1. Entrepreneur entices technology partner to join her firm, gives him **40%** of the equity.
2. Raises **$200,000** in equity from family and friends. The idea is valued post-money at **$1.0 million**.
3. Idea is technically feasible. Needs to hire **software engineers** to build a working prototype. Raises **$1 million** from angels on a **$2.5 million** post-money valuation. Establishes a **15%** option pool to provide equity to current engineers as well as future hires.
4. Prototype looks promising and company successfully raises **$3 million** of venture capital on a **$7 million** post-money valuation to start sales. The venture capitalist imposes the following terms: Company needs to hire an experienced CEO, CFO, and VP of Sales, giving the three options worth **10%, 3%**, and **7%**.
5. Sales growth is on plan, and the firm needs to ramp up to meet increasing demand. Raises **$10 million** of additional venture capital on a **$30 million** post-money valuation.
6. Firm receives acquisition offer from a large company (e.g., Microsoft, Cisco) for **$100 million in the large company's stock**.

Note that while our entrepreneur is being diluted, the increasing value of her firm offsets this dilution.

This example highlights a successful venture. Founders who distribute equity wisely grow the value of their firm, which leads to a higher return for all involved, even as dilution occurs. However, student entrepreneurs often make the mistake of giving too much founder stock to too many different people. If, for example, the firm started with five student founders with equal ownership and still progressed through each step, the final harvest value for each founder would be $1 million. While this sum is attractive, keep in mind that this growth projection likely takes five or more years, and in the early years, the founders will be paid below-market salaries (and probably no salaries until the angel round).

Also, if there is any kind of problem that leads to a lower valuation than projected here, the final payoff for the founders is greatly impacted. If, for example, the valuation that the firm receives when the first venture capital comes in is only $5 million versus $7 million, the entrepreneur (as sole initial founder) earns a harvest value of $2.8 million. If there were five initial co-founders who get equal shares, each would earn a bit less than $600,000 for many years of hard work and below-market pay. The lesson is to distribute equity wisely. Make sure that all co-founders will contribute throughout the entire time it takes to build and harvest the company and that each can increase the value of the company.

Event	Entr. Share	Co-Founder	Family/ Friends	Angels	Option Pool	CEO	CFO	VP Sales	VC Rnd1	VC Rnd2	Total	Valuation (000)	Ent's. Value
1	60%	40%									100%		
2	48%	32%	20%								100%	$1,000	$480
3	22%	14%	9%	40%	15%				43%		100%	$2,500	$540
4	8%	5%	3%	15%	6%	10%	3%	7%	43%		100%	$7,000	$562
5	5%	4%	2%	10%	4%	7%	2%	5%	29%	32%	100%	$30,000	$1,605
6	5%	4%	2%	10%	4%	7%	2%	5%	29%	32%	100%	$100,000	$5,349
Harvest Value for All Stakeholders	$5,349	$3,566	$2,229	$9,905	$3,714	$6,667	$2,000	$4,667	$28,571	$33,332			

Salary

Although equity can compensate for a below-market salary, most of your team will need at least a subsistence salary during the launch phase. The difficulty is trying to set that initial salary. You can start by researching the current market rate for the position you are trying to fill at online resources such as www.salary.com. The Web site provides general parameters for the position and then allows you to personalize your search by company size, industry, and other factors. For instance, an information technology director might earn anywhere from $155,000 to $208,000 in the Boston metropolitan area.[39] The person's salary would be adjusted by her previous work experience, the industry focus of your company, and other mitigating factors specific to the individual or your company. You can also double-check your market figure by looking at some of the Internet job sites like www.linkedin.com, www.monster.com and www.careerbuilder.com.[40] A scan of these sites found that a chief information technology officer position pays anywhere from $206,000 and $324,000.[41] The market rate is a reference parameter, and you'll adjust it by considering the person's expertise and perceived contribution to the company. A younger, less experienced co-founder will earn well below the market rate. A more senior, experienced co-founder with a long record of success might earn close to or above the market rate, but paying the market rate is probably impossible for a startup.

Once you know the market rate, you can negotiate a current salary and expected increases based on your company's improving cash flow. For instance, you might tie an increase to closing the next round of funding. Other increases might be linked to increasing cash flow due to improved sales. Instead of making firm commitments to future salary increases, consider using performance-based bonuses in the early years. This further aligns the team's efforts with the venture's overall goals and preserves cash flow. If team members successfully execute, the venture should have increasing sales, which in turn can lead to rapid growth in bonuses and other profit sharing. The key is to be creative and motivate your team to work toward common goals. That means deferred current income (lower salaries), with the promise of larger returns in the future (bonuses, appreciation of equity, and options).

Although startups should negotiate below-market salaries, it can be helpful to understand the implications of a fully loaded business model. When constructing your pro-forma financials, see what happens to your expected profitability if you paid everyone their market rates. All too often, entrepreneurs launch into a business expecting attractive profit margins only to realize that these margins are a mirage; once people are paid according to the market rate (say, in the fifth year), the profits disappear. Some entrepreneurs choose to promise market rates but defer payment until cash flow improves. In this case, they are creating a deferred liability that obligates the company to make up for the lower-than-market salary in the future. This means the market-rate salary is reflected in the income statement, the actual pay is shown on the cash flow, and the remainder appears on the balance sheet as a deferred liability. However you decide to compensate your team, be cognizant of the full range of possibilities, and keep in mind that you need to preserve cash flow in the early years to fund growth.

Other Compensation Considerations

In addition to equity and salary, as the owner of a company you will need to think through a number of other issues in overall compensation. You will be competing with companies of all shapes and sizes for the most skilled people in the workforce. Putting together a competitive compensation package means thinking beyond just the monetary side of compensation. For instance, while they may not be feasible in the earliest parts of the startup phase, as quickly as possible you will want to consider things like health and dental plans and retirement savings programs like 401(k)s. Even from the start, you will need to figure out a holiday and vacation package that makes sense for your company.

Every organization is different, and it's important to align your benefits package with the types of people you intend to hire. If your business will rely on recent college graduates, something like company-sponsored life insurance will probably be unnecessary. However, if your staff will be older, married people who have families, life insurance and a solid family healthcare plan will be essential. The key is that all of these benefits are strategic in nature. Your goal in developing a compensation package is to attract and motivate the best talent in the most cost-effective way possible. You should never underestimate the effect that a thoughtful benefits plan can have on employee satisfaction and loyalty. There are few things as powerful as having a workforce that feels they work for a great company.

External Team Members

Although your core team is critical to your venture's success, you will leverage the team's efforts by building a strong **virtual team**—that is, all those who have a vested interest in your success, including professionals you contract for special needs, such as lawyers, accountants, and consultants. It also includes those who have invested in your business, especially if they have valuable expertise. For instance, you'll be well served if you secure angel investors who are successful entrepreneurs in your industry. You may also be able to gain help from those who haven't financially invested in your firm but are interested in helping new businesses succeed, perhaps by serving on advisory boards for new companies. Finally, at some point you'll likely pull together a board of directors, which is required by law if you are incorporated. Let's examine each of these outside team members in more detail.

Outside Investors

When you are considering bringing on outside investors, whether in the form of angel investors or venture capitalists, never underestimate the value these team members can bring with their experience and wisdom. For many angel investors in particular, the experience of working with a startup is as much about the satisfaction of mentoring a young entrepreneur as it is about financial gain. Take, for example, the story of Norm Brodsky, the long-time entrepreneur and contributor to *Inc.* magazine. In describing his decision to invest in David Schneider's New York City restaurant, he said, "Yes, making money is important. I wouldn't go into a deal unless I thought I could get my capital back and earn a good return. But I don't really do this type of investing for the money anymore. I'm more interested in helping people get started in business. Whatever I make is a bonus on top of the fun I have being a part of it and the satisfaction I get from helping people like David succeed."

For an aspiring entrepreneur, finding an investor with that kind of an attitude is invaluable. As David Schneider put it, "I really liked the idea of having somebody I could go to who cared about this place as a business . . . . It's like he's always pushing people to better themselves. He wants you to move on, to expand, to grow."[42] In business, experience is the greatest competitive advantage, and an investor can bring that asset to a fledgling company. But Schneider's comments also point to another key benefit of having a strong investor on your side: You'll have someone to hold you accountable and keep you focused. Many entrepreneurs underestimate the challenge being your own boss can pose. When the going gets tough or decisions get complicated, it can be incredibly helpful to have someone prodding you forward. For all these reasons, choose carefully if you decide to raise capital through angel investors.

Lawyers

Every new venture will require legal advice. Although you may be able to incorporate on your own, other aspects of your venture will benefit from your attorney's guidance. As discussed earlier, your lawyer can draft an appropriate template for employee contracts. If your business is developing some intellectual property, you may wish to file a patent. The right attorney can help you search existing patents and decide which elements of your intellectual property are patentable. She will devise a suite of patents and then, if you deem it appropriate, help you patent your product in several important countries. Lawyers can also consult on the myriad of unforeseen issues that are likely to arise, which is why it is so essential to choose your attorney carefully.

When making a decision to hire a lawyer, consider several factors. For instance, a smaller firm is likely to offer lower billing rates, a factor that can be very important to a startup. However, small firms are often heavily dependent on a small handful of clients who make up the bulk of their business. For this reason, you may find that your company is a low priority for a small firm with several key accounts. In contrast, while a large firm may bill at a higher rate, it will almost always have someone available to answer your questions, and it will also offer the benefit of a large pool of lawyers with diverse areas of expertise to draw from. Since your legal issues may cover everything from employment law to intellectual property, a large firm isn't necessarily a bad choice. While you may pay more, you may also find that a larger firm is more willing or able to set up a flexible payment plan.

In addition, when choosing your lawyer, it is essential that you find someone whom you like, who shows an appreciation for and interest in your company, and, most importantly, who has deep knowledge of your industry. The last thing you want is to be paying several hundred dollars an hour to talk with someone who is distant or aloof. And as for hourly rates, yes, you should expect to pay a minimum of $150/hour—and likely much more than that. For this reason, it is critical that you do as much preparation and research as possible before you sit down with your attorney. Most firms bill in increments of as little as 10 minutes, so you need to use your time with an attorney as effectively and efficiently as possible. Also keep in mind that, while it is important to have a lawyer from the beginning to ensure that you avoid many of the classic mistakes, there is also a wide variety of free resources available to small businesses. These include everything from online templates for standard agreements and forms to nonprofit- and government-sponsored law centers that can provide low-cost or pro-bono advice. While you should always turn to your lawyer for the final word, you can save your company a lot of money by using the available resources to get some of the legwork out of the way. Just remember that, as your company grows, your time will become more valuable, and at some point, spending hours doing your own research becomes counterproductive.

When John Earle first started his apparel company, Johnny Cupcakes , intellectual property was the least of his worries, but as his brand grew in popularity, counterfeiting and piracy become rampant. In an effort to bootstrap the company, CFO, John's mother Lorraine, a former law office manager, used her knowledge of the law to write cease-and-desist letters to over 200 counterfeiters. Lorraine used her legal connections to cost-effectively trademark the Johnny Cupcakes logo and copyright designs. Lorraine explained, "People steal our name, our logo, our designs. In some countries, they're actually opening Johnny Cupcakes stores and selling our stuff."[43] Lorraine was able to use her past experience to save thousands of dollars on lawyer fees by doing the work herself and educating her son on legal matters during the process.

Accountants

It's often wise to hire an accountant to handle tax filings in the early years because you're likely to be too busy to do it yourself and too small to have an in-house person, such as a controller or CFO, to manage the process for you. Many of the same caveats about working with lawyers apply to accountants, although you may be well served by an accountant who is a sole proprietor. The nature of accountants' work is somewhat different from that of lawyers, and for this reason, you needn't work with a larger firm in your early years. Don't forget that an accountant is a trained business professional; beyond filing tax returns and keeping your filings up to date, an accountant can help you analyze the strengths and weaknesses of your company's financial performance. He may be able to help you find ways to improve cash flow, strengthen margins, and identify tax benefits that can save you money down the road. Furthermore, both lawyers and accountants represent another spoke in your network, as both groups frequently have a long list of business and professional contacts. These can include everything from potential partners and customers to angel investor networks and venture capital firms.

Board of Advisors

A board of advisors can be extremely beneficial to the early-stage company. Unlike a board of directors, a board of advisors has no fiduciary duty to shareholders. Instead, the goal is to offer a source of expert guidance and feedback to the lead entrepreneur. In choosing a board, you should look to enlist people with expertise in your field and a sincere interest in mentoring an emerging business. Good sources are your professors, current and former entrepreneurs, professional investors such as venture capitalists and angels, suppliers for your firm, and individuals who may have insight into your target customers. Beyond advice, this group can expand your personal network and provide leads to new customers or investors. In fact, board of advisor members will often become investors if your firm goes through a private placement.

One final note on boards of advisors relates to communication. Many first-time entrepreneurs struggle to strike the right balance between too much and too little communication. Keep in mind that, if you have developed a board of powerful advisors, they are busy individuals. Don't e-mail or phone them every time you have a question. Instead, accumulate questions and think about which ones are most critical to your firm and where the advisor can add the most value. Do some preliminary legwork to find alternative answers to these questions and options you might be inclined to pursue. If you are prepared, you will have a more productive conversation with your advisors, and they will be even more supportive of your future efforts.

The flip side to overcommunicating with advisors is touching base with them rarely—or only when you want help raising money. This type of communication suggests the entrepreneur is interested only in the advisor's network, but the advisor is less inclined to open up that network unless he has a strong understanding of the company's progress. Produce a monthly or bimonthly email newsletter that keeps all your important stakeholders, including your board of advisors, informed about the company's progress. This newsletter should be short and concise so that it will get read. More often than not, the newsletter will prompt an advisor to contact you with some useful input or connection to someone in her network. Properly managing your board of advisors will pay dividends, so don't neglect it.

Board of Directors

When incorporating a company, entrepreneurs must establish a board of directors whose purpose is to represent the interests of the equity holders. Thus, when you initially incorporate, the only shareholders might be you and your co-founders. Once you seek outside financing, it becomes important to fill out the board beyond the co-founders. Venture capitalists and more sophisticated angels often require representation on the board. A common board structure for the early-stage firm is five board members; these might include two insiders like the CEO and CFO, two members from the lead investors, and one outsider, who most often is selected with strong input from the investors. The outsider is often a person who has significant vertical market expertise and who can add value to the strategic operating decisions.

The board is in charge of governance and represents the shareholders. It meets quarterly to review the company's progress and its strategy going forward. The board will determine compensation for the company's officers and also oversee financial reporting. With the passage of the Sarbanes-Oxley Act, the responsibilities and potential liability of the board have greatly increased. While the legislation applies only to public companies, more and more small businesses are finding it necessary to align with the act if they hope one day to sell to a public company or go public themselves. It's a voluntary choice to do so, but the act's standards are rapidly becoming the "best practices" for accounting and financial control at well-managed companies. This means that developing a clear set of expectations, ethical standards, and procedures for board members is essential. Furthermore, you'll want to ensure that your board has at least one or two members who can be considered independent, which means that they are not susceptible to potential conflicts of interest. Board members should be encouraged to act in the best interest of all the shareholders, not just the principal owner.

We believe the entrepreneurial team should extend beyond the co-founders and early employees to include external individuals who can provide invaluable wisdom and input. Entrepreneurship is truly a team sport—the stronger your team, the stronger your bench, the more likely you'll not only survive but also thrive. The next section looks at some difficulties you might incur once the team is in place.

Keeping the Team Together

We've looked at the value of a well-functioning team. But not every team functions well, even if it's filled with superstars. Consider the Boston Red Sox, which had Major League Baseball's third highest payroll ($173 million) in 2012.[44] The team finished in last place in the American League East Division despite having all-star David Ortiz and power players such as Adrian Gonzalez, Josh Beckett, John Lackey, Kevin Youkilis, Dustin Pedroia, and Jacoby Ellsbury[45] Why has this happened? Common sense dictates that the team with the best talent should win, but a dysfunctional team often fails. The key here is chemistry: Sometimes the whole really is greater than the sum of the parts. Consider the Oakland A's of Major League Baseball. Although as of the writing of this book they have not won the World Series since 1989, they have consistently achieved a winning record despite having one of the lowest payrolls in the major leagues. In 2012, the Oakland A's had the second-best record (94-68) in the American League, and yet they spent 28% of what the winning New York Yankees spent on payroll.[46] The A's general manager, Billy Beane, argues that a manager can put together a winning combination as long as he understands the gaps in his team, works to fill those gaps, and focuses on finding players who match the team's culture and work ethic. While we're not advocating the statistical construction of teams, we do believe that understanding and effectively directing your team toward its ultimate goal can make all the difference in the world.

You can hardly overestimate the importance of culture and fit. The key to building and growing a successful team is establishing a company culture and working to bring in team members who subscribe to that culture. Culture starts at day one in any new venture and evolves from the way the founders interact among themselves and with other early employees. Picture culture as analogous to duck imprinting. When a duckling is born, she follows the first thing she sees, which is usually her mother. Likewise, when a person joins a company, she quickly acculturates to the environment she is in—or leaves shortly thereafter.

Once established, a company culture is incredibly difficult to change. So decide what type of culture you want, and then work to create it. Company culture is an enigmatic and amorphous thing, and the ways in which it affects organizational performance are not completely understood. It often filters down from the very top of the company, and thus it reflects the values and skills of the CEO and other leaders. If you want a company with an open, trusting environment, then you need to foster an open and trusting relationship with your direct reports. If you lead with fear and intimidation, this approach will filter its way down to all levels of your organization. The bottom line is that you need to think through the culture you want to create, decide on one you are comfortable with, and work daily to communicate the values behind that culture. The most successful cultures are those rooted in core values and beliefs that are a part of the company's mission, vision, and mantra.

Keep in mind that not everyone will fit the culture of your company. For many first-time entrepreneurs, this represents a source of frustration and internal conflict, but it shouldn't. There are people who like buttoned-up, conservative work environments and people who like laid-back, laissez-faire workplaces. One person's "unprofessional" atmosphere makes another person's ideal company. Don't fight this, but do recognize the culture you are trying to create and seek to hire people who will feel comfortable in it.

As a company grows, it's common for the culture to evolve. The classic example is the loosely organized startup culture where the pace of work is relentless, and as a result, a lot of misgivings are overlooked. Nine times out of 10, this culture will evolve toward a more structured "corporate" culture as the company gets bigger, and the chaos that was so critical to the early stage will begin to erode the company's success. Every startup will see certain elements of its culture evolve and certain elements stay the same year after year. The most important point is to make the change deliberate and recognize the long-term commitment needed to instill it.

Even if a venture has a strong culture, problems with the team are inevitable. Just as the best cure is prevention, the best way to keep your team functioning well is to avoid some of the common pitfalls. We will take a look at some of the problems that most new-venture teams face and then examine ways to avoid them.

Burnout

We've all heard the stories of startups during which the team ate and slept in the office for weeks at a time. A diet of pizza and Red Bull is synonymous with the crazed hours of the classic launch phase. The atmosphere is relaxed but energized, and the people are highly motivated by the fast-paced environment and the thrill of being on the cutting edge of an emerging technology.

While this approach works for many early-stage ventures, it's not for everyone, and it has its drawbacks. On top of the long hours, there's the uncertainty that your product will work as intended or that the market will respond to the product or service as you hoped. Every minor misstep seems to take on epic importance and increases the stress levels of your team. Moreover, your team members will notice that the balance between personal and professional life is out of whack, and they may start questioning whether this sustained effort is worth it. As these pressures increase, the risk of losing a critical team member mounts. It's important to manage and relieve these stresses as much as possible.

As the lead entrepreneur, you need to act as the coach of the team and keep the members focused on the end goal. This means that communication is critically important. Although email is the standard business communication form these days, in the startup phase, you should make a point of having daily face-to-face communication with every team member. Listen to each of them—not only about the progress of their assignments, but also about the stresses they may be feeling. Present them with regular updates on the overall progress of the venture and give them realistic progress reports on how things are going. It is far more damaging to withhold negative information they will ultimately discover for themselves. If they understand that the venture is falling behind schedule or that the product isn't functioning quite as planned, they can be energized to correct these problems.

New ventures also have planned stress-relieving activities, or bonding experiences, such as the Friday happy hour or the lunchtime basketball game. Get away from your workspace and share some downtime with each other. The upside of these extracurricular activities is the strong bonds it helps the team build. A startup can be like your college days, where you'll make some of your lifelong friends. Many new ventures also have stress relievers right in the workplace, such as foosball tables, dartboards, and other distractions so that individuals can break from their work for a few minutes and clear their minds. It's often a good idea to provide free soda, coffee, and snacks as well. These little perks are cost effective and build goodwill and camaraderie. Relieving stress will help keep your team strong and cohesive.

Family Pressure

If working long hours stresses your team members, it also stresses their families. Spouses and significant others complain to their partners about their never being home or their being too tired to pay attention to their families. Missing a child's ball games and school performances can create resentment. Stress at home can negatively affect performance and increase the risk of turnover. If spouses continually ask why their partners have left good-paying jobs for lower pay and the promise of a future payoff, your team members will question their own motives. So it's imperative that open communication occur on the home front as well.

Counsel your team members to set the expectations of their families even before they join your team. If a spouse is forewarned of the long hours, it minimizes the angst. It's also a good idea to include families in stress-relieving events on a regular basis. Company picnics are a nice way for spouses to connect with other spouses. In this way, they can develop an informal support group with people who are facing the same difficulties. In fact, some new ventures formalize these family support groups by organizing a few events that are spouse specific. It is important to remember and remind all involved that the long hours will subside and that, if the venture is successful, everyone will benefit.

Interpersonal Conflicts

In such a charged environment, interpersonal conflicts among team members are common. Resolve these disputes as quickly as possible, or they may escalate to the point where they become destructive. Lead entrepreneurs typically find that they spend as much time coaching and managing team issues as they do directly working on the business. If you find yourself in this situation, don't worry—this is a valuable and effective use of your time. If you can keep your team working together, you'll have more success than if you try to carry the burden all alone.

As the coach, you may be able to resolve some conflicts only by firing one of the team members. While firing is a necessary part of running a company, you need to be prepared for the inevitable disruption it will cause (although it can be therapeutic to those who remain if it removes some of the stress that the fired individual brought to the company). Depending on the person's agreement with the company, his departure may require a buyout of equity and a lump-sum settlement. That's why firing is usually undertaken only if the person is not only prone to interpersonal conflicts but also underperforming in some way (either not skilled enough to do the jobs required or shirking his responsibilities). First try to resolve the conflict by mediating between the parties, and be sure not to appear to be favoring either one. It may be prudent to hire an outside expert who is perceived as a neutral party. Whatever resolution you agree upon, make sure that it is implemented as planned.

CONCLUSION

Entrepreneurship is a team sport. The most critical task any lead entrepreneur undertakes is defining who should be on the team and then creating an environment in which that team can flourish. This chapter has identified what type of team members ventures might need, how to entice and compensate them, and how to build a strong, supportive culture. Maintaining a team requires ongoing effort, and many organizations find that team dynamics suffer when the firm experiences rapid growth. Chapter 14 revisits these issues and suggests ways that organizations can keep their entrepreneurial orientation.

YOUR OPPORTUNITY JOURNAL

Reflection Point	Your Thoughts...
1. What are your three strongest attributes?	
2. Talk to a close mentor and ask what he or she sees as your strengths. Do these match the attributes you identified above?	
3. What skills do you need to develop prior to launch? What skills can you develop during the launch and early stages of your company? Create a plan to develop those skills.	
4. Create an organization chart for your venture. Show positions to be filled immediately and those to be filled later (along with the dates of filling those positions). Create a staffing plan based on your organization chart.	
5. Think about the types of employees you'd like to hire. What kind of values are you looking for? Remember, this is the point at which you create your company's culture.	

WEB EXERCISE

Scan Monster.com, Salary.com and other job sites. Look at the postings for CEO and other key employees of early-stage companies in the industry that you are interested in pursuing. What skills are being sought? What level of previous experience is desired? How much are they offering for these key employees? Use this information to start creating your own staffing plan.

NOTES

1. 2012 10K Form, Microsoft.
2. Minniti, M., Bygrave, W., and Autio, E. *Global Entrepreneurship Monitor: 2005 Executive Report*. Wellesley, MA: Babson College and London Business School. 2006.
3. www.nrf.com/modules.php?name= Pages&sp_id=1244
4. "2010 Operations Report" by the National Restaurant Association and Deloitte & Touche LLP.
5. Lechler, T. Social Interaction: A Determinant of Entrepreneurial Team Success. *Small Business Economics*, 16: 263–278. 2001.

6   Ruef, M. Strong Ties, Weak Ties and Islands: Structural and Cultural Predictions of Entrepreneurial Team Success. *Industrial and Corporate Changes*, 11: 427–449. 2002.

7   Bird, B. *Entrepreneurial Behavior*. Glenview, IL: Scott Foresman. 1989.

8   Hofman, M. The Big Picture. *Inc.*, 25(11): 87–94. October 15, 2003.

9   www.crunchbase.com/company/etsy

10   www.nytimes.com/2007/12/16/magazine/16Crafts-t.html?_r=2&oref=slogin&ref=magazine&pagewanted=all

11   www.businessinsider.com/etsy-now-profitable-gets-a-new-ceo-2009-12

12   http://bits.blogs.nytimes.com/2012/07/18/one-on-one-chad-dickerson-ceo-of-etsy

13   http://www.facebook.com/press/info.php?founderbios.

14   Stone, Brad. "Is Facebook Growing Up Too Fast?" *New York Times*. March 28, 2009. www.nytimes.com/2009/03/29/technology/Internet/29face.html

15   www.foodshouldtastegood.com/about-fstg/our-story/timeline

16   www.foodshouldtastegood.com/about-fstg/in-the-news/2011

17   www.generalmills.com/Media/NewsReleases/Library/2012/February/food_taste_good_2_29.aspx

18   Drucker, P. Managing Oneself. *Harvard Business Review*, 83(1): 100–105. 2005.

19   *HRfocus*, 82(9): 8–9. September 2005.

20   McFarland, K. The Psychology of Success. *Inc.*, 27(11): 158–159. November 15, 2005.

21   Kuemmerle, W. A Test for the Fainthearted. *Harvard Business Review*, 80(5): 122–126. 2002.

22   Ibid.

23   www.eventuring.org/eShip/appmanager/eVenturing/ShowDoc/eShipWebCache Repository/Documents/FTNV-pp276-279.pdf.

24   Brief Profile of 2003 Inc. 500 Companies. *Inc.* 25(10). October 2003.

25   www.huffingtonpost.com/alexandra-wilkis-wilson

26   www.huffingtonpost.com/alexis-maybank

27   http://online.wsj.com/article/SB10001424052748703730804576313330486181732.html

28   www.forbes.com/sites/glassheel/2012/08/29/insider-secrets-of-gilt-groupes-alexandra-wilson

29   http://idobi.com/news/2007/08/johnny-cupcakes-you-need-to-know-me

30   http://idobi.com/news/2007/08/johnny-cupcakes-you-need-to-know-me

31   www.inc.com/magazine/20100501/my-son-the-entrepreneur.html

32   Hoffman, Claire. (2008) The battle for facebook. *The Rolling Stone*. www.rollingstone.com/news/story/21129674/the_battle_for_facebook/print

33   Spirrison, J. B. Startups Ponder Equity Compensation Conundrum. *Private Equity Week*. October 4, 1999, pp. 1–2.

34   Robbins, S. Dividing Equity Between Founders and Investors: How to Figure Out Who Gets What Percentage of the Business When Investors Come on Board. *Entrepreneur*. October 13, 2003.

35   Beyster Institute. *Employee Ownership Plans—"Keys to Success."* www.beysterinstitute.org/about_employee_ownership/keys_to.success.cfm.

36   Burlingham, B. The Boom in Employee Stock Ownership. *Inc.*, 22(11): 106–110. August 2000.

37   www.investopedia.com/articles/optioninvestor/09/expensing-esos.asp#axzz2Ex73uFMs

38   Ibid.

39   http://swz.salary.com/SalaryWizard/Information-Technology-Director-Salary-Details-Boston-MA.aspx

40   www.ebizmba.com/articles/job-Web sites

41   http://monster.salary.com/SalaryWizard/Chief-Information-Technology-Officer-Salary-Details-Boston-MA.aspx

42   Burlingham, B. Touched by an Angel. *Inc.*, 19(10): 46–47. July 1997.

43   www.inc.com/magazine/20100501/my-son-the-entrepreneur.html

44   http://content.usatoday.com/sportsdata/baseball/mlb/salaries/team

45   http://boston.redsox.mlb.com/bos/history/all_stars.jsp

46   http://espn.go.com/mlb/standings/_/group/5

47   Maurice M. Ohayon, Epidemiology of Insomnia: What We Know and What We Still Need to Learn, *Sleep Medicine Reviews*, 6(2):97–111. 2002.

48   National Sleep Foundation, 2005 Sleep in America Poll, Washington DC, March 2005.

49   Chronic insomnia, obstructive sleep apnea, restless leg syndrome, and narcolepsy are the major medical disorders associated with sleep problems.

50   Melinda Beck, When Sleep Leaves You Tired, *Wall Street Journal*, June 9, 2009.

51   The company sponsors all-hands pizza lunches every few weeks to which outside experts are invited to speak on subjects related to Zeo's business.

Zeo, Inc.

The more you know, the better you sleep.™

Newton, Massachusetts

As students at Brown University in 2003, Eric Shashoua, Jason Donahue, and Ben Rubin shared a problem common to students of every generation: sleep deprivation. Each tried to pack as much as possible into every day with the *least* possible amount of sleep. The result was predictable: They had trouble getting up in the morning and staying alert in class.

One of the three had, through his coursework, become aware of a study commissioned by NASA during the 1960s. That study focused on the human sleep cycle. It identified points in the cycle at which a person would be most alert if awakened. For the three friends, NASA's findings seemed to have practical utility. If they could wake up at the right point in their sleep cycles, they would be less groggy and more effective in the classroom. They could continue cheating the gods of sleep, but with fewer negative consequences. Reasoning that an effective solution would benefit the millions of people who, like them, were burning their candles at both ends, the three set out to build a company around that solution. "We saw ourselves as the target market," recalls Jason. "That market had to be large since companies were pushing caffeine products and special drinks, like Red Bull, to help people stay alert."

Six years on, the college friends were still together, but now as founding executives of Zeo, a business dedicated to a somewhat larger mission: to help people get a better night's sleep. During those years they had raised $14 million, invented a way to track sleep comfortably, and developed and launched a consumer product that was gaining nationwide awareness. And although they were sleeping better than they had in college, they were now dealing with other issues. Zeo was no longer a three guys' college project. It was now a fast-growing enterprise with an increasing number of employees with specialized skills, experiences, and reporting relationships. An older, seasoned CEO was at the helm, and the focus of the enterprise's energy had shifted from developing and launching a product to expanding sales and satisfying customers.

Unsurprisingly, this evolution in the company's life was affecting the founders and their roles in the company. To evolve with the company's needs and contribute as leaders, they had to continue to grow professionally, learn new skills, and step up to new challenges. How would the founders evolve and grow to meet the different needs of the company?

The Sleep Problem/Opportunity

Most people take sleep for granted. Yet 30–50% of the adult U.S. population reports difficulty in sleeping.[47] In a 2005 poll of adult Americans, 24% of respondents reported getting "a good night's sleep" only a few nights *per week*, and 13% reported getting that good night's sleep only a few nights *per month*. Another 13% told pollsters that they *rarely or never* had a good night's sleep.[48]

Sleep problems can have detrimental effects on a person's attentiveness, work and academic performance, and even relationships. Even so, only 8% of people speak with their primary care physicians about their sleep problems. And few doctors bother to ask. By one estimate, less than 20% of doctors ask patients how well they are sleeping as part of their annual physical exams. This "don't ask, don't tell" situation results in millions of people living with their sleep problems for years and years without relief.

For a minority of sleep-deprivation sufferers, the underlying cause can be traced to one or another medical condition.[49] The medical establishment has responded to these with various forms of clinical diagnoses and therapy. Its primary diagnostic tool is the sleep laboratory, a specially equipped room in which individual patients are observed and monitored by means of polysomnography (PSG)—the gold standard of sleep diagnosis. In the United States, a small number of board-certified sleep specialists (approximately 5,000) attend to the millions who suffer from medical conditions that interfere with normal sleep.

The majority of people with sleep problems, however, have no underlying medical issues. Their difficulties often stem from work or lifestyle choices. These individuals include students, hospital physicians and nurses, shift-workers, people struggling to meet deadlines, long-haul truck drivers, hard-driving professionals, and heavy consumers of caffeinated products and alcohol. Sleep deprivation for them often results in drowsiness and reduced cognitive performance, and a greater susceptibility to accidents at work and on the highway.

It was this market, estimated at 70 million people in the United States alone, that Zeo aimed to serve. From the beginning, the company has made it clear that its product is not intended for the diagnosis or treatment of sleep disorders and warned customers that "If you suspect that you may have a sleep disorder, consult your physician." Zeo did not intend to compete with medical devices, sleep laboratories, or medical practitioners.

Building the Company

When they formed Zeo in December 2003, Eric, Jason, and Ben knew little about sleep science or sleep medicine. Eric, a senior, was studying computer science and French; Jason, then a junior, was majoring in business and Chinese. Ben, a junior majoring in computer engineering, was recruited later through a campus job posting. Brown University, however, was a leading center for the study of sleep and sleep medicine, so the team worked hard to build relationships with the University's sleep experts and to learn from them and from other campus resources. In time they would expand their relationships and learning to a broader network.

Initially, the business opportunity was narrowly defined around the concept of Smart-Wake™, a technology used to track sleep and identify the optimal times for awakening someone refreshed and alert. To accomplish this, they would have to build a device capable of accurately monitoring and recording a person's sleep stages (wake, light sleep, REM, and deep sleep). They would do this by developing a comfortable, wireless sensing device that the customer would wear on his or her forehead during the night. The technical breakthrough that made this possible was a dry fabric sensor material developed by the team. The device itself would detect and transmit vital data to a bedside receiver/monitor, which would store and later array the information in a manner that a lay person could easily interpret. Ben initially estimated that he could develop a testable prototype over the school's Christmas break. In fact, the job took over two-and-a-half years.

Sleep Stages

People typically pass through various stages of sleep during the night. These include wake, light sleep, rapid eye movement (REM) sleep, and deep sleep. A person normally experiences repeated cycles of these phases during the night.

Light Sleep: Takes place between the transitions to the other phases of sleep and wakefulness. Usually accounts for the longest phase of the sleep cycle.

REM: Necessary for consolidating memories, learning, creativity, problem solving, and emotional well-being. A time when dreams occur.

Deep Sleep: Restorative phase in which the body secretes a growth hormone needed for development and physical repair. People generally feel most groggy when awakened from deep sleep. According to cognitive tests, they may experience impaired mental performance for up to 4 hours when abruptly awakened from deep sleep.

Early Financing

Many people responded affirmatively to the SmartWake™ concept. Eric recalls how he would talk about the project in the campus cafeteria. "Bystanders started to say, 'That's a great idea. Can I invest in your company?'" And many of them did in small amounts. This in turn led Eric to seek out private investors in the community, who invested larger amounts. Ultimately this allowed the group to get more serious efforts underway with a small seed round. In the very beginning, other non-dilutive funds were also sought:

- A $9,000 grant from the Slater Center of Rhode Island
- An $18,000 grant from the National Intercollegiate Inventors and Innovators Alliance
- $10,000 in cash and $10,000 in services from the Brown Entrepreneurship Program Business Plan Competition
- $25,000 in cash and $35,000 in services from winning the State of Rhode Island Business Plan Competition

By mid-2005, all three founders had graduated from Brown and were working full-time in the company, which needed more money. Their fundraising efforts shifted exclusively to angel investors. Responsible for fundraising efforts, Eric pitched to angel groups and individual investors all over southern New England, as well as within the Rhode Island business community and Brown University alumni. "This was hard to do," he says, "given our ages." Each rejection, however, encouraged him to dig for reasons and to refine his presentation. By the end of this 10-month period, with a second oversubscribed round, the company had raised a total to date of over $1 million from several groups and individuals.

Among Zeo's early investors was Sean Glass. Like the Zeo founding team, Glass had joined with other classmates (in his case, years earlier at Yale) to start a successful business while still an undergraduate. He learned of Zeo through a fellow angel investor, a Brown graduate who had already taken a small stake in new enterprise. Glass thought the company had a strong concept since there were few credible products in the consumer sleep market; as he put it, "People will go to great lengths to solve their sleep problems." Glass also saw a bit of himself and his company's co-founders in the Zeo team. And he liked what he saw. "Eric, Jason, and Ben had different personalities, but they clearly trusted each other in their roles. All were very well organized and open to learning."

Glass invested in 2005 as a member of an angel group. Still, he perceived some difficult hurdles ahead. "They would have to convince people that their product was scientifically valid, and that it really worked. It would also need to be priced right." And from the user's perspective, the headband monitor they were working on had to be comfortable and look good. Otherwise, "how many people will get into bed with their spouses wearing a weird-looking contraption on their heads?"

Advice and Credibility

Sleep science is a relatively new field. Research on the subject only began in the 1950s. As a result, the community of sleep specialists is small, and communication and collaboration is commonplace.

From the outset, the venture team understood the importance of tapping into this scientific community, drawing on its expertise, and gaining credibility by allying with key members. Most of the responsibility for this task fell to Ben Rubin, who, beginning at Brown University, cold-called key people, introduced himself and Zeo, and solicited their advice and support.

To his surprise and relief, these specialists did not automatically show him the door. Most, in fact, expressed genuine interest in the goal Zeo was pursuing. They were intrigued by the potential benefits that an inexpensive, self-administered measuring and monitoring system would bring to the millions of people who suffered from nonmedical-related sleep difficulties.

Each contact produced leads to other notables in the U.S. sleep science community. Before long, Ben and the team had assembled an informal group of sleep health advisers from several of the nation's leading medical institutions. In addition to this group, a key consultant, John Shambroom, joined Ben's development efforts. John brought a unique scientific and engineering background to the team, which included extensive experience in tracking brainwave patterns, critical to ongoing development. This initial group contributed invaluable technical guidance and gave the start-up venture much needed credibility in the eyes of potential investors. John would later join the company and expand this group into a formal board with semiannual meetings. Board members would represent the broad scope of sleep science: a psychologist, a specialist in circadian rhythms, a leading researcher, a clinical practitioner, and so forth (Exhibit 6.1).

EXHIBIT 6.1 Zeo Advisory Board

Chair: **Kenneth P. Wright Jr., PhD**
Director, Sleep & Chronobiology Lab,
University of Colorado, Boulder

Daniel Aeschbach, PhD
Assistant Professor of Medicine,
Harvard Medical School

Michael J. Breus, PhD
"The Sleep Doctor," author, WebMD® sleep
expert and AOL® wellness coach

Charles A. Czeisler, MD, PhD
Director, Division of Sleep Medicine,
Harvard Medical School

Phyllis C. Zee, MD, PhD
Professor of Neurology and Neurobiology and
Physiology Director,
Sleep Disorders Center
Northwestern University Medical School

John W. Winkelman, MD, PhD
Assistant Professor of Psychiatry,
Harvard Medical School and Medical
Director, Sleep Health Center of Brigham
and Women's Hospital

The team also sought business advice. It made a list of pioneers in fields related to Zeo, then approached each in turn. "It usually took a few calls to get through," says Eric, "but once we got past the gatekeepers, most of these people were very approachable."

I'd tell them that we were students who had started a company, that we admired what they had accomplished, and that we would appreciate their advice. I'd then ask, 'Could we meet with you for just a half hour or so?' This is how we met Colin Angle, founder of iRobot, and Sherwin Greenblatt, former president of Bose. Colin had started his company while a graduate student at MIT. We maintained an advisory relationship with these business leaders for over two years, then asked them to join our board, which they did.

A Coach/CEO

The three founders wanted to launch a consumer product company, first nationally and then internationally, and knew that they wouldn't have the best chance of success doing this on their own. Recognizing that they had never done this before, they wanted to find an expert who could help them achieve greater success, and from whom they could learn. So, with the proceeds of the final angel round closed in the summer of 2006, they set out to find an experienced person who could guide them through the important stages of final product development, launch, and growth. An executive search firm with an affinity for start-ups was engaged and asked to find qualified candidates for the CEO position. That firm's consultant met with the three founders and interviewed each extensively. What qualities and experiences were they looking for in a candidate? How would they describe their ideal candidate? How did they expect the person to work with them?

Eric, Jason, and Ben were of one mind. They wanted a CEO with an entrepreneurial outlook and a successful record in marketing consumer-health products. More than that, their ideal candidate would be a coach and mentor, helping each of them to develop his business and management skills. As they saw it, Zeo was growing from a small start-up into a real business; each founding member wanted to grow quickly into the new roles that operating such a business demanded.

Finding a person with the desired combination of experience and personal qualities was a tall order, but after several months of searching, the recruiter presented the team with several qualified candidates. The candidate they selected was Dave Dickinson, a man roughly twice their ages.

Dickinson's life path had been much different than those of Zeo's founders. As a teenager he had learned something of how entrepreneurial businesses work, and how they differ from bureaucratic organizations. His father had joined with former IBM veterans to develop a small company, and his work experiences were a frequent topic of conversation in the Dickinson household. Dave knew and admired the president of his father's new company.

I remember playing basketball with him when I was a junior in high school. And I still recall how much I wanted to be like him—to know everyone who worked for the company, to know their families, and to enjoy the freedom to get things done without dealing with committees and layers of bureaucracy. How many big company presidents play basketball with their employees' kids?

Despite his youthful attraction to small business life, Dickinson's career path went in the opposite direction. Armed with an MBA in marketing from Northwestern University, he worked for several giant consumer-health product companies: Procter & Gamble, Johnson & Johnson, Arm & Hammer, and Mead Johnson. In 1995, however, his entrepreneurial instincts were given a chance to express themselves. Dickinson's boss at Mead Johnson asked him to create a new product incubation unit, staffed by some 100 employees from marketing and R&D. "These were disciplines that never spoke to each other," he recalls. "At our Evansville [Indiana] headquarters the marketing people were in a building on one side of a four-lane road, and the R&D people were on the other side. No one ever crossed that road, except to eat lunch."

In accepting the assignment, Dickinson got permission to take over and renovate one floor of unused space in an old industrial building. He hired an architect to implement his vision of an open design in which communication and collaboration between marketing and R&D specialists would naturally occur. There would be no private offices, no cubicles. To further set the incubator apart from the rest of the company, he had the place painted in bright colors. Quotations by famous inventors adorned the walls. White boards and games were set out here and there to encourage interaction. A basketball hoop was mounted on a far wall. A phone booth was installed at the back of the space. "I told people that if they *really* needed to have a private conversation, they could use the phone booth."

The success of this interdisciplinary product incubator changed Dickinson's life in two important ways. First, it made him realize how much he enjoyed breaking free of corporate rules and routines, and building new things from scratch. Second, it led to an important new assignment. In 1998, he was asked to move to Boston and help initiate a novel kind of venture capital firm, jointly invested in by Bristol Myers Squibb (parent of Mead Johnson) and General Mills. Consumer health and wellness would be its investment focus. Dickinson recalls how that experience broadened his understanding of innovation, different business models, and the management challenges faced by young and inexperienced entrepreneurs. "I spent a lot of time helping the CEOs of these companies, particularly in the marketing area." He enjoyed sharing his knowledge with these CEOs and helping them with market development. "In many cases, I wished that I was them!" And, in 2001, he became the CEO of his first start-up, a biotechnology company initially incubated within Harvard Medical School.

Dickinson's background brought him into the sights of Zeo's headhunter in late 2006. He offered two unique qualities that Zeo needed: experience in developing, launching, and marketing consumer health products, and an open, mentoring personality. For Dickinson's part, Zeo represented an outlet for his entrepreneurial instincts.

Meetings between Dickinson, the founders, and Zeo's key investors were encouraging. The candidate met all of Zeo's expectations, and Dickinson liked what he saw in the venture and its principals. "You could see that these guys were insatiable learners, hungry for experience and knowledge. They were eager to learn from everyone—from people like me, from investors, and from their advisory board. There was no youthful arrogance."

It was a match. After doing due diligence on the venture and its technology, and in return for a reasonable salary and an equity stake vested over time, Dickinson joined the company as CEO in February 2007.

Beyond SmartWake

By the time Dave Dickinson joined the company, the team had raised over $1 million dollars around its SmartWake™ concept. With Dave now wearing the CEO cap, Eric could turn his full attention to the job of prospecting for additional investment capital and expanding Zeo's strategic connections for business development. Jason's focus would remain on potential customers: Who were they? What were their needs in a sleep product? How would they connect with Zeo and its evolving technology?

Ben's engineering training made him the logical person to handle product development. This would be no small job. The technology had to be capable of accurately sensing and monitoring sleep without all the paraphernalia and personal assistance needed in conventional sleep laboratories. It had to be affordable to the average consumer, and so simple that an untrained customer could operate it correctly. And it had to provide a scientifically valid measure of an individual's sleep. More than one sleep-specialist expert declared that meeting all of these requirements was impossible.

Undeterred, Eric, Jason, and Ben thought they had a solid venture concept in Smart-Wake™. If people understood their sleep cycles and awakened themselves at an optimal point (outside of deep sleep), they would be more rested and alert. And they would be happy with Zeo. Ben's work, bolstered by John Shambroom's background and expertise, would soon give them the technology they needed to make that happen. By early 2007, he had a working prototype that Jason could test on focus group participants. Those participants, mostly college students and young professionals, responded favorably to the prototype and to the proposition of wakening refreshed and on the ball. They had little interest or curiosity about their sleep stages, as recorded by the prototype. However, test subjects who represented the broader population sent the team a disturbingly different message: They had sleep issues that SmartWake™ failed to address.

> *The product said it took me 43 minutes to fall asleep. What can I do to get to sleep faster?*
> *I wake up at around 2 A.M. and cannot get back to sleep. How can I change that?*
> *Your device says that I get about one hour of deep sleep at night. Is that good or bad? What does it mean for my performance at work?*

People wanted answers to these and other questions, and they wanted *solutions* to their sleep problems. The crucial question was: *What can I do to get a better night's sleep?*

Feedback from potential customers revealed the limited nature of Zeo's initial value proposition. Sleep was a big issue for many people—it affected their relationships, health, and performance on the job, at school, and on the athletic field. Hundreds of companies, from pill makers to pillow and mattress manufacturers, were touting the importance of a good night's rest. Knowing the optimal time to wake up—the SmartWake™ proposition—was merely a small part of a much bigger issue. "SmartWake™ was attractive to the 30-and-under crowd," says Jason, "but that part of the total market was small compared to the people who were experiencing real pain because of their sleep patterns. Not waking up at the optimal time was nothing compared to the problems people experienced by not getting a good night's sleep—problems with drowsiness, their relationships, job performance, health, and so on."

The opportunity was clearly broader than initially conceived. But addressing it would require one big thing: practical and personalized solutions to common sleep difficulties. Recalls Jason, "We weren't sure that we had the expertise to help people sleep better. We wondered if this was too high a mountain to climb." Indeed, climbing that mountain would require at least another year of work—maybe two. As things stood, the company did not have enough cash to fund another year or more of development. Could more be raised? The initial product launch was scheduled for mid-2007. Would current investors agree to deferring that planned launch if it meant building a better product? Should they launch the product in its current state, and then develop an improved Zeo Version 2.0?

After much discussion, it was clear that the intelligent wake-up proposition would satisfy a market segment that was too small, given the expectations of the founders, their advisors, and investors. Quantitative testing with focus group participants (using product concept testing methodology introduced by Dave) confirmed the appeal of the product concept with sleep improvement capabilities. They also feared disappointment by customers. "We had no choice," says Jason, "but to step up to the larger concept. We might not have a real business otherwise." After seeing the market-testing numbers, Zeo's investors agreed.

Enter Venture Capital

Recognizing that their expanded value proposition would require substantial new capital, the team went back to its angel investors, including those who, because of oversubscription on the previous round, had not been able to participate. "But we quickly learned," says Eric, "that this approach would take too much time and was unlikely to produce the level of funding we needed." They decided to go after larger pools of capital, namely, venture money. "This is where our board members really helped with advice and introductions." iRobot founder Colin Angle introduced them to people at iD Ventures America, a quality venture firm that had financed his venture. iD Ventures led the company's Series B round; closing in 2008, even as the world financial system poised on the verge of collapse. Many deals were canceled during this period, but Zeo's went through. A later Series C round of financing, led by Trident Capital, closed in 2009, bringing total capital raised by Zeo to $14 million.

Zeo now had sufficient capital to exploit the large opportunity it had found and to hire the people it needed to scale up for commercial operations and launch.

The Go-to-Market Product

To fulfill its larger aims, the company had to develop both a more sophisticated sleep phase tracking product *and* an online, personal "sleep coach." Part educational tool, part motivational program, the go-to-market product Zeo would offer what potential customers had clearly asked for: a product package that revealed the user's sleep patterns, and an online coach that would help each customer discover the habits and behaviors that interfered with his or her night's rest. An interactive "7-Step Sleep Fitness Program"—which took a full year to develop—would teach users how to overcome sleep-robbing habits and behaviors. At launch, the final package (Exhibit 6.2) included the following:

- **A soft, lightweight headband containing Zeo's SoftWave™ sensor technology**. Worn during the night with the sensor against the forehead, this device accurately tracks the user's sleep patterns and transmits the data wirelessly to a bedside receiver/display. Unlike traditional methods of tracking sleep patterns, the sensor connects to the skin without gels or adhesives thanks to a unique patent-pending material developed by the company. (Tests-rated tracking results are comparable to the gold standard for assessing sleep.)

- **Bedside display unit**. The size of a clock radio, the bedside unit receives data transmitted from the headband sensor. Algorithms and artificial intelligence software determine the user's sleep phases throughout the night. A sleep graph summarizes each night's sleep stages. A "ZQ" score gauges the quantity, quality, and depth of each night's sleep. In addition, the user can see at a glance his or her total sleep time, how long it took to fall asleep, how often and how long he or she was awakened, and the total amounts of REM, light, and deep sleep.

- **Access to the personalized 7 Step Sleep Fitness™ Program**. This online coaching program analyzes the user's unique sleep patterns and lifestyle, and then recommends techniques for addressing factors that may be negatively affecting sleep. The program also provides regular assessments of user's sleep statistics to help track progress.

- **The SmartWake™ Alarm feature**. The headband sensors search for a natural awakening point—the optimal time to get out of bed in the morning, when the user transitions into and out of REM sleep and the brain is more active. The bedside unit's alarm will sound as early as a half hour before the user's set wake-up time, but never later than that time.

EXHIBIT 6.2 Product Hardware

The Zeo Headband, with dry fabric
sensor materials shown.

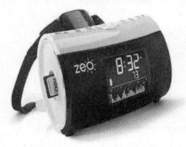

Zeo Receiver/Display Unit

Source: Zeo, with permission.

Using an SD (Secure Digital) memory card within the bedside display, the customer can use his or her personal computer to transfer accumulated sleep data to a personal online account, myZeo.com. The Web site (Exhibit 6.3) has interactive tools for understanding the data. It also provides cause-and-effect information on how and individual lifestyle choices—including exercise, diet, drinking, and stress—affected sleep.

Manufacturing of the physical product was outsourced to an Asian contract manufacturer. The price was eventually set at $249 for the product alone, and $349 for the deluxe package, which included the product, a year's supply of headband sensors, and unlimited access to the online 7Step coaching program. Sales would be made directly to customers via the Internet.

The Launch

As mid-2009 approached, the Zeo crew prepared for the product's official launch. Not having the public company financial resources common to consumer product launches, they needed a high ROI method to gain public exposure. So, working with a Boston-based PR firm, Schneider Associates, they devised an innovative plan to create media buzz. Dozens of reporters were invited to spend the night, courtesy of the company, at a brand-new five-star New York City hotel. Each was given a Zeo device that they would use during the night to record their sleep patterns.

The next morning, the overnight guests were treated to a breakfast in the hotel ballroom, where company personnel were on hand to help them understand their recorded sleep patterns from the previous night. After a brief presentation by Zeo, several scientific experts spoke on

EXHIBIT 6.3 | **Sleep Tools and Coaching Program Information**

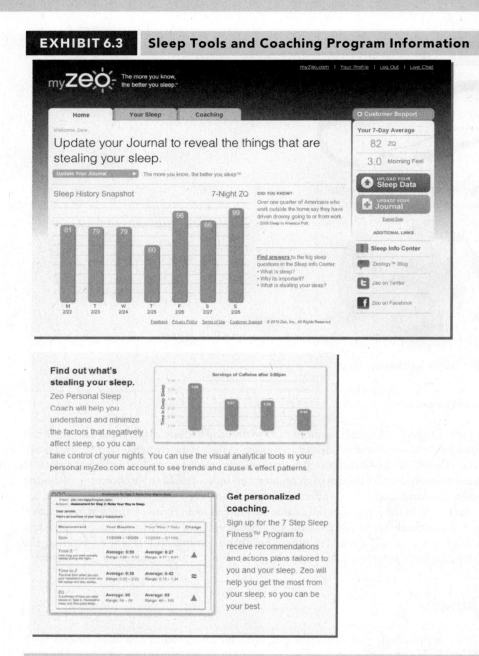

Source: Zeo, with permission.

the relationship between sleep and human health. Reporters then moved to "break out" tables where specific sleep-related topics such as sleep and human performance, methods for sleeping better, and so forth, were discussed. At one table, the trainer of the Boston Celtics entertained reporters' questions about sleep and athletic performance. "The idea," says Dave, "was to give reporters opportunities to pick up on many different story lines."

This hotel PR gambit and other launch PR efforts paid huge dividends almost immediately. The first big story about Zeo appeared within days in the *Wall Street Journal*. The *Journal's* health columnist, Melinda Beck, described how Zeo had helped her discover and understand her own sleep problems. "Finding out what's going on in your sleep generally requires spending the night in a professional sleep lab hooked up to lots of wires and monitors," she told millions of readers. "But I've been testing a new home-sleep monitor called the Zeo Personal Sleep Coach that lets people track their sleep patterns nightly in their own bedrooms."[50] She went on to describe her dismal ZQ score, how it responded negatively to tensions surrounding her column deadlines, and how it improved once she switched to decaffeinated coffee and kicked her dog out of the bedroom. In the article, she interviewed members of the company's advisory board and other Zeo users, who shared their positive experiences with the product, its coaching program, and how changes in daily habits affected their ZQ scores.

For the company, Beck's article could not have been more timely or beneficial. Orders began pouring in. Other positive articles quickly followed in the *New York Times, Forbes, USA Today, Popular Science, Woman's Day*, and other national periodicals. Ben and Jason soon found themselves interviewed on Fox TV, and America's primo TV pitchman, Regis Philbin, had himself filmed in bed wearing his Zeo headband and talking about his own sleep problems. More orders came in—at a time when consumer product sales in the United States were in the basement!

Over the next six months, the young company continued to score PR coups. One of the most significant of these occurred on December 14, 2009, at the height of the holiday gift-buying season. The nation's most popular morning TV program, *The Today Show*, watched by over six million Americans, ran four short story segments on Zeo's founders and their new product, with testimonials from a user, a leading sleep medical authority, and the TV network's own doctor/journalist. All praised the product. KaBoom! The sky began raining orders and Google identified Zeo as the most searched topic that day, even ahead of a Tiger Woods scandal story that was making headlines all over the media.

A Changing Company . . . Changing Roles

The product launch and subsequent media buzz marked a watershed for Zeo. The once-obscure little company was now on the map and receiving enormously positive feedback from reviewers. And the cash register was ringing.

Rather than relax, however, employees kept up a punishing pace of work. Says Eric, "With working many nights and weekends, there hasn't been a lot of time for friends and family, or—ironically—for sleep." The only married member of the founding team, Eric consciously tried to optimize the limited time he had available to spend with his spouse by focusing on communication. Jason Donahue echoed his partner's assessment of the work load. "We don't have a problem with absenteeism around here. Our problem is *presentee-ism*—people not going home."

Even before the June 2009 launch, however, Zeo had been changing. New people with deep and specialized experience had come onboard. Subsequent to Dickinson's joining the company, John Shambroom was hired as the initial VP of research, engineering, and operations, but was later asked to focus on the company's scientific and clinical platform as the VP of scientific affairs. Later, others were hired to head up e-commerce, finance and manufacturing, and engineering and product development. And as 2009 drew to a close, the team was searching for a specialist in direct-response TV advertising. "These people had technical skills we needed right away," says Dave Dickinson. "We couldn't wait months and years for our own people to develop them. And we'll do more of this as we grow." By late 2009, 19 people were on the payroll. Eight were on the management team, making the company strategically top-heavy in preparation for growth.

The launch and the addition of new people had an impact on the roles of the three founders. "We're now wearing fewer hats," said one. "Each of us is developing new skills and learning a lot from Dave." As an obliging mentor, Dave Dickinson made an effort to learn what each founder did innately well and then directed each into areas where he could make the greatest contribution and develop more skills. "To do this I actually used the same profile test for Eric, Jason, and Ben that their recruiter had used on me." Each person's tests results were shared with his colleagues, and this helped each person to better understand his strengths and weaknesses and those of his peers. "That exercise really developed trust, which made the rest of the effort easier."

For Jason Donahue, the post-launch period coincided with a major redirection of attention, from product development, sales, and customers to brand management and assuring high customer satisfaction. With Dave at the helm, Eric Shashoua shifted his primary attention to business development and to relationships that would help the company grow. He was now spending more time with Zeo's directors (Exhibit 6.4), the advisory board, the sleep-health community, and potential channel and product partners. Ben Rubin had once been in charge of technology development, product development, engineering and manufacturing. He was now focused on technology and its application to the company's next generation of sleep-related products.

While all acknowledged the necessity of these changes, it came not without some nostalgia. Ben commented that, "As the company has gotten bigger and our roles have become more specialized, we [the founders] have lost something. Each of us probably misses having a larger role." He notes that decision making has also changed. "The three of us can no longer sit down together for five minutes and make a decision. The process is now more complicated. That's good for the business but sometimes frustrating for us." As the same time, Ben is accepting of changing roles, seeing them as direct outcomes of choices the three of them had made.

> *If we had decided to be a smaller niche company, our roles would not have had to change nearly as much. Our decision to address a large consumer market had important consequences: It dictated our need for an experienced CEO, for more outside capital, for more employees with specialized know-how, and so forth. We have to recognize and accept the impact of our own decisions.*

EXHIBIT 6.4   Zeo Board of Directors

Colin Angle
CEO, iRobot Corporation

Ronald Chwang
Chairman and President, iD Ventures America

Peter Meekin
Managing Director, Trident Capital

W. Anthony Vernon
Former Company Group Chairman,
Johnson & Johnson

Dave Dickinson
CEO, Zeo Inc.

Sherwin Greenblatt
Former President, Bose Corporation

Eric Shashoua
Co-Founder & VP, Zeo Inc.

Any misgivings the founders had about their changing roles appeared to have taken a back seat to conscious efforts to grow into those new roles. Speaking for the group, Eric noted that they had surrounded themselves with experienced employees and routinely interacted with business advisors, investors, sleep-science specialists, and with other entrepreneurs. Jason pointed to books and blogs, and to events and seminars as important sources of learning and growth.[51] For his part, Ben acknowledged the benefit of having experienced and knowledgeable mentors on the board and outside the company.

After six years of building a company from scratch, the three founders were not intimidated by the challenge of taking on new roles and learning new skills. "We have a *just do it* attitude around here," said Jason. "Sometimes you have to learn under fire." He cited how Eric had successfully negotiated a deal with a direct-mail catalog company even though he had no experience in that area. "Eric talked to experts who understood the catalog business, then did it."

Case Questions

1. What are the advantages/disadvantages of founding a company with your friends?
2. How did the founders identify and entice stakeholders to join their board of advisors?
3. Why did the founders seek a new CEO? Would you do that or would you want to run the business yourself? What was the process they used to select the CEO?
4. How did the role of each founder change as the business grew?
5. How do you maintain the culture when the company is professionalizing with a large top management team?

J.B. Schneider and Antonio Turco-Rivas.

THE BUSINESS PLANNING PROCESS

The most important aspect of writing the business plan is not the plan itself, but all the learning that goes on as you identify your concept and then research the concept, the industry, the competitors, and, most importantly, your customers. The written plan has its place (as an articulation of all the learning you have achieved), but even a technically well-written plan does not necessarily ensure a successful new venture. *Inc. Magazine* finds that few if any of the fastest-growing companies in the country have a business model exactly the same as the one in their original written business plan: Of those that wrote a formal business plan, 65% admitted that the existing business was significantly different from their original concept.[1] But following a formal process can help ensure that you don't miss any important gaps in your planning process. As General Dwight D. Eisenhower famously stated, "In preparing for battle I have always found that plans are useless, but planning is indispensable."[2]

This chapter takes the view that the *process* undertaken in developing a tight, well-written story is the most important thing. Furthermore, our research indicates that students who write a business plan, even if it is for an entrepreneurship class, are far more likely to become entrepreneurs than students who haven't written a business plan.[3] Business planning isn't just writing; it's research, it's talking to others, it's iterative, it's a *learning* process. . . and given that, a three-ring binder that catalogs all your learning is the best place to start.

This chapter is written by Andrew Zacharakis.

The purpose of business planning is to tell a story; the story of your business. Thorough business planning can establish that there is an opportunity worth exploiting and should then describe the details of how this will be accomplished. During the dot-com boom of the late 1990s, many entrepreneurs and venture capitalists questioned the importance of business planning. Typical of this hyper-startup phase are stories like that of James Walker, who generated financing on a 10-day-old company based on "a bunch of bullet points on a piece of paper." He stated, "It has to happen quick in the hyper-competitive wireless-Internet-technology world. There's a revolution every year and a half now."[4] The implication was simple. Business planning took time—time that entrepreneurs didn't have.

April 2000 was a sobering wake-up call for investors and entrepreneurs who had invested in that dot-com boom. Previously, many entrepreneurs believed that all that was needed to find investors and go public was a few PowerPoint slides and a good idea. The NASDAQ crash in April dispelled those beliefs as people came to realize that the majority of these businesses never had the potential to produce profits. Today investors have learned from this lesson and demand well-researched market opportunities and solid business planning. Entrepreneurs have also learned the various benefits of a well-researched plan.

There is a common misperception that business planning is primarily used for raising capital. Although a good business plan assists in raising capital, the primary purpose of the process is to help entrepreneurs gain a deeper understanding of the opportunity they are envisioning. Many would-be entrepreneurs doggedly pursue ideas that will never be profitable because they lack a deep understanding of the business model. The relatively little time spent developing a sound business plan can save thousands or even millions of dollars that might be wasted in a wild goose chase. For example, for a person who makes $100,000 per year, spending 200 hours on a business planning process equates to a $10,000 investment in time spent ($50 per hour times 200 hours). However, launching a flawed business concept can quickly accelerate into millions in spent capital. Most entrepreneurial ventures raise enough money to survive two years, even if the business will ultimately fail. Assuming the only expense is the time value of the lead entrepreneur, a two-year investment equates to $200,000, not to mention the lost opportunity cost and the likelihood that other employees were hired and paid and that other expenses were incurred. So do yourself a favor and spend the time and money up front.

The business planning *process* helps entrepreneurs shape their original vision into a better opportunity by raising critical questions, researching answers for those questions, and then answering them. For example, one question that every entrepreneur needs to answer is, "What is the customer's pain?" Conversations with customers and other trusted advisors assist in better targeting the product offering to what customers need and want. This pre-startup work saves untold effort and money that an entrepreneur might spend trying to reshape the product after the business has been launched. While all businesses adjust their offerings based upon customer feedback, business planning helps the entrepreneur to anticipate some of these adjustments in advance of the initial launch.

Perhaps the greatest benefit of business planning is that it allows the entrepreneur to articulate the business opportunity to various stakeholders in the most effective manner. Business planning provides the background information that enables the entrepreneur to communicate the upside potential to investors. Second, it provides the validation needed to convince potential employees to leave their current jobs for the uncertain future of a new venture. Finally, it can also help secure a strategic partner, key customer, or supplier. In short, business planning provides the entrepreneur with the deep understanding she needs to answer the critical questions that various stakeholders will ask. Completing a well-founded business plan gives the entrepreneur credibility in the *eyes* of various stakeholders.

Think of the business plan as a compilation of learning (both literally and figuratively). Start with a three-ring binder divided into categories, and then start collecting information in each section. Write a synopsis for each of these sections that includes your interpretation of what

"The key to understanding your business opportunity is to get out there and talk to people. . . people who sell, distribute, make and use similar products—most importantly, the customer. Writing a business plan without this groundwork leads to assumptions that may not hold water. There's not much room for error in your key assumptions and this field research helps validate those assumptions."

Jim Poss, Founder and CEO
BigBelly Solar
www.bigbellysolar.com

Courtesy Gina Maschek

Gina Maschek, co-founder of Beyond Blossoms, shows off some of her flowers

"It's not the 40 page report with the appendices and the Excel worksheets that is important. It's the legitimate understanding of

what would be necessary to create the business. I think another thing that is valuable about a business plan that gets committed to paper is that it provides a touchstone and a point of reference for the entrepreneur to measure his progress against. If you say in your plan that you will sign up 500 customers in the first year and only sign up 50, that is far more revealing than having no plan and signing up 50. Without established targets and goals, it is very hard to gauge how you are doing. Falling short is not the problem—where you fall short, and identifying why, and then correcting course—that is where business planning is important."

Rob Adler, President
Financial Recovery
Technologies

"The business plan is relatively unimportant because the only thing you know for sure is that it WON'T be accurate with what actually happens. The planning, however, is hugely important. It helps identify the key assumptions that drive your business model, and the subsequent chain of assumptions you have built on top of the original assumptions. The more comprehensive the planning process, the better your ability to recognize and re-strategize the business going forward."

Dan Hermann, Founder and CEO
Lazy Bones
Mylazybones.com

"Business planning really helps you understand your business, especially the drivers of the business. For example, what happens if I tweak my customer retention rate? How does that change my customer acquisition cost, etc.? How does that prolong or shorten the time to break even. . . ? It gives you a basis to make important decisions."

Gina Maschek, Co-founder
Beyond Blossoms
www.beyondblossoms.com

the information means and how that implies that you should shape and reshape your concept. You can also compile all this information on your computer, but whatever method you choose to catalog it, the point is the same—you need a mechanism to start organizing your learning.

The Planning Process

Business planning literally begins when you start thinking about your new venture. In Chapter 3, we highlighted the opportunity recognition process. That is the genesis of planning. It progresses from there when you start sharing your thoughts with potential co-founders over a cup of coffee or lunch. It moves on from that point when you share the idea with your significant other, friends, family, colleagues, and professors, among others. At each interaction, you are learning about aspects of your business opportunity. Do your friends think they would buy this product or service (potential customers)? Have they said things along the lines of "This is just like XYZ Company. . . " (potential competitor)? Have they informed you of potential suppliers or other people you might want to hire or at least talk to or learn from? All these bits and pieces of information are valuable learning that you should document and catalog in your three-ring binder.

Once you acquire a critical mass of learning, it's time to start organizing your information in a meaningful way. First, write a short summary (less than five pages) of your current vision. This provides a road map for you and others to follow as you embark on a more thorough planning process. Share this document with co-founders, family members, and trusted advisors. Ask for feedback on what else you should be thinking about. What gaps do the people who read this summary see? What questions do they ask and how can you gain the learning necessary to answer those questions in a convincing and accurate manner? This feedback will provide a platform for you to attack each of the major areas important to launching and running a new venture.

Your planning process will focus on critical aspects of your business model; not coincidentally, these critical aspects map well to the typical format of a business plan (see Figure 7.1). Now that you have some feedback from your trusted advisors, you can begin attacking major sections of the plan. It really doesn't matter where you start, although it is often easiest to write the product/service description first. This is usually the most concrete component of the entrepreneur's vision. Wherever you begin, don't let the order of sections outlined in Figure 7.1 constrain you. If you want to start somewhere else besides product description, do so. As you work through the plan, you'll inevitably find that this is an iterative process. Every section of the plan interacts with the other sections, and as a result, you'll often be working on multiple sections simultaneously. Most important, keep in mind that this is *your* business planning process; this is your learning. You should follow whatever method feels most comfortable and effective.

Wisdom is realizing that the business plan is a "living document." Although your first draft will be polished, most business plans are obsolete the day they come off the presses. That means that entrepreneurs are continuously updating and revising their business plan—they recognize it is a learning process, not a finished product. You'll continue learning new things that can improve your business for as long as you're involved with the business, and the day you stop learning how to improve it is the day that it will start its decline toward bankruptcy.

I.	Cover
II.	Executive Summary
III.	Table of Contents
IV.	Industry, Customer, and Competitor Analysis
V.	Company and Product Description
VI.	Marketing Plan
VII.	Operations Plan
VIII.	Development Plan
IX.	Team
X.	Critical Risks
XI.	Offering
XII.	Financial Plan
XIII.	Appendices

■ **Figure 7.1**

Business plan outline

So keep and file each major revision of your plan, and occasionally look back at earlier versions for the lessons you've learned. Remember, the importance of the business plan for you isn't the final product but the learning that you gain from writing the novel of your vision. The plan articulates your vision for the company, and it crystallizes that vision for you and your team. It also provides a history—a photo album, if you will—of the birth, growth, and maturity of your business. Although daunting, business planning can be exciting and creative, especially if you are working on it with your founding team. So now let us dig in and examine how to effectively conduct the business planning process.

The Story Model

One of the major goals of business planning is to attract various stakeholders and convince them of the potential of your business. Therefore, you need to keep in mind how these stakeholders will interpret your plan. The guiding principle is that you are writing a story, and all good stories have a theme—a unifying thread that ties the setting, characters, and plot together. If you think about the most successful businesses in America, they all have well-publicized themes. When you hear their taglines, you instantly gain insight into the businesses. For example, when you hear "absolutely, positively has to be there overnight," most people think of Federal Express (FedEx) and package delivery. On top of that, they think of reliability, which is the quality FedEx wants to embody in the minds of its customers. Similarly, "Just do it" is intricately linked to Nike and the image of athletic excellence (see Figure 7.2).

A tagline is a sentence, or even a fragment of a sentence, that summarizes the essence of your business. It's the theme that every sentence, paragraph, page, and diagram in your business plan should adhere to—the unifying idea of your story. One useful tip is to put your tagline in a footer that runs on the bottom of every page. As you are writing, if the section doesn't build on, explain, or otherwise directly relate to the tagline, it most likely isn't a necessary component to the business plan. Rigorous adherence to the tagline facilitates writing a concise and coherent business plan. You might also want to put your tagline on your business card, company letterhead, and other collateral material you develop for the business. It's a reminder to you and your team about what you are trying to accomplish as well as an effective marketing tactic that helps build your brand.

Now let's take another look at the major sections of the plan (refer back to Figure 7.1). Remember that, although there are variations, most planning processes will include these components. It is important to keep your plan as close to this format as possible because many stakeholders are accustomed to this format, and it facilitates spot reading. If you are

Nike.	*Just do it!*
FedEx.	*When it absolutely, positively has to be there overnight*
McDonald's.	*I'm lovin' it*
Microsoft.	*Be What's Next*
Walmart.	*Save Money. Live Better.*
Twitter.	*Yours to Discover*
Facebook.	*Facebook helps you connect and share with the people in your life.*[5]
LinkedIn.	*Be great at what you do*[6]

■ **Figure 7.2**

Taglines

seeking venture capital, for instance, you want to make quick reading possible because venture capitalists often spend as little as five minutes on a plan before rejecting it or putting it aside for further attention. If a venture capitalist becomes frustrated with an unfamiliar format, it is more likely that she will reject it rather than trying to pull out the pertinent information. Even if you aren't seeking venture capital, the common structure is easy for other investors and stakeholders to follow and understand. Furthermore, the highlighted business plan sections in Figure 7.1 provide a road map for questions that you need to consider as you prepare to launch your business.

The Business Plan

Although it's the business planning *process* that's important, it is easier to discuss that process by laying out what the final output, the business plan, might look like. We will progress through the sections in the order that they typically appear, but keep in mind that you can work on the sections in any order that you wish. Business planning is an iterative process. Also, you may find it useful to refer to the P'kolino business plan at the end of this chapter as you read each of the following sections. You'll notice areas where the P'kolino plan follows our suggestions and areas where it doesn't. The most important point is that you evaluate the P'kolino plan's strengths and weaknesses based on how well it articulates the P'kolino story.

The Cover

The cover of the plan should include the following information: company name, tagline, contact person, address, phone, fax, email, date, disclaimer, and copy number. Most of the information is self-explanatory, but a few things should be pointed out. First, the contact person for a new venture should be the president or some other founding team member. Imagine the frustration of an excited potential investor who can't find out how to contact the entrepreneur to gain more information. More often than not, that plan will end up in the reject pile.

Second, business plans should have a disclaimer along these lines:

> *This business plan has been submitted on a confidential basis solely to selected, highly qualified investors. The recipient should not reproduce this plan or distribute it to others without permission. Please return this copy if you do not wish to invest in the company.*

Controlling distribution was, until recently, particularly important when seeking investment, especially if you did not want to violate Regulation D of the Securities and Exchange Commission, which specifies that you may solicit only qualified investors (high-net-worth or high-income individuals). In April 2012, President Obama signed into law the Jumpstart Our Business Startups (JOBS) Act, intended to encourage funding of U.S. small businesses by easing various securities regulations. The JOBS Act directs the SEC to lift the ban on general solicitation and advertising of private placements in securities (i.e., investing in startups). This was previously prohibited to avoid the requirement to register with the SEC (i.e., go public). Although in 2014, when this aspect of the JOBS Act goes into effect, you will be able to raise money by advertising the opportunity to the public, the act will still prohibit non-accredited investors from investing.[7]

The cover should also have a line stating which number copy it is. For example, you will often see on the bottom right portion of the cover a line that says "Copy 1 of 5 copies." Entrepreneurs should keep a log of who has copies so that they can control for unexpected distribution. Finally, the cover should be eye-catching. If you have a product or prototype, a picture of it can draw the reader in. Likewise, a catchy tagline draws attention and encourages the reader to look further.

Executive Summary

This section is the most important part of the business plan. If you don't capture readers' attention in the executive summary, it is unlikely that they will read any other parts of the plan. This is just like a book's jacket notes. Most likely, the reader will buy the book only if she is impressed with the notes inside the cover. In the same way, you want to hit your readers with the most compelling aspects of your business opportunity right up front. *Hook the reader.* That means having the first sentence or paragraph highlight the potential of the opportunity. For example:

> *The current market for widgets is $50 million, growing at an annual rate of 20%. Moreover, the emergence of mobile applications is likely to accelerate this market's growth. Company XYZ is positioned to capture this wave with its proprietary technology: the secret formula VOOM.*

This creates the right tone. The first sentence emphasizes that the potential opportunity is huge; the last sentence explains that Company XYZ has a competitive advantage that enables it to become a big player in this market. Too many plans start with "Company XYZ, incorporated in the state of Delaware, will develop and sell widgets." Ho-hum. This kind of opening is dull and uninspiring—at this point, who cares that the business is incorporated in Delaware (aren't they all?). Capture the reader's attention immediately or risk losing her altogether.

Once you have hooked the reader, you need to provide compelling information about each of the following subsections:

- Description of Opportunity
- Business Concept
- Industry Overview
- Target Market
- Competitive Advantage
- Business Model and Economics
- Team and Offering
- Financial Snapshot

Remember that you'll cover all these components in detail in the body of the plan. As such, we will explore them in greater detail as we progress through the sections. Given that, your goal in the executive summary is to touch on the most important or exciting points of each section. Keep it brief and make it compelling.

Since the executive summary is the most important part of the finished plan, write it *after* you have gained a deep understanding of the business by working through all the other sections. Don't confuse the executive summary included in the plan with the short summary that we suggested you write as the very first step of the business plan process. As a result of your research, the two are likely to be significantly different. Don't recycle your initial summary. Rewrite it entirely based on the hard work you have done by going through the business planning process.

Table of Contents

Continuing the theme of making the document easy to read, a detailed table of contents is critical. It should include major sections, subsections, exhibits, and appendices. The table of contents provides the reader a road map to your plan (see Figure 7.3). Note that the table of contents is customized to the specific business, so it doesn't perfectly match the business plan outline presented earlier in Figure 7.1. Nonetheless, a look at Figure 7.3 shows that the company's business plan includes most of the elements highlighted in the business plan outline and that the order of information is basically the same as well.

■ Figure 7.3

Table of Contents

Industry, Customer, and Competitor Analysis

Industry. The goal of this section is to illustrate the opportunity and how you intend to capture it. However, before you can develop your plot and illustrate a theme, you need to provide a setting or context for your story. Refer back to Chapters 2 and 3, where we described characteristics that create an attractive opportunity. In your plan, you'll need to delineate both the current market size and how much you expect it to grow in the future. In addition, you need to indicate what kind of market you're facing. History tells us that often the best opportunities are found in emerging markets—those that appear poised for rapid growth and that have the potential to change the way we live and work. For example, in the 1980s the personal computer, disk drive, and computer hardware markets revolutionized our way of life. Many new companies were born and rode the wave of the emerging technology, including Apple, Microsoft, and Intel. In the 1990s, it was anything dealing with the Internet. eBay, Google, and Facebook have leveraged the Internet and changed the way we live. Mobility is the word today.

The mobile industry is fundamentally changing how consumers spend money, from the homes we buy and the doctors we visit to how we select entertainment and modes of travel, from what we eat and drink to how we communicate and get to work each day. Mobile does not simply change our purchasing behavior but also the purchasing options themselves. Five major platforms dominate—Apple, Google, Amazon, Microsoft, and Facebook, although it is Apple and Google that have the real power because they have built eco-systems around their platforms. Now that sharing information is just a thumb swipe away, customers are openly sharing more than ever before. Mobile is closing the divide for brands and advertisers between their advertisement and its impact on a subsequent purchase. The long-term race is to control the platform over which this information sharing occurs. Having this knowledge is quite simply the most valuable currency in today's commerce. Total Global Mobile Revenues hit $1.5 trillion in 2012, over 2% of the world's GDP. The moment is rapidly approaching when mobile commerce will be *the* dominant form of commerce.[8]

Other important current trends include energy and environment, which have created a clean technology boom. According to *Clean Energy Trends 2012*, revenue from clean technologies grew 31% from $188 billion in 2010 to $246 billion in 2011 and is projected to grow to $386 billion by 2021.[9] Another market structure that tends to hold promise is a fragmented market where small, dispersed competitors compete on a regional basis. Many of the big names in retail revolutionized fragmented markets. For instance, category killers such as Walmart, Staples, and Home Depot consolidated fragmented markets by providing quality products at lower prices. These firms replaced the dispersed regional and local discount, office supply, and hardware stores.

Another key attribute to explore is industry economics. For example, do companies within the industry enjoy strong gross and net income margins? Higher margins allow for higher returns, which again leads to greater growth potential. This typically happens when the market is emerging and demand exceeds supply. So, again, you'll want to explore where the margins are today—and also where you expect them to go in the future.

You'll note that we keep referring to the future. A good market analysis will look at trends that are shaping the future. For instance, as the world continues to adopt wireless communication, more and more people are connected 24/7. What might this mean for your business? Another trend that has had tremendous ramifications on U.S. society is the life cycle of the baby boom generation. Over the last 50 years, business has responded to this generation's needs and wants. In the 1950s and 1960s, that meant building schools. In the 1970s and 1980s, it meant building houses and introducing family cars like the minivan. In the 1990s, it led to Internet concepts, as this group was more affluent and computer savvy than any generation before it. Today the baby boomers are approaching retirement. What opportunities does this trend portend? Identify the trends, both positive and negative, that will interact with your business.

You need to describe your overall market in terms of revenues, growth, and future trends that are pertinent. In this section, avoid discussing your concept, the proposed product or service you will offer. Instead, use dispassionate, arm's-length analysis of the market with the goal of highlighting a space or gap that is underserved. Thus, focus on how the market is segmented now and how it will be segmented into the future. After identifying the relevant market segments, identify the segment your product will target. Again, what are the important trends that will shape this segment in the future?

Customer. Once you've defined the market space you plan to enter, you'll examine the target customer in detail. As we discussed in Chapters 4 and 5, an accurate customer profile is essential to developing a product that customers truly want and marketing campaigns that they will actually respond to. Define who the customer is by using demographic and psychographic information. The better the entrepreneur can define her specific customers, the more apt she is to deliver a product that these customers truly want. Although you may argue that everyone who is hungry is a restaurant's customer, such a vague definition makes it hard to market to the core customer. For instance, since I'm a middle-aged man, my eating habits will be different from what they were when I was 20-something. I will frequent different types of establishments and expect certain kinds of foods within a certain price range. I'm beyond fast food, for example. Thus, you'd have very different strategies to serve and reach me than you would to reach younger people. Unless you develop this deep an understanding of your customer, your business is unlikely to succeed.

To help, companies often develop profiles of the different kinds of customers they target. For example, Apple has profiled its primary customer segments, which serve as an aid to help employees better understand their customers' needs. Their target customers come from households earning more than $60,000 annually, they have completed 4+ years of college study, one-third are between 18 and 34 years old, and 1 in 5 customers are self-employed.

A venture capitalist recently said that the most impressive entrepreneur is the one who comes into his office and not only identifies who the customer is in terms of demographics and psychographics, but also identifies that customer by address, phone number, and email. You can even go one step further by including letters of interest or intent from key customers who express a willingness to buy, once your product or service is ready. When you understand who your customers are, you can assess what compels them to buy, how your company can sell to them (direct sales, retail, Internet, direct mail), and how much it is going to cost to acquire and retain them as customers.

An exhibit describing customers in terms of the basic parameters and inserted into the text of your plan can be very powerful, because it communicates a lot of data quickly.

Too often entrepreneurs figure that, if they love their product concept, so should everybody else. Although your needs and wants are the best place to start, you must recognize that they may not be the same as everyone else's. So to truly understand your customers, you need to talk to them. Early in your conceptualization of your product or service, go out and interview potential customers (the appendix at the end of Chapter 5 provides some questions that might be useful). Keep your questions open ended and try not to direct the customer's answers. It is critical to *listen* at this stage rather than talking about your concept. After each customer interaction, go back and reevaluate your concept. Can you cost-effectively incorporate features that will make this product better fit the customer's need? After several individual conversations, run a focus group and then maybe a broader customer survey. At each step along the way, refine your concept and start to define the demographic and psychographic characteristics of your primary target audience. This process helps you create a better product that is more likely to gain customer acceptance than if you boldly (and blindly) charge ahead with your initial concept. As you get closer to launching, you'll likely have a beta customer use your product or service to further refine the concept. The key once again is that business planning is the *process*, not the output (written plan).

Competition. The competition analysis proceeds directly from of the customer analysis, and you should complete it using a competitive profile matrix. You have already identified your market segment, profiled your customer, and described what he wants. Armed with this information, you can begin to research how your direct and indirect competitors are meeting those needs. The basis of comparison will be the different product features and attributes that each competitor uses to differentiate itself from the pack. A competitive profile matrix not only

	My Concept	Big-Box Stores	Amazon	History Channel Web site	Museum Stores	Specialty Web sites
History book selection	2	3	1	3	4	3
Display of artifacts	1	5	5	5	3	5
History-related gift items	1	5	4	2	1	2
Videos/DVDs	1	4	3	3	5	2
Price	3	2	1	2	3	3
Atmosphere	1	2	5	5	4	5
Employee knowledge	1	4	5	5	2	5
Ease of shopping for specific items	2	2	1	1	3	4
Location	4	1	1	1	5	3
Ease of browsing	1	2	3	3	2	4

■ Figure 7.4

Competitive profile matrix

creates a powerful visual catch-point but also conveys information about your competitive advantage and is the basis for your company's strategy (see Figure 7.4).

The competitive profile matrix should be at the beginning of the section, followed by text describing the analysis and its implications. Figure 7.4 shows a sample competitive profile matrix for a new retail concept—a specialty store targeting the history enthusiast. The entrepreneur rates each competitor (or competitor type) on various key success factors using a five-point scale (with 1 being strong on the attribute and 5 being weak). Often entrepreneurs include product attributes such as the product color, dimensions, specifications, and so forth, but you should omit this unless you believe they are the main criteria customers will use to decide to buy your product over those of competitors. Instead, focus on the key success factors that often lead a customer to buy one product over another, such as price, quality, speed, and so on. It is also a good idea to list your own concept in the matrix. Up until this point, your plan has been painting a picture of the industry and market. By including your concept in the matrix, you begin to shift the focus toward your company and the opportunity you believe it can capture. In Figure 7.4, we can see that the entrepreneur expects to do well on most attributes, except for price and location. In describing the matrix, the entrepreneur would explain why the business is weak on those attributes and why it is better on the rest. Understanding the strengths and weaknesses of the business concept helps the entrepreneur to define the company's strategy.

Finding information about your competition can be easy if the company is public, harder if it is private, and very difficult if it is operating in "stealth" mode (it hasn't yet announced itself to the world). Most libraries have access to databases that contain a wealth of information about publicly traded companies (see Figure 7.5 for some sample sources), but privately held companies or "stealth ventures" represent a greater challenge.

The best way for savvy entrepreneurs to gather competitive information is through their network and trade shows. Who should be in the entrepreneur's network? First and foremost are the customers the entrepreneur hopes to sell to in the near future. Just as you are (or should be) talking to your potential customers, your existing competition is interacting with this group every day, and as a result, your customers are the best source of information about the "stealth" competition on the horizon. Although many entrepreneurs are fearful (verging on the brink of paranoia) that valuable information will fall into the wrong hands and lead to new competition that invalidates the current venture, the reality is that entrepreneurs who openly talk about their ideas with as many people as possible are far more likely to succeed. Take the risk. Talking allows entrepreneurs to get the kind of valuable feedback that can make the difference between success and failure in a venture.

Infotrac — Find an array of databases in the business, science, and social science disciplines.

Factiva — Search the world's leading business and news publications, including *WSJ* & *Barron's*.

LexisNexis — Find full-text articles on national and international news, business, company and financial information as well as the text of laws, codes, statutes, rulings, and law journal articles.

Dun & Bradstreet — Source of commercial information and insight on businesses. D&B's global commercial database contains more than 205 million business records and an international business directory.

Hoover's Online — Proprietary information about more than 40,000 public and non-public companies and 225,000 key executives. Contains in-depth industry analyses, information on a company's location, summary financials, top competitors, top officers and more.

CorpTech — The database contains details for more than 95,000 companies and 285,000 executives in 17 high-tech industry sectors. The data is compiled from primary research obtained from company sources to ensure current and accurate information .

RDS Business Reference Suite — The RDS Business Suite combines three business research staples — Business & Industry, Business and Management Practices and TableBase (available separately or as a collection) — to deliver a comprehensive research package featuring more than 1,400 global business sources. Linked databases providing data and full-text searching on firms.

Bloomberg — Integrates data, news, analytics, multimedia reports, email, and trading capabilities into a single platform.

Business Monitor International — Country risk, industry reports, and company coverage in global markets. Includes news, reports, and data.

Figure 7.5

Sample sources for information on public/private companies

Company and Product Description

The dispassionate analysis described in the previous section lays the foundation for describing your company and concept. In this section, you'll introduce the basic details of your company before moving on to a more detailed analysis of your marketing and operations plans.

You can begin by identifying the company name and where the business is incorporated. After that, you should provide a brief overview of the concept for the company and then highlight what the company has achieved to date. If you have reached any major milestones, be sure to list them, but don't worry if the business plan is your first step. Subsequent drafts will provide you with opportunities to showcase what you have achieved.

Once you have provided an introduction, take some time to communicate the product and its differentiating features. You can do this in writing, but keep in mind that graphic representations are visually powerful. You'll note in the P'kolino case at the end of this chapter that the photos create a powerful message, communicating much about how this concept is different from the existing alternatives. Highlight how your product fits into the customer value proposition. What is incorporated into your product, and what value-add do you deliver to the customer? Which of the customer's unmet wants and needs are fulfilled by your offering? In essence, you need to tell us why your product is better, cheaper, or faster and how that creates value for the customer. Your advantage may be a function of proprietary technology, patents, distribution, and/or design. In fact, the most powerful competitive advantages are derived from a bundle of factors because this makes them more difficult to copy.

Entrepreneurs also need to identify their market entry and growth strategies. Since most new ventures are resource constrained, especially for available capital, it is crucial that the lead entrepreneur establish the most effective way to enter the market. We discussed in Chapters 3 and 5 how to identify your core customer or primary target audience (PTA) based on an analysis of the market and customer sections. Focusing on a particular niche or subset of the overall market allows new ventures to effectively utilize scarce resources to reach those customers and prove the viability of their concept.

The business plan should also sell the entrepreneur's vision for the company's long-term growth potential. If the venture achieves success in its entry strategy, either it will generate internal cash flow that can be used to fuel continued growth, or it will be attractive enough to get further equity financing at improved valuations. The growth strategy should talk about the secondary and tertiary target audiences that the firm will pursue once it meets success with the core customer. For instance, technology companies might go from selling to users who want the best performance (early adopters) to users who want ease of use (mainstream market). Whatever the case, you should devote at least a paragraph or two to the firm's long-term growth strategy.

Marketing Plan

Up to this point, you've described your company's potential to successfully enter and grow in a marketplace. Now you need to devise the strategy that will allow it to reach its potential. The primary components of this section are descriptions of the target market strategy, product/service strategy, pricing strategy, distribution strategy, marketing communications strategy, sales strategy, and sales and marketing forecasts. Let's take a look at each of these subsections in turn.

Target Market Strategy. Every marketing plan needs some guiding principles. In targeting and positioning your product, you should lean heavily on the knowledge you gleaned from the customer analysis. For instance, product strategies often fall along a continuum whose endpoints are rational purchase and emotional purchase. For example, when a person buys a new car, the rational purchase might be a low-cost reliable option such as the Ford Focus. In contrast, some people see a car as an extension of their personality—and therefore might buy a BMW or an Audi because of the emotional benefits it delivers. Within every product space, there is room for products measured at different points along this continuum. You can also use this idea of a continuum to find other dimensions that help you classify your marketplace. These tools help entrepreneurs decide where their product fits or where they would like to position it, and once you have solidified your target market strategy, you can begin working on the other aspects of the marketing plan.

Product/Service Strategy. Building from the target market strategy, this section of the plan describes how you will differentiate your product from the competition. Discuss why the customer will switch to your product and how you will retain customers so that they don't switch to your competition in the future. You can create a powerful visual by using the attributes defined in your customer profile matrix to produce a product attribute map. This tool is a great way to illustrate how your firm compares to the competition. In creating it, you should focus on the two most important attributes, putting one on the x-axis and the other on the y-axis. The map should show that you are clearly distinguishable from your competition on desirable attributes.

Figure 7.6 shows the competitive map for the retail concept that focuses on the history enthusiast. The two attributes on which it evaluates competitors are atmosphere

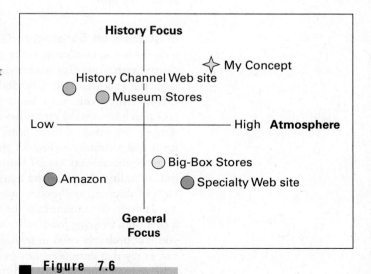

Figure 7.6

Product attribute map

(Is this a place where people will linger?) and focus (Does it have a broad topic focus, or is it specialized?). As you can see from Figure 7.6, our retail concept plans to have a high level of history specialization and atmosphere, which places it in the upper-right quadrant. From the product attribute map, it is easy to see how our retail concept will distinguish itself from the competition. The map implies that history specialization and atmosphere will attract history buffs and entice them to return time and again.

This section should also address what services you will provide the customer. What type of technical support will you provide? Will you offer warranties? What kind of product upgrades will be available and when? It is important to detail all these efforts because they will affect the pricing of the product. Many times entrepreneurs underestimate the costs of these services, which leads to a drain on cash and ultimately to bankruptcy.

Pricing Strategy. Pricing your product is challenging. Canvassing prevailing prices in the marketplace helps you determine what the perceived value for your product might be. If your product is of better quality and has lots of features, price it above market rates. We saw in Chapter 5 that a price-skimming strategy is best in the beginning, to gain a sense of what customers are willing to pay—that means pricing a bit higher than you believe the perceived value to be. It is always easier to reduce prices later than to raise them. Most importantly, if during the course of researching possible prices you find that you can't price your product well above what it will cost you to produce it, the business planning process will have saved you untold time and pain. You have two choices: redesign your concept or abandon it.

Remember to avoid "cost plus" pricing (also discussed in Chapter 5). First, it is difficult to accurately determine your actual cost, especially if this is a new venture with a limited history. New ventures consistently underestimate the true cost of developing their products. For example, how much did it really cost to write that software? The cost includes salaries and payroll taxes, computers and other assets, the overhead contribution, and more. Since most entrepreneurs underestimate these costs, they underprice their products. Second, we often hear entrepreneurs claim that they are offering a low price in order to penetrate and gain market share rapidly. One major problem with launching at a low price is that it may be difficult to raise the price later; it can send a signal of lower quality. In addition, demand at that price may overwhelm your ability to produce the product in sufficient volume, and it may unnecessarily strain cash flow.

Distribution Strategy. This section of your written plan identifies how your product will reach the customer. Since much of the cost of delivering a product is tied up in its distribution, your distribution strategy can define your company's fortune as much as or more than the product itself. Distribution strategy is thus more than an operational detail. For example, the e-commerce boom of the late 1990s assumed that the growth in Internet usage and purchases would create new demand for pure Internet companies. Yet the distribution strategy for many of these firms did not make sense. Pets.com and other online pet supply firms had a strategy calling for the pet owner to log on, order the product from the site, and then receive delivery via UPS or the U.S. Postal Service. The strategy was fantastic in theory, but in reality, the price the market would bear for this product didn't cover the exorbitant costs of shipping a 40-pound bag of dog food.

It's wise to examine how the customer currently acquires the product. If you're developing a new brand of dog food and your primary target customer buys dog food at Walmart, then you will probably need to include traditional retail outlets in your distribution plans. This is not to say that entrepreneurs are limited to a single-channel distribution strategy, just that to achieve maximum growth will probably require the use of common distribution techniques. While it may be appealing to take retail outlets out of this chain, re-educating customers about a new buying process can be prohibitively expensive and challenging.

Once you determine the best distribution channel, the next question is whether you can access it. The Walmart example is a good one. A new startup in dog food may have difficulty getting shelf space at Walmart. A better entry strategy might focus on boutique pet stores to build brand recognition. Once your product is well known and in high demand, retail stores like Walmart will be much more likely to carry your brand. The key here is to identify appropriate channels and then assess how costly it is to access them.

Marketing Communications Strategy. Communicating effectively to your customer requires advertising and promotion, among other methods. Since these tools are expensive, resource-constrained entrepreneurs need to carefully select the appropriate strategies. What avenues most effectively reach your core customer? Your options include mass advertising, target advertising (e.g., Google Adwords), and public relations. While mass advertising is often the most expensive approach, it is also one of the most effective tools for building a brand. In contrast, if you can identify your core customer by name, then direct mail may be more effective than mass media blitzes. Similarly, grassroots techniques such as public relations efforts geared toward mainstream media can be more cost effective.

Bo Fishback, Eric Koester, and Ian Hunter are serial entrepreneurs and the co-founders of Zaarly, a private company focused on developing a proximity-based, real-time, buyer-powered market platform. They knew that their marketing strategy needed to generate demand before their app was released. They employed a multifaceted approach to accomplish this through social media posts, open/closed social media groups, online blogging, and features in media such as the Huffington Post to establish thought-leadership. They then were interviewed on FOX Business, Bloomberg, and *Inc.* magazine, which led to numerous other online articles in well-known media. Marketing in this way, they attracted enough attention that Meg Whitman became a board member, and they raised $14.1 million in funding. Launching in 2011, Zaarly's marketing campaign ensured they had customers on day one, and after only 3.5 months, they had over 100,000 subscribers.

In contrast, the dot-com boom of the late 1990s offers striking examples of advertising failures, such as Computer.com's exorbitant media buy during the 2000 Super Bowl. The firm spent $3 million of the $5.8 million it had raised on three ads.[10] Needless to say, the gamble failed, and now it represents a textbook example of the importance of using advertising carefully.

As you develop a multipronged advertising and promotion strategy, create detailed schedules that show which avenues you will pursue and the associated costs (see Figures 7.7a and 7.7b). These types of schedules serve many purposes, including providing accurate costs estimates, which will help in assessing how much capital you need to raise. They also build credibility in the eyes of potential investors by demonstrating that you understand the nuances of your market.

Promotional Tools	Budget over 1 Year
Print advertising	$ 5,000
Direct mail	3,000
In-store promotions	2,000
Tour group outreach	1,000
Public relations	1,000
Total	$ 12,000

Figure 7.7a

Advertising schedule

Publication	Circulation	Ad Price for Quarter Page	Total Budget for Year 1
Lexington Minuteman newspaper	7,886	$ 500	$4,000
Boston magazine	1,400,000	$1,000	$1,000

■ **Figure 7.7b**

Magazine advertisements

Sales Strategy. The section on sales strategy provides the backbone that supports all of the subsections described so far. Specifically, it illustrates what kind and level of human capital you will devote to the effort. You should complete a careful analysis of how many salespeople and customer support reps you will need. Will these people be internal to the organization or outsourced? If they are internal, will there be a designated sales force, or will different members of the company serve in a sales capacity at different times? Again, a thoughtful presentation of the company's sales force builds credibility by demonstrating an understanding of how the business should operate.

Sales and Marketing Forecasts. Gauging the impact of sales efforts is difficult. Nonetheless, to build a compelling story, entrepreneurs need to show projections of revenues well into the future. How do you derive these numbers? There are two methods: the *comparable method* and the *build-up method*. After detailed investigation of the industry and the market, entrepreneurs know the competitive players and have a good understanding of their history. The **comparable method** models the sales forecast after what other companies have achieved and then adjusts these numbers for differences in things like the age of the company and the variances in product attributes. In essence, the entrepreneur monitors a number of comparable competitors and then explains why her business varies from those models.

In the **build-up method**, the entrepreneur identifies all the possible revenue sources of the business and then estimates how much of each type of revenue the company can generate during a given period of time. For example, a bookstore generates revenues from books and artifacts. Thus, a bookstore owner would estimate the average sales price for each product category. Then he might estimate the number of people to come through the store on a daily basis and the percentage that would purchase each revenue source. From these numbers, he could create a sales forecast for a typical day, which could then be aggregated into larger blocks of time (months, quarters, or years). These rough estimates might then be further adjusted based on seasonality in the bookstore industry. In the end, the bookstore owner would have a workable model for sales forecasts.

The build-up technique is an imprecise method for the new startup with limited operating history, but it is critically important to assess the viability of the opportunity. It's so important, in fact, that you might want to use both the comparable and the build-up techniques to assess how well they converge. If the two methods are widely divergent, go back through and try to determine why. The knowledge you gain of your business model will help you better articulate the opportunity to stakeholders, and it will provide you with invaluable insights as you begin managing the business after its launch. Chapter 8 provides more detail on how to derive these estimates.

While we know for certain that these forecasts will never be 100% accurate, it is essential to minimize the degree of error. Detailed investigation of comparable companies can help you accomplish this goal, as can triangulating your comparable method results with your build-up method results. However you go about building your forecast, always keep in mind that the smaller the error, the less likely your company will run out of cash. Beyond building credibility with your investors, rigorous estimates are also the single best tool for keeping your company out of financial trouble.

Operations Plan

The key in the operations plan section is to address how operations will add value for your customers. Here, you'll detail the production cycle and gauge its impact on working capital. For instance, when does your company pay for inputs? How long does it take to produce the product? When does the customer buy the product and, more importantly, when does the customer pay for the product? From the time you pay for your raw materials until you receive payment from your customers, you will be operating in a negative cash flow. The shorter that cycle, the more cash you have on hand and the less likely you are to need bank financing. It sounds counterintuitive, but many rapidly growing new companies run out of cash even though they have increasing sales and substantial operating profit. The reason is that they fail to properly finance the time their cash is tied up in the procurement, production, sales, and receivables cycle.

Operations Strategy. The first subsection of your operations strategy section provides a strategy overview. How does your business compare on the dimensions of cost, quality, time-liness, and flexibility? Emphasize those aspects that provide your venture with a comparative advantage. It is also appropriate to discuss the geographic location of production facilities and how this enhances your firm's competitive advantage. Your notes should cover such issues as available labor, local regulations, transportation, infrastructure, and proximity to suppliers. In addition, the section should provide a description of the facilities, discuss whether you will buy or lease them, and explain how you will handle future growth (by renting an adjoining building, perhaps). As in all sections detailing strategy, support your plans with actual data.

Scope of Operations. What is the production process for your product or service? Creating a diagram makes it easier for you to see which production aspects to keep in-house and which to outsource (see Figure 7.8a). Considering that cash flow is king and that resource-constrained new ventures typically should minimize fixed expenses on production facilities, the general rule is to outsource as much production as possible. However, there is a major caveat to that rule: Your venture should control aspects of production that are central to your competitive advantage. Thus, if you are producing a new component with hard-wired proprietary technology—let's say a voice recognition security door entry—it is wise to internally produce that hard-wired component. The locking mechanism, on the other

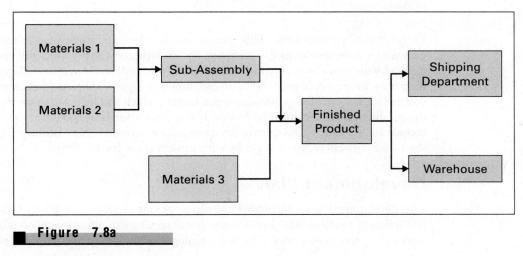

Figure 7.8a

Operations flow

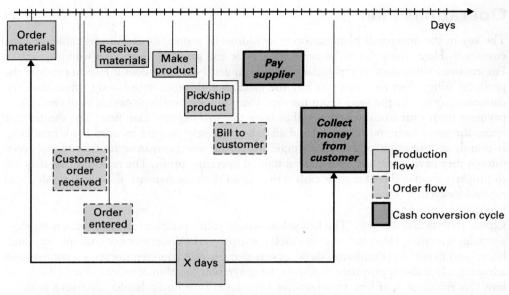

Source: Adapted from Professor Robert Eng, Babson College

Figure 7.8b

Operating cycle

hand, can be outsourced to your specifications. Outsourcing the aspects that aren't proprietary reduces fixed costs for production equipment and facility expenditures, which means you have to raise less money and give up less equity.

The scope of operations section should also discuss partnerships with vendors, suppliers, and partners. Again, the diagram should illustrate the supplier and vendor relationships by category or by name (if the list isn't too long and you have already identified your suppliers). The diagram helps you visualize the various relationships and ways to better manage or eliminate them. The operations diagram also helps identify staffing needs—for example, how many production workers you might need depending on the hours of operation and number of shifts.

Ongoing Operations. This section builds upon the scope of operations section by providing details on day-to-day activities. For example, how many units will you produce in a day and what kinds of inputs will you need? An operating cycle overview diagram graphically illustrates the impact of production on cash flow (see Figure 7.8b). As you complete this detail, you can start to establish performance parameters, which will help you to monitor and modify the production process into the future. If this plan is for your use only, you may choose to include such details as the specific job descriptions. However, for a business plan that will be shared with investors, you can get by with a much lower level of detail.

Development Plan

The development plan highlights the development strategy and also provides a detailed development timeline. Many new ventures will require a significant level of effort and time to launch the product or service. This is the prologue of your story. For example, new software or hardware products often require months of development. Discuss what types of features you will develop and tie them to the firm's competitive advantage. This section should also discuss any patent, trademark, or copyright efforts you will undertake.

Development Strategy.

What work remains to be completed? What factors need to come together for development to be successful? What risks to development does the firm face? For example, software development is notorious for taking longer and costing more than most companies originally imagined. Detailing the necessary work and what needs to happen for you to consider the work successful helps you understand and manage the risks involved. After you have laid out these details, you can assemble a development timeline.

Development Timeline.

A development timeline is a schedule that you use to highlight major milestone and to monitor progress and make changes. It's often useful to illustrate time lines as Gantt charts. Figure 7.9 illustrates a typical Gantt chart for a new business launching a history themed bookstore.

The timeline helps you track major events, delegate responsibilities for project tasks, and schedule activities to best execute those events. In addition to plotting future milestones, it is a good idea to illustrate which development milestones you have already achieved as of the writing of the business plan. Finally, keep in mind that, as the old adage says, "time is money." Every day your product is in development and not on the market, you lose a day's worth of sales. You will have to work hard to meet deadlines, especially in those industries where speed to market is critical.

Team

We mentioned in Chapter 2 that Georges Doriot would rather back a "grade-A man with a grade-B idea than a grade-B man with a grade-A idea." For this reason, the team section of the business plan is often the section that professional investors read right after the executive summary. This section is also critically important to the lead entrepreneur. It identifies the members responsible for key activities and conveys why they are exceptionally qualified to execute on those responsibilities. The section also helps you consider how well this group of individuals will work together. It is well established that ventures started by strong teams are much more likely to succeed than those led by weak teams.

Team Bios and Roles.

Every story needs a cast of characters, and the best place to start is by identifying the key team members and their titles. Often the lead entrepreneur assumes a CEO role. However, if you are young and have limited business experience, it is usually more productive to state that the company will seek a qualified CEO as it grows. In these cases, the lead entrepreneur may assume the role of Chief Technology Officer (if she develops the technology) or Vice President of Business Development. However, don't let these options confine you. The key is to convince your investors that you have assembled the best team possible and that your team can execute on the brilliant concept you are proposing.

A simple, relatively flat organization chart is often useful to visualize what roles you have filled and what gaps remain. It also provides a road map for reading the bios that follow. The bios should demonstrate records of success. If you have previously started a business (even if it failed), highlight the company's *accomplishments*. If you have no previous entrepreneurial experience, discuss your achievements in your last job. For example, bios often contain a description of the number of people the entrepreneur previously managed and, more importantly, a measure of economic success, such as "grew division sales by 20-plus percent." The bio should demonstrate your leadership capabilities. Include the team's resumes as an appendix.

Activity	12	11	10	9	8	7	6	5	4	3	2	1	Opening Month
10–12 Months Prior to Opening													
1) Finalize business plan and financials	▓												
2) Review plans with local bookstore/ specialty shop owners	▓	▓											
3) Fill in skill gaps with advisory board		▓											
4) Determine exact location possibilities		▓	▓										
7–9 Months Prior to Opening													
5) Register rights to business name			▓										
6) Seek funding from appropriate sources				▓									
7) Update business plan per feedback from potential financiers				▓									
8) Make initial contact with product vendors				▓	▓								
9) Contact POS/inventory vendors and store designers						▓							
4–6 Months Prior to Opening													
10) Determine exact store design							▓						
11) Finalize product vendors								▓					
12) Confirm funding									▓				
3 Months Prior to Opening													
13) Finalize store design plans									▓				
14) Open vendor/bank accounts										▓			
15) Place fixture orders										▓			
16) Finalize marketing plan and implement to announce store opening events										▓			
17) Submit merchandise orders with all vendors										▓			
1 Month Prior to Opening													
18) Contact local media re placement in local newspapers and magazines											▓		
19) Code merchandise category data in inventory management system											▓		
20) Recruit and train staff											▓		
21) Receive merchandise, fixtures, and complete setup of store											▓		
Opening Month													
22) "Soft opening" of store to assess customer response, training, and system functioning												▓	▓
Grand Opening of Store												▓	▓

Figure 7.9

Gantt chart

Advisory Boards, Board of Directors, Strategic Partners, External Members. Many entrepreneurs find that they are more attractive to investors if they have strong advisory boards. In building an advisory board, you want to create a team with diverse skills and experience. Industry experts provide legitimacy to your new business as well as strong technical advice. Other advisors should bring financial, legal, or management expertise. Thus, it is common to see lawyers, professors, accountants, and others who can assist the venture's growth on advisory boards. Moreover, if your firm has a strategic supplier or key customer, it may make sense to invite him onto your advisory board. Typically, these individuals are remunerated with a small equity stake and compensation for any organized meetings.

By law, most types of organization require a board of directors. While members of the advisory board can also provide needed expertise, a board of directors is different from an advisory board. The directors' primary role is to oversee the company on behalf of the investors, and to that end, the board has the power to replace top executives if it feels doing so would be in the best interests of the company. Therefore, the business plan needs to briefly describe the size of the board, its role within the organization, and any current board members. Most major investors, such as venture capitalists, will require one or more board seats. Usually, the lead entrepreneur and one or more inside company members, such as the Chief Financial Officer or a Vice President, will also have board seats.

Strategic partners may not necessarily be on your advisory board or your board of directors, but they still provide credibility to your venture. For this reason, it makes sense to highlight their involvement in your company's success. It is also common to list external team members, such as the law firm and accounting firm that your venture uses. The key in this section is to demonstrate that your firm can successfully execute the concept. A strong team provides the foundation that can ensure your venture will implement the opportunity successfully.

Compensation and Ownership. A capstone to the team section should be a table listing key team members by role, compensation, and ownership equity. A brief description in the text should explain why the compensation is appropriate. Many entrepreneurs choose not to pay themselves in the early months. Although this strategy conserves cash flow, it would misrepresent the individual's worth to the organization. Therefore, the table should contain what salary the employee is due. If necessary, that salary can be deferred until a time when cash flow is strong. Another column that can be powerful shows what the person's current or most recent compensation was and what she will be paid in the new company. Highly qualified entrepreneurs taking a smaller salary than at their previous job make an impressive point. While everyone understands that the entrepreneur's salary will increase as the company begins to grow, starting at a reduced salary sends the message that you and your team believe in the upside of your idea. Just be sure the description of the schedule underscores the plan to increase salaries in the future. In addition, it is a good idea to hold stock aside for future key hires and to establish a stock option pool for critical lower-level employees, such as software engineers. The plan should discuss such provisions.

Critical Risks

Every new venture faces a number of risks that may threaten its survival. Although the business plan, to this point, is creating a story of success, readers will identify and recognize a number of threats. The plan needs to acknowledge these potential risks; otherwise, investors will believe that the entrepreneur is naïve or untrustworthy and may possibly withhold investment. How should you present these critical risks without scaring your investor or other stakeholders? Identify the risk and then state your contingency plan. Critical risks are critical assumptions—factors that need to happen if your venture is to succeed as currently planned. The critical assumptions vary from one company to another, but some common categories are market interest and growth potential, competitor actions and retaliation, time and cost of development, operating expenses, and availability and timing of financing.

Market Interest and Growth Potential.

The biggest risk any new venture faces is that, once the product has been developed, no one will buy it. Although you can do a number of things to minimize this risk, such as market research, focus groups, and beta sites, it is difficult to gauge overall demand, and the growth of that demand, until your product hits the market. State this risk, but counter it with the tactics and contingencies the company will undertake. For example, sales risk can be reduced by mounting an effective advertising and marketing plan or by identifying not only a core customer but also secondary and tertiary target audiences that the company will seek if the core customer proves less interested.

Competitor Actions and Retaliation.

Too many entrepreneurs believe either that direct competition doesn't exist or that it is sleepy and slow to react. Don't rely on this belief as a key assumption of your venture's success. Most entrepreneurs passionately believe that they are offering something new and wonderful that is clearly different from what is currently on the market. They go on to state that existing competition won't attack their niche in the near future. Acknowledge the risk that this assessment may be wrong. One counter to this threat is that the venture has room in its gross margins to operate at lower-than-anticipated price levels and the cash available to withstand and fight back against such attacks. You should also identify the strategies you will use to protect and reposition yourself, should an attack occur.

Time and Cost of Development.

As mentioned in the development plan section, many factors can delay and add to the expense of developing your product. The business plan should identify the factors that may hinder development. For instance, during the extended high-tech boom of the late 1990s and into the new century, there has been an acute shortage of skilled software engineers. You need to address how you will overcome the challenge of hiring and retaining the most qualified professionals, perhaps by outsourcing some development to the underemployed engineers in India. Compensation, equity participation, flexible hours, and other benefits that the firm could offer might also minimize the risk. Whatever your strategy, you need to demonstrate an understanding of the difficult task at hand and assure potential investors that you will be able to develop the product on time and on budget.

Operating Expenses.

Operating expenses have a way of growing beyond expectations. Sales, administration, marketing, and interest expenses are some of the areas you need to monitor and manage. The business plan should highlight how you forecast your expenses (comparable companies and detailed analysis) and also lay out your contingency plans for unexpected developments. For instance, you may want to slow the hiring of support staff if development or other key tasks take longer than expected. Remember, cash is king, and your plan should illustrate how you will conserve cash when things don't go according to plan.

Availability and Timing of Financing.

We can't stress enough how important cash flow is to the survival and flourishing of a new venture. One major risk that most new ventures face is that they will have difficulty obtaining needed financing, both equity and debt. If the current business plan is successful in attracting investors, cash flow will not be a problem in the short-term. However, most ventures will need multiple rounds of financing. If the firm fails to make progress or meet key milestones, it may not be able to secure additional rounds of financing. This can put the entrepreneur in the uncomfortable position of having to accept unfavorable financing terms or, in the worst-case scenario, force the company into bankruptcy. Your contingency plans should identify viable alternative sources of capital and strategies to slow the "burn rate."[11]

A number of other risks might apply to your business. Acknowledge them and discuss how you can overcome them. Doing so generates confidence among your investors and helps you anticipate corrective actions that you may need to take.

Offering

Using your vision for the business and your estimates of the capital required to get there, you can develop a "sources and uses" schedule for the offering section of your business plan. The sources section details how much capital you need and the types of financing, such as equity investment and debt infusions. The uses section details how you'll spend the money. Typically, you should secure enough financing to last 12 to 18 months. If you take more capital than you need, you have to give up more equity. If you take less, you may run out of cash before reaching milestones that equate to higher valuations.

Financial Plan

Chapter 8 illustrates how to construct your pro-forma financials, but you will also need a verbal description of these financials. We will defer discussion of this section until the next chapter.

Appendices

The appendices can include anything and everything that you think adds further validation to your concept but that doesn't fit or is too large to insert in the main parts of the plan. Common inclusions would be one-page resumes of key team members, articles that feature your venture, and technical specifications. If you already have customers, include a few excerpts of testimonials from them. Likewise, if you have favorable press coverage, include that as well. As a general rule, try to put all exhibits discussed in the written part of the plan on the same page on which you discuss them so the reader doesn't have to keep flipping back to the end of the plan to look at an exhibit. However, it is acceptable to put very large exhibits into an appendix.

Types of Plans

So far in this chapter, we have laid out the basic sections or areas you want to address in your business planning process. The earliest drafts should be housed in a three-ring binder so you can add and subtract as you gain a deeper understanding, but at some point, you may want to print a more formal-looking plan.

Business plans can take a number of forms depending on their purpose. Each form requires the same level of effort and leads to the same conclusions, but the final document is crafted differently depending on who uses it and when they use it. For instance, when you are introducing your concept to a potential investor, you might send a short, concise summary plan. As the investor's interest grows and she wants to more fully investigate the concept, she may ask for a more detailed plan. Even though the equity boom of the late 1990s essentially equated entrepreneurship with venture capital, a business plan serves many more purposes than the needs of potential investors. Employees, strategic partners, financiers, and board members all may find use for a well-developed business plan. Most importantly, the entrepreneur herself gains immeasurably from the business planning process because it allows her not only to run the company better but also to clearly articulate her story to stakeholders, who may never read the plan. In sum, different consumers of the business plan require different presentation of the work.

Your three-ring binder is basically what we would call an *operational plan*. It is primarily for you and your team to guide the development, launch, and initial growth of the venture. There really is no length specification for this type of plan, but it's not unusual to exceed 80 pages. The biggest difference between an operational plan and the one you might present to a potential investor is the level of detail, which tends to be much greater in an operational plan. Remember, the creation of this document is where you really gain the deep understanding so important in discerning how to build and run the business.

If you need outside capital, a business plan geared toward equity investors or debt providers should be about 25 to 40 pages long. Recognize that professional equity investors, such as venture capitalists, and professional debt providers, such as bankers, will not read the entire plan from front to back. That being the case, produce the plan in a format that facilitates spot reading. The previous discussion highlighted sections that these readers might find useful. The key is to present a concise version of all the material you have produced in your planning process. Focus on what the investor values the most. Thus, operational details are often less important unless your competitive advantage derives from your operations. Our general guideline is that "less is more." For instance, we've found that 25-page business plans receive venture funding more often than 40-page plans (other things being equal).

You may also want to produce an expanded executive summary. These plans are considerably shorter than an operational plan or the 25- to 40-page plan discussed above—typically, no more than 10 pages. The purpose of this plan is to provide an initial conception of the business in order to test initial reaction to the idea. It allows you to share your idea with confidantes and receive feedback before investing significant time and effort on a longer business plan.

After you've completed the business planning process, rewrite the expanded executive summary. You can use this expanded summary to attract attention. For instance, send it to investors you have recently met to spur interest and a meeting. It is usually better to send an expanded executive summary than a full business plan because the investor will be more apt to read it. If the investor is interested, he will call you in for a meeting. If the meeting goes well, the investor often then asks for the full business plan.

Style Pointers for the Written Plan and Oral Presentation

Once you start writing plans for external consumption, the way you present the information becomes important. Not only do you need to capture the reader's attention with a well-researched opportunity, but also you need to present your case in a way that makes it easy and interesting to read. Too many business plans are text-laden, dense manifestos. Only the most diligent reader will wade through all that text. The key is to create visual catch-points.

Use a table of contents with numbered sections, as we described earlier in this chapter. Then use clearly marked headers and subheaders throughout the document. This allows the reader to jump to sections she is most interested in. Another way to draw the reader to important points is to use bulleted lists, diagrams, charts, and sidebars.[12] Your reader should be able to understand the venture opportunity by just looking at the visual catch-points of a plan. Work with your team and trusted advisors on ways to bring out the exciting elements of your story. The point is to make the document not only content rich but also visually attractive.

Some investors have no interest in a plan at all. Instead, they prefer to see an executive summary and PowerPoint slides, and they often read the PowerPoint slides instead of asking the entrepreneur to personally present those slides. We have already discussed executive summaries, so let's spend a few moments on PowerPoint slides. You should be able to communicate your business opportunity in 10 to 12 slides, possibly along the following lines:

1. Cover page showing product picture, company name, and contact information
2. Opportunity description emphasizing customer problem or need that you hope to solve
3. Illustration of how your product or service solves the customer's problem
4. Some details (as needed) to better describe your product
5. Competition overview
6. Entry and growth strategy showing how you get into the market and then grow
7. Overview of your business model—how you will make money and how much it will cost to support those sales
8. Team description
9. Current status with time line
10. Summary including how much money you need and how it will be used

The key to creating a successful presentation is to maximize the use of your slides. For example, graphs, pictures, and other visuals are more powerful and compelling than texts and bulleted lists. Entrepreneurs who create bulleted lists often use them as cue cards during an oral presentation and either stare at the screen behind them as they talk or continually look back and forth between the screen and their audience. In either case, this behavior might prevent you from creating a personal connection with your audience.

This connection is important because it conveys that you have confidence in your plan and that you have a strong command of the concept. A second problem with bulleted lists is that those in your audience will tend to read them, and their attention will be focused on the slide and not on what you are saying. Again, you want to create a strong personal connection with your audience. You should be able to use graphics to communicate the key points. Doing so will better engage your audience and make them more inclined to view your opportunity favorably.

CONCLUSION

The business plan is more than just a document; it is a process, a story. Although the finished product is often a written plan, the deep thinking and fact-based analysis that go into that document provide the entrepreneur the keen insights needed to marshal resources and direct growth. The whole process can be painful, but it almost always maximizes revenue and minimizes costs. The reason is that the process allows the entrepreneur to better anticipate instead of react.

Business planning also provides talking points so that entrepreneurs can get feedback from a number of experts, including investors, vendors, and customers. Think of business planning as one of your first steps on the journey to entrepreneurial success. Also remember that business planning is a process and not a product. It is iterative, and in some sense, it never ends. As your venture grows, you will want to come back and revisit earlier drafts, create new drafts, and so on for the entire life of your business. Keep your three-ring binder close by and continue to add to and revise it often. It is the depository of all the learning that you have achieved as well as your plans for the future. While preparing the first draft of your plan is tough, the rewards are many. Enjoy the journey.

YOUR OPPORTUNITY JOURNAL

Reflection Point	Your Thoughts...

Reflection Point

1. What data have you gathered about your opportunity?
   a. What do these data suggest as far as reshaping your opportunity?
   b. What new questions do they raise, and who should you talk to in order to answer these questions?
2. Who have you shared your vision with?
   a. Who have they referred you to?
   b. What new learning have you gained from these conversations?
3. What is your "tagline"?
4. Does your executive summary have a compelling "hook"?
5. Does your business planning process tie together well? Do you have a compelling, articulate story?

WEB EXERCISE

Scan the Internet for business plan preparation sites. What kinds of templates are available? Do these make it easier to write a plan? What is the downside, if any, of using these templates? What are the benefits? Find some sample plans online. These plans are often advertised as superior to "typical" plans. Are they better? What makes them better?

NOTES

1 Bartlett, S. Seat of Your Pants. *Inc.*, October 2002.

2 *The Quotations Page*. www.quotationspage.com/quote/36892.html.

3 Lange, J., Bygrave, W., and Evans, T. *Do Business Plan Competitions Produce Winning Businesses?* Paper presented at 2004 Babson Kauffman Entrepreneurship Research Conference, Glasgow, Scotland.

4 Thomas, P. Rewriting the Rules: A New Generation of Entrepreneurs Find Themselves in the Perfect Time and Place to Chart Their Own Course. *Wall Street Journal*, May 22, 2004, p. R4.

5 www.facebook.com

6 www.linkedin.com

7 www.sec.gov

8 www.chetansharma.com/research.htm

9 Makower, J., Pernick, R., and Wilder, C. *Clean Energy Trends 2008*. San Francisco, CA: Clean Edge, 2008.

10 Sacirbey, O. Private Companies Temper IPO Talk. *IPO Reporter*, December 18, 2000.

11 *Burn rate* is how much more cash the company is expending each month than earning in revenue.

12 A running sidebar, a visual device positioned on the right side of the page, periodically highlights some of the key points in the plan. Don't overload the sidebar, but one or two items per page can draw attention to highlights that maintain reader interest.

P'kolino

CASE

P'kolino™

Business Plan
May-2005

Prepared by:
J.B. Schneider &
Antonio Turco-Rivas N.

Contact Information:
Phone: (781) 497-0913
Email: jb@pkolino.com
        atrn@pkolino.com
Address:
600 West Cummings Park
Suite 5350
Woburn, MA 01801

Executive Summary

P`kolino, LLC

(pee-ko-lee-no)

Pkolino

QUICK FACTS:

Management:
J.B SCHNEIDER: President, Marketing
ANTONIO TURCO-RIVAS: Operations
Sales, Finance
RISD: Design and Development

Industry: Play at Home – Play Furniture

Business: Improving play at home with products like this:

Patents: Currently filing provisional patents

Law Firm: Brown Rudnick, and Berlack Israels LLP

Auditors: N/A

Current Investors: Founders

Financing Sought: $400K

Use of Funds: Manufacturing, Marketing and Product Development

Employees: Founders (2)

Clients: Conversations with specialty retailers (e.g. Museum of Modern Arts)

Exit Strategy: Acquisition by toy manufacturer, furniture retailer or furniture manufacturer

CONTACT INFORMATION:
600 West Cummings Park, Suite 5350
Woburn, MA 01801
Phone: (781) 497-0913
Email: jb@pkolino.com or
atrn@pkolino.com
Website: www.pkolino.com

Summary:
P'kolino is committed to improving play at home by developing and marketing innovative play products and accessories. P'kolino believes that play should be fun and that play is critical to a child's physical, mental and social development. We hear from parents that they believe this too. Our products,
- are designed for optimal usage by the child,
- grow and adapt to the child's stage of development, and
- integrate with toys and activities to encourage and enhance play.

P'kolino not only improves play at home but its business of "growing" products, toy integration and complementary accessories serves as the foundation for a solid business with recurring, high margin sales.

Strategy:
Our goal is for P'kolino to become synonymous with play at home, and to accomplish this we have designed a progressive growth strategy. Through research we determined that the basis for play, the play space and its furniture, are in need of improvement. We've identified four key areas for improvement:
- Existing play furniture hinders play because it is designed for miniature adults.
- Play furniture rapidly loses its value because children outgrow it.
- The child loses interest in the play furniture quickly because it has few applications.
- Play spaces are cluttered and unorganized

P'kolino addresses these needs by:
- Making play more productive by designing furniture for the ones who use it: children.
- Increasing the useful life of the furniture by designing it to grow with the child
- Maintaining interest in the furniture by increasing its uses. Add-on toy kits integrate with the table for unlimited uses.
- Organizing the play spaces by designing these toys kits to simply fold-up and store away in a child friendly storage unit.

We will build distinctive, high quality products and focus on developing a strong brand. P'kolino will first target the high-end market because it values the brand, its consumers are influencers, and it has the highest margins. We will grow by introducing additional products to the high-end markets and expanding with a different product line into the higher volume mid-market.

Distribution will primarily be direct, however we will partner with key retail showrooms to create familiarity with our products. A strong direct channel will enable us to develop extended relationships with our customers for repeat sales of upgrades, accessories and toy kits.

Market:
Play furniture is a $1.2 billion market. The High-end segment is $51million, growing at 9% and strong margins of 55% gross/20% net. The Mid segment is estimated at $300 million, growing at 8% per year and margins of 48% gross/14% net. The mass segment is estimated at $800 million, growing at 7% and margins of 37% gross and 5% net.

Operations:
Outsourcing manufacturing, and using a collaboration model for product development.

Management Background:
- Antonio Turco-Rivas: co-founder and Sales & Operations Manager is a Babson MBA 2005. Antonio is a proven entrepreneur who successfully launched two ventures. He has managerial and sales experience.

- J.B. Schneider: co-founder and Marketing & Product Development Manager is a Babson MBA 2005 with over 10 years of marketing strategy and communications experience for several Fortune 500 companies.

	Year 1	Year 2	Year 3	Year 4	Year 5
Revenues	612K	1783K	2922K	4168K	5793K
Expenses	643K	1761K	2806K	3786K	5093K
Net Profit	-31K	22K	116K	382K	700K
Head Count	4	7	13	14	14

Confidential Information
Business Plan - Dated May-2005
Woburn, Massachusetts – USA

<table>
<tr><td>**1**</td><td>**Mission Statement**</td></tr>
</table>

"P'kolino will develop innovative playroom furniture designed for the child to improve play"

"P'kolino is a product development and marketing company. Our goal is to improve play at home by developing and marketing innovative playroom furniture <u>designed for the child</u>. Our products will grow and adapt to the child's stage of development and integrate with toys and activities to encourage and enhance play."

<table>
<tr><td>**2**</td><td>**Industry Overview**</td></tr>
</table>

2.1 <u>Understanding the Playroom Market</u>

Four million children are born in the United States each year.[1] Thus, at any given time, there are 30 million children ages 8 or younger. This large base fuels the $38 billion children's toy and furniture market, currently growing at 13% per year (according to the industry trade publication "Playthings"). The playroom market (meaning the area of the house set aside for children's recreation and play) is part of this pie, and includes elements of both the furniture and the toy industry.

"Children's playroom furniture market is estimated at $1.2 billion, growing at 7% annually for the next five years"

P'kolino will compete in the children's playroom furniture space, estimated to be a $1.2 billion market, growing at 7% annually for the next five years (according to marketresearch.com). However, a playroom is not a playroom without toys. For this reason, P'kolino will develop furniture products and accessories designed to integrate with toys and activities to complete the playroom offering and enhance their play value.

Exhibit 2-A
The Playroom Market
(US$ Billions)

$1.2

$38

■ Toy + Furniture Market
□ Playroom Furniture

The dynamics of the playroom market are influenced by both the furniture and toy industry. An overview of each of these industries follows.

2.2 <u>Furniture Industry Highlights</u>

Households in the US spend over $24 billion a year on furniture and this figure is expected to grow at 2% per year according to the American Furniture Manufacturer Association (AFMA). The industry has traditionally been highly segmented, but because of lower margins fueled by intense competition from imports, it has started to consolidate. Last year, for example, products manufactured and imported from other countries (especially China) represented 45%[2] of total purchases.

---

[1] Source: U.S. Census Bureau – www.census.gov
[2] Source: US Department of Commerce – www.commerce.gov

Confidential Information
Business Plan - Dated May-2005
Woburn, Massachusetts – USA

Companies competing in this market are:
- Furniture Brands International, the largest maker of residential furniture and owner of brands like Henredon, Drexel, and Maitland-Smith (the company has over $2.3 billion in revenues).[3]
- Lay Z Boy ($1.9 billion in revenues).
- Ashley Furniture ($1.7 billion in revenues)
- and others; like Ethan Allen and local players.

These companies distribute products through a network of furniture centers, independent dealers (specialty retailers), national and local chains, and department stores.

According to the AFMA, children's furniture generated $4 billion in 2003, 90% related to children's bedroom furniture sales (cribs, changing tables, etc.) and the remaining 10% or <u>$400 million</u> to children's tables, chairs, storage and toys. Niche players have dominated this segment of the industry and according to the American Home Furnishings Alliance (annual publication) it is the fastest growing segment (8% in 2003).

"Children's furniture is the fastest growing segment in the Furniture Industry with 8% growth in 2003"
American Home Furnishing Alliance

We believe the Furniture Industry will continue to face strong competition from foreign manufacturers (selling at lower prices). Local manufacturers will have to invest in technology and compete on quality and speed. In the children's furniture market, the large companies have been traditionally focused on bedroom furniture. Niche players have been taking over the more specialized products - those requiring expertise in other areas - like child development (i.e. the playroom furniture).

Exhibit 2-B
Furniture Industry
(US$ Billions)

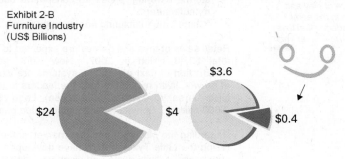

■ Furniture Industry ☐ Children's Bedroom ■ Children's Playroom

---

[3] Source: Hoovers Online – www.hoovers.com

Confidential Information
Business Plan - Dated May-2005
Woburn, Massachusetts – USA

2.3 Toy Industry Highlights

The Toy Industry accounted for $34 billion in 2003.[4] On both the manufacturing and retailing side it is a highly concentrated industry. For the past few years it has been growing at 5-9% per year, with almost 60% of the products being imported from other countries.[5]

According to "Playthings annual report" the Toy industry is highly seasonal with almost 70% of all toy purchases occurring during the Holiday season (Christmas).

The "Playthings annual report" for 2003 also stated the main forces driving the industry as follows:

Exhibit 2-C
The Toy Industry
(US$ Billions)

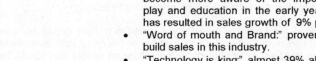

- "Educational toys:" after many ups and downs, it seems like American parents have become more aware of the importance of play and education in the early years. This has resulted in sales growth of 9% per year.
- "Word of mouth and Brand:" proven ways to build sales in this industry.
- "Technology is king:" almost 39% all of toys sales (in terms of US$) are video games or what they like to call "technology related products".
- "Merchant power:" Mass merchandisers, in particular Walmart (sells 25% of the toys sold every year in America), have taken the industry by storm, lowering prices to consumers but also lowering margins to manufacturers.
- "China:" manufacturing has gone overseas.

"Parents have become more aware of the importance of play and education in the early years... educational toys sales are up 9% per year"
"Playthings"

Retail sales of toys and games are expected to grow 4.3 percent per year to total $37.8 billion in 2007.[6] New video game technologies and the introduction of next generation systems are expected to be the main driver of growth. With respect to toys the leaders in the industry are Mattel ($4.9 billion in sales), Hasbro ($3.1 billion), Lego ($1.6 billion), and Leap Frog ($600 million).[7] Sony takes the lead in video games.

Regarding the playroom furniture market, some companies like Rubbermaid (using the Little Tykes brand) have developed; role-play toys, ride-on toys, sandboxes, activity gyms and climbers, and plastic juvenile furniture. These products are sold in toy stores (not furniture stores) and have been targeting the price sensitive consumer. Our research indicates that these types of

---

[4] Source: Industry trade publication "Playthings"
[5] Source: Industry trade publication "Playthings"
[6] Source: Marketreseach.com
[7] Source: revenues for Toy industry leaders from Hoovers Online

Confidential Information
Business Plan - Dated May-2005
Woburn, Massachusetts – USA

"$800 million in playroom furniture products are sold each year by Toy Industry related companies

products carry very low margins (average 5% profit margins).[8] To compete, companies like Brio, another strong player in this niche, sells low price train tables to encourage parents to buy their higher margins trains (they lose money on the furniture to sell the toy).

According to the Marketresearch.com industry report, of the $34 billion, $6 billion accounts for furniture products. However, this number includes car seats, play pens, strollers, etc. For playroom furniture, our research[9] indicates that approximately $800 million is sold each year.

Exhibit 2-D
Toy Industry
(US$ Billions)

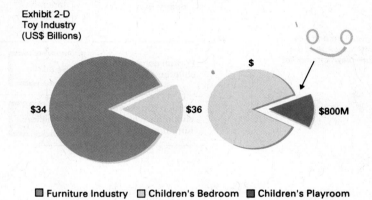

$34 $36 $ $800M

■ Furniture Industry   □ Children's Bedroom   ■ Children's Playroom

Our research concludes that large toy companies dominate the price-sensitive segment of the playroom furniture market. However for mid and high-end play furniture products, niche manufacturers and retailers like Pottery Barn Kids and Land of Nod have taken the lead.

---

[8] Sources: According to 10K fillings for the SEC and/or public financial statements from: Graco, Rubbermaid, Brio and others.
[9] Based on Marketresearch.com Industry Report and Sales of top ten manufactures of playroom furniture products

Confidential Information
Business Plan - Dated May-2005
Woburn, Massachusetts – USA

2.4 <u>How it all Comes Together (Furniture & Toy Industry)</u>

Furniture meets toys in the playroom; both Industries converge and influence the $1.2 billion market.

Exhibit 2-E
The Playroom Furniture Market
(US$ Billions)

"The Furniture and Toy industry converge in the furniture playroom market"

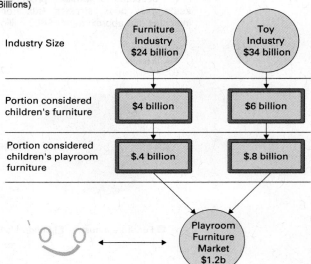

The Playroom furniture market (where P'kolino will compete) has inherited many of the competitive dynamics of its parent industries:

- Is growing at an average of 7% annually[10]
- Is highly seasonal (almost 70% of sales during the Holiday season)
- Almost 60% of the products are manufactured abroad[11]
- For highly price sensitive consumers the market is highly concentrated, but at mid and high-end income levels niche players dominate
- Word of mouth and brand are the main drivers of sales

---

[10] Source: Marketresearch.com Industry Report
[11] Based on the Management calculations, supported by AFMA information on Furniture Imports

Confidential Information
Business Plan - Dated May-2005
Woburn, Massachusetts – USA

2.5 Trends Influencing the Playroom Market

More children are being born: According to the latest statistics from the National Center for Health Statistics, women in the United States are having more children now than at any time in almost 30 years. During most of the 1970s and 1980s, the average birthrate was fewer than two children per woman, today that average has increased to 2.1 children. As a result of this trend, the population of children age 5 and under is expected to grow in 2004, and to experience gradually increasing annual percentage gains through 2010.

Mom's with more income and spending more: More women are having babies later in life, when their income tends to be higher and more stable. The birth rates for women in their 30s and older are at their highest level in three decades, up 2%-3% since 1990 for women in their 30s, and up more than 7% for women in their 40s.[12] As a result many of them are coming into the toy and furniture markets with higher disposable income than was previously the case.

"...More babies, more disposable income and more spending in children's furniture are also driving the playroom market"

Grandparents are spending more: According to the U.S. Census Bureau, greater longevity and higher disposable income of a growing U.S. population of grandparents is also boosting average per capita spending on home furnishings and toys for young children. There are about 70 million grandparents in the United States today. As a result of divorces and remarriages, many American children have six to eight adults in the "grandparent" role. According to the research firm Interep (supported by Simmons database), grandparents are spending over $60 billion on grandchildren each year.

More aware/educated parents: Parents these days are being bombarded by advice from experts about developing children's mental, physical, and social skills. Parents understand the value play has on this development and look for products to encourage it. In an interview with the trade publication Playthings (May 2002), Susan Oliver, executive director of the non-profit organization Playing for Keeps, explains:

"Parents with dollars to spend, typically those who have greater amounts of education, are increasingly aware of the connection between play and healthy development. There has been a lot of media coverage about brain development, with an emphasis on the critical role of a stimulating environment during the first three years of a child's life." As long as the market approach is toward kids learning more at a younger age, consumers will pay to get on the higher rung of the educational ladder"

---

[12] Source: U.S. Census Bureau – www.census.gov

Confidential Information
Business Plan - Dated May-2005
Woburn, Massachusetts – USA

"...The Power of Play program, continues to reach literally millions of people...play has a positive effect on children's overall well-being is instrumental in the child's development"

New laws: New safety legislation has propelled safer product designs as the industry and the media warn consumers not to use older products that do not meet current safety standards.[13]

Home remodeling: With new TV shows encouraging makeovers of home spaces, Americans are likely to spend more on home furnishing in 2005.

The Power of Play Campaign: Children appear to be growing up much faster; they look more mature and they know more about the world at younger and younger ages. Child development experts stress that despite appearances, a child is still a child. This message is a major focus of "The Power of Play" program, which continues to reach literally millions of people throughout our nation as a result of the second phase of broadcast and print public service announcements sponsored by the Toy Manufacturer Association.

The importance of this message was discovered as a result of a national survey conducted in 1999 on behalf of the American Toy Institute, the industry's charitable and educational foundation, recently renamed the Toy Industry Foundation. Ninety-one percent of the survey participants, made up of parents, teachers and child experts, stated that play has a positive effect on children's overall well-being and was instrumental in the development of a child's imagination, self-confidence, self-esteem, creativity, problem-solving and cooperation.

Toys March Up-market: A recent article in the Wall Street Journal (please refer to Appendix 11.1) explained the profit killing price war landscape for toy-making and retailing in the mass market, and highlighted how premium priced toys appear to be outgrowing the simpler less expensive versions.

David Shaw, the new owner of the FAO Schwarz retail stores stated "the admittedly small niche is a vibrant marketplace full of customers looking for something different from what's available at mass retail stores... is a niche that small retailers and catalogs dominate."

A customer commented as she visited one small specialty retailer in New York City "these toys aren't cheap... but they are really good-quality...I know my kids will love them."

---

[13] Source: The U.S. Public Interest Research Group

Confidential Information
Business Plan - Dated May-2005
Woburn, Massachusetts – USA

2.6 Playroom Furniture Market Structure and Competition

The Playroom Furniture Market has three main segments: mass ($800 million), mid ($300 million) and high-end ($51 million). These segments are derived from a market segmentation based on product quality, price, distribution channel and type of customer.

High-end segment: P'kolino will enter the playroom furniture market in this segment. This segment refers to exclusive products sold primarily through catalogs, interior-designer depots, trade events, specialty small retailers and direct from the designer/manufacturer. These products are expensive and branded with the designer's name. Most of these products are usually designed in Italy, Germany, Spain, Netherlands, among others European countries. Buyers are looking for something unique and beautiful. Interior designers are the main promoters in this segment; however, some specialty furniture boutiques have also begun to carry premium furniture for play. Furniture usually takes 6 to 8 weeks for delivery.

"P'kolino market entry strategy will be to target the High-end segment, a small but profitable spot"

Exhibit 2-F
Playroom Furniture Market (US$ MM)

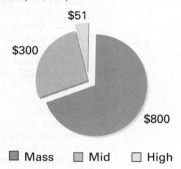

$51

$300

$800

☐ Mass   ☐ Mid   ☐ High

Customers in this segment are resorting to custom designed playroom solutions using interior designers; some of them even specialized on child-spaces. Customers are also buying from product boutiques that sell furniture as well as other children products (e.g. clothing, toys, and accessories). Small independents design firms (e.g. Truck Architecture) generally design the products sold in these stores. These design shops are usually niche players, who specialize in products such as hand painted furniture, or replications of classic styles. Their value to the boutique is the uniqueness of the product; you cannot find them at the mid or mass market stores.

To summarize, our main competitors in this market are the interior designers (custom made) and the niche product designers. They are often

Confidential Information
Business Plan - Dated May-2005
Woburn, Massachusetts – USA

small in size with limited reach and resources. According to our research this segment is growing at 9% per year with strong margins of 55% gross/20% net.[14]

Due to the distinctive characteristics of the High-end segment it is difficult to pinpoint a single market or list of the most prominent competitors. However, we will provide examples of the type of competition P'kolino will face as it enters the high-end segment:

- **Truck Architecture:** is a good example of a design firm. With offices in New York City and a team of 3 designers the company has developed high-end playroom furniture products with a very contemporary style. Truck has been in business since 2000, and sells its products through specialty retail stores, online retailers and in an affiliate web-based store (Offi). Truck founders Jennifer Carpenter, Jonathan Marvel and Rob Rogers have been successful with PR, and have managed to showcase its products in high visibility places like the Museum of Modern Arts (MoMA) Stores in San Francisco and New York.

- **Casakids – Roberto Gil:** Born in Buenos Aires, Argentina and educated at Harvard University, Roberto Gil trained as an architect before delving into furniture design. Gil's lines of children's furniture are very simple in terms of design and configuration. His products have been sold most recently at the Guggenheim Museum Store, Barney's New York, the Whitney Museum's Store Next Door, FAO Schwarz, SF MoMA, and The Land of Nod.

- **KidKraft, Inc:** Originally formed in 1968 as a manufacturer and supplier to the early-childhood sector, KidKraft began competing in the juvenile retail market in 1996. Today, KidKraft creates a wide array of room furnishings, gifts and toys, including licensed juvenile products. KidKraft (headquarter in Dallas, Texas) competes in other segments of the market as well. Its most recent line of products, hand-painted furniture pieces, is positioned at high-end price points. KidKraft has a strong distribution channel infrastructure for mid and mass market products, and is trying to leverage those channels to enter the high-end segment.

---

[14] Based on primary and secondary research – Interviews with industry experts.

Confidential Information
Business Plan - Dated May-2005
Woburn, Massachusetts – USA

"The mid segment is the sweet spot for P'kolino, with reasonable volume, high margins and less price sensitive customers...is driven by quality and looks, not price."

Mid-Segment: Retailers like Pottery Barn Kids, Bellini, Bombay Kids, Land of Nod and specialty catalogs have become the leaders in this segment. These companies are mainly furniture retail chains with products designed with a more conservative classic look and with better materials. The majority of the pieces are made from wood, normally targeting the family room and the child's bedroom. Some of the products are multipurpose (e.g. coffee table that is also a train table). Competition in this segment is considered "high" because of the limited number of players. Pottery-Barn, the market leader, is also the style setter for this segment. In contrast to the take-home approach of mass merchandisers, delivery of the product to the end customer usually takes up to 4 weeks.

Most of the products are sold by catalog, although Pottery-barn, Bellini and Bombay have all opened physical stores to showcase their children's product line.

Customers in this segment are looking for more exclusive designs and will trust companies like Pottery-Barn Kids, The Land of Nod, and Bellini because of their established reputations for high quality and visually appealing products. The largest threats for these companies are the copy-cats (e.g., Ikea and Target) as they manufacture very similar products priced 30-40% less. Copy cats are successful because the brand defining product attribute - beauty - is easily replicated.

According to our research, succeeding in this segment requires a strong brand. Our strategic differentiation in this market will be to offer compelling, customer driven attributes, leveraging the functionality of our products, a grow-with-your-child proposition and furniture integration with toys/activities. For P'kolino the mid-segment is the sweet spot (good margins and healthy volume).

According to AFMA, the mid-segment is growing at 8% per year and has been enjoying healthy margins of 48% gross and 14% net.

Key competitors in the Mid-Segment:

- **Pottery Barn Kids (PBK):** A subsidiary of Williams-Sonoma, Inc. is the largest player in this segment with over 87 stores, an online store-front and 4 to 5 catalog issues per year. According to 10k reports, revenues are split 50/50 between physical stores and direct channels. PBK competes with quality, design and brand and had revenues over $300 million last year. They entered the playroom furniture market with a number of products targeting the bedroom and family room spaces, as well as some toy like furniture pieces (e.g. kitchen play sets).

Confidential Information
Business Plan - Dated May-2005
Woburn, Massachusetts – USA

In a recent article in the <u>Wall Street Journal</u>[15] - "Williams-Sonoma: Seeing a Strong High-End Consumer," it was reported that:

"Furniture sales have increased to about 25% of total company sales from about 17% a year earlier, said Laura Alber, head of the Pottery Barn brand. "It's really a key strategic focus," Alber said. "Furniture seems to be a strong area of growth and one where we're very focused on driving profitability."

- **Bellini:** A manufacturer and specialty retail boutique chain that has been around for more than 15 years. They sell high-end European designed children's furniture and accessories. Bellini targets the big spenders with solid-wood juvenile furniture. The company franchises its retail concept and has stores nationwide. Some of its products could be considered high-end, but depending on the franchisee target, the store would more likely than not carry products at prices closer to the mid-segment. They have embraced the grow-with-your-child concept for bedroom furniture, but they are still very classic and basic in terms of their playroom offering.

- **Land of Nod:** The runner-up in terms of playroom furniture in this segment. The online-catalog based juvenile furniture store was recently acquired by Crate and Barrel. They are now in the process of opening stores following the PBK success; however, their business model is different. They sell products designed and manufactured by others. They are competing head to head with PBK in terms of design attributes, style and prices.

"The mass segment is highly concentrated, suffers low margins and uses mainstream toy distribution channels"

Mass-Segment: In this segment, furniture market characteristics more resemble those of toys than in the other segments. Together Brio, Imaginarium, Little Tykes and Fisher Price hold up to 58%[16] of the market share. Small independents that manufacture furniture products under licensed brands such as Dora the Explorer, Barnie, Barbie, Disney, etc, also hold a solid 20% market share[17].

This segment can be considered highly concentrated (few players) and price sensitive. Customers in this segment are buying playroom furniture the way they buy toys: at large discount stores (75%) like Walmart, Target, Kmart or large specialized retailers like Toys R Us.

Products like play tables and chairs are sold for less than $200. They are made of plastic or composite materials and in many cases branded with cartoon characters. The majority of the products are not designed to

---

[15] Wednesday August 25-2004, WSJ
[16] Source: Derived from individual sales from companies financial statements
[17] Source: "Playthings" Annual Report

Confidential Information
Business Plan - Dated May-2005
Woburn, Massachusetts -- USA

integrate with the toy or activity (toy/furniture integration) and competition seems to be based on price and brand, not on quality or looks. The noticeable exceptions are the train tables and some Lego tables. Brio for example, sells its train table almost at cost, but then makes a profit selling the trains.

Distribution and competitive dynamics in this segment mimic those of the toy industry in terms of levels of concentration (few players with large market shares), business cycle (70% of sales occurs during the holidays)[18] and barriers of entry (very low margins – competition based on volume). Most of the participants in this market have been losing money lately. On average, the mass segment margins have been 37% gross, and 5% profit.[19]

Some Key Competitors in the Mass-Segment:

- **Brio**: Based in Sweden, but with operations in Europe, Asia and the US. With $1.6B in sales,[20] the company has complemented its toy offering with some playroom furniture pieces (especially train tables) now representing about 1/3 of total sales. The company has a strong presence in the Nordic countries and has made an effort to penetrate the US market with products priced a little above the market average. Specialty stores and mass merchandisers have been carrying Brio products in small quantities because of its price point. Brio represents the "traditional wood based" products in this segment. High quality products and a reputation for delivering on educational play support its strong brand.

- **Little Tykes**: Subsidiary of Newell Rubbermaid, Little Tykes is the largest manufacturer of plastic based tables and chairs for this segment. With operations all over the world, Little Tykes has positioned its products as safe, durable and low price playroom furniture. Its products are sold in mass merchandise stores and according to the parent company's financial statements, the division has been struggling to maintain profitability because of higher raw material prices (oil based). In July 2004, the company sold its Little Tykes Commercial Play Systems (LTCPS) unit to PlayPower. Little Tykes had 28% gross and -2% profit margins in 2003.[21]

- **Imaginarium:** This Spain based company and Toys R Us affiliate since 2001 is the second largest manufacturer of play tables for this market segment. The relationship with Toys R Us guarantees shelf space in the stores to display its products and has even created barriers of entry to other manufacturers in that channel. The

"P'kolino will enter the mass-segment once it has penetrated the high and mid segments of the market and developed a strong brand"

[18] Source: Toy Industry Association Annual Report
[19] Source: Hoovers Online, SEC filings and Annual Reports from Mattel, Hasbro, Lego and LeapFrog
[20] Source: Brio Annual Financial Statements
[21] Source: Newell Rubbermaid Annual Report, SEC Filling, Hoovers Online

Confidential Information
Business Plan - Dated May-2005
Woburn, Massachusetts – USA

company has positioned its products similar to Brio but with a lower price tag and quality. The company has had a disappointing year in the U.S. according to the <u>Wall Street Journal</u>, but remains a competitor with a strong distribution channel and world-class product development capabilities.

The following summarizes the size and structure of the Playroom Furniture Market:

Exhibit 2-G The Playroom Furniture Market
Summary of Market Segments and Competitive Dynamics

The Furniture Playroom Market

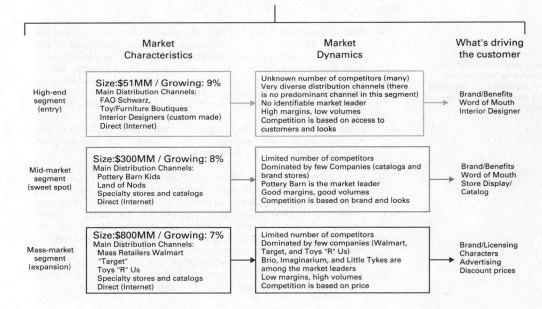

Confidential Information
Business Plan - Dated May-2005
Woburn, Massachusetts – USA

3	The Opportunity

Play is a child's work and education; it is how they learn and grow. Parents are more willing to pay for products that encourage or facilitate play as they become more educated about child development and the importance of play. Evidence of this trend is the growing spending on educational toys (growing at 9% for the last three years)[22], and playroom furnishings (growing at 7% per year[23]). P'kolino has identified a powerful opportunity that leverages this trend.

"Willingness to pay for products that encourage child development is on the rise."

Through our research we discovered that the basis for play - the play space and its furniture - is in need of improvement. We identified four key areas for improvement:

"The basis for play - the play space and its furniture – is in need of improvement"

- Existing playroom furniture compromises play because it is designed for miniature adults and not children.
- Playroom furniture loses its value fast because children quickly outgrow it. One size fits all in playroom furniture simply doesn't work.
- The child loses interest in the playroom furniture quickly because it has few applications.
- Lastly, and probably most obviously, play spaces are cluttered and unorganized.

"Parents want to know the right toy to buy"

We also discovered that parents are feeling the pressure of wanting to know the right toy to buy, at the right time to effectively support the development of their children.

4	Company and Product Description

4.1 Company and Description:

P'kolino, LLC is based in Woburn, MA and is a product design and marketing company. We believe play is an integral part of a child's healthy development and that current play furniture compromises play. It is our goal to improve the play experience at home. P'kolino currently has 4 product concepts under development through a partnership with the Rhode Island School of Design (RISD).

"P'kolino, improving play at home."

---

[22] According to Parents Magazine and LeapFrog SEC fillings
[23] *According to marketresearch.com*

Confidential Information
Business Plan - Dated May-2005
Woburn, Massachusetts – USA

4.2 The P'kolino Concept

P'kolino will address the opportunity in the play space by designing truly innovative play furniture and child development stage specific toy kits.

These solutions will have the following characteristics:

"P'kolino's playroom furniture is designed for the child and functional for the parent. It grows and adapts to the child's stage of development and integrates with toys/activities to encourage and enhance play"

1. We are making play more productive by designing playroom furniture for the ones who use it, the children. **Functional.**
2. We are increasing the useful life of the furniture by designing it to grow with the child through key stages of development. **Multi-purpose.**
3. We are maintaining interest in the furniture by increasing its uses. The furniture is designed to be a toy and to transform to different activities. This transformation is made possible by add-on toy kits that change the P'kolino table from activity to activity (for example: from a Lego table to a painting table to a train table and so on). **Multi-purpose.**
4. We are organizing the play space by designing the toy kits to simply fold-up and store away in a child friendly storage unit. **Functional.**

In addition to these key differentiators P'kolino's products will be safe, beautiful and fun, as these are necessary attributes to succeed.

These solutions also address the challenges parents have of selecting the right toys for the right stage because our toy kits will be packaged for specific stages of child development.

The "grow with the child" capabilities of our products will reduce our customers' total costs of ownership and provide us with opportunities for follow-on sales. Follow-on products will be in the form of developmentally appropriate toy kits, upgrade packages and accessories.

Confidential Information
Business Plan - Dated May-2005
Woburn, Massachusetts – USA

4.3 Product Description

P'kolino's first product line will include two different table designs, a storage unit, and toy kits. Constant product innovation is part of our strategy, and it will be supported with a product development effort in order to expand our current offering and include accessories and new products every year.

Initial Product line

Table A shows a very contemporary, style driven concept, with plenty of multifunctional (i.e., grow with the child) capabilities resulting from its unique modular design. It is composed of 7 separate pieces and designed to accommodate at least four stages of the child's development. This product will be the hub for the toy kits and the foundation of our playroom offering. The product is made of wood, high-density foam and fabric.

Note: the following are pictures of prototypes of Table A; the actual product may be different. They are presented here for the purpose of illustrating the concept.

Confidential Information
Business Plan - Dated May-2005
Woburn, Massachusetts – USA

Prototypes designed at risd for P'kolino

Packaging Mode

Toddler Mode

Infant Mode

Two table Mode

Toddler Mode

Toddler 1 Mode

Children Interacting with Table "A"

Table B shows a more playful design, with an almost endless array of configurations. This six-piece concept is designed around the belief that children can also play with the furniture itself. Most of the pieces are very light to facilitate child interaction and unit reconfiguration. This unit is intended for the more sophisticated parent, one that is willing to pay more for an exceptional product. This table is made of wood, high-density foam and fabric.

Note: *the following are pictures of prototypes of Table B; the actual product may be different. They are presented here for the purpose of illustrating the concept*

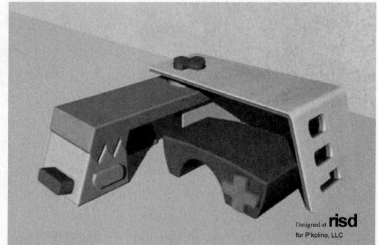

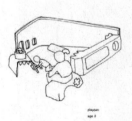

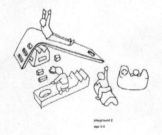

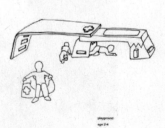

Prototypes designed at risd for P'kolino

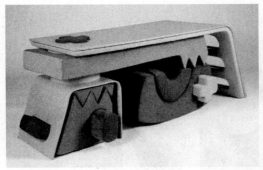

Packaging Mode

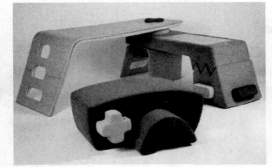

Table Mode

Table Mode

Playground Mode

Playground Mode

Table Mode

Children Interacting with Table "B"

  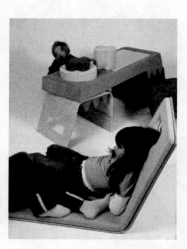

Confidential Information
Business Plan - Dated May-2005
Woburn, Massachusetts – USA

The Toy kits: These pieces are the link between the furniture and the toy. They are storage compartments that unfold on top of Table A to change the table top into an activity or toy /play enhancer. The inside of the toy kit will be designed to accommodate the requirements of a specific activity and child stage of development.

For example: if we wanted to convert the table into a toddler "Lego" table, the interior of the toy kit will have stage appropriate Lego plates attached; the unit itself will also hold the Lego blocks. When unfolded, it locks on top of Table A, transforming it into a toddler Lego table. When done, simply fold it up and store it in our storage unit.

Note: the following are pictures of prototypes of the Toy kits; the actual product may be different. They are presented here for the purpose of illustrating the concept

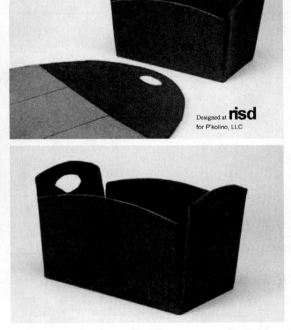

Designed at **risd**
for P'kolino, LLC

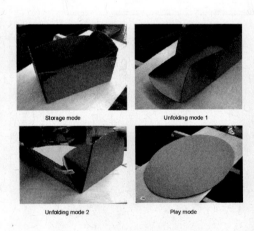

Storage mode

Unfolding mode 1

Unfolding mode 2

Play mode

Confidential Information
Business Plan - Dated May-2005
Woburn, Massachusetts – USA

The Storage Unit: this unit will hold up to 10 toy kits and is designed to fit the design style of Table A. It allows for ease of use and accommodates a child's height and strength. The unit is made out of wood, but the drawers will be light enough so that children can open them.

Note: *the following are pictures of prototypes of the storage unit; the actual product may be different. They are presented here for the purpose of illustrating the concept*

With capabilities of holding toy kits on top of the piece or in the drawers

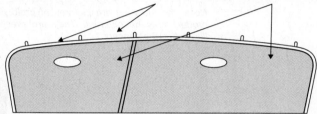

Storage Urti

Confidential Information
Business Plan - Dated May-2005
Woburn, Massachusetts – USA

Prototypes designed at risd for P'kolino

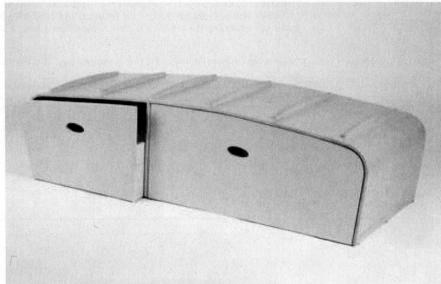

(See more pictures in the appendix)

Confidential Information
Business Plan - Dated May-2005
Woburn, Massachusetts – USA

4.4 Competitive Advantage

P'kolino product attributes can be summed up as follows:

- **Multi-purpose:** modifies for changes in activity and grows with children through their stages of development,
- **Functional:** designed to better fit how children use the product (i.e. not miniature adult furniture),
- **Educational**,
- **Fun**,
- **Safe** and
- **Beautiful:** visually appealing.

(Please refer to Appendix 12.2 for details on the product attributes).

"Our key differentiating benefits will be the increased functionality, the improved educational value and the multi-purpose nature of our products"

Exhibit 4-A
Key Product Attributes

multi-purpose

functional   educational

m
f   e
b   s   f

beautiful   safe   fun

Safety, beauty and fun are absolute necessities in this market. They are the attributes that most competitors have and ones that we will build our differentiating attributes on. Our key differentiating benefits will be the increased functionality, the improved educational value and the multi-purpose nature of our products. By focusing our product development on these key attributes we will have a clear competitive advantage.

Exhibit 4-B
Attribute Comparison Chart – P'kolino's Assessment (rankings: 1 is best in the category, 10 is the worst)

Competitors	Mkt. Segment	Educational	Safe	Multipurpose	Fun	Functional	Beautiful
P'kolino	High / Mid	2	3	1	2	1	3
Brio	Mass	3	5	2	3	7	7
Fischer-Price	Mass	1	2	3	1	6	8
Imaginarium	Mass	4	4	4	4	4	9
Little Tykes	Mass	5	1	6	5	2	10
Pottery Barn Kids	Mid	8	8	5	6	5	1
Land of Nod	Mid	7	7	7	7	3	2
Truck	High	9	10	8	10	8	5
Casa Kids	High	10	9	9	9	9	6
Videl	High	6	6	10	8	10	4

Confidential Information
Business Plan - Dated May-2005
Woburn, Massachusetts – USA

4.5 Our Strategy

Our strategy is designed to accomplish four key objectives:
1. Develop a strong brand → "owning the play-space at home"
2. Develop a solid customer base → " loyalty and recurring revenue"
3. Achieve predictable and sustainable growth → "good margins and repeat purchases"
4. Develop a culture of innovation → "capability of generating champion products"

"P'kolino targets the high-end segment because customers are market influencers, they value brand over price and offers better margins. P'kolino will later expand to the mid segment"

Overview:
To penetrate the children's play market we will need to target influential customers and develop a strong brand. From this position we will expand our product line and extend into new markets expanding our customer base. We will maintain long relationships with our customers by offering them development stage appropriate upgrades, toy kits and accessories. This will provide us with recurring and predictable revenue.

Market Entry:
P'kolino will first target the high-end playroom market because of its favorable characteristics:
• it values innovation and brand over price,
• its consumers are market influencers, and
• it offers the highest margins.

We will focus on establishing and building a reputation for high quality products and target consumers that want the best for their children. Through a mix of public relations and grassroots marketing we will establish our products in the high-end market. Concurrently, we will develop toy-kits and accessories that integrate and complement the furniture to deliver a complete play experience.

Growth Strategy:
Growth in the high-end market is limited due to its size. In order to increase our customer base for sales of additional P'kolino products we will need to expand into the larger mid-market segment. To do this we will leverage our high-end brand reputation and introduce lower cost tables and storage with similar attributes into the larger mid-market. We expect to execute this expansion in our third year of operation.

Exhibit 4-C
Market Penetration Strategy

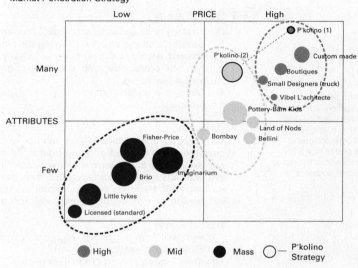

Growth will also be achieved by maintaining long term relationships with our customers to promote repeat purchases of upgrades, accessories and toy kits. Given the targeted age range (0-5 years) of our products and the average of over 2 children per household, a single customer relationship could last over 8 years with multiple sales per year. This will give us a recurring and predictable revenue stream. As we increase our customer base and product line the revenue from these repeat sales will increase dramatically.

Exhibit 4-D
Number of units sold per type of product

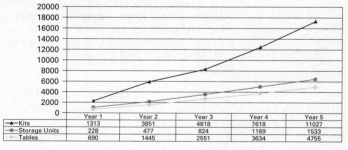

	Year 1	Year 2	Year 3	Year 4	Year 5
Kits	1313	3851	4818	7618	11027
Storage Units	228	477	824	1169	1533
Tables	690	1445	2551	3634	4755

Confidential Information
Business Plan - Dated May-2005
Woburn, Massachusetts – USA

Given the difficulties of the mass market, which include troubled distribution channels, intense price competition, and price sensitive customers, it is not currently part of our market extension plan. However, we will continue to evaluate it. Should conditions become more favorable, we may consider moving to this segment.

Continued product innovation is a key to this market penetration and expansion strategy. To achieve this we will focus internally on creating a culture of innovation through

• Proven product research and development methodologies,
• Creative work environments and employment arrangements, and
• Hiring proven talent that fits our dynamic, innovating culture.

5 Marketing Plan

Overview: We will bring this product to the market by targeting customers in the high-end market segment that want the best for their child. We will reach this audience through public relations, grassroots marketing, direct marketing and strategic distribution channels.

5.1 Understanding the Customer

Our primary customers will be parents who want the best for their children, and are willing and able to pay a premium for a better product.

"Our primary customers will be parents who want the best for their children, and are willing and able to pay a premium for a better product"

According to our research, our initial customers will be educated consumers who possess a strong desire to provide the best environment possible for their children to play at home. They are likely to spend a considerable amount of time researching the web for options, and have a strong bias toward friend and family recommendations (word-of-mouth).

We also see several key influencers in this purchasing decision, they are:
• "Authorities" – Experts in the field of child rearing/development. (e.g., Teachers, Care-givers, Publications).
• Children
• Grandparents
• Peers – Other parents

In addition to being influencers grandparents are also secondary customers. Grandparents are often richer than parents, more involved and

Confidential Information
Business Plan - Dated May-2005
Woburn, Massachusetts – USA

buy large gifts for their grandchildren. The percentage of buyers of relevant children's products that are grandparents.[24]
• Games and toys 26%
• Infant furniture 21%
• Children furniture 16%

There are nearly 60 million grandparents in the U.S. at present and they spend an estimated $30 billion per year on their grandchildren[25]. Although grandparents exercise significant purchasing power, they are likely to ask for parent consent before they buy our products; making the parent our core customer.

5.2 Target Customer Profile

The demographics of our primary target customer are:
• Household Income $150K+ *
• At least one child 0-5 years old.
• Female *
• College educated* (or higher)
• Live in the Northeast*
  *These demographics have the highest indexes for infant, toddler and pre-school purchases.[26]

Additionally these consumers are:
• Not price sensitive.
• More influenced by the product benefits.
• The "concerned" parent, those who genuinely want the best for their child.
• Visionaries; they see the benefits and are going to set the trend for others in this segment to follow

These parents are in parenting groups such as Mothers Forums and Play Groups, and enroll children in early developmental classes (e.g., Creative Movements). They subscribe to parenting magazines, read parenting books or consult with Child Development/Parenting Experts. As a result, they are influenced by "Authorities" either through reading they have done themselves or by first-hand interaction with teachers and caregivers.

Other customer segments in this market are the "competitive" and "compensating" parents. They have the same demographic profile but have different interests. They are the followers. The "concerned" educated parent sets the bar and these others follow.

[24] Source: Simmons data cited by Interep
[25] Source: Simmons data cited by Interep
[26] Source: Simmons Market Research Bureau, Fall 2002 Study of Media and Markets; Packaged Facts

Confidential Information
Business Plan - Dated May-2005
Woburn, Massachusetts – USA

As we move down market to the mid-market, the primary customer demographics and behaviors are the same except for the following.
- Household Income drops to $100K+.
- They are influenced by the premium market.
- Due to increased price sensitivity they are more pragmatic in their purchasing decisions.
- They are more likely to do their own research (more shopping around, talking to their friends). Word-of-mouth is very influential in this market.

5.3 Pricing Strategy

"Market Entry – High-end pricing strategy will be market-demand pricing"

Market Entry – High-end pricing strategy will be market-demand pricing to maximize per sale profit. We anticipate the following price ranges per product:

- Table A = $650
- Table B = $1200
- Storage Unit = $450
- Toy Kit = $50 (average)
- Providing contribution margins between 50-60%

Expansion to the mid market will require a different pricing strategy. Lower table prices (around $350) for better market penetration will increase the user/installed base and provide a larger marketing base for the toy kits and accessories.

5.4 Distribution Strategy

"P'kolino's distribution goal is to have over 85% of sales revenue come from channels direct-to-the-customer"

P'kolino's distribution goal is to have over 85%[27] of sales come from direct-to-the-customer channels within five years. We expect that we will have to start with a distribution mix of approximately 65% of our sales through retail. Retail channels will enable customer exposure to, and interaction with, the products. As the understanding of our products grows and the brand develops we will shift the distribution mix to direct channels.

Retail Stores: Retailers will be chosen based on their clientele. We will target non-traditional retailers that give P'kolino a "showroom" for its designs. For example, we will target The Museum of Modern Arts (MoMA) store which features uniquely designed and educationally beneficial products as one of our first outlets. This strategy will help us reach the right

---

[27] Other furniture merchants have proven success in direct channels. Land of Nod estimated at nearly 100% sales are direct; through catalog and web. Pottery Barn Kids – direct sales = 72% of its $392 million in revenue. As stated in the 11/18/04 Wall Street Journal "William Sonoma's, inc Third Quarter 2004 results."

customer and generate some exposure for our products. To encourage customer interaction with us we will offer a free Toy Kit to those who have purchased a table or storage unit through a retail channel. The customer will redeem the free kit through a direct channel (web or mail) so that we may capture relevant customer data. This customer data is critical to our direct marketing to support our migration of customers to the direct sales channels as well as to encourage future purchases.

Direct-to-the-Customer: The goal is to have 85% of our revenue come through direct channels (web, mail and phone). Based on the proven success of other furniture merchants in direct channels (Land of Nod estimated at nearly 100% sales from direct channels like catalogs and the web,[28] and Pottery Barn Kids direct sales equal 72% of its $392MM in revenue)[29] we believe this is achievable.

The primary direct channel will be through the internet as 70% of our target customers have high-speed internet access. We will also offer mail and phone orders.

We will build a website that provides consumers with an easy product review, selection and purchasing experience. Proliferation of high-speed internet access enables us to show the many benefits of our products through the latest multi-media tools (streaming video demonstrations of our products in the form of infomercials through the web).

5.5 Communication Strategy – Year 1

Overview: In the first year our communications strategy will focus on targeted marketing that can be directly attributed to sales. We will try many different tactics to determine what generates the best dollar spent to sales ratio. Additionally, we will build the brand through low cost, guerrilla marketing efforts such as pubic relations and grassroots marketing.

---

[28] Our estimate based on Land of Nods business model of direct sales and no retail store to date.
[29] As stated in the 11/18/04 WSJ's "William Sonoma's, inc Third Quarter 2004 results.

Confidential Information
Business Plan - Dated May-2005
Woburn, Massachusetts — USA

Exhibit 5-A   Marketing Communications Strategy

Marketing Initiative	Estimated Cost	Estimated Table Sales	Estimated Storage Sales	Estimated Toy Kit Sales	Total Units Sold	Marketing Cost/Sale
Public Relations	$5,000	30	10	57	96	$52
GrassRoots	$5,000	80	26	151	257	$19
Word-of-Mouth	$5,000	50	17	94	161	$31
Online	$25,000	80	26	151	257	$97
Advertising	$15,000	50	17	94	161	$93
Direct Marketing	$20,000	70	23	132	225	$89
Retail Marketing Exp.	$6,000	330	109	622	1061	$6
Total $	81,000	690	228	1300	2218	$37

Public Relations

Public Relations (PR) will be at the center of our communications plan. The first phase of this plan is to utilize the PR potential of cooperation with Babson, the #1 entrepreneurship program in the country, and RISD, the #1 school of design. We have brought together these school's PR departments and have agreements to promote the story at no cost to us. To that end, we are developing a video documentary of the product design process to be used as a PR asset for the schools and P'kolino. From this PR exposure we intend to interest target market publications (e.g. Parenting Magazine) in P'kolino's story.

The PR effort will be a company priority. Management will make constant and persistent efforts to get new and compelling stories to the media. We will become a source of information for key media authorities and eventually seek product placement opportunities. Management will also seek active relationships with key media personalities to support our brand and products.

Grassroots Marketing

Grassroots Marketing will be how we get the customers interacting with the product and start the word-of-mouth engine running. We will start this grassroots effort in Boston targeting Mother's Forums, Play Groups and Day Care Centers (e.g., Bright Horizons). We will expand this effort strategically through major cities in the Northeast. These customers will be driven to the direct channels for purchase.

Word-of-Mouth

As noted, word-of-mouth is a powerful tool is this market. We will encourage word-of-mouth by identifying key influencers in target markets and seeking to make them advocates of P'kolino products. Additionally, we will seek a child development expert endorsement to add additional

"Word-of-mouth is a powerful medium in this market."

Confidential Information
Business Plan - Dated May-2005
Woburn, Massachusetts – USA

credibility. Word-of-mouth (viral marketing) tools such as referral benefits and e-mail forwarding will also be used.

Email and Web

The Web (www.pkolino.com) will be a powerful online catalog and direct purchase channel. At pkolino.com we will have product pictures, descriptions and video demonstrations to give customers as near to a physical world shopping experience as possible. The web will also be a means for us to generate awareness through targeted e-mail, keyword search, banner advertising and enhanced web advertising tools (such as rich media and dynamic banners).

Retail Sales Marketing Materials

Collateral materials such as brochures and point of purchase displays will be necessary to support our sales through retailers. Initially we will have a brochure from the RISD product development process that we can use for early discussions. We will also develop a high quality flyer for the two tables and the storage system (Storage unit and Kit). High-quality brochures and catalogs will be developed for use by retailers and distributed through mail and grassroots marketing campaigns.

Advertising

Our advertising goal will be to increase awareness of P'kolino in the high-end market. Our advertising efforts will focus on media that reach a high concentration of our target customer. The advertising will be primarily in print media because of its ability to show our product for a relatively low cost. These ads will drive customers back to pkolino.com for more information or purchase.

Direct Mail

In the first year of operation and in preparation for the 2005 Christmas season we will run a direct mail test. This mailing will target high-end customers in the Northeast to keep resources and expenses to a minimum. A successful test would result in about 1+% purchase rate from mailed brochures. Should this test prove successful we will look to roll-out a larger direct campaign prior to the Christmas season.

5.6 Sales Strategy

The founders will serve as the sales force making direct calls to strategically identified retailers. It will be our strategy to focus on a select number of local retailers so the founders can manage these relationship and still focus on other priorities. When we expand into the mid-market (in year 3) we will hire a dedicated sales manager.

Confidential Information
Business Plan - Dated May-2005
Woburn, Massachusetts – USA

5.7 Sales and Marketing Forecast

We expect that sales will start slowly as our grassroots efforts and word-of-mouth campaign gain momentum. In the first year we expect to generate revenues of $600K based on table unit sales of 690 units. Most of these sales will be achieved through grassroots marketing efforts, web direct sales and two or three retailers in the Northeast. On average the company will spend $220 marketing dollars per each new customer, and each customer is expected to generate an average of $887 in revenues during the first year. Our expectation is that this number will drop to $451 in average revenue per customer per year as time passes.

Exhibit 5-B   Marketing Dollars per Customer

Customer Base	Year 1	Year 2	Year 3	Year 4	Year 5
New Customers	**690**	**1,445**	**2,551**	**3,634**	**4,755**
Customer Base	690	2,135	4,686	8,221	12,856
Customer Base Growth		409%	319%	275%	256%
Average Sales p/Customer	$887	$836	$624	$507	$451
Marketing $ p/ New Customer	$176	$246	$219	$237	$248
Marketing $ p/Customer	$176	$166	$119	$105	$92

5.8 Communications Strategy Years 2-5

In Year 2 P'kolino's communications strategy will be similar to Year 1 but with a greater focus on marketing tactics that will give us a broader reach to expand our customer base. It will also differ in that it will introduce tactics to reach existing customers for repeat purchases. We will:

- Continue our Public Relations efforts but target more national publications.
- Continue our grassroots events and word-of-mouth efforts but expand their scale.
- Look more to direct marketing, advertising and the web to increase brand awareness and drive sales.
- Begin relationship marketing and efforts to gain repeat sales from existing customers.

Year 2 will serve as preparation and learning for expansion into the mid-market where some of the guerrilla tactics may still apply but our marketing efforts will have to grow to a new scale.

In Years 3-5 we will continue to shift our marketing mix to media that enable us to reach more customers. However, it will be critical to do so in an increasingly targeted manner. Direct marketing (mail and web) will be our primary medium because of its ability to target precise customer segments,

Confidential Information
Business Plan - Dated May-2005
Woburn, Massachusetts – USA

gather marketing and purchase behavior data and enable us to maintain one-to-one communications for an extended customer relationship. With this data we can become increasingly efficient at acquiring and retaining customers and thus reducing our marketing expense per sale.

It will also be important for us to maintain some advertising presence to keep brand awareness high in the general market. This awareness is necessary to help the targeted marketing break through the clutter.

6	The Team

Antonio Turco-Rivas: co-founder and Sales & Operations Manager is a Babson MBA 2005 and father of one. He has successfully launched two technology ventures in Latin America. Antonio's background also includes two years as a Corporate Finance consultant for Venezuela's most important Investment Bank and two years as a special assets Manager at the fifth largest Latin American Bank in the U.S. Antonio is a proven entrepreneur, manager and sales professional.

J.B. (Joseph B.) Schneider: co-founder and Marketing & Product Development Manager is a Babson MBA 2005 and father of three, with over 10 years of marketing strategy and communications experience. J.B. has been a project manager and led key customer acquisition and retention programs for several Fortune 500 companies. He has also been an integral part of entrepreneurial ventures and their products and marketing development.

Rhode Island School of Design (RISD): RISD's Furniture Department is ranked #1 by the US News & World Report as the best graduate industrial design program in the world, and is recognized for the creativity and quality of its students. Currently 15 designers and one faculty member are actively designing the first versions of the P'kolino products.

Advisors: Individuals for these roles are currently being evaluated and will be filled at a later date.
- Child Development Expert
- Manufacturing Expert
- Juvenile Product Market Expert

Confidential Information
Business Plan - Dated May-2005
Woburn, Massachusetts – USA

7	Operations

7.1 Operations Strategy

P'kolino's core functions (design and marketing strategy) will be the main operational activities performed in-house. All other operational activities like manufacturing, packaging, shipping and some office/administrative and customer service functions will be outsourced.[30]

For manufacturing, the company has identified several manufacturers in the Bento Goncalves region in Brazil that are currently operating with underutilized (excess) capacity and have the technology and expertise to manufacture our products. We have partnered with one of these companies to manufacture our first line of products. AFECOM, our first manufacturing partner, produces over 140,000 furniture pieces per year and is well known in Europe and Latin America. Late in the 2nd year of operations, P'kolino will reexamine this strategy (when volumes increase) and evaluate alternative manufacturing options in Asia. P'kolino products are built with wood, high-density foam and fabrics. AFECOM's high density foam manufacturing technology, finishing quality, speed, volume requirements and logistic costs are better and more accommodating to P'kolino during this first stage.

The economics of the manufacturing process will be determined by our ability to negotiate with potential manufacturers. For the purpose of this document we will use industry averages.[31] For minimum orders of 150 units, the payment terms are 50% up front and 50% on shipment. For the first year of operations we plan to complete two 150 table orders. Production time is 4 weeks for prototypes and 10 weeks to manufacture and order shipment of the approved prototypes.[32]

Exhibit 7-A
Operations Cycle

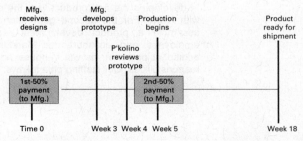

---

[30] Outsourcing cost for manufacturing, packaging, shipping are included in the Cost of goods sold, based on industry average (AFMA)
[31] Sources: AFMA – American Furniture Manufacturing Association
[32] Operations Cycle is a 14 week process for existing products, and an 18 week process for new products

Confidential Information
Business Plan - Dated May-2005
Woburn, Massachusetts – USA

Regarding the product development process for P'kolino, it takes 9 to 12 months to develop a new product (from concept to customer).[33]

Exhibit 7-B
P'kolino Product Development Process

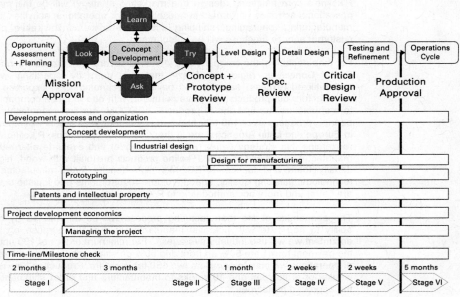

In developing the first product line, the company leveraged its relationship with RISD. For the second generation of products P'kolino will have to assemble a product development team composed of both full-time employees and collaborators. Marketing and sales will also require additional personal, as will in-house administrative and customer service responsibilities. Our staffing plan follows:[34]

---

[33] Based on the current P'kolino product development process.
[34] Salaries are based on Boston average salaries for the respective positions according to the Career Journal (Wall Street Journal online edition) salary search (Salaryexpert.com)

Confidential Information
Business Plan - Dated May-2005
Woburn, Massachusetts – USA

Exhibit 7-C
P'kolino Staffing Plan

Staffing Plan	Year 1	Year 2	Year 3	Year 4	Year 5
CEO	1	1	1	1	1
	$40,000	$70,000	$120,000	$150,000	$220,000
COO	1	1	1	1	1
	$40,000	$70,000	$120,000	$130,000	$130,000
Product Development Mgr.		1	1	1	1
		$69,680	$72,467	$75,366	$78,381
Product Development Staff		1	1	1	1
		$54,080	$56,243	$58,493	$60,833
Operations and Logistics Mgr.			1	1	1
			$64,896	$67,492	$70,192
Marketing Manager			1	1	1
			$80,038	$83,240	$86,570
Sales Manager	1	1	1	1	1
	$35,000	$70,000	$72,800	$75,712	$78,740
Sales and Marketing Staff			1	2	2
			$58,406	$60,743	$63,172
Direct Channel Support			1	1	1
			$64,896	$67,492	$70,192
Customer Service Staff			1	1	1
			$48,672	$50,619	$52,644
Office Administration		1	1	1	1
		$33,280	$34,611	$35,996	$37,435
Accounting				1	1
				$39,370	$40,945
Advisors	1	1	1	1	1
	$20,000	$31,200	$32,448	$33,746	$35,096
Total Headcount	**4**	**7**	**13**	**14**	**14**
Total Salaries	**$135,000**	**$398,240**	**$863,334**	**$989,010**	**$1,087,371**
Benefits	$20,250	$59,736	$129,500	$148,352	$163,106
Total Compensation	**$155,250**	**$457,976**	**$992,835**	**$1,137,362**	**$1,250,476**

Benefits are estimated as a percentage of salaries (15%). Eventual hires are considered in the financial statements for the product development, sales, and marketing efforts.

7.2 <u>Development Timeline</u>

Exhibit 7-D
P'kolino Timeline

Month/Activity	M1	M2	M3	M4	M5	M6	M7	M8	M9	M10	M11	M12	M13	M14	M15	M16	M17	M18	M19	M20	M21	M22	M23
Hire child development expert as advisor	▒																						
Secure funding	█	█	█																				
Launch RISD/BABSON PR campaign	▒	▒																					
Production 150 tables + storage + kits	█	█	█	█	█																		
Web site development		▒																					
Develop institutional sales channel			█	█	█	█	█	█	█	█	█	█											
Hire marketing/tech intern																							
Office relocation				█																			
Launch grassroot marketing campaign					▒	▒	▒	▒	▒														
Team focuses on sales						█	█	█	█														
Production 160 tables + storage + kits (2nd)					▒	▒																	
Collection efforts										█													
Production + 400 tables + storage + kits								▒	▒														
Hire Product Development Manager										█	█	█											
Hire Marketing Manager													▒	▒									
Web site improvements														▒									
Marketing campaign															█	█	█	█	█	█			
Production 500 tables + storage + kits														▒	▒								
Team focuses on sales																			█	█	█		
Collection efforts																						▒	▒

Confidential Information
Business Plan - Dated May-2005
Woburn, Massachusetts – USA

8	**Critical Risks**

- <u>Highly competitive market</u> – All segments of this market are highly competitive, and this is particularly true in the mid and mass segments. P'kolino will compete with a distinctive product and a different value proposition as a niche player. We will establish our brand in the high-end segment and then moving down to more competitive markets. However, the potential remains that competitors will identify our niche, before our brand has a foothold. We will rely on innovation and speed to compete if competitors attack our niche.

- <u>Copycats</u> – Intellectual property protection can be circumvented to produce competing and possibly cheaper version of our products. P'kolino will base its designs not only on beauty, but on improved usability to the end user (the child). Designing products that are better suited for children to play with, while creating identifiable differences and defining brand attributes that are more difficult to replicate.

- <u>Lawsuits</u> – Although we will take precautions to make our product safe for children it is possible that children may injure themselves while using one of our products. We will carry product liability insurance to protect us financially from such an event but the potential brand damage must be recognized.

- <u>Product defects and/or recall</u> – P'kolino will take precautions to develop durable, reliable and safe products using materials that have proven to stand the test of time. However, it is possible given the expected useful life of these products and the use by children that these products could break creating hazards for children. Should this occur and depending on the situation P'kolino may be obligated or feel it necessary to issue a recall of the defective product. Some manufacturers carry insurance in case the defect is caused by some error during the manufacturing process. We will further explore this possibility.

- <u>Sales lower than expected</u> – In case this happens P'kolino will have the capability of adjusting production volume and shifting strategy fairly quickly because of our size and structure. We will also retain sufficient cash to support an increase in the number of inventory days.

Preparation Questions

P'kolino is a children's furniture company that was launched in 2005. As you read the business plan, keep the following questions in mind:

1. Does the business plan tell a coherent and compelling story?
2. Does the plan capture all of the learning that Antonio and JB have accumulated?
3. What three questions do you think Antonio and JB need to answer through further planning before they launch the venture?
4. What are the three strongest aspects of the plan?
5. What areas need improvement?

This business plan was prepared by Antonio Turco-Rivas and J.B. Schneider in support of their business. The original drafts were prepared in the Entrepreneur Intensity Track taught by Professor Andrew Zacharakis. © Copyright P'kolino and Babson College, 2005.

Financial stock chart.

BUILDING YOUR PRO-FORMA
FINANCIAL STATEMENTS

Many entrepreneurs are intimidated by numbers, even after they've gone through the business planning process. They understand their concept, and they even have a good sense of the business model, but ask them to put together pro-forma financials or read an income statement and they have a panic attack.

You might feel that building your financials or understanding them isn't that important because you can always hire an accountant. Although an accountant is a useful advisor, in the pre-launch stage, the lead entrepreneur needs to understand the numbers inside and out. After all, the lead entrepreneur is the person who will be articulating her vision to potential employees, vendors, customers, and investors. If the entrepreneur is easily stumped by simple questions of profitability or costs, potential employees, customers, and other parties important to the new venture's success will lose confidence in the lead entrepreneur's ability to execute on the concept. Financial statements serve to bridge the entrepreneur's great idea and what that idea really means in terms of dollars and cents. So, although it can be painful, learn

This chapter is written by Andrew Zacharakis.

the numbers behind your business. The rewards of gaining this deep insight are often the difference between success and failure.

If for no other reason, the lead entrepreneur needs to understand the numbers so she can decide whether this business has the potential to provide her with a good living. It is too easy to get caught in a trap where a new venture is slowly draining away your investment or where you are working, in real terms, for less than the minimum wage.[1] The goal of this chapter is to give you an introduction to entrepreneurial financial planning. Unlike in existing businesses, which have an operating history, entrepreneurs must develop their financials from scratch. There are no previous trends in revenue and costs that you can use as a basis to project future revenues and costs. Yet the failure to come up with solid projections may cost you your initial investment as well as that of your investors. This chapter will help you generate sound projections.

Common Mistakes

In preparing this chapter, we sent an email to several acquaintances who are professional equity investors (either angels or venture capitalists). We asked them, "What are the most common mistakes you see when you review an entrepreneur's business proposal?" We wanted to know what "red flags" made them hesitant to believe that the business could survive and succeed. Here are the six mistakes they consistently cited.

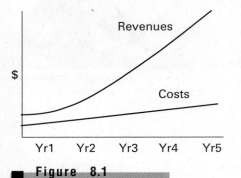

Figure 8.1

Hockey stick sales growth

1. **Not understanding the revenue drivers.** Entrepreneurs need to know what the leverage points are that drive revenues. They need to understand how many customers are likely to see the product, how many of those who see it will buy it, and how much, on average, they will buy each time. Although every entrepreneur claims his estimates are "conservative," 99% of the time entrepreneurs are overly optimistic in their projections. So avoid the "conservative" adjective; it strikes most sophisticated investors as naïve.

2. **Underestimating costs.** If you were to graph the revenue and cost projections of entrepreneurs over time, you would often see revenues growing in a "hockey stick" fashion, while costs slowly progress upward (see Figure 8.1). We often see revenue projections of $15 million after five years on costs of only $5 million. That is unbelievable. When we dig into those numbers, we often see that the firm has only five employees in year five. That assumes revenues per employee of $3 million, which is nearly impossible. Often entrepreneurs underestimate how much infrastructure they need in the way of employees and physical assets to achieve that level of sales. Entrepreneurs also underestimate the cost of marketing expenditures to acquire and retain customers. Poor projections lead to cash crunches and ultimately to failure.

3. **Underestimating time to generate revenues.** Pro-forma financials often show sales occurring immediately. Typically, a business will incur costs for many months before it can generate revenue. For instance, if you are opening a restaurant, you will incur rent, inventory, and labor costs, among others, before you generate a dime in revenue. Another "red flag" is how quickly revenues will ramp up. Often projections show the business at full capacity within the first year. That is rarely realistic.

4. **Lack of comparables.** Investors typically think about the entrepreneur's concept from their knowledge of similar businesses. They will compare your gross margins, net income margins, and other metrics to industry standards and selected benchmark companies. Yet many entrepreneurs' projections have ratios that far exceed industry standards, and when questioned about this above-average performance, they can't explain it. You need to understand your business model in relation to the industry and be able to explain any differences.

5. **Top-down versus bottom-up forecasting.** Investors often hear entrepreneurs claim that their revenues represent 3% of the market after year three. The implication is that it is easy to get that 3%. Investors know that, although it doesn't sound like much, the trick is how you get to that 3%. They want to see the process—the cost of acquiring, serving, and retaining the customer. Investors won't believe that you can get 3% without causing competitors to take notice and action.

6. **Underestimating time to secure financing.** The last pet peeve of investors is that entrepreneurs assume financing will close quickly. Whether entrepreneurs want to raise $25,000 or $1 million, they project it will happen in the next month. In reality, it often takes as long as six months to close a round of financing. Fred Adler, famed venture capitalist who invested in Data General, used to hand out t-shirts that said, "Happiness is a positive cash flow." Yet, if entrepreneurs are too optimistic about how quickly they can close a round of financing, they will quickly have negative cash flow, which often means they are out of business.

Understanding these pitfalls will help you generate realistic financials and, more importantly, enable you to convincingly articulate your business model so that you can sell your vision to employees, customers, vendors, and investors. Before we move on, here is a quick overview of financial statements.

Financial Statement Overview

You'll need to include three standard financial statements in your business plan: the income statement, the statement of cash flows, and the balance sheet. Most people first want to know why there are three statements. The reason is simple: Each one provides a slightly different view of the company. Any one alone is only part of the picture. Together they provide a detailed description of the economics of your company.

The first of these statements, the **income statement**, describes how well a company conducted its business over a recent period of time—typically, a quarter (three months) or a year. This indicator of overall performance begins with the company's revenues on the top line. From that accounting of sales, subtract the company's expenses. These include

- Cost of the products that the company actually sold
- Selling, marketing, and administrative costs
- Depreciation—the estimated cost of using your property, plant, and equipment
- Interest on debts
- Taxes on profits

The bottom line of the statement (literally) is the company's profits—called *net income*. It is important to realize that the income statement represents a measurement of business performance. It is *not* a description of actual flows of money.

A company needs cash to conduct business. Without it, there is no business. The second financial statement, the **statement of cash flows**, monitors this crucial account. As the name implies, the statement of cash flows concerns itself exclusively with transactions that involve cash. It is not uncommon to have strong positive earnings on the income statement and a negative statement of cash flows—less cash at the end of the period than at the beginning. Just because you shipped a product does not necessarily mean you received the cash for it yet. Likewise, you might have purchased something like inventory or a piece of equipment that will not show up on your income statement until it is consumed or depreciated. Many noncash transactions are represented in the income statement.

What is curious (and sometimes confusing to those who have never worked with financial statements before) is the way the statement of cash flows is constructed. It starts with the bottom line (profits) of the income statement and works backward, removing all the noncash transactions. For example, since the income statement subtracted depreciation (the value of using your plant and equipment), the statement of cash flows adds it back in because you don't actually pay any depreciation expense to anybody. Similarly, the cash-flow statement needs to include things that you paid for but did not use that period. For example, you might have paid for inventory that has not yet sold, or you might have bought a piece of equipment that you will depreciate over time, so you would need to put those items on the cash flow statement. After all these adjustments, you are left with a representation of transactions that are exclusively cash.

The **balance sheet** enumerates all the company's assets, liabilities, and shareholder equity. **Assets** are all the things the company has that are expected to generate value over time—things like inventory, buildings, and equipment; accounts receivable (money that your customers still owe you); and cash. **Liabilities** represent all the money the company expects to pay eventually. These include accounts payable (money the company owes its suppliers), debt, and unpaid taxes. **Shareholder equity** is the money that shareholders have paid into the company as well as the company's earnings so far. Where the income statement describes a process or flow, the balance sheet is a snapshot of accounts at a specific point in time.

All your assets come from a liability or shareholder equity. Therefore, the sum of the asset accounts must equal the sum of the liabilities and shareholder equity account.

$$\text{Assets} = \text{Liabilities} + \text{Shareholder Equity}$$

The assets are shown on the left side of the balance sheet, with the liabilities and shareholder equity on the right. The balance sheet *always* balances. If your balance sheet does not balance, you have made a mistake.

This is, of course, only a partial treatment of financial statements, but it should be enough for you to understand this chapter. We strongly recommend reading John Tracy's excellent book, *How to Read a Financial Report*.[2] It is a simple, short, and easy way for novices to quickly learn the basics. The remainder of this chapter will step you through a process to generate your financials.

Building Your Pro-Forma Financial Statements

Figure 8.2 previews the points we will cover. Think of this as a checklist in developing your financials. Rigorously completing each step will lead to better financial projections and decisions. Underlying these steps are two methods: the **build-up method** and the **comparable method**. Our advice is to go through all the steps in an iterative fashion so that you not only know the numbers but also "own the numbers."

Build-Up Method

Scientific findings suggest that people make better decisions by decomposing problems into smaller decisions. If you think about the business planning process, you are going through a series of questions that help you answer the big question: Is this an attractive opportunity? Thus, you evaluate the industry, the competition, the customer, and so forth. Based upon that analysis, you decide whether to launch the business. Constructing pro-forma financials is part of this process. In the build-up method, you look at the revenue you might generate in a typical day. You then multiple that day times the number of days you're open in a year to come up with your yearly revenue. You then do a similar exercise for costs. Doing your revenues and costs on a daily basis helps you come up with more realistic annual projections.

Build-Up Method

1. Identify all your sources of revenues
2. Determine your revenues for a "typical day"
3. Understand your revenue drivers
   a. How many customers you will serve
   b. How much product they will buy
   c. How much they will pay for each product
   d. How often they will buy
4. Validate driver assumptions
   a. Primary research (talk to customers, attend trade shows, etc.)
   b. Secondary research (industry reports, company reports, etc.)
5. Recombine. Multiply the typical day by the number of days in a year
6. Determine Cost of Goods Sold (COGS) for a typical day
7. Recombine. Multiply COGS by number of days in a year
8. Determine operating expenses by most appropriate time frame
9. Refine operating costs
10. Create preliminary income statement

Comparable Method

11. Compare revenue projections to industry metrics
12. Run scenario analysis
13. Compare common-sized cost percentages to industry averages

Building Integrated Financial Statements

14. Derive monthly income statements for first two years, yearly statements for year 3–5
15. Create balance sheet (yearly for year 1–5)
16. Create cash-flow statement (monthly for years 1 and 2, yearly for years 3–5)

Final Steps

17. Write a two- to three-page description of financial statements

■ **Figure 8.2**

Financial construction checklist

The place to start is the income statement; the other two statements are in part derived from the income statement. First, identify all your revenue sources (usually the various product offerings). Second, identify all your costs. Once you have the business broken down into its component parts, the next step is to think about how much revenue you can generate in a year, but we can decompose this estimate as well.

Revenue Projections

Instead of visualizing what you will sell in a month or a year, break it down into a typical day. For example, if you were starting the retail bookstore mentioned in the last chapter, you would estimate how many customers you might serve in a particular day and how much

Product/Service Description	Price	Units Sold/Day	Total Revenue
1. Books	$20	75 visitors*75%*1.5 books	$1,687.50
2. DVDs	$30	75 visitors*15%*1 DVD	337.50
3. Maps	$50	75 visitors*10%*1 map	375.00
4. Ancillary Items	$100	75 visitors*5%*1 globe	375.00
5. Other (Postcards, Magazines, etc.)	$5	75 visitors*20%*2 items	150.00
Totals			$2,925.00

Assumptions:
Traffic — 75 visitors a day

- Books — 75% of visitors will buy 1.5 books each
- DVDs — 15% of visitors will buy 1 DVD each
- Maps — 10% of visitors will buy 1 map each
- Globes — 5% of visitors will buy 1 ancillary item each
- Other — 20% of visitors will buy 2 misc. items

50% of sales will happen during the holiday season
30% of sales will happen during summer tourist season (May through September)

Figure 8.3

Revenue worksheet

they would spend per visit based on the types of books and ancillary items they would buy. Figure 8.3 illustrates the process. First, it details the product mix and the average price for each item — books, maps, and other ancillary products. Second, it estimates the traffic that the store will draw on a typical day. It lists the assumptions at the bottom of the schedule. Then it estimates how many people will come into the store to buy an item and how many items they will buy. The last column gives total revenue per day by product category.

Figure 8.3 highlights critical revenue assumptions, or what we might call *revenue drivers*. Simply put, going through this exercise tells you how you will make money. It also helps you understand how you might be able to make more money. In other words, what revenue drivers can you influence? A retail shop might be able to increase its daily sales by increasing the traffic coming into the store through advertising or by increasing the number of people who buy and how much they buy through up-selling — "Can I get you anything else today?" Although this thought exercise is invaluable, your estimates are only as good as your assumptions.

How do you strengthen your assumptions? How do you validate the traffic level, the percentage of customers who buy, and so forth? The answer is through research. The first place to start is by talking to people who know the business. Talk to bookstore owners, book vendors, mall leasing agents, and others in the industry. A good way to interact with these participants is at industry trade shows. The next thing to do is to visit a number of bookstores and count how many people come in, what portion buy, and how much they spend. Although you might feel conspicuous, there are ways to do this field research without drawing attention to yourself or interfering in the store's business. For example, you might go sit outside a bookstore and watch how many people who walk by enter the store and how many people come out of the store with a package. Finally, talk to your expected customers — avid readers in this example. Find out how often they buy history books. Ask them how much they spend on these items a month and where they currently buy them. By going through several iterations of primary research, you will sharpen your estimates.

In addition to conducting the research yourself, you can seek out secondary sources such as industry reports and Web sites. For example, there are lots of excellent resources on retail bookstore operations such as the Small Business Development Center's 2012 Bookstore Research Report[3] and the *Manual on Bookselling*, edited by Kate Whouley and published by the American Booksellers Association (ABA) in 1996. The ABA also publishes its annual *ABACUS Survey*, which provides detailed information on all sorts of financial metrics in the industry such as sales data on new and used books and operating costs.

Once you are comfortable that your assumptions are sound, you can then multiply the typical day by the number of days of operation in the year to arrive at yearly revenue estimates. This is a first cut. Clearly, a typical day varies by the time of the year. People do much of their shopping around the December holiday season. Therefore, most pro-forma projections for new companies typically show monthly income figures for the first two years. This allows the entrepreneur to manage seasonality and other factors that might make sales uneven for the business.

Cost of Goods Sold

Once you have your revenue projections, you next consider costs. An income statement has two categories of costs—cost of goods sold and operating expenses. **Cost of goods sold (COGS)** is the direct costs of the items sold. For a bookstore, COGS is the cost of inventory that is sold in that period. As a first cut, you might assume that COGS for a retail outlet would be around 50% (assumes a 100% markup). Since sales from Figure 8.3 were approximately $3,000 per day, COGS would be around $1,500.

As with revenue assumptions, you need to sharpen your COGS assumptions. Use a schedule similar to that in Figure 8.3 to refine COGS by product (see Figure 8.4). After some investigation at Hoovers.com, you find that the gross margin on books is only 27% for the likes of Amazon.com and Barnes & Noble. On other items you might sell, other companies' gross margins (for MTS and TransWorld Entertainment) are around 24%. Although these margins are lower than first estimated, these companies have a different business model—high volume, lower margins. Where will your bookstore operate? If it is high volume, your margins should be similar to these companies' margins. If you choose to offer a premium shopping experience, meaning a highly knowledgeable sales staff and unique historical artifacts, you would likely achieve higher margins. Remember that your financials need to mirror the story

Product/Service Description	Price	Gross Margin	Revenue	COGS
1. Books	$20	40%	$1,687.50	$1,012.50
2. Videos	$30	50%	337.50	168.75
3. Maps	$50	50%	375.00	187.50
4. Ancillary Items	$100	50%	375.00	187.50
5. Other (Postcards, Magazines, etc.)	$5	50%	150.00	75.00
Totals			$2,925.00	$1,631.25

Total Revenue	$2,925.00
COGS	1,631.25
Gross Profit	$1,293.75
Gross Profit Margin	44%

Figure 8.4

Cost of goods worksheet

you related in your business plan—be consistent. Figure 8.4 shows the price per item, the gross margin (revenue minus COGS) per item, and the revenue per item (from Figure 8.3) and then calculates COGS in dollar terms [revenue times (1 - COGS)]. Since the gross margins for items differ, the overall gross margin is 44%.

Operating Expenses

In addition to direct expenses, businesses incur operating expenses, such as marketing, salaries and general administration (SG&A), rent, interest expenses, and so forth. The build-up method forecasts those expenses on a daily, monthly, or yearly basis as appropriate (see Figure 8.5). For example, you might get rental space for your store at $30 per square foot per year depending on location. You might need about 3,000 square feet, so your yearly rent would be $90,000 (put in the yearly expense column). You'll pay your rent on a monthly basis, so you would show a rent expense of $7,500 in the month-to-month income statement. At this point, however, you are just trying to get a sense of the overall business model and gauge whether this business can be profitable; showing it on a yearly basis is sufficient.

Expense	Daily	Monthly	Yearly	Total
Store Rent			90,000	$90,000
Manager Salary			60,000	$60,000
Assistant Manager			40,000	$40,000
Hourly Employees	176			$63,360
Benefits	21		12,000	$19,603
Bank Charges			10,530	$10,530
Marketing/Advertising		1,000		$12,000
Utilities		333		$4,000
Travel			1,000	$1,000
Dues			1,000	$1,000
Depreciation		833		$10,000
Misc.			4,000	$4,000
				$0
Totals				$315,493

Assumptions:

Rent — 3,000 sq. ft. at $30/sq. ft. = $90,000
Hire 1 manager at $60,000/year
Hire 1 assistant manager at $40,000/year
Store is open from 9 a.m. to 7 p.m. daily, so 10 hours per day
Need 2 clerks when open and 1 clerk an hour before and after open
2 clerks × 10 hours × $8/hour + 1 clerk × 2 hours × $8/hour
Benefits are 12% of wages and salaries
Bank charges about 1% of sales
Advertising — $1,000/ month
Travel — $1,000/year to attend trade shows
Dues — $1,000/year for trade association
Depreciation — $100,000 of leasehold improvements and equipment, depreciated over 10 years using the straight-line method

Figure 8.5

Operating expenses worksheet

	Mon.	Tues.	Wed.	Thurs.	Fri.	Sat.	Sun.	Total
Store Hours	10:00–9:00	10:00–9:00	10:00–9:00	10:00–9:00	10:00–9:00	10:00–9:00	11:00–5:00	
Hours Open	11	11	11	11	11	11	6	72
Shift 1	9:30–1:30	9:30–1:30	9:30–1:30	9:30–1:30	9:30–1:30	9:30–1:30	10:00–2:00	
Shift 2	1:30–5:30	1:30–5:30	1:30–5:30	1:30–5:30	1:30–5:30	1:30–5:30	1:00–5:00	
Shift 3	5:30–9:30	5:30–9:30	5:30–9:30	5:30–9:30	5:30–9:30	5:30–9:30		
Shift 1 Hrs.	4	4	4	4	4	4	4	
Shift 2 Hrs.	4	4	4	4	4	4	4	
Shift 3 Hrs.	4	4	4	4	4	4	0	
Total Shift Hours	12	12	12	12	12	12	8	80
Staff Headcount								
Shift 1	2	2	1	2	1	4	3	
Shift 2	1	1	0	1	1	4	4	
Shift 3	1	1	1	2	4	4	0	
Total Staff	4	4	2	5	6	12	7	40
Total Hours Worked								
Shift 1	8	8	4	8	4	16	12	
Shift 2	4	4	0	4	4	16	16	
Shift 3	4	4	4	8	16	16	0	
	16	16	8	20	24	48	28	160
Mgr.	0	0	8	8	8	8	8	40
Asst. Mgr.	8	8	8	0	8	8	0	40

Total hourly employee hours/week = 160
Hourly rate $8/hour   8
Total wages per week $1,280
Total wages per year $66,560

Figure 8.6

Headcount table

Based on the first cut, your bookstore is projecting operating expenses of approximately $315,000 per year. However, the "devil is in the details," as they say, and one problem area is accurately projecting operating costs, especially labor costs. Constructing a headcount schedule is an important step in refining your labor projections (see Figure 8.6). Although the store is open on average 10 hours per day, you can see from the headcount table that Sunday is a shorter day and that the store is open 11 hours on the other days. The store operates with a minimum of two employees at all times (including either the store manager or the assistant store manager). During busier shifts, the number of employees reaches a peak of six people (afternoon shift on Saturday, including both managers). Looking at the calculation below the table, you see that the new wage expense is about $66,000, a bit higher than the first estimate. This process of examining and reexamining your assumptions over and over is what leads to compelling financials.

Just as you refine the hourly wage expense, you need to also refine other expenses. For example, marketing expenses are projected to be $12,000. Create a detailed schedule of how you plan on spending those advertising dollars. If you refer back to the last chapter, Figure 7.7a has a schedule of detailed expenses. This illustrates another point: *Financial analysis is really just the mathematical expression of your overall business strategy.* Everything you write about in your business plan has revenue or cost implications. As investors read business plans, they build a mental picture of the financial statements, especially the income statement. If the written plan and the financials are tightly correlated, investors have much greater confidence that the entrepreneur knows what she is doing.

Preliminary Income Statement

Once you have forecasted revenues and expenses, you put them together in an income statement (Figure 8.7). Figure 8.3 forecasted average daily sales of almost $3,000. You need to annualize that figure. You can expect the store to be open, on average, 360 days per year (assuming that the store might be closed for a few days such as Christmas and Thanksgiving). Note that the first line is called Total Revenues and then shows the detail that creates that total revenues line by itemizing the different revenue categories. COGS is handled in the same manner as revenues; you multiply the typical day by 360 days to get the annual total.

After adjusting the hourly wages per the headcount table (which also means adjusting employee benefits), take the operating expenses worksheet (see Figure 8.5) and put it into the income statement. If you believe that you can secure debt financing, put in an interest expense. However, for the initial forecasts, you may not yet know how much debt financing you'll need or can secure to launch the business, so leave out the interest expense until you derive a reasonable estimate. Next compute taxes. Make sure to account for federal, state, and city taxes as applicable. Note that the right column calculates the expense percentage of total revenues. This is called a *common-sized income statement*. Although you have been rigorous in building

Total Revenues	**$1,053,000**	**100%**
Historical Books	607,500	
Videos	121,500	
Maps	135,000	
Ancillary Items	135,000	
Other	54,000	
Total COGS	**$587,250**	**55.8%**
Historical Books	364,500	
Videos	60,750	
Maps	67,500	
Ancillary Items	67,500	
Other	27,000	
Gross Profit	**$465,750**	**44.2%**
Operating Expenses		
Store Rent	90,000	
Manager Salary	60,000	
Assistant Manager	40,000	
Hourly Employees	66,560	
Benefits	19,987	
Bank Charges	10,530	
Marketing/Advertising	12,000	
Utilities	4,000	
Travel	1,000	
Dues	1,000	
Depreciation	10,000	
Misc.	4,000	
Total Operating Expenses	**$319,077**	**30.3%**
Earnings from Operations	**$146,673**	**13.9%**
Taxes	**$58,669**	**5.6%**
Net Earnings	**$88,004**	**8.4%**

■ **Figure 8.7**

Income statement

up your statement, you can further validate it by comparing your common-sized income statement to the industry standards, which is where you start using the comparable method.

Comparable Method

How can you tell whether your projections are reasonable? In the **comparable method**, you look at how your company compares to industry averages and benchmark companies. The first thing to do is gauge whether your revenue projections make sense and then see whether your cost structure is reasonable. Comparables help you validate your projections. For instance, a good metric for revenue in retail is sales per square foot. The bookstore is projecting sales of $1 million in 3,000 square feet, which equates to $351 per square foot. Secondary research into the average per bookstore[4] and also into what one or two specific bookstores achieve is a good place to start.[5] For example, $351 is in line with independent bookstores ($350/square foot) but higher than Barnes & Noble ($297/square foot).

The projections seem reasonable considering that you will be selling certain items like maps, which have a much higher ticket price than books, but there are a couple of caveats to this estimate. First, it is likely to take a new bookstore some time to achieve this level of sales. In other words, the income statement that has been derived might be more appropriate for the second or third year of operation. At that point, the bookstore will have built up a clientele and achieved some name recognition.

Second, you should run some scenario analyses. Does this business model still work if your bookstore only achieves Barnes & Noble's sales per square foot ($297)? Also run a few other scenarios related to higher foot traffic, recession, outbreak of war (sales of books on Islam increased with September 11 and escalating tensions in the Middle East), and other contingencies. Having some validated metrics, such as sales per square foot, helps you run different scenarios and make sound decisions about whether to launch a venture in the first place and then about how to adjust your business model so that the venture has the greatest potential to succeed.

Other metrics that are easily obtainable for this type of establishment include *sales per customer* or *average ticket price*. Figure 8.3 shows expected sales of $2,925 per day from 75 unique store visitors. That translates into an average transaction per visitor of $39. However, not every visitor will buy; many people will just come in and browse. Figure 8.3 assumed that 75% of visitors would buy a book and a lower percentage would buy other items. If that percentage holds true, 56 people will actually purchase something each day. Thus, the average receipt is $52. This average ticket price is considerably higher than Barnes & Noble's rate of $27.

As with all your assumptions, you have to gauge whether a higher ticket price is reasonable. An entrepreneur might reason that the bookstore isn't discounting its books and is also selling higher-priced ancillary goods. Run scenario analyses again to see whether your bookstore survives if its average ticket price is closer to Barnes & Noble's. In other words, see what happens to the model overall when you change one of the assumptions—in this case, the average selling price.

After you're comfortable with the revenue estimate, you next need to validate the costs. The best way is to compare your common-sized income statement with the industry averages or some benchmark companies. It is unlikely that your income statement will exactly match the industry averages, but you need to be able to explain and understand the differences. Figure 8.8 looks at the common-sized income statements for your store and for Barnes & Noble. The first discrepancy appears in the COGS. Your store projects COGS of 56% of revenue, whereas Barnes & Noble is projecting 70%. Why would Barnes & Noble's COGS be so much higher? Upon further investigation, you find that Barnes & Noble includes occupancy costs like rent and utilities in COGS. If you add your store's $90,000 rent plus

	Our Specialty Bookstore		Barnes & Nobel (FY2007) (in millions)		Industry Average
Total Revenues	$1,053,000	100%	$5,410	100%	100%
Historical Books	607,500				
Videos	121,500				
Maps	135,000				
Globes	135,000				
Other	54,000				
Total COGS	$587,250	55.8%	$3,770	69.7%	60.0%
Historical Books	364,500				
Videos	60,750				
Maps	67,500				
Globes	67,500				
Other	27,000				
Gross Profit	$465,750	44.2%	$1,641	30.3%	40.0%
Operating Expenses					
Store rent	90,000				
Manager Salary	60,000				
Assistant Manager	40,000				
Hourly Employees	66,560				
Benefits	19,987				
Bank Charges	10,530				
Marketing/Advertising	12,000				
Utilities	4,000				
Travel	1,000				
Dues	1,000				
Depreciation	10,000				
Misc	4,000				
Total Operating Expenses	$319,077	30.3%	$1,432	26.5%	37.5%
Earnings from Operations	$146,673	13.9%	$209	3.9%	2.5%
Taxes	$58,669		$73		
Net Earnings	$88,004	8.4%	$136	2.5%	

Figure 8.8

Comparable analysis

$4,000 in utilities into COGS, COGS becomes 65% of revenue, which is still lower that Barnes & Noble's. However, COGS of 65% is in line with the specialty retail industry rate of 67%.[6] The reasoning for this discrepancy is similar to that for the higher ticket price. Your specialty bookstore's COGS is likely lower than Barnes & Noble's because it is not a discount bookseller (meaning it earns higher margins on every book sold than does Barnes & Noble). You also plan to sell other retail items that generate higher margins.

Since the gross profit margin is the inverse of COGS—revenue minus COGS—the explanation provided for COGS also holds for the gross margin. Barnes & Noble's gross margin is 30% versus 35% for your specialty bookstore (with rent included in COGS).

When you compare operating expenses for the two companies, you can see that your bookstore is projecting operating expenses to be 30% of revenue versus 27% for Barnes & Noble. However, we must once again adjust for the occupancy expense because you include occupancy in operating expenses, whereas Barnes & Noble includes it in COGS. With that adjustment, your operating expenses are about 21% of revenue, somewhat less than Barnes & Noble. We would want to investigate to see if we are underestimating the number of employees we will need. Or are we paying lower rent because we aren't in a high-profile location. The key is to determine if lower costs are reasonable or not.

Based on the comparable analysis, it appears that your projections are reasonable. Your earnings from operations are higher (13.9%) than Barnes & Noble's (3.9%) and the independent book store average (2.5%), but that may be explained by the higher gross margins and the fact that you haven't yet included any interest expenses. For example, if you use debt financing for any of your startup expenses, such as leasehold improvements, you will have an interest expense that would reduce your net income margin to be more in line with the comparable companies.

This exercise has primarily used benchmark companies, but industry averages also provide useful comparable information. The *Almanac of Business and Industrial Financial Ratios* published by CCH Group and *Industry Norms and Key Business Ratios* published by Dun and Bradstreet are excellent sources to use as starting points in building financial statements relevant to your industry. Specifically, these sources help entrepreneurs build income statements by providing industry averages for cost of goods sold, salary expenses, interest expenses, and other costs. Again, your firm will differ from these industry averages, but by going through scenario analyses and understanding your business model, you should be able to explain why your firm differs.

Building Integrated Financial Statements

Once you have a baseline income statement, the next step is to construct monthly income and cash-flow statements for two years (followed by years 3 through 5 on a yearly basis) and a yearly balance sheet for all five years. Five years is standard for many business plans because it usually takes new firms some time to build sales and operate efficiently. Five years also gives the entrepreneur a sense of whether her investment of time and energy will pay off. Can the business not only survive but also provide the kind of financial return to make the opportunity costs of leaving an existing job worthwhile?

The income statement, cash-flow statement, and balance sheet are the core statements for managing any business. Changes in one statement affect all others. Understanding how these changes affect your business can mean the difference between survival and failure. Many entrepreneurs will find their businesses on the verge of failure, even if they are profitable, because they fail to understand how the income statement is related to the cash-flow statement and balance sheet. How is that possible, you might ask?

Entrepreneurs need to finance rapid growth. For example, a bookstore needs to buy inventory in advance of selling to its customers. The owner needs to ensure that he has enough books and other products on hand that he doesn't lose a sale because a customer is frustrated that the book isn't in stock. (Americans are notorious for wanting instant gratification.) Yet having inventory on hand drains cash. If the bookstore expects sales of $500,000 in December, then it must have $280,000 worth of inventory at the end of November ($500,000 × 56%—the average COGS). How does the bookstore pay for this? Internal cash flow? Vendor financing? Equity? Having strong pro-forma financials helps the entrepreneur anticipate these needs far enough in advance to arrange the appropriate financing.

Tom Iverson shops for sale books at a Barnes & Noble book store March 16, 2006 in Arlington Heights, Illinois. Tim Boyle/ Getty Images, Inc

The bookstore example illustrates why a new business wants to show the income and cash-flow statements on a monthly basis for the first two years; there is likely to be seasonal fluctuations in demand for which you need to anticipate and plan. Moreover, the first two years are the most vulnerable period in a new venture's life. It takes time to build up your clientele (during which you earn lower revenues), learn how to efficiently operate (during which you have higher costs), develop a track record so you can secure vendor financing (remember the cash-flow implications), and understand seasonality (which will make demand vary). For instance, monthly projections allow the entrepreneur to anticipate and understand any seasonality that might happen in the business. In addition to the financing issue discussed previously, seasonality affects other key operations and decisions. For example, your bookstore will need to hire more salespeople during the holiday season. Integrated financials can help the entrepreneur plan for that hiring increase.

In sum, it is critical to show the first two years of pro-forma projections on a monthly basis because this is when a company is most vulnerable to failure. Monthly forecasts help you understand these issues and prepare for them. For years 3 through 5, yearly projections are sufficient because the further out one goes, the less accurate the projections become. Nevertheless, your longer-term projections communicate your vision of the upside potential of your opportunity. The exercise of going through the projection process is more important than the accuracy of the projections. The process helps you gain a deeper understanding of the business and whether you should pursue the opportunity.

As the bookstore example indicates, changes in one statement affect other statements. Figure 8.9 formally shows how the pro-forma financials are integrated. You can see that the income statement drives the balance sheet, which drives the cash-flow statement (although the cash from financing and uses of cash from the cash-flow statement feed back into the balance sheet). We'll briefly touch on how to move from our base income statement to a full set of pro-forma financial projections, but going into a step-by-step process is beyond the scope of this chapter.

Income Statement

The base income statement generated shows the level of operations that might be achievable in year 3 or 4. Thus, you need to make a number of adjustments to generate the other years. First, you need to create monthly statements for the first two years. That means you need to understand the seasonality of your business and the sales cycle. One mistake that many entrepreneurs make is showing revenues from the first day they launch the business. Remember

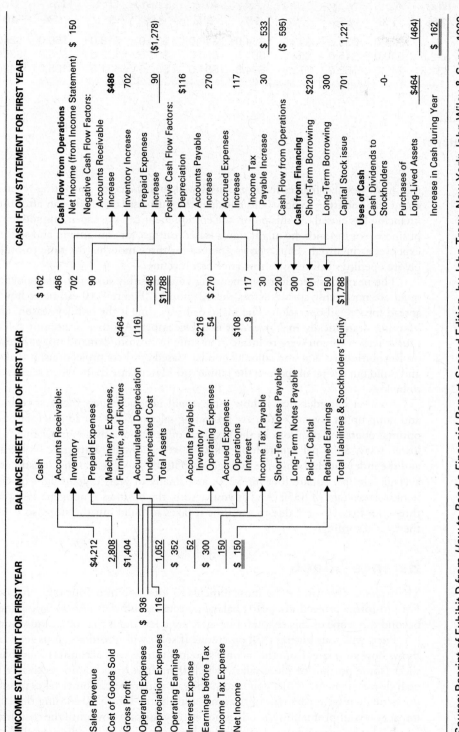

EXHIBIT D-MASTER EXHIBIT
(Dollar amounts in thousands)

INCOME STATEMENT FOR FIRST YEAR

Sales Revenue		$4,212
Cost of Goods Sold		2,808
Gross Profit		$1,404
Operating Expenses	$ 936	
Depreciation Expenses	116	1,052
Operating Earnings		$ 352
Interest Expense		52
Earnings before Tax		$ 300
Income Tax Expense		150
Net Income		$ 150

BALANCE SHEET AT END OF FIRST YEAR

Cash		$ 162
Accounts Receivable:		486
Inventory		702
Prepaid Expenses		90
Machinery, Expenses, Furniture, and Fixtures	$464	
Accumulated Depreciation	(116)	
Undepreciated Cost		348
Total Assets		$1,788
Accounts Payable:		
Inventory	$216	
Operating Expenses	54	$ 270
Accrued Expenses:		
Operations	$108	
Interest	9	117
Income Tax Payable		30
Short-Term Notes Payable		220
Long-Term Notes Payable		300
Paid-in Capital		701
Retained Earnings		150
Total Liabilities & Stockholders' Equity		$1,788

CASH FLOW STATEMENT FOR FIRST YEAR

Cash Flow from Operations		
Net Income (from Income Statement)		$ 150
Negative Cash Flow Factors:		
Accounts Receivable Increase	**$486**	
Inventory Increase	702	
Prepaid Expenses Increase	90	($1,278)
Positive Cash Flow Factors:		
Depreciation	$116	
Accounts Payable Increase	270	
Accrued Expenses Increase	117	
Income Tax Payable Increase	30	$ 533
Cash Flow from Operations		($ 595)
Cash from Financing		
Short-Term Borrowing	$220	
Long-Term Borrowing	300	
Capital Stock issue	701	1,221
Uses of Cash		
Cash Dividends to Stockholders	-0-	
Purchases of Long-Lived Assets	$464	(464)
Increase in Cash during Year		$ 162

Source: Reprint of Exhibit D from *How to Read a Financial Report,* Second Edition, by John Tracy. New York: John Wiley & Sons, 1983.

Figure 8.9

Interrelated financial statements

(000)												
Jan. 3%	Feb. 2%	Mar. 3%	Apr. 4%	May 6%	June 7%	July 9%	Aug. 8%	Sept. 5%	Oct. 3%	Nov. 10%	Dec. 40%	Year 100%
Year 1			$24.0	$36.0	$42.0	$54.0	$48.0	$30.0	$18.0	$60.0	$240.0	$552.0
Year 2 $22.5	$15.0	$22.5	$30.0	$45.0	$52.5	$67.5	$60.0	$37.5	$22.5	$75.0	$300.0	$750.0
Year 3 $31.5	$21.0	$31.5	$42.0	$63.0	$73.5	$94.5	$84.0	$52.5	$31.5	$105.0	$420.0	$1,050.0

■ Figure 8.10

Seasonality projections

that most new businesses incur expenses well in advance of generating revenue. In thinking about the bookstore, you would consider the business launched soon after the first round of financing has closed. At this point, the entrepreneur can start spending money to establish the business. For instance, he might sign a lease, contract for equipment, and so forth. Show those expenses as incurred. Thus, show expenses for three months (the time to build out the store before opening) before you show your first revenue.

The next consideration in generating your monthly forecasts is seasonality. Revenues in retail are not evenly spread across the 12 months. Figure 8.10 estimates how sales might be spread for a retail operation. The make-or-break time is the holiday season, and you see sales jumping dramatically in November and December. Another important spike might be the tourist season (if you were to locate your store in Boston, demand might jump if you focused on Revolutionary War and colonial goods). Based on these projections, it makes sense to lease and build out the retail space in the January to March time frame when sales levels are expected to be low.

Another consideration is how long it will take your new business to build its clientele and ramp up its revenues. You are projecting sales of $350 per square foot once you hit your optimal operating position. In the first year of operation, that number might be significantly lower—say, $200 per square foot, which is well below the Barnes & Noble average of $297 and the independent bookstore average of $350. In year 2, a reasonable estimate might be that average sales per square foot hit $250, and finally in year 3, you might hit the independent bookstore average of $350. And as you've seen, the business is not generating sales for the first three months of year 1 due to the time it takes to build out the store, so you need to adjust the sales accordingly.

Balance Sheet

The *balance sheet* can be the most difficult to integrate into your other financial statements. For pro-forma projections, yearly balance sheets are sufficient. Again, going into great detail is beyond the scope of this chapter, but there are a few items that often cause confusion.

First, will your business sell on credit? If so, it will record accounts receivable. Figure 8.9 shows how your sales from the income statement drive your accounts receivable on the balance sheet (some portion of those sales), which then drive an accounts receivable increase on the cash-flow statement. While you record the sale when the customer takes possession, you may not actually receive payment until some point in the future. Recording the sale has a positive impact on your profitability but does not affect your cash flow until the customer actually pays.

If your business is buying equipment, land, or a plant or is adding leasehold improvements, you will have an asset of plant and equipment. A common error is to show this as a capital expense, meaning that it appears in full on your income statement the moment you contract for the work. This assumes you will fully use that equipment within the year (or whatever length your income statement covers). To accurately reflect the acquisition of the asset, instead show the full outflow of money as it occurs on your cash-flow statement and then depreciate the cost per year of life of the asset on your income statement. You would also have an accumulated depreciation line item on your balance sheet showing how much of the asset has been used up. Referring back to Figure 8.5, you see the bookstore is projecting leasehold improvements of $100,000, which it expects to use up over 10 years ($10,000 per year or $833 per month).

Accounts payable acts in a manner similar to accounts receivable, except that it is a loan to your company from a supplier (see Figure 8.9). Once the new store is able to secure vendor financing on inventory, for example, it will show the COGS as it sells its books, but it may not have to pay the publisher until later (assuming that the book is a fairly fast-moving item). So the expense would show up on your income statement but not on your cash-flow statement—until you paid for it. Until then, it is held in accounts payable on the balance sheet.

The final problem area is retained earnings. Entrepreneurs know that the balance sheet should *balance*. A common error is to use the retained earnings line to make the balance sheet balance. Retained earnings is actually

Previous Retained Earnings + Current Period Net Income
— Dividends Paid during the Current Period

If you find that your balance sheet isn't balancing, the problem is often in how you have calculated accounts receivable or accounts payable. Balancing the balance sheet is the most frustrating aspect of building your pro-forma financial statements. Yet hardwiring the retained earnings will ultimately lead to other errors, so work through the balancing problem as diligently as possible.

Cash-Flow Statement

If you have constructed your financial statements accurately, the **cash-flow statement** identifies when and how much financing you need. You might want to leave the financing assumptions empty until after you see how much the cash-flow statement implies you need (see Figure 8.11). One of the many benefits of this process is that it will help you determine exactly how much you need, so as to protect you from giving up too much equity or acquiring too much (or not enough) debt. The bookstore cash-flow statement shows some major outlays as the store is gearing up for operation, such as inventory acquisition and equipment purchases. You can also see from the cash-flow statement that the business is incurring some expenses prior to generating revenue [($17,000) listed as net earnings]. This net earnings loss is reflected on the company's monthly income statement and is primarily attributable to wage expenses to hire and train staff.

You can see that in the first six months, the cash position hits a low of just over −$316,000. This is how much money you need to raise in order to launch the business. For a new venture, most of the money will likely be in the form of equity from the entrepreneur, friends, and family. However, the entrepreneur may be able to secure some debt financing against his equipment (which would act as collateral if the business should fail). In any event, once you recognize your financing needs, you can devise a strategy to raise the money necessary to start the business. To provide some buffer against poor estimates, you might raise $350,000. This amount would show up on both the cash-flow statement and the balance sheet.

Putting It All Together

Once you have completed the financial spreadsheets, write a two- to three-page explanation to precede them. Although you understand all the assumptions and comparables that went into building the financial forecast, the reader needs the background spelled out. Describing the financials is also a good exercise in articulation. If your reader understands the financials and believes the assumptions are valid, you have passed an important test. If not, work with the

	Month 1	Month 2	Month 3	Month 4	Month 5	Month 6
OPERATING ACTIVITIES						
Net Earnings	(17,000)	(12,882)	(2,244)	(7,079)	(1,277)	8,394
Depreciation	1,115	1,115	1,115	1,115	1,115	1,115
Working Capital Changes						
(Increase)/Decrease Accounts Receivable	0	(64)	(88)	40	(48)	(80)
(Increase)/Decrease Inventories	(104,562)	(19,605)	32,676	(39,211)	(65,351)	71,886
(Increase)/Decrease Other Current Assets	0	(230)	(316)	144	(172)	(287)
Increase/(Decrease) Accts Pay & Accrd Expenses	0	3,215	4,421	(2,010)	2,411	4,019
Increase/(Decrease) Other Current Liab	0	3,445	4,737	(2,153)	2,584	4,306
Net Cash Provided/(Used) by Operating Activities	(120,446)	(25,005)	40,301	(49,154)	(60,737)	89,354
INVESTING ACTIVITIES						
Property & Equipment	(101,000)	0	0	0	0	0
Other						
Net Cash Used in Investing Activities	(101,000)	0	0	0	0	0
FINANCING ACTIVITIES						
Increase/(Decrease) Short-Term Debt						0
Increase/(Decrease) Curr. Portion LTD						0
Increase/(Decrease) Long-Term Debt						0
Increase/(Decrease) Common Stock						0
Increase/(Decrease) Preferred Stock						0
Dividends Declared						0
Net Cash Provided/(Used) by Financing	0	0	0	0	0	0
INCREASE/(DECREASE) IN CASH	(221,446)	(25,005)	40,301	(49,154)	(60,737)	89,354
CASH AT BEGINNING OF PERIOD	0	(221,446)	(246,451)	(206,150)	(255,304)	(316,041)
CASH AT END OF PERIOD	(221,446)	(246,451)	(206,150)	(255,304)	(316,041)	(226,687)

Figure 8.11

Cash-flow statement

reader to understand her concerns. Continual iterations strengthen your financials and should give you further confidence in the viability of your business model.

This section of the business plan should include a description of the key drivers that affect your revenues and costs so that the reader can follow your pro-forma financials. This description is typically broken down into four main sections. First, the "overview" paragraph briefly introduces the business model.

The first subsection should discuss the income statement. Talk about the factors that drive revenue, such as store traffic, percentage of store visitors that buy, average ticket price, and so forth. It is also important to talk about seasonality and other factors that might cause uneven sales growth. Then discuss the expense categories, paying attention to the cost of goods sold and major operating expense categories, such as rent, interest expense, and so forth. Based on your description, the reader should be able to look at the actual financials and understand what is going on. The key focus here is to help the reader follow your financials; you don't need to provide the level of detail that an accountant might if he were auditing your company.

The next subsection should discuss the cash-flow statement. Here, you focus on major infusions of cash, such as equity investments and loan disbursements. It is also good to describe the nature of your accounts receivable and accounts payable. How long, for instance, before your receivables convert to cash? If you are spending money on leasehold improvements, plant and equipment, and other items that can be depreciated, you should mention them here. Typically, the discussion of the cash-flow statement is quite a bit shorter than the discussion of the income statement.

The final subsection discusses the balance sheet. Here, you would talk about major asset categories, such as the amount of inventory on hand and any liabilities that aren't clear from the previous discussion.

CONCLUSION

Going through these exercises allows you to construct a realistic set of pro-forma financials. It's a challenge, but understanding your numbers "cold" enables you to articulate your business to all stakeholders, so you can build momentum toward the ultimate launch of your business. Just as we said in the last chapter that the business plan is a live document, so too, are the financial statements a set of live documents. They are obsolete immediately after they come off the printer. As you start your launch process, you can further refine your numbers, putting in actual revenues and expenses as they occur, and adjusting projections based on current activity. Once the business is operating, the nature of your financial statements changes. They not only help you to assess the viability of your business model but also help you to gauge actual performance and adjust your operations based on that experience.

Although most entrepreneurs tell us that drafting the financials induces some pain, they also concede that going through the process is gratifying and rewarding. They learn to master new management skills, build their business, and protect their investment. So dig in.

YOUR OPPORTUNITY JOURNAL

Reflection Point	Your Thoughts...
1. What are your revenue sources? How can you influence these revenues (what are your drivers)?	
2. Identify some companies that you can benchmark. What are their revenue sources? How do they drive revenue?	
3. Refine your projections. Who can you talk to that is knowledgeable about your business (customers, vendors, competitors)? What secondary sources can you find (Hoovers.com, Robert Morris and Associates database)?	
4. Compare your common-sized financials to those of your benchmark company. Can you validate or explain differences between you and the benchmark company?	
5. Are there other metrics you can use (sales per employee or sales per square foot) to verify your projections?	
6. What happens to the viability of your business when you run some scenario analyses based on the different metrics you've identified?	

WEB EXERCISE

Look for some comparison metrics (the *Bizminer* site www.bizminer.com is useful, but see if you can find others). How do your sales per employee figures match the benchmark reports? How does your pro-forma balance sheet match up to some of the presented ratios? Can you explain any differences?

NOTES

[1] By minimum wage, we mean that the money the entrepreneur can take out of the business is less on an hourly basis than the minimum wage.

[2] Tracy, John. *How to Read a Financial Report*. Seventh edition. Hoboken, NJ: John Wiley & Sons, Inc. 2009.

[3] www.sbdcnet.org/small-business-research-reports/bookstore-2012

[4] 1999 ABACUS Financial Survey. Annual Survey conducted by the American Booksellers Association. http://bookweb.org.

[5] Look for publicly traded companies on your favorite database, such as http://SEC.gov.

[6] http://bizstats.com/otherretail.htm.

P'kolino Financials

We revisit the P'kolino business plan in this chapter. Study the financial projections and evaluate how realistic you think they are.

These financials were prepared by Antonio Turco-Rivas and J. B. Schneider in support of their business. The original drafts were prepared in the Entrepreneur Intensity Track taught by Professor Andrew Zacharakis.© Copyright P'kolino and Babson College, 2005.

Business Plan
May-2005

Prepared by:
J.B. Schneider &
Antonio Turco-Rivas N.

Contact Information:
Phone   (781) 497-0913
Email   jb@pkolino.com
          atrn@pkolino.com
Address:
600 West Cummings Park
Suite 5350
Woburn, MA 01801

9	Financial Plan

9.1 Basis of Presentation

This plan contains five-year projected financial information for our company. While management believes that the assumptions underlying the projections are reasonable, there can be no assurance that these results can be realized or that actual results will meet management expectations. It is important to notice that our first month of operations is expected to be April 2005, causing the holiday season to be reflected in the financial statement as the third quarter in our projections. Monthly financial statements for the first two years are available on request.

9.2 Income Statement Assumptions – Revenues

The number of tables sold each month is the main driver of revenues for P'kolino. This number is estimated based on the expected outcome of the marketing efforts the company has planned for each year. At the beginning the company will sell two different types of tables targeting the high-end segment of the market. However, at the beginning of the third year the company plans to introduce a third table that will target the mid segment.

For the Storage Unit, management assumes that 30% of those customers that purchase tables are likely to buy the Storage Unit as well. The Storage Unit is designed so that it holds up to 10 toy kits (three are offered as a bundled package with the Storage Unit).

Every time a new table is sold, a new customer has been gained. P'kolino projections assume that one out of every two customers will purchase one Toy Kit every 12 months for a period of 3 to 4 years. Gift purchases of the Toy Kits are also estimated as a percentage of the existing customer base. One out of every two existing customers will trigger (influence) one Toy Kit gift purchase every 12 months.

Accessories will enter the revenue stream at the 2nd year of operations. It is estimated that as the product line expands accessories will eventually represent up to 25% of our sales.

The numbers of new customers are expected to increase at an average rate of 35% for years 3,4 & 5 for products targeting the high-end segment and at 45% for those targeting the mid-segment of the market (as a benchmark Pottery Barn Kids sales increased 35% in 2004).

Exhibit 9-A
The Playroom Furniture Market

# Units	Year 1	Year 2	Year 3	Year 4	Year 5
Tables	690	1,445	2,551	3,634	4,755
Table A	449	939	1,268	1,712	2,311
Table B	242	506	683	922	1,244
Table C			600	1,000	1,200
Storage Unit	228	477	824	1,169	1,533
Toy Kits	1,313	3,851	4,814	7,618	11,027
Accessories	0	9,925	15,606	21,068	28,442

P'kolino will remain in the high-end segment of the market for its first 2 years of operations and has priced its products accordingly. All products are priced as a function of both their manufacturing costs and their marketing positioning strategies. At year 3 a $400 table with a 45% contribution margin will be introduced to the mid-segment.

Exhibit 9-B
Prices and Manufacturing Cost

Product	Selling Price	Manufacturing Cost	Contribution in US$	Contribution as % of Price
Table A	$650	$260	$390	60%
Table B	$1,200	$260	$940	78%
Table C	$300	$130	$170	57%
Storage Unit	$450	$140	$310	69%
Toy kit version 1	$30	$10	$20	67%
Toy kit version 2	$55	$26	$29	53%
Accessories	$60	$28	$32	53%

P'kolino will sell its products both online (direct) and through specialty retailers. Retailers are expected to markup our products by 50% (according to our primary research). Thus, our wholesale price will need to account for this markup. Management estimates that even though 80% (30% after year 2) of the units sold will be sold through retailers, only 23% of the revenue will come from this distribution channel. The percentage sold through retailers will drop over time as P'kolino gains brand recognition and further develops its direct distribution channel.

Exhibit 9-C
% of Revenues by Distribution Channel

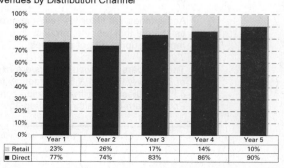

	Year 1	Year 2	Year 3	Year 4	Year 5
Retail	23%	26%	17%	14%	10%
Direct	77%	74%	83%	86%	90%

Confidential Information
Business Plan - Dated May-2005
Woburn, Massachusetts – USA

As stated earlier in this document the Toy kits and accessories are the main vehicles for generating recurrent revenue from existing customers.

Exhibit 9-D
Revenue Mix (% of revenue by type of product)

Revenue Mix	Year 1	Year 2	Year 3	Year 4	Year 5
Tables	79%	57%	54%	55%	54%
Storage	13%	9%	11%	11%	11%
Kits	8%	9%	6%	7%	8%
Accessories	0%	25%	28%	27%	27%

Revenues for P'kolino will increase significantly during the winter holiday season. As is the case in the toy industry, playroom products are seasonal and more than 50% of total revenues will be generated during this period. Summer will be the second best season because children are out of school and spending more time at home.

Exhibit 9-E
Seasonal Sales – Number of tables sold per month Year 1 & 2

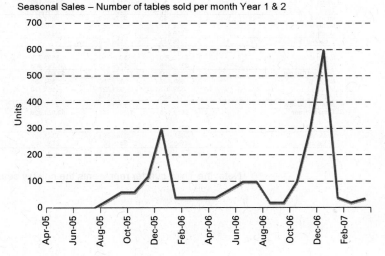

Exhibit 9-F
Revenue Forecast

Revenue per year	Year 1	Year 2	Year 3	Year 4	Year 5
Tables	**$481,501**	**$1,008,361**	**$1,589,988**	**$2,274,038**	**$3,134,920**
Table A	$220,101	$460,937	$711,113	$976,358	$1,354,885
Table B	$261,400	$547,424	$698,876	$997,680	$1,420,035
Table C	$0	$0	$180,000	$300,000	$360,000
Storage Unit	**$79,871**	**$167,267**	**$334,359**	**$474,521**	**$656,146**
Toy Kits	**$50,772**	**$158,621**	**$189,781**	**$310,663**	**$462,848**
Accessories	**$0**	**$449,603**	**$807,891**	**$1,109,235**	**$1,539,278**
Total Revenues	**$612,145**	**$1,783,851**	**$2,922,020**	**$4,168,457**	**$5,793,191**
Revenue Growth		191%	64%	43%	39%

Exhibit 9-G
Revenue Monthly Forecast

Monthly Revenues	Year 1	Year 2	Year 3	Year 4	Year 5
Month 1	$0	$39,182	$64,182	$91,560	$127,247
Month 2	$0	$67,346	$110,316	$157,373	$218,712
Month 3	$0	$101,212	$165,789	$236,510	$328,694
Total 1st Quarter	$0	$207,741	$340,287	$485,443	$674,653
Month 4	$0	$124,420	$203,804	$290,740	$404,062
Month 5	$25,314	$29,350	$48,076	$68,584	$95,316
Month 6	$50,627	$30,775	$50,411	$71,915	$99,945
Total 2nd Quarter	$75,941	$184,545	$302,292	$431,240	$599,323
Month 7	$50,627	$127,270	$208,474	$297,402	$413,320
Month 8	$102,680	$366,132	$599,739	$855,567	$1,189,040
Month 9	$255,986	$729,413	$1,194,808	$1,704,473	$2,368,823
Total 3rd Quarter	$409,293	$1,222,815	$2,003,020	$2,857,442	$3,971,183
Month 10	$36,602	$57,750	$94,596	$134,948	$187,547
Month 11	$39,453	$39,327	$64,420	$91,899	$127,719
Month 12	$50,856	$71,674	$117,405	$167,485	$232,766
Total 4th Quarter	$126,911	$168,751	$276,421	$394,333	$548,032
Total for year	**$612,145**	**$1,783,851**	**$2,922,020**	**$4,168,457**	**$5,793,191**
Average Revenue					
by Month	$51,012	$148,654	$243,502	$347,371	$482,766
by Quarter	$153,036	$445,963	$730,505	$1,042,114	$1,448,298

Note: the Third quarter represents the holiday season.

Confidential Information
Business Plan - Dated May-2005
Woburn, Massachusetts – USA

9.3 Income Statement Assumptions – Cost of Sales

Our business model assumes that manufacturing of all P'kolino products will be outsourced to Brazil and then eventually to an Asian manufacturer. The average cost of sales will be 47% of revenues. Cost of sales is estimated based on manufactured units.

Exhibit 9-H
Cost of Sales

Manufacturing Costs	Year 1	Year 2	Year 3	Year 4	Year 5
Table A	$116,610	$244,205	$329,677	$445,064	$600,836
Table B	$62,790	$131,495	$177,518	$239,650	$323,527
Table C	$0	$0	$84,000	$140,000	$168,000
Storage Unit	$31,878	$66,759	$115,325	$163,668	$214,652
Kits	$25,818	$85,988	$95,251	$157,954	$237,232
Accessories	$0	$277,900	$436,968	$589,907	$796,374
Other	$29,193	$54,504	$200,357	$219,636	$245,602
Total COGS	**$266.289**	**$860.851**	**$1.439.096**	**$1.955.879**	**$2.586.223**

9.4 Income Statement Assumptions – Expenses

Expenses for P'kolino are centered on three main areas: 1) Sales and Marketing, 2) General Administration Expenses and 3) Research and Development.

For the first year, sales and marketing expenses are close to 20% of sales. Developing our website, generating initial marketing materials and a direct mail campaign are the main uses of these funds. Again after year 3, marketing efforts intensify as P'kolino makes an effort to enter the mid-segment of the market with a new product.

Over time, General and Administration expenses converge towards the industry average. However, P'kolino's business model calls for a lean organization that concentrates on sales, product development and marketing. Management will make every effort to outsource all areas of the business not directly related to the core competency of the company. By year 5, the company will have 10 employees. The company will open an office at a business incubator during its first and second year of operations. P'kolino will relocate to a new facility by the end of year 2.

Product development (or R&D) is central to the P'kolino business model. It will require 10% of revenues during the first and second year and 9% on average thereafter (the R&D for the first year has been partially funded and executed prior to starting operations). During years 1&2 the company will

Confidential Information
Business Plan - Dated May-2005
Woburn, Massachusetts – USA

develop a table for the mid-segment of the market as well as new Toy kits and accessories.

Other expenses such as legal expenses, insurance, etc. are estimated based on industry averages.

Exhibit 9-I
Projected Financial Statements

	Year 1	%	Year 2	%	Year 3	%	Year 4	%	Year 5	%
Revenues	$612,145	100%	$1,783,851	100%	$2,922,020	100%	$4,168,457	100%	$5,793,191	100%
Cost of Sales	$266,289	44%	$860,851	48%	$1,439,096	49%	$1,955,879	47%	$2,586,223	45%
Gross Profit	**$345,856**	**56%**	**$923,000**	**52%**	**$1,482,924**	**51%**	**$2,212,578**	**53%**	**$3,206,968**	**55%**
Expenses										
Sales & Marketing	**$121,379**	**20%**	**$354,768**	**20%**	**$559,581**	**19%**	**$861,467**	**21%**	**$1,180,662**	**20%**
Salaries & Benefits	40,250	7%	80,500	5%	242,932	8%	322,503	8%	335,403	6%
Advertising	15,000	2%	50,000	3%	60,000	2%	150,000	4%	300,000	5%
Direct Mail Campaign	20,000	3%	150,000	8%	150,000	5%	250,000	6%	350,000	6%
Free Kit	15,008	2%	31,429	2%	42,429	1%	57,279	1%	77,327	1%
Web Expenses Marketing	25,000	4%	25,000	1%	35,000	1%	40,000	1%	60,000	1%
Other Marketing Expenses	6,121	1%	17,839	1%	29,220	1%	41,685	1%	57,932	1%
General and Administration	**$103,333**	**17%**	**$201,583**	**11%**	**$369,867**	**13%**	**$424,276**	**10%**	**$531,254**	**9%**
Salaries & Benefits	90,000	15%	178,250	10%	319,534	11%	367,276	9%	449,587	8%
Depreciation	1,333	0%	3,333	0%	10,333	0%	17,000	0%	21,667	0%
Rent & Utilities	5,000	1%	10,000	1%	20,000	1%	20,000	0%	35,000	1%
Corporate Office	7,000	1%	10,000	1%	20,000	1%	20,000	0%	25,000	0%
Product Development (R&D)	**$61,000**	**10%**	**$227,324**	**13%**	**$288,017**	**10%**	**$318,938**	**8%**	**$450,095**	**8%**
Salaries & Benefits		0%	142,324	8%	148,017	5%	153,938	4%	160,095	3%
Testing	1,000	0%	5,000	0%	10,000	0%	15,000	0%	20,000	0%
Product Development	60,000	10%	80,000	4%	130,000	4%	150,000	4%	270,000	5%
Other Expenses	**$91,304**	**15%**	**$112,096**	**6%**	**$120,551**	**4%**	**$129,211**	**3%**	**$169,830**	**3%**
Legal	15,000	2%	20,000	1%	25,000	1%	25,000	1%	25,000	0%
Relocation		0%	10,000	1%		0%		0%		0%
Other	1,000	0%		0%		0%		0%		0%
Insurance	15,304	3%	44,596	2%	73,051	3%	104,211	2%	144,830	3%
Interest	60,000	10%	37,500	2%	22,500	1%		0%		0%
Total Expenses	**$377,016**	**62%**	**$895,771**	**50%**	**$1,338,016**	**46%**	**$1,733,892**	**42%**	**$2,331,841**	**40%**
Profit Before Taxes	**($31,160)**	**-5%**	**$27,229**	**2%**	**$144,908**	**5%**	**$478,686**	**11%**	**$875,127**	**15%**
Taxes		0%	5,446	0%	28,982	1%	95,737	2%	175,025	3%
Net Income	**($31,160)**	**-5%**	**$21,783**	**1%**	**$115,926**	**4%**	**$382,949**	**9%**	**$700,102**	**12%**

Confidential Information
Business Plan - Dated May-2005
Woburn, Massachusetts – USA

9.5 Balance Sheet Assumptions

P'kolino outsources manufacturing of their products allowing it to minimize investment on fixed assets. Inventory is assumed at 45 days (meaning 8 inventory turns per year, equal to the industry average according to Hoover's online database). Management believes it will be able to maintain this level due to its emphasis on direct distribution.

Accounts receivable will average 30 days due to expected receivables from sales to retailers. Direct sales will have limited receivables, occurring mostly by credit card.

Table designs will be considered intangible assets and supported by constant product development efforts.

Accounts payable will be 25 days during the first few years because vendors will require most of our purchases to be paid in advance. Over time, accounts payable will lengthen as we develop a credit history.

Exhibit 9-J
Projected Balance Sheet Statements

	Year 1	Year 2	Year 3	Year 4	Year 5
ASSETS					
Cash	$ 289,628	$ 133,388	$ 106,278	$ 338,241	$ 1,036,185
Accounts Receivable	$ 50,856	$ 71,674	$ 92,140	$ 131,444	$ 182,677
Inventory	$ 70,582	$ 91,338	$ 138,210	$ 197,167	$ 274,016
Total current assets	**$ 411,066**	**$ 296,400**	**$ 336,629**	**$ 666,852**	**$ 1,492,879**
Net fixed assets	$ 6,595	$ 18,476	$ 37,357	$ 44,571	$ 47,119
Fixed Assets	*$ 8,000*	*$ 24,000*	*$ 54,000*	*$ 79,000*	*$ 104,000*
Fixed Assets Acum. Deprec.	*$ 1,405*	*$ 5,524*	*$ 16,643*	*$ 34,429*	*$ 56,881*
Other assets	$ 6,103	$ 8,601	$ 11,057	$ 15,773	$ 21,921
Net Intangibles	$ 50,700	$ 50,700	$ 50,700	$ 50,700	$ 50,700
Patents + Intangibles	$ 50,700	$ 50,700	$ 50,700	$ 50,700	$ 50,700
Total assets	**$ 474,463**	**$ 374,177**	**$ 435,743**	**$ 777,897**	**$ 1,612,619**
LIABILITIES					
Accounts and trade notes payable	$ 42,719	$ 60,206	$ 77,398	$ 110,413	$ 153,449
Income Taxes payable	$ -	$ 5,446	$ 28,982	$ 95,737	$ 175,026
Other	$ 12,205	$ 17,202	$ 22,114	$ 31,547	$ 43,843
Total current liabilities	**$ 54,924**	**$ 82,854**	**$ 128,493**	**$ 237,697**	**$ 372,317**
Convertible LT debt	$ 400,000	$ 250,000	$ 150,000	$ -	$ -
Total liabilities	**$ 454,924**	**$ 332,854**	**$ 278,493**	**$ 237,697**	**$ 372,317**
	$ -	$ -	$ -	$ -	$ -
Paid-in capital	$ 50,700	$ 50,700	$ 50,700	$ 50,700	$ 50,700
Retained earnings	$ (31,161)	$ (9,377)	$ 106,550	$ 489,499	$ 1,189,602
Total liabilities and net worth	**$ 474,463**	**$ 374,177**	**$ 435,743**	**$ 777,897**	**$ 1,612,619**

9.6 <u>Funding Assumptions</u>

The company will fund its operations through equity and convertible long-term debt. Founders have issued $50.7K worth of equity. Proceeds will be used to pay for the product development of the initial product line. Additional funding will come in the form of long-term convertible debt (convertible into equity at the lender's discretion) for up to $400K over the next five years, at a 15% annual interest rate. Friends and family will be the primary investors initially.

Exhibit 9-K
Use of Funds (average)

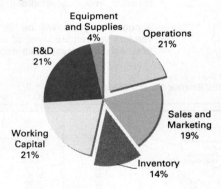

Confidential Information
Business Plan - Dated May-2005
Woburn, Massachusetts – USA

9.7 Cash Flow Assumptions

Investments will maintain positive cash flow the first 2 years. After this period, P'kolino estimates that it will generate enough cash from operations to repay the long-term debt and finance future growth.

Exhibit 9-L
Projected Cash Flow Statements

	Year 1	Year 2	Year 3	Year 4	Year 5
Net Income	$ (31,161)	$ 21,784	$ 115,927	$ 382,950	$ 700,102
Accounts receivable (increase)	$ (50,856)	$ (20,818)	$ (20,467)	$ (39,304)	$ (51,233)
Inventory (increase)	$ (70,582)	$ (20,755)	$ (46,873)	$ (58,956)	$ (76,849)
Depreciation	$ 1,405	$ 4,119	$ 11,119	$ 17,786	$ 22,452
Other Liabilities	$ 12,205	$ 4,996	$ 4,912	$ 9,433	$ 12,296
Accounts Payable	$ 42,719	$ 17,487	$ 17,192	$ 33,015	$ 43,036
Tax payable	$ -	$ 5,446	$ 23,536	$ 66,756	$ 79,288
Operating Cash Flow	$ (96,270)	$ 12,259	$ 105,346	$ 411,680	$ 729,092
Purchase of PPE	$ (8,000)	$ (16,000)	$ (30,000)	$ (25,000)	$ (25,000)
Other Assets	$ (6,103)	$ (2,498)	$ (2,456)	$ (4,716)	$ (6,148)
Change Intangibles	$ (50,700)	$ -	$ -	$ -	$ -
Cash from Investing	$ (64,803)	$ (18,498)	$ (32,456)	$ (29,716)	$ (31,148)
Convertible LT debt	$ 400,000	$ (150,000)	$ (100,000)	$ (150,000)	$ -
Issued Stock	$ 50,700	$ -	$ -	$ -	$ -
Cash from Finance	$ 450,700	$ (150,000)	$ (100,000)	$ (150,000)	$ -
Change in cash	$ 289,628	$ (156,240)	$ (27,110)	$ 231,963	$ 697,944
Cash Flow:	$ 289,628	$ 133,388	$ 106,278	$ 338,241	$ 1,036,185

9.8 Breakeven Analysis

Exhibit 9-M
Breakeven vs. Revenues

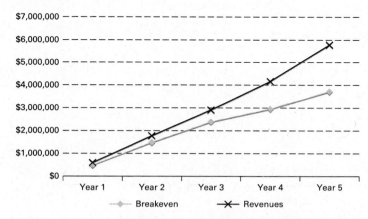

Preparation Questions

1. How do the common-sized income sheet ratios compare to industry standards? Can you explain the variances in a way that makes the projections seem sound?

2. How do the revenues per employee compare to industry standards? Again, can you explain the variances?

3. Do the financial projections accurately capture all the expenses that are implied in the written plan (refer back to previous chapter)?

4. Is the proposed financing sufficient to cover the company's cash flow needs? What happens if sales are not as high or quick to materialize as expected?

Vittorio Zunino Celotto/Getty Images

Grameen Bank Founder and Nobel Peace Prize Laureate Muhammad Yunus speaks during the lecture 'A world without poverty' on February 1, 2010 in Milan, Italy.

FINANCING ENTREPRENEURIAL VENTURES WORLDWIDE

A new business searching for capital has no track record to present to potential investors and lenders. All it has is a plan—sometimes written, sometimes not—that projects its future performance. This means that it is very difficult to raise debt financing from conventional banks because they require as many as three years of actual—not projected—financial statements and assets that adequately cover the loan. Thus almost every new business raises its initial money from the founders themselves and what we call informal investors: family, friends, neighbors, work colleagues, and strangers; a few raise it from lending institutions, primarily banks; and a miniscule number raise it from venture capitalists, who are sometimes called *formal investors*. This chapter examines funding from entrepreneurs themselves, informal investors, and venture capitalists in the United States and throughout the world. Chapter 10 will explain how to raise equity capital, and Chapter 11 will look at nonequity sources of financing, including banks.

Before we examine conventional means of financing startups in medium- and higher-income nations, we'll begin by looking at how many would-be entrepreneurs eking out subsistence livings in some of the most impoverished regions of the world are being financed by microcredit organizations.

This chapter is written by William D. Bygrave.

Entrepreneurial Financing for the World's Poorest

"To 'make poverty history,' leaders in private, public, and civil-society organizations need to embrace entrepreneurship and innovation as antidotes to poverty. Wealth-substitution through aid must give way to wealth-creation through entrepreneurship."[1] But the challenge is, "Where do nascent entrepreneurs living in poverty get any money to start a micro-business?" In Africa, for instance, 600 million people live on less than $3 per day based on purchasing power parity (PPP). For China, the number may be 400 million and for India 500 million.[2]

In the developing world, 1.4 billion people (one in four) were living below US$1.25 a day in 2005, down from 1.9 billion (one in two) in 1981. Poverty has fallen by 500 million since 1981 (from 52% of the developing world's population in 1981 to 26% percent in 2005), and the world is still on track to halve the 1990 poverty rate by 2015. But at this rate of progress, about a billion people will still live below $1.25 a day in 2015.[4]

Conventional banking is based on the principle that the more you have, the more you can borrow. It relies on collateral, which means that a bank loan must be adequately covered by assets of the business or its owner—or in many cases, both. But half the world's population is very poor, so about 5 billion people are shut out of banks. For example, fewer than 10% of adults in many African countries have bank accounts. Even in Mexico, the number of families with bank accounts is less than 25%.

La Maman Mole Motuke lived in a wrecked car in a suburb of Kinshasa, Zaire, with her four children. If she could find something to eat, she would feed two of her children; the next time she found something to eat, her other two children would eat. When organizers from a micro-credit lending institution interviewed her, she said that she knew how to make chikwangue (manioc paste) and that she needed only a few dollars to start production. After six months of training in marketing and production techniques, Maman Motuke got her first loan of US$100 and bought production materials.

Today Maman Motuke and her family no longer live in a broken-down car; they rent a house with two bedrooms and a living room. Her four children go to school consistently, eat regularly, and dress well. She currently is saving to buy some land in a suburb farther outside the city and hopes to build a house.[3]

Microfinancing

In 1976, in the village of Jobra, Bangladesh, Muhammad Yunus, an economist, started what today is the Grameen Bank. This was the beginning of the microfinance concept, which is best known for its application in rural areas of Bangladesh but which has now spread throughout the world. Yunus believes that access to credit is a human right. According to him, "one that does not possess anything gets the highest priority in getting a loan." Even beggars can get loans from the Grameen Bank. They are not required to give up begging but are encouraged to take up an additional income-generating activity, such as selling popular consumer items door to door or at the place of begging.[5] The bank provides larger loans, called *microenterprise loans*, for "fast-moving members." As of June 2009, almost 1.9 million Bangladeshis had taken microenterprise loans. The average microenterprise loan was US$360, and the biggest was US$23,209 to purchase a truck. The Grameen Bank total loan recovery rate is 97.81%, which is remarkable because the bank relies entirely on personal trust and not collateral.[6]

Microfinancing is now available in many nations. It is generally agreed that it is a powerful tool in the fight to reduce poverty in poorer nations. The following is a microfinance success story from Mexico, excerpted from an article in *The Financial Times*.[7]

Oscar Javier Rivera Jimenez stands on the corrugated steel roof of his warehouse and surveys the urban wasteland around him. "We constructed all of this with the money from Compartamos," he says. "Before, there was nothing. We built it ourselves. That made it possible. And the help of God as well, which is the secret of everything." Compartamos is Latin America's biggest provider of microfinance—small loans aimed at budding entrepreneurs, targeted at areas of severe poverty.

Mr. Rivera, who set up his business six years ago in the municipality of Chimalhuacan, one of the poorest slums on the outskirts of Mexico City, is one of Compartamos' most successful clients. Starting at the age of 21 by delivering parts on a tricycle—much of the area lacks paved roads, while both water and electricity supplies are unreliable—he now controls an impressive warehouse, where builders can buy an array of different girders. He recently opened a second branch about a mile away. He now has nine employees, four from outside the family—showing that his brand of enthusiastic entrepreneurship might yet rescue the neighborhood.

Compartamos ("Let's share" in Spanish) started life as a nongovernmental organization, and gained its seed capital from multilateral funds. Now with more than 300,000 clients, its next plan is to convert itself into a bank, so that it can take in savings and also start to offer life insurance. Its portfolio grew by 58% last year, and Carlos Danel and Carlos Labarthe, its joint chief executives, intend to keep that growth going. By 2008, they aim to have one million clients. Compartamos' average loan is for $330,[8] and as is typical of microcredit elsewhere in the world, only 0.6% of its loans are 30 or more days late.

Microcredit for the Poorest of the Poor

The first Microcredit Summit Campaign was held in 1997. Its aim was "to reach 100 million of the world's poorest families, especially the women of those families, with credit for self-employment and other financial and business services by the year 2005."

In November 2006, the campaign was relaunched to 2015 with two new goals: (1) working to ensure that 175 million of the world's poorest families, especially the women of those families, are receiving credit for self-employment and other financial and business services by the end of 2015 and (2) working to ensure that 100 million families rise above the US$1 a day threshold, adjusted for purchasing power parity (PPP), between 1990 and 2015.[9] The campaign defines the "poorest" people as those who are in the bottom half of those living below their nation's poverty line, or any of the 1.2 billion people (240 million families) in the world who live on less than US$1 per day based on PPP.

In November 2011, to coincide with the release of the *State of the Microcredit Summit Campaign Report 2012* (SOCR 2012), the Microcredit Summit Campaign announced that more than 137.5 million of the world's poorest families received a microloan in 2010—an all-time high, according to a report released today by the Microcredit Summit Campaign. Assuming an average of five persons per family, these 137.5 million microloans affected more than 687 million family members, which is greater than the combined populations of the European Union and Russia. SOCR 2012 provides the data shown in Figure 9.1.[10]

Figure 9.2 shows the relationship between the number of families living in absolute poverty in each region (living on under US$1 a day, adjusted for PPP) and the number of poorest families reached in each region at the end of 2010. Of the 137.5 million poorest clients reached at the end of 2010, 82.3% (113.1 million) were women. The growth in the number of very poor women reached has increased from 10.3 million at the end of 1999 to 113.1 million at the end of 2010. This is almost a 1,001% increase in the number of poorest women reached from December 31, 1999 to December 31, 2010. The increase represents an additional 102.9 million poorest women receiving microloans in the last 11 years.

In the following sections, we will examine how entrepreneurs in all financial circumstances, from the poor in developing nations to the well-off in developed nations, raise money to start their new businesses.

Entrepreneurs and Informal Investors

Self-funding by entrepreneurs, along with funding from informal investors, is the lifeblood of an entrepreneurial society. Founders and informal investors are sometimes referred to as the **Four Fs**: founders, family, friends, and foolhardy investors. One of the most noteworthy findings of the Global Entrepreneurship Monitor (GEM) studies is the amount and extent of

Year	Number of Institutions Reporting	Total Number of Clients Reached	Number of "poorest" clients reported
12/31/97	618	13,478,797	7,600,000
12/31/98	925	20,938,899	12,221,918
12/31/99	1,065	23,555,689	13,779,872
12/31/00	1,567	30,681,107	19,327,451
12/31/01	2,186	54,932,235	26,878,332
12/31/02	2,572	67,606,080	41,594,778
12/31/03	2,931	80,868,343	54,785,433
12/31/04	3,164	92,270,289	66,614,871
12/31/05	3,133	113,261,390	81,949,036
12/31/06	3,316	133,030,913	92,922,574
12/31/07	3,552	154,825,825	106,584,679
12/31/09	3,589*	190,135,080	126,220,051
12/31/10	3,652	205,314,502	137,547,441

Source: Maes, J. P. and Reed, L. R. *State of the Microcredit Summit Campaign Report 2012*. Microcredit Summit Campaign. 2012. p.35.

Figure 9.1

Growth in the implementation of microcredit, 1997– 2010

	Asia	Africa/ Middle East	Latin America/ Caribbean	Eastern Europe & Central Asia
Number of Poorest Families	182.4	79.8	9	3.4
Number Reached by Microfinance	125.5	8.9	2.9	0.13
Percent Coverage	69%	11%	32%	4%

Source: Maes, J. P. and Reed, L. R.. *State of the Microcredit Summit Campaign Report* 2012. Microcredit Summit Campaign. 2012. p.39.

Figure 9.2

Microfinancing by region, 2010 (in millions)

funding by the Four Fs. The prevalence rate of informal investors among the adult population of all the GEM nations combined is 3.6%, and the total sum of money they provide to fund entrepreneurship is equal to 1.2% of the combined gross domestic product (GDP) of those nations. The entrepreneurs themselves provide 65.8% of the startup capital for their new ventures; assuming that the remainder of the funding comes from informal investors, the funding from entrepreneurs and informal investors combined amounts to 3.5% of the GDP of all the GEM nations.

The informal investor prevalence rate among the GEM nations participating in the 2009 study is shown in Figure 9.3. Among the G7 nations, the United States and France have the highest prevalence rates (both 3.8%), and the United Kingdom has the lowest (1.1%). The annual amount of funding provided by informal investors as a percentage of the GDP of the GEM 2009 nations is shown in Figure 9.4. The total amount of funding is the product of the number of informal investors and the average amount that each investor provides annually. A nation with a high prevalence rate and a high average amount per informal investor relative to its income per capita—China, for instance—ranks high in Figure 9.4. Russia, on the other hand, ranks low because its prevalence rate and the average amount per informal investor relative to its income per capita are both low. Of course, it is to be expected that in general the wealthier a nation, the higher the average amount per investor.

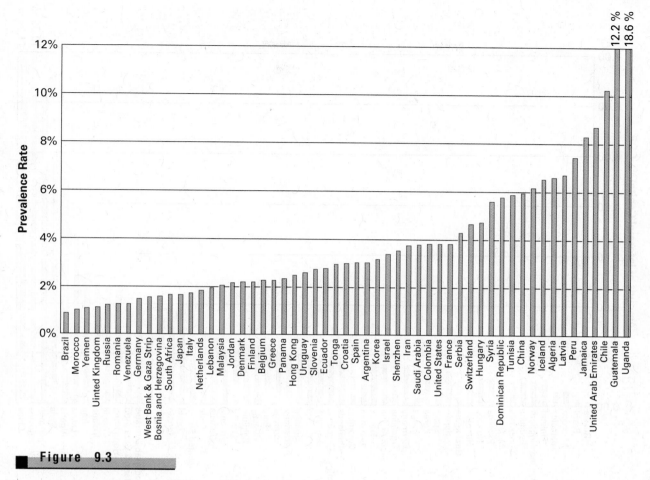

Figure 9.3

Informal investor prevalence rate, 2009

Nonetheless, there is considerable variation, as we can see in Figure 9.5, which compares the average amount per investor with GDP per capita. Informal investors in nations above the trend line provide more investment per capita than predicted, and those below the trend line provide less; for example, Japan and the Netherlands provide more, and Norway, Finland, and the United States less. However, the amount of informal investment in a nation is only one side of the financing equation; the other side is the startup funding needed by entrepreneurs.

Amount of Capital Needed to Start a Business

The amount of capital that entrepreneurs need to start their ventures depends, among other things, on the type of business, the ambitions of the entrepreneur, the location of the business, and the country where it is started. In the United States, the average amount required to start a business is $62,594, with entrepreneurs providing 67.9% of the funding. For all the GEM nations combined, the average amount needed to start a business is $53,673, and as expected, more is needed for an opportunity-pulled venture ($58,179) than for a necessity-pushed one ($24,467). The amount needed to start a business is highest in the business services sector ($76,263) and lowest in the consumer-oriented sector ($39,594). The businesses that need the most startup capital are those created with the intent to grow and hire employees. For

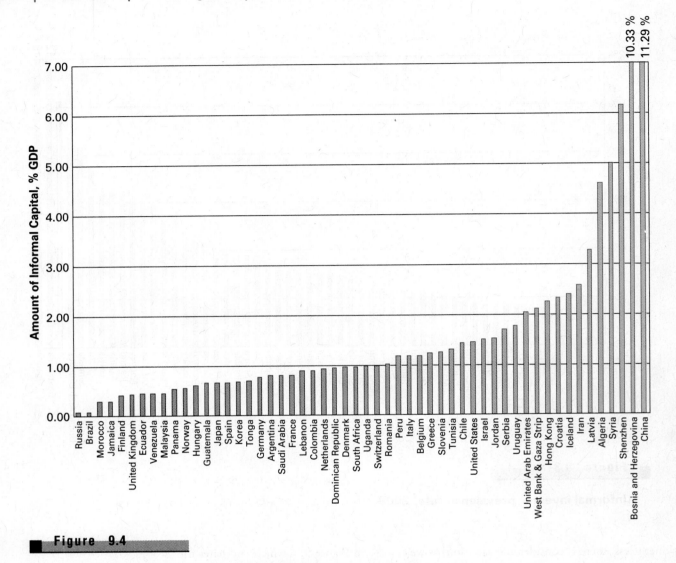

Figure 9.4

Annual informal investment as a percentage of GDP, 2009

example, nascent businesses that expect to employ 10 or more persons five years after they open require an average of $112,943 of startup money. Business started by men require more capital than those started by women ($65,010 vs. $33,201); a partial explanation is that women are more likely than men to start necessity-pushed businesses, which are more likely to be consumer-oriented and less likely to be business services.

To put nations on an approximately equal footing on the basis of wealth, we plot the amount of funding needed to start a business against a nation's GDP per capita, as seen in Figure 9.6. Entrepreneurs in countries falling below the trend line have a comparative advantage over entrepreneurs in countries above the trend line because it costs less to start a business relative to the income per capita in those countries, all other things being equal. This finding partially explains why the United States and Canada have the highest total entrepreneurial activity (TEA) rates among the G7 nations and Italy the second-lowest rate. It might also explain to some extent why Norway has a higher TEA rate than its Scandinavian neighbors Sweden and Denmark.

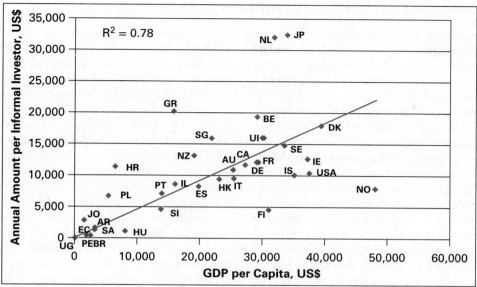

R^2 is the proportion of the variation that is explained by the trend line. An R^2 of 0.78 indicates that 78% of the variation in annual amount per informal investor is explained by GDP per capita.

Figure 9.5

Annual amount per informal investor vs. GDP per capita (US$)

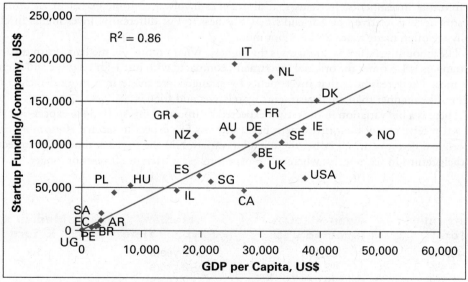

R^2 is the proportion of the variation that is explained by the trend line. An R^2 of 0.86 indicates that 86% of the variation in startup funding per company is explained by the GDP per capita.

Figure 9.6

Startup funding per company vs. GDP per capita (US$)

Characteristics of Informal Investors

Entrepreneurs provide 65.8% of their startup capital; hence, others, principally informal investors, provide the remaining 34.2%. Who are informal investors? We can categorize them as follows: close family and relatives of the entrepreneurs (49.4%) are first; next are friends and neighbors (26.4%); these are followed by other relatives (9.4%), work colleagues (7.9%), and strangers (6.9%), as shown in Figure 9.7. Strangers—the foolhardy investors among the Four Fs—are usually called *business angels*.

Using GEM data for the United States, Bygrave and Reynolds[11] developed a model that predicted whether or not a person was an informal investor. They found that the informal investor prevalence rate among entrepreneurs was 4.3 times the rate among nonentrepreneurs. With just one criterion, whether someone was an entrepreneur, their model correctly classified 86% of the entire population as being or not being informal investors. And with just two criteria, whether a person was an entrepreneur and that person's income, the model correctly identified an informal investor 56% of the time across the entire population, of whom slightly less than 5% were informal investors. Looked at another way, the model was 11 times better than a random choice at singling out an informal investor from the entire adult population. In general, this means that entrepreneurs in search of startup funding should target self-made entrepreneurs with high incomes. More specifically, they should first talk with the entrepreneurs among their close relatives, friends, and neighbors.

Financial Returns on Informal Investment

What financial return do informal investors expect? The median expected payback time, as you can see in Figure 9.7, is two years, and the median amount returned is one times the original investment. In other words, there is a negative or zero return on investment for half the informal investments. It seems that altruism is involved to some extent in an informal investment in a relative's or a friend's new business.[12] Put differently, investments in close family are often made more for love, not money.

The amount invested by strangers is the highest. What's more, the median return expected by strangers is 1.5 times the original investment, compared with just 1 for relatives and friends. The most likely reason is that investments by strangers are made in a more detached and businesslike manner than are investments by relatives and friends.

There is a big variation in the return expected by informal investors: 34% expect that they will not receive any of their investment back, whereas 5% expect to receive 20 or more times the original investment. Likewise, there is a big variation in the payback time: 17% expect to get their return in six months, whereas 2% expect to get it back in 20 years or longer.

Relationship: Investor-Investee	Percent Total	Mean Amount Invested US$	Median Payback Time	Median X Return
Close family	49.4%	23,190	2 years	1 x
Other relative	9.4%	12,345	2 years	1 x
Work colleague	7.9%	39,032	2 years	1 x
Friend, neighbor	26.4%	15,548	2 years	1 x
Stranger	6.9%	67,672	2–5 years	1.5 x
	100.0%	24,202	2 years	1 x

Figure 9.7

Relationship of informal investor to investee

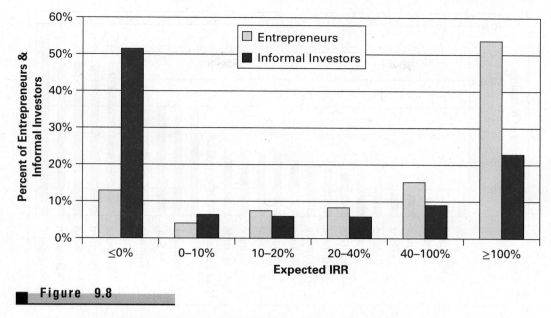

Figure 9.8

Expected IRR for entrepreneurs and informal investors

Entrepreneurs are much more optimistic about the return on the money that they themselves put into their own ventures: 74% expect the payback time to be two years or sooner, and their median expected return is 2 times their original investment, while 15% expect 20 or more times that investment.

The expected **internal rate of return** or **IRR** (compound annual return on investment) is calculated from the expected payback time and the times return for informal investors and entrepreneurs who reported both (see Figure 9.8). The returns expected by entrepreneurs are almost the reverse of those expected by informal investors: 51% of informal investors expect a negative or zero return, and only 22% expect a return of 100% or more; by contrast, only 13% of entrepreneurs expect a negative or zero return, but a whopping 53% expect a return of 100% or more.

Supply and Demand for Startup Financing

Is the amount of funding sufficient to supply the external capital that entrepreneurs need to finance their new ventures? The average amount of an informal investment ($24,202) is more than the average amount of external financing that entrepreneurs need ($18,678). So for those entrepreneurs who are successful in raising money from informal investors, the amount on average more than meets their needs. But is there enough informal investment to supply all the nascent entrepreneurs in a given country?

The percentage of nascent businesses that could be funded with the available informal investment, assuming it all went to nascent businesses, is shown in Figure 9.9. Singapore has the highest percentage of nascent businesses that could be funded and Brazil the lowest. Of course, not all nascent businesses deserve to get funded. Without knowing the merits of each nascent business, and hence whether or not it deserves to be funded, we cannot say if the available informal investment is adequate. But it seems likely that a country with enough informal investment to fund 40% or more of all its nascent entrepreneurs probably has sufficient informal investment because, in the end, the majority of new businesses never become viable in the long-term,[13] failing to produce a satisfactory return on investment for either their owners or their investors.

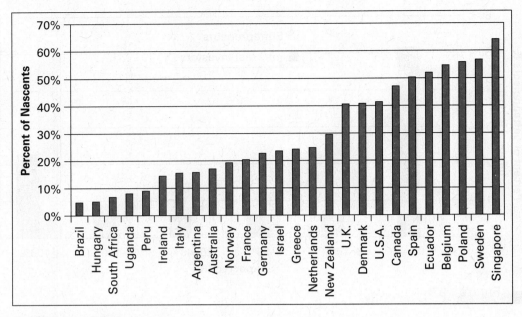

Figure 9.9

Percentage of nascent businesses that could be funded by available informal investment

However, just because a country has sufficient startup capital overall does not mean that every deserving nascent business gets funded. An entrepreneur's search for startup capital from informal investors is a haphazard process. If an entrepreneur is unable to raise sufficient money from relatives, friends, and acquaintances, there is no systematic method of searching for potential investors who are strangers. Granted, there are organized groups of informal investors (*business angels*) in many nations, but the number of companies they finance is tiny in proportion to the number of entrepreneurs who seek capital. In addition, most business angel networks in developed nations look for high-potential startups that have prospects of growing into substantial enterprises of the sort that organized venture capitalists would invest in at a subsequent round of funding.

Venture Capital

By far the rarest source of capital for nascent entrepreneurs is venture capital.[14] In fact, nascent companies with venture capital in hand before they open their doors for business are so rare that even in the United States—which has almost two-thirds of the total of classic venture capital[15] in the entire world—far fewer than one in 10,000 new ventures gets its initial financing from venture capitalists. In general, venture capital is invested in companies that are already in business rather than in nascent companies with products or services that are still on paper. For example, out of 3,698 U.S. businesses in which $26.5 billion of venture capital was invested in 2012, only 1,163 received venture capital for the first time, and of those, relatively few (274) were seed-stage companies. From 1970 through 2012, the venture capital industry invested $556 billion in 41,000 companies at all stages of development.[16] It is estimated that over the same period, informal investors provided more than a trillion dollars to more than

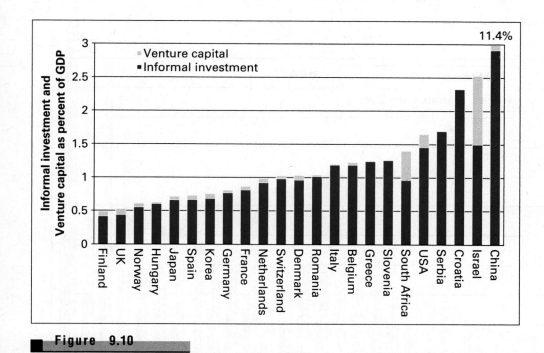

Figure 9.10

Informal investment and venture capital as a percentage of GDP, 2008

10 million nascent and baby businesses. In every nation, there is far more informal investment from the Four Fs than formal investment from venture capitalists (see Figure 9.10).

Classic Venture Capital

While classic venture capitalists finance very few companies, some of the ones that they do finance play a very important—many say a crucial—role in the development of knowledge-based industries, such as biotechnology; medical instruments and devices; computer hardware, software, and services; telecommunications hardware and software; Internet technology and services; electronics; semiconductors; nanotechnology; and clean technology (cleantech). Venture capitalists like to claim that the companies they invest in have the potential to change the way in which people work, live, and play. And, indeed, an elite few have done just that worldwide; some famous examples are Intel, Apple, Microsoft, Federal Express, Cisco, Genentech, Amazon, eBay, Google, Facebook, and Twitter.

It's not by chance that almost all the venture-capital-backed companies with global brand names are American; rather, it is because the United States is the predominant nation with respect to classic venture capital investments. In 2008, 74% of all the classic venture capital invested among the G7 nations was invested in the United States. The amount of classic venture capital as a percentage of GDP for the GEM nations is shown in Figure 9.11. Israel, which of all the GEM nations has a venture capital industry most like that in the United States, has the highest amount of venture capital in proportion to its GDP (1.1%), while Italy has the lowest among the G7 nations.

While 74% of the classic venture capital invested in the G7 nations was in the United States, only 36% of the companies that received that investment were there because the amount invested per company in the United States was $8.9 million compared with an average of $1.7 million per company in the other G7 nations. Figure 9.12 shows the amount invested per

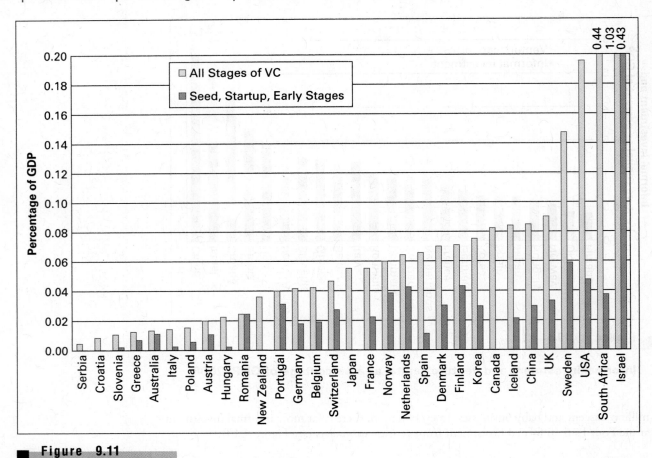

■ Figure 9.11

Classic venture capital investment as a percentage of GDP, 2008

company for all the GEM nations, including the G7. It is hard to see how companies in Japan, for example, which received on average $972,000 of venture capital, can hope to compete in the global market against companies in the United States that received $8.9 million. It is just as costly to operate a company in Japan as in the United States, if not more so; in fact, entrepreneurs work just as long hours in the United States as they do in Japan. Furthermore, the home market where startups initially sell their products and services is more than twice as big in the United States as in Japan. Although the average amounts of venture capital per company in Germany ($1.4 million) and the United Kingdom ($3.2 million) are higher than in Japan, these amounts still appear to be wholly inadequate in comparison with the United States. And when the nominal amount of venture capital per company is adjusted for purchasing power, the gap between the United States and the other G7 nations is even wider. China and the United States are almost equal in the amount invested per company in nominal dollars, but when purchasing power is considered, China tops the United States by almost 100%.

Since the main purpose of classic venture capital is to accelerate the commercialization of new products and services, U.S. companies have a very considerable advantage in the global marketplace. What's more, successful U.S. companies can build on their venture capital backing by subsequently raising very substantial financing with initial public offerings (IPOs) in the stock market.

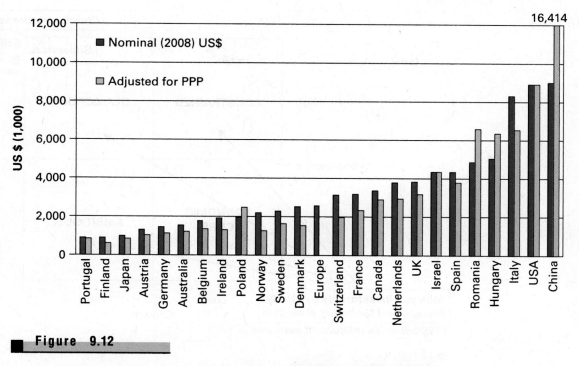

Figure 9.12

Classic venture capital investment per company, 2008

About 80% of the venture capital invested in the United States finances high-technology companies; by contrast, only 29% of the venture capital invested in the other G7 nations, except Canada, is in high-technology companies. Seventy-three percent of the venture capital invested in high-technology companies at all stages from seed through buyouts in the G7 nations goes to companies in the United States. But when the investment is narrowed down to classic venture capital, the proportion invested in U.S. high-technology companies increases to an estimated 80%, with the U.S. share of classic venture capital invested in biotechnology at 81% and in computer hardware and software at 83%. When it comes to investment in all stages of consumer-related companies, the situation is reversed—only 13% of them are in the United States and 87% are in the other G7 nations.

Importance of Venture Capital in the U.S. Economy

One way of classifying young ventures is by their degree of innovation and their rate of growth[17] (see Figure 9.13). In the bottom left quadrant of the figure are companies that are not very innovative and grow comparatively slowly. They provide goods and services that are the core of the economy; for the most part, they have lots of competitors, and they grow at the same rate as the economy. In the upper left quadrant are companies that are innovative but that are not fast growing because for one reason or another they are constrained—often because they are started and managed by entrepreneurs with limited ability. In the bottom right quadrant are companies that are not particularly innovative but that outpace the growth rate of many of their competitors because they are run by ambitious entrepreneurs with superior

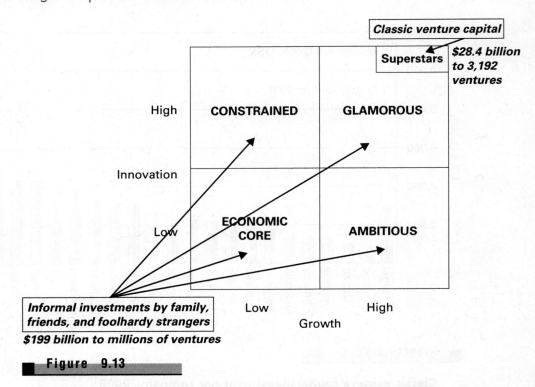

Figure 9.13

Financing entrepreneurial ventures in the United States, 2008

management skills. And in the top right quadrant are companies that are innovative and have superior management; among them are the superstar companies that attract media attention.

Informal investment goes to companies in all quadrants. In contrast, classic venture capital goes only to the companies in the uppermost corner of the glamorous quadrant. They are the companies with potential to become the superstars in their industries—and in a few instances, to be central in the creation and development of a new industry segment. By and large, they are led by entrepreneurial teams with excellent management skills. The companies are usually already up and running when the first venture capital is invested, although in a few rare instances venture capital is invested before the company is operational. Looked at another way, classic venture capital accelerates the growth rate of young superstar companies; it seldom finances nascent entrepreneurs who are not yet in business. A relatively sophisticated subset of informal investors, business angels, invests primarily in the glamorous companies, especially those with the potential to become superstars. Business angels are often entrepreneurs themselves, or former entrepreneurs, who invest some of their wealth in seed- and early-stage businesses. Angel investment frequently precedes formal venture capital.

If venture capital dried up in the United States, there would be no noticeable change in the number of companies being started because so few have venture capital in hand when they open their doors for business, whereas everyone has funding from one or more of the Four Fs. But in the long-term, the effect on the economy would be catastrophic because venture-capital-backed companies generate a disproportionate number of good-paying jobs and create many of the new products and services. Those companies make a major contribution to the U.S. economy. For instance, by 2010, venture-capital-backed companies accounted for 11% of jobs in the U.S. private sector and 21% of its GDP (see Figure 9.14).[18]

Venture-capital-backed companies employ a high proportion of high-tech workers in the United States. They accounted for 90% of software, 74% of biotechnology, 72% of semiconductor, 54% of computer, and 48% of telecom jobs in 2010.

	2000	2010	2000–2010 Annual Growth
Jobs	8.7 Million	11.9 Million	2.9%
Sales	$1.5 Trillion	$3.08 Trillion	6.8%

**Top 5 States by Employment at
Venture-Capital-Backed Companies
Headquartered in the State in 2010**
California 2,887,063
Texas 1,129,551
Pennsylvania 783,527
Washington 778,579
Massachusetts 775,151

Source: National Venture Capital Association

■ **Figure 9.14**

Economic Benefits of Venture-Capital-Backed Companies

Venture-capital-backed companies, adjusted for size, spend over twice as much on R&D as other companies. In particular, small firms in the venture-dominated information technology and medical-related sectors are big spenders on R&D.

Mechanism of Venture Capital Investing

The formal venture capital industry was born in Massachusetts at the end of World War II when a group of investors inspired by General Georges Doriot, a legendary professor at the Harvard Business School, put together the first venture capital fund, American Research and Development. They did so because they were concerned that the commercial potential of technical advances made by scientists and engineers at the Massachusetts Institute of Technology during World War II would be lost unless funding was available to commercialize them. The fledgling venture capital industry grew and evolved; eventually, the most common form of organization for U.S. venture capital funds became the limited partnership.

The mechanism of venture capital investing is shown in Figure 9.15.[19] At the center of the process are the general partners of venture capital funds, which are limited partnerships with a 10-year life that is sometimes extended. The general partners of venture capital funds raise money from limited partners. In return for managing the partnership, the general partners receive an annual fee of 2% to 3% of the principal that has been paid into the fund. The general partners then invest money in portfolio companies in exchange for equity. If all goes well, the investment in the portfolio companies grows, and the equity is eventually harvested, usually with an IPO or a trade sale to a bigger company. The capital gain on the harvest is shared 80%—20% between the limited partners and the general partners once the limited partners have received back all the principal they put into the limited partnership. The general partners' share is called the *carried interest*, which is usually 20%. Sometimes gatekeepers (formally called *investment advisors*) are employed by limited partners to advise them on what venture capital funds they should invest in and to watch over an investment once it has been made. The gatekeeper's fee is approximately 1% of the capital invested.

Georges Doriot (1899–1987) founded the venture capital industry when he started American Research and Development in Boston in 1946. His venture capital firm made many seed-stage investments, the most famous of which was $70,000 for 77% of the startup equity of Digital Equipment Corporation. (1979 photo)

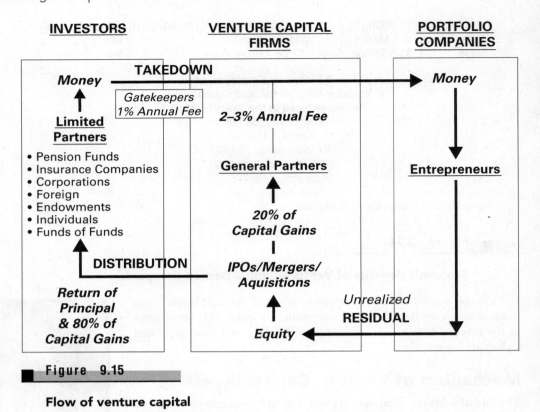

Figure 9.15

Flow of venture capital

Historically, the biggest portion of the money invested by limited partners came from pension funds—in both the public and the private sectors—with the balance coming from funds of funds, endowments, foundations, insurance companies, banks, and individuals; however, in 2009, funds of funds overtook pension funds as the top provider.

Kleiner Perkins Caufield and Byers: A Legendary Venture Capital Firm

Eugene Kleiner and Tom Perkins formed their venture capital firm, then known as Kleiner Perkins, in 1972. Kleiner was one of the founders of Fairchild Semiconductor, and Perkins was a rising star at Hewlett-Packard. It is probably the most successful venture capital firm ever. Today it is known as Kleiner Perkins Caufield and Byers (KPC&B). Headquartered on Sand Hill Road in the heart of Silicon Valley. Since 1972 it has invested in more than 400 companies, among them AOL, Amazon, Compaq, Genentech, Intuit, LSI Logic, Netscape, Sun, and Google.

In 2008, KPC&B raised a $700 million fund, Kleiner Perkins Caufield & Byers XIII. The limited partner investors in the 13th fund since 1972 are largely the same ones that have invested in KPC&B funds over the last 25 years or so. This family of funds has been so successful that it is virtually impossible for new limited partners to invest because the general partners can raise all the money they need from the limited partners who invested in previous funds. The $700 million was to be invested by the general partners over three years, mainly in early-stage companies with innovations in greentech, information technology, and life sciences.

As we've mentioned, each venture capital partnership (called a *venture capital fund*) has a 10-year life. If a venture capital fund is successful, measured by the financial return to the limited partners, the general partners usually raise another fund four to six years after the first fund. This, in essence, means that successful venture capital firms generally have two to four active funds at a time, since each fund has a life of 10 years.

Financial Returns on Venture Capital

A rule of thumb for a successful venture capital fund is that, for every 10 investments in its portfolio, two are big successes that produce excellent financial returns; two are outright failures in which the total investment is written off; three are walking wounded, which in venture capital jargon means that they are not successful enough to be harvested but are probably worth another round of venture capital to try to get them into harvestable condition; and three are living dead, meaning that they may be viable companies but have no prospect of growing big enough to produce a satisfactory return on the venture capital invested in them.

Approximately 3,000 of the 41,000 or so companies (about 7%) financed with venture capital between 1970 and 2012 have had IPOs.[20] Of the others that were harvested, mergers and acquisitions were the most common exit. In comparatively rare instances, the company's managers bought back the venture capitalist's investment.

The highest return on a venture capital investment is produced when the company has an IPO or is sold to or merged with another company (also called a *trade sale*) for a substantial capital gain. In general, however, trade sales do not produce nearly as big a capital gain as IPOs do because most trade sales involve venture-capital-backed companies that aren't successful enough to have an IPO. For instance, one way of harvesting the walking wounded and living dead is to sell them to other companies for a modest capital gain—or in some cases, a loss. The average post-IPO valuation of venture-capital-backed companies that went public in the five years through 2011 was $777 million[21] compared with an average valuation of $142 million for those that were exited through mergers and acquisitions.[22]

The overall IRR to limited partners of classic venture capital funds, over the entire period since 1946 when the first fund was formed, has been in the mid-teens. But during those six decades, there have been periods when the returns have been higher or lower. When the IPO market is booming, the returns on venture capital are high, and vice versa. The returns of U.S. venture capital are shown in Figure 9.16. Over the 20-year horizon, seed- and early-stage funds outperformed balanced and expansion- and later-stage ones. This is what we might have expected because the earlier the stage of investment, the greater the risk, and hence, the return should be higher to compensate for the risk. The seed- and early-stage risk premium was spectacular for the 20-year horizon (39.7% versus 12.5% for expansion- and later-stage

Investment Horizon IRR (%) through September 30, 2012					
Fund Type	**1 Year**	**3 Years**	**5 Years**	**10 Years**	**20 Years**
Seed/Early Stage	8.4	12.9	4.5	4.9	39.7
Later/Expansion Stage	5.4	17.1	8.1	10.3	12.5
Multi Stage	7.5	9.4	3.0	6.8	13.9
All Venture Funds	7.7	12.2	4.5	6.1	28.8
NASDAQ	29.0	13.7	2.9	10.3	8.7
S&P 500	30.2	13.2	1.1	8.0	8.5

Source: Cambridge Associates LLC. U.S. Venture Capital Index® and Selected Benchmark Statistics

■ **Figure 9.16**

Venture capital IRRs and NASDAQ and S&P 500 Returns

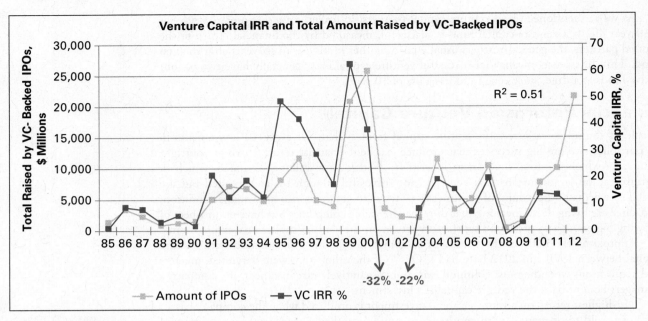

Figure 9.17

Venture capital year-to-year IRR and total raised by venture-capital-backed IPOs

funds) because the 20-year horizon includes the years 1999 and 2000, which were the peak of the Internet bubble, when year-to-year returns on all venture capital funds were 62.5% and 37.6%, with returns on seed- and early-stage funds being far higher. However, the 3, 5, and 10 year returns on seed- and early-stage funds underperformed expansion- and later-stage funds; but in the most recent year, 2012, seed- and early-stage funds outperformed expansion- and later-stage funds.

The importance of the IPO market for venture capital is demonstrated in Figure 9.17, which shows the year-to-year IRRs of venture capital and the total amount of money raised by IPOs of companies backed with venture capital. This shows a close correlation between the two lines: when the IPO market is thriving, as it was in 1999 and early 2000, the returns on venture capital are high. Not only do lucrative IPOs directly produce spectacular returns on venture capital invested in the companies going public, but also they indirectly raise the returns on acquisitions and mergers because IPO market valuations tend to set the valuations of all private equity deals. For instance, in 2000 during the Internet bubble, the average valuation for a venture-capital-backed merger/acquisition was $338.4 million, but by 2002, after the bubble burst, the average valuation fell to $52.2 million.

Google's spectacular IPO in the third quarter of 2004 boosted the confidence of the venture capital industry. Some industry leaders expected that it would herald the start of a new cycle in venture capital investing, with more money being invested in seed- and early-stage businesses. What they were hoping for was another revolutionary innovation that would fire up the enthusiasm of investors such as personal computers did at the beginning of the 1980s and the Internet and the World Wide Web did in the late-1990s. They hoped it would be nanotechnology, but a boom never materialized; next they bet on clean technology; and in 2012 they had high hopes for social media.

Clean technology attracted a lot of venture capital, with the amount invested increasing more than 10-fold from $0.4 billion in 2004 to $4.5 billion in 2011. Silicon Valley's preeminent venture capital firm, Kleiner Perkins Caufield & Byers, recruited Al Gore as a partner.

According to Gore, who was cited for "informing the world of the dangers posed by climate change" when awarded the 2007 Nobel Peace Prize, clean technology will be "bigger than the Industrial Revolution and significantly faster."[23] But an IPO boom in clean technology stocks had not yet occurred by the end of 2012. What's more in 2012 there were some highly visible failures of venture-capital-backed clean technology companies such as Solyndra in solar power and A123 in lithium ion batteries. Returns were dreadful—huge losses in some cases such as A123—for small investors who had bought stock in the few clean technologies that had gone public. Lack of small investor interest in clean technology stocks meant a paucity of IPOs in that sector, which depressed venture capital returns.

Then in 2012 venture capitalists believed that social media companies would be the next big thing that could rival the Internet boom. After all, Facebook—the most famous social media company—claimed to have about 1 billion users worldwide when it went public in May 2012. Unfortunately, as you will read in the next chapter, Facebook's IPO went awry for investors—especially small ones—who bought the stock at the IPO and had lost half the value of their investment four months later. Although those who held on to their stocks recovered most of their investment by July 2012, Facebook's IPO did not turn out to be a get-rich-quick bonanza like the Internet IPO boom, and it made small investors wary of IPOs.

So in 2012 venture capitalists were still waiting for an IPO boom to boost their returns, which had been unsatisfactory for 10 years because limited partners such as pension funds that provided money to venture capital partnerships could have earned as good a return or maybe better by investing in NASDAQ stocks. Limited partners took notice of the inadequate returns from venture capital and cut the money they commited to new venture funds for four consecutive years from 2007 to 2010; the amount increased in 2011, but was 41% less than the amount in 2006. And venture capitalists became less. . . what else. . . venturesome in 2012 because they invested in 38% fewer seed-stage companies than in 2011 and the amount they invested in them was the lowest since 2003.

Venture Capital in Europe

Since the mid-1990s, venture capital grew rapidly, as most nations strived to emulate the impact that classic venture capital was having on the U.S. economy. It has happened before: at the end of the 1960s, when the United States enjoyed a boom in classic venture capital, and again at the start of the 1980s, when the rest of the world marveled at the success of the personal computer industry and the emerging biotech sector in the United States. Unfortunately, in both instances it turned out to be a false dawn. Returns on classic venture capital outside the United States were—to say the least—disappointing, and classic venture capital floundered.

One of the principal reasons for the failure of classic venture capital in Europe at the start of the 1990s was the failure of the secondary markets after the general stock market crash of October 1987. The Unlisted Securities Market in London, the Second Marché in Lyon, the Marché Hors-Cote in Paris, the Mercato Restrito in Milan, and the Secondary Market in Brussels had been significant contributors and enabling factors for the introduction of venture capital in those European countries in the early 1980s because they provided ready markets for floating IPOs of venture-capital-backed companies. Unfortunately, those European secondary markets, unlike the NASDAQ in the United States, did not recover, and so they faded, which left European venture capitalists without their favorite and most bountiful exit route from their investments: IPOs.[24]

In the late 1990s, markets for IPOs in Europe started to prosper, especially the AIM in the United Kingdom, but just as in the United States after 2001, it again became very difficult to float venture-capital-backed IPOs in Europe; consequently, classic venture capital returns fell and investments declined. Once more it demonstrated that classic venture capital cannot do well without a robust IPO market.

Factors Affecting Availability of Financing

The three fundamental elements of an entrepreneurial society are an abundance of would-be entrepreneurs, plenty of market opportunities for new ventures, and sufficient resources—of which financing is a major component—for entrepreneurs to launch their new ventures.[25] Numerous environmental and societal factors affect the three basic elements, and in combination with the basic elements, they determine the degree of entrepreneurial activity in a region. We will now look at how financing correlates with entrepreneurial activity and the factors that affect the availability of financing. Because GEM includes many nations, we can see how informal investment and venture capital are related to environmental, societal, and governmental factors.

Total Entrepreneurial Activity and Informal Investing

The prevalence of informal investors correlates positively with the overall TEA index and three component TEA indices—opportunity, market expansion potential, and high job growth potential. And the amount of informal investment as a percentage of GDP correlates positively with two TEA indices—necessity and high job growth potential. Those correlations are convincing evidence that nations with more informal investing have more entrepreneurial activity, but they do not separate cause from effect. Informal investing and entrepreneurship depend on each other: Informal investment facilitates entrepreneurship, and entrepreneurship brings about a need for informal investment.

Factors Affecting Informal Investing

Money for informal investing comes from a person's after-tax income and savings, which more often than not are accumulated from after-tax income. Thus, it seems reasonable to hypothesize that the higher the rate of taxation, the less likely that a person will have discretionary money to invest, and vice versa. In many nations, especially developed ones, the biggest taxes are social security, income taxes, indirect taxes such as sales tax on goods and services, and taxes on capital and property.

For all the GEM nations, the prevalence rate of informal investors is negatively correlated with social security taxes and with taxes on capital and property. For nations with an income of at least $5,000 per capita, the amount of informal investment per GDP correlates negatively with social security taxes, the highest marginal income tax rate, indirect taxes, and taxes on capital and property. Stated another way, nations with higher taxes on individuals have lower rates of informal investing. High tax rates inhibit informal investing.

Factors Affecting Classic Venture Capital

In contrast to informal investing, the amount of classic venture capital as a percentage of GDP does not correlate with taxes on individuals or corporations. The explanation is that only a small proportion of classic venture capital comes from individuals and corporations. Far more comes from pension funds, which are essentially investing money that has been entrusted to them by others, and hence, they are not directly affected by taxes nearly as much as individuals are.

The amount of classic venture capital as a percentage of GDP correlates with the amount of informal investment as a percentage of GDP. This occurs because almost all companies start out with informal investment; then, if they show superstar potential, they attract classic venture capital. Thus, vigorous informal investing paves the way for robust classic venture capital investing. So, although there is no direct link between classic venture capital investment and taxation, there is an indirect link via informal investors, who are influenced by how much they pay in taxes.

As we pointed out earlier, there is a correlation between the returns on venture capital and the IPO market in the United States. In turn, this correlation means that the amount of venture capital provided by limited partners depends on the IPO market because, when the returns on venture capital are good, limited partners put more money into venture capital funds, and vice versa. In 2008, for instance, when the one-year return on venture capital dropped precipitously, commitments of new money by limited partners fell 21%.

CONCLUSION

Financing is a necessary but not a sufficient ingredient for an entrepreneurial society. It goes hand in hand with entrepreneurs and opportunities in an environment that encourages entrepreneurship.

Grassroots financing from the entrepreneurs themselves and informal investors is a crucial ingredient for an entrepreneurial society. Close family members and friends and neighbors are by far the two biggest sources of informal capital for startups. Hence, entrepreneurs should look to family and friends for their initial seed capital to augment their own investments in their startups. Many entrepreneurs waste a lot of valuable time by prematurely seeking seed capital from business angels and even from formal venture capitalists—searches that come up empty-handed almost every time. Entrepreneurs must also understand that they themselves will have to put up about two-thirds of the initial capital needed to launch their ventures.

YOUR OPPORTUNITY JOURNAL

Reflection Point	Your Thoughts...
1. How much equity financing do you need to get your business launched? When do you need it?	
2. Where will you get your initial financing? How much money can you invest from your personal resources (savings, second mortgage, etc.)?	
3. Create a strategy for other equity financing. Build a list and rank order Four F funding sources. Estimate how much each of these investors might be able and willing to invest.	
4. Do you think your business has the potential to raise formal venture capital (high-tech, high-innovation, high-growth prospects, first-rate management team, etc.)? If so, when might you be ready for venture capital? How much would you raise?	

WEB EXERCISE

What can you learn about equity financing on the Web? Search for some investor/entrepreneur matching sites (e.g., www.angelinvestmentnetwork.ca). Do you think these services are effective? Would they work for your business? What can you learn about venture capital on the Web? Look at www.pwcmoneytree.com/moneytree/index.jsp. What regions and sectors are receiving the most money? Which venture capital funds are the most active? Are they investing in your sector?

NOTES

1 Prahalad, C. K. Commentary: Aid Is Not the Answer. *The Wall Street Journal. August* 31, 2005. p. A8.

2 Ibid.

3 www.microcreditsummit.org/about/what_is_microcredit.

4 World Bank. *New Data Show 1.4 Billion Live on Less Than $1.25 a Day, but Progress Against Poverty Remains Strong.* August 26, 2008. www.worldbank.org.in/WBSITE/EXTERNAL/COUNTRIES/SOUTHASIAEXT/INDIAEXTN/0,,contentMDK:21880805~pagePK:141137~piPK:141127~theSitePK:295584,00.html.

5 Yunus, M. Grameen Bank *at a Glance*. Dhaka, Bangladesh: Grameen Bank. 2004.

6 www.microcreditsummit.org/involve/page1.htm.

7 Authers, John. Major Victories for Microfinance. *Financial Times. May* 18, 2005.

8 www.accion.org/moreaboutmicrofinance.

9 www.microcreditsummit.org/about/about_the_microcredit_summit_campaign.

10 Maes, J. P. and Reed, L. R. *State of the Microcredit Summit Campaign Report* 2012 Microcredit Summit Campaign. http://mcs2015.org/2012_Report_English

11 Bygrave, W. D., and Reynolds, P. D. Who Finances Startups in the U.S.A.? A Comprehensive Study of Informal Investors, 1999–2003. In S. Zahra et al., eds., *Frontiers of Entrepreneurship Research* 2004. Wellesley, MA: Babson College.

12 Bygrave, W. and Bosma, N. 2009, Investor Altruism: Financial returns from informal investments in businesses owned by relatives, friends, and strangers. To be published in Minniti, M. (Ed) *The Dynamics of Entrepreneurial Activity*, Oxford University Press.

13 Headd, Brian. *Business Success: Factors Leading to Surviving and Closing Successfully.* Center for Economic Studies, U.S. Bureau of the Census, Working Paper #CES-WP-01-01. January 2001.

14 Venture capital data were obtained from the following sources: National Venture Capital Association Yearbooks, European Venture Capital Association Yearbooks, Australian Venture Capital Association, Canadian Venture Capital Association, IVC Research Center (Israel), and South African Venture Capital and Private Equity Association.

15 Classic venture capital is money invested in seed-, early-, startup-, and expansion-stage companies.

16 *Venture Impact 2009, p 9*. National Capital Venture Association & The MoneyTree Report by PwC and NVCA based on data from Thomson Reuters. Data updated through 2012.

17 Kirchhoff, B. A. In W. D. Bygrave, ed., *The Portable MBA in Entrepreneurship*. New York: Wiley, 1994, p. 429.

18 *Venture Impact: The Economic Importance of Venture Capital Backed Companies to the U.S. Economy.* Fourth edition. National Venture Capital Association. www.nvca.org/index.php?option = com_docman&task = doc_download&gid = 359&ItemId = 93.

19 Bygrave, W. D. *Venture Capital Investing: A Resource Exchange Perspective.* Dissertation, Boston University, 1989.

20 National Venture Capital Association. www.nvca.com/def.html.

21 *National Venture Capital Association: Yearbook 2012.* New York: Thomson Venture Economics.

22 Ibid.

23 Al Gore's Next Act: Planet-Saving VC. February 12, 2008. http://money.cnn.com/2007/11/11/news/newsmakers/gore_kleiner.fortune.

24 Peeters, J. B. *A European Market for Entrepreneurial Companies. In William D. Bygrave, Michael Hay, and J. B. Peeters, eds.,* Realizing Investment Value. London, England: Financial Times/Pitman. 1994.

25 This is excerpted from Financing Entrepreneurs and Their Businesses, presented by William D. Bygrave at the Entrepreneurial Advantage of Nations Symposium at the United Nations Headquarters, New York, April 29, 2003.

CASE # DayOne

In an uncharacteristic show of frustration, Andrew Zenoff nearly tossed the phone into its cradle on his desk when his latest funding lead—number 182—had decided not to invest. With the 2003 winter holiday season in full swing, the 38-year-old seasoned entrepreneur knew that his fundraising efforts would now fall on deaf ears until after the New Year holiday.

Andrew stared out from the open office at a group of young mothers in the retail area—all cradling newborns—chatting with the nursing staff and with each other as they waited for the morning lactation class to begin.

> *Those new moms out there need us; that's why we're doing well despite a terrible location, a recession, and no money for advertising! So why can't I seem to convince investors what a great opportunity this is?! Am I—along with my staff and all of our satisfied customers—suffering from some sort of collective delusion?*

He closed his eyes, breathed deeply, and calmed down. After all, he quickly reminded himself, his San Francisco–based DayOne Center—a one-stop resource for new and expectant parents—was doing just fine as it approached its third year of operations. What Andrew and his team were being told, though, was that, before funds would flow, they would need to provide additional proof of concept—a second center, sited and scaled to match the DayOne business plan. The chicken-egg challenge, of course, was that they would need about a million dollars to build that proof. Andrew leaned back to consider his best options for moving forward.

My Brest Friend

A graduate of Babson College in Wellesley, Massachusetts, Andrew was no stranger to entrepreneurial mountain-climbing. For three years, he had strived to build a national distribution channel for My Brest Friend, the most popular nursing pillow in a fragmented market. By 1996, he had secured an overseas manufacturer, office space in a San Francisco warehouse, and a few volume accounts that were yielding a decent—but far from satisfying—cash flow. He was still wrestling with the issue of how to educate the buyer about the advantages of his product when suddenly his venture had come under siege:

> *A nursing pillow company that was not doing well somehow thought that I had copied their design. There was no infringement, but they sued us anyway, and I decided to fight. The owner of this company was a woman with kids, and as the suit dragged on, my lawyers convinced me that, if this thing went to trial, a jury might side with her instead of a guy who has no kids and has never been married. If she won, they'd get an injunction against me, and that would be the end of my business.*
>
> *That year I switched law firms three times, spent over $250,000 on legal fees, and ended up paying a settlement in the low six figures. I was emotionally drained, and nearly entirely out of cash, but I had managed to save my business.*

A Question of Distribution

Following that painful settlement in the spring of 1997, Andrew set about to devise a more effective delivery model for his nursing pillow enterprise. He soon came to the realization that the solution he was looking for didn't exist:

This case was prepared by Carl Hedberg under the direction of Professor William Bygrave. © Copyright Babson College, 2004. Funding provided by the Frederic C. Hamilton Chair for Free Enterprise. All rights reserved.

We definitely had the best product in the category. The problem was that people needed to be educated to that fact—either outright or through trusted word of mouth. The various channels I had worked with—big retailers, hospitals, Internet sites, catalog companies, lactation consultants—each offered only a certain facet of what a new parent needed, and so none of them had been really efficient at delivering my product to the marketplace. What it needed was a combination of education, retailing, and community.

Later that summer, Andrew got a call from one of his customers, Sallie Weld, Director of the Perinatal Center at the California Pacific Medical Center. An active promoter of My Brest Friend, Sallie had come to a frustrating juncture in her own career:

During the mid to late 1990s, I had spent a lot of time and energy setting up a new type of perinatal center. New moms were coming in asking for support and advice on various products—breast pumps in particular. When we started carrying pumps, that sort of opened up a Pandora's Box; now people wanted other products to go with the pumps. Andrew's pillow, for example, was the best on the market, so we started carrying that.

And after a couple of years, this retail aspect of our childbirth and parenting education program began to turn a profit—and the minute it did, the hospital got greedy. They told us that we were not going to be able to hire more trained staff to handle the increased demand for our consults, and they said that all of our retailing profits would be channeled back into the general fund to support other departments. That was incredibly frustrating. I knew I was onto something, though, and I started a consulting business to help other perinatal centers. The problem was, they couldn't pay much for my services. That's when I decided to give Andrew a call.

They agreed to meet at Zim's Restaurant, an aging diner in the upscale Laurel Hill neighborhood of San Francisco. It was a meeting that would change their lives.

DayOne—Beginnings

In August 1997, Sallie and Andrew met at Zim's for coffee and carrot juice, respectively. Sallie explained that no single service provider had ever been able to adequately serve the various needs of new moms:

A hospital setting would seem to be the natural place to set up an educational support and product center for these women, but the bureaucracy just won't let that happen. There are also plenty of examples where nurses have tried to offer outside consulting services to new mothers, but while that's a great thought, they never seem to get very far without the business and retail component. And retailing without knowledgeable support is just products on a shelf.

After 90 minutes of brainstorming, the pieces suddenly fell into place. Andrew had found the unique distribution model he'd been searching for:

I said to Sallie, "Let's move these hybrid health-services retailing ideas into a private care center outside of the hospital—a retail center that could provide new and expecting parents with everything they needed in one place." We'd be backing up the hospitals and supporting women at a critical and emotionally charged period in their lives.

This was like a lightning bolt of a vision for both of us, and at that moment, we decided that we were going to build a national chain of these centers. That was the beginning of DayOne.

Having already built one business from scratch, Andrew noted that he wasn't surprised that it was months before they were ready to take a material step:

I had told Sallie that, even though this sounded great, she shouldn't think about quitting her job at the hospital until I had a chance to lead us in an exercise to see if this business was a viable idea. I conducted a ton of focus groups, and every week Sallie and I would get together to talk about what I had learned—and what kind of center DayOne would be. After about nine months, in the summer of 1998, we decided, yes, this makes sense; let's do it.

Seed Funding

Andrew called investor Mark Anderssen, a shareholder and an active supporter of My Brest Friend. When Mark seemed receptive to the DayOne concept, Andrew paid him a visit:

> *I flew to Norway to meet with him in person. I was sure that after we opened up one of these, we'd be able to attract enough capital to start a chain. I figured that we would need about $300,000 to fund the next year and a half; we would be writing the business plan and working on the build-out requirements so that, when we were ready, we could move through the construction process quickly and get it opened. He said great and put up about half the money to get us started.*

As Sallie focused in on staffing requirements and retail offerings, Andrew began writing the plan, defining the target market (see Exhibit 9.1), designing the space, and looking for the right retail location: upscale, ground floor, easy parking, with excellent signage potential.

That summer, about a year after their momentous meeting of the minds, the Zim's restaurant block fell to the wrecking ball to make way for a brand new office and retail complex. Andrew saw that the location was close to the hospitals, was in a vibrant retail area, had good stroller accessibility, and offered lots of parking. When the developer pointed out the street-level retail availability on the blueprints, Andrew saw that it was precisely where Zim's had been; DayOne would be growing up in the exact spot where Andrew and Sallie had had their first meeting.

Andrew secured the space with a sizable deposit, engaged the architects, and scheduled a contractor to handle the build-out. With their sights now set on an April 2000 Grand Opening, Sallie left her job to become DayOne's first paid employee. Everything was on schedule and proceeding as planned. Then, suddenly, nothing was.

Scrambling to Survive

In January, Andrew contacted his funding partner for the other half of the seed funding allocation. The investor, who had recently suffered some losses in high tech, explained that he would be unable to extend any more money. Andrew was in shock:

> *Things were already rolling along; I had architects working, Sallie and two assistants on payroll, a huge locked-in lease—and now, suddenly, with the bills mounting up, we were out of capital!*

Andrew had been pitching the DayOne vision to other investors all along, and that same week an individual came forward with a substantial amount of money to invest. Andrew explained that, while the promise of cash got him motivated, he soon concluded that this wasn't just about the money:

> *This investor approached me and said that since I clearly understood the baby industry, he could get me a million and a half bucks for an Internet company. So I spent four weeks trying to figure out how I could do this on the Internet. Then I realized that, even though I probably could come up with something, it wouldn't really provide new parents with what they needed. And so I went back to them and said that I can't do it; it's not in line with my values and my beliefs.*

EXHIBIT 9.1	Business Plan Excerpt: The Market

The Center for New & Expectant Parents

The Market

According to the United States Department of Health and Human Services, women in the United States are having more children than at any time in almost 30 years. With four million births annually—more than half are first-time parents—the United States produces more than 2.2 million potential new customers each year. Indeed, the current baby boom is projected to continue until 2018. Spending an average of $8,100 on baby-related products and services during their baby's first year (excluding primary medical care), new parents represent more than $17.8 billion in annual purchasing power.

In recent years, the size of the juvenile products industry alone—i.e., products for babies 0–18 months—has grown to $16 billion annually. The company plans to reach the most commercially attractive part of this market—approximately 1,350,000 first-time parents each year with a college education and at least middle-income households. Additionally, the company expects to reach the market of more than 1,000,000 second-time parents annually, who comprise 25% of DayOne's target customer base.

The percentage of women in the United States who choose to breastfeed their babies continues to rise dramatically each year. According to a 2001 survey of 1.4 million mothers, the prevalence of breastfeeding in the United States is at the highest rate ever recorded, with 69.5% of new mothers now initiating breastfeeding, and 32% still breastfeeding at 6 months. (*Breastfeeding Continues to Increase into the New Millennium*, Pediatrics, Vol. 110, No. 6, Dec. 2002.) Moreover, 78.3% of college-educated mothers with household incomes of greater than $50,000 breastfeed versus a national average of 59.2%, and 59.2% of second-time mothers are breastfeeding.

As an ever-increasing number of studies confirm the advantages of breastfeeding for babies' immune systems and intellectual development, DayOne expects the incidence of breastfeeding to remain on the rise. Indeed, according to the U.S. Department of Health and Human Services, 75% of all first-time mothers will try to breastfeed their child compared to less than 50% only 15 years ago.

More than two-thirds of breastfeeding women experience difficulty during breastfeeding and seek outside help. The majority of these problems surface after the brief hospital stay, when access to hospital-based lactation consulting programs is no longer available. Most mothers first turn to their pediatricians and OBGYNs, who are increasingly referring first-time mothers to lactation consultants because they lack the time and specific expertise. DayOne provides pediatricians, OBGYNs, and new mothers with a high-availability support solution.

There are numerous other market factors that favor DayOne's solution:

- The existing market is highly fragmented. In order to receive necessary services, products, and support, new and expectant parents must navigate between baby specialty stores, catalogs, Internet sites, hospitals, and independent childbirth educators and lactation consultants.
- Pregnant women and new mothers desire community for support, information, and the opportunity to share common experiences.
- Hospitals continue to downsize, reducing staffs and shortening the duration of maternity visits, forcing new mothers to rely on outside sources for needed support and services.
- Baby specialty stores continue to disappear off of the retail landscape in the face of big-box operators, reducing the personal touch that new parents seek.

Although he was now sure that the DayOne model wouldn't work as a Web business, Andrew saw that there still might be a way to leverage the red-hot Internet space to garner the funding he so desperately needed:

> I met with a big online company that was doing baby-related things and told them that I thought their model had issues; first-time parents need to touch and feel and learn before they buy. I suggested that in order to survive long-term, they would need to partner with a bricks-and-mortar business like the kind we were building.
>
> Well, at the time their stock was worth several hundred million; those two guys told me that they were doing just fine and that they had no interest in what we were doing at DayOne. You know, a year later, they were out of business.

DayOne centers were designed to be a key distribution channel for Brest Friend products, so Andrew aggressively leveraged resources at his wholesale venture in an effort to keep the flagship store on schedule. That had worked well for a while, but ever since Andrew began working long hours to open DayOne, sales of his nursing pillows had fallen precipitously. It was now achingly clear that, if this innovative distribution concept failed, My Brest Friend would be facing a long road back.

By March 2000, DayOne had amassed $200,000 in payables that Andrew couldn't begin to cover—at least not in the near term. Two architectural firms had already walked out on the project when they became aware that the startup was suffering from a severe funding gap. Andrew convinced the third one to come on board by pointing out that he himself wasn't drawing a salary—that his partner Sallie had resigned from a good job at the hospital to do this, and that they had already begun to interview and hire additional staff. This was real; they would find a way. That's just about the time that things began to get really ugly.

Nightmare on the Second Floor

By mid-March, DayOne had endured 45 days without cash, and Andrew had spoken with nearly 50 investors, without success. The landlord called. Construction, it seemed, was behind schedule—a fact that, under the circumstances, suited Andrew just fine. When the landlord requested a face-to-face meeting as soon as possible, Andrew was pretty sure that the guy wasn't calling him in to apologize a second time for the occupancy delay:

> The landlord tells me that because of our financial position, they are not going to let us have a ground floor space; he's afraid that DayOne couldn't cover the rent. He says the only space they have for us is on the second floor—end of story. I said, "I don't know what to do; I don't have the money. I need to get out of this lease." He said, "Well, you're on the second floor, and you can't get out of the lease." Great; a lease for a top-floor space that I couldn't pay for.

Andrew returned the following day with a stronger argument:

> I said look, you can't squeeze blood from a stone. And anyway, I am out of this lease because your building has taken so long to deliver that my investors have backed out! I told him that I can't honor the lease because he hadn't honored his deal. He didn't really respond to me, but we both knew that I was all done.

Andrew was trying to visualize how he was going to break this devastating news to his partner Sallie when he received an astounding call on his cell phone:

> I had been pitching the business plan to everyone I could think of and hadn't gotten anywhere. All of a sudden here was an investor calling to say that he and three others were interested in

putting up $150,000 apiece. $450,000 was about half of what I would need to open, and a lot less than the $1.5 million I was trying to raise as a first round. But it was a start; I pushed the "Go" button again.

I went back to the real estate guy and said, "You know, you're right; even if this is on the second floor, this is my space. I'll keep it." That's when he told me that he had already rented out half of our space to someone else. So, not only were we going to be way in back on the second floor with half the space we needed, but also we were now going to have to pay to completely reconstruct our architectural drawings.

Understanding that he was still a half a million dollars shy of what they would need to open the doors, Andrew continued to dole out just enough money to keep his various service providers on board. In June, the landlord informed him that the building was now ready for occupancy—meaning that the first $10,000 monthly rent payment was due. Andrew made sure to pay that bill on time, and in full.

Grand Opening

The construction business, like many trades, was a close-knit community of craftspeople and professionals. It was not surprising, then, that word was out on the slow-paying, underfunded project up on Laurel Hill that had already gone through three architectural firms and at least that many plan revisions. After a long search, Andrew located a contractor who apparently was not aware of DayOne's precarious financial situation. Along the way, he had signed up another minor investor, so when construction began in August 2000, DayOne had $480,000 on hand. In late November—as the build-out neared completion—the contractor suddenly announced that he would not release the occupancy permits until he and his crew were paid in full for the work they had completed. Andrew recalled that it was another one of those pivotal moments:

I owed these guys something like $200,000, and I didn't have anything left. I just wanted to get to the opening party in January because I felt that, if we got enough people to come and enjoy it and get excited about what we were doing, we'd be able to raise the money we needed. I convinced the contractor to let us open, and at that party, two different guests pulled me aside and said that they wanted to invest. One woman wired me $50,000 the following Monday without so much as glancing at the business plan. I got another $50,000 from a couple who had just had their baby. When we officially opened later that week, the contractor was paid in full, but we were again out of money.

As they had always planned to do, Andrew and Sallie called the area hospitals to let them know that DayOne was open for business and ready to serve. Andrew recalled that the response from the medical community took them completely by surprise:

One reason we thought we could make do with a second-floor location was because our plan had always been to drive traffic by being the type of place that medical professionals would want to send their patients. Instead, hospital directors were telling us that they considered us to be the competition and that they were going to tell all the docs in San Francisco not to support our efforts in any way.

With no help from the hospitals, ineffective signage, cramped facilities (see Exhibit 9.2), and no capital for marketing and advertising, Sallie and Andrew were faced with a harsh reality: Either customers would love the experience enough to spread the word, or their business would quickly wither and die.

EXHIBIT 9.2 | **Signage and Facility**

Delivering a Unique Customer Experience

DayOne immediately began attracting a base of young, mostly affluent new and expectant moms seeking advice on everything from the latest baby carriers to sore nipples. Many signed up for the $99 annual membership on the spot to take advantage of discounts offered on programs and workshops (see Exhibit 9.3). Some dropped by out of curiosity or with specific

EXHIBIT 9.3   DayOne Membership Flyer

DayOne Membership

The Center For New & Expectant Parents

Why DayOne Membership?

A DayOne Membership provides a valuable opportunity for customers to save money, receive personalized attention, fully access our many resources, and connect with a community of new and expectant parents, seven days a week.

DayOne Membership Includes All of the Following:

- 40% Savings on DayOne Value Packages
- 30% Savings on Parent Groups
- 30% Savings on Workshops
- 25% Savings on Classes
- 20% Savings on Lactation Consultations
- Special Membership Prices on Selected Retail Items
- Unlimited Use of Resource Library
- Free Book & Video Rental
- Unlimited Use of Precision Baby Weigh Station
- Unlimited Use of Changing Stations
- In-Store Internet Access
- An Easy Way to Register for Classes & Purchase Products

DAY ONE MEMBERSHIP
Annual renewal fee $49

$99

Memberships are non-refundable

www.DayOneCenter.com • 3490 California St. San Francisco, CA 94118 • 415.440.DAY1 (3291)

questions for the professional staff. Sallie quickly established a ground rule that she felt struck a fair balance between the needs of these mothers and the need to advance the business:

> When someone comes in with a question, we have a 10-minute rule. If your question is so involved that one of us cannot answer it in 10 minutes, then you need to make an appointment, and we need to charge you.[1] Ideally, these are people who are members, but many times, if they are not, we can convert them by giving them those 10 minutes and maybe recommending some classes or products right there on the shelves that might be just what they were looking for. And they leave here thinking, wow, where else can I go where I can get that kind of knowledgeable service without having to be a member first?

Sallie noted that, because of their customer-care orientation, she and her nursing staff were always looking out for ways to help—without first trying to calibrate whether a particular act of humanity or assistance would generate profits for the business. Pointing to a basic plastic and metal chair in the corner of her office, Sallie said that she wasn't surprised to see that simple kindness had its rewards:

> Our favorite story is about that chair. We like new moms to be sitting up straight when they first start nursing—versus a rocking chair. I had one mom—not a member—who said every time she came in for a consult that the only way she could breast feed was in that type of chair. Every time she came in she said it, so finally I said, "Hey, why don't you take the chair home with you until you're feeling more comfortable with the whole process?" She looked at me and said, "Really?"
>
> So she took the chair home. The next day she became a member, she bought a breast pump from us instead of the one she was eyeing on eBay, and she went around telling all of her friends that we lent her that chair. She brought it back a few weeks later and has become one of our best customers.
>
> What goes around comes around, and when we give a little bit, it's such a shock to them that they've gotten good service. I have this rule that if there's a mom hanging out in the rocking chair area, one of us goes over and asks if we could get her a glass of cold water. I swear it's like you've just offered them a million dollars! They'll start to ask you questions, and it almost always turns into a sale. It's so funny—and a bit pathetic—that nobody ever thinks about these moms; everybody talks to, and about, the baby.
>
> That's what we do differently. We make them feel good, knowing that if we take care of them, they'll take care of the baby. And all of that is definitely good for business.

Despite an encouraging level of customer interest and loyalty right from the start, the retailing side of the business continued to struggle. Andrew knew what the problem was:

> The thing is, I am not a retailer. So everything we did early on was shooting from the hip. Sallie had some experience selling retail products at the hospital, but she was better on the service side. We had hired one retail buyer who lasted two months; didn't know what she was doing. Then another; same thing. The problem was, these people knew a lot about retailing, but we needed somebody who also understood the baby industry.

DayOne had begun to cover its operating expenses by the end of the summer of 2001, but the business was still in dire need of funding. As the capital markets continued to deteriorate that year, fundraising became an even more arduous task than ever before. While the 9–11 terrorist attacks on the East Coast hurt retail sales and drove potential investors further underground, satisfied clients continued to drive new customers to the center.

---

[1] Personal consulting service was offered at $89/hour, a competitive rate in the Greater Bay area.

In January 2002, the retail buyer that Andrew and Sallie had been searching for showed up on their doorstep. Ten-year retailing veteran Jennifer Morris had come over from The Right Start, the largest chain of specialty stores for infants and children in the United States. She recounted how she was drawn to the new venture and alluded to why her predecessors might have been overwhelmed by the task:

> *I found out about DayOne through working at The Right Start in San Francisco. I would either see a DayOne tote bag or customers would tell me all about it. I started to investigate and found out that DayOne is not the kind of place you'd stumble onto. I was immediately attracted to the energy in this place; from the customers, the staff, the nurses, to the classes and the workshops, everyone just really seemed to love it.*
>
> *The biggest challenge for us is trying to be a one-stop shop. We have quite a few product categories (see Exhibit 9.4), and I buy from over 100 vendors—sometimes just one item from one vendor. A lot of those decisions are made by listening to our customers. If they come in with a terrific product, we can then go research that item and bring it in. We have no limits on that, really; we carry products from New Zealand, from Australia—from all over the world. If there's a great new product out there, we'll find it.*

EXHIBIT 9.4	Retail Product Offerings
Category	**Approximate Profit Margins**
Maternity Products	40%
Infant Clothing	54%
Nursing Clothes	52%
Breastfeeding Equipment	50%
Gifts	55%
Baby Accessories	47%
Infant Safety & Health	57%
Book Sales	42%
Toys	53%
Preemie Clothing	53%
Skin Care	47%
Hardgoods	44%
Bras	51%
Food & Beverages	10%

Sallie pointed out that in a similar way, she and the nursing staff were always looking for instructors and programs [2] that would distinguish DayOne as a premiere care center:

> *We search for the best and invite them to teach their classes here. More and more, though, the good ones come looking for us. We have started a lot of fresh and exciting workshops, but almost immediately other places in town copy what we're doing. Sometimes I wonder how long we can keep it fresh and exciting, but then again, that's what we thrive on.*

The DayOne team began its second year of operations finding ways to trim overhead, enhance the customer experience, and refine the retail operations. To further this effort, Andrew

---

[2] In addition to a core of standard classes and support groups dealing with childbirth, breastfeeding, and exercise, the center offered other workshops such as Infant & Child CPR, Infant Massage, Musical Play, First Foods, and Practical First Aid & Safety.

tapped New York–based Stephen Cooper—an expert in retailing and finance—to serve as the company's Chief Operating Officer.

By early summer, the company—which in May had been honored with a "Best of SF" accolade (see Exhibit 9.5)—was signing up a steady stream of new members. Many of those clients were now being referred to the facility by local physicians who were quietly ignoring the sentiments of their hospital administrators. One such referral was Lisa Zoener, a new mom who said that she found out about DayOne from her obstetrician:

> *I have told lots of people about this place; it's definitely a word of mouth type of thing. My husband and I drop a ton of dough here on baby vitamins and other stuff. DayOne products are definitely higher priced than in other stores, but I'm already here for the classes—and a lot of us feel that buying DayOne products is a way to support what they're trying to do here. I don't find the second floor to be a problem—there is a parking garage right downstairs. It was full today, though.*

EXHIBIT 9.5 | *SF Weekly* **Best of 2002 Feature**

Best Place to Go After You've Had a Baby

Day One

Your new baby has finally arrived. You're excited, anxious, sleep-deprived, and frankly a little concerned that medical professionals have let you leave the hospital with this newborn. You've forgotten everything you learned in parenting classes, and nothing you were told in childbirth class has happened the way they said it would. In short, you need support, reassurance, help, *something* ... and not from your mother-in-law. Look no more. Strap the little bundle into a carrier and get yourself to the knowledgeable, calm, and compassionate folks at Day One. As a business, the center is an odd mix: a retailer of higher-end baby tools and accessories, a lending library of books and tapes, the home of parenting classes, and a kind of lounge to hang out and nurse, chat, change diapers, or just get the heck out of your living room. As if all of that were not enough, Day One has medical scales to monitor your baby's weight and lactation consultants to help mother and baby get the hang of nursing. An annual membership is only $99, which also gets you a 5 percent discount on merchandise. The center is open seven days a week to fulfill its mission: "to provide new and expectant parents with a single-source, time-efficient solution for the essentials needed during this special and often challenging time of life." A brilliant idea that we're glad has finally arrived.

Details

Address: 3490 California (at Locust), Suite 203, 440-3291.

sfweekly.com | originally published: May 15, 2002

Although he now had actual operating figures, a slew of customer testimonials, and an appropriate town picked out for the second DayOne, Andrew was still unable to raise the money he would need to proceed with those expansion plans. Then, in November, Andrew received a call that he was sure would change everything.

The Saudi Connection

Unknown to the DayOne staff, one of their very satisfied new moms was the daughter of a Saudi prince. Her father, Samir, was visiting from his home in London and, through her experience, had learned a lot about what DayOne was doing. Andrew described their two-hour meeting at the center:

> *Samir said that he had an eye for businesses and that he thought what we were doing was brilliant. He said that he was the president of a multinational conglomerate out of London and Saudi Arabia; he wanted to fund our U.S. rollout and also help us export it to other countries.*

Andrew sent the prince on his way with a detailed business plan. Due diligence indicated that Samir was indeed who he said he was, so Andrew's excitement grew when the Saudi called a week later to say that he wanted to take it to the next level. That next step was having a colleague of his—a woman based in Arizona who had run four different billion-dollar retail businesses—work as his eyes and ears to determine the best way to move the venture forward.

Ann Pearson, 60, a self-described workaholic and leading advisor to a separate $5-billion new venture fund, spent the entire day at the center and was thrilled with the concept. She explained that to move ahead, she and Andrew would need to build a business plan that would warrant her stamp of approval. Andrew recalled that that's when the real work began:

> *For the next three months, Ann was flying here every few weeks, and Steve, our COO, was flying in from New York for three days at a time. She had us rewrite an entirely new business plan to sort of grind down to the nitty-gritty every aspect of the business so that she felt that she could put her stamp on it. We spent hundreds of hours, many tens of thousands of dollars. She was like this manic corporate raider–type, driving us really hard.*

Along the way, Andrew had begun to notice that Ann didn't seem to have a high regard for his DayOne staff and kept implying that, before the business could begin its rollout, management changes would have to be discussed. It was bad enough when she suggested that Samir's daughter—a junior investment banker—might make a good choice for CFO, but when Ann began to infer that Andrew might not make the cut as CEO, he'd heard enough:

> *We had gotten into these heavy negotiations, and we had also started getting into huge fights. Ann ended up being an absolute animal; she wanted to drive everyone out of the business and take it over. But if you know me, I am not somebody who is going to get pushed around like that, and I wasn't going to sell out for anything. Then, all of a sudden, Samir calls and says that he's not interested anymore.*

It was nearly mid-spring of 2003 by the time Andrew turned away from that mirage—and several more months before the next major investor prospect would surface. The DayOne team now had a positive operating income for the center (see Exhibit 9.6), a detailed business plan with five-year pro-formas (see Exhibits 9.7–9.10), proven managerial performance, and, as always, a need for investment capital.

EXHIBIT 9.6	DayOne Income Statement—San Francisco Actuals		
	2001	**2002**	**2003**
Retail Sales			
Product Sales	$ 533,676	$687,492	$816,000
Memberships	55,566	62,774	76,050
Total Retail Sales	$589,242	$750,266	$892,050
Total Service Sales	181,761	222,947	272,000
TOTAL SALES	771,003	973,213	1,164,050
Total Cost of Retail Sales	288,569	346,213	434,627
Total Cost of Service Sales	196,144	156,680	190,624
TOTAL COST OF SALES	484,713	502,893	625,251
Gross Margin Retail Sales	300,673	404,053	457,423
Percent of Sales	51.0%	53.9%	51.3%
Gross Margin Service Sales	(14,383)	66,267	81,376
Percent of Sales	−1.9%	29.7%	29.9%
TOTAL GROSS MARGIN	286,290	470,320	538,799
Percent of Sales	37.1%	48.3%	46.3%
TOTAL CENTER EXPENSES	426,134	374,684	417,852
CENTER EBITDA	**(139,844)**	**95,636**	**120,947**
Percent of Sales	−18.1%	9.8%	10.4%

EXHIBIT 9.7	Five-Year Income Statement Projections—Rollout				
	Year 1	**Year 2**	**Year 3**	**Year 4**	**Year 5**
Total Stores	**2**	**6**	**14**	**26**	**42**
New Stores	**2**	**4**	**8**	**12**	**16**
RETAIL SALES					
Product Sales	$1,904,000	$3,581,614	$10,713,896	$24,506,943	$46,011,931
Memberships	201,050	398,000	1,226,000	2,804,000	5,282,000
Total Retail Sales	2,105,050	3,979,614	11,939,896	27,310,943	51,293,931
Total Service Sales	647,000	1,250,800	3,713,000	8,470,000	15,882,000
TOTAL SALES	**2,752,050**	**5,230,414**	**15,652,896**	**35,780,943**	**67,175,931**
COST OF SALES					
Total Cost of Retail Sales	1,025,629	1,913,567	5,785,809	13,276,595	24,956,361
Total Cost of Service Sales	393,484	623,048	1,694,132	3,735,912	6,859,763
TOTAL COST OF SALES	**1,419,113**	**2,536,615**	**7,479,941**	**17,012,507**	**31,816,124**
GROSS MARGIN					
Gross Margin Retail Sales	1,079,421	2,066,047	6,154,087	14,034,348	26,337,570
Percent of Sales Gross	51.3%	51.9%	51.5%	51.4%	51.3%
Margin Service Sales	253,516	627,752	2,018,868	4,734,088	9,022,237
Percent of Sales	39.2%	50.2%	54.4%	55.9%	56.8%
TOTAL GROSS MARGIN	**1,332,937**	**2,693,800**	**8,172,956**	**18,768,436**	**35,359,807**
TOTAL CENTER EXPENSES	**1,011,450**	**1,752,576**	**4,762,754**	**10,787,758**	**20,177,895**
CENTER EBITDA	**321,486**	**941,224**	**3,410,202**	**7,980,678**	**15,181,913**

EXHIBIT 9.8	Five-Year Cash Flow Projections—Rollout				
	Year 1	Year 2	Year 3	Year 4	Year 5
Operating Activities					
Net Income	(974,692)	(592,920)	971,764	4,522,301	11,111,776
Adjustments for Non-Cash Items					
FFE	—	—	—	—	—
Leasehold	102,857	308,571	720,000	1,337,143	2,160,000
Pre-Opening Costs	18,571	55,714	130,000	241,429	390,000
Product Promotions					
Total Adjustments for Non-Cash Items	121,429	364,286	850,000	1,578,571	2,550,000
Changes in Working Capital	—	—	—	—	—
Current Assets	—	—	—	—	—
Current Liabilities	(312,188)	—	—	—	—
Net Changes in Working Capital	(312,188)	—	—	—	—
Net Cash—Operating Activities	**(1,165,452)**	**(228,634)**	**1,821,764**	**6,100,873**	**13,661,776**
Investing Activities					
Investing Activities	—	—	—	—	—
FFE	(720,000)	(1,440,000)	(2,880,000)	(4,320,000)	(5,760,000)
Leasehold	(130,000)	(260,000)	(520,000)	(780,000)	(1,040,000)
Pre-Opening Costs	(300,000)	(600,000)	(1,200,000)	(1,800,000)	(2,400,000)
Inventory	(120,000)	(240,000)	(160,000)	(240,000)	(320,000)
Security Deposits					
Net Cash—Investing Activities	**(1,270,000)**	**(2,540,000)**	**(4,760,000)**	**(7,140,000)**	**(9,520,000)**
Financing Activities					
Proceeds from Class B Unit Offering	—	—	—	—	—
Founder Investment	—	—	—	—	—
Payments on Notes Payable and LT Debt	(624,758)	—	—	—	—
Common Stock Repurchases	—	—	—	—	—
Proceeds from Exercised Stock Options	—	—	—	—	—
Net Increase (Decrease) in Short-Term Debt	—	—	—	—	—
Net Cash—Financing Activities	(624,758)				
Inc/(Dec) in Cash Equivalents	(3,060,210)	(2,768,634)	(2,938,236)	(1,039,127)	4,141,776
Cash and Equivalents Beginning Balance	7,232	(3,052,978)	(5,821,612)	(8,759,847)	(9,798,975)
Cash and Equivalents at Ending balance	(3,052,978)	(5,821,612)	(8,759,847)	(9,798,975)	(5,657,199)

EXHIBIT 9.9	Five-Year Balance Sheet Projections—Rollout				
	Year 1	**Year 2**	**Year 3**	**Year 4**	**Year 5**
Total Stores	**2**	**6**	**14**	**26**	**42**
New Stores	**2**	**4**	**8**	**12**	**16**
ASSETS					
Cash	$ (2,632,978)	$ (4,621,612)	$ (5,994,847)	$ (5,093,975)	$ 1,257,801
Other Current Assets	$ 25,316	$ 25,316	$ 25,316	$ 25,316	$ 25,316
Total Current Assets	(2,607,662)	(4,596,296)	(5,969,531)	(5,068,659)	1,283,117
Inventory	416,516	1,016,516	2,216,516	4,016,516	6,416,516
Fixed Assets					
Leasehold	1,352,424	2,792,424	5,672,424	9,992,424	15,752,424
Accumulated Depreciation	(102,857)	(411,429)	(1,131,429)	(2,468,571)	(4,628,571)
Net Leasehold	1,249,567	2,380,995	4,540,995	7,523,853	11,123,853
Security Deposit	172,000	412,000	572,000	812,000	1,132,000
Pre-Opening Expenses	130,000	390,000	910,000	1,690,000	2,730,000
Accumulated Depreciation	(18,571)	(74,286)	(204,286)	(445,714)	(835,714)
Net Pre-Opening Expenses	111,429	315,714	705,714	1,244,286	1,894,286
Total Fixed Assets	1,532,995	3,108,710	5,818,710	9,580,138	14,150,138
TOTAL ASSETS	$ (658,150)	$ (471,070)	$ 2,065,694	$ 8,527,996	$21,849,772
LIABILITIES					
Short-Term Liabilities					
Trade Payables	—	—	—	—	—
Trade—Zenoff Products	—	—	—	—	—
Van—Note Payable	—	—	—	—	—
Other Payables	13,806	13,806	13,806	13,806	13,806
Total Current Liabilities	13,806	13,806	13,806	13,806	13,806
Long-Term Liabilities	—				
Accrued Compensation					
Notes Payable	—				
Total Long-Term Liabilities	—	—	—	—	—
TOTAL LIABILITIES	13,806	13,806	13,806	13,806	13,806
EQUITY					
Retained Earnings—Prior Year	(1,454,355)	(2,009,048)	(1,821,967)	714,797	7,177,099
Retained Earnings—Current Year	(554,692)	187,080	2,536,764	6,462,301	13,321,776
Additional Paid-In Capital	1,064,304	1,064,304	1,064,304	1,064,304	1,064,304
Partnership Earn/(Loss)	272,787	272,787	272,787	272,787	272,787
Total Equity	(671,957)	(484,876)	2,051,888	8,514,190	21,835,965
TOTAL LIABILITIES AND EQUITY	$ (658,151)	$ (471,070)	$ 2,065,694	$ 8,527,996	$ 21,849,771

EXHIBIT 9.10 Five-Year Corporate	Year 1	Year 2	Year 3	Year 4	Year 5
Executive					
CEO	175,000	175,000	200,000	200,000	200,000
Chairman			150,000	150,000	150,000
COO	150,000	175,000	200,000	200,000	200,000
CFO	75,000	100,000	125,000	150,000	150,000
Office and Finance					
Controller			90,000	90,000	90,000
Finance Clerk		85,000	40,000	40,000	40,000
IT Manager			85,000	85,000	85,000
Inventory Manager			85,000	85,000	85,000
Office Clerk	40,000	40,000	40,000	40,000	40,000
Office Clerk			40,000	40,000	40,000
Service					
Service Director	45,000	95,000	100,000	200,000	200,000
Service Manager				75,000	150,000
Service Assistant			40,000	80,000	80,000
Marketing					
Marketing Director		100,000	125,000	125,000	125,000
Marketing Assistant			45,000	80,000	80,000
Operations					
Operations Director			100,000	100,000	100,000
Operations Manager		60,000	60,000	120,000	180,000
Operations Assistant			40,000	40,000	40,000
Operations Assistant				40,000	40,000
Operations Assistant					40,000
Purchasing					
Buyer			60,000	60,000	120,000
Assistant Buyer			40,000	80,000	120,000
Total Salaries	485,000	830,000	1,665,000	2,090,000	2,410,000
Benefits Load (15%)	557,750	954,500	1,914,750	2,403,500	2,771,500
Increase (2%)		11,155	19,090	38,295	48,070
Total Corporate Payroll	1,042,750	1,795,655	3,598,840	4,531,795	5,229,570

Prove It—Again

The DayOne plan called for opening 42 centers in five years, but so far the team found itself in a holding pattern around its flagship location. Andrew thought it ironic that, by overcoming challenges and making compromises to get the first store open, they had developed a business that investors seemed unwilling to accept as a proof of concept:

> *We are now one of the most trusted brands in San Francisco. People love us. Investors are saying, well, this first center has done great for what it is, but your plan talks about a center that would be on the ground floor with street-side visibility, have support from the hospitals, and be in a bigger, more appropriate space. So because we are talking about a bigger center with bigger economics, they don't want to take the risks.*

Andrew estimated that he was going to need about $1.3 million to pay off current debt and open up a center that was more reflective of the business plan model (see Exhibit 9.11). That second DayOne would be sited in an affluent town about 35 miles to the south:

EXHIBIT 9.11	**Typical Center—Development Budget**	
PRE-OPENING COSTS		
Store Build-Out (~3,800 sq. ft.)		418,000
6 Months Management Salary		110,000
Pre-Opening Expenses		65,000
Operations Consultant—Travel		10,000
Operations Consultant		30,000
Real Estate Acquisition		10,000
Inventory		155,000
Security Deposit		40,000
Miscellaneous		50,000
Total Pre-Opening Costs		888,000
CORPORATE OVERHEAD		
Legal, Acctg, Other Prof Fees		15,000
Payroll and Benefits		225,000
FFE		10,000
Insurance		20,000
Utilities & Rent/Whse		12,000
Miscellaneous		20,000
Total Corporate Overhead		302,000
TOTAL CASH REQUIREMENTS		1,190,000

Palo Alto would be the next spot. It's in our back yard, and it's got the right demographics. It would be a bigger center, with more space, twice as many classrooms; twice the business, twice the sales.

Sallie noted that, because of the rave reviews her group had received, some investors wondered aloud if that magic could be replicated in other centers:

We have a great reputation in the community, and we set a tone here of warmth; we respect these women. Can we find as good a staff for Palo Alto, and can we train them well enough? Absolutely. Sure, it won't ever be what we have here, but it doesn't have to be to make the business work. I have no doubt that in every community we choose to locate in we can find qualified, caring nurses who would love the chance to do what we are doing here.

She paused—and then added:

We hit bumps, and then we move on. And all the while we keep refining this model; the quality of our workshops, the way we work; it's all so much better than it was even one year ago. So it will happen; I'm sure of it—this struggle is for a reason. Andrew is big on that; it's all about the journey, not the destination.

Moving Forward

Andrew checked his cash-on-hand balance. After three years, he had still not taken a dime of salary, and yet he had to smile as he penned this particular company check. The cabinetry work at the facility had cost $85,000, and with this disbursement, Andrew would be making good on his promise to pay those guys—not quickly—but in full. There were plenty of others who were still waiting, but in time, they would be paid as well.

The phone rang, and on the other end was a young venture capitalist whose partner's pregnant wife had heard about DayOne from her sister's friend's pediatrician....

Preparation Questions

1. What more can the members of the DayOne team do to build credibility and improve their chances of securing the capital they need to implement the business plan?

2. What other options might be considered for raising the funds needed to move the company ahead?

3. Imagine Andrew has approached you as a potential investor. Has DayOne proven the model yet? What are your concerns? Would you invest?

Jim Poss and BigBelly© solar-powered trash compactor.

RAISING MONEY FOR STARTING AND GROWING BUSINESSES

You've developed your business idea and written a business plan in which you have forecast how much money you'll need for your new venture. Now you're wondering where you will get the initial money to start your business and the follow-on capital to grow it. In this chapter, we discuss the mechanics of raising money from investors, including business angels, venture capitalists, and public stock markets. First, we revisit the Jim Poss case, which you studied in Chapter 3, to examine how Jim scraped together the resources to start his business.

Jim Poss, BigBelly Solar

During the second year of his MBA studies, Jim enrolled in Babson's Entrepreneurship Intensity Track, which is for students who want to develop a new venture that they will run full time as soon as they graduate. Jim's first product, the BigBelly® is an automatic, compacting trash bin powered by solar energy. The innovative BigBelly dramatically cuts

This chapter is written by William D. Bygrave.

emptying frequency and waste handling costs, trash overflow, and litter at outdoor sites with high traffic and high trash volume. The BigBelly's target end users, such as municipalities and outdoor entertainment venues, face massive volumes of daily trash and very high collection costs. By the time he graduated in May 2003, Jim had a company, originally named Seahorse Power Company, and a business plan, and he was developing a prototype.

While still in school, Jim won $1,500 worth of legal services at an investors' forum held by Brown Rudnick Berlack Israels, LLP, a leading Boston law firm. Jim used this as part payment for the legal fees associated with his patent application. He invested $10,000 from his savings in BigBelly Solar (BBS) and was awarded $12,500 through the Babson Hatchery Program. He recruited two unpaid Olin College engineering students to help with the design, manufacture, and testing of the prototype. Jim then developed a partnership with Bob Treiber and his firm, Boston Engineering, from which he received a "ton of work" pro bono and free space in which to assemble and test the prototype. Vail Ski Resort ordered a BigBelly and paid Jim the full purchase price ($5,500) in advance. In fact, he presold nearly half the first production run, and there was a 50% down payment with each order.

Jim's parents invested $12,500. A business angel invested $12,500. Spire Corporation, a 30-year-old publicly traded solar energy company, invested $25,000. Jim won the Babson Business Plan Competition, which brought in $20,000 in cash, which he shared among the team members—the first compensation they had ever received from the project. The award also brought in $40,000 worth of services and lots of publicity. Over the next year, Jim raised $250,000 with an "A" round of private investment from 17 individuals and companies, in amounts ranging from $12,500 to $50,000 with convertible debt. By the fall of 2005, BBS had sold about 100 compactors. In November 2005, Jim closed a round of equity financing.

As of 2012, BigBelly Solar had sold trash compactors to more than 1,000 customers across the United States and 30 other countries. The purchase price of a BigBelly had decreased to $3,900 in 2009 (before any bulk discounts).[1] BBS added wireless SMS text capabilities to its most recent compactors to alert trash collectors when the bins reach capacity. Among BigBelly Solar's most notable customers are the City of Philadelphia, the U.S. Forest Service, Harvard University, the Boston Red Sox, the Chicago Transit Authority, and PepsiCo.

Bootstrapping New Ventures

Jim Poss is a typical example of how an entrepreneur bootstraps a startup by scraping together resources, including financing, services, material, space, and labor. In Chapter 2, you read about how Steve Jobs and Stephen Wozniak at Apple and Sergey Brin and Larry Page at Google raised their capital. Jobs and Wozniak developed their first computer, Apple I, in a parent's garage and funded it with $1,300 raised by selling Jobs' Volkswagen and Wozniak's calculator. They then found an angel investor, Armas Markkula, Jr., who had recently retired from Intel a wealthy man. Markkula personally invested $91,000 and secured a line of credit from Bank of America. Brin and Page maxed out their credit cards to buy the terabyte of storage that they needed to start Google in Larry's dorm room. Then they raised $100,000 from Andy Bechtolsheim, one of the founders of Sun Microsystems, plus approximately $900,000 from family, friends, and acquaintances. Both Apple and Google subsequently raised venture capital and then went public.

There is a pattern in the initial funding of BigBelly Solar, Apple, and Google that is repeated over and over in almost every startup. The money comes from the Four Fs introduced in Chapter 9: First, the founders themselves dip into their own pockets for the initial capital; next they turn to family, friends, and foolhardy investors (business angels). If their companies grow rapidly and show the potential to be superstars (see Figure 9.13 in Chapter 9), they raise venture capital and have an initial public offering (IPO) or are acquired by a bigger company. The money from family and friends might be a loan or equity or a combination of both, but when it is raised from business angels, from venture capitalists, or with an IPO, it will be equity. Before they raise money in exchange for equity, entrepreneurs must know the value of their companies, so they know how much equity they will have to give up. Before we discuss the mechanics of raising money, let's examine how to value a company.

Valuation

There are four basic ways of valuing a business:

- Earnings capitalization valuation
- Present value of future cash flows
- Market-comparable valuation
- Asset-based valuation

No single method is ideal because the value of a business depends among other things on the following:

- Opportunity
- Risk
- Purchaser's financial resources
- Future strategies for the company
- Time horizon of the analysis
- Alternative investments
- Future harvest

The valuation of a small, privately held corporation is difficult and uncertain. It is not public, so its equity, unlike that of a public company, has very limited liquidity or probably none at all; hence, there is no way to place a value on its equity based on the share price of its stock. What's more, if it is an existing company rather than a startup, its accounting practices may be quirky. For instance, the principals' salaries may be set more by tax considerations than by market value. There may be unusual perquisites for the principals. The assets such as inventory, machinery, equipment, and real estate may be undervalued or overvalued. Goodwill is often worthless. There might be unusual liabilities or even unrecognized liabilities. Perhaps the principals have deferred compensation. Is it a subchapter S or limited liability corporation or a partnership? If so, tax considerations might dominate the accounting.

When valuing any business, especially a startup company with no financial history, we must not let finance theory dominate over practical rule-of-thumb valuations. In practice, there is so much uncertainty and imprecision in the financial projections that elaborate computations are not justified; indeed, they can sometimes lead to a false sense of exactness.

The following sections describe the four methods to determine the valuation.

> *"The engine that drives enterprise is not thrift, but profit."*
> —*John Maynard Keynes*

Earnings Capitalization Valuation

We can compute the value of a company with the earnings capitalization method as follows:

$$\text{Company Value} = \text{Net Income}/\text{Capitalization Rate}$$

This method is precise when net income is steady and very predictable but not useful when valuing a company, particularly a startup, whose net income is very uncertain. Even for an existing small business, the method is fraught with problems: For example, should the net income be that for the most recent year, or next year's expected income, or the average income for the last five years, or . . . ? Hence, we seldom use the earnings capitalization method for valuing small, privately held businesses.

Present Value of Future Cash Flows

The present value of a company is the present value of the future free cash flows, plus the residual (terminal) value of the firm:

$$PV = \sum_{t=1}^{N} (FCF_t)/(1 + K)^t + (RV_N)/(1 + K)^N$$

where K is the cost of capital, FCF_t is the free cash flow in year t, N is the number of years, and RV_N is the residual value in year N.

$$
\begin{aligned}
\text{Free Cash Flow} = &\ \text{Operating Income} \\
&- \text{Interest} \\
&- \text{Taxes on Operating Income} \\
&+ \text{Depreciation \& Other Noncash Charges} \\
&- \text{Increase in Net Working Capital} \\
&- \text{Capital Expenditures (Replacement \& Growth)} \\
&- \text{Principal Repayments}
\end{aligned}
$$

Free cash flow is cash in excess of what a firm needs to maintain its optimum rate of growth. A rapidly growing, high-potential firm will not generate any free cash flow in its first few years. In fact, entrepreneurs and investors want it to use excess cash to grow faster. Therefore, we determine the value of such a firm entirely by its residual value.

Market-Comparable Valuation (Multiple of Earnings)

This valuation method is the company's net income (NI) multiplied by a ratio of the market valuation to net income (P/E) of a comparable public company, or preferably the average for a number of similar public companies. Ideally, the comparable companies should be in the same industry segment as the company that we are valuing. If the company is private, we usually discount its valuation because its shares are not liquid.

$$\text{Total Equity Valuation} = NI \times P/E$$

For a public company, the total equity valuation is the same as the market capitalization. If we substitute net income per share (earnings per share or EPS) for total net income in this formula, we have the price per share instead of market capitalization.

Variations on this method use earnings before interest, taxes, depreciation, and amortization (EBITDA) multiplied by the ratio of price per share to EBITDA per share of comparable companies, or simply the operating income (EBIT) multiplied by the ratio of price per share to EBIT per share.

The NI × P/E method is the most common technique for valuing rapidly growing companies that are seeking investment from professional investors such as venture capitalists or that are going public. For a fast-growing company with no free cash flow, NI × P/E is the same as the residual value, RV_N, in the equation in the previous section.

Asset-Based Valuation

There are three basic variations on the asset-based method:

- Modified (adjusted) book value
- Replacement value
- Liquidation value

Modified book value is appropriate for an established company that is stable or growing slowly. In this case, the value of the company is its book value, which is paid-in equity plus retained earnings or, looked at another way, assets minus liabilities. The problem with taking the book value on the existing balance sheet is that it assumes that accounting records accurately reflect the economic value of the assets and the liabilities. Unfortunately, the accounting of most businesses distorts the economic value of an organization—none more so than private, closely held companies. Hence, we must make adjustments to assets and liabilities before we can determine an accurate value. The major weakness of the modified book value is that it reflects the past instead of the future. It is static, not dynamic, because it is based on existing assets and liabilities rather than future earnings.

Replacement value is appropriate when someone is considering whether to set up a similar business from scratch or to buy an existing business.

Liquidation value is appropriate for a business that has ceased to be a going concern. It might be in bankruptcy, or it might simply be a business for sale that no one is willing to buy as a going concern. Just as the name implies, the valuation of the business is what someone is willing to pay for the assets.

Example of Market-Comparable Valuation

Here is a simplified illustration of market-comparable valuation, which is the most commonly used method for valuing a potential superstar company that is trying to raise venture capital:

Bug-Free Web Software (BFWS), a 12-month-old Internet software company, has successfully beta-tested its product and is seeking $4 million of venture capital to go into full-scale production and distribution. BFWS is forecasting sales revenue of $50 million with net income of $5 million in five years. What percentage of the equity will the venture capitalists require?

To value this company and estimate the amount of equity that the venture capitalists will need to get their required rate of return (internal rate of return or IRR), we need the following:

1. Future earnings (NI)
2. Comparable price-to-earnings ratio (P/E)
3. Amount being invested (at time 0) (INV_0)
4. Risk-adjusted cost of capital (IRR)
5. Number of years before the investment will be harvested (N)

BFWS's financial projections forecast that the net income in five years will be $5 million, so NI is $5 million and N is 5 years. What is the P/E? The P/E will be the average for public companies that are comparable to BFWS. In general, P/E ratios are determined by the rate of growth of a company and of the industry segment the company is in. This is illustrated in Figure 10.1.

In the bottom left corner are companies in slow-growing industries; they grow at approximately the same rate as the industry—for example, automobile manufacturers. If the company is growing faster than the overall industry, its P/E should be higher than the industry average, and if it is growing slower, its P/E should be lower than average (of course,

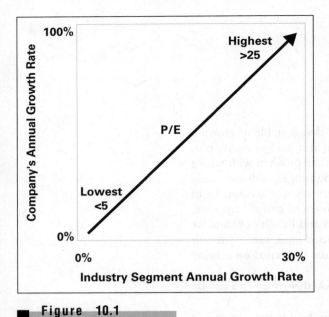

Figure 10.1

Price to earnings

if a company is losing money, its NI is negative, so it does not have a positive P/E ratio, in which case you might use a multiple of revenues). In the upper right corner are rapidly growing companies in high-growth industry segments, which is where BFWS expects to be. As we will see when we discuss venture capital later in this chapter, P/E ratios for superstar software/Internet companies in the top right corner are sometimes much higher than 25, but when valuing a very young company such as BFWS with no history of sales and income, venture capitalists will be conservative and use a P/E of approximately 20.

Using BFWS's financial projections, the future value of the company in five years will be as follows:

$$FV_5 = NI_5 \times (P/E)_5$$
$$FV_5 = NI_5 \times (P/E)_5 = \$5 \text{ million} \times 20 = \$100 \text{ million}$$

We now want to calculate the percentage of the equity that the venture capitalists will need to get their required IRR. The expected return depends on the risk involved. In general, the younger the company, the greater the risk. Figure 10.2 shows the expected IRR for the various stages of a company in which the investment is being made.

A *seed-stage* company is one with not much more than a concept; a *startup* company is one that is already in business and is developing a prototype but has not sold it in significant commercial quantities; a *first-stage* company has developed and market-tested a product and needs capital to initiate full-scale production. *Second-stage* and *third-stage/mezzanine* financings fuels growing companies; and *bridge* financing may be needed to support a company while it is between rounds of financing, often while it waits to go public.

BFWS has a prototype that has successfully passed its beta test and now wants to go into full-scale production, so it is classified as being at the startup stage, where the expected IRR is 60%. Now we need to find out what percentage of BFWS's equity the venture capitalists will need to meet a 60% return. Figure 10.3 shows the percentage of the equity needed to produce a return of 60% on a $4 million investment for various future values (from $20 million to $100 million) and holding periods (from two to eight years).

The future value of BFWS is expected to be $100 million in five years; hence, the venture capitalist will require 42% of BWFS's equity.

The market-comparable valuation formula is as follows:

$$\text{Percentage of Equity} = \frac{INV_0 \times (1 + IRR/100)^N \times 100}{NI_N \times (P/E)_N}$$

Company Stage	Expected Annual Return (IRR)
Seed	80%
Startup	60%
First-stage	50%
Second-stage	40%
Third-stage/Mezzanine	30%
Bridge	25%

Figure 10.2

Expected IRR of investors by stage of investment

Holding Period	Future Value, $million				
Years	20	40	60	80	100
2	51%	26%	17%	13%	10%
3	82%	41%	27%	20%	16%
4	NA	66%	44%	33%	26%
5	NA	NA	70%	52%	42%
6	NA	NA	NA	84%	67%
7	NA	NA	NA	NA	NA
8	NA	NA	NA	NA	NA

■ Figure 10.3

Percentage of equity to produce a 60% IRR on a $4 million investment

Applying this formula to BFWS:

$$\text{Percentage of Equity} = \frac{4,000,000 \times (1 + 60/100)^5 \times 100}{5,000,000 \times 20} = 42\%$$

There is a lot of uncertainty in this computation: Will BFWS achieve the net income it has forecasted? If so, will it reach it in five years, or longer? Will the price-to-earnings ratio for comparable public companies be 20, or higher? Or will it be lower? Will the window for floating IPOs be open in five years, or will it be shut and delay BFWS's IPO? Any of these contingencies will affect the IRR when the venture capitalists harvest their investment in BFWS. Occasionally, a venture-capital-backed company does better than expected. However, more often than not it does not meet its financial forecast; consequently, the actual IRR is usually less than expected.

Asset-Based Valuation Example

Most companies are ordinary rather than glamorous superstars. In this section, we'll examine how to value an ordinary company that does not have the potential to attract venture capital or go public.

Suppose you want to become an entrepreneur by buying out an ordinary business—let's call it XYZ Corporation—that is well established in an industry that is growing about as fast as the overall economy and is an average performer. You will probably hope to buy it for its *modified book value*. The balance sheet for XYZ Corporation is shown in Figure 10.4. It lists the assets and liabilities as they are reported on the latest financial statements. The reported book value (total shareholder equity) is $5,159,000. In the second column are the adjustments that the accountants make to bring the assets and liabilities to actual market value; the footnotes explain the adjustments. The third column shows the restated numbers, which are the reported values (column 1) plus the adjustments (column 2). The restated book value is $6,309,000. That is probably what the seller will ask for the company.

Here are the critical questions the buyer should ask before buying an existing business:

- ▣ What is the growth rate of the industry?
- ▣ By how much is the company's growth rate above or below the industry average?
- ▣ What adjustments need to be made to the income and cash-flow statements and the balance sheet to reflect how the new owners will operate the business?
- ▣ How do the adjusted earnings and cash flows compare with industry averages?
- ▣ How does the balance sheet compare within industry averages (especially debt to equity)?

Assets	As Reported	Adjustments	Restated	Liabilities	As Reported	Adjustments	Restated
Cash	1,500		1,500				
Accounts Receivable (net) (1)	3,300	(100)	3,200	Capitalized Leases	500		500
Inventory (2)	3.419	450	3,869	Long-Term Debt	600		600
TOTAL CURRENT ASSETS	8,219	350	8,569	TOTAL LIABILITIES	4,860	100	4,960
Land and Buildings (3)	1,000	750	1,750				
Machinery & Equipment (4)	750	200	950	SHAREHOLDER EQUITY			
Other Assets (5)	50	(50)	0				
				Capital Stock	500		500
TOTAL ASSETS	10,019	1,250	11,269	Retained Earnings (7)	4,659	1,150	5,809
LIABILITIES							
Accounts Payable	1,700		1,700	TOTAL SHAREHOLDER EQUITY	5,159	1,150	6,309
Short-Term Debt	1,410		1,410				
Accruals (6)	650	100	750				
TOTAL CURRENT LIABILITIES	3,760	100	3,860	TOTAL LIABILITIES & SHAREHOLDER EQUITY	10,019	1,250	11,269

RESTATEMENT NOTES:

(1) Deduct $100 K for uncollectible receivables
(2) LIFO reserve adjustment of inventory to fair market value
(3) MAI appraisal of land & building reflect value of $950 K
(4) Machinery & equipment appraisal reflects current market value of $950 K
(5) Other assets were principally goodwill from expired patents—deduct
(6) Investigation found accruals unrecorded of an additional $100 K
(7) The net pretax effect of change in (1) through (6)

Figure 10.4

XYZ balance sheet adjusted to reflect fair market value of assets and liabilities. ($000s)

◉ How is the purchase being financed, and how will that change the income and cash-flow statements and balance sheet?

◉ How will the new owner's strategies affect the company's future performance?

When these questions have been answered, the buyer should make five-year pro-forma financial statements and do some sensitivity analysis of the critical factors such as sales revenue, cost of sales, and interest and repayment of both the old debt the buyer takes over and any new debt added to help finance the purchase of the business.

Financing a New Venture

The first financing for your new business will come from you and your partners if you have any. It will be cash from your savings and probably from your credit card. According to the GEM study (see Chapter 9), the average amount of startup financing for a new business in the United States is about $60,000, of which about 70% is provided by the entrepreneurs themselves. Perhaps you will also contribute tangible assets such as intellectual capital, like software and patents, and hard assets such as computer equipment. As the company gets under way, you will also be contributing to your company financially by working very long hours for substantially less than the salary you could get working for someone else; seven-day work weeks and 12-hour days are not unusual for entrepreneurs starting up businesses.

Before you turn to family and friends for startup money, you should look at all the possibilities of getting funding from other external sources, just as Jim Poss did. Sources might include the following:

- Services at reduced rates (some accounting and laws firms offer reduced fees to startup companies as a way of getting new clients)
- Vendor financing (getting favorable payment terms from suppliers)
- Customer financing (getting down payments in advance of delivering goods or services)
- Reduced rent from a landlord (some landlords, such as Cummings Properties in Massachusetts,[2] offer entrepreneurs reduced rents or deferred rents for the first six months or perhaps a year)
- An incubator that offers rent and services below market rates
- Leased instead of purchased equipment
- Government programs such as the Small Business Innovation Research awards for technology companies

You probably should talk to a bank. But keep in mind that banks expect loans to be secured by assets, which include the assets of the business and its owner or of someone else, such as a wealthy parent, who is willing to guarantee the loan with personal assets. The U.S. Small Business Administration (SBA) can help when you are unable to secure a bank loan through personal or business assets. When a bank believes that issuing a loan to your small or prospective business would be too risky, you may ask it to apply for an SBA guarantee. If the SBA approves your lender's request, it will guarantee 50%–85% of the loan. You will need to secure the remaining percentage through other means, but SBA support makes you a much more attractive borrower. The SBA will not help you to repay your loan, but in the event that you or your business defaults on the loan, the administration will reimburse the lender for a portion of the remaining principal. If you and your business fit the required criteria, the overall amount that the SBA will guarantee depends upon how you plan to use the proceeds.[3] In 2012, the SBA program provided more than $100 million in loans per day to small businesses.[4] However, even if you qualify for an SBA loan, you will have to guarantee the loan personally, and the bank granting the loan will expect that at least 25% of the startup financing will be owners' equity. This means that, if you want to borrow $75,000 under the SBA program, you must have $25,000 invested in the company. The SBA figure of $100 million loaned per day is impressive, but most of that money goes to existing businesses rather than new companies. An excellent SBA loan FAQ sheet can be found athttp://web.sba.gov/faqs/faqindex.cfm?areaID=19.

There is more information on SBA resources in Chapter 11.

Informal Investors

After you have exhausted all the other potential sources of financing, you should turn to informal investors for help with the initial funding of your new business. As you read in the preceding chapter, informal investors are by far the biggest source of startup financing after the entrepreneurs themselves. In the United States, informal investors provide more than $100 billion per year to startup and young businesses.[5] Approximately 50% of informal investment goes to a relative's business, 28.5% to a friend's or neighbor's, 6.1% to a work colleague's, and 9.4% to a stranger's.[6] In this section, we will look at informal investors who are inexperienced when it comes to funding startup companies; in the next section, we will look at an important subset of informal investors, business angels, who are more sophisticated.

Half of all informal investors in the United States expect to get their money back in two years or sooner, according to the GEM study. This suggests that they regard their money as a short-term loan instead of a long-term equity investment. We are using the term *investment* loosely in this context because it may be more like a loan rather than a formal investment. Whether it is a loan or an equity investment, the downside financial risk in the worst case is the same because, if the business fails, the informal investors will lose all their money. It is important to make clear to informal investors what the risks are. If you have a business plan, you should give them a copy and ask them to read it. But assume that they probably will not read it thoroughly; hence, you should make sure you have discussed the risks with them. A guiding principle when dealing with family and friends is not to take their money unless they assure you they can afford to lose their entire investment without seriously hurting their standard of living. It may be tempting to borrow from relatives and friends because the interest rate is favorable and the terms of the loan are not as strict as they would be from a bank, but if things go wrong, your relationship might be seriously impaired, perhaps even ended.

How should you treat money that a relative or friend puts into your business in the early days? At the beginning, the business has no operating experience, and it is very uncertain what the outcome will be. Thus, it is extremely difficult—maybe impossible—to place a valuation on the fledgling venture. It is probably better to treat money from friends and family as a loan rather than as an equity investment. As in any loan, you should pay interest, but to conserve cash flow in the first year or two, make the interest payable in a lump sum at the end of the loan rather than in monthly installments. You should give the loan holders the option of converting the loan into equity during the life of the loan. In that way, they can share in the upside if your company turns out to have star potential, with the possibility of substantial capital gains for the investors.

When you are dealing with relatively small amounts of money from relatives and friends—especially close family such as parents, brothers, and sisters—you may not need a formal loan agreement, particularly if you ask for money when you are under pressure because your business is out of cash. But at a minimum, you should record the loan in writing, with perhaps nothing more than a letter or a note. If you want something more formal, Virgin Money US sets up loan agreements for small businesses with informal investors.[7] A documented loan agreement could be important if you subsequently start dealing with professional investors such as sophisticated business angels and venture capitalists.

Crowdfunding. The JOBS (Jumpstart Our Business Startups) Act of 2012 and its amendment the Crowdfund Act, enables startups and small and mid-sized businesses to use SEC-approved crowdfunding portals to raise money from anyone online. The crowdfunding provision creates an exemption that will let a company sell up to $1 million in unregistered stock every 12 months to an unlimited number of investors who need not be accredited.

The transaction must go through an intermediary, either a broker or a funding portal. The intermediary must register with the SEC and a self-regulatory organization, make sure investors understand the risks, and conduct a background check on the company's officers, directors, and large shareholders. They are also supposed to make sure investors don't exceed their investing limit. The most one person can invest in all crowdfunded securities combined in one year is: The greater of $2,000 or 5% of annual income or net worth (excluding a home) if the person's annual gross income or net worth is less than $100,000, or 10% of annual income or net worth, up to $100,000, if the person's income or net worth is at least $100,000.[8]

Crowdfunding or crowd financing of a business in exchange for equity will be legal as soon as the SEC promulgates its rules,[9] which originally were expected to be announced in Janaury 2013, but were delayed[10] and had not been released by August 2013.

Crowdfunding has been used to finance not just businesses but a diversity of endeavors including disaster relief, movie production, and political campaigns. An early example was in 1997, when fans underwrote an entire U.S. tour for the British rock group Marillion, raising $60,000 in donations by means of a fan-based Internet campaign. The idea was conceived and managed by fans without any involvement by the band.[11]

Entrepreneurs were using crowdfunding before the JOBS Act but were not allowed to give equity in exchange for cash; instead they usually gave a product or service. For example, Impossible Instant Lab raised $559,232 from 2,509 backers to support the development and production of a device that will "transform your digital iPhone images into real instant photographs that you can touch, caress, and share with friends." In return for their cash, backers were to receive the product at a discounted price or free depending on their level of financing; estimated delivery date was February 2013. Fundraising commenced on September 10, 2012, and when it closed 28 days later, had raised more than twice the original goal of $250,000.[12] The shipping date was subsequently rescheduled to August 29, 2013. The company's founder and CEO Doc Florian Kaps 'retired' on July 3, 2013.

The Crowdfund Act, when it is put into effect, has the potential to trigger a revolution in the way that entrepreneurs raise funds for their new ventures. Not surprisingly, financial entrepreneurs have already set up crowdfunding platforms in advance of the SEC regulations. Funding platforms will take a percentage of the money that they raise online for a company. Portals such as Crowdfunder.com and WeFunder.com are claiming that they already have millions of dollars committed for investing in startups.[13] But it remains to see how many entrepreneurs successfully raise capital through crowdfunding portals. Not all entrepreneurs are enthusiastic about soliciting small investments online. A 2012 survey found that only 9% of Inc. 500 CEOs were likely to raise money that way while 72% were not.

Business Angels

In the previous chapter, you saw that informal investors are most likely to be entrepreneurs. In the case of the funding of Apple, Google, and many other companies not as famous, such as BigBelly Solar, wealthy entrepreneurs play a key role in the funding of many new ventures. We call those types of informal investors **business angels**.

Business angels fund many more entrepreneurial firms than venture capitalists do.[14] Angels invest in seed-stage and very early-stage companies that are not yet mature enough for formal venture capital or companies that need financing in amounts too small to justify the venture capitalist's costs, including evaluation, due diligence, and legal fees.

We do not know how many wealthy persons are business angels, but we do know that Securities and Exchange Commission (SEC) Rule 501 defines an "accredited investor" as a person with a net worth of at least $1 million, or annual income of at least $200,000 in the most recent two years, or combined income with a spouse of $300,000 during those years. According to Forrester Consulting, the number of households in the United States that fit that profile is approximately 630,000.[15] So that is the number of business angels qualified to invest in private offerings governed by SEC rules.

Angels on Broadway: The Color Purple[16]

The term *angel* was first used in a financial context to describe individual investors who put up money to produce new plays and musicals in the theater. Putting together a new theatrical production is not unlike starting up a high-potential business. It costs between $10 million and $12 million to produce a Broadway musical. Occasionally, a show is a gigantic success, for example, *Cats*, but more often than not it either fails or is mediocre. Seventy-five percent of Broadway shows fail.[17] It is said that you can make a killing on Broadway, but you can't make a living—in contrast to Wall Street, where you can make a steady living with an occasional killing.

The musical version of *The Color Purple* opened on Broadway in December 2005—eight years after producer, Scott Sanders, first recognized the opportunity of producing a musical stage version of Stephen Spielberg's 1985 movie, in which Oprah Winfrey was one of the stars. Oprah called it one of the greatest experiences of her life. After Sanders persuaded the author,

the production, attending rehearsals and management meetings. Then when the show was fully financed,

Peter Kramer/Getty Images

Author Alice Walker (L), Producer Scott Sanders, TV Personality Oprah Winfrey and actor LaChanze at the curtain call for *The Color Purple* at the Broadway Theater on December 1, 2005 in New York City.

Alice Walker, to allow him to produce a musical based on her 1982 Pulitzer Prize–winning novel, Walker wrote to Oprah in 1997 and asked her "to do a little angel work for the show." But there was no response from Oprah until July 2005.

In the meantime, Sanders had raised almost all the $11 million needed to put the show on Broadway. He put in some of his own money; then in 2002 he raised $2 million from AEG Live—a strategic partner—with a commitment for another $2 million of follow-on investment. With the initial $2 million he produced a month-long trial run of *The Color Purple* in Atlanta to sold-out audiences and standing ovations in 2004. This attracted Roy Furman, a Wall Street financier and frequent Broadway angel, who had worked with Sanders in the past. Furman agreed to raise half the $11 million that Sanders needed and made a seven-figure investment himself. Furman took an active interest in

Oprah called. She agreed to allow Sanders to put, "Oprah Winfrey presents *The Color Purple*" on the theater marquee. To make room for Oprah to invest $1 million, other investors' commitments were trimmed. Oprah also offered to feature a couple of songs from the musical on her hugely successful TV show. A book endorsement by Oprah almost guaranteed a place on the best-sellers list; Sanders and Furman hoped that by featuring *The Color Purple* on her show, Oprah would help to make it a Broadway hit.

Sanders and Furman estimated that if the average audience was 75% of full capacity in the 1,718-seat Broadway Theatre, *The Color Purple* would pay back the original investment in 12 months. Five months after its opening, *The Color Purple* was grossing more than $1 million a week, making it one of the top five shows on Broadway. The show recouped its investment within the first year and grossed more than $100 million before it closed on Broadway in 2008.[18]

Searching for Business Angels

Most nascent entrepreneurs do not know anyone who is a business angel, so how should they search for one? The good news is that today there are "formal" angel groups, which are angels who have joined together to seek and invest in young companies. Most of them are wealthy entrepreneurs; some are still running their businesses, while others are retired. Angel investor groups have been around for many years, but they started to proliferate in the late 1990s when it seemed as if everyone was trying to make a fortune by getting in early on investments in Internet-related startups. Although many angels lost a lot of money on their investments when the Internet bubble burst, angel groups continued investing in seed- and early-stage companies, albeit at a much reduced rate.[19]

Angel groups have different ways of selecting potential companies to invest in. A few groups consider only opportunities that are referred to them, but most welcome unsolicited business plans from entrepreneurs. They evaluate the plans and invite the entrepreneurs with the most promising ones to make a presentation to the group at one of their periodic (usually monthly) meetings. A few of those presentations eventually result in investments by some of the angels in the group. Some groups charge the entrepreneurs a fee to make a presentation, and a few even require a fee when an entrepreneur submits a business plan. The size of each investment ranges from less than $100,000 to as much as $2 million—and in a few instances, considerably more.

Important as angel groups have become, they comprise only a few thousand investors compared with hundreds of thousands of business angels who invest on their own. Entrepreneurs are much more likely to raise money from angels who invest individually rather than in packs. Unfortunately, individual business angels are very hard to find. Searching for them requires extensive networking. But according to Bill Wetzel, professor emeritus at the University of New Hampshire who pioneered research into angel investing and who started the first angel investment network as the forerunner of ACE-Net (Angel Capital Investment Network), "Once you find one angel investor, you have probably found another half dozen."[20]

Consider how other entrepreneurs found business angels. Steve Jobs and Stephen Wozniak found Armas Markkula through an introduction by a venture capitalist who looked at Apple and decided it was too early for him to invest. Sergey Brin and Larry Page were introduced to Andy Bechtolsheim by a Stanford University faculty member. Jim Poss worked for Spire Corporation and got to know Roger Little, founder and CEO of Spire and a leading expert on solar power; he met another of his angel investors at a wind energy conference sponsored by Brown Rudnick. When a leader in an industry related to the one the new company is entering becomes a business angel, it sends an important signal to other potential investors. For instance, once Andy Bechtolsheim had invested in Google, Brin and Page soon put together $1 million of funding. And Jim Poss's parents said they would invest only if Roger Little invested.

Types of Business Angels

Business angels range from silent investors who sit back and wait patiently for results, to others who want to be involved in the operations of the company, as a part-time consultant or as a full-time partner. Richard Bendis classifies business angels in the following categories: entrepreneurial, corporate, professional, enthusiast, and micromanagement.[21]

Entrepreneurial angels have started their own businesses and are looking to invest in new businesses. Some have realized substantial capital gains by taking their companies public or merging them with other companies. Others are still running their businesses full-time and have sufficient income to be business angels. In general, entrepreneurial angels are the most valuable to the new venture because they are usually knowledgeable about the industry, and just as important, they have built substantial businesses from the ground up and so understand the challenges that entrepreneurs face. They can be invaluable advisors and mentors. Armas "Mike" Markkula is a famous example of a business angel who had made his fortune in two entrepreneurial companies, first Fairchild and then Intel. He had "retired" at the age of 38 when Steve Jobs and Stephen Wozniak were introduced to him. He invested in Apple; worked with Steve Jobs to write Apple's first business plan; secured a bank line of credit; helped raise venture capital; recruited Michael Scott, Apple's first president; and then became president himself from 1981 to 1983. According to Stephen Wozniak, "Steve [Jobs] and I get a lot of credit, but Mike Markkula was probably more responsible for our early success, and you never hear about him."[22]

Corporate angels are managers of larger corporations who invest from their savings and current income. Some are looking to invest in a startup and become part of the full-time management team. Corporate angels who have built their careers in big, multinational corporations can be a problem for a neophyte entrepreneur because they know a lot about managing companies with vast resources but have never worked in a small company with very limited resources. Here is an example of what might go wrong: A fish-importing wholesaler was started and run by two young men. The company grew fast, but it ran out of working capital. Two angels, one of them a marketing executive with a huge multinational food company, invested $500,000 on condition that the young company hire the marketing executive as its marketing/sales vice president. Very soon there was a clash of cultures. The founders continued to work 12-hour days, while the new vice president was traveling first class and staying in fancy hotels when he made sales trips. Within a year, the business angels took control of the company. The two founders left, and a year later it closed its doors.

Professional angels are doctors, dentists, lawyers, accountants, consultants, and even professors who have substantial savings and incomes and invest some of their money in startups. Generally, they are silent partners, although a few of them, especially consultants, expect to be retained by the company as paid advisors.

Enthusiast angels are retired or semiretired entrepreneurs and executives who are wealthy enough to invest in startups as a hobby. It is a way for them to stay involved in business without any day-to-day responsibilities. They are usually passive investors who invest relatively small amounts in several companies.

Micromanagement angels are entrepreneurs who have been successful with their own companies and have strong views on how the companies they invest in should be run. They want to be a director or a member of the board of advisors and get regular updates on the operations of the company. They do not hesitate to intervene in the running of the business if it does not perform as expected.

There is no ideal type of business angel. And in general, most entrepreneurs cannot pick and choose because it is so hard to find business angels who are prepared to invest. But just as a wise angel will carefully investigate the entrepreneur before investing, likewise a smart entrepreneur will find out as much as possible about a potential business angel. There is probably no better source of information than other entrepreneurs in whom the angel has previously invested. Ask the business angel whether he or she has invested in other entrepreneurs and whether you may talk with them.

Putting Together a Round of Angel Investment

If you're raising a round of investment from business angels, you'll need a lawyer knowledgeable in this area because there are various SEC rules that you need to comply with. The SEC Web site has a good brochure on private placements that you should read.[23] Most private placements by startup entrepreneurs are made under Regulation D, Rule 504, dealing with offerings up to $1 million; fewer are made under Rule 505, dealing with offerings up to $5 million. (There is a brief explanation of these in Chapter 12 on legal and tax issues.)

The first thing you'll want to do is place a value on your startup. Valuation of a seed-stage company is more art than science. It's also very subjective, with entrepreneurs placing a substantially higher value than business angels. Informed business angels will determine the value based on similar deals made by other angels and venture capital firms. The comparable-market valuation method will provide a back-of-the-envelope estimate to see whether the company has a chance of meeting the business angel's required return.

In general, business angels are satisfied with a lower return than venture capitalists are because, unlike venture capitalists, they have only minimal operating costs and they do not have to pay themselves carried interest on any capital gains. You saw in Chapter 9 that venture capitalists charge as much as 3% per year on the money they invest, and on top of that, they deduct carried interest of 20%—sometimes more—from the capital gain they pass on to their investors. So, to produce a return of 25% for their investors, venture capitalists need to get a return of 35% or more from their investment portfolio. According to Wainwright, business angels expect an IRR of 15% to 25%, with a payback time between five and seven years.[24] A Massachusetts Institute of Technology (MIT) study found that the business angels expected returns between 3:1 and 10:1 on their investments and that actual returns ranged from losses on 32% of their investments to higher than 10:1 on 23%.[25] The same MIT study found that business angels were evenly split between preferring IPOs and acquisitions as their exit strategy; none preferred a buyback. In practice, 27% of business angel investments ended with an IPO, 35% with an acquisition, and 5% with a buyback, and 32% were losses.

While financial returns are very important to business angels, they also invest for nonfinancial reasons. These include a desire to give back and mentor budding entrepreneurs, to be involved in startups without total immersion, to have fun, to be part of a network of other business angels, to stay abreast of new commercial developments, to be involved with the development of products and services that benefit society, and to invest in entrepreneurs without the pressure of being a full-time venture capitalist.[26]

Most angel investments are for preferred stock convertible into common stock on a 1-to-1 ratio. Preferred stock gives investors priority rights over founders' common stock, which relates to liquidation and voting. The potential problem with convertible preferred stock is that it sets a valuation on the stock at the first round. If that valuation turns out to be higher than the venture capitalist's valuation at the second round, negotiations between the venture capitalist and the entrepreneur will be difficult. The shortfall might even be a deal breaker.

Jim Poss placed a pre-money valuation of $2.5 million on BigBelly Solar when he was raising his first round of funding from business angels. He raised $250,000, so the post-money valuation was $2.75 million. Investors would have owned 9.1% (250,000/2,750,000 × 100%) of the equity if Jim had issued stock. But instead of stock, he issued convertible debt. Some seed-stage companies that expect to get venture capital investment in later rounds of financing use convertible debt rather than convertible preferred stock. **Convertible debt** is a bridge loan that converts to equity at the next round of investment, assuming that it is an equity round. Convertible debt securities allow the next-round investors, who are usually venture capitalists, to set the value of the company and provide the first-round angel investors with a discount. Business angels would like to get a 30% discount, but actual discounts range from 10% to 30%. Convertible debt has the advantage over convertible preferred stock because it reduces or eliminates squabbling over the valuation between venture capitalists and the entrepreneur on behalf of the angels.[27]

The major conditions of a proposed deal are spelled out in a term sheet. Three examples of business angel term sheets are found in *Venture Support Systems Project: Angel Investors*.[28]

Venture Capital

Over the four years from 2009 to 2012, a total of 4,393 companies received venture capital for the first time—for a yearly average of only 1,098 companies—and most of those were not seed- or startup-stage companies.[29] The reality is that a person has a better chance of winning $1 million or more in a lottery than getting seed- or startup-stage venture capital.[30] It is extremely rare that entrepreneurs have venture capital in hand when their new businesses begin operating.

Venture capital is almost always invested in companies that are already in business and have demonstrated the potential to become stars or, better yet, superstars in their industry. Nothing excites venture capitalists more than a company with a product or service that is already being bought by satisfied customers. Venture capital accelerates the commercialization of new products and services; it seldom pays for the initial development of concepts. It is also important to keep in mind that the bulk of venture capital in the United States goes to high-technology-based companies. In 2012, for example, 44% of the companies that received venture capital were in the information technology sector (including the 25% that were Internet-related), 26% were in medical/life sciences, 12% were classified as cleantech; only 16% were not high-technology companies.[31]

Candidates for Venture Capital

Here, in order of importance, are the six top factors venture capitalists look at when evaluating a candidate for investment:[32]

1. Management team
2. Target market
3. Product/service
4. Competitive positioning
5. Financial returns
6. Business plan

Management Team. We've said that the crucial ingredients for entrepreneurial success are a superb entrepreneur with a first-rate management team and an excellent market opportunity. Entrepreneurs should have most of the startup team identified before they approach venture capitalists. If they are sufficiently impressed with the progress a startup company has made, venture capitalists will sometimes help recruit a key member of the team. They will even help recruit a new CEO if they have reservations about the lead entrepreneur's ability to build a rapidly growing company with the potential to go public. The best venture capitalists have extensive contacts with potential candidates for management positions in their portfolio companies.

Target Market. The target market should be fragmented, accessible, and growing rapidly. The Internet triggered a stampede of venture capital investing in the late 1990s because it promised to become a huge market with many different segments; there were no dominant players in the new segments, and the segments were readily accessible to new entrants.

" . . . there's plenty of technology, market opportunity, and venture capital, but too few great entrepreneurs and teams [in 2004]."[33]
— *John Doerr, legendary venture capitalist, Kleiner Perkins Caufield & Byers*

Product/Service. The product or service should be better than competing products or services, and it should be protected with patents or copyrights, as appropriate. It does not have to be the first product in its market segment. For example, Google was not the first Web search engine; it simply was superior to the existing ones. Again, it is important to stress that a company with a working prototype—or better yet, satisfied customers—has a much better chance of raising venture capital than does an entrepreneur with just an idea and a business plan.

Competitive Positioning. There is no dominant competitor in the market niche. Distribution channels are open. And the company has an experienced marketing manager with expert knowledge of market segment. SolidWorks positioned its CAD/CAM software in a niche where it was difficult for well-established competitors, especially Parametric Technology, to move in without cannibalizing their business models.

Financial Returns. The potential financial return is important, but classic venture capital does not depend on sophisticated financial computations. Venture capitalists have a rule of thumb for early- and expansion-stage companies—they will invest only if the company has the potential to return at least seven times their investment in five years—in venture capital jargon, "seven x" in five years. A 7x return in five years produces an IRR of 47.6%; a 10x return in five years produces an IRR of 58.5%.

Business Plan. Every entrepreneur seeking money from business angels or professional venture capitalists must have a competent written business plan. But no matter how good a business plan may be, it will not impress investors nearly as much as a product or service that is already being sold to customers. Too many entrepreneurs spend too much effort refining and polishing their business plans rather than implementing their businesses.

Ideal Candidates for Venture Capital

The *ideal* candidate for a first round of venture capital meets the following criteria:

- CEO/lead entrepreneur has significant management and entrepreneurial experience with demonstrated ability to manage a rapidly growing company in a fast-paced industry segment.
- Vice president of engineering is recognized as a star in the industry (if it is a technology-based business).
- Vice president of marketing has a proven track record.
- Some members of the top management team have worked together before.
- The product/service is better than those of its competitors.
- Intellectual capital such as patents and copyrights is protected.
- The market segment is fragmented, growing rapidly, and expected to be big.
- There are no dominant competitors.
- The company has satisfied customers.
- The company projects sales of $50 million in five years.
- The gross income margin is expected to be better than 60%, with a net income margin better than 10%.
- The amount of investment is between $5 million and $10 million.
- The company has the potential to go public in five years.
- Potential return of 7x or higher.
- IRR of 60% or higher.

Actual Venture-Capital-Backed Companies

Venture-capital-backed companies that have IPOs are the cream of the crop, so by examining profiles of companies at the time they go public, we can see how the best companies measure

	Medians			
	Internet	Software	Hardware	Semiconductor
Marketing and Operations				
Market Growth Rate	135.7%	23.5%	37.5%	15.5%
Annual Sales Growth Trend (all years)	87.0%	54.3%	55.7%	24.7%
Sales Growth Trend (12 months)	93.3%	45.9%	54.3%	30.1%
Annualized Sales Revenue	$9,720,000	$23,396,000	$27,268,000	$39,940,000
Gross Margin	72.7%	75.6%	39.1%	42.2%
Profit Margin	−36.7%	3.4%	−0.5%	7.9%
Net Income (last year)	($2,414,530)	$308,000	($639,000)	$1,495,000
Net Income (last quarter annualized)	($3,462,921)	$1,644,000	$2,140,000	$3,226,000
R&D Ratio	27.0%	18.4%	14.5%	14.6%
# of Employees	124	134	92	213
Financial				
IRR	506.9%	124.8%	148.0%	30.5%
Times Return	7.16	6.67	10.71	4.94
Years from 1st VC Investment to IPO	0.96	2.53	4.04	5.00
Time from Incorporation to IPO	5	8	7	11
Price/Share 1st Round of VC	$1.25	$1.50	$1.13	$2.79
IPO Price	$14	$12	$10	$11
P/E Ratio	70	54	32	26
Size of IPO	$34,000,000	$27,600,000	$22,320,000	$29,130,000
Market Capitalization after IPO	$163,488,290	$105,510,812	$89,244,768	$77,468,542

■ **Figure 10.5**

Venture-capital-backed public companies

up to the ideal. Figure 10.5 shows the results of a study of 122 venture-backed-companies that went public in the years 1994–1997,[34] when the stock market indices were rising but before the Internet bubble (which ran from the end of 1997 to the beginning of 2001).

The management of those companies came close to the ideal. For instance, half of the top management teams had a combined 114 years of experience or more. Seventy-one percent of the companies had at least one founder with previous startup experience. And in about two-thirds of the companies, two or more founders had worked together before starting their present venture.

Market and operating performance at the time of the IPO was quite different among the industry segments (see Figure 10.5). The industry segments appear in order of their maturity from left to right, with the Internet being the least mature and the semiconductor the most mature. Much of the difference between companies in the four industries is explained by the maturity of their industry segment. The Internet market segments were growing much faster than were the semiconductor ones, as was the annual growth rate of sales revenue. There was a big difference between the characteristics of Internet and semiconductor companies.

Internet companies had the least sales revenue at the time of the IPO and semiconductor companies the most. None of the four segments attained the ideal of at least $50 million in annual sales revenue. Not one of the industry segments met the net income margin of at least 10% prescribed for the ideal, but the Internet and software companies exceeded the gross margin requirement of at least 60%, whereas the hardware and semiconductor companies fell short. In all segments except the Internet, the annualized net income improved dramatically in the quarter before the IPO.

However, despite the shortcomings on sales revenue and net income, the venture capitalists met their hoped-for times return on the first round of venture capital in all industries except semiconductors. And their IRR handily topped their expectations. The median IRR for Internet companies was a whopping 507% because they went public only one year after they received their first round of venture capital. In contrast, five years elapsed for semiconductor companies between the first round of venture capital and the IPO. So, although the times return in the semiconductor segment was almost 5 compared with just over 7 in the Internet segment, the IRR in semiconductors was only 30.5% because the longer an investment is held, the lower the IRR. The P/E ratios were 70 for the Internet companies that were profitable, 54 for software, 32 for hardware, and 26 for semiconductors. The differences in the P/E ratios mainly explain the differences in market capitalization among the different industry segments.

What does this mean for entrepreneurs who are seeking venture capital? First, there is not one set of ideal criteria for a company, but there are tendencies based on the industry sector. Second, the management team must be excellent. Third, the faster the growth of the industry and the growth of the company, the more likely it is to get the attention of venture capitalists. Fourth, entrepreneurs should focus on sales growth rather than profitability in the first few years and then show a profitability spurt in the year before the IPO. Fifth, on average, companies are several years old and have developed products or services before they get their first venture capital investment.

Dealing with Venture Capitalists

The first big challenge for an entrepreneur is reaching a venture capitalist. It is easy to get names and contact information for almost every venture capital firm from the Internet and subscription data sources such as VentureXpert.[35] However, venture capital firms pay much more attention to entrepreneurs who are referred to them than to unsolicited business plans that arrive by mail or email. Entrepreneurs are referred to venture capitalists by accountants, lawyers, bankers, other entrepreneurs, consultants, professors, business angels, and anyone else in contact with venture capitalists. But most of them are reluctant to recommend an entrepreneur to a venture capitalist unless they are confident that the entrepreneur is a good candidate for venture capital.

Entrepreneurs should be wary of "finders" who offer to raise venture capital for the entrepreneur. Most venture capitalists do not like dealing with finders because they charge the company a fee based on the amount of money raised—a fee that comes out of the money the venture capitalists invest in the company. What's more, it's the entrepreneur, not the finder, who has to deal with the venture capitalists.

If the entrepreneur is fortunate enough to find a venture capitalist who would like to learn more about the new business, a meeting will take place at either the company's or the venture capital firm's office. The first meeting is usually an informal discussion of the business with one of the partners of the venture capital firm. If the partner decides to pursue the opportunity, he or she will discuss it with more of the partners; if they like the opportunity, they will invite the entrepreneur to make a formal presentation to several partners in the firm. This meeting is the crucial one, so it is important to make as good a presentation as possible. Not only are the venture capital partners assessing the company and its product or service, but also they are carefully scrutinizing the entrepreneur and other team members to see whether they have the right stuff to build a company that can go public.

If the venture capital partners like what they see and hear at this meeting, the firm will pursue the entrepreneur with the intent to invest and will begin its due diligence on the entrepreneur, other team members, and the company. Entrepreneurs who get to this stage will be evaluated as never before in their lives. It is not unusual for a venture capital firm to check dozens of references on the entrepreneur. Any suggestion of dubious conduct by the entrepreneur will be investigated. After all, the entrepreneur is asking the venture capital

VENTURE CAPITAL IS "RELATIONSHIP" CAPITAL

Brook Byers and Ray Lane, talking about how Kleiner Perkins Caufield & Byers helps entrepreneurs:[36]

Brook Byers (referring to Kleiner Perkins Caufield & Byers' network): It's not keiretsu, it's relationship capital.

Ray Lane: Whether you call it a network, a Rolodex, keiretsu, or whatever, it is something that entrepreneurs crave, because they're looking for help. As Brook said, money is not a differentiator in our business, but they're looking for help. Either you have knowledge in their domain, and you can help them get from startup to a company that actually gets something in the market, or you help them scale through relationships. In this world, at least in the enterprise world, it helps to know somebody.

firm to trust him or her with several million dollars that in most cases is not secured by any collateral. All entrepreneurs should get a copy of their credit reports and be prepared to explain any delinquencies.

Entrepreneurs who get to this stage may be wondering whether the venture capital firm is the right one for them and be tempted to approach other venture capital firms to see what they might offer. But instead, they should conduct due diligence on the venture capital firm. Ask for a list of the entrepreneurs the firm has invested in and permission to speak with them. Here are some things to look for.

Value Added. The best venture capitalists bring more than money to their portfolio companies.[37] They bring what they call *value added*, which includes help with recruiting key members of management, strategic advice, industry contacts, and professional contacts such as accountants, lawyers, entrepreneurs, consultants, other venture capitalists, commercial bankers, and investment bankers.

Patience. Some venture capital firms, especially newer ones with relatively inexperienced partners, are more likely to get impatient when a portfolio company fails to meet expectations. Studies of venture-capital-backed companies that have not yet gone public or been acquired find that approximately 50% to 60% of them have changed CEOs at some time after the first round of venture capital;[38] only 18% of those that have had IPOs have changed CEOs.[39] Another indication of lack of patience is a venture capital firm quick to invoke covenants in the investment agreement, which contains a couple of hundred pages. There are all manner of covenants in those agreements, and it is not unusual for a company to violate one or perhaps more. An experienced venture capitalist will usually waive a covenant unless the violation is so severe that it jeopardizes the viability of the company.

Deep Pockets. Will the firm have enough money to invest in follow-on rounds of venture capital if the company needs them? Venture capital firms that have been in business for a long time have established a reputation of producing good returns for their limited partners, so they are able to raise new funds from time to time. In contrast, a young venture capital firm with only one small fund without a proven track record of producing satisfactory returns for its limited partners will have difficulty raising a second fund.

Board of Directors. Does the venture capitalist sit on the board and regularly attend meetings? How often does the board meet? And how many boards does the venture capitalist serve on? A rule of thumb is that a venture capitalist should not be on more than half a dozen boards of portfolio companies.

Accessibility. Is the venture capitalist readily available when the entrepreneur needs advice? Conversely, does the venture capitalist interfere too much in the day-to-day running of the company?

Negotiating the Deal

The valuation of the company is probably the biggest issue to be negotiated. Generally, the entrepreneur's valuation is higher than the venture capitalist's. Entrepreneurs can make valuations of the company based on computations like the one earlier in this chapter for

BFWS; they can also talk to other entrepreneurs who have recently received venture capital. In general, venture capitalists have more information about pricing than entrepreneurs do because they know the valuations of similar deals that have been recently completed, and those will be the basis for the valuation.

Let's return to BFWS. The entrepreneur's calculations show that the venture capital firm will be looking for 42% of the equity after it has put in its $4 million. Hence, the company will be worth $9.42 million ($4 million/0.42) after the money has been invested—what is called the *post-money valuation*. The pre-money valuation is thus $5.42 million ($9.42 million − $4 million).

The venture capitalist knows that comparable deals have been valued at $4 million pre-money. So the venture capitalist needs 50% of the equity post-money. After negotiations, the entrepreneur and the venture capitalist settle on a pre-money valuation of $4.5 million for BFWS, which means that the venture capitalist will get 47.1% of the equity, with a post-money valuation of $8.5 million, and the entrepreneurs and any angel investors who have already put money into BFWS will be left with 52.9%. The venture capitalists will expect that a pool of stock, about 15% of the issue, will be reserved for key employees who will be hired in the future.

The next step is for the venture capitalist to provide a *term sheet* listing the main conditions of the deal. (You can find samples on the Web.[40]) The term sheet will specify how much money the venture capital firm is investing, how much stock it is getting, a detailed listing of all the stock issued or reserved for stock options *before* the venture capital is invested—and *after*. The venture capitalists will in almost every case get convertible preferred stock. The rights of the preferred stock will be spelled out; they will include dividend provisions, liquidation preferences, conversion rights (usually one share of preferred stock converts to one share of common stock), antidilution provisions, voting rights, and protective provisions.

The term sheet will also have clauses covering information rights, such as a requirement for the company to supply timely unaudited quarterly and audited annual financial statements, board membership, a description of how the venture capital will be used, employment agreements, stock registration rights, and terms under which management can sell stock privately. It will also specify the date when the deal will close.

Term sheet provisions are subject to negotiation. But the sheet will contain a date and time when the venture capitalist's offer will expire unless the entrepreneur has accepted the offer in writing.

Follow-On Rounds of Venture Capital

It is quite likely that there will be subsequent rounds of venture capital. In 2012, for instance, 1,163 companies received first-round venture capital financing and 2,535 received follow-on financing in the United States. Let's see what might happen in a second round of financing for BFWS.

Two years after the first round of venture capital, BFWS has met its milestones set out in its business plan, so the venture capitalists are happy. They had expected that the company would go public to raise more money, but the IPO window is closed (as it was in 2002 and 2003, after the Internet bubble burst and investors lost their appetite for IPO stocks not only of Internet-related companies but also of information technology companies in general). BFWS estimates it needs $6 million to stay on its rapid-growth trajectory for the next two years, when it hopes the IPO window will again be open.

When a company has met its milestones, its valuation has increased. It's not unusual for venture capitalists to agree to a valuation three times what it was at the first round. BFWS will be talking both to its present venture capitalists, who will be eager to invest in a second round, and to other venture capitalists so as to get more than one valuation. We'll assume the deal will be struck at a pre-money valuation three times the post-money valuation of the first round, or $25.5 million (3 × $8.5 million). The post-money valuation will be $31.5 million.

So the venture capitalist will get an additional 19% of the stock for his $6 million investment at the second round of financing. If all goes well and the IPO window opens up during the next two years, BFWS expects to go public.

Harvesting Investments

When business angels or venture capitalists put money into a business, there has to be a way they can realize their investments at a future date. This is called the exit or harvest for the investor. There are three ways to exit an investment: an initial public offering, an acquisition, and a buyback of the investor's stock by the company itself. We've mentioned that most investors prefer an IPO because it produces the highest valuation in most cases—but not in every case. An acquisition is the second choice. And a buyback is a distant third because in almost every instance it produces a mediocre return.

One of the questions neophyte entrepreneurs seeking external equity financing most often ask is, "Can I buy back the investors' equity?" The answer is, "In principle yes, but in practice it is extremely unlikely." Buybacks are rare because a successful and rapidly growing company needs all the cash it can get just to keep on its growth trajectory. It has no free cash to buy out its external investors. A firm doing a buyback is more likely to be one of the living dead for which an IPO or acquisition is not feasible, but somehow the company arranges a refinancing in which it buys back the stock owned by the original investors. Sometimes a venture capital agreement includes a redemption (buyback) clause that allows the venture capital firm to exit its investment by selling it back to the company at a premium if an IPO or acquisition does not occur within a specified time period.

Initial Public Offering

Only a miniscule number of companies raise money with a firm commitment IPO.[41] Over the period 2009–2012, 189 venture-capital-backed companies went public, which averages out at only 47 IPOs per year.[42] (In 2011, 35% of all IPOs were by venture-capital-backed companies.) As we saw in the previous chapter, roughly 7% of companies backed with venture capital have gone public since 1970. Figure 10.6 shows the funding filters that most venture-capital-backed companies must pass through to get to an IPO.

Without doubt, IPOs are glamorous and generally yield the biggest returns for the pre-IPO investors, but in the long run, they're not always satisfactory for the entrepreneurs and the management team, for a variety of reasons. Granted, many entrepreneurs such as Bill Gates (Microsoft), Larry Ellison (Oracle), Robert Noyce and Gordon Moore (Intel), Bernie Marcus and Arthur Blank (Home Depot), and Sergey Brin and Larry Page (Google) took their companies public and never looked back, but that is not always the case.

Joey Crugnale took his small chain of brick-oven pizza restaurants, Bertucci's, public in 1991 at $13 per share. But he was unable to satisfy Wall Street's appetite for ever-increasing sales and earnings. By 1998, Bertucci's stock, which at one time peaked at $25, was languishing at $6. Crugnale decided that he wanted to take his company private so that he would be free from the continual scrutiny of investors. He made an offer to buy out the investors for $8 per share. He knew that, once he proposed to buy back the company, there was a possibility other companies might bid for it, but he assumed that was very unlikely because he founded the company and he ran it. He soon found out his assumption was wrong. Quite unexpectedly, New England Restaurant Company handily topped his offer with a bid of $10.50 per share. Crugnale agonized over it but decided not to make a counteroffer. He walked away from Bertucci's a wealthy man at 46, but with a feeling of loss because he no longer was running the business he had built from scratch into a chain of 84 restaurants in 11 states and the District

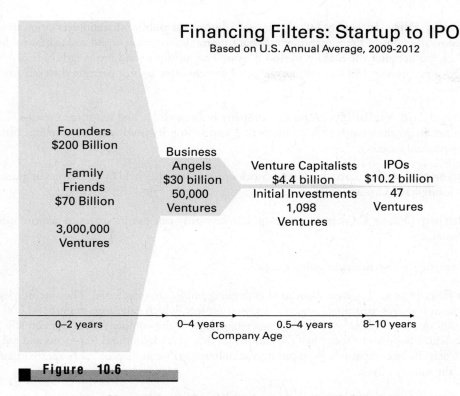

Financing Filters: Startup to IPO
Based on U.S. Annual Average, 2009-2012

Founders
$200 Billion

Family
Friends
$70 Billion

3,000,000
Ventures

Business
Angels
$30 billion
50,000
Ventures

Venture Capitalists
$4.4 billion
Initial Investments
1,098
Ventures

IPOs
$10.2 billion
47
Ventures

0–2 years   0–4 years   0.5–4 years   8–10 years
Company Age

■ **Figure 10.6**

Financing filters: Three Fs to IPO based on 2009– 2012 data

of Columbia. He sometimes regrets taking Bertucci's public instead of keeping the company private and building his personal wealth from the cash flow that his restaurants were generating.

Crugnale has subsequently started Cajun-Mexican, Latin-fish, and Italian restaurants—each one with several outlets—hoping to repeat his success with Bertucci's. So far it has eluded him. But he consoles himself with the knowledge that it took several years before Bertucci's was a hit. However, one thing he knows for sure is that his restaurants will not go public. "I have no investors, I own everything myself, so I don't have to answer to anybody. . . . There are no restrictions, and I like that freedom."[43]

Pros and Cons of an IPO

The following are the upsides of going public.

Financing. The principal reason for a public offering is to raise a substantial amount of money that does not have to be repaid. For example, the average amount of money raised by the 189 venture-capital-backed companies that floated IPOs during the period 2009–2012 was $215 million. The average post-money valuation of the companies that went public in 2010 was $497 million; on average, the companies sold 20.4% of their equity at the IPO.

Follow-On Financing. A public company can raise more capital by issuing additional stock in a secondary offering.

Realizing Prior Investments. Once a company is public, shareholders prior to the IPO know the value of their investment. What's more, their stock is liquid and can be sold on the stock market after the **lockup period** is over. The lockup period is a length of time after the IPO date (usually 180 days) when the prior shareholders are not permitted to sell any of their stock.

Prestige and Visibility. A public company is more visible and has more prestige. This sometimes helps the company with marketing and selling its products, outsourcing, hiring employees, and banking.

Compensation for Employees. Stock options presently held by employees or granted in the future have a known value.

Acquiring Other Companies. A public company can use its shares to acquire other companies.

And here are the downsides of going public.

High Expenses. Expenses associated with going public are substantial. They include legal and accounting fees, printing costs, and registration fees, which can range from $100,000 to $400,000 or more. Those expenses are not recoverable if the company does not actually go public, which happens to about half the companies that embark on the IPO process and fail to complete it. If the company does go public, the underwriter's commission takes approximately 7% of the money raised.

Public Fishbowl. When a company goes public, SEC regulations require that it disclose a great deal of information about itself that until then has been private and known only to insiders. That information includes compensation of officers and directors, employee stock option plans, significant contracts such as lease and consulting agreements, details about operations including business strategies, sales, cost of sales, gross profits, net income, debt, and future plans. The IPO prospectus and other documents that have to be filed with the SEC are in the public domain; they are a gold mine for competitors and others that want to pry into the company's affairs. At the peak of the Internet bubble in November 1999, Cobalt Networks went public; its market niche was inexpensive thin servers for small and mid-sized organizations. Before the IPO, the inexpensive thin-server market hadn't attracted much competition from big companies such as Dell, IBM, Hewlett-Packard, and Sun Microsystems. However, after Cobalt's spectacular IPO, they became aware that the niche was growing rapidly. Ten months later Sun announced it was acquiring Cobalt.

Short-Term Time Horizon. After an IPO, shareholders and financial researchers expect ever-increasing performance quarter by quarter. This expectation forces management to focus on maximizing short-term performance rather than on achieving long-term goals.

Post-IPO Compliance Costs. To meet SEC regulations, a public company incurs accounting costs it never had when it was private. Those can amount to $100,000 or more annually.

Management's Time. After an IPO, the CEO and the CFO have to spend time on public relations with the research analysts, financial journalists, institutional investors, other stockholders, and market makers—so named because they make a market for the company's stock. This is a distraction from their main job, which is running the company for optimal performance. Some public companies have executives whose main job is dealing with investor relations.

Takeover Target. A public company sometimes becomes the target of an unwelcome takeover by another company.

Employee Disenchantment. A rising stock price boosts the morale of employees with stock or stock options, but when it is sinking, it can be demoralizing—especially when an employee's options go "underwater" (the stock price falls below the options price). Underwater options can make it difficult to motivate and retain key employees.

The Process of Going Public

Before a company can have an IPO, it must file a registration statement with the SEC to ensure that the prospectus discloses everything the public needs to know before deciding whether to buy its shares. The IPO cannot go forward until the SEC has approved the registration statement. A delay sometimes wreaks havoc on a company's finances if the IPO window closes suddenly. When the Internet bubble burst, many CEOs who had anticipated using the proceeds from IPOs to finance their companies were unable to float public offerings. Some companies were sold at fire-sale prices, and others shut their doors with huge losses to private investors, especially venture capital firms.

Entrepreneurs with serious aspirations to take their companies public should be farsighted and run their companies from the beginning as if they will have a future IPO. In practice, this means their accounting and law firms should be well-known national firms with lots of clients who have had IPOs. Of course, this is more expensive than starting out with small, local firms, but it will pay off in the long run if there is an IPO or acquisition by a public company.

When a company decides it's time to go public, the first step is to select an investment banker. This is where professional advisors such as accounting firms, law firms, and venture capitalists are valuable. Studies have shown that companies backed by leading venture capital firms and taken public by leading underwriters have the highest market capitalizations.[44] Leading investment bankers are not shy. They aggressively pursue companies that they would like to take public. Banks compete for a company's IPO in what's called a *beauty contest* or *bake-off*. They present their credentials to the company's CEO and board of directors and place a preliminary valuation on the company using the market-comparable (NI × P/E) method. The company usually selects the underwriter that has had the most success with IPOs in the same industry during the previous few years. If the company selects more than one underwriter, the bank managing the IPO is the *lead underwriter*, and the other banks are called the *syndicate*.

As soon as the underwriter has been selected, the IPO process begins in earnest with an "all-hands" meeting in which the key players—including the lead underwriter, accounting and law firms, and company executives—decide what they will do and when. They then prepare the prospectus with all the information the SEC deems the public needs to know before investing. This document includes details of the offering, what the company plans to do with the proceeds, the company's financial history and its future strategy, information about company management, and the company's industry niche, especially its competition. Risks are spelled out in detail. The preliminary prospectus is colloquially called the *red herring* because on the front page is a notice printed in red stating that some information is subject to change—in particular, the price per share and the number of shares to be offered. After filing the preliminary prospectus with the SEC, the company waits for the SEC, the National Association of Securities Dealers (NASD), and perhaps state securities organizations to review the documents for any omissions or problems that it must correct before the IPO can proceed. A *quiet period* lasts from the moment the company files the preliminary prospectus with the SEC until 25 days after the IPO. During this time, the company is forbidden to distribute any information about itself that is not contained in its prospectus.

Once the preliminary prospectus has been approved, the lead underwriter and the CEO embark on a whirlwind tour of leading financial centers such as New York, San Francisco, Los Angeles, Chicago, Boston, and perhaps overseas centers such as London, Paris, Frankfurt, Hong Kong, and Tokyo. The purpose of the tour, or "road show," is to promote the upcoming IPO and gauge the level of interest from potential investors. During the road show and immediately after, the underwriter builds a book of investors who say they want to buy the stock. The underwriter and the company meet the day before the IPO and use the order book to set the price of the stock and the size of the offering. The more the stock is oversubscribed, the higher the price will be. The underwriter commits to deliver the agreed-upon proceeds to the company regardless of whether it sells all the stock at the offering price. This commitment creates tension between the company, which is pushing for a high price, and the underwriter, which wants to set a price that will enable it to sell all the stock at the offering price. Once the price had been set, the company distributes stock to the banks in the syndicate, which then allocate it to their clients.

The underwriter hopes the price at the end of the first day's trading will be about 15% higher than the offering price; this is known as the *first-day pop*. The number of shares in the offering multiplied by the pop is known as *money left on the table*; it is the additional amount of money the company would have received if the offering price had been the same as the first day's closing price (academic researchers refer to it as *underpricing*). During the Internet bubble, when the public's appetite for Internet-related stocks was insatiable, first-day pops of more than 100% were not unusual.

If the share price shoots up and stays there, some companies have a secondary public offering and raise more money, usually before the 180-day lockup expires and the market is flooded by insiders selling shares and depressing the price. Sycamore Networks, for example, raised $284 million at its IPO in October 1999. It had a first-day pop of almost 400%. About five months later, with the stock about 500% above its IPO price, it had a secondary offering and raised about $1.2 billion.

But sometimes an IPO falls short of expectations, as, for example, Facebook's on May 18, 2012. What had been ballyhooed in advance as "the IPO of the century" turned out to be the flop of the decade for investors who bought Facebook shares at the offering price of $38 and saw them fall below $18 by September 2012. Many factors may have contributed to the Facebook IPO fiasco: the underwriter, Morgan Stanley, overvalued the stock when it set the price at 107 times trailing 12-month earnings; they sold too many shares; 25% of the shares were allocated for retail investors instead of the more usual 15%; information in the prospectus may have been too optimistic—even misleading—and last minute amendments that lowered revenue and profit expectations reached financial institutions but not small investors; insiders sold too much stock at the IPO; the lockup period of 90 days was unusually short compared with the traditional 180 days; Zinga, which accounted for 19% of Facebook's 2011 revenue, released disappointing earnings and revenue in July 2012; Mark Zuckerberg, Facebook's CEO, who had been prominent in the pre-IPO road show, shied away from the investment community in the IPO aftermath when he should have been boosting investor confidence; and trading errors on Nasdaq, where Facebook is listed, may have caused some first-day losses.[45]

The SEC launched a review of all the participants in the IPO to see if any material information in the prospectus was omitted or misrepresented. While the Senate Banking Committee looked into the matter, and held meetings with a range of involved parties including Facebook, Nasdaq, Morgan Stanley, and the SEC.

Irate investors filed lawsuits. But a fortunate few that had invested in Facebook when it was still a private company and cashed in their shares for $38 at the IPO had no complaints: Goldman Sachs sold 24.3 million shares, which raised $924 million at the IPO price, doubling its original investment. Greylock Partners made 18 times its initial investment, selling 7.6 million shares for $289 million. Microsoft sold 6.6 million shares, which raised $249 million, more than quintupling its initial stake.[46] Alas, as is often the case with IPOs, the losers were small investors who bought their shares at $38.

Venture capitalists in general had been anticipating that Facebook's IPO would trigger an investor stampede for social media IPOs and enable them to exit their investments with lucrative returns in much the same way that Netscape's spectacular IPO had heralded the Internet gold rush in 1995. They were sorely disappointed. But not Accel Partners, Facebook's lead venture capital investor, whose $12.2 million stake in 2005 was valued at $10 billion at the IPO—a 800-fold return over seven years, which is an IRR of approximately 160%.

BFWS Goes Public

Let's return to our example. Two years after raising its second round of venture capital and five years after it was founded, the IPO window for software companies is open, so BFWS decides to go public. It has exceeded its forecasts and has revenue of $75 million, with net income of $8.33 million. Revenue is growing at 50% per year. It wants to raise $50 million gross with an IPO. Based on the prevailing industry P/E ratio of 30, the investment bank values the company post-IPO at $250 million ($8.33 million × 30). To raise $50 million, BFWS will have to sell 20% of its equity (50/250 × 100). That leaves the existing stockholders with 80% of the company.

Everyone should be happy with the return on their investments. At the IPO price, the $4 million of first-round venture capital is worth $64.8 million (16.2× return and IRR of 100%), and the $6 million of second-round venture capital is worth $38.1 million (6.3× return and IRR of 152%). The founders and the original investors hold stock worth $72.9 million, and the stock option pool is worth $24.3 million. The original founders and stockholders own 29.1% of BFWS, the venture capitalists 41.1%, the stock option pool 9.7%, and the public 20%. And the company receives the proceeds of $50 million minus the underwriters' 7% commission; that is $46.5 million.

Selling the Company

By far the most common way for investors to realize their investment, if a company has done well and chooses not to go public, is to sell the business to another company. A company is usually bought by a bigger company for strategic reasons, such as when a big pharmaceutical company buys out a young biotech company that has developed a promising drug but lacks the resources and experience to take it through the Food and Drug Administration (FDA) approval process or to market it, once it receives FDA approval.

A Strategic Acquisition: LowerMyBills.com

Matt Coffin started LowerMyBills.com in 1999. His vision was to provide consumers with a free, one-stop Internet destination to obtain better deals on all their recurring monthly expenses, including mortgages, utilities, automobile loans, insurance, and credit cards. LowerMyBills.com attracts customers for mortgage lenders and others by advertising on a wide variety of Web sites, including Yahoo!, AOL, and MSN. Consumers who click through on mortgage ads, for example, are taken to the LowerMyBills.com Web site, where they enter information relevant to the mortgage approval process. The Web site matches this against the lending criteria of the clients of LowerMyBills.com and passes qualifying leads on to several different lenders. The lenders contact the consumer, who can choose the most appropriate offer. LowerMyBills.com is paid for every lead it passes to a lender.

In the last quarter of 2001, LowerMyBills.com posted its first profit. By 2005, it had a leading position in the U.S. market. The company, based in Santa Monica, California, was

Steve Goldstein/The New York Times/Redux Pictures

Matt Coffin, Founder, LowerMyBills.com.

financed with $12 million, first from business angels and then from venture capital firms. Coffin, who still owned 25% of the equity, commented:[47]

> By 2004, I knew personally that I was way in the money, but I also knew that I had 99% of my net worth tied up in the business. Back when the Internet crashed, I had a bunch of friends that had started online companies that had gone up and come down fast. One guy who had turned down an offer for $700 million went bankrupt a year later.
>
> Investment banks were calling me like crazy to say it was time for us to go public. We looked at the possibility of raising additional capital from new investors—recapitalize with new shareholders so that current stakeholders could get some liquidity. There was also the option of selling to a corporate buyer, while staying on in some sort of earn-out arrangement.
>
> The team hired an investment bank, gave nine presentations, and within short order had received eight offers from corporate buyers ranging from two to four hundred million dollars. Private equity firms that were interested in a partial buyout were putting forward valuations that averaged half of what the acquirers were offering. This decision was about a lot more than finance.

> Every employee owns stock in this business, and they have worked really hard to get us to this point. We did need some sort of harvest, but I also knew that we still had a lot of growth ahead of us, and every option has its own set of risks and potential ramifications.

Coffin was in the enviable position of having a business that was growing rapidly in an industry segment that was expanding extremely quickly. LowerMyBills.com had 176 employees. On a pro-forma basis, sales in the year ended March 31, 2005, were $120 million, with operating profit of $26 million. Clearly, the company could have gone public, but Coffin decided to explore being acquired by a strategic partner. In May 2005, LowerMyBills.com was acquired by Experian, then a member of GUS, plc, the British retail and services group. Here are excerpts from a press release by GUS plc:[48]

Acquisition of LowerMyBills.com by Experian

GUS plc, the retail and business services group, today [May 5, 2005] announces that Experian has acquired 100% of the share capital of LowerMyBills.com, a leading online generator of mortgage and other loan application leads in the United States. LowerMyBills.com is complementary to Experian's existing direct-to-consumer activities and operates in large, fast-growing markets. The purchase price is $330 million, plus a maximum performance-related earn-out of $50 million over the next two years. Further strong growth in sales and profit is expected in the current financial year and beyond. The acquisition is being funded from GUS' existing banking facilities. The acquisition is expected comfortably to exceed GUS' financial target of generating a double-digit post-tax return on investment over time.

Experian is establishing leading positions in various markets in connecting consumers with companies via the Internet. Its strategy is to offer a wide range of products that assist consumers in managing the financial aspects of key life events such as moving house or buying a car. Experian enables consumers to find financial products and services that best suit their needs, while helping companies to find new customers quickly and effectively. As well as LowerMyBills.com, the newly formed Experian Interactive operation includes Consumer Direct (selling credit reports, scores, and monitoring products to consumers) and MetaReward and Affiliate Fuel (both of which generate online leads for clients).

This acquisition is attractive because:

LowerMyBills.com operates in large, fast-growing markets. More than 20 million American households take out a new mortgage each year. In 2004, home lenders spent $22 billion on acquiring customers, an amount which has grown by over one-third in the last five years. Of the $22bn, about $1 billion is currently spent online and this is growing by about 30% a year. For example, Experian estimates that the percentage of mortgages originated online will treble between 2003 and 2008.

LowerMyBills.com has a strong market position. LowerMyBills.com is the most visited home loan service on the Internet. In a highly fragmented market, it is one of only two players of scale with its online leads generating more loans than any individual lending institution. It has strong relationships with more than 400 lenders, including five of the top ten mortgage providers in the United States.

Over time, LowerMyBills.com will benefit from the skills, expertise, and client relationships within Experian:

Consumer Direct, MetaReward, and LowerMyBills.com all work in the same Internet space and can share expertise and traffic. Combined, these businesses have more than 29 million visitors to their Web sites each month; and there are also benefits of LowerMyBills.com working more closely with Experian's Credit business. The introduction of Experian's modeling and analytical capabilities will allow it to improve the quality of leads passed to lenders. Experian will also be able to sell LowerMyBills.com's services to its existing financial services clients, where it has strong relationships.

Don Robert, Chief Executive Officer of Experian, commented:

"This acquisition represents a step-change in building Experian's direct-to-consumer activities. With LowerMyBills.com, we will now assist consumers in making the most cost-effective financial services decisions, while also providing our lender clients with high-quality leads for new borrowers. The strategic fit could not be better and we are delighted to welcome the talented people of LowerMyBills.com to Experian."

Why Be Acquired?

The acquisition of LowerMyBills.com by Experian is a very good example of what the seller and the acquirer are seeking from a strategic acquisition. The following are the advantages and disadvantages of an acquisition from the perspective of the seller.

Management. By selling the company rather than going public, the managers can stay focused on what they do best—continuing to build the company—rather than having to spend a lot of time on public relations with the financial community. Also, they probably will not be as driven by quarter-by-quarter results as they would be if the company were public. For example, LowerMyBills.com will have a relatively small effect on Experian's net income; it can probably focus on rapid sales growth rather than optimizing quarterly profits for the next few years.

Founder and CEO. Selling a company the entrepreneur has built from nothing into a thriving enterprise can be traumatic. Edward Marram (co-author of Chapter 13 of this book) sold his company, Geo-Centers, in 2005. He said his head told him that it was the right thing to do, but his heart told him not to do it. After all, he was selling a company he started from nothing in 1975 and built into an organization with 1,100 employees. When a company is private, the CEO reports only to a board of directors, but when it is acquired, he or she has to report to a boss; if the acquirer is a big company, that boss may report to a boss. It can be very frustrating for the CEO/founder who has been making all the important decisions to find that his or her ideas have to be approved by a hierarchy before they can be implemented.

Company. Experian has very deep pockets; it will be able to provide capital to LowerMyBills.com if it needs it.

Investors. Acquisitions are often paid for in cash rather than stock. Thus, investors get cash immediately after the deal is completed, unlike in a public offering, when pre-IPO investors have stock they cannot sell for 180 days, meaning they face the risk that the stock will go down before they can sell it. Of course, if the company is bought with the acquirer's stock instead of cash and if there are restrictions on the sale of the stock, there is still a risk that the stock price will go down before the investors can sell it.

Entrepreneur and Employee Stock. If it is a cash transaction, as it was in the LowerMyBills.com acquisition, the entrepreneurs and employees get cash immediately. The potential disadvantage is that they no longer hold stock, so they have no upside potential if the company continues to do well. True, there is usually an *earn-out*, which is additional compensation to be paid in a few years if the company meets targets specified at the time of the acquisition. In the case of LowerMyBills.com, the earn-out is $50 million compared with $330 million paid when the acquisition was completed. It is well worth getting the earn-out, but it is only 15.2% more, so it might not be enough to motivate key employees to stay.

Employment Agreement. Key employees will have an employment agreement that forbids them to compete with the company for a specific number of years—usually no more than two—if they leave. That will probably be the same agreement they had with the company before it was acquired. However, the CEO and top management will almost certainly be required to sign new noncompete agreements as part of their employment contracts with the acquirer.

Culture. Initially, the acquirer will not interfere in the management of the purchased company, but eventually it will probably want to put in its own management system and maybe its own executives in a few key positions. When it does that, there is a risk there will be a clash of cultures.

Expenses and Commissions. The expenses and investment banker's commission are substantially lower for an acquisition than for an IPO.

CONCLUSION

When an entrepreneur accepts money from a financially sophisticated investor such as a business angel or a venture capitalist, there has to be a future harvest when the investment can be realized. Generally, that harvest occurs when the company is acquired; occasionally, it happens when the company goes public. The harvest is primarily for the investors rather than the entrepreneurs. If entrepreneurs are not careful, they can give would-be investors the impression that they themselves are planning to exit the company at the harvest. That is not what professional investors like to hear. They want to invest in entrepreneurs whose vision is to build a business and continue building it after the harvest, not in entrepreneurs who are in it to get rich quick. Remember that Bill Gates made almost all his huge fortune by the appreciation of Microsoft's stock after its IPO; so did Microsoft employees and investors who held onto their stock for many years after the IPO.

> "I hate it when people call themselves 'entrepreneurs' when what they are really trying to do is launch a startup and then sell or go public, so they can cash in and move on. They're unwilling to do the work it takes to build a real company, which is the hardest work in business." Steve Jobs[49]

After a long negotiation between a Boston-area entrepreneur and a venture capitalist for seed-stage financing of a medical device company, the venture capitalist asked the entrepreneur, "Where do you personally want to be in 10 years' time?" The entrepreneur replied that he hoped he would have built a $200 million company that was the leader in its market niche and that he would still be the CEO. The venture capitalist immediately shook the entrepreneur's hand and said, "You have your money." The entrepreneur was very surprised because it seemed to him that the venture capitalist already knew about how big the company might become if things went well, so he asked what triggered the spontaneous decision to invest. The venture capitalist replied, "If you had said, 'retired to a house on the beach in Maine,' we would not have invested. We want entrepreneurs who are focused on building businesses for the long haul, rather than short-term personal wealth." The venture capitalist added, "Congratulations, you have just completed the most difficult selling job you will ever do. You have convinced a venture capitalist to invest in a seed-stage company."

YOUR OPPORTUNITY JOURNAL

Reflection Point	Your Thoughts...
1. How can you bootstrap your venture? What services can you get for free or at reduced rates? What equipment can you lease or buy used?	
2. In the last chapter, you created a funding strategy. Now think about how you will gain access to angels and venture capitalists. Who can make introductions on your behalf?	
3. What valuation method makes the most sense for your company? What comparable companies can you refer to as you prepare your valuation?	
4. Imagine your harvest. What companies might likely acquire you? How can you prepare for that future acquisition?	
5. Is there a possibility that your company could go public (high-growth industry)? What do you need to do to prepare for that?	

WEB EXERCISE

Identify several companies that you can use as comparables in a valuation. What P/E ratios currently prevail across the companies? Can you explain the variance in P/Es? Which comparable company is yours most similar to? Where does its P/E fall in the range? Compute a valuation for your firm. What adjustments should you make?

NOTES

1 Gross, Daniel. *BigBelly: A Solar Powered Garbage Solution?* Newsweek Web Exclusive. September 10, 2009. www.newsweek.com/id/215120.

2 Cummings Properties works with local colleges and universities to promote entrepreneurship. Cummings helps sponsor several local business plan competitions and also provides special rate packages for new businesses growing out of college programs. The following site has links to colleges with Cummings Properties sponsorship programs: www.cummings.com/how_to_lease_space.htm#entrep.

3 Be sure to review the SBA options carefully because so many exist. The majority of loan guarantees fall within the 7(a) classification. These loans can be used for a wide variety of reasons, and the SBA will guarantee up to 85% of the loan or $1.5 million. Additional options exist if the capital will be used to improve your building or to fund working capital or if you fit certain sociological criteria. www.sba.gov/financialassistance/borrowers/guaranteed/index.html.

4 http://www.sba.gov/content/sba-loan-dollars-fy-2012-reach-second-largest-total-ever-3025-billion-second-only-fy-2011

5 Bygrave, W. D., and Reynolds, P. D. Who Finances Startups in the U.S.A.? A Comprehensive Study of Informal Investors, 1999–2003. In S. Zahra, et al., eds., *Frontiers of Entrepreneurship Research* 2004. Wellesley, MA: Babson College, 2004.

6 Ibid.

7 Virgin Money US. www.virginmoneyus.com. Although borrowing money from relatives, friends, and business associates is common, very little has been written about how to do it well. Virgin Money US is a pioneering company that has developed a set of products and services to facilitate these transactions (see www.virginmoneyus.com). Based in Waltham, Massachusetts, the company manages loans between relatives, friends, and other private parties in over 45 U.S. states and offers information online you can use to get financing quickly. Generally, the process works like this:

1. Identify a lender and agree on financing terms, such as loan amount, interest rate, and term.

2. Formalize the loan with a legally binding document, such as a promissory note.

3. Create a system for repayment that is affordable for you and reassures your lender that the loan will eventually be repaid.

Virgin Money has found a way to keep private loans on track by restructuring them if your business goes through difficult times along the way. Tracking the payments during a restructuring is critical in order to deduct the interest as a business expense. The company can also help you develop a credit rating for your business by reporting the performance of private loans to credit bureaus. By structuring your private financing in a businesslike manner, you will be able to demonstrate to your investors that you are serious about your endeavor.

8 www.sfgate.com/business/networth/article/Crowdfunding-awaits-key-rules-from-SEC-4264631.php#ixzz2LNR9Nb4J

9 http://techcrunch.com/2012/04/04/crowdfunding-is-a-go/

10 www.sfgate.com/business/networth/article/Crowdfunding-awaits-key-rules-from-SEC-4264631.php#ixzz2LNR9Nb4J

11 http://en.wikipedia.org/wiki/Crowd_funding#cite_note-5

12 www.kickstarter.com/projects/impossible/impossible-instant-lab-turn-iphone-images-into-rea

13 www.inc.com/eric-markowitz/new-era-how-the-crowdfunding-landscape-will-evolve.html

14 Sohl, Jeffrey. *The Angel Investor Market in 2008: A Down Year in Investment Dollars but Not in Deals*. Center for Venture Research. March 26, 2009. www.wsbe.unh.edu/files/2008_Analysis_Report_Final.pdf. National Venture Capital Association/PricewaterhouseCoopers. *MoneyTree Report*^{TM}. October 20, 2009. www.nvca.org/index.php?option=com_docman&task=doc_download&gid=496&ItemId=93.

15 Wainwright, F. *Note on Angel Investing*. Case # 5 001. Hanover, NH: Tuck School of Business at Dartmouth, Center for Private Equity and Entrepreneurship. 2005.

16 Excerpted from *The Making Of The Color Purple, Business Week*. November 21, 2005, pp. 105–112.

17 Seitz, Patrick. What's a Dream Team's DNA? Businesses Could Learn Some Team Dynamics from Broadway, Scientists. Investor's Business Daily, June 6, 2005.

18 www.playbill.com/news/article/114543-Broadways-The-Color-Purple-Will-Close-Feb24.

19 As of the writing of this book, a comprehensive list of angel groups can be found at www.inc.com/articles/2001/09/23461.html.

20 http://activecapital.org.

21 Cited in David R. Evanson and Art Berof. Heaven Sent: Seeking an Angel Investor? Here's How to Find a Match Made in Heaven. *Entrepreneur*. January 1998.

22 www.failuremag.com/index.php/site/print/steve_wozniak_interview.

23 www.sec.gov/info/smallbus/qasbsec.htm. Section 6.

24 Wainwright, F. *Note on Angel Investing*. Case #5 001. Hanover, NH: Tuck School of Business at Dartmouth, Center for Private Equity and Entrepreneurship. 2005.

25 *Venture Support Systems Project: Angel Investors*. Release 1.1. Cambridge, MA: MIT Entrepreneurship Center, February 2000.

26 Ibid.

27 Ibid.

28 Ibid.

29 *NVCA Yearbook 2009*.

30 www.lottery.state.mn.us/qanda.html#0.

31 PricewaterhouseCoopers/National Venture Capital Association MoneyTree™ Report, Data: Thomson Reuters

32 Baccher, Jagdeep. Venture Capitalists' Investment Criteria in Technology-Based New Ventures. Dissertation. University of Waterloo, 2000.

33 www.siliconbeat.com/entries/2004/11/13/qa_with_kleiner_perkins_caufield_byers.html.

34 Bygrave, W. D., Johnstone, G., Lewis, J., and Ullman, R. Venture Capitalists' Criteria for Selecting High-Tech Investments: Prescriptive Wisdom Compared with Actuality. *Frontiers of Entrepreneurship Research* 1998. Wellesley, MA: Babson College, 1998. www.babson.edu/entrep/fer/papers98/XX/XX_A/XX_A.html.

35 www.venturexpert.com/VxComponent/vxhelp/VentureXpert_Fact_Sheet.pdf.

36 www.siliconbeat.com/entries/2004/11/13/qa_with_kleiner_perkins_caufield_byers.html.

37 Rosenstein, J., Bruno, A. V., Bygrave, W. D., and Taylor, N. T. CEO Appraisal of Their Boards in Venture Capital Portfolios. *Journal of Business Venturing*, 8(2): 99–113, 1993.

38 Rosenstein, J., Bruno, A. V., Bygrave, W. D., and Taylor, N. T. How Much Do CEOs Value the Advice of Venture Capitalists on Their Boards? *Frontiers of Entrepreneurship Research*, 1990. *Wellesley*, MA: Babson College. 1990. Bygrave, W. D., Marram, E., and Scherzer, T. Boards *of Directors of Venture-Capital-Backed Companies*. Presentation at Babson-Kauffman Entrepreneurship

Research Conference, Boulder, Colorado, June 2002. Summary published in *Frontiers of Entrepreneurship 2002*. Wellesley, MA: Babson College, 2002.

39 Bygrave, W. D., Johnstone, G., Lewis, J., and Ullman, R. Venture Capitalists' Criteria for Selecting High-Tech Investments: Prescriptive Wisdom Compared with Actuality. *Frontiers of Entrepreneurship Research* 1998. Wellesley, MA: Babson College, 1998. www.babson.edu/entrep/fer/papers98/XX/XX_A/XX_A.html.

40 www.netpreneur.org/funding/anatomy_term_sheet.pdf.

41 In a firm commitment IPO, an underwriter guarantees to raise a certain amount of money for a company; in contrast, with a best efforts offering, an underwriter does its best to sell as many of the shares as it can at the offering price. Firm commitment offerings are far superior to best efforts offerings. All IPOs that are listed on the NASDAQ, the New York Stock Exchange, and the American Stock Exchange are firm commitment offerings. The statistics given in this book refer to firm commitment offerings.

42 *NVCA Yearbook 2012*

43 McGinn, Daniel. Reinventing Mr. *Bertucci. January* 18, 2004. www.boston.com/news/globe/magazine/articles/2004/01/18/reinventing_mr_bertucci?mode=PF.

44 Bygrave, W. D., and Timmons, J. *Venture Capital at the Crossroads*. Boston: Harvard Business School Press, 1992.

45 www.bloomberg.com/news/2012-10-10/facebook-fought-sec-to-keep-mobile-risks-hidden-before-ipo-crash.html

46 Ibid.

47 Matt Coffin. *143-T06A-U*. Wellesley, MA: Babson College, 2006.

48 Excerpted from www.experianplc.com/en/news/company-news/2005/05-05-2005.aspx.

49 Isaacson, Walter. *Steve Jobs*. New York: Simon & Schuster, 2011, p. 569.

MetaCarta: Growing a Company, Do We Take the VC Money?

Doug Brenhouse leaned back in his office chair and took a moment to himself away from the turmoil involved with the biggest decision of his professional life. Should he and his two co-founders, John Frank and Erik Rauch, accept the funding and terms that Sevin Rosen and its syndicate of three other VC firms had on the table? Three years after creating MetaCarta, a software startup building a product that converts unstructured textual information into maps (geographic search versus the text searches of Google), the team needed money, but who should they take money from and what were the implications of those investors? The current deal, if accepted, would dramatically change both the ownership structure as well as the day-to-day control of the company. Doug wondered if the team was ready to relinquish so much control over the growth of their firm.

Doug's History

Doug Brenhouse's background was a combination of entrepreneurship and engineering. In his family, owning a small business was "the norm." His father was a partner in a wood products manufacturing company. Two of Doug's uncles owned a women's clothing store chain and the other was an independent home builder. One of his aunts was an independent insurance agent, and many of his friends' parents also had businesses of their own. With entrepreneurs to his left and right, Doug considered that he too would eventually pursue his entrepreneurial ambitions. It was just a question of when the time would be right.

In 1996, Doug earned a bachelor's degree in mechanical engineering with a minor in management from McGill University. After graduation, he joined Active Control Experts, Inc., a small company that designed piezoelectric actuators in Cambridge, Massachusetts. The company used specialized ceramics that produce an electric current when physical force is exerted onto them. The technology applied to vibration dampening in aviation, sound production in speakers, and physical shock absorption in sporting goods, such as skis[1] and mountain bikes.[2] The company had been founded only four years earlier and retained its startup culture. In 1997, *Inc. Magazine* named Active Control Experts the 79th fastest growing private company in America.[3] Doug learned a lot working for an early stage entrepreneurial company and thought that this experience was preparing him for his own venture. After three years with the company, Doug wanted to explore the option of founding his own company.

In 1999, Doug enrolled in Babson College's MBA program. As he was about to enter his second year, Babson created a new program where students could apply their studies directly to launching a new venture. Doug stated, "Babson was a natural fit. In addition to the standard business education, I was able to walk the path of the first seven months of a business while actually starting one." Doug spent the early part of the program trying to figure out what kind of business to start. Doug looked at a variety of opportunities. Doug recalled:

This case was written by Andrew Zacharakis and Brian Zinn with support from The John H. Muller, Jr. Chair in Entrepreneurship at Babson College.

[1] BUSINESSWIRE, "ACX Technology Enables World's first Electric Snowboard," November 3, 1997.

[2] Sally McGrane, "Maybe an Electric Ski Would Help" *New York Times*, December 3, 1998. http://tech2.nytimes.com/mem/technology/techreview.html?res=9B0DEFD6153BF930A35751C1A96E958260

[3] www.inc.com/inc5000/2007/company-profile.html?id=1998079

One of the best places to see what kind of opportunities were emerging was the MIT 50k Business Plan Competition. There was a social mixer at the beginning of the year. Everyone was gathering around big dishes of food. It was almost like speed dating, just trying to meet as many people as you could. Here, I met my business plan competition team [John Frank and Erik Raush]. John was a very charismatic guy. It seemed like [his idea] was more than just putting together some students for a business plan competition. I could sense that John was going to launch this business regardless of the outcome of the 50kv.[4]

Pattie Maes,[5] Founder and Director of MIT Media Lab's Fluid Interface Group, had advised John to go find a partner with business expertise. Serendipitously, John and Doug had come to the MIT 50k looking for the same thing; someone with complementary skills to partner with. Through this introductory social event, the three member founding team was established.

Erik's and John's Backgrounds

Erik Rauch was a brilliant scholar and somewhat eccentric. He had a peculiar hobby of recording in his journal places with odd names, such as Hopeulikit, Georgia, and North Pole, Arkansas. His fascination with places and maps helped him see the potential that would eventually be MetaCarta. He enrolled in Yale University in 1992, earning the Morton B. Ryerson Scholarship. During his time there, he excelled at computer science and related mathematics. Erik was a research assistant in both Yale's Mathematics and Computer Science Departments. His work included writing an algorithm for floating-point variable optimization and using computer programming for fractal geometry simulation. Erik graduated from Yale in 1996. He went on to work in the Theoretical Physics Department at IBM's T.J. Watson Research Center and to study graduate-level computer science at Stanford University, before beginning his work towards a PhD in artificial intelligence at MIT.

John Frank began his pursuit of scientific expertise at Yale University, earning his bachelor's degree in physics in 1999. While at Yale, he completed an internship with IDEO, a renowned design and innovation consulting firm. He was also the Team Director of "Team Lux—Yale Undergraduates Racing with the Sun." This was a student-led team that built and raced a solar-powered vehicle in the 1,250 mile Sunrayce 97 competition, finishing ninth out of 56 teams. After graduating from Yale, John began his doctoral studies in physics at MIT. At MIT, he first conceived of the software applications that would shape the next 10 years of his life and also enlisted Erik's help to build the software.

John's Idea

John Frank encountered a problem for a class he was taking at MIT. He was doing a project on how trees affected rainfall in the South Pacific. To conduct this research, he had to compare the vegetation on an island to a variety of other climatic features of each geographic area he examined. He needed to locate all the weather station information on each island and no matter what Internet search he tried to construct, he couldn't get access to all of the data he needed. John thought, wouldn't it be great if I could take a map, put it on top of the island and use that as the filter? Then I could find everything about this geography and get back the

---

[4] Doug Brenhouse, interviewed by authors, Wellesley, MA, February 4, 2011. All quotes in case are from this interview.

[5] http://en.wikipedia.org/wiki/Pattie_Maes

information that I need and I would not have to know the names of all the different knolls and hills and stations that people refer to when they write about that location.

Traditional search engines can use specific text, such as the name of a city or river, to relate locations with other search terms. John wanted to create software that could search through online information and unstructured documents and identify which specific geographic location that document is referring to. This would include associating a mention of the "Potomac River" with the states that it runs through, as well as recognizing that a reference to "approximately 200 miles northeast of New York City" should most likely be connected with the area near Boston, Massachusetts. In other words, this search engine would build maps based upon textual data. The initial program they developed was able to produce locations on a map based upon search terms. For example, if you wanted to search wine, a map would be generated that showed all the locations related to wine. You could even search in different languages. The maps[6] below illustrate different results based upon a search term.

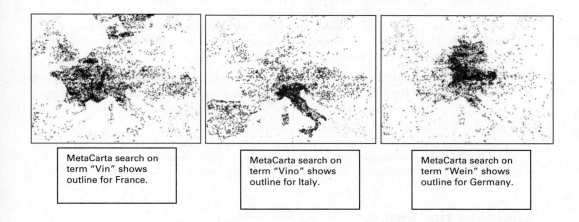

MetaCarta search on term "Vin" shows outline for France.

MetaCarta search on term "Vino" shows outline for Italy.

MetaCarta search on term "Wein" shows outline for Germany.

John possessed solid programming skills, but he needed someone with superior expertise to develop his concept into potentially revolutionary software. He brought his idea to Erik Rauch. John and Erik had known each other from their time at Yale. Knowing Erik's experience with doctoral-level artificial intelligence programming, John enlisted his help.

Forming a Founding Team

Doug, John, and Erik understood that their collective ability to work together was crucial to the success of the venture. According to Doug:

It is very much like getting married. You have to "date" for a while and really like the person that you are going to "marry." We ended up "dating" for four months or so before deciding that the business was worth pursuing and incorporating. We spent a lot of time together. Both socially and working on the business. Both were equally important. We got to know each other's friends and family pretty quickly. On the "work" side, it was like feeling around in the dark. We were doing a lot of research into what business models might make sense, what other companies were doing, how we packaged what we had and pitched it to investor—there was a lot of trial and error and we got to see how we each dealt with different situations, where each other's strengths and weaknesses were, and as it turned out, we complemented each other incredibly well.

---

[6] http://en.wikipedia.org/wiki/Erik_Rauch

Things were moving fast. The trio incorporated MetaCarta in January and started to raise money. This violated the MIT 50k rules and the team was initially disqualified until one of MetaCarta's advisors convinced the 50k committee to let the team compete. Unfortunately, Doug and his partners did not win, but the competition was another opportunity for the three students to test their "fit" as a team. With John and Erik providing the technical expertise and Doug articulating the business proposition, the team chemistry was strong and Doug knew this was the opportunity he was looking for.

Dynamics of the Founding Team

All three of the founding members shared science and engineering backgrounds. From this common foundation, their skills branched out in different directions:

> *[We had] very complementary skills. Erik was very technical. Big brain, it made sense for him to be pursuing a PhD in Artificial Intelligence. John spanned the gamut: very capable, very good at explaining technology. His father was a CEO of a variety of businesses. Besides good DNA, I think that he picked up a lot at the dinner table about how to be charismatic and how to run a business. My skills, though I have an engineering background, were much more on the business side, running and managing the business.*

The MetaCarta founders needed to decide how to structure their fledgling team before attempting to develop the idea into a business. They anticipated the need for help from more experienced executives in later stages. Their initial titles reflected that expectation:

> *We all fit into our roles extremely well. We intentionally took on roles where we expected "C" level [hires] to come on. We had these grand visions of growth of the company. I took a VP role and John took the President role thinking that a CEO and a COO would [join at a later date]. Erik was initially Chief Scientist. He was continuing his PhD studies and was part time.*

Dividing the Equity

John, Doug, and Erik arranged a division of equity in the company before they had a concrete valuation of the business. If they had waited until after starting the process of seeking financing to decide how to share ownership among the founders, it could have been a much more complicated decision. By agreeing soon after their initial formation of the company simplified the decision because factors such as the influence of the investors, the complexity of proposed investment deal terms, and changing priorities of all the involved parties did not confuse the decision.

> *We all recognized our equity positions were reliant on the value over time and not their immediate worth. We all had the mindset of vesting [the equity] over a period of three years. We realized that if the team dynamics didn't work, for whatever reason, there would be enough equity to entice [a new hire] to fill the role.*

The Business Model

MetaCarta's original business model was to allow free access to its search product online. The company would monetize its service through Internet advertising.

> *This was 2000. The dot-com boom was well underway. Internet advertising was tremendous and what made the most sense was that you could create a geographic search engine. Then folks who advertise on the Internet, like McDonalds or Nike, might be willing to pay more for their*

advertisement on a map that was driving real purchasers into their physical stores. The story was resonating with early investors and we raised $100,000. Everything was going as planned, but then came the dot-com bust and the stock market fell apart practically overnight and there was [no longer the same level of] Internet advertising dollars. So the idea of selling Internet advertising at a premium disappeared. We thought, "Now, what should we do?" We thought hard and long and changed the business model.

Instead of providing a free search engine to the public, the MetaCarta team thought the capability would be useful as an enterprise search engine. . . government agencies, Fortune 500 companies. . . while the new business model did not target as large of a market, the core customer was clear and the value proposition meant that the customer should be willing to pay for the product.

Difficulty Raising Capital

Now the team had to raise money based on this different business model. Getting money on the new business model was difficult. The angel investor community and venture capital firms had recently been shaken by the stock market crash, resulting in a plunge in early stage investing. The chart below shows total dollars invested per year by VCs and angels. As can be seen, 2001–2003 was not a strong period relative to the recent past to raise capital. The team's new mantra became, "There is no bad time to start a business," but Doug wondered if they were deluding themselves.

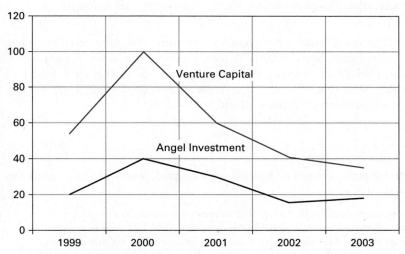

Angel data from Jeffrey Sohl, University of New Hampshire, Center for Venture Research. Venture Capital data from **Thomson ONE** Banker [New York, NY] : Thomson Financial

MetaCarta needed capital at precisely the time when it was most difficult for a software company to find funding.

It was incredibly hard work. We talked to everybody that we possibly could. It was all about getting to the next conversation and not getting discouraged. This was a time where the Internet bubble had crashed. A bunch of folks were sitting around not interested in spending their money on technology, but still wanted to get together [for angel investor meetings] for social reasons. We went and pitched, and some of the guys were asleep. They would ask questions that were intended, it seemed, to derail the opportunity. There was lots of criticism and very little [of it] was constructive. We would go to talk to people and they would look you in the eye and say, "We just don't get it. We think that you guys are idiots. This doesn't make any sense to me." I remember that we went to one local VC firm and we pitched to them. We were explaining one of our potential markets, oil and gas, to them and why [that was so attractive]. We already had Chevron interested as an investor and potential customer. The venture capital folks asked, "Why do people in the oil and gas industry need to read documents?" This person at a prominent venture capital firm in Boston just could not comprehend why this technology would be important.

Alternative Financing: DARPA

In October 1957, the Soviet Union launched Sputnik, the first human-built object to orbit the Earth. Military experts at the time believed that the technology that launched Sputnik was the first step in developing intercontinental nuclear missiles.[7] The United States hoped to launch a satellite of its own within six months, albeit one far smaller than Sputnik. In addition to the U.S. satellite project, the federal government created DARPA (Defense Advanced Research Projects Agency). This agency's mission was to provide research and funding to develop technologies that could be used by the US military and, in some cases, the public as well.

Because of the difficulty in securing conventional financing, MetaCarta explored an unconventional funding source: DARPA. Doug and his team were successful in securing $500,000 in funding.

DARPA funding was a big step for us. It allowed us to move out of John's living room and into an office and add a few talented people to the team. We also started taking small salaries for ourselves.

Getting the DARPA money was a big boost to the team. Not only could they pay themselves and hire more talent, but the DARPA money came in the form of a grant. No dilution. Furthermore, DARPA provided credibility to the team and their project. John and Doug soon realized that while this infusion was welcome, they needed more. The company was continuing to grow quickly and that required additional financing.

Angels

Although the angel investment community had still not recovered, John and Doug decided to go back to solicit angel investment.

We ended up raising money from family, friends, and business connections. We also got introductions to local software luminaries in the Boston area, some from MIT, and some from different angel groups in town. Pitching to angels was starting to wear on us. We often left those meetings asking ourselves, "Why did we do this again? Right, because this is what we do." At the end of the day, we ended up meeting some great people in Boston, who introduced us to some other great people. As we managed to pick up one, then two, then four, then eight, we managed to bring together a great group of investors in Boston. The same was true for New York. We ended up hooking up with three partners from Goldman Sachs. One introduced us to another, who introduced us to [the third]. We had a contingent in Boston and a contingent in New York. They were great to work with.

---

[7] Jorden, William J. Soviet Fires Earth Satellite Into Space; It Is Circling the Globe at 18,000 M.P.H.; Sphere Tracked in 4 Crossings Over U.S. *New York Times*. Oct 5, 1957. www.trumanlibrary.org/museum/sputnik1.htm

Valuing the company at such an early stage presented a challenge for the founding team. Even after identifying interested investors, terms of the deal would shape the company's future. If John, Doug, and Erik demanded too high a valuation, some investors would lose interest. Too low of a valuation would lead to an erosion of their founders' equity as financing rounds progressed. Once the first investor in a particular round would come to an agreement with the founders on the terms of the deal, the other potential investors interested in the round would be faced with a "take it or leave it" ultimatum. Furthermore, most early stage investors, including both angel investors and venture capitalists, write clauses into their investment contracts that prevent such dilution, often at the expense of the founders.

MetaCarta and the angel investors reached a compromise that is common for early stage investments: convertible debt. In the fourth quarter of 2001, the investors contributed $1 million with an 8% accruing interest rate.

> The debt was convertible at a discount to the next round or at a fixed valuation, which was $4 million in eighteen months. We figured that if we made it to that date, then we would be successful enough to be worth this valuation. The first money we raised was in the fourth quarter of 2001. It converted in 2003.

Therefore, if MetaCarta did not raise any additional capital before November 1, 2003, then the company would be valued at $4 million before the angel investment of $1 million of debt was converted to equity. With the $4 million "pre-money" valuation (value before the additional equity investment is added) and the original $1 million, the company's post-money valuation would be $5 million at the conversion. This would give the angel investors 20% ownership of the company, if MetaCarta did not raise a venture capital round of investment before that conversion.

The second qualifying event in the contract was a venture capital round of funding. If MetaCarta were to raise a venture capital round of financing, then the $1 million initial investment plus any accrued interest would convert to stock at a 20% discount to the price paid by the venture capitalists. Convertible debt allows the next round of investors to set the price and the valuation, but makes sure that the first investors receive a benefit for taking the increased risk of investing earlier.

Going Back for More

Although the company had sold their product to several government customers at this point, like many startups, the cash burn rate was faster than expected. Product development was proceeding briskly but to keep on track, MetaCarta needed more money. In the second quarter of 2002, MetaCarta founders approached the task of finding more growth capital from two directions. First, they contacted the company's existing angel investors. These individuals had not been anticipating the next round of financing until 2003. Nonetheless, the MetaCarta executive team had found its angel investors primarily from successful professionals from the software and technology communities in Boston and New York. Not only were these investors more open to initial investment in a software startup, but given the company's success to date, the experienced investors understood the requirements to keep MetaCarta growing. Whereas investors who were only familiar with more traditional businesses may have balked at the idea of MetaCarta asking for additional angel funding, the technology minded financiers of this company did not shy away. The company raised a second angel round in 2002, from its original investors.

The second direction for raising capital was much more arduous. In-Q-Tel is the venture arm of the U.S. Central Intelligence Agency. Based upon MetaCarta's product's potential for government use, the founders approached In-Q-Tel.

> *In-Q-Tel is a very interesting source of capital. They are the venture arm of the U.S. Central Intelligence Agency (CIA). They were very prestigious in that the government customer base that we were focusing on views companies that receive money from In-Q-Tel as vetted technologies. From a technology perspective, having due diligence done by them was second to none. So, we spent a long time talking with them, showing them what we had, and convincing them to take a look. They took a look and they liked what they saw. Once we got their seal of approval that the technology that we had was exceptional, they agreed to invest. There was a bunch of nuances around what they received for their investment . . . We structured the deal such that it was very good for both of us . . .*
>
> *The company was now two years old, In-Q-Tel had come in in a significant way, we had the DARPA funding, the angel backing, and customers that were really positive on us.*
>
> *In-Q-Tel's backing was really important. We were able to "wave that flag." We were able to say that we had hit all these milestones that we had said that we were going to hit. We were able to walk into any meeting and say that we had taken money from In-Q-Tel and that they had already vetted the technology. Here is the name of the person to go talk to. He was part of the CIA. It was the best possible seal of approval. It was a lot of work to get it. We had been pursuing them for long time. It was early 2001 when we started [talking to In-Q-Tel] and took us a year and a half until they invested. And we were actively pursuing them for that whole time.*

And More Money

While happy about the product development and growth in customers, Doug could not believe how fast they were burning capital. Alas, another year later and MetaCarta was in need of more capital. Based upon the success of previous fundraising and the increasing traction with customers, several venture capital firms expressed interest, but the fundraising environment in 2003 was still tight. Sevin Rosen Funds, one of the leading VC firms in the country with such notable investments as Compaq, Ciena and Electronic Arts, was very interested. Considering that Sevin Rosen was in Texas and the Silicon Valley, Kevin Jacques, a venture partner at Sevin Rosen, enlisted a Boston firm to also participate, Solstice Capital. After several months, Kevin Jacques put an offer on the table. Sevin Rosen and a syndicate of other venture firms would invest $6.5 million into MetaCarta at a pre-money valuation of $6.5 million. Doug, John, and Erik realized that would require 50% of the equity and give the investors the majority of the shares.

The venture syndicate also wanted to include an option pool to entice future hires and reward strong performance from the existing employees. While Doug, John, and Erik agreed that an option pool was necessary and understood that they too would be eligible for option grants, they also realized that this would further dilute their current equity. As is common, the VCs wanted the shares to come out of the founders' and earlier round investors' stakes. Doug recounted:

> *The $6.5 pre-money valuation resulted in a cram down to the angels, which was unfortunate. We were upset that our early backers were being offered a lower share price than they paid. Also, we as founders were struggling with the amount of dilution, grappling with the notion that although the piece may have been smaller, the potential size of the pie was now much bigger.*

The table below shows MetaCarta's capitalization over time, assuming they would take the Sevin Rosen money. The co-founders debated. *Should we take the money? The impact on our ownership and that of the previous investors is pretty severe.* They also questioned whether the short-term hit on the value of the investors and on themselves would be erased by the growth that the new capital would enable. MetaCarta could seek different venture capital sources, but the process between the initial meeting and closing the deal was likely to take months and the outcome might very well be the same, especially if economic conditions worsened. What should they do? The co-founders decided to sleep on it and decide in the morning.

MetaCarta Capitalization Table

	Date,	Invest/ Capital	Share Price	Shares	Value	Pre- Money	Post- Money	
Pre-Round Financing								
Founders						100%	100%	
DARPA	2001	$500		0	$0	0%	0%	Grant, no equity implications.
Angel, First Investment	2001	$1,000		0	$0	0%	0%	Convertible debt
Total		$1,500		0	$0	100%	100%	
Series A								
Founders			$0.64	6,250	$4,000	100%	63%	
Angel, First Investment			$0.51	2,109	$1,080		21%	Converted to equity at 20% discount. Note principal plus interest (8%) buys equity at 80% discount off share price
Angel, Second Investment Plus In-Q-Tel	2002	$1,000	$0.64	1,563	$1,000		16%	
Total		$1,000		9,922	6,080		100%	
Series B (proposed)								
Founders			$0.33	6,250	$2,063	63%	16%	
Angel, First Investment			$0.33	2,109	$696	21%	5%	
Angel, Second Investment			$0.33	1,563	$516	16%	4%	
Option Pool			$0.33	9,775	$3,226		25%	
Sevin Rosen and Other VCs	2003	$6,500	$0.33	19,697	$6,500		50%	
Total		$6,500		39,394	$13,000	100%	100%	

Case Questions

1. Why has this deal attracted venture capital?
2. Should MetaCarta take the Sevin Rosen offer?
3. How was the valuation determined? Is there anything MetaCarta could do to improve the valuation?
4. What would you, as an angel investor think about the current terms? What, if anything, can you do about it?

Rick Cochran, founder of Mobile Medical International Corporation, SBA Small Business Person of the Year, 2011.

DEBT AND OTHER FORMS OF FINANCING

Entrepreneurs at small, growing firms, unlike finance treasurers at most *Fortune* 500 companies, do not have easy access to a variety of inexpensive funding sources. In the entire world, only a handful of very large firms have access to funding sources such as asset-backed debt securitizations, A-l commercial paper ratings, and below-prime lending rates. Most financial managers of small- to medium-sized firms are constantly concerned about meeting cash-flow obligations to suppliers and employees and maintaining solid financial relationships with creditors and shareholders. Their problems are exacerbated by issues concerning growth, control, and survival. Moreover, the difficulty of attracting adequate funds exists even when firms are growing rapidly and bringing in profits.

This chapter describes various financing options for entrepreneurs and identifies potential financing pitfalls and solutions. We also discuss how these issues are influenced by the type of industry and the life cycle of the firm and how to plan accordingly.

Getting Access to Funds—Start with Internal Sources

Entrepreneurs requiring initial startup capital, funds used for growth, and working capital generally seek funds from *internal* sources. Managers or owners of large, mature firms, in contrast, have access to profits from operations as well as funds from external sources.

This chapter is written by Joel Shulman.

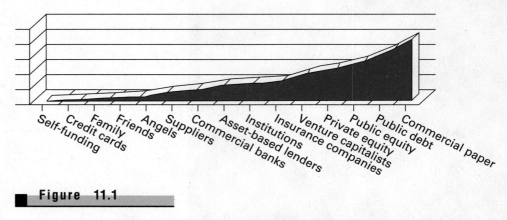

Figure 11.1

Sources of outside funding: Levels of funding and firm maturity

We distinguish internal from external funds because internal funding sources do not require external analysts or investors to independently appraise the worthiness of the capital investments before releasing funds. External investors and lenders also don't share the entrepreneur's vision, so they may view the potential risk/return trade-off in a different vein and demand a relatively certain return on their investment after the firm has an established financial track record.

Figure 11.1 shows a listing of funding sources and approximately when a firm would use each. In the embryonic stages of a firm's existence, as we've discussed, much of the funding comes from the entrepreneur's own pocket, including personal savings accounts, credit cards, home equity lines, and other assets such as personal computers, fax machines, in-home offices, furniture, and automobiles.

Soon after entrepreneurs begin tapping their personal fund sources, they may also solicit funds from relatives, friends, and banks. Entrepreneurs would generally prefer to use other people's money (OPM) rather than their own because, if their personal investment turns sour, they still have a nest egg to feed themselves and their families. The need to protect a nest egg may be particularly acute if the entrepreneur leaves a viable job to pursue an entrepreneurial dream on a full-time basis. The costs to the entrepreneur in this case include

- The opportunity cost of income from the prior job
- The forgone interest on the initial investment
- The potential difficulty of being rehired by a former employer (or others) if the idea does not succeed

Add to this the embarrassment of having to beg for a new job while paying off old debts, and the prospective entrepreneur quickly realizes that the total cost of engaging in a new venture is very high. Family and friends may volunteer to fund the entrepreneur's project in the early stages and often will do so without a formal repayment schedule or specified interest cost. However, the funds are far from free. Total costs—including nonfinancial indirect costs, such as family pressure, internal monitoring, and strained relations—are probably extremely high. Moreover, family and friends make poor financial intermediaries, since they have limited financial resources, different repayment expectations, and narrow loan diversification. This will contribute to the entrepreneur's desire to get outside funding from a traditional source as soon as possible. The question is, "Where can you go before a bank will give you money?"

Start with Credit Cards and Home Equity Lines

Entrepreneurs who require an immediate infusion of cash often don't have the luxury of time to await the decision of a prospective equity investor or credit lender. They're prone to tapping their personal credit cards for business purchases or borrowing against a low-interest-bearing home equity line of credit. According to a Federal Reserve report,[1] at the end of 2008, consumers had personal credit outstanding close to $2.6 trillion, with approximately one-third applied to revolving credit (credit cards). Nonrevolving credit includes personal credit associated with loans for automobiles and vacations but does not include home equity lines. This credit, which is derived from commercial banks, finance companies, credit unions, and savings institutions, is for personal consumption. Presumably, entrepreneurs have applied some of it to their businesses. Many banks set up credit cards for either personal or business use. And "points" systems that provide credit toward frequent-flyer miles or future purchases may give consumers an economic incentive to maximize their use of credit cards, whether for personal or business purposes. Home equity lines of credit (HELOCs) are another important way in which consumers provide funding for their businesses. In mid-2009, there was over $600 billion in outstanding HELOCs, according to the Federal Reserve.[2] Several studies have shown that many entrepreneurs use HELOCs to raise capital. For example, in August 2008 a Rasmussen Report found 30% of respondents use home loans for funding. And another study by the Small Business Research Board found 54% of entrepreneurs use home equity.[3]

Laugh at Your Own Risk

Back in 2000, Adam Lowry and Eric Ryan did not plan on going into the comedy business, but they seemed to make everyone laugh. They both lived in the Bay Area, the Internet start-up capital of the world. Yet potential investors thought they were crazy for trying to start up their company called Method, a household products company that would sell soap and cleaning supplies from environmentally friendly ingredients in cool packaging. They pooled together $100,000 in personal savings to start. By the spring of 2001, Lowry and Ryan had hired Alastair Dorward as CEO. And they were $300,000 in debt, split among the three partners' credit cards. By this time, the tech-bubble had burst, and all of a sudden venture capitalists were no longer laughing at their idea. In late 2001, the partners received a term sheet for $1 million. To celebrate, the partners took their investors, lawyers, and accountants out to dinner. The three entrepreneurs' credit cards were all declined. Thank goodness Lowry knew the owner of the restaurant. Lowry said, "We convinced him we were good for it—that the guy over there was about to give us a million bucks." As of 2009 sales were "north of $100 million" and the company had 130 products sold in more than 8,000 stores.[4]

Cash Conversion Cycle

One of the most important considerations in setting up a business is deciding when to pay the bills.

The business operating cycle for a traditional manufacturer begins with the purchase of raw materials and ends with collections from the customer. It includes three key components: the inventory cycle, the accounts receivable cycle, and the accounts payable cycle. The **inventory cycle** begins with the purchase of the raw materials, includes the work-in-process period, and ends with the sale of the finished goods. The **accounts receivable cycle** then begins with the sale and concludes with the collection of the receivable. During this operating cycle, the business generally receives some credit from suppliers.

The **accounts payable cycle** begins with the purchase of the raw materials or finished goods, but it ends with the payment to the supplier. The vast majority of organizations, particularly manufacturing operations, experience a gap between the time when they have to pay suppliers and the time when they receive payment from customers. This gap is known as the **cash conversion cycle (CCC)**. For most companies, the credit provided by suppliers ends long before the accounts receivables are paid. This means that, as companies grow sales levels, they need to get external financing to fund working capital needs. One of the primary causes of bankruptcy is the inability to finance operations, shutting down potentially successful ventures.

Some companies generate payments from customers before they need to pay their suppliers. Their cash conversion cycle is negative, although from a cash-flow perspective it is very positive. Your industry's typical cash conversion cycle is one of the most important things you should find out about your overall financing scheme. It makes a big difference to your chances for success and growth—if you are fortunate enough to receive payments before providing the service or paying your supplier.

Negative Cash Conversion Cycle

In 2000, a Babson College sophomore by the name of Siamak Taghaddos set up a new venture, Grasshopper, that provided emerging growth companies with a professional telephone-answering service. Virtually all Taghaddos's sales were generated through an automated system that he created on the Internet. Customers paid upfront monthly fees ranging from $9.95 to $39.95 that were charged automatically to their credit cards. Taghaddos paid his own expenses a few weeks later. This negative cash conversion cycle enabled him to grow exponentially with little need for external capital (since he initially leased the equipment required for the service).

By his senior year, Taghaddos was generating over $500,000 in revenues and outearned all but a handful of his professors. Two years after his graduation, he had revenues over $5 million and 20 employees and was named, along with his partner David Hauser, by *Business Week* as one of the top five entrepreneurs in the United States under the age of 25. Although this successful entrepreneur clearly generated the majority of his growth based on unique skill and marketing insight, had he not established a company with a negative cash conversion cycle, it's likely that his meteoric growth would have been constrained due to a severe cash crunch.

Working Capital: Getting Cash from Receivables and Inventories

The timing of collection of accounts receivable and payment of accounts payable is a key determinant in whether a firm is cash rich or cash poor. For example, an increase in net working capital (that is, current assets minus current liabilities) doesn't necessarily translate into an increase in liquidity. One reason is that increases in net working capital often result from increases in operating assets, net of increases in operating liabilities. These operating assets, such as accounts receivable or inventory, are usually tied up in operations, and firms don't commonly liquidate them (prematurely) to pay bills, typically paying with liquid financial assets, such as cash and marketable securities, instead. Thus, we can use only liquid financial assets to assess a firm's liquidity.

Further, corporate insolvency usually results when the firm fails to service debt obligations or callable liabilities on time. We can estimate corporate liquidity fairly accurately by taking the difference between liquid financial assets and callable liabilities, referred to as the *net liquid balance*. The net liquid balance is actually a part of net working capital. *Net working capital* is easy to calculate in one of two ways:

- Take the difference between current assets and current liabilities (as described earlier), or
- Take the difference between long-term liabilities, including equities, and long-term assets (such as fixed assets).

The first formula is often misinterpreted to be the difference between two liquid components, whereas the second definition suggests that the residual of long-term liabilities minus long-term assets is used to finance current assets, some of which may be liquid. The second definition also enables us to analyze the current assets and liabilities as consisting of both liquid financial/callable components and operating components.

Net working capital is actually the sum of the working capital requirements balance. This suggests that only a part of net working capital is liquid. Clearly, as a small firm grows, current operating assets will increase. If current operating liabilities don't increase at the same rate as the increase in current operating assets (which is true when an entrepreneur pays suppliers before receiving payment from customers), then the entrepreneur will find that the firm's net liquid balance will decrease (assuming the firm does not increase its long-term funding arrangements). This may be true even though the firm is generating paper profits. As long as the increase in working capital requirements *exceeds* the increase in profits, then the firm will find itself reducing its liquidity levels.

This highlights one of the fundamental weaknesses of the traditional liquidity ratios, such as the current ratio or quick ratio. These ratios include both liquid financial assets and operating assets in their formulas. Since operating assets are tied up in operations, including these assets in a liquidity ratio is not very useful from an ongoing-concern perspective. Note the difference between a liquidity perspective and a liquidation perspective. A liquidation perspective assumes that in the event of a crisis, the firm may sell assets off in order to meet financial obligations, while a liquidity perspective assumes that the firm meets its financial obligations without impairing the viability of future operations. From an ongoing perspective, a new ratio—*net liquid balance* to *total assets*—may be more indicative of liquidity than either the current ratio or the quick ratio.

Using Accounts Receivable as Working Capital

Accounts receivable—that is, the money owed to the company as a result of sales made on credit for which payment has not yet been received—are a major element in working capital for most companies. And they are one of the reasons we can assert that *working capital* is not the same as *available cash* and that the timing of short-term flows is vitally important.

If a company is selling a major part of its output on credit and giving 30 days' credit, its accounts receivable will be about equal to sales of 30 days—that is, to one-twelfth of its annual sales—if sales are reasonably stable over the year. And if the company's collection policies are so liberal or ineffective that in practice customers are paying an average of, say, 45 days after they are billed, accounts receivable are no less than one-eighth of annual sales. Investment in accounts receivable is a use of funds. The company has to finance the credit it is giving to its customers by allowing its money to be tied up in this way instead of being available for investment in productive uses. Therefore, accounts receivable, like cash, have an opportunity cost.

The magnitude of a company's accounts receivable obviously depends on a number of factors:

- The level and the pattern of sales
- The breakdown between cash and credit sales

- ☑ The nominal credit terms offered
- ☑ The way these credit terms are enforced through a collection policy

We'll discuss each of these factors in detail in the following sections.

The Sales Pattern

The basis of all receivables and collections is clearly *actual net sales*— that is, sales sold minus any returns. From actual sales come the assumptions about receipts from future cash sales and collections of future credit sales. These are the key inputs in forecasting cash flow, as discussed later in this chapter. Techniques for forecasting future sales fall into two broad groups:

- ☑ Techniques that use external or economic information
- ☑ Techniques that are based on internal or historical data from the company's own past sales

Most managers are more familiar with the techniques in the second group than they are with economic forecasting. The methods for forecasting from historical data range from the very simple (such as a straightforward moving average) to fairly sophisticated models. For instance, variations on exponential smoothing make it possible to take into account both long-term trends in the company's sales and seasonal variations. Simply put, although the more sophisticated techniques are useful, no forecasting method based *only* on historical sales data is completely satisfactory. You cannot be sure that either total industry sales or the company's share of the sales will be the same as they have been; you must consider a variety of external factors.

Methods of forecasting environmental change also fall into two broad groups. One group is primarily concerned with *forecasting the future performance of the economy as a whole*, particularly future levels of the gross national product (GNP) and the national income. These *GNP models*, as they are called, are highly complex, computer-based models. Their construction may be beyond the capabilities of most entrepreneurs, but you can easily purchase their output. The other group is more concerned with *forecasting sales for individual industries and products*. One way to do this is to identify economic time series to use as leading indicators to signal changes in the variable being forecast. Again, this technique is best wielded by an experienced economist with a computer. The important point for the entrepreneur is that forecasting techniques are becoming progressively less of an art and more of a science.

Cash versus Credit Sales

The relative proportions of cash sales and credit sales may make an important difference to expected cash flows. Unfortunately, this is a variable over which most entrepreneurs have little control. For example, a company in retail sales can certainly take steps to increase its cash sales, either by banning credit entirely or by offering a discount on cash sales. But a company selling primarily to other corporate organizations—other manufacturing companies, wholesalers, distributors, or retail chains—has few cash sales. Its best hope is to set its credit terms to encourage prompt payment, but the sales will still be credit sales, not cash sales.

Credit Policies

Credit policies boil down to two general questions:

- ☑ To whom should we give credit?
- ☑ How much credit should we give?

These two questions are closely interconnected. The business needs to evaluate most potential credit sales on their own merits, and this is costly and time consuming. In fact, the salaries and overhead of the credit analysts are likely to be the largest single item in the cost of giving credit to customers.

How much freedom a company has in setting the terms on which it will grant credit depends very much on its *competitive position*. For example, an organization in a monopolistic position has considerably more flexibility than does one that faces aggressive competition. But real monopolies are rare. Most companies approach such a position only during very short periods, after they have introduced radically new products and before their competitors have had time to introduce similar ones. A company in such a position may be tempted to take advantage of it through product price, but it is likely to tighten up its credit policy as well. The advantage of restricting credit will be fairly short-lived, but the damage to customer relations could continue for a long time.

Nevertheless, economic factors do play an important part in credit policy. The key issue is *elasticity of demand* for the entrepreneur's product (we assume that the credit terms are a component of the overall price as the customer sees it and that customers will resist a reduction in credit, just as they will resist a price increase). If demand for a product is *inelastic*— that is, if an increase in price or a restriction in the terms of credit will produce a relatively small drop in demand, with the result that net sales revenues actually increase—then there is some potential flexibility in the terms of sale. Even here, however, it will be the industry as a whole that enjoys this flexibility; individual companies will probably have to accept general industry practice. If demand for a product is *elastic*, on the other hand, there will be little room to change the terms of the sale at either the company or the industry level.

Finally, a company operating below full capacity or below its optimal output may well be tempted to offer unusually generous credit terms in order to stimulate demand. The key question then is whether the cost of the additional funds tied up in accounts receivable will be more than offset by the additional sales and reduced operating costs. Alternatively, a company working at full capacity, with its product back-ordered, is in a position to tighten up on its credit policies to reduce its investment in receivables.

Setting Credit Terms

The terms of credit include both the *length of time* given before payment is due and the *discount* given for prompt payment. Terms expressed as "2/10, net 30" mean that payment is due within 30 days (from the date of the invoice) and that the payer can deduct 2% from the bill if he makes the payment in 10 or fewer days. Some companies, on the other hand, set their net terms as payment by the end of the month following the month in which the sale is invoiced. Obviously, this latter policy is considerably more generous than "net 30" and is likely to result in a much larger investment in receivables.

An entrepreneur's failure to take advantage of cash discounts available on its accounts payable may be a very expensive mistake, equivalent to borrowing short-term funds at 36%. Is it an equally serious mistake for a company to offer the same terms to its customers? The answer is that it depends on whether giving a cash discount really does speed up collections and whether the *opportunity cost* of the funds that would otherwise have been locked up in receivables justifies the reduction in net sales revenues.

For example, assume that an entrepreneur's terms are 2/10, net 30 and that 25% of its customers actually take advantage of this discount. Annual sales are $36 million, of which $9 million are discounted, and the company recognizes profits when the sales are made. The discount's cost, therefore, is 2% of $9 million, or $180,000. Assuming that 25% of the customers pay in 10 days and the rest pay in 30, the average collection period (including both discount and nondiscount sales) is 25 days, giving average accounts receivable of $2.5 million, as shown in the following equation:

$$\$36,000,000/(360/25) = \$2,500,000$$

If the company did not give a discount, none of its customers would pay within 10 days, and the average collection period would fall from 25 to 30. In that case, average accounts receivable would be $3 million:

$$\$36,000,000/(360/30) = \$3,000,000$$

The question is, then, whether the added return the company makes on the $500,000 by which the discount policy has reduced the average accounts receivable exceeds $180,000, the cost of the discount policy. As this represents a return on investment of more than 36%, the answer is probably no.

A change in the net terms, however, is likely to make a greater difference to the average accounts receivable balance than giving or withholding a discount for prompt payment. Even if you give terms of 2/10, net 30, you can assume that a relatively small percentage of customers will take advantage of the discount. But if you change the net terms from 30 days to 45, doubtless a high percentage of customers *will* take advantage. Going back to the previous example and assuming that 25% of customers pay within 10 days and the rest at the end of 45 days, the average payment period now is approximately 36 days [(10 × .25) + (45 × .75)], and the average accounts receivable is $3.6 million, as shown:

$$\$36,000,000/(360/36) = \$3,600,000$$

In this example, we assumed that, if the net terms are set at 30 or 45 days, everyone who does not take advantage of the discount for prompt payment will pay by the end of the net period. This is unrealistic. Many entrepreneurs and the companies they do business with make a practice of reducing their requirements for funds by paying all their bills late. True, the most commonly offered terms are 2/10, net 30, but a survey revealed that the actual experience of U.S. companies is that their average receivables run between 45 and 50 days. A company's accounts receivable depend not only on the terms of credit offered but also on how well those terms are enforced through the company's collection policy.

Collection Policies

Some of a company's accounts receivable will be paid sometime after the theoretical time limit has expired. Others will never be paid at all and will have to be written off as bad debts. Neither of these variables is completely within the company's control, but both can be controlled to some extent.

The collection techniques of companies selling directly to the ultimate consumer are often highly standardized and even automated. The firms store master records of customers in computer data files and periodically search for overdue accounts. Each customer whose account has been outstanding for more than the net terms receives a series of increasingly stronger letters asking for payment. A system like this provides little opportunity to match the collection technique to the particular customer and situation. The average amount owed is probably small, however, and more individualized techniques are hard to justify in such circumstances.

When an entrepreneur's firm sells primarily in the industrial market and its customers are businesses, it will look at each individual case and determine how best to collect. If the other company is able to pay, the entrepreneur should rigorously attempt to secure payment before the situation becomes any worse. The methods include:

◼ Refusing any further orders or supplying only for cash

◼ Threatening legal action

◼ Actually undertaking legal proceedings, using a specialized collection agency

If the other company is already in serious financial trouble, however, an all-out collection attempt may simply force the customer into insolvency, followed by liquidation or reorganization. The wisest approach in this case may be to continue to give credit, or at least not to try to collect existing receivables, in the hope of keeping the other company in business.

But if your company is one of a number of creditors, you gain nothing by being generous unless the other creditors are willing to do the same. Otherwise, you are simply subordinating your claims to those of others and increasing the chance that the debt will never be paid at all.

It's safe to say that collection procedures are expensive and therefore are justifiable *only when the expected results exceed the cost*. Collection operations are, in fact, an excellent demonstration of the economists' law of diminishing returns. For a given volume of overdue accounts, the first few thousand dollars spent on collection will probably produce worthwhile results. But further expenditure is likely to yield less and less return.

How much should you be willing to spend on collection? The answer depends on the reduction you expect in accounts receivable and the return you'd expect if these additional funds were available for reinvestment in productive operations. Assume that you can reduce overdue accounts receivable $250,000 by hiring an assistant for $25,000. To cover the assistant's salary, you need to earn at least a 10% return on the funds released from accounts receivable. This represents a fairly reasonable rate of return and should be attainable. However, consider all the other nonwage costs of hiring an assistant, including FICA taxes, health care, and benefits, which could easily push the costs of the assistant up another $10,000, or 40%. Whenever you consider reducing excess receivables, examine the size and scope of the collection attempts and judge whether the costs justify the expenditure.

Setting Credit Limits for Individual Accounts

Another method of reducing overdue accounts and limiting bad debts is setting limits to the credit allowed on individual accounts. Again, as in collections, entrepreneurs need to distinguish between *sales to individual consumers* and *sales to corporate buyers*. An entrepreneur selling directly to consumers clearly cannot afford to undertake a thorough credit investigation of each one (unless the product being sold is a very expensive item, such as a boat or an automobile) and will set fairly arbitrary limits on the basis of limited information. But if the customers are business organizations, the setting of credit limits requires more thorough analysis, especially when the firm adds a new customer to its files and when it suspects an existing customer's circumstances have deteriorated.

Dun & Bradstreet offers resources and business reports through its Web site (www.dnb.com). You can check others' business credit ratings and your own business credit information. These ratings range from "high" to "limited" and include an estimate of the company's financial strength, usually based on net worth. If more detail is needed, Dun & Bradstreet and other agencies sell reports that include information about a company's principal officers, any past bankruptcies, and, most important, the company's credit history in relationship to its existing suppliers.

There are a number of other sources of information:

- Some industry associations operate credit advisory services for the benefit of their members.
- Companies selling directly to the consumer can get information from local credit bureaus.
- Commercial banks are also a useful source of credit information. An entrepreneur considering an extension of credit to a customer can ask her bank to carry out a credit investigation, which the bank will do by approaching the customer's bank for information about the customer.

You can cut short much of the work of appraising the creditworthiness of new customers by using external sources of information, but monitoring accounts receivable and deciding whether to increase credit limits or ban further credit represent a continuing task for your own staff. The decisions are often difficult. No company likes to turn down orders. Once again, you face a trade-off: the potential profit on the sale versus the cost of financing increased receivables and the probability of bad debt. Since the cost of the latter far exceeds the cost of the former, most entrepreneurs are very careful about granting credit.

The two major determinants of the credit decision are the character of the individual creditor or management of the creditor firm and the capacity of the firm to repay the loan. Entrepreneurs will find that the same simple set of guidelines they use in extending credit to customers is what banks use in extending credit to entrepreneurs. They're known as the Five Cs of credit:

- *Character* refers to the customer's integrity and willingness to repay the financial obligation.
- *Capacity* addresses the borrower's cash flow and ability to repay the debt from ongoing business operations.
- *Capital* is the borrower's financial net worth; consequently, a wealthy borrower may be a desirable customer even if her annual cash flows are relatively low.
- *Collateral* refers to the resale value of the product in the event repossession becomes necessary.
- *Conditions* refer to national or international economic, industrial, and firm-specific prospects during the time period of the credit.

The credit-granting decision is only part of the entrepreneur's concern. Another important task is monitoring accounts receivable balances. Since receivables tied up in operations may represent a large opportunity cost, either in lost investment returns or in greater borrowing balances, entrepreneurs are careful not to let the accounts receivable balances get too large.

Although the opportunity costs for accounts receivable may be quite large, the largest current asset balances are usually in inventories. As the entrepreneur's business grows, inventory balances rise, and resulting operating cash flows decline. You need to monitor both accounts receivable and inventories and keep the levels as low as possible without interfering with profitable sales. This is especially true if you have a shortage of capital or credit limitations.

Inventory

Inventory represents the most important current asset of most manufacturing and trading companies, yet money invested in inventory doesn't earn a return. In fact, it costs money to maintain inventories. Some inventory will be devalued or become a total loss because it deteriorates or becomes obsolete before it can be used or sold. These costs can easily add up to 20% or more of the inventory value annually. Since the money tied up in inventory might otherwise be invested profitably, the real costs plus the opportunity costs of carrying inventory may add up to 30%, 40%, or even more. As with accounts receivable, the dollar amount of inventory depends on when the entrepreneur chooses to recognize profit: Is it at the time of production or the time of sale? A strong argument can be made for valuing inventories at cost or market, whichever is lower. Given uncertainty about how much cash flow the inventory will actually generate, a conservative approach to valuation is best.

Entrepreneurs usually also want to keep inventory levels as low as possible, not only to reduce the inventory carry charges such as storage costs and insurance but also to ensure that as little capital as possible is tied up in inventory.

But carrying too little inventory also incurs heavy costs. These include:

- The costs of too frequent reordering
- The loss of quantity discounts
- The loss of customer goodwill or plant efficiency due to items being unavailable when needed

You'll want to weigh these costs against those of carrying excessive inventory in order to be able to judge the optimal level of inventory.

The control of investment in inventories is particularly important to t*he management of working capital*. Inventories are likely to represent your largest current investment and to be the least liquid of your current assets. Marketable securities can be turned into cash in a matter of hours, and most accounts receivable will usually be collected within the next 30 days. But three months' supply of inventory will take three months to turn into cash, if forecasts of demand or usage prove accurate. If your forecasts were optimistic, you might need even more time. The alternative—an immediate forced sale—is hardly attractive. You can sell marketable securities for their market value and sell, or factor, receivables for something like 80% of their face value. But inventories, other than some raw materials for which a ready market always exists, traditionally sell for little more than 10% of their acquisition cost in a forced sale. Thus, controlling a company's investment in inventory is of critical importance to managing your working capital.

One Company's Old Inventory Is Another's Treasure

Patrick Byrne could not raise money from any of the 50 venture capital firms to which he pitched his idea. His investment banker closed 181 out of 182 deals in 1999, and Overstock.com was the only deal that did not receive an investment. Byrne then got his break when a company named Miadora.com, an online jewelry e-tailer that received over $51 million in venture capital, was about to go bankrupt. The venture capitalists needed someone to purchase and liquidate the inventory fast. Overstock.com was officially born. Over the next few months, Overstock.com liquidated 18 different companies, all backed by venture capitalists. And Byrne finally received some venture capital backing himself.[5]

Overstock.com has grown from $1.8 million in revenue in 1999 to over $1.1 billion by 2012.

Sources of Short-Term Cash: More Payables, Less Receivables

Entrepreneurs usually don't have all the cash they need all the time. Very often an entrepreneurial firm needs to build up its inventory, thus reducing cash levels. Or an entrepreneur's customers may place unusually large orders, thus increasing accounts receivable financing or reducing company cash levels. This section describes the many ways entrepreneurs obtain additional short-term cash to restore their cash balances to the required levels.

As a rule, entrepreneurs look for short-term cash at the lowest possible rates. For example, an entrepreneur faced with a cash shortage might look first to her company's suppliers because they extend credit to the company by collecting for goods and services after supplying them. The entrepreneur can enlarge this credit by paying bills more slowly—and also obtain additional cash by collecting from her customers more quickly.

Cash from Short-Term Bank Loans

Although supplier financing is convenient, it is often cheaper to pursue bank financing if possible. Entrepreneurs faced with a severe cash shortage may also try to convert into cash two of their working capital assets: accounts receivable and inventory. An entrepreneur may pledge her accounts receivable to a finance company in exchange for a loan, or she may sell them to a factoring company for cash. Similarly, an entrepreneur may pledge her inventory (often using a warehousing system) in exchange for a loan.

Cash from Trade Credit

Trade credit is one important and often low-cost source of cash. Nearly all entrepreneurs make use of trade credit to some degree by not paying suppliers immediately for goods and services. Instead, companies bill the entrepreneur, and the entrepreneur pays in 10 days, 30 days, or more. From the time the supplier first provides the goods or services to the time the customer finally pays for them, the supplier has, in effect, loaned the entrepreneur money. The sum of all these loans (bills) represents an entrepreneur's trade credit. By paying bills more slowly, an entrepreneur can increase the amount of these loans from his suppliers.

One way to take more time to pay bills (or stretch payables) is to stop taking discounts. For example, if your company normally takes advantage of all prompt-payment discounts, such as 2% for payment within 10 days, you can increase your company's cash by passing up the discount and paying the bill in the expected 30 days. Of course, this is an expensive source of cash. If you lose a 2% discount and have the use of the funds for 20 more days, you've paid approximately 36% interest (annual rate) for using the money.

In practice, though, the interest cost wouldn't really be 36% because, by forgoing discounts and aggressively stretching payables, you wouldn't pay the bill in 30 days. Instead, you might try to pay it in 60 days. Now the equivalent interest rate is only about 15% (50 days' extra use of the money for 2%).

This brings up the subject of late payments. Many entrepreneurs don't consider 30 days (or any other stated terms) a real deadline. Instead, they try to determine the exact point at which further delay of payment will bring a penalty. For example, if a company pays too slowly, the supplier may take one of the following actions:

- Require payment in full on future orders
- Report the company to a credit bureau, which would damage the company's credit rating with all suppliers
- Bring legal action against the company

Many cash managers believe, however, that as long as they can pay company bills just before incurring any of these penalties, they maximize their company's cash at little or no cost. The *hidden costs* of this approach include such risks as a damaged reputation, a lower credit limit from suppliers, higher prices from suppliers to compensate for delayed payment, and the risk of exceeding the supplier's final deadline and incurring a penalty.

Cash Obtained by Negotiating with Suppliers

If an entrepreneur wants more credit and would like to stretch out her payables, very often she can negotiate with her suppliers for more generous credit terms, at least temporarily. If she and her supplier agree on longer credit terms (say, 60 or 90 days), she can get the extra trade credits she needs without jeopardizing her supplier relations or credit ratings. One way suppliers compete is through credit terms, and you can use that fact to your advantage.

Some suppliers use generous terms of trade credit as a form of sales promotion that may well be more effective than an intensive advertising campaign or a high-pressure sales team. The credit may be a simple extension of the discount or net terms, or it may take a modified form such as an inventory loan.

Cash Available Because of Seasonal Business Credit Terms

If the entrepreneur is in a highly seasonal business, as many types of retailers are, he will find large differences in credit terms in different seasons. For example, as a retailer, he might be very short of cash in the fall as he builds up inventory for the holiday selling season. Many suppliers will understand this and willingly extend their normal 30-day terms.

Furthermore, some suppliers will offer exceedingly generous credit terms in order to smooth out their own manufacturing cycle. Consider a game manufacturer that sells half its annual production in the few months before Christmas. Rather than producing and shipping most of the games in the late summer, this manufacturer would much rather spread out its production and shipping schedule over most of the year. To accomplish this, the manufacturer may offer seasonal dating to its retail store customers. **Seasonal dating** provides longer credit terms on orders placed in off-peak periods. For example, the game manufacturer might offer 120-day terms on May orders, 90-day terms on June orders, and so on. This will encourage customers to order early, and it will allow the game manufacturer to spread out production over more of the year.

Advantages of Trade Credit

Trade credit has two important advantages that justify its extensive use. The first advantage is convenience and ready availability; because it is not negotiated, it requires no great expenditure of executive time and no legal expenses. If a supplier accepts a company as a customer, it automatically extends the usual credit terms even though it may set the maximum line of credit low at first.

The second advantage (closely related to the first) is that the *credit available from this source automatically grows as the company grows*. Accounts payable are known as a spontaneous source of financing. As sales expand, production schedules increase, which in turn means that larger quantities of materials and supplies must be bought. In the absence of limits on credit, the additional credit becomes available automatically simply because the firm has placed orders for the extra material. Of course, if the manufacturing process is long and the company reaches the deadline for the supplier's payment before selling the goods, it may need some additional source of credit. But the amount needed will be much less than if no trade credit had been available.

Cash Obtained by Tightening Up Accounts Receivable Collections

Rapidly growing accounts receivable tie up a company's money and can cause a cash squeeze. However, these same accounts receivable become cash when collected. Some techniques—such as lockboxes and wire transfers—enable firms to collect receivables quickly and regularly. But how can the firm increase the rate of collection temporarily during a cash shortage?

The most effective way is simply to *ask for the money*. If the entrepreneur just sends a bill every month and shows the amount past due, the customer may not feel a great pressure to pay quickly. But if the entrepreneur asks for the money, with a handwritten note on the statement of account, a phone call, or a formal letter, the customer will usually pay more quickly. Of course, more aggressive collection techniques also have costs, such as the loss of customer goodwill, the scaring away of new customers, the loss of old customers to more lenient suppliers, and the generation of industry rumors that the company is short of cash and may be a poor credit risk.

The entrepreneur can also *change his sales terms* to collect cash more quickly. Options include the following:

1. *Introduce, increase, or eliminate discounts.* A company can initiate a discount for prompt payment (for example, a 2% discount for payment within 10 days). Similarly, a company with an existing discount may increase the discount (for example, increase the discount from 1% to 2%). Finally, a company can eliminate the discount altogether and simply demand cash immediately or upon delivery (COD). Companies will have difficulty instituting these measures if competitors offer significantly more lenient credit terms.

2. *Emphasize cash sales.* Some entrepreneurs, particularly those selling directly to consumers, may be able to increase their percentage of cash sales.

3. *Accept credit cards.* Sales made on bank credit cards or on travel or entertainment cards are convertible within a couple of days into cash. The credit card companies charge 3% to 7% of the amount of the sale for this service.

Obtaining Bank Loans Through Accounts Receivable Financing

One approach to free up working capital funds is to convert accounts receivable into cash more quickly through aggressive collection techniques. However, if you fear aggressive collection may offend customers and cause them to take their business to competitors, you may decide to convert accounts receivable to cash through a financing company, using either pledging or factoring. The following sections describe both methods. In practice, finance companies and banks offer many variations on them.

Pledging

Pledging means using accounts receivable as collateral for a loan from a finance company or bank. The finance company then gives money to the borrower, and as the borrower's customers pay their bills, the borrower repays the loan to the finance company. With this form of accounts receivable financing, the borrower's customers are not notified that their bills are being used as collateral for a loan. Therefore, pledging is called *non-notification financing.* Furthermore, if customers do not pay their bills, the borrower (rather than the finance company) must absorb the loss. Thus, if the customer defaults, the lender has the right of recourse to the borrower.

A finance company will not usually lend the full face value of the accounts receivable pledged. Typically, a company can borrow 75% to 90% of the face value of its accounts receivable if it has a good credit rating and its customers have excellent credit ratings. Companies with lower credit ratings can generally borrow 60% to 75% of the face value of their receivables. Pledging receivables is not a cheap source of credit. It's used mostly by smaller companies that have no other source of funds open to them.

Pledging with Notification

Another form of pledging is called **pledging with notification**, in which the borrower instructs its customers to pay their bills directly to the lender (often a bank). As checks from customers arrive, the bank deposits them in a special account and notifies the borrower that money has arrived. Here, the lender controls the receivables more closely and does not have to worry that the borrower may collect pledged accounts receivable and then not notify it. The company loses under this system, however, because it must notify its customers that it has pledged its accounts receivable, which can reduce its credit rating.

Factoring

Factoring is selling accounts receivable at a discount to a finance company known as the *factor.* The factor takes over credit checking and collection. If the factor rejects a potential customer as an unacceptable credit risk, the company must either turn down the order or insist on cash payment.

The fees that factors charge vary widely. They include

- An interest charge, usually expressed on a daily basis for the time the bill is outstanding
- A collection fee, usually in the range of an additional 6% to 10% (on an annual basis)
- A credit-checking charge, either a percentage of the invoice or a flat dollar amount

The factor keeps a hold-back amount to more than cover these various fees and charges, deducts the total from the hold-back amount, and sends the remainder to the company.

Recourse

Factoring may be with or without recourse. *Factoring without recourse* means that, if the customer doesn't pay its bill (it is a true deadbeat), the factor must absorb the loss. *Factoring with recourse*, on the other hand, means that, if the customer doesn't pay the bill within a prenegotiated time (for example, 90 days), the factor collects from the selling company. The company must then try to collect from the customer directly.

Naturally, a factor charges extra for factoring without recourse, typically 6% to 12% (on an annual basis) added to the interest rate it charges the selling company. For factoring without recourse, factors generally come out ahead because they minimize bad-debt expense by carefully checking each customer's credit. Nevertheless, the selling company might prefer factoring without recourse for two reasons:

- The company does not have to worry that any bills will be returned. In this way, factoring without recourse is a form of insurance.
- The factor expresses the extra charge for factoring without recourse as part of the daily interest rate. This daily interest rate may look very small.

Most factoring is done with notification. This means the customer company is notified and instructed to pay its bill directly to the factor. When factoring is without notification, the customer sends payment either directly to the supplier or to a post office box. In general, factoring is more expensive than pledging. On the other hand, factors provide services, such as credit checking and credit collection, that a company would otherwise have to carry out itself. For a small company, using a factor is often less expensive than providing the same services for itself.

Obtaining Loans against Inventory

An entrepreneur's inventory is an asset that can serve as collateral for a loan, providing needed cash without jeopardizing access to the inventory. There are four basic ways to use inventory as security for a loan, depending on how closely the lender controls the physical inventory:

1. *Chattel mortgage*, in which specific inventory is used to secure the loan
2. *Floating (or blanket) lien*, in which the loan is secured by all the borrower's inventory
3. *Field warehousing*, in which the lender physically separates and guards the pledged inventory right on the borrower's premises
4. *Public warehousing*, in which the lender transfers the pledged inventory to a separate warehouse

Obtaining "Financing" from Customer Prepayments

Some companies are actually financed by their customers. This situation typically occurs on large, complex, long-term projects undertaken by defense contractors, building contractors, ship builders, and management consulting firms. These companies typically divide their large projects into a series of stages and require payment as they complete each stage. This significantly reduces the cash they require, compared with firms that finance an entire project themselves and receive payment on completion. In some companies, customers pay in advance for everything they buy. Many mail-order operations are financed this way.

Choosing the Right Mix of Short-Term Financing

The entrepreneur attempts to secure the required short-term funds at the lowest cost. The lowest cost usually results from some combination of trade credit, unsecured and secured bank loans, accounts receivable financing, and inventory financing. Although it is virtually impossible to evaluate every possible combination of short-term financing, entrepreneurs can use their experience and subjective opinion to put together a short-term financing package that will have a reasonable cost. At the same time, the entrepreneur must be aware of future requirements and the impact that using certain sources today may have on the availability of short-term funds in the future. In selecting the best financing package, the entrepreneur should consider the following factors:

- The firm's current situation and requirements
- The current and future costs of the alternatives
- The firm's future situation and requirements

For small firms, the options may be somewhat limited, and the total short-term financing package may be less important. On the other hand, larger firms may face myriad possibilities. Clearly, the short-term borrowing decision can become quite complex, but choosing the right combination of options can be of significant financial value to the entrepreneur's firm.

Traditional Bank Lending: Short-Term Bank Loans

After an entrepreneur has fully used her trade credit and collected her receivables as quickly as competitively possible, she may turn to a bank for a short-term loan. The most common bank loan is a *short-term, unsecured loan* made for 90 days. Standard variations include loans made for periods of 30 days to a year and loans requiring collateral. Interest charges on these loans typically vary from the prime rate (the amount a bank charges its largest and financially strongest customers) to about 3% above prime.

Commercial banks are the most important suppliers of debt capital to small firms, supplying more than 80% of lending in the credit line market and more than 50% in other markets, such as commercial mortgages and vehicle, equipment, and other loans. After banks tightened their standards for loans of all kinds in the wake of the 2008 banking crash, it has been more difficult for small businesses, and according to the Federal Reserve's annual survey of senior loan officers, banks have not eased their tougher standards as of 2012.[6] Bank loans to small businesses peaked at $711.5 billion in 2008, but fell to $606.9 billion by the end of June 2011.[7]

Very often, an entrepreneur doesn't immediately need money but can forecast that she will have a definite need in, say, six months. The entrepreneur will not want to borrow the required money now and pay unnecessary interest for the next six months. Instead, she will formally apply to her bank for a *line of credit*, which is an assurance by the bank that, as long as the company remains financially healthy, the bank will lend the company money (up to a specified limit) whenever the company needs it. Banks usually review a company's credit line each year. A line of credit is not a guarantee that the bank will make a loan in the future. Instead, when the company actually needs the money, the bank will examine the company's current financial statements to make sure that actual results coincide with earlier plans.

Banks also grant *guaranteed lines of credit*, under which they guarantee to supply funds up to a specified limit regardless of circumstances. This relieves the company of any worries that money may not be available when it's needed. Banks usually charge extra for this guarantee, typically 1% a year on the unused amount of the guaranteed line of credit. For example, if the bank guarantees a credit line of $1 million and the company borrows only $300,000, the company will have to pay a commitment fee of perhaps $7,000 for the $700,000 it did not borrow.

In return for granting lines of credit, banks usually require that an entrepreneur maintain a *compensating balance* (that is, keep a specified amount in its checking account without interest). For example, if an entrepreneur receives a $1 million line of credit with the requirement that she maintain a 15% compensating balance, the entrepreneur must keep at least $150,000 in her demand account with that bank all year. The bank, of course, does not have to pay interest on this demand account money, so the use of this money compensates it for standing ready to grant up to $1 million in loans for a year. Of course, when the bank actually makes loans, it charges the negotiated rate of interest.

Maturity of Loans

The most common time period, or maturity, for short-term bank loans is 90 days; however, an entrepreneur can negotiate maturities of 30 days to one year. Banks often prefer 90-day maturities, even when the entrepreneur will clearly need the money for longer than 90 days, because the three-month maturity gives the bank a chance to check the entrepreneur's financial statements regularly. If the entrepreneur's position has deteriorated, the bank may refuse to renew the loan and thus avoid a future loss.

Entrepreneurs, on the other hand, prefer maturities that closely match the time they expect to need the money. A longer maturity (rather than a series of short, constantly renewed loans) eliminates the possibility that the bank will refuse to extend a short-term loan because of a temporary weakness in the entrepreneur's operations.

Interest Rates

The rates of interest charged by commercial banks vary in two ways:

1. The general level of interest rates varies over time.
2. At any given time, different rates are charged to different borrowers.

The base rate for most commercial banks traditionally has been the *prime rate*, which is the rate commercial banks charge their very best business customers for short-term borrowing. This is the rate that makes the news every time it changes. Congress and the business community speculate about the prime's influence on economic activity because historically it has been the baseline for loan pricing in most loan agreements. "Prime plus two" or "2% above prime" was a normal statement of the interest rate on many loan contracts. However, as the banking industry has begun to price its loans and services more aggressively, the prime is becoming less important and compensating balances less popular.

The current trend in loan pricing is *to price the loan at a rate above the marginal cost of funds* as typically reflected by the interest rates on certificates of deposit. The bank then adds an interest rate margin to the cost of funds, and the result is the rate charged to the borrower. This rate changes daily in line with the changes in money market rates offered by the bank. As liability management becomes more of a way of life for bankers, the pricing of loans will become a function of the amount of competition, both domestic and international, that the banker faces in securing loanable funds. As a result of this competition for corporate customers and enhanced competition from the commercial paper market, large, financially stable corporations are often able to borrow at a rate below prime.

The interest borrowers pay depends on several factors:

- ◙ The dollar amount of the loan
- ◙ The length of time involved
- ◙ The nominal annual rate of interest
- ◙ The repayment schedule
- ◙ The method used to calculate the interest

The various methods used to calculate interest are all variations of the simple interest calculation. *Simple interest* is calculated on the amount borrowed for the length of time the loan is outstanding. For example, if you borrow $1 million at 10% and repay in one payment at the end of one year, the simple interest is $1 million times 0.10, or $100,000. In the *add-in interest* method, the lender calculates interest on the full amount of the original principal and immediately adds it to the original principal, calculating payments by dividing principal plus interest by the number of payments to be made. If there is only one payment, this method is identical to simple interest. However, with two or more payments, this method results in an effective rate of interest greater than the nominal rate. Continuing with the add-in interest example, if you repaid the $1 million loan in two six-month installments of $550,000 each, the effective rate is higher than 10% because you don't have the use of the funds for the entire year.

The *bank discount method* is common in short-term business loans. Generally, there are no immediate payments, and the life of the loan is usually one year or less. Interest is calculated on the amount of the loan, and the borrower receives the difference between the amount to be paid back and the amount of interest. In our example, the lender subtracts the interest amount of $100,000 from the $1 million, and you have the use of $900,000 for one year. If you divide the interest payment by the amount of money you actually used ($100,000 divided by $900,000), the effective rate is 11.1%.

If the loan were to require a compensating balance of 10%, you have the use of the loan amount less the compensating balance requirement. The effective rate of interest in this case would be 12.5% minus the interest amount of $100,000 divided by the funds available, which is $800,000 ($1,000,000 minus $100,000 interest and minus a compensating balance of $100,000). The effective interest cost on a *revolving credit* agreement includes both interest costs and the commitment fee. For example, assume the TBA Corporation has a $1 million revolving credit agreement with a bank. Interest on the borrowed funds is 10% per annum. TBA must pay a commitment fee of 1% on the unused portion of the credit line. If the firm borrows $500,000, the effective annual interest rate is 11% [(0.1 × $500, 000) + (0.01 × $500, 000) divided by $500,000].

Because many factors influence the effective rate of a loan, when evaluating borrowing costs, use only *the effective annual rate* as a standard of comparison to ensure that you compare the actual costs of borrowing.

Collateral

To reduce their risks in making loans, banks may require collateral from entrepreneurs. Collateral may be any asset that has value. If the entrepreneur does not repay the loan, the bank owns the collateral and may sell it to recover the amount of the loan.

Typical collateral includes both specific high-value items owned by the company (such as buildings, computer equipment, or large machinery) and all items of a particular type (such as all raw materials or all inventories). Banks use blanket liens as collateral when individual items are of low value, but the collective value of all items is large enough to serve as collateral.

The highest level of risk comes in making loans to small companies, so it's not surprising that a high proportion of loans made to small companies—probably 75%—are secured. Larger companies present less risk and have stronger bargaining positions; only about 30% of loans made to companies in this class are secured.

One aspect of protection that most banks require is *key person insurance* on the principal officers of the company taking out the loan. Because the repayment of the loan usually depends on the entrepreneur's or managers' running the company in a profitable manner, if something should happen to them, there may be some question about the safety of the loan. If the officer or officers die, the proceeds of the key person policy are paid to the bank in settlement of the loan.

When making loans to very small companies, banks often require that the owners and top managers personally sign for the loan. Then, if the company does not repay the loan, the bank can claim the signer's personal assets, such as houses, automobiles, and stock investments.

Applying for a Bank Loan

To maximize the chances of success in applying for a bank loan, make personal visits to the bank, and make quarterly delivery of income statements, balance sheets, and cash-flow statements to sustain good relationships.

You'll need to conduct the actual process of obtaining bank credit (whether a line of credit or an actual loan) on a personal basis with the bank's loan officer. The loan officer will be interested in knowing the following information:

- How much money the company needs
- How the company will use this money
- How the company will repay the bank
- When the company will repay the bank

You should be able to fully answer these questions and support your response with past results and realistic forecasts.

Restrictive Covenants

Bank term loans are negotiated credit, granted after formal negotiations take place between borrower and lender. As part of the conditions, the bank usually seeks to set various restrictions, or **covenants**, on the borrower's activities during the life of the loan. These restrictions are tailored to the individual borrower's situation and needs; thus, it is difficult to generalize about them. This section introduces some of the more widely used covenants and their implications. All are (at least to some degree) negotiable; it is wise for the financial executive to carefully review the loan contract and try to moderate any overly restrictive clause a bank may request.

The restrictive covenants in a loan agreement may be

- *General provisions* found in most loan agreements and designed to force the borrower to preserve liquidity and limit cash outflows
- *Routine provisions* found in most loan agreements and normally not subject to modification during the loan period
- *Specific provisions* used according to the situation to achieve a desired total level of protection

Let's look at each in more detail.

General Provisions

The most common of all general provisions is a requirement relating to the *maintenance of working capital*. This may simply be a provision to keep net working capital at or above a specified level. And if the company is expected to grow fairly rapidly, the required working capital may be set on an increasing scale. For example, the bank may stipulate that working capital is to be maintained above $500,000 during the first 12 months of the loan, above $600,000 during the second, above $750,000 during the third, and so on. If the borrower's business is highly seasonal, the requirement for working capital may have to be modified to reflect these seasonal variations.

The provision covering working capital is often set in terms of the borrower's current ratio—current assets divided by current liabilities—which must be kept above, for example, 3 to 1 or 3.5 to 1. The actual figure is based on the bank's judgment and whatever is considered a safe figure for that particular industry. Working capital covenants are easy to understand and very widely used. Unfortunately, they are often of rather doubtful value. As we discussed earlier in this chapter, a company may have a large net working capital and still be short of cash.

Another widely used covenant is *a limit on the borrower's expenditures for capital investment*. The bank may have made the loan to provide the borrower with additional working capital and does not wish to see the funds sunk into capital equipment instead. The covenant may take the form of a simple dollar limit on the investment in capital equipment in any period. Or the borrower may be allowed to invest up to, but not more than, the extent of the current depreciation expense. This provision may prove to be a serious restriction on a rapidly growing company. And clearly, any company will find such a covenant damaging if the maximum expenditure is set below the figure needed to maintain productive capacity at an adequate and competitive level.

Most term loan agreements include *covenants to prevent the borrower from selling or mortgaging capital assets without the lender's permission*. This may be extended to cover current assets other than the normal sale of finished goods, in which case the borrower is prohibited from factoring accounts receivable, selling any part of the raw material inventory, or assigning inventory to a warehouse finance company without the bank's express permission.

Limitations on additional long-term debt are also common. The borrower is often theoretically forbidden to undertake any long-term debt during the life of the term loan, although in practice the bank usually allows new debt funds to be used in moderation as the company grows. The bank may extend the provision to prevent the borrower from entering into any long-term leases without authorization.

One type of covenant that clearly recognizes the importance of cash flows to a growing company is a *prohibition of or limit to the payment of cash dividends*. Again, if dividends are not completely prohibited, they may be either limited to a set dollar figure or based on a set percentage of net earnings. The latter approach is obviously the less restrictive.

Routine Provisions

The second category of restrictive covenants includes routine provisions found in most loan agreements that usually are not variable. The loan agreement ordinarily includes the following requirements:

- The borrower must furnish the bank with periodic financial statements and maintain adequate property insurance.

- The borrower agrees not to sell a significant portion of its assets. A provision forbidding the pledging of the borrower's assets is also included in most loan agreements. This provision is often termed a *negative pledge clause*.

- The borrower is restricted from entering into any new leasing agreements that might endanger the ability to repay the loan.

- The borrower is restricted from acquiring other firms unless prior approval has been obtained from the lender.

Specific Provisions

Finally, a number of restrictions relate more to the borrowing company's management than to its financial performance. For example:

- Key executives may be required to sign employment contracts or take out substantial life insurance.
- The bank may require the right to be consulted before any changes are made in the company's top management.
- Some covenants prevent increases in top management salaries or other compensation.

Restrictive covenants are very important in term loans. If any covenant is breached, the bank has the right to take legal action to recover its loan, probably forcing the company into insolvency. On the other hand, covenants may protect the borrowing company as well as the lender, in that their intention is to make it impossible for the borrower to get into serious financial trouble without first infringing one or more restrictions, thus giving the bank a right to step in and apply a guiding hand. A bank is very reluctant to force any client into liquidation.

Equipment Financing

Capital equipment is often financed by intermediate-term funds. These may be straightforward term loans, usually secured by the equipment itself. Both banks and finance companies make equipment loans of this type. The nonbank companies charge considerably higher interest rates; they are used primarily by smaller companies that find themselves unable to qualify for bank term loans. As with other types of secured loans, the lender will evaluate the quality of the collateral and advance a percentage of the market value. In determining the repayment schedule, the lender ensures that the value of the equipment exceeds the loan balance. In addition, the loan repayment schedule is often made to coincide with the depreciation schedule of the equipment.

One further form of equipment financing is the *conditional sales contract*, which normally covers between two and five years. The buyer agrees to buy a piece of equipment by installment payments over a period of years. During this time, the buyer has the use of the equipment, but the seller retains title until the payments have been completed. Companies unable to find credit from any other source may be able to buy equipment on these terms. The lender's risk is small because it can repossess the equipment at any time if the borrower misses an installment. Equipment distributors who sell equipment under conditional sales contracts often sell the contract to a bank or finance company, in which case the transaction becomes an interesting combination of equipment financing for the buyer and receivables financing for the seller.

The credit available under a conditional sales contract is less than the full purchase price of the equipment. Typically, the buyer is expected to make an immediate down payment of 25% to 33% of the full cash price, and only the balance is financed. The cost of the credit given may be quite high. Equipment that is highly specialized or subject to rapid obsolescence represents a greater risk to the lender than widely used standard equipment, and the interest charged on the sale of such specialized equipment to a small company may exceed 15% to 20%.

Obtaining Early Financing from External Sources

It's almost impossible for a brand-new company to get a conventional bank loan because it has no trading history and usually no assets to secure the loan. Even after a young company is up and running, it is still difficult to get a bank loan. Many entrepreneurs overlook the possibility of getting an SBA-guaranteed loan.

SBA-Guaranteed Loans[8]

The U.S. Small Business Administration (SBA) administers three separate loan programs. The SBA sets the guidelines for the loans, while its partners (lenders, community development organizations, and microlending institutions) make the loans to small businesses. The SBA does not make direct loans but works with thousands of lenders and other intermediaries. The SBA guarantees these loans, thereby eliminating some of the risk to the lending partners. The SBA guarantees 85% of a loan under $150,000 and up to 75% of a loan greater than that figure. Interest rates on SBA-guaranteed loans are negotiated between the borrower and the bank, but they are subject to SBA maximums and generally cannot exceed 2.75% over the prime rate for loans greater than $50,000. The bank has to pay a one-time guarantee fee of 2% to 3.75% of the principal; that fee is usually passed on to the borrower.

To qualify for SBA loan assistance, a company must be operated for profit and fall within size standards. It cannot be a business engaged in the creation or distribution of ideas or opinions, such as newspapers, magazines, and academic schools, or in speculation or investment in rental real estate. SBA-guaranteed loans can be used for the following purposes:

- Expand or renovate facilities
- Purchase machinery, equipment, fixtures, and leasehold improvements
- Finance receivables and augment working capital
- Refinance existing debt (for compelling credit reasons of benefit to the borrower)
- Provide seasonal lines of credit
- Construct commercial buildings
- Purchase land or buildings

Applying for an SBA Loan

The bank will require your company to have adequate paid-in equity, which usually means that the owners have invested sufficient money in the company that the debt-to-equity ratio will be no more than 4:1. Put another way, if you are seeking a $100,000 loan, your paid-in equity must be at least $20,000. For a startup company, the bank will also expect that the paid-in equity will be cash. Another important condition is that everyone who owns 20% or more of the company must provide personal guarantees.

You'll have a better chance of getting a loan in a timely manner from a bank that processes lots of SBA loans rather than one that processes only a few. Visit the SBA Web site (www.sba.gov) and click on "Find Resources," then on the state where your business is located (e.g., Maine), then on "District Office" (e.g., Portland); then on "Name of State District Resource Guide" (e.g., Maine District Resource Guide). Download the District Resource Guide (title: *Small Business Resource*). *Small Business Resource* provides lots of useful information on the SBA resources, especially SBA loan programs. Near the end of *Small Business Resource* is a list of the SBA Top Lenders.

Once you've selected a bank:

- Prepare a current business balance sheet listing all assets and liabilities and the net worth. Startup businesses should prepare an estimated balance sheet including the amount invested by the owner and others.
- Prepare a profit-and-loss statement for the current period and the most recent three fiscal years. Startup businesses should prepare a detailed projection of earnings and expenses for at least the first year of operation.

- ☑ Prepare a personal financial statement of the proprietor and each partner or stockholder owning 20% or more of the business.

- ☑ List collateral to be offered as security for the loan.

- ☑ List any existing liens.

- ☑ State the amount of the requested loan and the purposes for which it is intended.

If your loan request is refused, contact the local SBA office regarding other loans that may be available from the SBA.

SBA National Small Business Person of the Year, 2011

Rick Cochran left a job at an advanced medical equipment provider to establish his first venture, Outpatient Services of America, a consulting firm specializing in planning and developing ambulatory surgery centers. His plan evolved in 1994, when he researched and created an initial design for a mobile surgery unit and established Mobile Medical International Corporation (MMIC), working from his basement in Walden, Vermont with a staff of five. By 1995, he had the capital, and by 1996, he had his prototype.

At first, he provided temporary solutions for hospitals undergoing renovations, but he was able to expand the business into broader commercial, military, and emergency response applications worldwide.

During one rough patch in 1999, much of his core team—inspired by Cochran's perseverance, optimism, and faith—worked without pay when financing ran dry and the company nearly closed its doors. They were reimbursed later, when the company rebounded. The company also secured financing support from three SBA-backed loans in 1997, 2005, and 2008.

MMIC's products include mobile surgical hospitals built into a semi-sized tractor-trailer and an inflatable hospital ward that fits into a trailer pulled by a Humvee. To date, MMIC has 22 mobile healthcare units in its product line, including Mobile Breast Care Centers, Mobile Intensive Care, Mobile Laboratory/Pharmacy, Mobile CT Scan/Dental/Ophthalmology, Mobile Ophthalmology, and Mobile Endoscopy Units.

Today, MMIC's staff has grown to 54, and net income—just $9,835 in 2008—rose in 2010 to $1.68 million on gross revenues of more than $14 million.[9]

Planning Cash Flow and Planning Profits

Although there is a relationship between them, cash flows are not the same as profit. **Profit** is an accounting concept designed to measure the overall performance of the company. It is a somewhat nebulous concept, open to variations in measurement techniques and accounting conventions, each of which produces somewhat different results, which are then open to different interpretations.

In contrast, **cash flows** are not always a direct measure of a company's performance. For example, take two opposite extremes: a young, profitable company sinking as many funds as it can get into a new venture and an old, unprofitable company heading for bankruptcy. The results in terms of cash flow are likely to be the same: *declining cash balances*. A company can earn a handsome profit and have a net cash outflow in the same month if it pays for new capital equipment in that month. It can equally well show substantial loss and an increased cash balance in one month if the results of new financing or the proceeds from the sale of substantial fixed assets are received in that month.

However, the concept of *cash* is not nebulous: Either the company has a certain amount of cash or it does not. And a lack of cash is critical. A company can sustain losses for a time without suffering, but a company that has no cash is insolvent and in imminent danger of bankruptcy, no matter what its profit picture may be.

Thus, many financial transactions that do not enter into the calculation of profit—such as buying new fixed assets, getting additional financing, and paying dividends—do enter into cash flows. Similarly, some transactions that enter into the determination of profit—notably, the deduction of depreciation and the amortization of expenses—do not directly enter into cash flows (although there are cash-flow benefits related to taxes) because they are noncash transactions with no effect on cash balances.

Many entrepreneurs and bankers are becoming increasingly interested in a concept called *free cash flow*. Free cash flow is equal to the firm's cash flow from operations minus investments in capital expenditures that are required to maintain the company's competitiveness. For example, a firm that has $1,500,000 in cash from operations and that spends $2,000,000 in property, plant, and equipment has a *negative* free cash flow of $500,000 ($1,500,000−$2,000,000). This implies that the firm does not have surplus funds from operations, as it is, in fact, borrowing in order to maintain appropriate levels of capital investments.

Another term that is becoming more common is *pretax undedicated cash flow*. Undedicated cash flow is equal to free cash flow plus tax plus interest expense. Undedicated cash flow, or "raider" cash flow, is emerging as an important variable in appraising the investment attraction of engaging in leveraged buyouts, restructuring, and mergers of publicly owned companies. Prospective buyers (raiders) often add back interest and taxes so that they can get the broadest possible picture of the company's available cash. Then the investors determine how they could redirect the cash flows. Since the prospective buyers are going to be owners and not passive shareholders, they are more concerned about having control of the cash than about operating profits. Often much of the operating cash flow is devoted to servicing debt after the transaction. As the firm begins to service the debt arrangement, the equity in the company automatically grows.

CONCLUSION

Working capital is often misinterpreted as being synonymous with *firm liquidity*. In fact, only a part of net working capital is liquid; the balance of net working capital is tied up in firm operations. *Liquidity* is largely a function of a firm's growth and the timing of receipts and payments. In situations where payments are made to suppliers before customers pay, growth in sales generally results in lower liquidity.

Preparing a cash-flow forecast assists entrepreneurs in assessing the timing and maturity of funding needs. With a cash-flow forecast, the entrepreneur can more easily determine the type of funding to procure and the small, growing firm's ability to grow with available funds. This includes efficiencies in accounts receivable, inventories, payables, and accruals. To the extent that entrepreneurs can successfully negotiate with customers and suppliers, they will be able to manage future growth. However, small firms are rarely afforded the benefits associated with growth funded exclusively through internal cash generation. The more common occurrence includes external debt sources, leasing, cash innovations, and governmental programs for small firms. Such is the fate of the small business entrepreneur. Early growth stages result in large funding requirements and huge risks for those who can't meet payroll and supplier demands. However, once an entrepreneur has negotiated for a level of funds from external sources, including bank financing, privately placed debt, leasing options, and other financing innovations, that entrepreneur has a better chance for long-term corporate survival.

YOUR OPPORTUNITY JOURNAL

Reflection Point	Your Thoughts...
1. What sources of capital do you have? Are you willing to take on a home equity loan? Use your personal credit cards? How much of a "nest egg" do you need to feel comfortable pursuing a new venture?	
2. What do you expect your cash conversion cycle to be? Is there a way to improve it? What accounts receivable terms are common in your industry? How should you manage accounts receivable?	
3. How much inventory does your business need to carry to avoid stock-outs? What terms can you get on inventory (accounts payable)?	
4. Can you finance your accounts receivable? What means (bank loans, factoring, etc.) are most available to you? Can you get loans on your inventory?	
5. What short-term loans are needed for your business (e.g., line of credit)? When will you be bank creditworthy?	

WEB EXERCISE

Visit the SBA Web site (www.sba.gov). The Web site has useful information on a number of startup issues. Take a look at the SBA loan programs. What steps do you need to undertake to qualify for these programs?

NOTES

[1] *Federal Reserve Statistical Release: Consumer Credit.* February 2009. www.federalreserve.gov/releases/g19/current/g19.pdf.

[2] *Federal Reserve Statistical Release: Assets and Liabilities of Commercial Bank in the US.* www.federalreserve.gov/releases/h8/Current.

3 *Financial Services for Small Businesses in the U.S.* Rockville, MD: Packaged Facts, March 2008, p. 272.

4 Excerpted from R. McCarthy, N. Heintz, and B. Burlingham. Starting Up in a Down Economy. *Inc.* May 1, 2008. www.inc.com/magazine/20080501/star ting-up-in-a-down-economy.html

5 O'Malley, T. 50 VCs Say No and I Still Did It. *American Venture*, p. 36. December 2005.

6 Federal Reserve. July 2012 Senior Loan Officer Opinion Survey on Bank Lending Practices.

7 Williams, Victoria. *Small Business Lending in the United States, 2010–2011.* U.S. Small Business Administration, Office of Advocacy, Office of Economic Research, 2011.www.sba.gov/advocacy/7540/173967

8 Excerpted from the SBA Web site. www.sba.gov.

9 www.sba.gov/sites/default/files/National %20Small%20Business%20of%20the %20Year.pdf

FEED Resource Recovery

It was the spring of 2006 and Shane Eten had just won a $20,000 sustainability award at the highly competitive Rice University Business Plan Competition. Shane was already thinking about how he would use the $20,000. This wasn't the first time his idea, Feed Resource Recovery (**feed**), had won or placed well in a business plan competition—he'd finished second at the Babson College, second at the University of Colorado, and second at the UC–Berkeley competitions. Although the prize money and services in kind were helpful, Shane knew that he couldn't successfully launch his business on prize money alone. Shane estimated that he would need $150,000–$250,000 to build the anaerobic digester prototype and much more money after that to scale production and sell the system across the country. Where would he get the money?

Based upon his success in the business plan competitions and through strong personal networking, Shane had talked to several venture capitalists and they all expressed strong interest in the business. Potential investors seemed to be coming out of the woodwork, but still Shane was uneasy. How much of the company would he have to give up if he was going to secure their investments? Even from his preliminary conversations with the venture capitalists, he knew that the valuation[1] of the company was only going to be part of the problem. He was discouraged by the grim prospect of having to jump through hoops, answering the venture capitalists endless list of questions. He figured it would take at least six months of battling back and forth over equity and shares during which time the venture capitalists would be looking over his shoulder, and all this before a prototype was ever built. Furthermore, several of the venture capitalists were saying "this is a great idea, come back when you have a prototype built," so Shane wasn't even sure if they were really interested or just talking. But what other choice did he have? How could he raise the substantial amount of funding that he would require to assemble a team and build a working prototype? And how could he accomplish all of this without giving up all rights to his idea? The task was daunting and the answers were scarce.

From Athlete to Entrepreneur: The History of Shane Eten

Shane Eten was born in Philadelphia and lived in a number of places while his father attended medical school. The family eventually settled in Cape Cod, Massachusetts, where his father and mother started a family-owned medical practice. Living near the sea inspired Shane's father.

> *My father built a sailboat in our back yard. He started when I was in sixth grade. He told me he was going to build a sailboat and sail it around the world. He was probably a little crazy, but he actually built a thirty-six foot trimaran.[2]*

For as long as Shane could remember, his father had a dream of building the sailboat. He would wake Shane up early in the morning on weekends and make him help work on the boat, sometimes working 12-hour days. After several years of effort, they successfully launched it and saw it sail.

This case was prepared by Reuben Zacharakis-Jutz under the direction of Professor Andrew Zacharakis. © Copyright Babson College. Funding provided by the John H. Muller Chair in Entrepreneurship. All rights reserved.

[1] The valuation of a company is broken into two parts. The pre-money valuation is how much the company is deemed to be worth prior to the investment. The post-money valuation is the pre-money valuation plus the investment. The percentage of equity that the investor receives is the investment/post-money valuation. The percentage that the entrepreneur retains is the pre-money valuation/post-money valuation.

[2] A trimaran is a fast pleasure sailboat with three parallel hulls.

Although at the time I really hated working on that boat, looking back I realize that it was a very important part of my childhood because it taught me the importance of hard work and taking a dream you have and making it reality.

Like many boys, Shane was more interested in playing sports than school. He always enjoyed the team aspect and the competitive nature that came with athletics. His goal was to play Division I basketball in college. Hampered by knee injuries but still wanting to pursue his dream of playing college basketball, Shane chose to attend Trinity College, a Division III school, and play ball there. Unfortunately, his knees never fully recovered from a series of knee surgeries, so Shane never had a chance to play in college.

At Trinity, Shane majored in psychology and graduated in 2000. Although he enjoyed studying psychology, Shane didn't want to pursue a career in the field, but he didn't know exactly what he wanted.

I really didn't enjoy school and to continue down the psychology career path would require me going back to school almost immediately. I like getting out there and getting my hands dirty with real work. In the field of psychology, I would have been doing a lot of research and theoretical education-based work. I wasn't ready for that. I wanted to get out in the world and make something happen.

After graduating from Trinity, Shane went on many interviews and eventually found a job working for an up-and-coming computer company, Angstrom Microsystems. Angstrom Microsystems built supercomputers from off-the-shelf components and Linux software. Shane loved working for this fast-growing entrepreneurial company because his job was never the same day-to-day. He had the opportunity to work with many different aspects of the business. His original job was working with vendors. Then he moved his way up to product development, and finally he settled in customer account management. While Shane was with Angstrom, the company grew from $500,000 to $15 million in sales in his first eight months. With the hands-on experience he gained and the opportunity of being able to see how so many aspects of a company worked, Shane realized:

Entrepreneurship is fun and, most importantly, competitive. There's a real science to starting a company. It was at this time that I first started thinking about building my own company.

Unfortunately, Angstrom's success was short-lived as the market took a turn for the worse when one of Angstrom's largest customers stopped growing. The CFO of Angstrom left for a position at a candle company. He called Shane and convinced him to come along for the ride. The position that Shane had been offered was 180 degrees different from his job at Angstrom and an opportunity to test his abilities in a new way. Although Shane liked the tech industry, he decided to give it a shot. So at age 24 he started as a manager of a candle manufacturing plant.

It was a drastic change. Laurence Candle Company was a 60-year-old, third-generation company, and I was managing people mostly older than me—some who had been working there for 30 years.

He was forced to get on the floor and get dirty learning the process of making candles.

The Laurence Candle Company was struggling because its product was very similar to another established brand, Yankee Candle. The company needed new ideas so Shane raised his hand and asked if they would give him a shot at designing a new line of candles. After doing a bunch of market research and going to trade shows to see what was out there, he launched a new line of candles made from a new type of wax made out of soy. Soy wax was environmentally friendly because the wax was made from an all-natural crop; it was considered renewable and therefore sustainable. The soy wax candle line took off. Not only was soy cheaper than traditional paraffin wax, but also it could be sold as all-natural for 30%–40% more than traditional candles. Sales jumped instantly. It saved the company.

> There was a new consumer emerging at this time, and if you could say that it was all-natural, then you could say that it was sustainable or noble. This new brand of customer was willing to pay a premium for environmentally friendly products.

Shane put in 60- to 70-hour workweeks developing the line of soy candles. He also started research on adding biodegradable plastic wrappers to the candles. It was at this point that Shane knew if he was going to put in this much time and effort toward an idea, the next time it would be for himself and his own company.

Working for small companies, Shane had learned a lot about how the business world worked, but he knew that he needed a stronger foundation in accounting and working with numbers. If he was going to be successful in starting and managing his own ventures, he was going to have to go back for an MBA. At 28 years of age, he decided it was time to go back to school. Soon after he applied, Shane was accepted to Babson College.

The CleanTech Industry

Shane entered Babson with a goal of finding an idea to launch his own business. He was intrigued with opportunities in the Clean Technology space, especially around combating global warming. Investment and growth in the CleanTech industry exploded in 2007, passing the record set in 2006 in the first three quarters.[3] Exhibit 11.1 shows an explosive upward investment trend.[4]

The increased growth and investment in the CleanTech industry has been brought on not only by the large price increases in gas and other fossil fuels but also by the raised awareness of global warming by prominent figures such as former Vice President Al Gore. Gore's work with the United Nations Intergovernmental Panel on Climate Change, his winning the Nobel Peace Prize, and his involvement in the Academy Award–winning documentary *An Inconvenient Truth* have brought to light the serious issues of climate change and global warming. These works have also brought legitimacy and an increased interest in the CleanTech industry.

> Taken at face value, the surprisingly entertaining An Inconvenient Truth *provides an idealistic, persuasive, and compelling dissection of the perils of global warming. Frightening and timely, the smartly organized documentary is an urgent plea for responsibility and action as well as an impassioned call to heed the ominous warnings of science.*[5]
>
> Gore's words resonated with Shane. As Gore stated:
>
> But along with the danger we face from global warming, this crisis also brings unprecedented opportunities. What are the opportunities such a crisis also offers? They include not just new jobs and new profits, although there will be plenty of both, we can build clean engines, we can harness the sun and the wind; we can stop wasting energy; we can use our planet's plentiful coal resources without heating the planet.

---

[3] November 28, 2007. *CleanTech Venture Investments by US Firms Break Record in 2007*. National Venture Capital Association (NVCA). Thompson Financial Press Release. Retrieved January 30, 2008, from http://nvca.org/pdf/CleanTechInterimPR.pdf.

[4] Ibid.

[5] Ogle, C. June 9, 2006. Seeing Entertaining Documentary Makes You Want to Save the World. *Miami Herald* online movie review. Retrieved January 30, 2008, from http://ae.miami.com/entertainment/ui/miami/movie.html?id=616935&reviewId=20952.

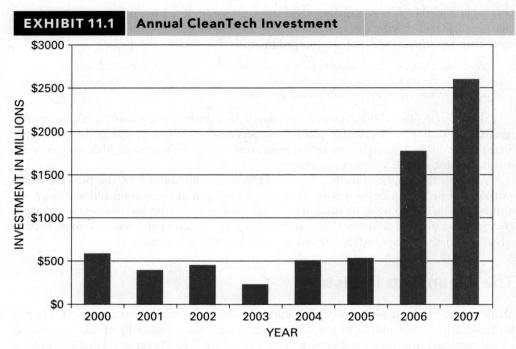

EXHIBIT 11.1 **Annual CleanTech Investment**

Source: National Venture Capital Association..

The procrastinators and deniers would have us believe this will be expensive. But in recent years, dozens of companies have cut emissions of heat-trapping gases while saving money. Some of the world's largest companies are moving aggressively to capture the enormous economic opportunities offered by a clean energy future.

But there's something even more precious to be gained if we do the right thing. The climate crisis also offers us the chance to experience what very few generations in history have had the privilege of knowing: a generational mission; the exhilaration of a compelling moral purpose; a shared and unifying cause; the thrill of being forced by circumstances to put aside the pettiness and conflict that so often stifle the restless human need for transcendence; the opportunity to rise.[6]

Consumers and the public in general are expecting companies to be more eco-friendly; they want to see real efforts made toward carbon reduction and recycling. This has encouraged companies to race toward new technologies in order to capture a piece of this new market. One example of the efforts that mainstream companies are making is Google's recent pledge to become a carbon neutral company.

Google today announced a new strategic initiative to develop electricity from renewable energy sources that will be cheaper than electricity produced from coal. The newly created initiative, known as RE<C, will focus initially on advanced solar thermal power, wind power technologies, enhanced geothermal systems and other potential breakthrough technologies. RE<C is hiring engineers and energy experts to lead its research and development work, which will begin with a significant effort on solar thermal technology, and will also investigate

---

[6] Excerpt from Gore, A. 2006. *An Inconvenient Truth: The Planetary Emergency of Global Warming and What We Can Do About It.* Paramount Classics.

enhanced geothermal systems and other areas. In 2008, Google expects to spend tens of millions on research and development and related investments in renewable energy. As part of its capital planning process, the company also anticipates investing hundreds of millions of dollars in breakthrough renewable energy projects which generate positive returns.[7]

Another example is Walmart. Although Walmart has faced much criticism for its energy consumption and pollution practices, the company has invested large amounts of money in green technologies. For example, Walmart installed solar power in 22 of its super centers, which accounts for roughly 1% of the U.S. super centers. Walmart has also made other green commitments promising to decrease its carbon footprint. It has pledged to eventually run off 100% of renewable energy sources. In the short run, company officials say they will adapt old stores to be 25% more efficient and new stores 30% more efficient.[8]

The increased interest in clean technology has attracted many investors. Exhibit 11.2 shows the distribution of investment in the CleanTech industry by subcategory.[9]

EXHIBIT 11.2	U.S. CleanTech Investment by Industry

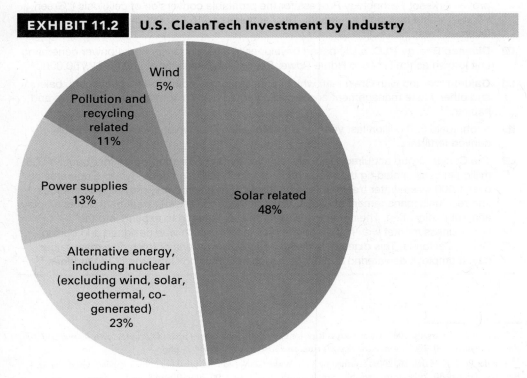

Wind 5%
Pollution and recycling related 11%
Power supplies 13%
Solar related 48%
Alternative energy, including nuclear (excluding wind, solar, geothermal, co-generated) 23%

Source: National Venture Capital Association.

[7] Fuller, J. November 27, 2007. *Google's Goal: Renewable Energy Cheaper than Coal Creates Renewable Energy R&D Group and Supports Breakthrough Technologies.* Google Press Center, Mountain View, CA. Retrieved January 30, 2008, from www.google.com/intl/en/press/pressrel/20071127_green.html.

[8] Walmart. *Environmental Overview.* Retrieved January 30, 2008, from www.walmartstores.com/GlobalWMStoresWeb/navigate.do?catg=345.

[9] NVCA 2007.

With the wealth of interest by angel investors and venture capitalists alike, many new companies have hit the ground running and have found success. This explains the high interest that Shane has received from these investors. The CleanTech Venture Network estimates that over 240 CleanTech companies could be positioned for a liquidity event between 2007 and 2009.[10] A small niche within the CleanTech sector known as waste conversion technologies is beginning to catch on. One such example is Converted Organics Inc. Converted Organics, based in Boston, is a development-stage company dedicated to producing a valuable all-natural, organic soil additive through food waste recycling. Started in 2003, Converted Organics Inc. is a five-employee operation that has just recently gone public raising $9.9 million in an IPO and has a market capitalization of $14.3 million.[11] Other examples of recent transactions involving waste conversion providers are noted in Exhibit 11.3.

| **EXHIBIT 11.3** | **Sample Investments into CleanTech Companies** |

- **BlueFire Ethanol, Inc.** is established to deploy the commercially ready, patented, and proven Arkenol Technology Process for the profitable conversion of cellulosic ("Green Waste") waste materials to ethanol. They acquired a $15,000,000 investment from Quercus Trust.[12]

- **Disenco Energy PLC**, a UK-based developer of a revolutionary home power generating unit known as the Disenco Home Power Plant, closed their initial IPO for $2,750,000.[13]

- **Oakleaf** merged with Greenleaf, which rents stationary compactors, containers, balers, and other waste management and recycling equipment to commercial businesses and haulers.[14]

- Scotts paid $20 million last year for **Rod McLellan Co.**, which focuses on naturally derived fertilizers.[15]

- The Carlyle Group acquired residuals recycler **Synagro Technologies** for about $447.5 million in cash, including the assumption of ~$310 million in debt. Synagro operates at over 1,000 wastewater treatment plants throughout the country, providing operations and residuals management services. Many of these wastewater treatment plants employ anaerobic digestion. The company is using this experience to expand into the agribusiness market with its first operational facility, which was designed and built in Chino, California. This digester is designed for 225 wet tons of fresh cow manure per day. It employs dewatering and onsite cogeneration using Capstone Micro turbines.[16]

---

[10] Parker, N. February 14, 2007. CleanTech Is Ripe for Growth. *Israel Venture Capital & Private Equity Journal (IVCJ)*. Retrieved January 30, 2008, from www.altassets.com/casefor/sectors/2007/nz9921.php.

[11] Van der Pool, L. March 16, 2007. Spurned by VCs, Waste Conversion Startup Goes Public. *Boston Journal Online*. Retrieved January 30, 2008, from www.bizjournals.com/boston/stories/2007/03/19/story8.html.

[12] January 8, 2008. *BlueFire Ethanol Closes $15.5 Million in Financing*. BlueFire Press Release. Retrieved January 30, 2008, from http://bluefireethanol.com/pr/45/.

[13] February 26, 2007. *Disenco Energy PLC Closes IPO for US$2,750,000 and Lists on the TSX Venture Exchange*. PR Newswire Europe Ltd. Retrieved January 30, 2008, from www.prnewswire.co.uk/cgi/news/release?id=191571.

[14] July 26, 2004. *Greenleaf Compaction, Inc. Has Merged with Oakleaf Waste Management*. Oakleaf News Releases. Retrieved January 30, 2008, from www.oakleafwaste.com/oakleaf/news/releases/2004/072604_2.asp.

[15] Lambert, E. September 4, 2006. *Organic Miracle Needed*. Retrieved January 30, 2008, from www.forbes.com/forbes/2006/0904/066.html.

[16] January 29, 2007. *The Carlyle Group to Acquire Synagro Technologies for $5.76 per Share*. Carlyle Group News. Retrieved January 30, 2008, from www.carlyle.com/News/NewsArchive/2007/item7052.html.

Roots of Feed Idea

At Babson, the entrepreneurship professors stress the importance of opportunity and an entrepreneur's fit to that opportunity. So Shane thought he should leverage his past experience and start his own candle line. However, copyright laws and low profit margins discouraged him. Next he looked at biodegradable packaging lines.

> When I had an idea, I would do research for maybe three weeks, and see who else was out there, if the product was feasible, and who the customers were.... I would usually find a really big obstacle. Or I just found a company that does this or a big brand that does this or someone that tried to start it and it didn't work. And when I got to biodegradable plastic, I realized there was no way to compost it, so it wasn't as environmentally friendly as I had first imagined. But during this search, I came across composting technology. This seemed like a big idea and a big opportunity. The key with composting that makes it so unique is that someone is getting paid for their raw materials, which is basically trash. Companies paid to have trash hauled away, so that meant composters could get their raw material for free or even be paid to take it away.

Shane started doing research into the composting industry and was intrigued by waste conversion technology. He looked at gasification,[17] plasma arc,[18] aerobic composting,[19] and finally anaerobic digestion.[20] Anaerobic digestion caught his eye. Anaerobic digestion was a relatively proven and cheap technology, and it seemed the most viable option. Next Shane began to look at the waste stream market. He wanted to know who the largest waste producers were, what kind of waste they produced, and what the competition looked like in those industries. He looked at households and small restaurants and found that in most cases they would not generate enough waste to justify an onsite digester and the cost of transporting the waste to a central location would be prohibitive. After further research, Shane found that the food waste produced by processing plants and supermarkets turned out to be the most promising. This was because they both were producing large amounts of food waste and the volume was concentrated in a single location (see Exhibit 11.4).

> Babson is great because there are tons of ideas floating around. The professors give us the tools to analyze whether an idea is an opportunity. You start with a problem, and if there's a problem, there's potentially an opportunity. So you have a bunch of students running around with two-page summaries on their ideas, sharing their thoughts, and seeking feedback during breaks from class. The school also has a "Rocket Pitch" event where you get three minutes to convince the audience that your idea has real potential. It takes a lot of work to learn how to pitch your concept in three minutes, but that process really helps you understand the issues around the idea.

---

[17] **Gasification** is a process that converts organic material or biomass into gasses or liquid fuels by a combination of high temperatures and reduced oxygen supply. (Schilli, J. Using Gasification to Process Municipal Solid Waste. Environmental and Resource Management Group of HDR: *HDR Innovations*, Vol. 12.)

[18] **Plasma arc gasification** is a process in which solid waste is shredded and fed into a furnace where extreme electrical charges bring the temperature above 3,000 degrees. After an hour or so, waste material breaks down into its molecular building blocks, leaving three marketable byproducts: a combustible synthesis gas, or syngas, that can be converted into steam or electricity; metal ingots that can be resold and melted down again; and a glassy solid that can be processed into material for floor tiles or gravel. (Durst, S. March 5, 2007. PROBLEM NO. 3: WASTE DISPOSAL. *Fortune*, Vol. 155, Issue 4, p. B-4.)

[19] **Aerobic composting** is the process of decomposing organic waste using microorganisms and an aerobic or oxygenated environment. (Pace, M., Miller, B., and Farrell-Poe, K. October 1, 1995. *The Composting Process*. Utah State University Extension. AG-WM 01.)

[20] **Anaerobic digestion** is a biochemical process in which particular kinds of bacteria digest biomass in an oxygen-free environment. Several different types of bacteria work together to break down complex organic wastes in stages, resulting in the production of "biogas." (Retrieved April 1, 2008, from www.oregon.gov/ENERGY/RENEW/Biomass/biogas.shtml #Anaerobic_Digestion.)

Shane's two-page opportunity was about the company he wanted to start, which he called Biospan. He would build a large anaerobic digester that would be at a centralized plant, and he would collect food waste from restaurants, grocery stores, and even homes to feed the digester and produce compost and biogas. The basic idea made sense—taking waste and producing a usable byproduct. Shane decided that this idea was worth investing time and effort to really understand it. Shane applied to Babson's Entrepreneur Intensity Track (EIT)[21] program with the idea of launching this business.

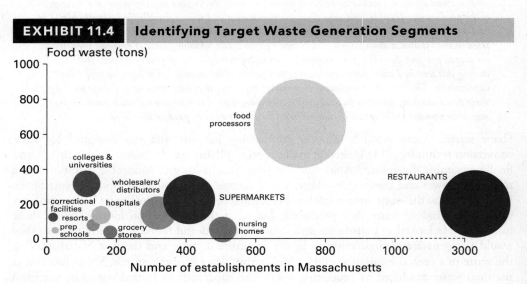

EXHIBIT 11.4 **Identifying Target Waste Generation Segments**

Source: Feed Business Plan.

Through the EIT program, Shane met with a venture capitalist who asked him tough questions like "How are you going to get six million dollars to build a big plant and how are you going to keep Waste Management from doing it bigger and better than you?" Six million dollars was a lot of money, and Shane didn't like the idea of competing with a company like Waste Management who did $13 billion in revenue each year. By asking the right questions, Shane also realized that a large centralized plant was inefficient. Transporting the waste to the plant and then sending the energy back to users added costs, used energy (gasoline for dump trucks), and wasn't as "Green" as a decentralized unit located where the waste was produced.

Shane then began to look at the industry and who might gain the greatest benefit from a mobile anaerobic system. Food processors, like large pig and chicken farms, already were starting to use anaerobic digestion systems. After more research, Shane found that grocery stores looked like the best option. They already were sorting their waste and sending it to composters, and the volume was low enough to discourage large players from entering. This seemed like a great marketplace for his decentralized systems.

You didn't have to ask them to change their habits. They were already sorting their waste, and the system could be implemented on location without disrupting their day-to-day operation.

Shane wanted to get into the industry as efficiently as possible, so he started to look for existing anaerobic systems that he could adapt to his target. He couldn't find any systems

---

[21] EIT is a curriculum focused on deep business planning and launch of a business during the final year of a student's education.

that could handle high solid content; they were mostly set up for human or animal waste. Furthermore, those companies building these systems were targeting larger scale, centralized plants, not smaller, decentralized systems that Shane envisioned. Many people, mainly the business professionals in anaerobic digestion, were saying that decentralized systems would be too small to be effective. In Europe, they were already using anaerobic digestion for food waste but only on a large scale. From the previous business models and the waste industry's frame of mind, the onsite model was not seen as profitable, but with the increases in energy prices and raised awareness in green tech, it started to make more sense. Shane believed if the technology could be produced, the idea would be easy to market in a food retail industry where the profit margins were razor thin and competition fierce.

The Product

The **feed** system, known as the R2, would utilize anaerobic digestion (AD), a clean, safe, and proven technology, to turn biodegradable waste into fuel (biogas) for a distributed electricity generation unit. AD is the breakdown of organic material by microorganisms in the absence of oxygen. Although this process occurs naturally in landfills, AD usually refers to an artificially accelerated operation that processes organic waste to produce biogas and a stable solid residue. People have been turning waste into biogas for hundreds of years, and many developing countries rely on small-scale AD systems for cooking. AD has grown rapidly in Europe, mostly in large centralized plants using advanced technologies. The R2 is a combination of the cheap, compact systems of India and China and the large-scale, expensive, and technologically sophisticated systems of Europe: a fully automated system that enables the customers to process waste and generate energy onsite without changing current waste disposal behavior.

> The decentralized nature of our system meant that you could place the R2 (see Exhibit 11.5) at the back of the store right in the same space that the organic waste dumpster currently occupied. It was critical to our potential customers that this system didn't require more space or alter the footprint of the current store (see Exhibit 11.6).

EXHIBIT 11.5	The R2 System: Compact Onsite Waste Conversion for Supermarkets

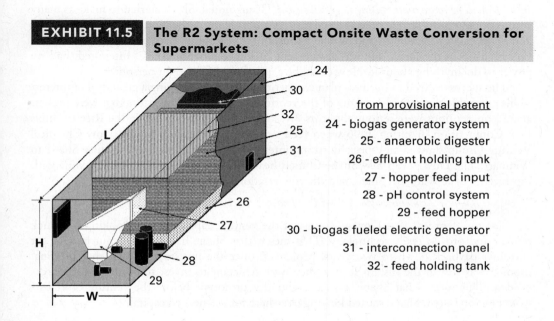

from provisional patent

24 - biogas generator system
25 - anaerobic digester
26 - effluent holding tank
27 - hopper feed input
28 - pH control system
29 - feed hopper
30 - biogas fueled electric generator
31 - interconnection panel
32 - feed holding tank

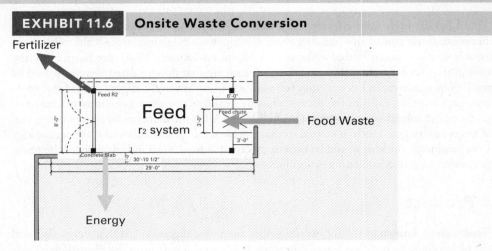

Source: Feed Business Plan.

The automation is made possible by the integrated control technology that operates the patented pH-balancing unit to continually optimize system performance. Other novel and patented ideas that differentiate the system include an integrated biogas generator unit, a gravity-fed system that increases efficiency while reducing cost and complexity, a multi-tank system for system reliability and flexibility, and pH balancing of the waste stream to handle diverse waste. Other than biogas, the R2 produces nutrient-rich compost that could potentially be sold to farmers. The projected price that the grocery store would pay for its R2 was around $300,000.

Lots of Interest

Craig Benson, a professor at Babson, told Shane that the best way to attract investors was to go and talk to the biggest customer you could find. *"If you can find a customer for your product, investors will be more than willing to get on board,"* Craig noted. Shane started to make as many connections as possible. He called several grocery store chains in the Northeast, including Stop and Shop, Shaw's, Walmart, and Whole Foods, but it was always hard get in front of anyone very high up in the ranks. He was always sent to someone who, even if interested, had no power to do anything about it. How could he get in front of the right person?

The success of **feed** in business plan competitions was also bringing a great deal of interest to his anaerobic digester idea. Many of the venture capitalists and investors that were present at the competitions were serious about its investment possibilities. During the Rice Business Plan Competition in spring 2006 when **feed** won the sustainability award, Dow Chemical Venture Group showed an especially strong interest and said they could introduce Shane to Walmart. The Dow group flew Shane to their headquarters and put him on the phone with top executives at Walmart. Shane said the conversation went something like this:

> *Does it have a 24-month payback time? I said no and they basically hung up.*

The problem was that Dow and most of the venture capitalists were looking for quick returns and proven ready technology. That meant that Shane had to figure out how to get customer payback down to two years. Moreover, once the investors realized that the final product was still in the distant future, they were reluctant to invest the time and resources needed. This meant that Shane needed to build a prototype before the venture capitalists would be interested. Shane started looking elsewhere for the needed capital.

Through the grapevine Shane heard about a Massachusetts Technology Collaborative (MTC) grant for onsite energy providers. To be eligible you needed to meet a set power output and find a buyer for the electricity that would sign on to the project. The MTC grant would then pay a certain amount of money for each kilowatt you could generate from the green energy method. Shane had a connection through a friend of the family at Ring Brothers grocery store, a small local grocery store on Cape Cod. Ring Brothers agreed to sign on as the company sponsor and **feed** won the grant for $195,000.

The grant required that **feed** first run a feasibility study before it could actually start to build the prototype, and the grant provided $20,000 for the research study. So Shane took a look at how much actual food waste Ring Brothers produced and found that they weren't producing enough waste to make the system feasible for the required energy output of 50 kw that was needed for the grant. Without the proper energy production output, they were forced to tell MTC that they were not going to be eligible for the $195,000 grant.

Team Building

Based upon his experience with Ring Brothers and the knowledge that he needed to build a prototype, Shane realized that he didn't have the skill set to do this venture on his own. He needed some technical expertise on the founding team. Shane knew that he would need an engineer to run the actual research and production of the first prototype. He needed someone who could take over a large part of the company and have the ability to get things done without supervision. A friend of Shane's who worked at Raytheon told him that he worked with a young engineer who fit the profile that Shane was looking for.

Ryan Begin specialized in product development at Raytheon, where he led a multidisciplinary team of engineers in the integration of advanced missile defense hardware. While Ryan enjoyed the big paycheck, he was looking for something different. Before Raytheon, Ryan had worked on multiple renewable energy and non-energy products through Clarkson University and other private organizations.

> I wanted to get out of the large corporation and saw the feed concept as really interesting. It was in the green space, where I had done some work before. But most importantly, I could be on the ground floor of something potentially huge.

When they met, Shane knew that he had found the business partner he was looking for and that Ryan would be a strong addition to the team.

> Ryan has the unique ability to get his hands dirty in putting the prototype together, but at the same time he is also very smart and brings a lot of expertise to the table. He has a great work ethic, and he's the kind of guy that works so hard and is so driven that he makes you feel guilty if you're not working just as hard.

After their initial meeting, Ryan began to run some of the numbers Shane had presented him regarding the biogas and electricity production of the suggested system. Although he found that many of numbers were on the high end of possibility, they still were within the range of having some real potential.

> I could see that some of Shane's projections were off by a lot, but the potential was there. Also the fact that he already had interested customers and investors reaffirmed my feelings that this could be a great opportunity for me.

Ryan was leaving a high-paying job at Raytheon with stability and benefits for a job with a new company and little or no salary.

I had a choice to make, I could continue to take the safe route with Raytheon, or I could put it all on the line to test my skills and have the chance to do something big and exciting. I didn't feel like I was doing any real engineering at Raytheon. Being able to lead product development within the renewable energy field was very appealing to me. I could also see that Shane had real business savvy and really believed strongly in his idea and had what it would take to sell it.

To entice and reward Ryan, Shane agreed to take him on as a co-founder and to give him some founder's shares. After some back and forth on the amount of stock Ryan would receive in the company, they settled on 20% of the founder's shares and the goal of paying a salary once they had raised a significant amount of investment.

EXHIBIT 11.7 **Feed Income Statement Projections**

Income Statement Years 1 to 5 ($)

	Year 1		Year 2		Year 3		Year 4		Year 5	
NET REVENUES	320,000	100%	1,880,000	100%	6,555,000	100%	13,985,000	100%	24,345,750	100%
COST OF REVENUE	332,800	104%	1,440,629	77%	4,939,057	75%	8,794,486	63%	15,538,904	64%
GROSS PROFIT	(12,800)	-4%	439,371	23%	1,615,943	25%	5,190,514	37%	8,806,846	36%
OPERATING EXPENSES										
Sales & Marketing	29,600	9%	96,400	5%	315,150	5%	521,550	4%	838,373	3%
Salaries & Benefits	0	0%	0	0%	58,500	1%	102,000	1%	108,000	0%
Initial Branding Efforts	20,000	6%	40,000	2%	60,000	1%	0	0%	0	0%
Other	9,600	3%	56,400	3%	196,650	3%	419,550	3%	730,373	3%
Research & Development	14,600	5%	190,900	10%	349,300	5%	727,550	5%	1,062,373	4%
Salaries & Benefits	9,600	3%	90,900	5%	249,300	4%	527,550	4%	862,373	4%
Product Development	5,000	2%	100,000	5%	100,000	2%	200,000	1%	200,000	1%
General and Administration	17,067	5%	171,100	9%	485,790	7%	742,417	5%	1,048,495	4%
Salaries & Benefits	0	0%	103,500	6%	300,690	5%	405,600	3%	504,000	2%
Depreciation	667	0%	4,000	0%	9,000	0%	11,667	0%	11,667	0%
Rent & Utilities	0	0%	6,000	0%	15,000	0%	15,450	0%	15,914	0%
Legal Feed	10,000	3%	20,000	1%	30,000	0%	30,000	0%	30,000	0%
Other	6,400	2%	37,600	2%	131,100	2%	279,700	2%	486,915	2%
Total Operating Expenses	61,267	19%	458,400	24%	1,150,240	18%	1,991,517	14%	2,949,241	12%
EARNINGS FROM OPERATIONS	(74,067)	-23%	(19,029)	-1%	465,703	7%	3,198,997	23%	5,857,605	24%
TAXES	0	0%	0	0%	(149,043)	-2%	(1,279,599)	-9%	(2,343,042)	-10%
NET EARNINGS	(74,067)	-23%	(19,029)	-1%	316,660	5%	1,919,398	14%	3,514,563	14%

Next Steps

With the start of a team and a strong customer interest, Shane and Ryan knew they had to build a functioning prototype. They had run some preliminary numbers and put together some pro-forma financials (see Exhibits 11.7–11.9 for pro-forma financials). They showed that **feed** needed investment now. Where could they get the $250,000 dollars needed to build the prototype (see Exhibit 11.8)? While most venture capitalists wouldn't invest at this stage, there were a few who might—but at what valuation and how long would it take to close the deal? Shane also could raise the money through family and friends, but this would take time as well. Shane and Ryan were anxious to get started, but they knew if they couldn't build a prototype, **feed** would never get off the ground.

EXHIBIT 11.8	Feed Balance Sheet Projections					
	Begin	**Year 1**	**Year 2**	**Year 3**	**Year 4**	**Year 5**
ASSETS						
CURRENT ASSETS						
Cash	250,000	174,926	140,904	866,314	3,127,462	7,174,275
Accounts Receivable		1,200	10,159	40,000	234,000	772,000
Inventories		0	0	60,000	130,000	331,200
Other Current Assets		204	1,224	60,000	130,000	276,000
Total Current Assets	250,000	176,330	152,287	1,026,314	3,621,462	8,553,475
PROPERTY & EQUIPMENT	0	1,500	16,000	29,250	32,500	31,250
TOTAL ASSETS	250,000	177,830	168,287	1,055,564	3,653,962	8,584,725
LIABILITIES & SHAREHOLDERS' EQUITY						
CURRENT LIABILITIES						
Short-Term Debt	0	0	0	0	0	0
Accounts Payable & Accrued Expenses		1,693	10,159	522,000	1,131,000	2,401,200
Other Current Liabilities		204	1,224	60,000	130,000	276,000
Current Portion of Long-Term Debt	0	0	0	0	0	0
Total Current Liabilities	0	1,897	11,383	582,000	1,261,000	2,677,200
LONG-TERM DEBT (less current portion)	0	0	0	0	0	0
STOCKHOLDERS' EQUITY						
Common Stock	250,000	250,000	250,000	250,000	250,000	250,000
Preferred Stock	0	0	0	0	0	0
Retained Earnings		(74,067)	(93,096)	223,564	2,142,962	5,657,525
Total Equity	250,000	175,933	156,904	473,564	2,392,962	5,907,525
TOTAL LIABILITIES & EQUITY	250,000	177,830	168,287	1,055,564	3,653,962	8,584,725

EXHIBIT 11.9 Feed Cash-Flow Projections

	Year 1	Year 2	Year 3	Year 4	Year 5
OPERATING ACTIVITIES					
Net Earnings	(74,067)	(19,029)	316,660	1,919,398	3,514,563
Depreciation	500	5,500	11,750	16,750	21,250
Working Capital Changes					
(Increase)/Decrease Accounts Receivable	(1,200)	(8,959)	(29,841)	(194,000)	(538,000)
(Increase)/Decrease Inventories	0	0	(60,000)	(70,000)	(201,200)
(Increase)/Decrease Other Current Assets	(204)	(1,020)	(58,776)	(70,000)	(146,000)
Increase/(Decrease) Accts Pay & Accrd Expenses	1,693	8,466	511,841	609,000	1,270,200
Increase/(Decrease) Other Current Liab	204	1,020	58,776	70,000	146,000
Net Cash Provided/(Used) by Operating Activities	(73,074)	(14,022)	750,410	2,281,148	4,066,813
INVESTING ACTIVITIES					
Property & Equipment Other	(2,000)	(20,000)	(25,000)	(20,000)	(20,000)
Net Cash Used in Investing Activities	(2,000)	(20,000)	(25,000)	(20,000)	(20,000)
FINANCING ACTIVITIES					
Increase/(Decrease) Short-Term Debt	0	0	0	0	0
Increase/(Decrease) Curr. Portion LTD	0	0	0	0	0
Increase/(Decrease) Long-Term Debt	0	0	0	0	0
Increase/(Decrease) Common Stock	0	0	0	0	0
Increase/(Decrease) Preferred Stock	0	0	0	0	0
Dividends Declared	0	0	0	0	0
Net Cash Provided/(Used) by Financing	0	0	0	0	0
INCREASE/(DECREASE) IN CASH	(75,074)	(34,022)	725,410	2,261,148	4,046,813
CASH AT BEGINNING OF YEAR	250,000	174,926	140,904	866,314	3,127,462
CASH AT END OF YEAR	250,000 174,926	140,904	866,314	3,127,462	7,174,275

EXHIBIT 11.10 Startup Capital Needed to Build Prototype

Components of Digester	$150,000
Engineering Salaries	75,000
Other/Misc	25,000
Total	**$250,000**

Preparation Questions

1. Is **feed** an opportunity?
2. Where can Shane raise the necessary money to build the prototype?
3. What are the implications on valuation for the different sources?

melking/iStockphoto

Halloween pumpkin leaf bags.

LEGAL AND TAX ISSUES, INCLUDING INTELLECTUAL PROPERTY

Why, When, and How to Choose an Attorney

Many enthusiastic entrepreneurs are so excited about where they're going that they forget to consider where they've been. They're surprised to learn that there may be serious limitations imposed upon their freedom of action arising out of their former employment. Some of these limitations may be the result of agreements signed by the entrepreneur while employed in her former position. Others may be imposed as a matter of law, without any agreement or even knowledge on the part of the employee. These considerations are among many that suggest that entrepreneurs obtain an early consultation with an appropriate attorney.

This chapter was written by Richard Mandel, Kirk Teska, and Joseph S. Iamdioio,

Unfortunately, many people perceive engaging an attorney as an unnecessary expense when beginning a new venture. However, the earlier you can consult a professional, the more likely your business will avoid costly mistakes. For example, without an attorney to advise you with regard to the drafting of a partnership or stockholders' agreement (described later in this chapter), the remaining partners may have no way of retrieving the share of the business owned by the estate of a founder who has left the business for a "better opportunity." Or the entrepreneur may be confronted by a large income tax bill for his receipt of "sweat equity."

The laws in the United States do not officially recognize legal specialties. In practice, however, the U.S. legal profession has become highly specialized. Thus, most patent attorneys do very little else, and most good litigation attorneys concentrate on litigating. The representation of startups and small businesses has become a specialty as well.

An attorney experienced in the problems of startups will be aware of the myriad issues that should be covered in a stockholders or partnership agreement and the other unique problems facing entrepreneurs. He or she will be able to advise among the various choices of legal entities available to entrepreneurial enterprises as well as to advise with regard to any residual obligations owed by an entrepreneur to previous employers. Most general corporate lawyers, representing larger, more established enterprises, are simply not as familiar with issues such as these. In addition, attorneys who practice in the start-up world will be familiar with these companies' unique cash-flow problems and may be willing to work out installment payments or other arrangements to ease the strain on tight start-up cash flow.

Leaving Your Present Position

Corporate Opportunity

The **corporate opportunity** doctrine is an outgrowth of the traditional obligation of loyalty owed by an agent to a principal. In its most common form, it prohibits an officer or director of a corporation, a partner in a partnership, or a person in a similar position from identifying a business opportunity that would be valuable to his company and using that information for his own benefit or the benefit of a competitor.

Thus, when the president, director, and effective owner of 66% of a corporation formed for the purpose of pursuing contracts to provide air transportation to Germany discovered such an opportunity, withheld such knowledge from his board and formed another corporation to pursue and obtain such a contract, he was held liable despite his claim that the original corporation might not have had adequate financial resources to deliver the service.[1] Generally, in order to discharge his legal obligation to the corporation of which he is a director, he would be required to disclose the opportunity to his board and allow the board to decide (without his participation) whether the corporation will make the purchase. Only after the corporation has been fully informed and decided *not* to take advantage of the opportunity may the director use that information for himself. Even then, as the new owner of a competitor, he would be required to resign his director position with the previous business.

The scope of this **duty of loyalty** is normally adjusted by the law to reflect the individual's position within the business. While the president and members of the board may be required to turn over knowledge of all opportunities that may be in any way related to the business of the company, lower-level employees probably have such an obligation only with regard to opportunities that are directly relevant to their positions.

Recruitment of Fellow Employees

Another aspect of the duty of loyalty owed by an employee to an employer is the legal requirement that the employee not knowingly take action designed to harm the employer's business. This is, perhaps, pure common sense. We would not expect the law to countenance a paid salesperson's regularly recommending that customers patronize a competitor, nor would we expect the law to endorse an engineer's giving his best ideas to another company. Similarly, courts have held that it is a breach of the duty of loyalty to solicit and induce fellow employees to leave their jobs.

Once again, the likelihood that a court would enforce this obligation against an employee depends to some extent on the nature of the employee's activities and her position in the company. Generally, two budding entrepreneurs need not fear reprisals for their having convinced each other to leave. Nor would there be much likelihood of liability if they convinced another employee to leave with them, especially if these conversations took place after working hours. However, if either of them worked in the human resources department, where their job descriptions would include recruiting and retaining employees, this same activity might well expose them to liability. Further, if their plan included the wholesale resignation of a relatively large number of employees, such that the company's ability to continue to efficiently function might be compromised, a court might be more likely to intervene with an injunction or other relief. Thus, when the president of a publishing company agreed to join a competitor and spent the remainder of his employment convincing 16 of his fellow employees to leave with him, he was found to have violated his fiduciary duty to his original employer.[2]

Noncompetition

More general than any obligation not to recruit fellow employees is the obligation not to compete with one's employer. Like most of the obligations we've already discussed, this duty is derived from the fiduciary relationship between employer and employee—specifically, the duty of loyalty. How can we justify accepting a paycheck from our employer while we are simultaneously establishing, working for, or financing a competing business?

The law imposes this duty not to compete on all employees, officers, directors, and partners while their association with the employer remains in effect. Unlike the obligation to protect proprietary information discussed below, however, the non-compete duty does not extend to the period after the termination of the relationship. To extend the obligation, the employer must obtain the employee's contractual promise.

We can analyze noncompetition agreements along many different dimensions, like the scope of the obligation. In an extreme case, an employee may have agreed not to engage in any activity that competes with any aspect of the business his former employer engaged in, or planned to engage in, at the time of the termination of the employee's association with the company. At the other end of the spectrum, the employee may have agreed only to refrain from soliciting any of his former employer's customers or (somewhat more restrictively) from dealing with any of the same, no matter who initiated the contact. We can also measure such agreements by the length of time they extend beyond the termination of employment and by their geographic scope.

Such measurements are important because, in the employment context, many states take the position that non-compete agreements contravene basic public policies, such as encouraging competition and allowing each individual to make the best use of his talents. A few such states (such as California) actually refuse to enforce all noncompetition agreements. Most, however, purport to enforce only those deemed reasonable, recognizing the employer's interest in protecting its business and goodwill. Only those restrictions that prevent likely harm to the employer's legitimate interests will be enforced.

Thus, a company could not enforce an agreement not to compete throughout New England against a salesman whose territory extended only to portions of Maine, New Hampshire, and Massachusetts.[3] Furthermore, although a manufacturer may be able to enforce such an agreement against an officer, salesperson, or engineer who has either direct contact with customers or knowledge of the company's processes and products, it might not be able to enforce the same agreement against a bookkeeper, whose departure would have little effect on the company's goodwill. Even the officer, salesperson, or engineer might be able to resist an agreement that purports to remain in effect beyond the time that the employer might reasonably need to protect its goodwill and business from the effects of new competition.

Another factor that may affect the enforceability of a noncompetition agreement is whether the employer agrees to continue part or all of the former employee's compensation during the noncompetition period. Similarly, a noncompetition agreement that might be unenforceable against an employee might nonetheless be enforceable against the seller of a business or a major stockholder having his stock redeemed. Finally, some courts that find the scope or length of a noncompetition agreement objectionable nonetheless enforce it to the maximum extent they rule acceptable. Others take an all-or-nothing approach.

Intellectual Property

Yet another potential complication arising out of an entrepreneur's previous employment is the possible use of information or technology belonging to the former employer. Such information need not be subject to formal patent or copyright protection to be protected from such use. And usually, by the time an entrepreneur has developed a viable business, she will have created a body of proprietary information of her own. At that point, she will be forced to turn her attention to protecting that information from use by competitors, employees, and end users who have failed to pay for the privilege. Thus, an in depth discussion of intellectual property rights would be advisable at this juncture.

Entrepreneurship and **intellectual property** (IP) go hand in hand. Intellectual property refers to creations of the mind, such as inventions; literary and artistic works; and symbols, names, images, and designs used in commerce. Business intellectual property includes patents, trade secrets, trademarks, and copyrights.

Patents protect inventions. **Trade secrets** cover proprietary information, whether it's in the form of a recipe, a customer list, or a unique way of conducting business. **Trademarks** are key in differentiating a business's products and services from those of others as well as in franchising arrangements. **Copyrights** protect authors' original creations, including literary, musical, artistic, software, and other intellectual works.

Investors need to be assured not only that a business has considered IP but also that it has implemented a plan to protect the company's crown jewels. And because IP protection costs money, it is necessary to budget for and manage it.

There are few guarantees in the area of IP. Not every patent application is granted; a name you've chosen for your company might not be available or be registrable as a trademark for a variety of reasons. Sometimes entrepreneurs must take risks. To do that wisely, entrepreneurs must understand the IP environment, which is slow to change in its legal underpinnings but continually being pushed to keep up with technological advances.

Even when it's successful, however, protecting IP is not the endgame. A patent, for example, doesn't generate revenue—it's just a document. A patent taken out for a great new idea is nothing unless people are willing to pay for that idea implemented in a product or service. Timing can play a crucial role in IP, just as it does in exploiting an entrepreneurial opportunity.

Finally, IP is everywhere. Just because a business isn't about technology, don't be misled into thinking it won't ever face IP issues. Patents today cover non-engineering subject matter such as holders for floral bouquets; trademark law is invoked in Internet search engines, pop-up ads, and Web sites in general; and even users of another company's products, for example, can be sued for patent infringement.

The Basics: What Is Protectable and How Should It Be Protected?

When someone conceives a new idea or designs a new product or method, two of the first questions to arise are these: Can I protect this? Can I keep competitors from copying this?

There are very practical reasons for protecting a new idea. Investors are loath to put money into a venture that cannot establish a unique product niche. Stockholders will challenge a corporation's investment of its resources in a program that can be easily copied once it is introduced to the market. All the time, effort, and money you invest in perfecting a product, as well as advertising and promoting it, may be wasted if imitators can enter the market on your heels with a product just like yours. Moreover, the imitators can cut prices because they have not incurred the startup expenses you had to endure to bring the idea from conception to a mass-producible, reliable, and appealing product or service.

The next question is, "Does my new product infringe the IP rights of anyone else?" Only by understanding the basics of IP can that be answered.

Once it is determined that a new idea, product, or method is eligible for one or more forms of IP protection—*patent, trade secret, trademark, or copyright*—secure the rights as quickly as the budget allows. A single product can qualify for different forms of protection, each obtained in a different manner and providing a different set of rights. For example, consider computer software. It will be marketed under a brand name and will be accompanied by a set of instructions. What is protectable, and how should it be protected? Where might others have IP that must be considered? The following sections provide information to help answer these questions.

Patents

Although there are actually three different kinds of patents, the kind usually used to protect an invention is a **utility patent**. Think utility patent whenever you think "better, cheaper, faster." But don't confuse invention in the patent sense with "eureka"-type ideas. Most patents are simple combinations of well-known components. Consider the following example.

Aerogel is listed in the Guinness Book of World Records as the world's lightest substance. A block of aerogel as big as an adult male weighs less than a pound but can support a small car. Recently, numerous companies have been patenting new uses for aerogel—as insulation, in fuel cells, and as building structures, just to give a few examples. Engineers at those companies didn't invent aerogel—a Stanford University researcher discovered it in the early 1930s. Still, the Patent Office will readily grant patents for new uses of aerogel.

Technically speaking, utility patents cover these classes of inventions:

- ▣ Chemical inventions include new compounds, new methods of making old or new compounds, new methods of using old or new compounds, and new combinations of old compounds. Assays, biological materials and methods, drugs, foodstuffs, drug therapy, plastics, petroleum derivatives, synthetic materials, adhesives, pesticides, fertilizers, and feeds are all protectable.

- ▣ General/mechanical inventions include everything from gears and engines to tweezers and propellers, from zippers to Jacques Cousteau's scuba regulator. For example, complex textile-weaving machines, space capsule locks and seals, and diaper pins are all protectable.

- ▣ Electrical inventions include everything from lasers to light switches, from the smallest circuit details to overall system architectural concepts.

Computer software is also patentable in various forms:

- ▣ Application programs, such as the software that runs in a computer used to control a chemical-processing plant or a rubber-molding machine, are patentable.

- Software for running a cash management account at a brokerage house or bank is patentable.

- Internal or operations programs that direct the handling of data in the computer's own operations are patentable.

Obtaining a Utility Patent. There is no rule that patents cover only remarkable inventions. Instead, the basic requirement for a utility patent is that the idea be different in some way from what came before. Most importantly, patent protection can be broad: The owner of the patent has the right to exclude others from making, using, selling, offering for sale, or importing the patented invention during the term of the patent. This "monopoly" lasts for 20 years from the date of filing. On average, though, given that a patent application takes about three years to process through the Patent Office, the patent term is usually about 17 years from the date the patent is granted.

The patenting effort begins when the inventor or inventors conceive of an invention. Typically, a registered patent attorney acting on the inventor's behalf prepares a patent application and files it in the U.S. Patent and Trademark Office. From the date the application is filed, there is a patent pending. There are no real legal rights associated with "patent pending." Full protection applies only if and when the Patent Office agrees that the invention is patentable and issues the patent. But with patent pending, a would-be competitor doesn't always know exactly what will be patented or when, and thus, he must proceed with caution in making the decision to offer the same or a similar product.

The patent application must contain a complete and understandable explanation of the invention. It doesn't have to be a nuts-and-bolts instruction manual. It is enough to convey the inventive concept so that a person "skilled in the art" can make and use the invention without undue experimentation. Further, the explanation must contain a full description of the best mode known by the inventor for carrying out the invention. For example, the inventor cannot use the second-best version or embodiment of the invention as an illustration for the patent application disclosure and keep secret the best embodiment. That could make the resulting patent invalid.

The *timing* of the filing is critical. In the United States, the patent application must be filed within one year of the first public disclosure, public use, sale, or even offer for sale of the product, or the filing will be barred and the opportunity to obtain a patent lost forever. This is known as the one-year period of grace. And if patent protection is beneficial in foreign countries, a patent application must be filed in the United States <u>before</u> any public activity occurs.

Market testing, exhibitions, or even use by the inventor himself can be a public use sufficient to activate the one-year period. One exception is a public use for experimental purposes. The test for whether a public use is an excepted experimental use is rigorous. The inventor must show that it was the operation and function of the invention that was being tested, not the appeal or marketability of the product employing the invention. Further, he should establish some evidence of the testing. For example, if samples were sent to potential customers for evaluation, it would be good to show that the customers returned filled-out evaluation forms and that the inventor considered and even made changes based on those evaluations.

The idea is that an inventor should be given only one year in which to file her patent application after she has begun to commercially exploit or to attempt to commercially exploit her invention. And it is not just an actual sale that triggers the one-year period: An offer for sale is sometimes enough, even if the sale is never consummated.

Criteria for Obtaining a Utility Patent. A patent "application" is not a form to be filled out. Instead, each patent application is unique, although all patent applications contain the same three basic sections:

- Drawings showing an embodiment of the invention

- A written description of the invention referring to the drawings akin to an engineering specification
- One or more claims—hybrid legal and technical language that "captures" the invention in words

June 23, 1964   J. S. KILBY   3,138,743

MINIATURIZED ELECTRONIC CIRCUITS

Filed Feb. 6, 1959   4 Sheets—Sheet 1

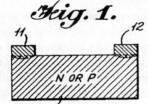

Fig. 1.

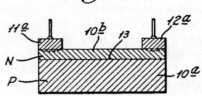

Fig. 1.ᵃ

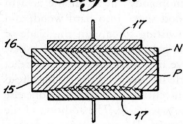

Fig. 2.

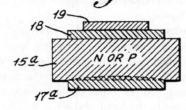

Fig. 2.ᵃ

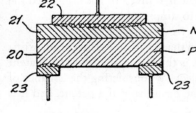

Fig. 3.

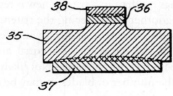

Fig. 5.

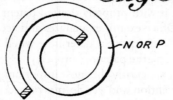

Fig. 5.ᵃ

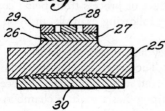

Fig. 4.

INVENTOR

Jack S. Kilby

BY

Stevens, Davis, Miller & Mosher
ATTORNEYS

Integrated circuit patent, 1958 (#3138743)

The definition of the patented invention—the protected property—is not what you disclose in the drawings and the specification portion of the application; these are only descriptions of one or more specific embodiments or versions of the invention. Instead, the coverage of the patent is defined by the third part of the application, the legal claims.

To qualify the invention for a patent, the claims must describe something both novel and unobvious. *Novelty* is a relatively easy standard to define: If a single earlier patent, publication, or product shows the entire claimed invention, the invention is not novel, and no patent will be issued. *Obviousness* is somewhat more difficult to grasp, and, worse, the test for obviousness is fairly subjective: Are the differences between the invention and all prior knowledge (including patents, publications, and products) such that the invention would have been obvious to a person having ordinary skill in the art? If so, the invention is not patentable even if it is novel.

Obviousness is a somewhat subjective determination, but many ideas have ultimately been deemed patentable even though they were originally rejected as obvious by an examiner of the U.S. Patent and Trademark Office. In one notable case, Anita Dembiczak came up with the idea of a plastic leaf bag configured to look like a giant Halloween-style pumpkin when stuffed with leaves. The U.S. Patent and Trademark Office essentially concluded that, since leaf bags were well known and pumpkins drawn on paper lunch sacks were also well known, the idea of a pumpkin leaf bag was obvious and therefore not patentable. Not so, said the Court of Appeals for the Federal Circuit: The Patent Office failed to prove there was any motivation to combine the idea of a Halloween pumpkin with a leaf bag. As a result, the patent for the leaf bag pumpkin was issued.

Consider another example of what "novelty" and "unobvious" mean in the area of patentability. Suppose a person is struggling to screw a wood screw into hard wood, and he realizes the problem is that he cannot supply enough twisting force with the blade of the screwdriver in the slot in the head of the screw. So he gets the bright idea of a new screwdriver with two shorter, crossed blades, which will give increased surface-area contact with two crossed slots in the head of the screw. The result: He has invented the Phillips head screwdriver, for use with a Phillips head screw. Certainly, the invention is "novel": No one else had made that design before. It is also "unobvious" and thus patentable. The addition of the second blade and has resulted in a wholly new screwdriver concept. The concept is patentable.

Now suppose another party, seeing the patent issued on this double-blade Phillips head, comes up with an improvement of her own. Her invention is to use three crossed blades (cutting the head of the screw into six equal areas). This design may not be patentable. Certainly it is novel, but is it unobvious? Not likely. Once the first inventor has originated the idea of increasing the number of blades, it may be obvious to simply add more blades.

Drafting the Patent Claims.

Once you have decided that a patentable invention exists, you must protect it with properly drafted patent claims. It is the claims that the U.S. Patent and Trademark Office examiner analyzes and accepts or rejects in considering the issuance of the patent; it is the claims that determine whether someone has infringed a patent, and it is the claims that define the patented property.

Claims, then, are clearly the most important part of a patent. It is no good to have claims that cover the invention and yet do not protect your product or process from being copied by competitors. Does this sound contradictory? Study the following example and you will understand.

Suppose an entrepreneur meets with a patent attorney and shows the attorney a new invention for carrying beverages on the slopes while skiing. The invention eliminates the risk of smashing glass, denting metal, or squashing a wine skin, and it also eliminates the need to carry any extra equipment: It's a hollow ski pole. The ski pole has a shaft, a chamber, and a handle. The handle has a threaded hole opening into the hollow shaft. Partway down the inside of the hollow shaft is a plastic liner that creates a chamber for holding liquids; this plastic liner is sealed to the shaft. The chamber is closed by a threaded plug. The entrepreneur wants to patent this invention, and so he assists the patent attorney in writing a description of the ski pole. They write the following claim:

A hollow ski pole for carrying liquids, comprising:

- a hollow shaft.
- a plastic liner inside the shaft to define a chamber for containing liquid.
- a handle on the shaft.
- a threaded hole in the handle that opens into the chamber.
- a threaded plug for sealing the threaded hole.

The patent application is filed. The U.S. Patent and Trademark Office examines the application and three years later issues the patent with that claim. The inventor is happy: The claim describes exactly what the entrepreneur markets and sells. But not happy for long—because a competitor comes out with a similar hollow ski pole that doesn't use a liner. The competitor simply welds a piece of metal across the inside of the shaft to make a sealed chamber. The competitor has avoided infringing the patent because there is no liner, which was one of the requirements of the patented claim. Still another competitor replaces the threaded plug with an upscale mahogany cork. Again, the patent is not infringed because there is no threaded plug, as required by the claim. Patent claims are akin to requirements, and a competitor who can sell a competing product without meeting all the claim requirements doesn't infringe the patent.

You can avoid this problem by exploring the various ways in which you can build your product before you file the patent application. You may need input from sales, marketing, engineering, and production people as well as from the inventor. After a thorough study, a better claim might emerge as follows:

A hollow ski pole for carrying liquids, comprising:

- a hollow shaft.
- a chamber in the hollow shaft for containing a liquid.
- a handle on the shaft having a hole opening into the chamber.
- a closure for the hole in the handle.

Now the liner and the threaded plug are not required. This claim, then, would likely be good enough to keep competitors at bay. There is a limit to how broadly you can word the claim, however. Eventually, if it becomes broader and broader and does not specify the ski pole or hollow shaft, it may apply to a bottle or a pot with a cover, and the patent will not be obtainable—it is not new. Careful claim drafting is thus critical.

If you don't remember anything else about patents, remember this: It's the claims that matter.

Provisional Patent Applications. Provisional patent applications are also available. People like provisionals because they don't have to include patent claims—indeed, a paper, specification, or report can be filed as a provisional. Be careful, though. In one case, a product embodying an invention was sold in the spring of 1996, a provisional application for the invention was filed in the spring of 1997, and a full patent application was filed in the fall of 1997. But, the provisional failed to adequately describe the invention actually claimed in the full patent application. The result? The patent was held invalid because the provisional failed to provide the necessary disclosure and thus the one-year deadline had been missed.

Provisionals have found favor because they are typically less expensive than full patent applications and allow companies to advertise "patent pending." In fiscal year 2012, over 160,000 provisional patent applications were filed.[4] But as the above case proves, provisionals are only as good as the details they contain. If you don't actually draft the legal claims for the invention, you should at least envision them to ensure that the provisional application adequately supports the claims you file later in the full utility application.

Design Patents. Another type of patent is the design patent. Hockey uniforms, ladies' dresses, computer housings, automobile bodies, buildings, shoes, and game boards are all protectable with design patents. But this type of patent covers only the *appearance* of the product, not the idea, underlying concept, or functionality of the product. What you see is what you get. Design patents are generally less expensive to obtain than utility patents but typically also offer far less protection.

Managing Patent Costs. Patents are expensive: Plan on spending between $15,000 to $25,000 to prepare and file a patent application and between $8,000 and $12,000 to prosecute the patent application. Prosecution is what occurs in the two to three years following filing of the application as you attempt to convince the Patent Office that the invention is worthy of a patent in the face of inevitable rejections. Foreign patents can cost over $10,000 per country in filing fees alone. But you have to put these costs in perspective. Consider the price of a mold for a plastic part, for example, or the cost of a marketing study undertaken by a consultant. Because of the potential value of a patent, the cost of filing is often well worth it. If, for example, Gillette's patent for the five-bladed Fusion razor can really be used to stop all competitors from introducing razors with similarly manufactured five blades, the cost of the Gillette patent and even the cost of patent litigation (typically $1 million or more) is well worth the protection afforded, especially given the enormous cost of Gillette's advertising campaigns surrounding the Fusion razor.

On the other hand, some patents may not have enough potential value to provide a return on the investment. Consider a patent for aerogel used as an insulating liner in deep-sea oil-well piping. If other insulating materials work as well or almost as well, the patent might not be worth the cost—unless it is worth something to advertise "the only deep-sea oil-well piping with aerogel!"

The problem is that, at the time the patenting decision must be made, the value of the patent might be hard to measure. Big companies regularly file for numerous patents and have a yearly IP budget in the millions of dollars. Entrepreneurial companies cannot typically afford those costs and thus must be particularly adept at planning and managing patents and other IP, all the while remembering the deadlines and the fact that the value of a given patent is measured by its claims. Finally, don't forget to make sure your new product or service doesn't infringe someone else's patent.

Trade Secrets

One benefit of trade secrets is they can cover everything patents cover—and much more. A trade secret is defined as knowledge, which may include business knowledge or technical knowledge that is kept secret for the purpose of gaining an advantage in business over one's competitors. Customer lists, sources of supplies of scarce materials, or sources of supplies with faster delivery or lower prices may be trade secrets. Certainly, secret processes, formulas, recipes, techniques, manufacturing know-how, advertising schemes, marketing programs, and business plans are all protectable.

Another benefit of trade secrets is there is no standard of invention to meet, as there is with a patent. If the idea is new in this context and if it is secret with respect to this particular industry or product, then it can be protected as a trade secret. Also unlike the case for patents, trademarks, and copyrights, there is no formal government procedure for obtaining trade secret protection. Protection is established by the nature of the secret and the effort to keep it secret.

Finally, a trade secret can be protected forever against disclosure by all those who have received it in confidence and from all who would obtain it by theft for as long as the knowledge or information is kept secret.

The key disadvantage of trade secrets is that, unlike the case with patents, there is no protection against discovery by fair means, such as accidental disclosure, independent inventions, and reverse engineering. Many important inventions, such as the laser, the integrated circuit, and the airplane, were developed more or less simultaneously by different persons. Trade secret protection would not permit the first inventor to prevent the second and subsequent inventors from exploiting the invention as a patent would.

But don't be misled into thinking trade secrets are a fallback position to patents or that they offer "free protection." Consider the feature of the Windows program that allows you to open two files at the same time, display them on the screen, and drag content from one into the other. Nice feature, but it cannot be a trade secret. Why not? Because you and everyone else can see the feature in operation every time you use it. Microsoft even advertises it. It's not a secret. Any competitor of Windows can write code that affords the same functionality. Microsoft's exact code that carries out that functionality is secret, to be sure, but even that is not "free" protection when you consider the overhead costs Microsoft incurs to ensure the code is always kept under wraps and that its numerous employees and consultants are subject to secrecy agreements.

Many companies use both approaches, filing a patent application and during its pendency keeping the invention secret. When the patent is ready to be issued, the company reevaluates its position. If the competition is close, they let the patent issue. If not, they abandon the patent application and rely on trade secret protection. But patent applications are now published 18 months after their earliest filing date, voiding trade secret protection unless the filer takes active steps to prevent publication (such as an agreement not to file an application for the invention in any foreign country).

Despite the problems with trade secrets, some have been appraised at a value of many millions of dollars, and some are virtually priceless. For example, Coca-Cola claims that its formula is one of the best-kept trade secrets in the world. Known as "Merchandise 7X," it has been tightly guarded since it was invented over 100 years ago. It is known by only two persons within the Coca-Cola Company and is kept in a security vault at the Trust Company Bank in Atlanta, Georgia, which can be opened only by a resolution from the company's board of directors. The company refuses to allow the identities of those who know the formula to be disclosed or to allow the two to fly on the same airplane. While some of the mystique surrounding the Coca-Cola formula may be marketing hype, it is beyond dispute that the company possesses trade secrets that are carefully safeguarded and extremely valuable.

Secrecy is essential to establishing trade secret rights; without it, there is no trade secret property. There are four primary steps for ensuring secrecy:

1. Negotiate confidential disclosure agreements with all employees, agents, consultants, suppliers, and anyone else who will be exposed to the secret information. The agreement should bind them not to use or disclose the information without permission.

2. Take security precautions to keep third parties from entering the premises where the trade secrets are used. Sturdy locks, perimeter fences, guards, badges, visitor sign-in books, escorts, and designated off-limits areas are just some of the ways that a trade secret owner can exercise control over the area containing the secrets.

3. Stamp specific documents containing the trade secrets with a confidentiality legend and keep them in a secure place with limited access, such as a safe, locked drawer, or cabinet.

4. Make sure all employees, consultants, and others who are concerned with, have access to, or have knowledge about the trade secrets understand that they are trade secrets, and make sure they recognize the value to the company of this information and the requirement for secrecy.

Bruno Vincent/Getty Images

Managing director of Apple Corps, Neil Aspinall leaves the Royal Courts of Justice during a break for lunch on March 29, 2006 in London. The Beatles' record label Apple Corps sued Apple Computer over use of the Apple name and logo in the music business which they said was in breach of a 1991 agreement.

Trade secret owners rarely do all these things, but they must do enough so that a person who misappropriates the secrets cannot reasonably excuse his conduct by saying that he didn't know or that no precautions were ever taken to indicate that something was a trade secret. This is important because, unlike patents, trade secret protection provides no "deed" to the property.

Trade secret misappropriations generally fall into one of two classes: someone who has a confidential relationship with the owner violates the duty of confidentiality, or someone under no duty of confidentiality uses improper means to discover the secret.

Trade secret theft issues frequently arise with respect to the conduct of ex-employees. Certainly, a good employee will learn a lot about the business during her employment. And some of that learning she will take with her as experience when she leaves. We cannot prevent that. The question is, "Did she simply arrive smart and leave smarter, or did she take certain information that was exclusively the company's?"

For example, in May 2012, CBS Broadcasting, Inc. brought suit against the American Broadcasting Companies, Inc. and related defendants alleging, among other things, misappropriation of CBS' trade secrets. Specifically, CBS alleged that ABC's new television show, *Life in a Glass House*, was developed using confidential, proprietary information related to the behind-the-scenes development, filming, and production of CBS' hit reality series *Big Brother*. It is further alleged that ABC obtained access to those trade secrets from 19 former CBS employees who had previously worked on *Big Brother* but had been hired by ABC to develop *Glass House*.

ABC, on the contrary, denies that any trade secrets have been employed in the production of *Glass House*. It points out that *Big Brother* has been on the air for 13 years and is one of approximately 400 reality shows to be broadcast during that period. It is highly unlikely, asserts ABC, that there is anything still secret about the production and editing of a reality show that could have been transferred to ABC by the former CBS employees.

In summary, trade secrets can be valuable, but they are not a form of "free protection," nor is protection available for secrets that can be discovered. Still, many investors rank trade secrets as at least as important as patents when they make an investment decision in a startup company.

Trademarks

Trademarks are the stuff of advertising. Technically speaking, trademark protection is obtainable for any word, symbol, or combination thereof that is used on goods to indicate their source. Any word—even common words such as "look," "life," and "apple"—can become a trademark, so long as the word is not used descriptively. "Apple" for fruit salad might not be protectable, but Apple for computers certainly is, and so, too, is Apple for a record company.

Common forms such as geometric shapes (circles, triangles, squares), natural shapes (trees, animals, humans), combinations of shapes, and colors may also be protected. Even the single color pink has been protected as a trademark for building insulation. Three-dimensional shapes such as bottle and container shapes and building features (for example, McDonald's golden arches) can serve as trademarks.

While people generally speak only of trademarks, that term also encompasses other types of marks. A trademark is for products. A **service mark** is a word or symbol or combination used in connection with the offering and provision of services. Blue Cross/Blue Shield, Prudential Insurance, and McDonald's are service marks for health insurance services, general insurance services, and restaurant services, respectively. McDonald's is a service mark (fast-food restaurant services) and also a trademark (the McDonald's brand Big Mac hamburger).

If you use any such name or feature to identify and distinguish your products, then think trademark protection. Ownership of a trademark allows you to exclude others from using a similar mark on similar goods that would be likely to confuse consumers as to the source of the goods. This right applies for the duration of ownership of the mark—that is, as long as the owner uses the mark.

Trademarks can be more valuable to some companies than patents and trade secrets combined. Consider the sudden appearance and abrupt increase in the worth of trademarks such as Cuisinart, Häagen-Dazs, and Ben & Jerry's. Consider also the increased value that a trademark name such as IBM, Microsoft, or GE brings to even a brand-new product. But don't be misled—trademarks and service marks protect the *names* of products and services, not the products and services themselves.

You can establish a trademark, unlike a patent, without any formal governmental procedure. You acquire ownership of a trademark simply by being the first to use the mark on the goods sold in commerce. It remains your property as long as you keep using it. And keep using it you must—because nonuse for a period of three years or more may constitute abandonment.

The mark should not be too descriptive of the goods on which you use it, and it is best to select a mark that is arbitrary and fanciful with respect to the goods. The reason is that every marketer, including a competitor, has the right to use a descriptive term to refer to its goods. Therefore, no one can secure exclusive rights to descriptive marks.

If a name is too descriptive, you cannot register it, and competitors may freely use it as is or in a slightly modified form. The more descriptive the mark, the less advertising required to inform consumers what the product is for. But so descriptive a mark enjoys a much lower level of protection.

On the other hand, a highly protectable arbitrary mark (Exxon, Kodak) requires significant expenditures in advertising dollars in order to inform consumers what the product or service associated with the mark actually is. Pick trademarks that are suggestive enough to adequately inform consumers but that are not too descriptive. Examples of marks held to be too descriptive include "Beer Nuts," "Chap-Stick," "Vision Center" (for an optical clinic), "Professional Portfolio System" (stock valuations), "5 Minute" (glue that sets in five minutes), "Body Soap" (body shampoo), "Consumer Electronics Monthly," "Light Beer," and "Shredded Wheat." The trademark Windows itself has more than once been the subject of legal action in which evidence existed that "windows" was descriptive before Microsoft adopted it.

A trademark owner should also take care to prevent the mark from becoming generic, as happened to Aspirin, Cellophane, Linoleum, and other product names. Thus, it is not proper to refer to, for example, a xerox—the correct form of description is a Xerox brand photocopier.

It is wise to research a proposed new mark to be sure the mark is clear before you use it; that is, verify that no one else is already using or has registered the same or a similar mark on the same or similar products. It's confusing to customers and expensive to change a mark and undertake the costs of all new printing, advertising, and promotional materials when you later discover that your mark has previously been used by another company. Moreover, in a due diligence study, whether at the time someone invests in your entrepreneurial company, at the time you make a public offering, or during a sale or merger, you can be sure a trademark search will be conducted. If you plan to enter foreign markets, make sure your mark does not mean something unintended in a foreign language.

Registering a Mark. Although trademarks don't have to be registered, there are significant benefits that make it worthwhile. You can register in individual states, or you can obtain a federal registration. A state registration applies only in the particular state that granted the registration and requires only use of the mark in that state. A federal registration applies to all 50 states, but to qualify, you must use the mark in interstate or foreign commerce. A distinct advantage of federal registration is that, even if you initially use a mark only locally—say, in New England—you can establish federal protection in all 50 states. Without a federal registration, you may later be blocked from using your mark in other states if a later user of the same mark, without knowledge of your use of the mark, federally registers it.

Also, you can file an application to register a mark that is not yet in use. After the U.S. Patent and Trademark Office examines the application and determines that the mark is registrable, you must show actual use within six months. The six-month period can be extended if good cause is shown. Nevertheless, before registration, even before actual use, the mere filing of the application establishes greater rights over others who actually used the mark earlier but did not file an application for registration.

A typical search and registration costs between $1,500 and $3,500 per mark. Given these fairly low costs, entrepreneurial companies regularly seek federal registration for all trademarks and service marks. A search increases the odds your registration will be successful, since the Trademark Office primarily evaluates two things: Is the mark too descriptive, and is it too similar to another already registered mark? If the answer to both these questions is "no," the registration is typically issued about a year after you file the trademark application.

Ownership of a Mark. Be careful with your trademark properties. You cannot simply sell a trademark by itself or transfer it like a desk, car, patent, or copyright. You must sell it together with the business or goodwill associated with the mark, or the mark will be considered abandoned.

Claiming ownership of a mark can be an important business decision. When Cuisinart started selling its food processors, it promoted them vigorously under the trademark Cuisinart. A good part of the business's success was due to the fact that the manufacture of the machines was contracted out to a quality-conscious French company, Robot Coupe, which had been making the machines for many years before they became popular among U.S. consumers under the mark Cuisinart. When price competition reared its head, Cuisinart found cheaper sources. Robot Coupe owned no patents and had no other protection. Cuisinart began selling brand X under the name Cuisinart, and a wild fight ensued through the courts and across the pages of major newspapers in the United States—but to no avail. The whole market had been created under the name Cuisinart, and Cuisinart had the right to apply its name to any machine made anywhere by anyone it chose. Robot Coupe, whose machine had helped create the demand for food processors, was left holding its chopper.

Copyright

Copyrights cover all manner of writings, and the term *writings* is very broadly interpreted. It includes books, advertisements, brochures, spec sheets, catalogs, manuals, parts lists, promotional materials, packaging and decorative graphics, jewelry, fabric designs, photographs, pictures, film and video presentations, audio recordings, architectural designs, and software.

Exact copying is not always required in order to engage in infringement. For example, you can infringe a book without copying every word; the theme itself may be protected. One example exists in the software area, where using the teachings of a book to write a program has resulted in copyright infringement of the book by the computer program. In another case, a program was infringed by another program even though the second program was written in an entirely different language and for an entirely different computer. Copyright, then, can sometimes be a good source of protection, but be careful: It doesn't generally protect engineering, inventions, marketing or advertising ideas, or business plans. The good news is that a copyright registration is easy to obtain, protection lasts a long time, and it is inexpensive (typically less than $500). But unless your business is related to some form of the arts (music, movies, books, photography) or software, copyright usually only offers very limited protection because ideas and functionality are not generally protected by copyright.

Copyright registration is not compulsory, but it bestows a few valuable benefits. If the copyright owner has registered the copyright, special damages can be recovered. This can be a real advantage in copyright cases where actual damages can be difficult and expensive to prove or actual damages are limited.

Registration simply requires filling out the proper form and mailing it to the Copyright Office with the proper fee and copies of the work to be registered. Accommodations are made for filing valuable or difficult deposit copies; for example, deposits for large computer programs may consist of only the first and last 25 pages. Further, if the program contains trade secrets, there is a provision for obscuring those areas from the deposit, since the Copyright Office's records are public. The Copyright Office doesn't really check to make sure the material is copyrightable; provided the form is filled out correctly, the Copyright Office will stamp it and you have a registration.

Figure 12.1 summarizes a few key aspects of the different avenues of IP protection.

International Protection for Intellectual Property

Obtaining protection for patents, trademarks, and copyrights in the United States alone is no longer sufficient in the modern arena of international competition and global markets. International protection often needs to be extensive and can be quite expensive, but there are ways to reduce and postpone the expense in some cases. You will want to consider protection in countries where you intend to market the new product or where competitors may be poised to manufacture your product.

A patent in one country does not protect the product in any other country: You must protect a novel product or method by a separate patent in each country. In addition, different countries have different conditions that you must meet to obtain any patent protection. The first and most important restriction is the time limit within which you must file an application to obtain a patent in a country or else forever lose your right to do so.

Patent Filing Deadlines.

Not all countries are the same with respect to filing deadlines. There is no period of grace in any other country but the United States, and each country has a slightly different view of what constitutes making an invention public. In Japan, for example, public use before the filing of an application bars a patent only if the public use occurred in Japan; in France, any public knowledge of the invention anywhere bars the patent.

Thus, whereas the United States allows a business one full year to test market its new product (see the earlier discussion), most other countries require that the patent application be filed before any public disclosure—that is, before the owner can begin to determine whether the new product will be even a modest success. Meeting this requirement is not inexpensive, especially when the U.S. dollar is down against the currencies of other major countries.

How to Extend Patent Filing Deadlines.

There are ways around having to file immediately in all foreign countries. If you file in the United States and then file in another country within one year of that date, the U.S. filing date applies as the filing date for that country. In this way, by filing one application for the invention in the United States, you can preserve your initial U.S. filing date for up to one year and then immediately make the

	Patents	**Trade Secrets**	**Trademarks**	**Copyright**
Subject Matter	Inventions and innovation, i.e., new products, features, and functionality	Only what can be kept secret	Names of companies, their products and services	Works of authorship, i.e., the arts and software
Cost	Expensive: $10–20K per patent per country	Depends on the volume of those secrets and the number of employees and consultants; definitely not "free"	Moderate: $1–3K per mark	Inexpensive: less than $500
Government Review	Yes—extensive and mandatory	No	Yes—moderate and optional but a good idea	Yes—but it is a rubber stamp
Term of Protection	On average, 17 years from issuance	Potentially forever—as long as the secret is kept secret	Potentially forever, as long as the mark is used	Long time—100 years
How Long to Achieve Protection	A fairly long time: 3–5 years	Immediately	Immediate—when the mark is used; registration takes about a year	Immediate, and registration takes only about a month
Pros	Can provide very broad protection even when an infringer didn't know about your patent	No government review; protects things not protectable by patents	Cost is moderate and the odds of achieving a registration can be determined beforehand	Inexpensive and immediate
Cons	Value is commensurate with the claims; high level of government scrutiny; strict time requirements	Cannot be used if the "secret" really isn't; others have the right to discover the secret on their own	Only protects names—not the products or the services themselves	Outside of software and the arts, copyright usually doesn't offer extensive protection

Figure 12.1

IP considerations

invention public through advertising, published articles, and sales. If within one year the product appears to be a success, you can then file in selected foreign countries, even though the prior public use of the invention would ordinarily bar your filing in those countries.

You can even delay up to 20 or even 30 months before incurring the costs of filing in individual countries. By filing a special Patent Cooperation Treaty (PCT) patent application in a specially designated PCT office within one year of your U.S. filing and by designating certain countries, you can preserve your right to file in those countries without further expense for 20 or 30 months after the U.S. filing date. That will provide an additional 8 or 18 months for test marketing the product. This does introduce the extra cost of the PCT application filing, but if you are considering filing in, say, six or more countries, it may be well worth the cost for three reasons:

- It delays the outflow of cash that you may not presently have or may require for other urgent needs.

- It provides for a uniform examination of the patent application.

- If the product proves insufficiently successful, you can decide not to file in any of the countries designated under the PCT and save the cost of all six national application filings.

Another cost-saving feature of international patent practice is the European Patent Convention (EPC), which is compatible with a PCT filing and which enables you to file a single European patent application and designate any one or more of the European countries in which you wish the patent to issue.

A number of international treaties affect trademark rights and copyrights as well. A "European" trademark registration is now available, for example, known as a Community Trade Mark (CTM). A single registration will cover the entire European Union (EU)—with the benefit of a single filing, you obtain plenary protection. However, there are certain drawbacks. For example, a single user in any country of the EU could block registration everywhere, and cost considerations make a CTM filing uneconomical unless you seek trademarks in at least three countries. Registration is also now possible simultaneously in the United States and other foreign countries via a treaty known as the Madrid Protocol.

Choice of Legal Form

Another important issue all entrepreneurs will confront is what legal form they should choose to operate their new venture. Many choices are available.

The most basic business form is the **sole proprietorship**, owned and operated by one owner who is in total control. No new legal entity is created; the individual entrepreneur just goes into business, either alone or with employees, but without any co-owners.

If there is more than one owner of the business, the default mode is the **general partnership**. This is the legal form that results when two or more persons go into business for profit, as co-owners, sharing profits and losses.

Another choice available to entrepreneurs is the **corporation**. This form is created by state government, as a routine matter, upon the entrepreneurs' filing an application and paying a fee. It is a separate legal entity, with legal existence apart from its owners, the stockholders.

A variation of the corporate choice is the **subchapter S corporation**. If a corporation passes a number of tests, it may elect to be treated as a subchapter S corporation, a designation that affects only its tax status. In all other respects, a subchapter S corporation is indistinguishable from all other corporations.

An increasingly popular form of business entity is the **limited liability company (LLC)**. This entity is owned by "members" who either manage the business themselves or appoint "managers" (either outsiders or a subset of the members) to run it for them. All members and managers have the benefit of limited liability (as they would in a corporation) and, in most cases, are taxed similarly to a subchapter S corporation without having to conform to the S corporation restrictions described later in this section.

Another possible legal form is a hybrid of the corporate and partnership forms, known as the **limited partnership**. Such a business would have one or more general partners, who would conduct the business and take on personal risk, and one or more limited partners, who would act as passive investors (similar to stockholders with no other interest in the business). Due to the availability of the limited liability company, this form of entity has over time faded into use in only a niches such as venture capital firms; it is no longer attractive to most businesses.

Also available is the **limited liability partnership (LLP)**, which is the entity of choice for many law firms, accounting firms, and the like, but is not widely used by other businesses.

Finally, a **not-for-profit entity** will typically take the form of a corporation or trust and elect nonprofit status as a tax matter. Although many startups do not make a profit, nonprofit status is available only to certain types of activities, such as churches, educational institutions, social welfare organizations, and industry associations. If an organization so qualifies, its income is exempt from taxation (as long as it doesn't stray from its exempt purpose), and if certain

	Control	Liability	Taxation	Administrative Obligations
Sole proprietorship	Owner has complete control	Unlimited personal liability	Not a separate taxable entity	Only those applicable to all businesses
Partnership	Partners share control	Joint and several unlimited personal liability	Not a separate taxable entity	Only those applicable to all businesses
Corporation	Control distributed among shareholders, directors, and officers	Limited personal liability	Separate taxable entity unless subchapter S election	Some additional
Limited liability company	Members share control or appoint managers	Limited personal liability	Not a separate entity unless affirmatively chosen	Some additional

Figure 12.2

Comparison of various business forms

additional tests are met, contributions to it may be tax deductible. All profits must be devoted to the company's exempt purpose; none may be distributed as dividends to private parties.

Although we can compare these forms of business on an almost endless list of factors, the most relevant include control issues, exposure to personal liability, tax factors, and administrative costs. We discuss these in detail in the following sections, and Figure 12.2 provides an overview of the issues and how they play out in the most relevant business forms.

Control

Since there is only one principal in the sole proprietorship, he wields total control over all issues. In the general partnership, control is divided among the principals in accordance with their partnership agreement (which need not be written but should be, to encourage specificity). The parties may decide that all decisions must be made by unanimous vote, or they may adopt a majority standard. More likely, they may require unanimity for a stated group of significant decisions and allow a majority vote for others.

Regardless of how power is allocated in the partnership agreement, in the eyes of third parties, each of the partners will have a free hand to contract with outsiders, subject only to the internal consequences of the partner's breaching his agreement with the others. This is also true for the consequences of torts committed by any partner acting in the course of partnership business.

A corporation, regardless of whether it has elected subchapter S status, is controlled by three levels of authority. Broadly speaking, the stockholders vote, in proportion to the number of shares they own, on the election of the board of directors, the sale or dissolution of the business, and amendments to the corporation's charter. In virtually all cases, these decisions are made either by the majority or by two-thirds of the votes cast. Thus, any group of stockholders owning a majority of the voting stock, can elect the entire board.

The board of directors in turn makes all the long-term and significant policy decisions for the business as well as electing the officers of the corporation. Votes are virtually always decided by majority. The officers, consisting of a president, treasurer, and secretary at a minimum, run the day-to-day business of the corporation and are the only level of authority that can bind the corporation by contract or in tort. It is not uncommon for the corporation's attorney to act as secretary, since the attorney presumably has the expertise to keep the corporate records of the company in an accurate manner.

The limited liability company can operate much like a general partnership. All members can share in control to the extent set forth in their agreement, known in most states as an *operating agreement*. However, members may choose to appoint one or more "managers" to control most of the day-to-day operations of the business.

Personal Liability

Should the business incur current liabilities beyond its ability to pay, must the individual owners risk personal bankruptcy to make up the difference? This unhappy result need not occur only as a result of poor management or bad business conditions. It could just as easily be brought about by an uninsured tort claim from a customer or a victim of a delivery person's careless driving.

In both the partnership and the sole proprietorship, the business is not recognized as a legal entity separate from its owners. Thus, the debts of the business are ultimately the debts of the owners if the business cannot pay. This unlimited liability is enough to recommend against these forms for virtually any business, with the exception perhaps of the one-person consulting firm, all of whose liability will be the direct result of the wrongdoing of its owner in any case.

If this unlimited liability is uncomfortable for the founders, imagine what it would mean to an investor. The investor no doubt has significant assets to lose and will likely have only limited control over the business decisions that may generate liability. This risk is made even worse by the fact that all partnership liabilities are considered joint and several obligations of all partners. Thus, the investor will be responsible for full payment of all partnership liabilities if the founders have no significant assets of their own.

The answer to this problem lies in the corporation and the limited liability company, both of which afford limited liability to all owners. If the business ultimately becomes insolvent, its creditors will look only to business assets for payment; any shortfall will be absorbed by the unfortunate creditors.

This solution is not quite as all-encompassing as it sounds. To begin with, creditors know these rules as well as entrepreneurs do. Thus, large or sophisticated creditors, such as banks and other financial institutions, will insist upon personal guarantees from the owners of the business before extending credit.

In addition, the law allows creditors to "pierce the corporate veil" and go after the owners of a failed corporation or LLC under certain conditions. The first situation in which this can occur involves a business that was initially underfunded or "thinly capitalized." A business should start out with a combination of capital and liability insurance adequate to cover the claims to which it might normally expect to be exposed. As long as the capital was there at the outset and has not been depleted by dividends or other distributions to owners, causing insolvency, the protection of the separate entity survives even after the capital has been depleted by unsuccessful operation.

The second situation that may result in the piercing of the corporate (or LLC) veil is the failure of the owners to treat the corporation or LLC as an entity separate from themselves by

- Failing to use *Inc., Corp., LLC*, or a similar legal indicator when dealing with third parties, or

- Commingling business and personal assets in a personal bank account or allowing unreimbursed personal use of corporate assets, or

- Failing to keep business and legal records and hold regular directors', stockholders', or members' meetings.

Taxation

Income taxes, both personal and corporate, that will be paid as a result of starting up and operating a business are an important consideration in the choice of the legal entity for a new venture. The ideal entity from the perspective of income taxes should do the following:

- Minimize or eliminate any personal income tax that might result from receipt of founder stock
- Maximize the tax shelter for the investors when the business has an annual loss
- Minimize taxes paid by the business, founders, and investors when the business has an annual profit
- Minimize capital gains taxes payable by the founders and investors if they sell all or some of their stock

No entity accomplishes all the above income tax considerations and at the same time shields the owners from liabilities incurred by the business. Although various forms of partnership might be more favorable tax shelters for the investors, operating businesses are almost always set up as a corporation or limited liability company for reasons that we have examined and will examine in the remainder of this and the next section.

Entrepreneurs are often warned about the *double taxation* that arises when a corporation makes a profit, pays income tax on it, and then distributes part or all of its profit after tax as a dividend to its stockholders, who in turn pay income tax on that dividend; this means that the same money is taxed twice (although potentially at a reduced dividend rate the second time).

In reality, however, double taxation is more a myth than a legitimate threat to the small business. In fact, in most cases, it presents an opportunity for significant economic savings. To begin with, most small corporations lower or even eliminate their profit by increasing deductible salaries and bonuses for their owners up to the limit deemed "unreasonable" by the Internal Revenue Service. The owners then pay only their own individual income tax on the money.

On the other hand, if it is necessary to retain some of these earnings, the start-up corporation will normally pay income tax at a lower rate than the stockholders would have, since tax will be imposed at the lowest marginal corporate rate rather than the stockholders' highest rate. When the corporation is later sold, the stockholders will be taxed at favorable capital gain rates, and the corporation will have had the use of the money in the meantime to create greater value. Thus, it is the rare small corporation that will actually pay double tax.

Furthermore, if the corporation meets certain eligibility requirements, it can elect, under subchapter S of the Internal Revenue Code, to be taxed essentially as if it were a partnership. Whatever profit or loss it may generate will appear on the tax returns of the stockholders in proportion to the shares of stock they own, and the corporation will file only an informational return. To take advantage of this option, the corporation must have 100 or fewer stockholders, all of whom must be individuals (with some exceptions) and either resident aliens or citizens of the United States. The corporation can have only one class of stock (with the exception of classes based solely on different voting rights) and is ineligible to participate in most multiple-entity corporate structures. Note there is no size limit on subchapter S eligibility.

The subchapter S election can be very useful in a number of circumstances. For example, if the business is expected to be profitable and investors insist upon a share of those profits, one cannot avoid double taxation by increasing salaries and bonuses. Since an investor performs no services for the business, any compensation paid to him would automatically be deemed "unreasonable." But under subchapter S, since there is no corporate tax, a dividend to the stockholders would be taxed only at the stockholder level.

If the business were to become extremely successful, the founders could reap the rewards without fear that their salaries might be attacked as "unreasonable," since, again, there are no corporate compensation deductions to disallow. An early subchapter S election can also avoid double taxation should the corporation eventually sell all its assets and distribute the proceeds to the stockholders in liquidation.

Furthermore, if the business is expecting losses in the short term, the investors might be able to use their share of the losses (determined by percentage of stock) to shelter other income subject to the passive loss rules of the Internal Revenue Code.

After having considered all of this, the founding entrepreneurs might wish to form a corporation, elect subchapter S treatment, and arrange their affairs such that, when an angel investor contributes his investment, he can make as much use of short-term losses as possible. However, since profits and losses in an S corporation must be allocated in accordance with stock ownership and only one class of stock is allowed, any disproportionate allocation of losses to the investor would have to be accompanied by a disproportionate allocation to him of later profits. More creative allocations of profit, loss, and control could be accomplished in a general (or limited partnership), but one or more of the owners would have to accept exposure to unlimited liability in those entities.

Limited liability companies were designed for just this circumstance. If structured carefully, they afford the limited liability and "pass-through" tax treatment of the S corporation, while avoiding the S corporation's restrictive eligibility requirements. Freed from these restrictions, limited liability companies can use creative allocations of profit, loss, and control that would constitute prohibited multiple classes of stock in the S corporation context.

The LLC is not the solution for all situations, however. The investor may have little ability to use losses due to a lack of material participation in the business as required by the Internal Revenue Code's passive loss rules. Worse yet, the investor would certainly not be enthusiastic at the notion of "phantom income" when the company's financial performance turns positive and the company begins to retain earnings.

Initial Investment of the Founders

As a general rule, founders normally arrange the issuance of their equity in the venture for very little tangible investment. After all, they intend to look to investors for working capital, and their investment will be the services they intend to perform for the business.

Of practical concern, however, is the fact that any property (including stock or LLC membership interests) transferred to an employee in exchange for the employee's services is considered taxable income under the Internal Revenue Code. Thus, whenever equity is issued to founders in exchange for services (so-called "sweat equity"), they may face an unexpected tax liability as a result.

In the LLC context, the Internal Revenue Service will, in most cases, value the ownership interest granted to the partner or member as equivalent to the amount credited to the capital account. Thus, as long as a noncontributing owner's capital account begins at zero and grows only to the extent of future profits, there will be no current taxation at the time of issuance.

However, in the corporate context, at approximately the same time that the founders are receiving their stock for minimal investment, the investors will be putting in the real money. Since the investors will be paying substantially more for their stock than the founders are paying for theirs, the Internal Revenue Service will likely take the position that they are getting a bargain in exchange for the services they are providing to their company. Thus the founders may be facing an unexpected income tax on the difference between the price per share of the investors' stock and the price of theirs.

One way to solve this problem is to postpone the investor's investment until the founders can argue for an increase in the value of the corporation's stock. Aside from the essentially fictional nature of this approach, most founders probably cannot wait that long. Instead, the parties must design a vehicle for the investors sufficiently different from the founders' interests to justify the higher price. This is taken care of in the LLC context by the difference in capital accounts. In the corporate context some form of preferred stock will serve the purpose (although the issuance of preferred stock would render a corporation ineligible for subchapter S status, as it would then have more than one class of stock).

How does all this inform the choice of entity? Essentially, the pass-through form exposes the investor to potential "phantom income" if the company does well, while failing to provide practical use of losses on his personal return if the company loses money. On the other hand, preferred stock in a C corporation provides the liquidation, dividend, participation, and conversion privileges the investor desires without the risk of phantom income. And from the founders' point of view, issuance of preferred stock to their investor has the benefit of solving their potential income tax problems. The parties will therefore likely agree on the C corporation as the best choice of entity unless the investor is looking for current distributions of profit instead of the company's retaining profits to fuel further growth.

Administrative Obligations

Start-up businesses should obtain an Internal Revenue Service federal identification number. On the state level, the business should obtain a sales and use tax registration number, both to facilitate reporting and collection of such taxes and to qualify for exemption from such taxes when it purchases items for resale. A nonprofit entity has 18 months to file for and secure nonprofit status from the Internal Revenue Service. Furthermore, all business entities will incur a certain amount of additional accounting expense, specifically for the calculation and reporting of taxable profit and loss.

Corporations and limited liability companies, however, bring some additional administrative burden and expense. They must file an annual report with the state government in addition to their tax return. This document usually reports only the business's current address, officers, directors, managers, and similar information, but it is accompanied by an annual maintenance fee. The fee, in addition to any income tax that the state may levy, must be paid to avoid eventual involuntary dissolution by the state.

In addition, corporations are sometimes formed under the laws of one state, while operating in another. In particular, the state of Delaware has a corporate law particularly sympathetic to management that has also been thoroughly interpreted by its long history of complex corporate litigation. Although these are questionable advantages in the context of a small business (where management and stockholders are generally the same people), Delaware does offer a method of calculating its fees that does not penalize a corporation for having a large number of authorized shares. This allows a corporation whose compensation strategy includes stock grants or stock options to use much larger numbers of shares in these grants, creating a psychological appearance of generosity that may not mathematically exist. Even corporations that have not adopted such a strategy often form in Delaware merely to share in an appearance of sophistication.

In all such cases, the corporation must pay not only initial and maintenance fees to the state of Delaware (or whichever state is chosen for formation), along with the costs of maintaining an address for service of process there, but also initial and annual maintenance fees to qualify to do business in each state in which it actually operates. Many large, national concerns pay these fees in virtually all 50 states.

Choosing a Name

The choice of a name for a business may seem at first to be a matter of personal taste, without many legal ramifications. However, since the name of a business may ultimately be the repository of its goodwill, the owner should choose a name that will not be confused with the name of another business.

Although partnerships and sole proprietorships need not do so, corporations and limited liability companies obtain their existence by filing charters with the state. As part of this process, each state will check to see whether the name of the new entity is "confusingly similar" to the name of any other entity currently registered with that state. Some states will also deny the use of a name they deem misleading, even if it is not similar to the name of another entity.

Stockholders' and Operating Agreements

The owners' respective investments will normally be memorialized in an operating agreement in the case of an LLC and in a combination of a stock purchase agreement, charter amendments, and stockholders' agreement in the case of a corporation. In a partnership, very similar provisions allocating equity interests and rights to distributions of profit and cash flow would appear in a Partnership Agreement. In all these cases, however, the parties would be well advised to go beyond these subjects and reach written agreement on a number of other potentially thorny issues at the outset of their relationship.

Negotiating Employment Terms

The founders should reach agreement with the investor about their commitment to provide services and the level of compensation for doing so. It would be very unusual for the founders to forgo compensation solely to share the profits of the business with their investor. For one thing, what would they be living on in the interim? For another, the profits of the business are properly conceived of as the amount left over after payment of the expenses of the business—including reasonable compensation to its employees. Thus, the founders should negotiate employment terms into the operating or stockholders' agreement, setting forth their responsibilities, titles, compensation, and related issues.

This is especially important in the case in which any individual founder may hold only a minority interest in the corporation (depending upon the voting rights given to the preferred stock). She may wish to foreclose the possibility that the other owners may ally and employ a majority of the shares to remove the founder as a director, officer, or employee of the company. Given the lack of any market for the shares of this corporation, such a move would essentially destroy any value the shares had for the holder in the short run.

Although a concise description of each party's obligations and rewards is still advisable to avoid dispute, this negative scenario would be illegal in a partnership (in the absence of serious misconduct by the party being removed), since the majority partners would be violating the fiduciary duty of loyalty imposed upon each partner toward the others under partnership law. Although no such duty formally exists among stockholders in a corporation, many states (not including Delaware) have imported the fiduciary duties of partners to the relationship among the founders of a closely held corporation. Similar doctrines have been developed for LLCs. Thus, in many states, were a founder to be removed without cause from her employment and corporate positions, she would have effective legal recourse even in the absence of a stockholders' agreement.

Disposition of Equity Interests

As for other items that might be covered in the agreement among the founders and investors, many address the disposition of equity held by the owners under certain circumstances.

Transfer to Third Parties. To begin with, although sale of stock in a close corporation or LLC is made rather difficult by federal and state securities regulation and the lack of any market for the shares, transfers are still possible under the correct circumstances. To avoid that possibility, stockholder and operating agreements frequently require that any owner wishing to transfer equity to a third party must first offer it to the company and/or the other owners, who may purchase the equity, often at the lower of a formula price or the amount being offered by the third party.

Disposition of Equity upon the Owner's Death.

Stockholder and operating agreements should also address the disposition of each owner's equity upon death. Again, it is unlikely that each owner would be comfortable allowing the deceased owner's stock to fall into the hands of the deceased's spouse, children, or other heirs, although this may be more acceptable in the case of a pure investor. Moreover, should the business succeed over time, each owner's equity may well be worth a significant amount upon death. If so, the Internal Revenue Service will wish to impose an estate tax based on the equity's value, regardless of the fact that it is an illiquid asset. Under such circumstances, the owner's estate may wish to have the assurance that some or all of such equity will be converted to cash so the tax may be paid. If the agreement forbids free transfer of the equity during lifetime and requires that the equity be redeemed at death for a reasonable price, the agreement may well be accepted by the IRS as a persuasive indication of the equity's value, thus also avoiding an expensive and time-consuming valuation controversy.

Any redemption provision at the death of the owner, especially one that is mandatory at the instance of the estate, immediately raises the question of the availability of funds. Just when the business may be reeling from the effects of the loss of one of its most valuable employees, it may be expected to scrape together enough cash to buy out the deceased's ownership. To avoid this disastrous result, many of these arrangements are funded by life insurance policies on the lives of the owners. This would be in addition to any key person insurance held by the business for the purpose of recovering from the effects of the loss. In structuring such an arrangement, however, the parties should be aware of two quite different models.

The first, and more traditional, model is referred to as a *redemption agreement*. Under it, the business owns the policies and is obligated to purchase the equity upon death. The second model is referred to as a *cross-purchase agreement* and provides for each owner to own insurance on the others and to buy a proportional amount of the deceased's equity. Figure 12.3 illustrates the primary differences between the two forms of agreement. While a cross-purchase is more complicated, especially if there are more than a few stockholders, it has significant benefits compared with a redemption agreement.

Disposition of Equity upon Termination of Employment.

Stockholder and operating agreements normally also address disposition of equity upon events other than death. Repurchase of equity upon termination of employment can be very important for all parties. The former employee whose equity no longer represents an opportunity for employment

	Effect on Tax Basis	Effect on Alternative Minimum Tax	Need for Adequate Corporate Surplus
Redemption agreement	No stepped-up basis	Risks accumulated current earnings preference for larger C corporations	Needs adequate surplus
Cross-purchase agreement	Stepped-up basis	No risk	Surplus is irrelevant

■ **Figure 12.3**

Comparison of stock redemption agreement and stock cross-purchase agreement

would like the opportunity to cash in her investment. The company and other owners may resent the presence of an inactive owner who can capitalize on their later efforts. Thus, both operating and stockholder agreements will normally provide for repurchase of the interest of a stockholder or member who is no longer actively employed by the company. This, of course, applies only to stockholders or members whose efforts on behalf of the company were the basis of their participation in the first place. Such provisions would not apply to a pure investor, for example.

This portion of the agreement presents a number of additional problems peculiar to the employee-owner. For example, the company cannot obtain insurance to cover an obligation to purchase equity upon termination of employment. Thus, it may encounter an obligation to purchase the equity of the former employee at a time when its cash position will not support such a purchase. Furthermore, courts uniformly prohibit repurchases that would render the company insolvent. Common solutions to these problems commit the company to an installment purchase of the affected equity over a period of years (with appropriate interest and security) or commit the remaining owners to make the purchase personally if the company is unable to do so for any reason.

Furthermore, these agreements frequently impose penalties upon the premature termination of a stockholder or member's employment. For example, normally the investor is relying on the efforts of the founders in making his investment. Should the founders be entitled to a buyout at full fair market value if he or she simply decides to walk away from the venture? Often these agreements contain so-called vesting provisions that require a specified period of service before repurchase will be made at full value.

Such provisions, in addition to providing incentive to remain with the company, have complicated tax implications as well. As discussed earlier, if an employee receives equity for less than fair market value, the discount would be considered taxable compensation. The Internal Revenue Code provides that compensation income with regard to unvested equity is not taxed until the stock is vested. But at that time, the amount of income is measured by the difference between the price paid for the equity and its value *at the time of vesting*. The only way to avoid this result in the corporate context is to file an election to pay the tax on the compensation income measured at the time of the purchase of the equity, even though the equity is not then vested and may have little or no current value. And that election must be filed within 30 days of the receipt of the stock, not at the end of the year. This tax problem does not normally arise in an LLC so long as there is no initial contribution to the founders' capital accounts.

Distributions of Company Profits. Stockholder and operating agreements may also include numerous other provisions peculiar to the facts and circumstances of the particular business. Thus, pass-through entities often provide for mandatory distributions of profit to the members or stockholders at least in the amount of the tax obligation each will incur as a result of the profits of the business. Other agreements might include provisions to resolve voting deadlocks between owners, since otherwise a 50-50 split of voting stock might paralyze the company. Various types of arbitration provisions might avoid this problem.

Redemption Provisions. Further, some stockholder or operating agreements provide investors with the right to demand repurchase of their equity at some predetermined formula price at a designated future time, so they will not be forever locked into a minority investment in a closely held company. Conversely, some such agreements provide the company with the right to repurchase such equity at a predetermined price (usually including a premium) should the capital no longer be needed. Other agreements protect investors against being left behind if the founders sell their equity to third parties. The presence or absence of all these provisions depends, of course, on the relative negotiating strengths of the parties.

Legal and Tax Issues in Hiring Employees

Employees as Agents of the Company

Employees are agents of the company and, as such, are governed by many of the agency rules that already affect the relationships of partners to a partnership and officers to a corporation. Thus, employees have the duty of loyalty to the company and obligations to not compete while employed, to respect confidentiality, and to account for their activities.

Possibly more interesting is the potential of employees to affect the business's relationships with third parties, such as customers and suppliers. Here, the rules of agency require that a distinction be drawn between obligations based on contractual liability and those resulting from non-contractual relationships such as tort actions.

Employees are authorized to bind their employers to contracts with third parties if such actions have either been expressly or impliedly authorized. Thus, if a company hires a sales manager and informs her that she has the authority to close any sale up to $50,000, she may wield that authority without further consultation with her principals. She also has the implied authority to do whatever is necessary to close such deals (such as sign a purchase order in the company's name, arrange delivery, and perhaps even alter some of the company's standard warranty terms).

However, the employee has authority that often extends beyond that expressly or impliedly given her. To illustrate this, suppose this sales manager decides to close a sale for $100,000. This goes beyond her express authority and is not within her implied authority since it was expressly prohibited. Yet, from the point of view of the customer, the company's sales manager appears to have the authority to close all sales transactions.

Unless the customer has been informed of the limitation imposed on the employee, he has no reason to think that anything is wrong. The law vindicates the customer in this situation by providing that the employee has apparent authority to conclude contracts within the scope of authority she appears to have due to actions of her employer. Since she was put into that position by her employer and the employer has not informed the customer of the limits imposed on the employee, the employer is bound by the employee's actions.

Outside the contract arena, the employee's power to bind the employer is based on similar considerations. The employer, under the doctrine of *respondeat superior* (or vicarious liability), is responsible for any actions of the employee occurring within the scope of her employment. Thus, if the sales manager causes a traffic accident on her way to a sales call, the employer is responsible for damages. This imposition of liability is not, in any way, based on the employer's fault. It is liability without fault imposed as a result of the economic judgment that employers are better able to spread losses among customers and insurance companies. Consistent with this approach, employers are normally not liable for the tort or criminal actions of employees *outside* the scope of their employment, such as actions occurring after hours or while the employee is pursuing his own interests. Furthermore, employers are normally not liable for the torts or criminal actions of agents who are not employees (so-called independent contractors), since they are more likely to be able to spread these costs among their own customers and insurers.

However, employers should not take this as an invitation to avoid all liability (and employee benefits, payroll taxes, withholding, etc.) by the wholesale hiring of independent contractors. To begin with, the labeling of a potential employee as an independent contractor is not necessarily binding by law. Courts will look at the level of control exerted by the employer and other related factors to make this determination. For example, in a very high profile case, Microsoft was forced to enter into a $97 million dollar settlement agreement with the IRS as a result of having misclassified thousands of "independent contractors."[5]

In addition, many activities of employers are considered nondelegable (such as disposal of hazardous waste). Employers cannot escape the consequences of such activities by hiding behind independent contractors.

Similarly, someone's status as an employee (or, for that matter, as an independent contractor) does not relieve him of responsibility for tortious or criminal acts. Notwithstanding any liability of the employer, the agent is always still jointly responsible for his own wrongful acts.

Employment Discrimination

In addition to these common-law considerations, there are, of course, a number of statutory rules of law that govern the employer-employee relationship. Perhaps the best known of these are the laws prohibiting employment discrimination. Title VII of the Civil Rights Act of 1964, the Age Discrimination in Employment Act, and laws protecting disabled and pregnant employees collectively prohibit employment discrimination on the basis of sex, race, national origin, religion, age, and disability. They do not, as yet, prohibit discrimination on the basis of sexual orientation, although a number of state and local laws do.

Prohibited discrimination can occur not only in hiring but also in promotion, firing, and conditions of employment. In fact, sexual discrimination has been found in cases of sexual harassment that created a "hostile environment" for the employee.

These statutes are exceptions to the age-old common law concept of employment at will that allowed employers to hire and fire at their whim, for any reason or no reason at all. This rule is still in force in situations not covered by discrimination laws and, of course, not involving employment contracts. Notwithstanding that rule, however, courts in many states have carved out exceptions to employment at will for reasons of public policy, such as cases involving employees fired for refusing to perform illegal acts or employees fired in bad faith to avoid paying commissions or other earned compensation to the employee. Furthermore, courts in some states have been willing to discover employment contracts hidden in employee manuals or personnel communications that employers may not have thought legally binding.

Employment Agreements

The attraction of employment agreements comes, in the main, from their protection against firing without cause. Thus, a major item of negotiation will likely be the length of the contract. Courts have universally held that an employee cannot be forced to work for an employer against her will. Thus, an employment contract is essentially a one-way street. The employee is promised employment for a period of time, with accompanying salary, bonus, and incentive provisions, but she can leave the company at any time without consequence (unless legally enforceable consequences are specifically provided). As a result, employers would be well advised to avoid employment agreements with their employees whenever possible and, if forced to grant one, at least to obtain some accompanying benefit for the company.

Such benefit usually comes in the form of the noncompetition and proprietary information covenants discussed at the beginning of this chapter. For example, a software engineer may promise, in exchange for a two-year employment agreement, not to work in the computer sales industry for a year after the termination of his employment. Yet, as mentioned, proprietary information obligations exist quite apart from any employee agreement, and courts may refuse to enforce noncompetition provisions against the employee.

Raising Money

Although it is analyzed in greater detail elsewhere in this book, raising money from potential investors involves another set of complex legal issues that deserve mention here.

Most businesspeople are aware of the fact that both federal and state law regulates the offer and sale of securities, but many believe that these statutes apply only to the offerings of large corporations. Small companies, they believe, are exempt from these acts. Unfortunately, this is a dangerous misconception. In fact, these laws (specifically, the federal Securities Act of 1933, the federal Securities Exchange Act of 1934, and states' "Blue Sky" statutes) apply to all issuers and their principals.

Further, some businesspeople who are aware of the reach of these acts nevertheless believe that they only apply to issuers of equity securities, mainly stock. This, too, is a misconception. All these statutes apply to issuers of "securities" not just stock. Securities include, in addition to stock, most debt (other than very short-term loans or loans for very specific purposes such as real estate mortgages), options, warrants, LLC membership interests, and any other form of investment in which the investor buys into a common enterprise and relies on the efforts of others for the investment's success.

In general, then, the securities laws prohibit the offering of securities to the public without prior (and very expensive) registration with the Securities and Exchange Commission (SEC). The SEC also punishes fraudulent activities in connection with such offerings, including not only affirmatively false statements but also mere nondisclosure of material facts about the investment. Due to the complex and expensive nature of registration, these laws provide exceptions to the registration requirement in specific circumstances, but even these offerings are generally subject to the antifraud provisions of the laws. Thus, the challenge to entrepreneurs is to identify provisions in the securities laws that will offer them an exemption from registration, understanding that they must still provide sufficient disclosure to potential investors (in the form of either an "offering circular" or, in appropriate circumstances, an unlimited opportunity to perform due diligence) to avoid "antifraud" liability.

The most popular exemption from registration under the federal act is the *private placement exemption*, which excuses from registration transactions "not involving a public offering." The SEC has relied in part on this exemption to issue regulations designed to facilitate the raising of capital by small businesses in small offerings. Thus, as of this writing, Regulation D under the act exempts from registration any offering of under $1,000,000 of securities. Above that amount, the regulation requires increasing levels of disclosure (still short of full registration, however) and limits the number of offerees to 35 plus an unlimited number of *accredited* investors. For these purposes, accredited investors are certain institutions, as well as individuals with net worth or annual income at levels that argue a need for less protection. In addition, at this writing, many small companies are awaiting implementation of a new "crowdfunding" exemption that should allow certain companies to make use of the Internet to accept relatively small investments from large numbers of unrelated investors.

Of course, exemption from registration under the federal act does not necessarily grant exemption under state acts. In fact, offerings made to investors in a number of states require attention to the Blue Sky statutes of each such state. Fortunately, however, federal law has preempted state regulation in offerings beyond a certain size, and even in the absence of preemption, virtually all state statutes contain similar exemptions for private placements, typically exempting offerings to 25 or fewer persons.

Thus, most entrepreneurs will likely be able to seek out the investment they will ultimately need without the necessity of registering with either the federal or state governments. However, it cannot be overemphasized that they remain subject to the antifraud provisions of these acts. Thus, they will be well advised to seek professional assistance in identifying the applicable statutory exemptions, drawing up a comprehensive offering circular for their offering if appropriate, and disclosing all that an investor would need to know about their company to make an intelligent investment decision.

CONCLUSION

Considering all the legal and tax pitfalls described in this chapter, you may be tempted to ask whether any entrepreneur would choose to go down the road of the startup if fully aware of the complications lying in wait. But not to be aware of these matters is to choose consciously to play the game without knowing the rules. These issues are there regardless of whether the entrepreneur prepares for them. Surely you are much more likely to succeed in a venture for having taken the time to become aware of the legal and tax issues facing the entrepreneur.

YOUR OPPORTUNITY JOURNAL

Reflection Point	Your Thoughts...
1. What fiduciary duty do you have with your current employer? Does your proposed new venture rely on proprietary information belonging to your previous employer? Are you materially interfering with your previous employer's business by recruiting away key employees?	
2. When should you engage an attorney? What criteria will you use in your decision?	
3. What legal form should you choose for your new company (sole proprietorship, corporation, etc.)? What criteria will you use in your decision?	
4. What will you name your company? Have you registered your name with the state government? Are there other companies using the same or similar name (check the U.S. Patent and Trademark Office database)?	
5. What provisions should you have in your shareholders' agreement? What kind of salary will you draw? When will you draw it? What provisions do you have for disposition of equity (e.g., death, termination, etc.)?	
6. What type of equity sharing (if any) will you implement with your key employees?	
7. What type of insurance is needed to protect your company? When will you secure this insurance?	
8. What is the crucial intellectual property of your company? How will you protect it?	

WEB EXERCISE

Many Web sites offer legal form templates (e.g., shareholder agreements). Studying these templates helps you talk with your lawyer and can reduce your legal fees (time spent with lawyers), especially if you draft the documents and then have the lawyer approve them (rather than having your attorney draft the documents from scratch). Search out Web sites that offer legal templates.

NOTES

[1] Klinicki v Lundgren, 67 Or App 160, 678 P2nd 1250 (1984).

[2] Bancroft Whitney Co. v Glen, 64 Cal 2nd 327, 411 P2nd 921 (1966).

[3] All Stainless Inc. v Colby 364 Ma 773 (1974).

[4] USPTO 2012 Annual Report, p. 175.

[5] Vizcaino v. Microsoft Corp., 120 F.3d 1006 (9th Cir. 1997), cert. denied, 522 U.S. 1098 (1998).

Tessera

For nearly a year, Tessera, Inc, a venture-backed company in San Jose, had been trying to get an agreement with a Fortune 500 company that seemed intent on ignoring Tessera's patent claims on a key technology used in semiconductor chips. In less than a decade after its founding, Tessera held over 80 issued patents involving the interconnection of silicon chips in a highly miniature form factor. The semiconductor industry, while not lawless, was a ruthlessly competitive frontier where only the strong (and quick) survived. It wasn't surprising, therefore, that this intellectual property (IP) challenge[1] had followed on the heels of industry knowledge that Tessera was struggling financially—and in the midst of a top-down reorganization and leadership change.

It was January 2000, and the company was at a critical strategic crossroads. Some industry players perceived that Tessera had neither the will nor the resources to take decisive action against a major firm like Multinational Semiconductor Inc. A successful legal response at this juncture could send a clear message across the globe that Tessera was prepared to defend its IP rights against all comers.

That strategy was not without significant risk, however, and the Tessera leadership did have alternatives to consider. Still, with smaller firms beginning to ignore Tessera IP as well, it was time to make some fundamental strategic decisions.

Relieving Pain with a Breakthrough Approach

For years, the number of transistors on a silicon chip had been following Moore's Law quite neatly; doubling every 18 to 24 months while the unit cost declined. By the late 1980s, demand for high performance, reliable, palm-sized (and smaller) electronic devices was taking off, but design manufacturers were being constrained by the chip package—the physical interface between the silicon die and the circuit board. Peripherally, leaded silicon packaging and interconnection technologies had simply reached their practical limit—both in terms of their bulk volume and related unfavorable heat dissipation characteristics.

Due to the challenges in fabricating functional, delicate, fine-pitch metal leads on these packages, assemblers were now seeing the yields on their boards dropping to unacceptable levels. In addition, with standard multi-chip arrays, it was often not possible to test for, and identify, defective chip components until the interrelated system within the device was fully assembled. For this reason, completing non-working parts typically represented a significant cost of production.

In 1990, a pair of engineering entrepreneurs came out of IBM during a period when that company was undergoing major restructuring and changes in its core business strategies. Tom DiStefano and Igor Khandros had a vision of a new way of packaging semiconductor

This case was prepared by Carl Hedberg under the direction of Professor David Kerns of Olin College and John Carlson of System Change, Inc. Funding provided by Babson and Olin Colleges. © Copyright Babson College, 2007. All rights reserved.

Tessera has neither authorized nor participated in the preparation of this case. The information contained in this case is provided solely by the authors and not by Tessera, and Tessera does not confirm or deny the accuracy of any such information.

[1] Intellectual property (IP) includes patents, trademarks, copyrights, and trade secrets; patents and patent applications are key assets for most technology-based companies and often enhance valuation. Patents provide the legal right to exclude others from making, using or selling the patented invention.

chips addressing this bottleneck in the integrated circuit (IC) semiconductor industry. They founded Tessera in New York to develop silicon packages that were virtually the same size as the chip itself.[2] Their ideas then had to be translated into a new technical approach and set of business processes that semiconductor companies could embrace.

The entrepreneurs bootstrapped their venture for nearly two years before securing a seed investment from a venture capital firm in Silicon Valley—on the condition that Tessera relocate to the West Coast. The partners agreed without hesitation, and were soon developing a research lab in San Jose that would double as a pilot manufacturing line in the same location.

Also in the works were plans for a manufacturing facility in Singapore to service the low-volume production needs of giant IC clients. Once their process technology proved itself, the partners expected large volume players to purchase patent licenses from Tessera as a way of refining their own CSP manufacturing capabilities. In anticipation of this evolution, Tom and Igor had diligently sought to protect every aspect of their intellectual property, primarily through patents.[3]

In late 1992, Igor left the company to start-up FormFactor, a manufacturer of semiconductor wafer probe cards. Tom served as Tessera's CEO until John Smith was hired a year later. John Smith was a veteran of Mostek, a large semiconductor company, and a founder of Dallas Semiconductor. Under his direction, Tessera continued to advance its original strategy of continuous research and development to maintain a pipeline of patent filings covering all aspects of their segment, including materials, equipment, and manufacturing processes.

By the mid-1990s, the company had secured CSP-based licensing agreements with a few major IC makers—most notably Intel. Although royalty payments would not begin unless or until the licensee deployed the technology, the agreements with these multinationals included "modest" up-front license fees that represented a substantial inflow to a small company like Tessera.

Despite its leading position in the CSP space, Tessera was struggling with how best to move forward. Patricof & Co., the venture group that had led the three previous rounds of funding, attracted a new lead investor for the series-D—a $30 million round that brought total funding to just under $65 million.[4] That round was achieved in 1997 when a large Swedish investment firm committed the bulk of the required funding.

A year later the company was in need of an additional $30 million. Once again, current investors sought to include additional investors. With Tessera revenue just barely over $3 million, Patricof & Co felt they needed to look for ways to strengthen what they continued to believe was a venture with the potential to be a significant star in their portfolio. There was a sense that new management initiatives were needed, and Tessera's Board became involved in orchestrating some changes.

---

[2] Their concept, which would become known as Chip Scale Packaging (CSP), provided a physical and an electrical interface between the chip and the system. The chip was designed to operate in a stacked configuration, with connections between the semiconductor chip and a circuit board underneath, and within the periphery of the chip itself. The CSP protected the chip from breakage, contamination, stress from heating and cooling, and in addition, allowed for the testing of individual module components.

[3] In the United States (since 1995), patents expired 20 years from date of filing. It typically took three to six years to obtain a patent, construct the licensing agreement, and realize a flow of revenue. With high technology, patents were often rendered obsolete by new ideas and innovations long before the expiration deadline.

[4] Funding was as follows: Series A; $1.4 million, Series B; $8.5 million, Series C; $20.7 million, Series D; $33.9 million. Total funding for the four rounds was $64.6 million.

Moving In

Rein Narma, a veteran electronics executive, had been a Tessera board member since 1991. Rein had seen a lot. Raised and educated in Soviet-controlled Estonia following World War II, he escaped to Germany after the communists killed his father. There he served as an interpreter at the Nuremburg trials, and in the early 1960s, his affiliation with the United Nations brought him to America. A few years later, Rein leveraged his educational background[5] to enter the private sector with Ampex and then General Instrument, a diversified consumer electronics firm based in New York.

After leaving his management position at General Instrument, Rein worked with Lou Patricof in assessing the technology and business potential of ventures that Patricof had invested in. Rein was involved in and intrigued by Tessera, and in the early 1990s was offered a seat on the Board of Directors.

In the early summer of 1998, Patricia Cloherty, a Tessera board member and limited partner at Patricof & Co., asked Rein if he knew of anyone who could jump in at Tessera in an operational and financial capacity to help the company's management and Board sort through its business options and help the company in an interim management capacity when the company's CFO resigned. Rein asked John Carlson, an experienced executive whom he'd mentored at General Instrument, to have a look. John was excited by the opportunity to work with Rein again on a company he often talked about:

> *I was in my late twenties when I first started to work with Rein. He was well into his 50s at the time, and we developed sort of a father-son relationship. He is a really wonderful man who taught me so much. He was also a great role model: a top manager with a solid understanding of business, technology, and people. Very few executives master all three.*

At General Instrument, John had contributed to operational and financial management in multiple business units, and had global experiences in GI's semiconductor business. When he got to Tessera's California headquarters, he could see that all was not well:

> *Understandably, the leadership had taken a lot of time and money to think through the steps, and to create their process technologies. There was a lot of equipment involved, and lots of trial and error. They now had a ton of valuable IP in place, but they had begun to go off in different directions with no defined business model. The company was involved in manufacturing, licensing, and even acquiring some advanced materials for research. When we got there, they were losing nearly $2 million a month. There was a real concern that the Series-E would be a down round.[6]*

Although quite a few industry heavyweights had taken licenses with Tessera, they had done so largely as an "insurance policy" in the event the CSP technology did emerge as the prevailing process. As a result, licensing revenues were nearly three years off projections, with operating losses well over $10 million per year. John commented:

> *One reason why many companies don't become pure IP licensing businesses is because it takes a lot of money, and it's a long ramp. A patent royalty model is like setting up a tollgate. You've got to go out and encourage people to use it, you've got to get them comfortable with any new process technologies that are required, and then you have to wait for the tollgate to fill. It can take a good three to five years before the money begins to flow in on any one agreement. And of course,*

---

[5] Rein attended the Technical University of Tallinn, Estonia.

[6] Down round: A round of financing where investors purchase stock from a company at a lower valuation than the valuation placed upon the company by earlier investors.

there is always the possibility that [a better process or technology] will come along. Then your IP becomes virtually worthless.

The good news: Tessera's technology was beginning to catch on. To help fuel the rate of adoption, the company had set up a pilot production line at its research labs in San Jose to work on improvements and to act as a training facility for licensees. John explained that process training was a critical aspect of the plan:

> *With a new technology like this, you have to train and educate. The San Jose lab was in fact a small-scale version of the low-volume production facility that was later set up in Singapore, and Tessera was bringing in groups from the Far East to see [the CSP production line] in operation.*
> *They had also developed a whole set of management education training programs to go with that, so when a company took a license for the technology, Tessera could offer it a one-week training program in the proprietary process. Quite brilliantly, I think, manufacturers were given licenses that included the rights to all future patents in this technology.*

By the mid-1990s, Tessera had amassed an impressive technology portfolio and was arguably the dominant, driving force in this fast-growth segment. The leadership, however, was deeply split as to how to best leverage their strategic assets.

On the manufacturing side, founder and CTO Tom Distefano was focused on developing a reliable pipeline for "flex" materials in anticipation of a growing demand. These materials (primarily thin polymide fused with copper lines), represented the backbone of CSP technologies, and Tom was taking steps to promote and expand the industry. To that end, he founded a magazine, *Chip Scale Review*, and organized a trade show, *Chip Scale International*. In early 1998, Tom had expressed his concerns to San Jose's Metroactive News:[7]

> *There was a fear that we would—and could—run out of supplies; absolutely. It's a chicken-and-egg thing; we had to build a marketplace for our supplies to ensure that we could build our product.*

CEO John Smith, on the other hand, was leaning more toward a licensing model based on the IP they already had in place. Middle management was in disarray—confused about who was in charge, and whose strategy they ought to be trying to implement. The Board was divided as well. In late 1998, John Carlson, working closely Chris Pickett, Tessera's head of IP, began to push for changes.

A New CEO

In the midst of this difficult atmosphere of divided leadership and spirited internal debate, Tom decided to leave the company. In mid-1999, the Board brought in new leadership. John Smith would now serve as CTO, and Bruce McWilliams, as the company's new CEO; they were charged with thinking through how to design, plan, and execute an IP business model in a very competitive industry.[8] John Carlson helped orchestrate some initial turnaround actions during that difficult period.

---

[7] www.metroactive.com/papers/metro/02.05.98/growth-9805.html

[8] Bruce had come over from S-Vision, a silicon chip-based display company that he co-founded in 1995. Earlier, Bruce had been a Senior Vice President at Flextronics International, an electronic manufacturing services company that had acquired nCHIP Inc., an advanced packaging manufacturer that Bruce had co-founded in 1989. Bruce had received a B.S., an M.S., and a Ph.D. in Physics from Carnegie Mellon University.

The company was still bleeding cash, so the first thing we did was to reduce the staff count. Being super intelligent, Tom had attracted and hired the best talent. These were all great, dedicated people, so we had to sort through and figure out who we couldn't live without. We ended up laying off 40 of the 150 employees. It was a terrible time. The whole place was churning over who was going to be next to go.

We also wrote off certain equipment and reassessed the value of three manufacturing lines, two in San Jose and one in Singapore, and made important operational improvements. Because of our need to focus, both the company's trade show and magazine were sold-off and removed from being supported by company staff. We initially decided to keep the Singapore facility open as part of Tessera's low-volume production capability. We completed an equipment lease that brought in over $3 million. We paid a high rate for that, but it gave the company short-term cash as we looked to close the Series E round.

Later that year, John was asked to step back in as CFO. He discovered that his new boss, CEO Bruce McWilliams, was a master at turning IP into cash. John recalled that Bruce has added a whole new strategic capability to the company:

Tessera was developing licensing partnerships by working with companies to set up manufacturing capabilities. Instead of waiting for the larger semiconductor companies to fall into line, Bruce targeted smaller firms in the Far East as candidates for taking licenses. They were also charged for Tessera's help in setting up their manufacturing lines. These licenses added important incremental revenues from both licensing fees and services, and of course, critical cash inflows.

We'd be talking about how in the world we were going to make our numbers, and he'd say; "let's have a look in the drawer" [Tessera's diverse patent portfolio] and create deals with technology we owned, but which wasn't part of our core business. One of these assets was the company's Two Metals production line which we then outsourced to another company. Unlike anyone I ever worked for before, Bruce understood that Tessera's non-core assets had their greatest value when "packaged." Bruce's package deal involved a license for using the technology with rights to certain patents, plus transfer of critical talent, equipment and a facility. These arrangements created near-term revenues through license fees and service revenues, while off-loading operating costs, a critical move to bring the company closer to profitability.

By the fall of 1999, the business had begun to stabilize somewhat, but the venture capital community was still not stepping up for the next round of funding. While the Internet boom era of the late 1990s had investors focused on dot-com plays that were ramping towards IPOs in a matter of months, their primary reluctance was likely that Tessera was now facing a threat to its very existence.

Frontier Provocations

Tessera's significant organizational and financial challenges had not gone un-noticed in the industry. Soon after Tom had resigned, Multinational Semiconductor, Inc (MSI) began importing semiconductor chip assemblies that clearly seemed to involve Tessera IP.[9] John said no one had been surprised by this rather blatant patent rights infringement:

It was pretty obvious that Tessera was struggling. There was a lot of industry talk about how Tessera was going down, that we were in financial distress; like, you don't have to worry about

---

[9] Tessera sought royalties under its U.S. Patent Nos. 5,679,977, "Semiconductor Chip Assemblies, Methods of Making Same and Components for Same" ('997 patent); 5,852,326, "Face-Up Semiconductor Chip Assembly" ('997 patent); and 5,347,159, "Semiconductor Chip Assemblies with Face-Up Mounting and Rear-Surface Connection to Substrate."

Tessera anymore. This is a fiercely competitive industry, and any sign of weakness can be disastrous. So while all these rumors were flying, MSI decides not to pay a license fee on a class of CSP patents we held. I called them up and one person said, yeah we'll get back to you; we're going to send the check. Then all of a sudden another guy calls back to say that no payment will be forthcoming.

In April 1999, Tessera had filed a formal request for those payments. MSI seemed intent on forcing Tessera into either taking legal action or backing down. Even worse, smaller manufacturers had begun to test Tessera's ability and resolve to police and enforce its patent protections. John compared the situation to a lawless frontier:

It's like the Old West. When the bad guys came into town, the good guy knew that he had to take on—not just any of them—but the meanest, baddest hombre in the bunch. Only by defeating the most dangerous threat would Tessera have any chance with the others. We were feeling that unless we took on and won against MSI, the patent licensing component of our business model would be badly weakened.

John added that the Tessera team harbored no illusions about what it would take to fight an infringement suit against a powerful firm like Multinational Semiconductors:

Patent enforcement can be an expensive and risky path for a small company. A firm like MSI will commission its lawyers to do relentless discovery, and they'll be asking for every possible document they can think of. That would mean we'd have to have a team of paralegals making copies of all of this stuff, which costs a fortune and is a major distraction. There is no limit to a large firm's legal budget, so its strategy would be to wear Tessera down—make it too expensive for us to pursue a legal resolution.
One option was to align with an equally powerful competitor that might relish the opportunity to take on MSI. Those firms were out there, but partnerships and acquisitions take time to put together. And of course, when it finally did go to trial, there wasn't any guarantee that we'd win—with or without a solid partner. If the court decision went against us, we would have spent a lot of money, and ended up with no IP—losing all possibility of future royalty revenue.

Given these challenges, Tessera continued to work on reaching a negotiated settlement with MSI. In the meantime, the company got a boost from a creative approach to fund-raising.

Dialing for Dollars

Robert Young had served as a member of the Tessera board of directors since 1991, and was named Chairman in 1996.[10] Seeing that efforts to attract a new lead venture capitalist had stalled out, in October 1999 he set up a conference call with a private network of well-moneyed

---

[10] At the time, Bob Young was the Chief Executive Officer of Curl Corporation, an Internet infrastructure software company. From 1986 to 1997, Mr. Young had served as a Managing Director at Dillon, Read & Co. Inc., an investment bank. He received a B.S. in Chemistry from the University of Delaware and a Ph.D. in Physical Chemistry from the Massachusetts Institute of Technology.

individuals. John Carlson as CFO was on the team that assembled in New York to field due diligence queries:

> These were high-net-worth people calling in with their top advisors. We had no idea who we were talking to. Bruce gave the presentation and we all took questions. We were saying that Tessera planned to protect its intellectual property rights, but that a legal showdown was not necessarily in the cards. The feeling was that with another $30 million of capital in-hand and progress being made in creating revenues and cutting the company's cash burn, perhaps negotiations would work after all. Having money in the hand puts a company in a much stronger negotiating position to take legal action, as well, if it came down to that.
>
> We had also made a fundamental decision to price a flat round at five dollars a share [equivalent to the previous round]. It worked; the checks started coming in—$500,000 here, a million there.

Having received $12 million in private funding in fairly short order, plus $10 million from Patricof & Co. and prior investors, the need for a lead investor was overcome. A new venture capital firm joined in with $5 million, and when the funding commitments reached $29.4 million, some industry-insiders put in $5 million to bring the amount raised to just under $35 million. Flush with a "survival chest" of capital, the team now returned to the task of solidifying their fundamental strategic plan.

A Critical Juncture

The patent challenge with MSI had become a defining moment in the company's long evolution. John Carlson noted the real question was not so much about whether to take on a large competitor in court, as it was about what sort of business they wanted to be:

> Going head to head with MSI over this is certainly on the table, but that process would create a tremendous number of distractions, like legal discovery, interviewing employees, and of course, endless documentation and meetings with lawyers.
>
> If we choose to avoid this confrontation, we could keep focusing on new technologies, and on keeping a stream of new patents in the pipeline. We could use the capital [that Tessera would allocate to fight MSI] to advance new technologies within the CSP space . . . get ahead of the curve, and keep on licensing . . .
>
> We could also leverage Bruce's tactic of generating incremental revenues off our technology by collaborating with some of these companies that are encroaching on our IP—maybe concentrate on building technology specific to certain mainstreaming applications like cell phones; own that space, as it were. . . . Eventually MSI, and the others, might come around; and if they didn't, we'd be in a stronger position to take legal action.

With the clock ticking on their patent protections, and with the number of bold infringements against their IP increasing exponentially, Tessera's leadership was well aware that anything less than a decisive strategy at this juncture could mark the beginning of the end. One seasoned industry observer put it this way:

> Tessera virtually created this industry segment, but that doesn't mean they couldn't lose it all—or even worse, become a marginalized player; forever struggling to get back in the game. At this point, they are bleeding cash and must move quickly. If they get it right; I suspect they'll be using some of that Series-E round to gear up for an IPO. But if they get it wrong . . . well, they wouldn't be the first high-potential tech venture to crash and burn in [Silicon Valley] . . .

Preparation Questions

1. Discuss the various options open to Tessera in dealing with MSI's challenge, and the strengths /weaknesses of each approach. Which path would you recommend and why?

2. Discuss the use of technology licensing as a primary revenue driver in an entrepreneurial enterprise. Are there any public companies (other than Tessera, which had an IPO in 2003) that rely on licensing as their principal revenue source? What are some key requirements and competencies for success with that strategy? What are some potential pitfalls?

3. Discuss the importance of teaching and training in the process of getting the marketplace to accept a new manufacturing method or technology. How did Tessera use training in promoting the adoption of CSP? Identify and describe at least one other technology-based company that utilized a strong teaching and training strategy and/or prototyping facilities to accelerate conversion to their new technology.

4. What factors do you believe contributed to Tessera's success in obtaining short-term revenue by licensing its existing patents in non-core areas?

5. It took a relatively long time for the semiconductor industry to adopt Tessera's technologies. What factors may have contributed to this delayed response?

6. Using the Internet, briefly summarize Tessera's history from the time of the MSI challenge to the present. Enumerate any additional lessons to be learned from the Tessera story, particularly those not previously emphasized.

Scott Eisen/Bloomberg/Getty Images

Yankee Candle Company

ENTREPRENEURIAL GROWTH

While entrepreneurship begins with an opportunity, sustainable success comes from creating an organization that can execute on that opportunity. However, as organizations start to gain more sales and customers, managing growth becomes a critical challenge that, if not handled appropriately, can lead to venture failure.

Why do entrepreneurs fail to manage growth? Often they have limited time and resources to spend on organization building. They're constantly fighting fires in the business's day-to-day operations or they're chasing too many opportunities, leaving little time for planning. Entrepreneurs without organizational or business skills may retreat into something they do know and are more comfortable doing, like product development. They may hire salespeople or engineers to handle sales and technical support before bringing in someone with organizational and business skills. But eventually growth overwhelms the operation. In order to survive and continue to grow, entrepreneurs need to pay attention to the requirements of a firm in its growth phase. They cannot neglect the planning and preparation required for long-term success.

Many believe that entrepreneurial skills and managerial skills are mutually exclusive and operate at different phases of the firm's life. Entrepreneurial skills *are* critical during the venture's launch, while managerial skills become increasingly important thereafter.

This chapter is written by Donna J. Kelley and Edward P. Marram.

> The objectives of any entrepreneur wishing to create a sustainable enterprise should include building an efficiently operating organization while developing an organization-wide entrepreneurial capability.

Yet the organization will need to retain its entrepreneurial spirit as it grows. It can't function over the long term by simply managing what it has previously created. Customer needs inevitably change. Competitors eventually offer superior products or services. Economic conditions, politics, technology, and a variety of other external shifts will create a constantly changing opportunity set that leads to new possibilities while rendering old opportunities obsolete.

It's no wonder that half the businesses started today will not be around in eight years. And far fewer firms will continue to grow and stay profitable—as few as one in seven.[1] What distinguishes those firms that not only survive but also thrive? Entrepreneurs and leaders who build an efficient operating organization, while maintaining the organization's entrepreneurial ability.

Making the Transition from Startup to Growth

During startup, the business opportunity is taking shape, but as yet there are no significant sales. The founders are acquiring resources and organizing initial operations—and they do everything. At the other end, in the mature stage and beyond, the business must deal with the problems of a well-established organization. Systems and structures can become entrenched and the culture can impede efforts to grow further, leading to decline. In this chapter, we look at how entrepreneurs operate once they've started and, we assume, their companies have reached a point of initial success with their opportunity. The primary task beyond this startup stage is to create a professional organization capable of managing its current growth, while setting the stage for continued entrepreneurship to ensure the organization can sustain growth as it matures and avoid decline.

The chapter is organized around four driving forces in the growth stages: leadership, the opportunity domain, resources and capabilities, and execution. Before we get to this discussion, let's review a key decision every entrepreneur must consider beyond startup: whether to sell, maintain, or grow the venture.

Looking Forward: The Choice to Grow, or Not,... or Sell

Figure 13.1 presents post-startup options for an entrepreneurial business. Each option presents at least two alternatives for the founder.

If a new venture is successful in generating sales, entrepreneurs can reap capital gains by finding a suitable buyer. If the entrepreneur decides to sell the business, she may stay with the acquiring company, or she may leave and either seek other employment or start another company. The first situation is perhaps the most common; the entrepreneur sells to reap a capital gain but stays on with the organization for several years to help in the transition. When Doug Brenhouse and John Frank, founders of MetaCarta (the case we covered in Chapter 10) sold their company to Nokia in 2010, John remained with the company. The buyer wants the entrepreneur to stay in order to reduce risk.

A typical acquisition might give the entrepreneur one-third of the price in cash, one-third in the acquiring company's stock (vested over the term of an employment contract), and one-third in an earn-out that is tied to the performance of the acquired company. If the acquired company meets certain milestones, the entrepreneur earns the full amount of the earn-out. If it falters, the entrepreneur's earn-out is at risk. Thus, the entrepreneur has an incentive to work hard after the acquisition takes place.

If a company is publicly traded, on the other hand, it is easier for the entrepreneur to sell and leave. Jim Clark, who co-founded Silicon Graphics in 1981, sold his remaining interest in the company in 1994 and left. He subsequently went on to co-found Netscape with

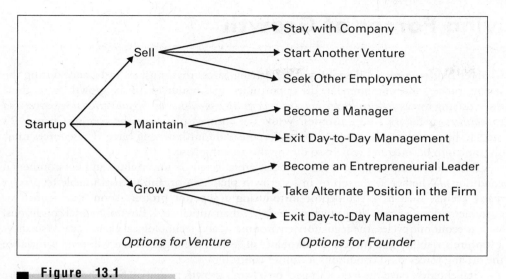

Figure 13.1

Post-startup options

Marc Andreessen. When selling a business, the founders often have contractual agreements to consider, like restrictions on their activities if they exit; for example, non-compete clauses may place limitations on their next venture. If you sell your business, the acquirer will prohibit you from starting a new, directly competing business.

When maintaining a business, the entrepreneur is faced with two basic choices. He can continue to lead the organization or exit day-to-day operations. Google co-founders Sergey Brin and Larry Page started the company up in 1998. They both stayed as co-presidents until 2001, when they recruited former Sun Microsystems and Novell executive Eric Schmidt as Chairman and CEO. They recognized they needed someone with experience and business acumen to grow the company.[2] Having an experienced CEO freed Brin and Page to focus on the aspects of the business they had the most passion for. Brin headed up the technology group at Google, while Page ran the products group.[3]

While our focus is on growing a business, it's true that many entrepreneurs choose to operate lifestyle businesses that pay enough salary for them to have a comfortable lifestyle, with less risk and complexity. These firms usually aren't large or successful enough to be sold, and the entrepreneurs don't have the desire to grow the business. One of the authors of this chapter, for example, was working with an ergonomics consulting company that hired her to grow the business. They explored a number of options, but growth would mean hiring more employees and moving out of the founder's basement. The founder decided he preferred the flexibility, lower risk, and greater control associated with staying small. After two engineers who had worked with him part-time finished college and moved on to other jobs, he maintained the business as a one-person operation, outsourcing any additional expertise, and keeping his commute to "a walk downstairs." What this example illustrates is that the decision to grow (or not) is multifaceted. It should take into account not only the ability to grow (the company could capture more customers if it were larger) but also the desires of the entrepreneur.

We'll now assume the company is currently growing, and the owner chooses to sustain a growing organization rather than selling or maintaining a lifestyle business. We'll focus on the founder as CEO, although most of the concepts also apply in the case where the founder is replaced. We next present our model of driving forces in the entrepreneurial firm's growth stages.

A Model of Driving Forces of Growth

Chapter 2 offers a model describing three driving forces that must be in balance during the startup process: the entrepreneur, the opportunity, and resources. In the growth stage, these three driving forces shift to *leadership, the opportunity domain,* and *organizational resources and capabilities,* as Figure 13.2 illustrates. While the business plan is at the core of Chapter 2's model, the growth model has *execution* as its core and fourth driving force. These forces must all come into balance and remain so during the growth phase.

Both the startup and the growth models are affected by uncertainty and environmental conditions. Whether at startup or in its growth phase, an organization is unable to predict many events, such as a competitor introducing a superior product soon after launch or customers adopting a product much more slowly than anticipated. Environmental conditions, such as economic cycles, the regulatory environment, and technological change, can also affect a venture's viability and success. In all phases of its life, the organization will need to balance the driving forces amid conditions it cannot control.

Stakeholders have the largest impact on a firm's growth potential. **Stakeholders** are those having a stake in the venture's success, like investors, customers, suppliers, and employees. As a new venture grows, it accumulates a range of insiders and outsiders who become increasingly dependent on the firm and exert heavy influence on its decisions. The organization will need to balance the current needs of these stakeholders with its need to think about how to sustain itself over the long term.

The 2009 bankruptcy of General Motors, then the world largest automobile maker, serves as a clear-eyed example of stakeholder interests running at odds with a company's growth model. GM reported an $8.6 billion loss in 2005. Bankruptcy court filings came four years later, the same year GM lost the title of world's largest automaker to Toyota. Why? Too many stakeholders were vested in maintaining the status quo. GM continued to pay out quarterly dividends to investors at $0.25/share even when its share price was trading below $5.00,[4] in what may have been an effort to "keep up appearances."[5] GM's labor force, the United Auto Workers (UAW) union stonewalled GMs innovation and growth initiatives to avoid job elimination and decreased pay and benefits. At one point, GM found itself actually paying its workers not to work. GM retained the car lines Saab and Saturn, although they had rarely

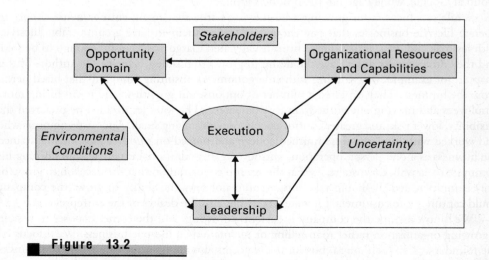

Figure 13.2

Driving forces of growth

been profitable. Generous pensions and healthcare plans, as well as rock-solid job security provided little incentive for GM management to rock the boat and substitute short-term pain for long-term sustainability.[6] In what amounted to a 30-year slow-motion car crash, GM's debts mounted and eventually GM was crushed by the weight of its own complacency, or more appropriately, by the entrenched inertia of GM's own stakeholders. Today, GM has reemerged from bankruptcy and again became a publicly traded company, with its stock ticker history wiped clean. What remains to be seen is if new leadership (installed by GM's largest shareholder—the U.S. government) can succeed in changing the stale management culture and renegotiating the labor relations that led to GM's downfall. In 2011, a reborn General Motors reclaimed the title of world largest automaker, earning $7.6 billion in profits. However Toyota, renowned for its efficiency, surpassed GM again in 2012, calling into question if GM has truly brought its growth model and its stakeholder interests back into alignment.

The Growth Process

Figure 13.3 shows the challenges associated with the four driving forces outlined in Figure 13.2, and the key imperatives the firm needs to address to achieve overall balance among the forces.[7] The table differentiates between a venture's early and later growth stages. This distinction is important because the problems facing a company at an early stage of growth are different from those it faces later, and therefore the decisions and solutions will change. By knowing where the organization stands in the life cycle, an entrepreneur can tell which problems are normal and which require special attention. For example, while an entrepreneur needs to focus her firm's strategy during early growth, she will need to look toward expansion in later growth stages.

Execution

The growth model has execution at its core. Execution depends on the other components in the model—leadership, the opportunity domain, and organizational resources and capabilities—but it has the most direct link to profits. The startup is commonly loosely managed, with few controls, very little performance assessment, and a lack of responsibility for outcomes. It often puts an emphasis on sales over profits, with chasing a new customer taking priority over considering the costs of serving that customer, for example. Growth will soon overwhelm operations, however, leaving the company capable only of reacting to inventory outages, overdue collections, diminishing cash flows, and delivery restrictions by suppliers. In addition, uncontrolled growth can lead to poor coordination between activities such as sales and inventory planning.

Without an adequate system of controls, the company can't optimize its decision making and prevent the waste of resources. One example of a startup that failed quickly because it did not understand cost monitoring, and therefore the inherent weaknesses of its own cost structure, was Webvan; one of the first online grocery retailers. Webvan was started by none other than Louis Borders, the successful founder of Borders Books. Borders felt that he could reduce the costs of selling groceries through automated warehousing and online ordering an allow him to offer the convenience of home delivered groceries to consumers. The low margins (2–3%) of the U.S. grocery business required Borders to find customers willing either to pay handsomely for the convenience or to buy in greater volume than they currently did. Neither requirement was likely to be met by cost-conscious consumers who normally shopped once a week, filling their refrigerators each time. Therefore, Borders needed to keep his costs much lower than the competition, and to do this he first needed to monitor them effectively.

| | Early Growth | | Later Growth | |
	Challenges	Key Imperatives	Challenges	Key Imperatives
Execution	Emphasis on sales over profits. Reactive orientation (fighting fires). Rapid growth overwhelms operations. Inadequate systems and planning leads to inefficiency, poor control, and quality problems. Informal communication and processes create confusion and lack of accountability.	Develop basic systems to manage cash, control receivables, inventory, and payables. Develop simple budgets and metrics to track performance and expenditures.	Profit orientation can constrain later growth. Organization outgrows initial systems and planning structure. Difficulties with coordination and control as decentralization increases.	Upgrade and formalize systems for control and planning for the longer term/future—before they are needed. Proactive planning replaces reactive approach. Maintain balance between control and creativity; ensure processes don't constrain innovation.
Opportunity Domain	Tendency to over-commit, pursue many diverse opportunities. Lack of clear strategy for how the venture competes.	Develop a focused strategy that leverages the company's unique value. Maintain the consistency of this strategy with all company activities (such as product development, marketing, operations).	Original opportunity domain may provide fewer opportunities for growth. Competitive pressures and changes in the market may threaten current businesses.	Establish competitive uniqueness and move beyond "one-product" orientation. Expansion into the periphery with products and markets. Also, develop strategy for future that provides new momentum and long-run effectiveness. Anticipate/respond to changes in industry/market environment.
Organizational Resources and Capabilities	Financial and human resources constrained as rapidly expanding sales require more people and financing. Generalized skills increasingly incapable of handling increased complexity.	Get profitability and cash flow in check. Tap early financing sources. Hire people with specialized expertise. Protect intellectual property.	Insufficient resources for growth.	Maintain bootstrap mentality. Manage cash for internal growth resources. Secure growth financing.
Leadership	Company outgrows entrepreneur's abilities. Entrepreneur unable to delegate. Internally promoted managers often lack adequate skills.	Start the process of delegating responsibility to others. Promote/hire functional managers/supervisory-level managers. Invest in management training.	Management lacks the managerial sophistication required for the increasing size and complexity of a growing organization. Inadequate communication throughout organization. Tensions between professional management and entrepreneur, between new and old managers and employees.	Recruit key professional management talent. Build fully functioning Board of Directors. Ensure leadership team shares in strategic planning and preserves entrepreneurial capability. Create decentralized reporting structure.

Figure 13.3

Challenges and key imperatives for managing growth

Webvan's cost control focus was on its warehouse operations, at the expense of its other costs, and it was this blind spot that eventually killed the business.

Webvan had a fast and promising start. In its first six months of business in San Francisco, it had over $13 million in sales, and by the end of its first year it had acquired over 47,000 subscribers (customers). However, the average cost of customer acquisition was high at $210, and the average customer order was low at only $81. Compounding this problem was the fatal fact that Webvan was acquiring customers who lived in suburbs, which drove an average delivery cost of $18, which was the heaviest contributor to the total average order handling and fulfillment cost of $27. Webvan was not only spending too much to acquire customers, but it was acquiring customers that were too expensive to serve because they lived in less densely populated areas that required $100,000 trucks driven by drivers earning $25–$35/hour. Making matters worse, after eventually discovering the problem caused by delivery costs, Webvan imposed a $4.50 deliver charge for orders under $50 to offset their costs, which had the negative effect removing any monetary incentive for customers to order more than $50. This charge did nothing but help hold the average customer order around $81/order, which was far below the $103 average order necessary for Webvan's automated warehouse and ordering system to be cost effective. Webvan eventually applied the $4.50 delivery charge to orders under $75 (still below its required average order size!), but it was too late. Webvan was encumbered by customers that were too expensive acquire, too expensive to serve, and who were incentivized to order in low volumes that made even its efficient automated warehouse operations too expensive. Webvan eventually shut its doors after only two years, having burned through $1.2 billion of its investors' money.[8]

With only so many hours in a day and so many days in a week, it is hard to step back, develop and implement new processes, hire and train people, and ensure everything functions adequately. Yet these control tasks are essential to creating an organization that can continue to thrive and grow. Therefore, your most critical first task in transitioning beyond startup is to create an efficient operation. This will eventually overlap with your efforts to sustain an entrepreneurial organization, but the firm will first need to catch up to its burgeoning growth—then it can set the stage for creating new sources of growth in the future. The key objectives for a control system should be to institute controls, track performance, and manage cash.

Instituting Controls

Your first **control system** in early growth should be relatively simple. The organization should quickly and easily be able to get it up and running and train people to use it. With a simple system, there's less that can go wrong, and as employees and managers get accustomed to control practices, you can upgrade the system later to handle a larger and more complex organization. You can also implement the system stepwise—for example, by starting with components having the greatest gap between actual and desired performance or with those that are easiest to put in place and therefore will have immediate impact.

An effective control system includes the following (all of which were covered in detail in Chapter 11):

- Accounts receivable and collections policies
- An inventory management system
- Account payable policies
- Assessment of performance and expenditures
- Metrics to track trends in cash, receivables, inventory, payables, expenditures, and performance

Managing costs requires both making decisions about expenditures and instituting controls that monitor spending. A growing firm's selling and administrative costs often expand rapidly with its escalation in sales. This expenditure is often appropriate because you need marketing to generate sales and administrative overhead to support the burgeoning organization. Yet you do need to monitor these areas to determine effectiveness and detect overspending. For example, certain advertising approaches may be more effective than others, or they may work in one region but not another.

As the company begins to sell more and more products in multiple markets, you will want to analyze its performance in different product or market segments, along with how effectively it is spending its resources. You need to understand what each product costs and whether you are truly making a profit. All the costs going into each product are those costs, both variable and fixed, that would disappear if the product were discontinued. What remains after these costs are deducted from the selling price contributes toward company overhead and profit.

You can also develop performance metrics to aid in decisions about investments and expenditures. Performance measures in an early-stage company are designed less for evaluating actual outcomes against a plan (as they would be in a more stable, established organization) than for helping in entrepreneurial decision making. As the company's operations expand, managers can develop metrics to help them answer the following questions:

- Which products or markets generate the highest revenues and margins?
- Which customers or customer groups are reliable accounts (make timely payments, are at low risk of default)?
- How effective are our expenditures in areas such as marketing and sales, and does this differ across markets?

Tracking Performance

Tracking performance is integral to one of the core functions of an entrepreneur, decision making. A performance tracking system is what separates decision making under uncertain conditions from merely guessing. Decisions must be sound as well as timely. A performance tracking system is about much more than simply key performance metrics, or KPIs. It is about investing the right dose of organizational effort into a simple, flexible, but deliberate plan to create and sustain a common operating picture that allows everyone in the company to see the critical variables of your business, your market, and your competition. While tracking systems will vary as greatly as companies do, there are basic criteria that the best systems all possess.

- They identify decisions that require a true "this or that" choice, including those under most likely, best case, and worse-case scenarios.
- For each decision, they determine the latest point in time at which the decision remains relevant to an outcome (the latest time any performance information would be of value).
- For each decision, they determine what specific questions must be answered to support a decision. They include what must be answered about the market, your own firm, and your competition.
- For each question, they determine the specific metrics (both qualitative and quantitative) needed to formulate an answer.
- They determine where, when, and how to measure each metric, and the name(s) of those responsible for measuring it.
- They remain simple so that tracking performance does not itself degrade performance.
- They assign someone responsibility for running the tracking system (using the entrepreneur as the *last choice*).

Successful entrepreneurs are careful not to invest excessive effort in tracking the activities of their competition too early on. They focus on finding, and delivering value to, their customers, and keeping their own business in order. Reliable information about your competition's future actions often takes more time and resources to collect than many startups can spend. Focus on tracking how you are creating value for, and relationships with, your customers and how you are running your business; track just what is needed to effectively deal with your competition when they get in your way. A simple, but deliberate performance tracking system supports a focus on timely action and excellent execution, because when you can efficiently determine where you stand, you will have more time and energy left to apply towards getting to where you want to be.

How do you determine what's good or bad when examining key metrics? For some financial ratios, published sources can provide industry averages for comparison. Entrepreneurial firms, however, often adopt policies that differ from those of more stable, established firms, such as spending on marketing while building brand awareness. Thus, it may be more useful to look at trends in metrics over time; for example, an increase in your collection period for receivables could indicate a relaxing in collection efforts, or a decrease in inventory turns could indicate you are at increasing risk of stock-outs. If you see significant changes and they are not the result of policy shifts in your firm, look for causes and consider making adjustments in policy.

One key point is to make performance measures as simple and inexpensive to track as possible, while providing information that helps you make better decisions. One very successful consulting firm had simple but useful measures. The entrepreneur tracked performance through his "B-Report." The B-Report was a simple Excel spreadsheet, with each consultant occupying a row, and columns representing every week of the year. If consultants expected to bill in a given week, they put a "B" in the column. If they did not, they left it blank. If the entrepreneur did not see a lot of B's, he knew he had a problem.

Performance measures for a growing organization should be as simple and inexpensive to track as possible, while providing information leading to better decision making.

The company can also develop simple budgeting practices to estimate cash and inventory needs, schedule production, determine staffing requirements, and set sales and profitability goals. It should upgrade and formalize these controls, metrics, and budgets as it moves toward later growth. But more importantly, these tools should evolve to provide the best information possible in aiding the company's decision making. The value they provide should more than justify the time and effort spent to develop and maintain them.

There may be times when it's appropriate to slow the pursuit of new growth in order to give the company room to improve its ability to manage growth. Some indicators that your company is growing at an uncontrollable rate are:

- *Your workforce is stretched too thin*, and you and/or the founding team are allocating too much time hiring/training new employees at the expense of providing the necessary leadership to existing employees.

- *The percentage of your cash flows from operations is declining against your cash flows from financing*, particularly debt. At this point, your cash conversion cycle, a measure of sustainability, is too long and/or getting longer. You may need to borrow money to sustain operating activities. Growth under these conditions can exacerbate this problem and leave your business unable to respond to unforeseen costs.

- *Profit margins are shrinking as sales are climbing.* Tight margins equate to a need to run an efficient operation, or have large amounts of cash on hand that are rarely found in a rapidly growing startup. Under these conditions the line between making a profit or incurring losses is very thin, and the overall risk posed by further growth may outweigh the benefits.

- *You are doing other peoples' jobs.* As the tempo of business increases, you are finding it harder to delegate effectively and doing more things yourself instead, which can lead to a breakdown in the organization's structure.

Albercan Drilling Supply	2011	2012	2013	Increase 2011–2013
Days sales outstanding	39	45	53	37%
Days in inventory	44	86	98	122%
Days in payables	36	38	53	48%
Cash conversion period	47	92	98	108%

■ Figure 13.4

Albercan cash conversion analysis

◉ *Customer complaints, in proportion to increases in sales, are increasing.* This means your company is not learning from your customers. Startups must "learn in order to earn." All companies receive complaints; the best companies embrace this feedback to refine their business to avoid scaling an inefficient business, or a business that does not yet understand its customer.

◉ *Your accountant is nervous.* While accountants in a startup should never be at ease, as the leader you must demonstrate the judgment required to recognize when the accountant's "worry-meter" is pegged, slow down, and listen to their counsel.[9]

Joel Kolen, former president of Empress International Ltd., a seafood distributor, emphasizes that:

> By taking a break from growth and putting in controls such as those at a large company, an entrepreneur can ease the growth transition and ensure that the qualities that helped build the company don't get lost in the rush to fill new orders.[10]

Managing the Cash Cycle

It takes money to make money. Most entrepreneurs know this, and while most pay attention to "how much?" successful entrepreneurs focus on "how fast?" The **cash cycle** shows the amount of time that passes between cash outlays and cash inflows during the company's sales process. It also shows the relationship between three key measures: days in payables, days in inventory, and days sales are outstanding. Let's use Albercan Drilling Supply to illustrate the cash cycle—and how better controls can conserve resources. Albercan's sole business was the sale of drill pipes and collars to drilling contractors in the local area. In 2013, as the company was growing, it seemed to have a constant need for cash. At the same time, its bankers were hesitant to extend more credit. A review of the key measures in Figure 13.4 shows that all have increased substantially in two years, more than doubling the cash conversion period.

As Figure 13.5 illustrates, the cash conversion period extends from the time of cash outlay (to suppliers) to cash inflow (from customers). Looking at this diagram, you can imagine how an increase in sales would actually decrease cash inflows in the short term. The company would need to borrow money to cover the costs associated with this increase in sales until cash comes in 98 days later. In the meantime, as it makes additional sales, the company would need to cover these costs. When cash finally comes in, the company would likely need that cash for more inventory!

Another problem revealed in this analysis is the length of time Albercan takes to pay suppliers. If typical payment terms are 30 days (whereas Albercan is paying in 58 days), the company may be testing its relationship with suppliers. This could lead them to refuse to ship additional product until Albercan pays past invoices, or in the worse case, they might refuse to do business with the company.

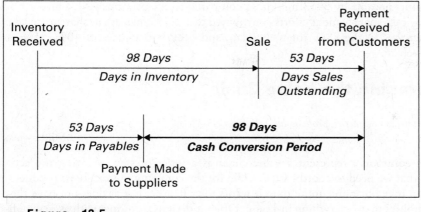

Figure 13.5

Cash conversion period for Albercan: 2013

The easy solution would be to borrow from a bank or other debt source, preferably using a revolving line of credit that allows the company to draw funds as needed and pay them back when it receives cash. These are short-term loans designed to cover shortfalls such as this. Borrowing can get expensive, though, so why not think about reducing the average cash conversion period? This is much more difficult, but it instills a sense of resource parsimony that boosts a company's efficiency. What if Albercan can reduce its days in inventory to 60 and its days' sales outstanding to 40? We'll also assume Albercan needs to reduce days in payables to 45. This all leaves a cash conversion period of 55 days, as Figure 13.6 shows. Not only will that reduce the period of time the company would need to borrow, but also it would reduce the average amount needed, because cash comes in more quickly and is therefore available for more inventory.

The cash management practices Flextronics International Ltd., a Singaporean firm ranked as one of the largest global electronics manufacturing services firms by revenue in FY2010 ($24 billion),[11] provides insight into the impact that changes in your cash conversion cycle have on your company. By the end of FY2010, Flextronics had succeeded in cutting its cash conversion cycle in half from 22 days in the previous year, to an industry-leading 11 days. This was largely accomplished by reducing its accounts receivable by $121 million and increasing

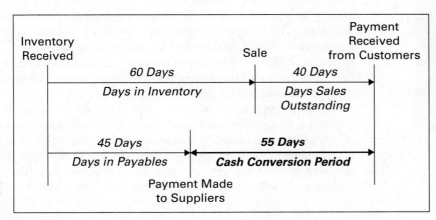

Figure 13.6

Adjusted cash conversion period for Albercan: 2013

its accounts payable by $413 million as compared to the previous year. During FY2010, the company cash management efforts contributed to a 267% increase in share price, as compared with increases in the Dow Jones, Nasdaq, and S&P 500 indices of 40%, 55%, and 40%, respectively.[12]

Leveraging the Value Chain

"Amateurs talk tactics, professionals talk logistics"

-Military maxim

We commonly represent a value chain as a series of steps showing the activities and entities that we need to coordinate in order for the company to execute its product or service. A startup may outsource more than it wants to at first because it does not have the resources or capabilities to do everything in-house. Often it designs a product with as many off-the-shelf parts as possible to minimize design and tooling charges. On the other hand, the firm may need to take on some value chain activities because there is no reliable or ready source for them; this is particularly true for new products or services for which there is little infrastructure. Alternatively, value chain players may not cooperate, leaving the company to, for example, sell its product direct rather than creating channel conflict for distributors who deal with more stable, older companies.

Courtesy Andrew Kardon

Andrew Kardon, founder of Joe Shopping

As the company grows, you should decide which value chain positions are capable of creating the most value and for which you can establish unique advantage.

For example, when Andrew Kardon founded Joe Shopping, a social networking site for bargain shoppers, he chose to handle all of the site development in house. "I don't need someone else to do my job," he wrote. He asked why he should pay someone else to do something that the staff he already had could do. Kardon was trying to develop a comparison-shopping engine from scratch, which would entail combining huge volumes of data feeds of various qualities into an easily searchable product database. This effort cost Kardon many hours and a lot of money, and in the end it worked, but not at the level of quality that he needed. Kardon dismissed outsourcing initially because he wanted to integrate the product search with the social networking across the whole site and the entire shopping experience. He simply wanted to control it all, but he quickly saw that full control came with a price. After his initially disappointing results, he outsourced development to a company that already had a search engine that was equal or better than what Kardon could have hoped for had he continued for another year trying to develop it himself. The cost of outsourcing this work came in at less than $100 a month. Outsourcing allowed Kardon to cut back on salaries, which at the time was his largest single expense.[13]

Outsourcing can enable a growing company to focus on those activities it can perform particularly well and those underlying its source of competitive advantage. It makes sense to outsource those activities other companies can do more reliably and less expensively, like the shopping networking site just mentioned. But recognize that, while moving activities outside reduces the steps the firm performs in-house, it will also reduce the control you have over those activities—and often consume substantial time just for managing the relationship. The firm will therefore need to weigh some considerations, such as how it will maintain quality and how responsive the value chain partner needs to be in reducing or increasing production in response to fluctuations in sales.

Maintaining the Entrepreneurial Organization

With all this talk about efficiency and controls, it's hard to imagine how anything entrepreneurial can happen. That is sadly the case with many companies. A history of success creates preferences for recreating the past rather than building toward the future. Efficiency in current operations often does not accommodate new initiatives, like those requiring different sales channels or different value chain partners. Customers want the company to improve the products they know best rather than forcing them to change their behavior and endure the switching costs of adapting to a new product.

How, then, can a well-run organization maintain the ability to create new businesses? It's primarily a combination of the remaining driving forces of the growth model: how leadership views and manages its opportunity domain and the organization's people and resources.

Opportunity Domain

While a startup is focused on shaping an opportunity and bringing it to life, as the organization grows, its leadership needs to define a strategic arena that guides decisions on how it competes in its industry and creates value for its targeted markets. An organization defines this arena through a balance of the unique capabilities it builds and its ability to differentiate itself in its competitive environment. This balance then guides decisions about how the company markets and sells its products and about which opportunities it pursues in expanding its business.

The impact of Stonyfield Farm's strategic focus can be seen in many aspects of its business. Stonyfield positioned itself as producing high-end yogurt products with quality, natural ingredients. It first sold its product through natural food and specialty stores, building a plant to better control its supply of hormone-free milk. The firm's marketing consisted of developing awareness and word of mouth by educating consumers about the quality of the product, promoting the company's social and environmental mission, and building a loyal following through plant tours, newsletters, and other customer relationship–focused programs. Stonyfield introduced new yogurt flavors, low-fat yogurt, and frozen yogurt. Its strategic focus shaped its distribution, manufacturing, marketing, and product development activities.

A focused strategy in early growth helps to guide the firm through the maze of opportunities that materialize once it experiences initial success. All too often, a startup chases diverse opportunities without defining what it can do distinctly well. During early growth, define your firm's core focus and develop capabilities around this, spending your limited resources and time close to this core, just as Stonyfield focused on building awareness of its unique brand and strengthening this brand with new yogurt flavors.

In later growth, your company has established its competitive uniqueness and can now leverage this, while training a strategic eye on the future. It may continue to extend its advantage in its current position by, for example, upgrading its products. Over time, however, opportunities will eventually diminish in a particular product space, and you will need to combine incremental extensions with expansion into the periphery. A company may create a next-generation product that includes improvements and new features for existing customers, while exploring new products and new markets. A restaurant chain can start offering Sunday brunch to its customers, for example, or it can launch a catering business.

Pay attention, however, to new developments in the industry and market environment. These may determine where you should best focus your strategic efforts at specific points in time. For instance, you may emphasize a current product to gain maximum returns before competition comes in. Or you may seek new ground if the market is becoming crowded by large competitors or if a technology foundation is becoming obsolete.

Yankee Candle Company illustrates how a company can expand over time within an existing product/market space and into the periphery. The company traces its origins to young Michael Kittredge's home operation, which soon expanded to an old paper mill. The company grew its sales of candles through gift shops and expanded into the international market through distributors. It started selling online and through catalogs. The company also opened its own retail stores, including a flagship store in South Deerfield, Massachusetts, which serves as a tourist destination, with a candle museum, a restaurant, and sales of toys, gifts, home accessories, and other products, along with candles of all shapes and sizes.

A Cautionary Note on Expanding Through Acquisitions: The Channing Bete Setback

Channing Bete enjoyed years of success with its information pamphlets providing advice on a range of topics, from managing diabetes to handling bullies. The company had a broad range of customers that included schools, hospitals, and government agencies. With its acquisition of Developmental Research Programs, Channing Bete set the stage for expanding from its single business of publishing printed information to a consulting operation focused on helping youth steer clear of drug use, delinquency, and pregnancy.

A few years later, revenues from the largest division of the acquired business fell 21.4%, and the division was shut down. A customer commented that Channing Bete's contributions to the business were little more than cosmetic but increased costs substantially. Losses spread to the core business, and the company fired one-fifth of its workforce. Tension mounted within the company as changes were imposed, such as replacing "flextime" with a 9-to-5 workday, even while the company touted its family-friendly culture. One former employee commented that the company got in over its head; it put a great deal of money and energy into the acquisition, neglecting lines of business that had been profitable.

Adapted from Bete Consulting Bet Falls Short: Move Brings Losses, Firings, Retrenchment, by Sunshine Dewitt. *Daily Hampshire Gazette*, July 18, 2005, Vol. 219, No. 271, pp. A1 and D1. Reprinted with the permission of the *Daily Hampshire Gazette*. All Rights Reserved.

While this expansion continued, the company entered the home fragrance market with products such as electric home fragrancers, room sprays, potpourri, and bath care products. The primary target audience was still women ranging in age from 20 to 60. However, the

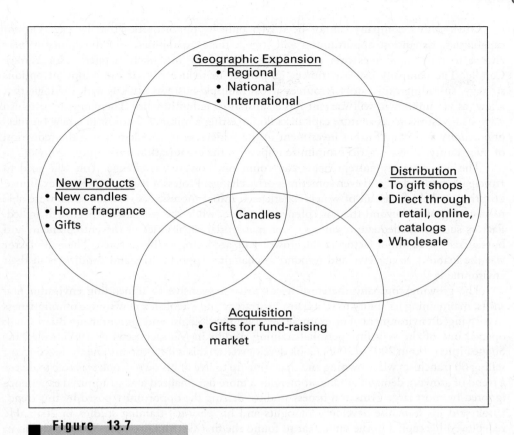

Figure 13.7

Yankee Candle's opportunity domain

company started to test new markets through its acquisition of GBI Marketing, a distributor of selected gift products (including Yankee Candle products) to fundraising organizations.

As Figure 13.7 shows, Yankee Candle has taken a multipronged approach to expanding its business: geographic expansion, new products, new distribution methods, and acquisition. There is a common logic surrounding all these methods, extending from core elements relating to its original product: candles. You've probably encountered small, single-operation candle shops. The Yankee Candle example[14] shows how a seemingly slow-growth business can become a high-potential venture with sales revenue surpassing $785 million in 2011.

As a company grows, it may experience stagnating growth in its core business but see little opportunity for expansion into the periphery. It may need to make drastic shifts in its business. As Channing Bete's experience illustrates (see the box on expanding through acquisitions), however, the company should make these forays outside the periphery carefully.

Acquisitions can provide inroads into new businesses for a company, but this undertaking requires an underlying logic. While Channing Bete attempted to move from publishing to consulting, Yankee Candle was already in the gift market when it made its acquisition. The central precept is the connection between organizational resources and capabilities and the opportunity domain, as illustrated in Figure 13.2. The growing organization should not consider external opportunities that simply appear attractive unless it has some particular ability to pursue them better than do competitors.

Obviously, a company cannot be driven only by opportunities that leverage current capabilities. Expansion opportunities will stretch these capabilities, and the company may choose to build new ones over time. Think about how this likely happened for Yankee Candle. The company can experiment or partner to reduce risk. It can adopt an options strategy, spreading exploratory resources across multiple business options with the logic that a few, as yet unknown, will warrant more substantial commitments. The company can also stage its investments, as venture capitalists do, investing a minimal amount in a new business opportunity and tying further investment to the achievement of milestones or the reduction of uncertainty. These practices minimize impact on the organization until more is known.

The one certainty entrepreneurs can count on, however, is change. You will need to anticipate, respond to, and even sometimes drive change. Professor Richard Osborne examined 26 privately held firms, all of which experienced initial success. Six of these firms were able to sustain growth beyond the entrepreneurial phase, while the rest saw their growth stalled. Factors such as inadequate resources, poor managerial capabilities of the entrepreneur, and bureaucracy were minor factors in the growth stall, according to this research. The main factor was the inability to perceive and respond to changing opportunities and conditions in their environment.[15]

The growing company therefore needs to be responsive to impending environmental shifts, maintaining its ability to transform its strategy and establish a new source of uniqueness in a changed environment. For example, exercise physiologist and entrepreneur Brian Cook opened one of the very first personal-training studios in Massachusetts in 1995, called In-Shape Fitness. From 2001 to 2006, Cook developed franchises for a one-on-one studio concept, selling 60 franchises while owning and operating up to five of his own. Cook was able to detect a trend of growing demand among women for a more personalized and customized experience ignored by most large gyms and fitness studios. Seizing the opportunity posed by this trend, Cook sold his franchise-development rights and his personal-training studios in 2006. He redeployed his capital in the same year to found the first Get In Shape For Women studio in Bedford, MA as a complete fitness program for women, combining such activities as cardio and weight training for women with nutrition information for a healthy diet and accountability through personal trainers that work with up to four women at time. He hit directly where the untapped demand had been growing, and in less than 5 years had grown his franchise to over 100 studios in 18 states nationwide, producing revenues of $2.4 million in 2011.[16]

As your company grows, its strategic planning efforts will benefit from the input of others inside and outside the company with critical knowledge that can influence the company's direction. Customers, particularly lead users, can provide information about market needs. Specialist employees who are close to markets and technologies can identify future opportunities. The firm can institute a function that gathers and monitors outside information and examines external trends and opportunities.

Organizational Resources and Capabilities

A bootstrap mentality does not end once the company is launched and successful; it is a lasting orientation toward maximizing value from resource parsimony.

Efforts to finance growth internally go hand in hand with controls. By improving its cash flow, your growing company can better avert a cash crisis and avoid being at the mercy of reluctant or expensive lenders or investors. You may even be able to self-finance some of its future growth, reducing reliance on more expensive sources of funding. The key lesson is this: A bootstrap mentality does not apply just to starting a company; it is a lasting orientation that maximizes returns through resource parsimony.

Obtaining Financial Resources for the Growing Company

Shortening operating cash cycles and increasing margins are vital for conserving cash. They essentially represent costless financing. The rapidly growing organization, however, will likely need to tap additional sources to finance its growth. Not only will you need financing to support accelerating sales, but also new policies, such as granting customer payment terms or taking on bulk orders, as well as investments in new products or services, will create a drain on cash.

Despite its success and future prospects, however, a company early in its growth cycle may have only certain options available. For example, a bank would not typically extend credit to a firm with little operating history and fluctuating sales. But as we discussed in Chapter 11, a supplier who is motivated to make a sale and gain a loyal, growing customer might. After a company has been established for a year, a bank might be willing to loan monies against a portion of its receivables, based on the founders' good credit, or with signed guarantees, perhaps requiring loan covenants to maintain certain numbers or ratios.

It's therefore useful to think in terms of stages when financing growth. Sources closed to the firm earlier in its life may open up later. Undertake periodic surveys of the firm's current financing options, and consider any changes that may open up new and cheaper financing sources. In this way, you may recognize new opportunities for refinancing at lower rates.

As we covered in Chapters 9, 10, and 11, sources of financing for early growth include:

- Investment from key management
- Founder loans
- Family and friends
- Angel investors
- Venture capital
- Loans on assets, such as receivables, inventory, and equipment
- Equipment leases
- Credit cards

As the company moves into later growth and undertakes expansion efforts, such as selling internationally or launching new products or services, it will need financing from sources more appropriate for higher-risk and longer-term investment. Banks typically will not loan substantial funds, unsecured, for riskier expansion efforts that won't generate returns for quite some time. The firm will likely need to rely on equity sources.

But there are other ways to finance future growth. Look to strategic partners who may provide more favorable financing terms. You may also decide to expand by franchising. Take the risks of these financing modes into consideration: For example, potential customers who compete with your strategic partner may view a relationship with you as too risky because your partner has some control over your firm or has greater access to information that could unfavorably affect the customer. Determine your resource needs by your firm's range of value chain activities. Reducing activities to those considered core to the business and achieving better coordination throughout the chain can reduce your resource requirements and risk, as we detailed in the execution section.

Intangible Resources and Capabilities

Resources at startup include people, but the focus is on acquiring capital, since the key human resource is the founder or founding team. As the company grows, it accumulates capital, to be sure, and fixed assets. But it also builds intangible assets—resources such as the proprietary knowledge underlying its products and services and the skills of the organization's people. You should have addressed intellectual property considerations early on, before early growth—even before starting the business. But this should also be an ongoing process requiring continual legal advice and subsequent actions to protect technologies, processes, and creative work through trade secrets, copyrights, trademarks, and patents (see Chapter 12).

Starting in early growth, you'll need to develop or hire people with specialized skills. Generalist skills are important at startup: Everyone should be able to pitch in and help with shipping, inventory control, marketing, and so forth. As volume increases and the business becomes more complex, it becomes harder to maintain efficiency and effectiveness with generalist skills. Now you will need to hire specialists in areas such as marketing, inventory management, accounting and finance, and logistics.

An organization also develops capabilities that define what it is good at. These are processes that coordinate and integrate the organization's tangible and intangible resources to create unique sources of value. Just like inventory and equipment, they lead to revenues for a company. Think about businesses or organizations that are familiar to you and about what they do best. McDonald's has efficient processes to deliver fast, low-priced meals. Microsoft delivers transformative computer operating systems and software. These transactions translate to capabilities. Now think about whether these organizations would be good at doing something totally different in their industry. Could McDonald's open a high-end restaurant? Will Microsoft's expansion into the tablet PC and smartphone market be a success? Possibly, but not easily. But there are opportunities to expand into the periphery with their capabilities. For example, McDonald's began to offer salads in an attempt to attract more health-conscious, but also convenience-minded and price-conscious, eaters. In 2008, McDonald's rolled out McCafé, which offers specialty coffees such as cappuccino, lattes, and mochas and directly competes with Starbucks.[17] In 2012, in another effort to increase sales from existing customers who are becoming more health conscious, McDonald's rolled out a completely new "Favorites under 400" menu to make it simpler for customers to select items based on their calorie content. In 2012, Microsoft released "Surface," its first tablet PC, and the Windows smartphone; both designed to run on the new Windows 8 OS, enabling the first ever-complete integration of Microsoft's Office products into mobile devices.[18]

Your capabilities need to be consistent with your firm's strategic focus. As the opportunity domain section of this chapter reveals, organizations define their strategy both through detecting where the opportunities are for unique advantages in the external competitive environment and through building and leveraging a set of unique capabilities. McDonald's needs to have processes that optimize efficiency and cut costs out of its operations. Microsoft needs to be constantly imagining and developing the next breakthrough operating systems and software applications, then integrating them into seamless eco-systems that help lock customers in. Think again about the capabilities Stonyfield Farm and Yankee Candle needed as they started and expanded their businesses.

Sustained growth in a changing environment requires constant attention to identifying what the company does best and matching that with the potential for unique value in the competitive environment. Your company may be good at user-friendly innovations. If it does this better than rivals and users are willing to pay a premium for that, then leverage it—ensuring the right people and systems are in place to maximize the value you can gain from this capability.

Meanwhile, you need to monitor the uniqueness and value of your company's capabilities over time. If competitors duplicate this ability or customers shift toward more technically complex solutions, reassess what your company does best. Renew key capabilities periodically. A research study of telecommunications and computer startups found that high levels of innovativeness at founding did not translate to higher growth seven, eight, or nine years out. And simply forming alliances didn't help. But those building internal technology capabilities beyond founding were more likely to achieve a higher level of sustained growth.[19]

Leadership

Figure 13.8 summarizes some key differences between entrepreneurs, managers, and entrepreneurial leaders. The entrepreneurial leader plays a distinct role, critical for sustaining a growing organization.

Starting the Delegation Process

The entrepreneur typically starts out doing everything. She answers phones, ships product, designs advertisements—in essence, performing just about all the activities needed to ensure the organization gets product sold and out the door. But sometime in early growth, the organization will outgrow her ability to keep up. She will have neither the time nor the expertise to deal with the range of challenges a burgeoning business presents. The following are symptoms revealing that the organization has outgrown the entrepreneur's capacity.

- The volume of decisions multiplies. The entrepreneur is working harder but accomplishing less.

- Decisions become more difficult to make: more complex and specialized. The entrepreneur increasingly wonders whether she has made the right decision.

- Everyone is still pitching in and doing everything, but more and more, something critical slips by or mistakes occur.

- If the entrepreneur is not directly involved in the task, no progress can happen.

Starting in early growth, the entrepreneur must delegate responsibilities to others in the organization. The process of delegation is mapped out in Figure 13.9.

Entrepreneur	Manager	Entrepreneurial Leader
Locates new ideas	Maintains current operations	Leverages core business while exploring new opportunities
Starts a business	Implements the business	Starts businesses within an ongoing organization
Opportunity driven	Resource driven	Capability and opportunity driven; leverages capabilities and builds new ones to expand opportunity domain
Establishes and implements a vision	Plans, organizes, staffs, controls	Establishes a vision and empowers others to carry it out
Builds an organization around the opportunity	Enhances efficiency of organization	Maintains entrepreneurial ability as organization grows; ensures culture, structure, systems are conducive to entrepreneurship; removes barriers
Leads and inspires others	Supervises and monitors others	Develops and guides entrepreneurial individuals; bridges between individuals and groups with diverse expertise and orientation
Orchestrates change in the competitive environment	Maintains consistency and predictability	Orchestrates change in both the organizational and competitive environment

Figure 13.8

The entrepreneur vs. manager vs. entrepreneurial leader

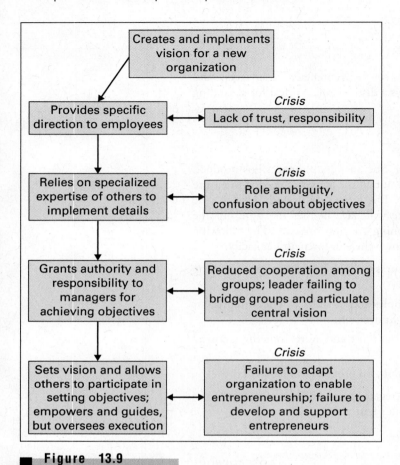

Figure 13.9

Transition from entrepreneur to entrepreneurial leader

As Figure 13.9 shows, the entrepreneur starts out assigning specific tasks to others. As delegation proceeds, she passes responsibility for achieving objectives to specialists, and then managers, without needing to understand or know about the underlying mechanics. Then the setting of objectives moves to others: experienced managers and teams close to the activity. This process enables the entrepreneur to spend less time on the day-to-day details of everything and focus on what she does best, while those most qualified make decisions. At the same time, the entrepreneur needs to oversee execution by providing guidance to managers and using metrics to evaluate progress, but she may need to step in when necessary, particularly when initiatives meet with resistance.

Delegation, while necessary for surviving the entrepreneurial growth phase, is typically difficult for the entrepreneur to accomplish. She may continue to attempt to do everything herself, but she's increasingly unable to do so. Faced with these challenges, the entrepreneur may revert back to what she does best, ignoring tasks she has neither the comfort level nor the capability to deal with. A technical entrepreneur may retreat to developing new products, while ignoring the company's inability to pay bills on time. What's bad is not the entrepreneur doing what she does best—it's having no one pay attention to the company's most critical problems.

Employees may not have a problem with the lack of delegation because they may prefer that the entrepreneur make decisions that they can then carry out. Then they don't need to take responsibility for outcomes. On the other hand, in allowing employees to take responsibility for decisions, the entrepreneur also needs to let them make mistakes and learn from them, circumstances neither the employees nor the entrepreneur may feel comfortable with. The entrepreneur cannot continue to be the "go-to" guy, however, when the volume of decisions mushrooms and she becomes increasingly less qualified to provide direction in many areas.

As the entrepreneur delegates, she will need to put in place managers who can be responsible for executing in specialized areas. Then, in her leadership role, she must develop the ability to inspire people with a range of expertise to organize, communicate, collaborate—and be creative in both running an efficient operation and pursuing entrepreneurial ideas.

First-Level Management

In early growth, the first set of supervisors can come from within. In some sense, they deserve to be promoted because they have been with the company since its early days and have contributed to its success. They were willing to chip in whenever and wherever needed, they have worked closely with you, the entrepreneur, and they therefore understand your vision and the purpose of the organization. They may also have the respect of their peers.

Assess whether these people have the potential to become managers, however, and whether they can develop their abilities through training and experience. There are a few things you should do: (1) set expectations up front, including setting personal performance goals; (2) provide coaching, mentoring, and training; and (3) periodically assess behavior and performance. But developing managers takes time. If the venture is late forming its management structure and is therefore playing catch-up, if internal and external conditions are rapidly changing, or if the learning gap between current employees and needed management is too wide, then allowing managers to learn on the job is too risky. You will need to hire from the outside.

Hiring from the outside has its own hazards because the workers, particularly those who have been there from the beginning, may not respect these outsiders. First, act as a broker between the employees and management during this transition. This includes advising the new manager and recognizing the cooperation and contributions of employees. The latter can mean acknowledging accomplishments through personal contact or making these visible around the organization. In addition, you (and your managers) can ensure employees have a satisfactory career path by promoting them and moving them into jobs in which they increasingly feel engaged and challenged.

Where possible, employ a mix of externally hired managers and internally promoted managers. Again, broker between these internal and external managers during the transition by setting expectations, advising and coaching, and monitoring behavior. By achieving cooperation among internal and external managers, you're more likely to accomplish broad cooperation across the organization. Also reinforce the authority of your new managers, whether they originate from the inside or the outside. For example, route to them employees who have always gone directly to you.

From Delegation to Decentralization

What starts as a process of delegation in early growth evolves into a decentralized reporting structure as the organization approaches later growth. As functions become more specialized and the product and service offering broadens, responsibility and decision making are best left to those with the expertise and day-to-day involvement in specific areas.

A decentralized structure can also aid communication flow throughout the organization, which increasingly becomes challenged as the organization grows. While closeness to the entrepreneur in early stages helps everyone understand her vision and the organization's objectives, the complexity and changes a growing organization experiences can create confusion about direction and purpose. Communication and understanding need to happen among the members of the management team, who then ensure consistent information flow throughout their areas.

Professional Management and Boards

In later growth, the organization needs to ensure it has a leadership team in place: professional managers who share in the organization's strategic planning process and have the capability to balance the need for efficient operations with the benefits of maintaining its entrepreneurial edge. Once the organization has created control systems, a management structure, and a strategic focus, it needs to look toward its future. This job becomes increasingly complex and requires those with experience and track records. Employees who have been promoted into managerial positions are not likely to be qualified for the organization's top levels. Consequently, professional managers typically come from the outside.

With the introduction of a leadership team, the organization itself becomes more professional. This is a major change, even more so than the shift from startup to early growth.

Some employees will leave, but others will make this transition. The practices you put in place to integrate managers and employees and insiders and outsiders during early growth will be critical to your introduction of a professional management team.

By carefully selecting members of the board of directors, you can provide alternative perspectives and depth and breadth of experience. The board should include experts from outside the firm who can become key participants in the strategic planning process. What's important for the firm is a proactive, rather than a reactive, approach to seeking ways to extend and build value. The composition of the company's board of directors will typically undergo changes as the firm emerges from its startup phase. Initially, the board may be informal—occupied by those unlikely to have high-level experience but able to provide support to the entrepreneur in her early endeavors. In early growth, boards typically evolve to include those able to provide operational guidance—for example, retired bankers, investors, and lawyers.

As the company professionalizes, the board should be more useful for strategic purposes, with members having a broader and visionary view of the market and industry—for example, other CEOs, industry experts, and senior executives in related businesses. While many investors require representation on the board of directors, avoid stakeholders who can control the firm for their benefit through board positions, such as suppliers, customers, and the company's lenders.

Supplement the skill and experience of the company's leadership and board of directors with the skill and experience of advisory boards and consultants. For example, you may assemble a group of technology experts from universities, government labs, and corporations to examine industry technological trends, or you may bring in a marketing consulting firm to determine tactics for expanding into overseas markets.

Coordinating the Driving Forces

The driving forces model shows a link among the three elements: organizational resources and capabilities, opportunity domain, and leadership. And at the core of this is execution: ensuring the most efficient and effective coordination of these activities in a way that enhances the organization's profitability. Capabilities and the opportunity domain interact: Capabilities define where the company can best play, and opportunities extend capabilities. Leadership maps out a particular opportunity domain with its strategic focus and modifies this focus over time, as the industry and market environment changes and the company seeks future growth. Leadership also ensures its capabilities and opportunity domain are in balance. But as the organization grows, a key concern for its leaders is how to manage its people and maintain its entrepreneurial capabilities, as the next section illustrates.

Leading People; Developing Entrepreneurs

The most common "people mistakes" an entrepreneurial firm makes are preparing people inadequately and maintaining the wrong people as the organization grows. Early in the business's life, organization members do their jobs and pitch in wherever needed. It is more important for the lean team to maintain the flexibility and broad skills needed to accomplish a lot with a little. Early in the game, it is not yet apparent these employees lack the skills needed to scale up the organization. It is difficult to think about training to develop future skills when growth is consuming everyone's time.

As the need for specialists and managers arises, the tasks you expect of some employees may exceed their abilities, and you may need to place them in other roles—or even fire them if necessary. Other employees may be able to rise up to the challenges presented and assume these new functions and responsibilities. The process of adapting to these new roles takes time, however. The company will often need to do some hiring from the outside. You will have to deal with reduced motivation from setbacks or crises at the same time that employees struggle with adapting to new employees and higher-level managers coming from the outside, both of whom lack the shared experiences gained through the organization's history.

The second tier of employees, beyond the founding group, is often said to be more like 9-to-5ers who tend to view working there as a job. But in most companies, there are entrepreneurs in the mix. While we often think that ideas come from anywhere or that anyone can be creative if given a chance, the reality is that some people don't have the stomach for ambiguity and risk. And in many companies, the entrepreneur remains the sole entrepreneurial engine.

Our research on corporate entrepreneurship suggests the organization's leaders need to:

- Identify those exhibiting passion for entrepreneurship.
- Develop their ability to work under conditions of high ambiguity.
- Ensure they have the inclination and credibility to convince others in the organization to contribute and commit to their projects.
- Facilitate, support, and guide their efforts, while also providing them with sufficient freedom and empowerment.
- Recognize their contribution to the company's innovation and growth ambitions.
- View failure as a risk associated with entrepreneurship and an opportunity for learning, therefore ensuring that well-intentioned failures are not punished.

We suspect these practices are also critical in smaller organizations. One study reports that human resource practices like training and development distinguish high-growth firms from more slowly growing ones.[20]

CONCLUSION

Starting a business is a risky endeavor, but staying in business can be just as challenging. As the entrepreneurial firm grows beyond founding, it needs to ensure its organization is capable of managing growth. We have outlined a driving forces model that integrates leadership, opportunity domain, and resources and capabilities—and has execution at the core. The entrepreneur should understand and anticipate the challenges associated with building and managing a growing organization at different stages, prepare the organization to execute effectively at each point, and set the stage for a healthy future.

These efforts, however, must not distance the company from its entrepreneurial roots. Growing companies struggle not just with such concerns as having fewer resources than big companies but also with coordinating an increasingly bigger and more complex business. The team members must work to prevent the organization from becoming a bureaucracy that inhibits entrepreneurship. They must continually foster entrepreneurial actions even when this is their biggest challenge. They have to consciously work on preserving and maintaining their entrepreneurial spirit, and if they lose it, they have to rejuvenate the company and rekindle entrepreneurship before it's too late.

YOUR OPPORTUNITY JOURNAL

Reflection Point	Your Thoughts...

1. What are your personal growth objectives for your venture? Is a "lifestyle" business going to meet your personal goals? Or a high-potential venture?

2. What will your role within the company be at various stages of growth? Do you want to remain the CEO? Are you more interested in another aspect—say, CTO?

3. What skills will you need to develop as the company grows to satisfactorily fulfill the roles you aspire to? Which of these skills can you learn on the job? Which skills might need further education or other outside development?

4. What kind of controls can you establish early in your venture's life? How will these help you manage cash and other key components of your business?

5. Which aspects of your business should you keep in-house and which should you outsource? How do you protect your competitive advantage?

6. What is your strategic focus for early growth? How do you leverage what you do really well? What are some possible peripheral growth opportunities for later in your venture's life?

7. What are your organization's key resources and capabilities? What should they be in the future? How do you build toward those resources and capabilities?

8. What is your leadership plan? When and which responsibilities will you delegate? How will you promote people in your organization? When might you need to go outside to hire?

WEB EXERCISE

Identify three companies that have experienced successful, rapid growth in your industry. Study their Web sites and search for articles about the companies. Can you discern their strategic focuses early in their growth cycles? What are the core areas that they are leveraging? How do their growth strategies change later in their lives? What are some peripheral markets/customers they are going for? Have they grown by acquisition? How has that worked out?

NOTES

1   Zook, C., and Allen, J. *The Facts about Growth*. New York: Bain Company. 1999.

2   Quinn, J. Google Founders Have "Grown Up" says CEO Eric Schmidt. Telegraph.co.uk. May 10, 2008. www.telegraph.co.uk/finance/newsbysector/media technologyandtelecoms/2789659/Google-founders-have-grown-up-says-CEO-Eric-Schmidt.html.

3   More recently, Schmidt has become Executive Chairman and Page is CEO.

4   www.bloggingstocks.com/2008/11/21/if-a-stocks-below-5-its-likely-to-dive

5   www.dividend.com/news/2012/the-biggest-dividend-stock-disasters-of-all-time

6   online.wsj.com/article/SB10001424052748704113504575264641145227612.html?KEYWORDS=Lesson. . .

7   Additional resources on growth stages can be found in the following references:

   ◉ Adizes, Ichak. *Managing Corporate Lifecycles*. Paramus, NJ: Prentice Hall, 1999.

   ◉ Churchill, Neil C. The Six Key Phases of Company Growth. In S. Birley and D. Muzyka (Eds.), *Mastering Enterprise*. London, England: Pitman Publishing, 1997.

   ◉ Flamholtz, Eric G., and Randle, Yvonne. *Growing Pains: Transitioning from an Entrepreneurship to a Professionally Managed Firm*. San Francisco, CA: Jossey-Bass, 2000.

   ◉ Greiner, Larry E. Evolution and Revolution as Organizations Grow. *Harvard Business Review*, 76(3): 55–63, 1998.

   ◉ Harper, Stephen C. *The McGraw-Hill Guide to Managing Growth in Your Emerging Business*. New York: McGraw-Hill, 1995.

8   www.venturenavigator.co.uk/content/153

9   www.startups.co.uk/is-your-business-growing-too-fast.html

10 Kolen, Joel, and Jaffe, Susan Biddle. Knowing When to Take a Breather: Controlling Company Growth. *Nation's Business*, 83(11): 6, November 1995.

11 www.circuitsassembly.com/cms/component/content/article/159/10901-ems-top-50

12 www.google.com/url?sa=t&rct=j&q=no table%20startup%20%22cash%20conversion%20cycle%20%22restructuring%20&source=web&cd=6&cad=rja&ved=0CFEQFjAF&url=http%3A%2F%2Fphx.corporate-ir.net%2FExternal.File%3Fitem%3DUGFyZW50SUQ9Nzg2MTh8Q2hpbGRJRD0tMXxUeXBlPTM%3D%26t%3D1&ei=Vd76UNG4KtCr0AHqiYDYBg&usg=AFQjCNH4jQSFFN4q4F7yYJ5KLPDC8U26VQ&bvm=bv.41248874,d.dmQ

13 (Andrew Kardon blog): http://blog.bestvendor.com/2012/08/outsourcing-is-a-startups-best-friend

14 www.secinfo.com/d12Pk6.phtj.htm#_8

15 Osborne, Richard L. Second Phase Entrepreneurship: Breaking Through the Growth Wall. *Business Horizons*, 37(1): 80–86, 1994.

16 www.inc.com/profile/get-in-shape-for-women

17 www.nytimes.com/2012/05/06/magazine/how-mcdonalds-came-back-bigger-than-ever.html?pagewanted=all&_r=0, and also its Web site www.mcdonalds.com/us/en/food/food_quality/nutrition_choices.html, and www.huffingtonpost.com/2012/07/23/mcdonalds-favorites-under-400-calories_n_1695885.html

18 www.microsoft.com

19 Kelley, Donna, and Nakosteen, Robert. Technology Resources, Alliances and Sustained Growth in New, Technology-Based Firms. *IEEE Transactions on Engineering Management*, 52(3): 292–300, 2005.

20 Barringer, B., Jones, F., and Neubaum, D. A Quantitative Content Analysis of the Characteristics of Rapid-Growth Firms and Their Founders. *Journal of Business Venturing*, 20: 663–687. 2005.

CASE

Lazybones

Sitting in his Cambridge townhouse, Dan Hermann mulled over the latest performance report for his company, Lazybones, a laundry delivery service for college students. The unit[1] in Boulder, Colorado, was performing well, and he could see the positive results of the company's hiring and training initiatives. The Boston, Massachusetts, store was bringing in decent revenues, but it had just lost its manager. Over the coming weeks, Dan would need to be onsite quite a bit to work with new staff. Meanwhile, the Storrs, Connecticut, location (Lazybones' newest unit) was well below expectations. So in addition to overseeing four other stores and giving extra attention in Boston, Dan needed to spend time in Storrs assessing why that site couldn't get off the ground.

On the surface, the Lazybones store operations were straightforward: collect dirty laundry from college students, clean it, and then deliver it back to their dorm or apartment in less than 24 hours. The process, fine-tuned at their Syracuse, New York, and Madison, Wisconsin, flagship locations, worked flawlessly. Dan and his co-founder, Reg Mathelier, could monitor each unit remotely via webcam. They also used a barcode tracking system to feed a comprehensive reporting system for each store: the daily dashboard performance monitor. In fact, Dan lived in Boston and Reg lived in Chicago, far from most of the operating units. Yet as the company grew, the workload and processes were becoming more complicated. Dan was rethinking his growth objectives:

I hope I didn't mess up a good thing. I'm making less money, working twice as many hours, and I'm rapidly approaching 40 years old. The hours I put in now have more meaning to me. I've got more at stake today than I had when we were a startup. How should I evaluate that?

Dan's business, prior to adding the new locations, generated a consistent flow of cash and allowed him and Reg to earn a nice living. The business had evolved to the point where it did not require much time or effort to maintain a return. It had become an annuity of sorts, and Dan was free to pursue additional projects, like earning his MBA at Babson College. Dan faced the dilemma that many successful lifestyle entrepreneurs face: Should he keep the business as it is, or should he grow it? Perhaps it was the excitement of his classes at Babson, but Dan felt the itch to grow the Lazybones franchise and the two stores in Boston and Boulder were steps in that direction. Unfortunately, it was proving to be more work than Dan had expected.

Courtesy Dan Hermann

The Syracuse, New York, unit

Take It to the Cleaners

It was May 1993, and like many other recent college grads, Dan Hermann and Reg Mathelier needed jobs. But neither saw himself in a corporate position. They both had an urge to start their own company; they just needed an idea. The inspiration came from an unlikely

---

This case was prepared by Sara Gragnolati under the direction of Professor Andrew Zacharakis.

[1] A unit, also called a store, is where Lazybones executes all of its laundry activities.

place. . . their own personal negligence. As stereotypical undergraduates, Reg and Dan were not too diligent with cleanliness. A close friend took note and offered to do their laundry in exchange for a small fee. The two friends started to realize that, if they had bemoaned doing their laundry, so, too, would many of the thousands of undergraduate students at their alma mater, the University of Wisconsin at Madison.

The barriers to entry in laundry service were low. With a loan of $12,000 from friends and family, the two newly minted graduates traded in their laid-back academic lifestyle for the sweat and tears needed to launch Lazybones, a laundry delivery service targeted at college students. Their strategy was simple: Appeal to the parents of incoming and returning students and offer a fee-based subscription program. Each subscription covered the weekly pick-up and drop-off of a prepaid amount of laundry. Any overage was billed by the pound.

Dan explained:

> The laundry is picked up, separated into lights and darks, washed with top-quality detergent and softeners, dried, meticulously folded, packaged in brown paper, and delivered back to the student within 24 hours of pick-up. Parents loved the idea. Now their kids, even if they were hundreds of miles from home, would have clean clothes when they went out in public and, God forbid, be wearing clean underwear if they should be rushed to the emergency room following an accident. Parents willingly prepaid for the semester to bring a little bit of "mom" to college with the kid.

Although they had a rudimentary business plan—Dan laughs when he thinks about how rough and incomplete it was—they mostly learned the business on the job. They started with three home-grade washers and dryers and went out and solicited their first customers. They quickly realized that their service speed was too slow and their prices too low. What they lacked in business experience the two compensated for with diligence. They were literally willing to do whatever it took to get Lazybones off of the ground.

> When we first started, we were working day and night, seven days a week. Reg and I knew that our service was going to be based on our quality. We would rewash clothes or hand scrub stains if needed.

The first year was a struggle for survival. Dan and Reg worked around the clock, and they were constantly on the verge of going out of business. They often used credit cards to finance the business over the first few years, especially during the summer, when the business basically came to a halt as students returned home. Fortunately, Dan and Reg found a complementary summer business to ease the cash-flow famine. While school was out of session, Lazybones stored student possessions (TVs, furniture, etc.) that the students did not want to lug home and back. Three years passed before either founder took home any money. But by year five, they were turning a profit. The whole process was an exercise in logistics, with a steep learning curve.

> We were constantly operating about 30% to 40% over what our actual logical capacity to do laundry was, given our facility, equipment, and staff. Yet we still weren't making money. But we were learning fast and having fun with the challenge of it. The demand for our service exceeded our ability to deliver, and we viewed this as an indicator that, if we hung in there and made adjustments, we would be onto something.

Six years into the business, Reg and Dan decided it was time to expand. After a friend conducted some market research, they identified Syracuse University as an ideal fit; the school charged a high tuition and possessed a large student base with a more-than-adequate amount of disposable income. Dan moved to Syracuse to oversee the opening. They soon received an endorsement from the school, which set up a direct pipeline to acquiring customers. Within a year and a half, the new location was breaking even.

Once a location hit profitability, the unit economics became attractive (see Exhibit 13.1 for the Unit Profit and Loss Statement). Customers loved the service, and many parents had approached Dan and Reg about possibly franchising Lazybones to other locations. Dan reflected:

> Expanding campus to campus meant we would not be able to add a lot of locations in close proximity to one another. Hiring good managers became even more important, as they would potentially need to operate [in] states away from our corporate office location in Massachusetts. Turnover was even more of a stress and an expense. I started to view franchising as the way to go.

The Industry

In 2009, the non-coin-operated laundry industry represented $9.6 billion of business, with the services sector occupying 21.5% of the total market.[2] Within the services arena, two segments exist: commercial customers, including hotels and hospitals, and noncommercial customers, such as the college-student base that Lazybones targets. This put Lazybones' direct market size at $1.0 billion.

The industry, in 2009, was highly fragmented and mature and had reached a sales plateau, with revenues declining by 2.1% from the previous year.[3] This was a market dominated by owner-operated businesses. Just 6% of the industry was composed of companies with 20 or more employees.[4] And from that portion, 5.4% of the market share went to the largest competitors: National Drycleaning Inc.,[5] Dry Clean USA, and Hangers America[6] franchises. Because of its narrow customer segment, though, Lazybones did not compete directly with these three companies.

While sales for the overall market waned, the services segment exhibited increases due to the growing tourism, hospitality, and retail fashion trades.

On the college campuses, Lazybones saw very little competition. Most of its competitors operated at only one school or city—mom-and-pop type players. There were few companies that serviced multiple schools. The most comparable competition, University Laundry in Texas and Soapy Joe's out of Maryland, did not have facilities in close proximity to any current Lazybones location. And while some colleges owned their own internal laundry service for students, enough institutions of higher learning did not offer a comparable service to provide significant competition for Lazybones.

Absentee Owner

> We grew very quickly in Syracuse, but when we made the transition from me being on hand to me being an absentee owner, we saw many challenges. All of a sudden we realized that we were the glue that held everything together and kept the quality at its highest level. We had to implement systems to sustain the business, or we would be forever tied to the day-to-day.

For the first three years, the two founders were tirelessly at work improving the business and evaluating their progress. Efficiency was a priority. Growing the business beyond its existing locations was far from their minds. They focused solely on developing the quality that

---

[2] IBISWorld. *IBISWorld Industry Report: Non Coin-Operated Laundromats and Dry Cleaners in the US.* August 2009.

[3] Ibid.

[4] Ibid.

[5] Parent company: DCI Management Group Ltd.

[6] Parent company: Cool Clean Technologies.

EXHIBIT 13.1 Model Store 5-Year Income Statement

Month	July	Aug	Sept	Oct	Nov	Dec	Semester	Jan	Feb	Mar	Apr	May	Jun	Semester
Laundry Revenue	$—	$2,907	$6,056	$7,994	$6,056	$1,211	$24,225	$36,338	$4,845	$2,423	$2,423	$2,423	$2,423	$48,450
Storage Revenue	$—	$—	$—	$—	$—	$5,281	$5,281	$—	$—	$—	$1,320	$5,281	$6,601	$13,202
Other Revenue							$—							$—
Total Revenue	$—	$2,907	$6,056	$7,994	$6,056	$6,492	$29,506	$36,338	$4,845	$2,423	$3,743	$7,703	$6,601	$61,652
Cost of Goods Sold	$—	$517	$1,593	$3,014	$4,090	$4,306	$13,519	$3,819	$4,329	$4,583	$4,838	$5,093	$5,093	$27,754
Gross Profit	$—	$2,390	$4,463	$4,980	$1,966	$2,187	$15,986	$32,518	$516	$(2,161)	$(1,095)	$2,611	$1,508	$33,898
Gross Profit %							54%							55%
Selling, General & Administrative	$14,526	$14,526	$12,776	$11,026	$11,026	$11,776	$75,659	$11,776	$11,776	$11,776	$13,526	$15,276	$14,526	$78,659
EBITDA	$(14,526)	$(12,136)	$(8,313)	$(6,046)	$(9,060)	$(9,590)	$(59,672)	$20,742	$(11,260)	$(13,937)	$(14,622)	$(12,666)	$(13,018)	$(44,761)
Interest Expense	$585	$580	$575	$570	$565	$559	$3,434	$554	$549	$544	$538	$533	$528	$3,246
Net Ordinary Income	$(15,111)	$(12,716)	$(8,888)	$(6,616)	$(9,625)	$(10,149)	$(63,106)	$20,187	$(11,809)	$(14,481)	$(15,160)	$(13,199)	$(13,546)	$(48,007)
Net Profit Margin		-437%	-147%	-83%	-159%	-156%	-214%	56%	-244%	-598%	-405%	-171%	-205%	-78%

Year	Year 1	Year 2	Year 3	Year 4	Year 5
Laundry Revenue	$72,675	$169,575	$290,700	$387,600	$484,500
Storage Revenue	$18,483	$25,084	$46,207	$72,611	$99,015
Other Revenue	$—	$—			
Total Revenue	$91,158	$194,659	$336,907	$460,211	$583,515
Cost of Goods Sold	$41,274	$91,416	$158,218	$216,124	$274,030
Gross Profit	$49,884	$103,243	$178,689	$244,087	$309,485
Gross Profit %	55%	53%	53%	53%	53%
Selling, General & Administrative	$154,317	$137,191	$142,423	$147,716	$153,131
EBITDA	$(104,433)	$(33,947)	$36,265	$96,371	$156,354
Interest Expense	$6,680	$5,894	$5,034	$4,094	$3,065
Net Ordinary Income	$(111,113)	$(39,841)	$31,231	$92,277	$153,289
Net Profit Margin	-122%	-20%	9%	20%	26%

was needed to sustain Lazybones. Eventually, Dan and Reg were able to get the business to the point where it required only 25 hours per week from each of them. At this stage, Lazybones was teetering between a lifestyle business and a growing business. With time on his hands, Dan decided he needed to figure out how to expand the company.

In September 2003, Dan started in the part-time evening MBA program at Babson College. Through his coursework, Dan's entrepreneurial spirit was sparked again. He started to realize the potential for growth in his business. Dan recalled his first conversation with Reg about growing:

> Reg, now a family man, wasn't necessarily open to the stress that would come along with growing Lazybones. Nonetheless, he was on board. He would have been fine with keeping it a lifestyle business. But he could see my vision. His practicality balanced me, and we both knew we had to have a plan if it was going to work.

Although Dan and Reg wanted to increase revenues and profits at their existing locations, they recognized that real company growth could be fueled only by campus-to-campus expansion.

Now living in the Boston area, Dan decided to oversee the opening of a local outlet in August 2008. This new facility would service Boston-area universities, such as Boston University and Babson College. In addition, Dan and Reg decided that it was time to take a risk and test the company's potential to grow. Through careful research, they decided to also open a store in Boulder to service the University of Colorado. Dan pointed out:

> We needed to push our systems to see how far they could go. Could we really succeed with Lazybones in any location in the United States? It was a gamble, for sure, but we had to know [to what] extent we could take this business. If we couldn't succeed in Boulder, we would have to restrategize our growth plans.

In regard to Boulder, Dan and Reg decided to hedge their bets by relocating their seasoned Wisconsin manager to run the new store. He had been very successful at handling the Madison location and had proven that he was trustworthy. Dan and Reg needed to know that the manager for this new store, so far away from where they were located, could be relied on.

During the first year, laundry sales in Boulder were much slower than projected. Dan and Reg came to realize that they had sent an operations specialist into a startup environment. Also, the manager did not know the town or the university. Last, they really needed someone who knew how to sell. Fortunately, revenues from the summer storage rentals came in higher than expected and helped to give the location a financial boost for the close of its first year. Despite the bump in revenue, Dan and Reg knew that they had to make a change if this store was going to succeed. They made the extremely difficult decision to replace their experienced manager, who had been a loyal employee of the company for many years, with someone new.

The problematic management situation in Boulder, in addition to simultaneous manager recruitment activities in three other locations, was the impetus for designing a structured training program. This was a step in the right direction: Lazybones needed more structure and metrics.

Ironing Out the Details

Just about a year prior to the Boston and Boulder openings, Dan met Joel Pedlikin during an MBA evening course at Babson. They developed a friendship, but it was not until they learned about franchising, through a finance course, that Joel's interest in joining the company peaked. During their Entrepreneurship class in the fall of 2008, Dan and Joel solidified their goal to grow Lazybones, which was now in its 15th year of operation. With Reg's full support,

Dan and Joel thoroughly explored franchising and the role it could play in growing Lazybones. The possibility of expanding the business to the point at which they could sell it intrigued them. The pair worked on a business plan during their Entrepreneurship class to investigate the feasibility of a franchising growth plan.

Dan and Joel identified a few areas of the business that needed to be improved in order to better position the company for growth, franchise development, and eventual acquisition. Following a typical franchising growth strategy, Dan and Joel planned on opening several more company stores. They wanted to prove that the process could be replicated and to iron out the unit management and monitoring details. Once they had seven to 10 company stores, the management team would start franchising Lazybones.

Dan (left) and Joel in front of a Lazybones delivery van

By May 2009, Joel had become a partner and full-time member of the Lazybones team. It was time to put their diligent research and planning into motion. The first step of the plan was to showcase the successful new company stores. Dan and Joel started by revamping their staffing strategy. Summer 2009 was the first year that the company implemented a hiring strategy. To successfully manage multiple locations, they needed the right people supervising company-owned stores. They realized they had to be thorough. Joel describes the transition:

> Our locations were first run by inexperienced managers, who had little more than a high school education. After 16 years, this method had worked for the status quo. To grow, we needed to have different qualifications and the benefits in place to attract the right applicants. So this past year, we put a lot of time and resources into this area.

The new plan included writing formal job descriptions and developing an interview process to screen potential employees. The company would hire only recent alumni of a location's target school for the role of manager. The rationale for this requirement was that an alumnus would understand the market and have potential contacts with university administrators, granting him, or her, a better chance to receive a university endorsement. Also, college graduates were culturally better suited to market and sell the Lazybones services to the company's target customers. Dan and Joel implemented incentives for the manager to grow the business locally. To minimize the potential for missteps, every candidate would go through both phone and in-person interviews, and at least two executives would thoroughly interview the best managerial candidates.

Eventually, Dan and Joel realized that, although they had been tracking metrics, it did little good unless the store managers had direct access to the same data. Lazybones implemented the Dashboard, which allowed both the executive team and the managers to view performance comparisons, work efficiencies, payrolls, and sales statistics on a daily basis (see Exhibit 13.2).

The University of Connecticut shop, in Storrs, Connecticut, was opened in August 2009. That same month they hired new managers for Boulder and Boston based on the new hiring priorities that Dan and Joel had created.

Franchising

Once Dan and Joel proved that they could replicate Lazybones' business model, both managers became certain of the company's future growth through franchising. The primary benefit of this mode of growth is that the franchisees finance each new location, thereby minimizing the

| EXHIBIT 13.2 | Performance Dashboard |

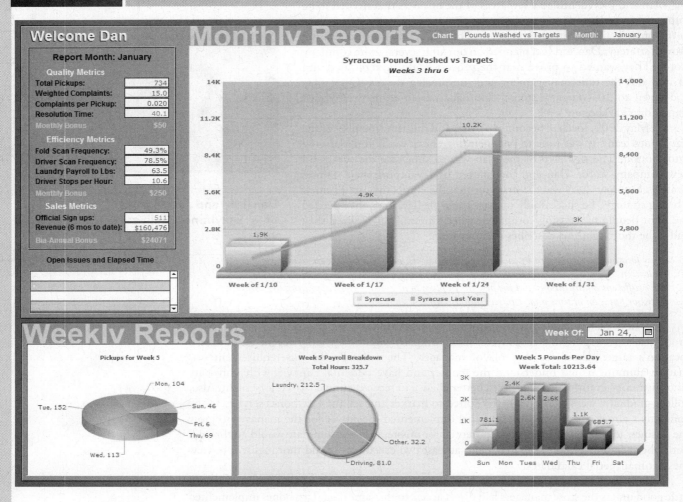

need for Lazybones to raise outside capital from investors or banks. In addition, the franchisee would be each new store's manager. Therefore, the head of each new location would have a strong financial incentive to grow the business, which would contribute positively to both the franchisee's and Lazybones' bottom line.

Between 2003 and 2008, U.S. franchise units, across all industries, grew over 4.5%, compounded annually.[7] This growth totals about 16,000 new units across approximately

[7] Johnson, Darrell M. The State of Franchising. *Franchising World*. 41(5):28–31.

3,000 franchised brands.[8] However, access to funding curbed the growth rate significantly, starting in the third quarter of 2008.

Franchising companies make money through three streams: an initial franchise fee, royalty rates, and advertising contributions. Initial franchise fees typically run from $10,000 to $100,000, with personal service franchises averaging $22,150.[9] This fee covers only the right to use the company name, plus training and manuals. The franchisee is responsible for property, equipment, inventory, and staffing. The royalty income is earned either monthly or quarterly and represents a fixed percentage of the franchisee's revenue. The franchisee also pays a fixed ratio, based on revenues, toward any nationwide advertising campaign run by the franchisor.

Dan and Joel identified the benefits to franchising:

> It's [a] faster method for growth and can spread our name nationally. This rapid growth will position us to be an attractive acquisition in the future.

Dan and Joel planned on setting the franchise fee at $35,000. This price was higher than the service industry mean, but the owners believed they could justify the premium with above-average benefits, such as high unit revenues and profits, a proven business model, and location exclusivity.

Lazybones would also receive monthly royalties of 7% on revenue. Again, this was higher than the service industry norm, which was 5.5%. Joel said:

> We are confident that our franchisees will make larger net margins with Lazybones than with most franchises. For instance, dry cleaners and laundromats average net margins between 3% and 6%, while Lazybones has historically achieved 15% and 20%. Asking for a 1.5% higher contribution in exchange for a three to five times improvement in net margins is a very fair exchange.

Franchisees will also pay 1% of their monthly revenue to Lazybones' national advertising fund. Corporate executives along with three franchisee representatives will manage the accounts.

Dan and Joel predicted that the company would be ready to franchise once it reached seven to 10 locations, under the condition that a majority of sites made a profit and none operated at a loss. But what challenges would they face in the transition? How could they maintain brand consistency, especially when it comes to service quality? When so much of the business depends upon the skills of the manager, how would Dan and Joel help to ensure the managing franchisees' success?

Vision for the Future

As of December 2009, Lazybones had five locations. They were still shy of their 7–10 store goal—a milestone they felt they should reach before adopting the franchise model. It was imperative that Lazybones provide proof of concept to prospective franchisees.

Before they could worry about where to open next, the Lazybones partners had to get each of their current locations to break even, or, even better, to operate at a profit. In Boston, for example, they had 155 laundry customers. The first and only urban location, Boston's

---

[8] Ibid.

[9] Blair, Roger, and LaFontaine, Franchine. *The Economics of Franchising*. Cambridge, England: Cambridge University Press, 2005, pp. 57–71. The 2001 number has been adjusted to 2008 with inflation rates.

operating costs were much higher than those of the other sites due to the driving, labor, and marketing expenses needed for functioning in a major city. To increase revenues at this location, the local manager wanted to start servicing residential customers, as opposed to exclusively students. But this process would require some major adjustments to their core operations, including evening pick-ups and deliveries and an upgraded company Web site.

Dan was previously committed to expanding Lazybones and harvesting the value he had created by selling the business. However, growth was proving to be difficult on many levels. Opening additional stores required a tremendous amount of his time, and the new endeavors were draining profits from the successful locations. He worried that perhaps he had talked his partner Reg into going down the wrong road. Maybe they should have stuck with their established successful locations and the nice leisurely life it had been providing for them. That route would mean cutting ties with Joel, who joined the management team only because of the perceived growth potential. Dan had plenty to think about as he prepared for a meeting with Reg and Joel.

Preparation Questions

1. Should Dan grow Lazybones or maintain it as a lifestyle business?
2. If he chooses growth, is franchising the best way forward?
3. What are the advantages and disadvantages of franchising versus other means of growth?
4. Lay out a five-year plan for growth at both the corporate and the individual location levels (that is, show how you can increase revenue per store).

Cheap energy drove the expansion of suburbia. With exploding world populations, social entrepreneurship seeks new ways of living and protecting resources.

SOCIAL ENTREPRENEURSHIP

INTRODUCTION

Just imagine a world where malaria is eradicated, saving 655,000 lives each year[1] and where entrepreneurs in developing countries have access to 5 billion potential individual investors and lenders through access to the Internet. Imagine car-free cities that dramatically reduce respiratory disease, where food is grown locally in vertical farms and buildings are made of "green concrete" made by capturing the CO_2 emitted from coal or natural gas power plants. By the year 2020, some of these things will be possible due to dramatic changes in technology, demographics, and socio-politics. Now, further imagine a world where women in the developing world have equal access to education, resulting in a dramatic slowing of population growth and increasing economic well-being. A world where human potential is no longer ignored or marginalized based on one's race or economic background, but maximized for the benefit of all. Imagine people around the world with the ability to afford to meet their basic needs without the need for government handouts or subsidies.

Many of these social, environmental, and technological changes will be possible because of social entrepreneurs. Social entrepreneurs will be essential to creating this new future

This chapter written by Brad George and Candida Brush.

by solving complex problems, both social problems that have economic consequences, and economic problems that have social impact. The intersection of social and economic problems and outcomes is more prevalent today than ever. There is a new world order, characterized by global interconnections and interdependence of business, society, communities, regions, and countries. In particular, technological innovation, decreasing natural resources, shifting demographics, social changes, and political unrest contribute to the complexity of problems as well as the opportunities for solutions (see box). These changes in the global environment require solutions that meet the needs of many stakeholders, and take into account both social and economic outcomes. This is the world of social entrepreneurship.

Turning Tragedy Into Opportunity

In recent years the planet has seen an increase in violent weather patterns. The human toll of these events has increased with increasing population. In addition, other factors such as deforestation in Haiti have increased the impact of these events on society. At the same time, global and social media have raised our awareness of these problems and inspired social entrepreneurs to take action.

Realizing that access to clean drinking water is an enormous problem following these events, Tricia Compas-Markman and her professor at Cal Poly, Dr. Tryg Lundquist, invented a personal water treatment bag that can be carried as a backpack and provides individuals with the ability to collect and treat their own water, making it safe to drink. The bags are easy to transport and one pallet of DayOne Waterbags can produce 26 times more drinking water than one pallet of water bottles. Tricia went on to found DayOne Response in order to make their invention commercially available.[2]

The Rise in Social Entrepreneurship

With these global changes, it is not surprising that there is a rise in the number of people creating ventures that have both social and economic goals. For example, a 2010 study by the Global Entrepreneurship Monitor found that fewer startup entrepreneurs in the United States focused primarily on economic goals (about 40%, down from almost 50% in 2008). About 7.5% of entrepreneurs indicated that they were pursuing primarily social goals, a slight increase from the 5% in 2008, while those emphasizing both social and economic goals increased from 42% to 46%.[3] And these trends are not limited to new ventures or the United States.

This increased emphasis and awareness of sustainability and social purpose creates opportunities for social entrepreneurs to find new ways to achieve these goals. Why is there a rise in social entrepreneurship? In part, it is because the assumptions upon which new ventures were created have changed. Until the 1990s, energy was relatively inexpensive, labor was widely available and in some countries, very cheap. Access to credit to start businesses was relatively easy, either through credit cards or small loans, and information to start a business only required a computer, cell phone, and Internet hookup. Further, the drivers of opportunities were usually due to technology or market forces. But, more recently, the drivers of entrepreneurial opportunities have shifted, creating new assumptions and conditions for venture creation. In particular, as global social and environmental issues increasingly affect a larger portion of the world, many drivers of entrepreneurial opportunities have shifted from simply market dynamics to more complex environmental and social catalysts. Wicked problems, those that require multiple stakeholders and complex solutions, are more often driving new ventures.[4] For instance, healthcare in a barrio in a Latin American country might be driven by a configuration of the healthcare system, immigration policies, drug importation, and contaminated water. The solution requires social and economic goals and outcomes. In other words, the traditional business model of identifying the opportunity, analyzing the industry, creating the business plan, raising money from investors, and scaling the business may not always work. Furthermore, stakeholders are increasingly active and better equipped to communicate and coordinate with each other, making it necessary to consider a wider variety of goals for any organization. As noted by Lee Scott, CEO of Walmart:

> *We thought we could sit in Bentonville, take care of customers, take care of associates—and the world would leave us alone. It doesn't work that way anymore."[5]*

With the increasing importance and emphasis on social entrepreneurship, it is important for any aspiring entrepreneur to have a basic understanding of some of the key elements involved. In this chapter, we begin by considering the definition of social entrepreneurship, and then provide a typology of different types of ventures to illustrate different options for positioning your venture in the social context. We then show how a venture can move across the typology with different variations of social and economic purpose and impact. Finally, we will discuss ways in which you can measure the success of your venture beyond simply economic success.

Popular Definitions of Social Entrepreneurship

	Author(s)
Process-Oriented Definitions	
Social entrepreneurship is an innovative, social value creating activity that can occur within or across the nonprofit, business, or government sectors.	Austin, Stevenson, and Skillern, 2006[8]
The activities and processes undertaken to discover, define, and exploit opportunities in order to enhance social wealth by creating new ventures or managing existing organizations in an innovative manner. Social wealth is defined broadly to include economic, societal, health, and environmental aspects of human welfare.	Zahra, Rawhouser, Bhawe, Neubaum, & Hayton, 2008[9]
Social entrepreneurship is about applying practical, innovative, and sustainable approaches to benefit society in general, with an emphasis on those who are marginalized and poor.	The Schwab Foundation for Social Entrepreneurship[10]
Entrepreneur-centric Definitions	
Social entrepreneurs are the change agents for society, seizing overlooked opportunities by improving systems, inventing new approaches, and creating sustainable solutions to transform society for the better. Social entrepreneurs are constantly searching for superior ways to solve the problems that plague society.	The Skoll Foundation[11]
Social entrepreneurs play the role of change agents in the social sector, by (i) Adopting a mission to create and sustain social value (not just private value), (ii) Recognizing and relentlessly pursuing new opportunities to serve that mission, (iii) Engaging in a process of continuous innovation, adaptation, and learning, (iv) Acting boldly without being limited by resources currently in hand, and (v) Exhibiting a heightened sense of accountability to the constituencies served and for the outcomes created.	Dees, 1998[12]
Social entrepreneurs are individuals with innovative solutions to society's most pressing social problems.	Ashoka[13]

SOCIAL ENTREPRENEURSHIP DEFINED

What exactly is social entrepreneurship? The fact is that almost everyone has his or her own personal definition of social entrepreneurship, what it means, what's included, or where it applies. Further, there are multiple terms used, some of which convey the same thing—for instance, green entrepreneurship, social venture, social enterprise, nonprofit startups, environmental entrepreneurship, social innovation, sustainability, corporate social responsibility, ethics, social justice, and the list can go on and on.

Definitions of social entrepreneurship vary both in content and approach. Some of the most common definitions are shown in the box on definitions of social entrepreneurship. There are *process-based* definitions that focus on actions such as value creation, opportunity recognition, opportunity exploitation, and resource mobilization. Then there are *entrepreneur-centric* definitions that focus on describing those that engage in social entrepreneurship. For example, Ashoka, a premier organization that invests in social entrepreneurs, defines a social entrepreneur as an individual with innovative solutions to society's most pressing social problems. Similarly, the Skoll Foundation, which also invests in social entrepreneurs for systemic change, identifies social entrepreneurs as society's change agents—pioneers of innovation that benefit humanity. Further confusing this definitional debate is the contextual placement of environmental entrepreneurship, also known as green, sustainable, or eco-preneurship. There are a variety of definitions in this area—environmental entrepreneurship is the early adoption of environmentally responsible practices and products[6] or environmental entrepreneurship is process of discovering, evaluating and exploiting economic opportunities that are present in environmentally relevant market failures.[7]

A SOCIAL ENTREPRENEURSHIP TYPOLOGY

In order to clarify the landscape of social entrepreneurship, we simplify the definitional debate by proposing that the process of entrepreneurship is the same across all entrepreneurial ventures. In other words, the activities of "creating or identifying an opportunity, acquiring the resources and building the team to create something of economic and social value"[14] apply across entrepreneurship of all kinds and contexts including corporate ventures, family enterprises, technology licensing, franchising, and of course, social ventures. While the process of entrepreneurship can be thought of as the same across all entrepreneurial ventures, most definitions focus on the fact that social entrepreneurship and social ventures are unique in their purpose and outcomes. Babson Professors Neck, Brush, and Allen map the landscape of entrepreneurship, which reflects the variety of traditional and social ventures.[15] This typology is based on two dimensions, *venture mission* and *impact*.

Every entrepreneurial venture has a mission or purpose. This purpose or reason for being is to solve a problem and almost always has both economic and social/environmental dimensions. The mission is the guide for strategy, policies, and the approach that the firm uses to reach customers, manage employees, and interact in the marketplace.[16] For example, here are three mission statements reflecting varying degrees of social and economic purpose. The first two have primarily an economic or social purpose while the third illustrates a combination of social and economic factors.

> *Our mission to revolutionize car rental distribution globally by reducing distribution costs in the industry while maintaining high margins and increased revenue for our customers and suppliers worldwide. In turn, our aim is become the largest distributor of car rental globally.*[17]
> —CarTrawler

We work with people and partners to develop innovative and long-lasting solutions to the water, sanitation, and hygiene problems in the developing world. We strive to continually improve, to experiment with promising new ideas, and to leverage resources to multiply our impact.[18]

—Water for People

Ben & Jerry's is founded on and dedicated to a sustainable corporate concept of linked prosperity. Our mission consists of three interrelated parts:

> ***Social Mission****: To operate the Company in a way that actively recognizes the central role that business plays in society by initiating innovative ways to improve the quality of life locally, nationally and internationally.*

> ***Product Mission****: To make, distribute, and sell the finest quality all natural ice cream and euphoric concoctions with a continued commitment to incorporating wholesome, natural ingredients and promoting business practices that respect the Earth and the Environment.*

> ***Economic Mission****: To operate the Company on a sustainable financial basis of profitable growth, increasing value for our stakeholders and expanding opportunities for development and career growth for our employees.*

> *Underlying the mission of Ben & Jerry's is the determination to seek new and creative ways of addressing all three parts, while holding a deep respect for individuals inside and outside the company and for the communities of which they are a part.*[19]

—Ben & Jerry's

The outcomes of business are both social and economic, but these may vary in the degree to which social and economic performance is measured.[20] For example, the international coffee company Starbucks spends significant time and effort to ensure that the producers of its coffee beans, the farmers in Central America, follow ethical guidelines. They approve and train third party organizations to ensure the ethical sourcing of their coffee according to C.A.F.E. Practices.[21] Likewise, TisTik, a small jewelry retailer in Cambridge, MA works to support artisans from the founder's home country of Mexico and ensure that they are fairly paid for their work. It also sells products made by prisoners in an effort to help them earn money so that they are better able to support themselves upon their release.

There are four specific types of entrepreneurial ventures, plus a hybrid form (Figure 14.1). *Traditional Ventures* (quadrant 1) focus primarily on economic mission and economic impact—financial performance is the primary metric. These ventures have no explicit social mission beyond running a good and profitable business through the exploitation of market-based opportunities. *Social Consequence Ventures* (quadrant 2) are similar to the traditional venture except that many of their practices have social outcomes, yet these social outcomes are not the reason for the firm's existence but it is an outcome of doing business. The popular term, corporate social responsibility, most closely aligns with the Social Consequence Venture. *Social Purpose Ventures* (quadrant 3) are founded on the premise that a social problem will be solved, yet the venture is for-profit and the impact on the market is typically perceived as economic. The fourth type of venture is the *Enterprising Nonprofit* (quadrant 4). *Enterprising Nonprofits* have earned income activities which very much apply the general principles of entrepreneurship.[22] Additionally these organizations focus on growth and economic sustainability and may be funded by venture philanthropists. Finally,

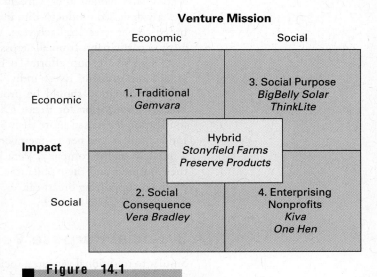

Figure 14.1

Typology of Ventures[23]

there are *hybrid forms* that have a combination of behaviors and characteristics that are found in more than one type. The next section provides examples of each type of venture and their strategies.

1. Traditional Venture

Traditional ventures are those that we are most commonly familiar with. These are firms whose primary mission and outcomes are economic. While it can be argued that all firms have some social outcomes through the creation of jobs and other benefits, traditional ventures view these as byproducts rather than primary outcomes. Their main focus is on maximizing revenues and profits by recognizing and capturing opportunities in the market. An example of this would be Gemvara. The company, founded by two undergraduate students, sells customized jewelry online. The company follows more of a traditional business model, whereby customers design jewelry online and the company creates the design and sends it direct to the customers. As they describe it,

> Gemvara isn't a traditional jeweler. We have the crazy idea that you deserve jewelry that's uniquely you. That's made only for you. . . . We make your design the way you would (if you were a master metalsmith with a lot of time on your hands.)"[24]

The company has a traditional economic goal orientation and measures success based on economic factors such as revenue growth, profitability and returns on investment.

2. Social Consequence

Social consequence ventures are those that have an economic mission, but also have a firm commitment to social impact, sometimes at the expense of economic returns. Take for example, Vera Bradley (the case from Chapter 2). Guided by founders, Patricia Miller and Barbara Bradley Baekgaard, Vera Bradley has earned a reputation as a leader in the gift industry. While on vacation in March 1982, Patricia and Barbara were awaiting a flight in Atlanta when they noticed a definite lack of feminine-looking luggage. The longtime friends wasted no time in correcting this situation. Within weeks, these dynamic women had created a company, named after Barbara's mother, capable of marketing and manufacturing their cleverly designed products. But, instead of just creating a company, they are also committed to breast cancer research. Each year, Vera Bradley sponsors a golf and tennis tournament, which attracts participants from all across the United States to Fort Wayne, Indiana.

"This is a group effort. To break a million dollars for breast cancer research is truly an accomplishment! Every individual, company or foundation, whether they made a $5 or $20,000 donation should be proud to be part of this success," says Catherine Hill, Vera Bradley Foundation for Breast Cancer Foundation Development Director. Since 1998, the foundation has raised more than $15 million, and presently endows a chair in oncology, Dr. Linda Malkas, and her 16-member research team at the Indiana University Cancer Center. As a publicly traded company, Vera Bradley has a strong economic mission, but the impact of their business and their philanthropic activities has strong social outcomes. Retail stores sell products supporting breast cancer, several of their designs are in pink and if purchased, profits go to breast cancer research.

3. Social Purpose Venture

Similar to traditional ventures, social purpose ventures firms that seek to make profits, but that were started with a specific social mission. The opportunity they are addressing has a specific social or environmental aspect to it. Essentially, they are looking for a profitable means of addressing a social issue. Jim Poss, as you recall from the case in chapter 3, started Big Belly

Solar in 2003. He went to Babson College to start a company, specifically an environmental company. While doing an independent study on the trash industry, Jim recognized that trash pickup and hauling represented an enormous waste of fuel and labor and that the burning of that fuel had significant environmental consequences. From there he developed the concept for BigBelly, which is a solar powered trash compactor for use in rural and urban settings. He founded BigBelly in 2003 with a mission to reduce fossil fuel consumption through innovative cost-saving approaches to inefficient, everyday problems. Today, BigBelly Solar is changing the concept of waste collection by implementing on-site solar compaction systems. The flagship product, the BigBelly, can be found around the world, reducing pollution by cutting down the frequency of trash collection trips.

BigBelly has an explicit social/environmental mission, "We are committed to improving the environment and economies of the world by utilizing an efficient approach," but the venture is a for-profit business, seeking to grow and be financially sustainable. The company believes that it cannot solve social problems without economic success.

"Our BigBelly product was so successful, we changed our name to BigBelly Solar and refocused the company around a central business proposition: Saving fuel is environmentally and fiscally sound." Another example is ThinkLite, a lighting company founded by Enrico Palmiero and Dinesh Wadhwani, two Babson College dorm mates. They got the idea for their company from an ad for an energy-efficient light bulb. They thought they could sell businesses on going green by putting the bottom-line savings up front, rather than the environmental benefit. ThinkLite, founded in 2009, manufactures custom energy-saving light systems. Recognizing that high costs often prevent firms from choosing more environmentally friendly products, ThinkLite uses a unique business model that eliminates the upfront costs by having the customer only pay for the energy it saves. Clients typically pay ThinkLite about 40% of the estimated two- to three-year savings. By eliminating the initial purchase and installation costs, ThinkLite reduces the financial risk to its customers. As ThinkLite describes it,

> Thinklite is a global lighting efficiency company dedicated to helping businesses and governments go green without having to incur the upfront costs and difficulties associated with the change.[25]

ThinkLite licenses its technologies from private laboratories in Germany, uses components from Korea, designs them in Boston, and assembles them in China. After ThinkLite installs the lighting system, the client's lighting bill drops on average by 50 to 80%, Wadhwani says. The company has about 100 clients, including AT&T, Kodak, and Babson College, as well as smaller businesses ranging from restaurants to offices. ThinkLite uses different efficient lighting technologies depending on the application, and tailors its design to adapt to the current lighting fixtures and infrastructure already in place, thereby making an effective and efficient retrofit possible for any type of facility.[26] As with BigBelly Solar, ThinkLite has a clear environmental mission, but uses a unique business model to drive economic returns.

4. Enterprising Nonprofit

As mentioned previously, enterprising nonprofits are firms offering products or services that generate revenue and income like other entrepreneurial ventures, but in this case that income is put to use to address a social problem rather than returned to investors or the owners. Sometimes social entrepreneurship is equated with nonprofits, but we contend that ventures that rely strictly on donations for their funding operate under entirely different principals than other entrepreneurial ventures and therefore they are not included in our typology. Enterprising nonprofits are driven by a social mission and focus on social outcomes as measures of their performance, but like other ventures they need to find ways to generate revenue and grow their business as a means of increasing their social impact.

One Hen is a nonprofit organization whose mission is to "provide education resources that engage children." The business was built around a book about a young West African boy who received a small loan to buy a hen, and then became an entrepreneur. He gradually moved from poverty to economic sustainability. It is the story of how the world can be changed, one person, one family, and one community at a time. The founders, including the author, created a board game based on the book in order to help students learn about business and finance in a fun, creative way. From there the business has expanded into additional enrichment curriculum that includes One Hen micro-finance for kids and the Good Garden: Food Security for Kids. One Hen focuses on micro-finance, which is the practice of providing financial services—such as working capital loans, insurance, and savings—to those at the poverty level. Such basic financial tools help necessity entrepreneurs to build and run their businesses, stabilize consumption, shield them from risk, and find a way out of poverty. The venture generates revenue through the sales of the book and donations, but provides lessons plans, the board game, and other teaching materials free to educators because the primary focus of their venture is to reach as many children as possible. One Hen is an enterprising nonprofit, an entrepreneurial solution to a serious social problem that is focused on social impact.

Another example would be Kiva. Kiva is an organization that provides micro-lending around the world. Their mission, "to connect people through lending for the sake of alleviating poverty,"[27] allows individuals to make micro-loans to working poor to enable them to have a business and work themselves out of poverty. Kiva is the world's first person-to-person micro-lending Web site, empowering individuals to lend directly to unique entrepreneurs around the globe. The organization works this way—individuals browse entrepreneurs' profiles on the site, choose someone to lend to, and then make a loan, helping a person they have identified to make great strides toward economic independence and improve life for themselves, their family, and their community. The loan period is usually six to 12 months, and the lender can receive email journal updates and track repayments. Then, when the loan is repaid, the lender can lend to someone else in need. Kiva partners with existing expert microfinance institutions. Kiva is a nonprofit with a social mission and clear social impact, but the organization is also enterprising in the way that it innovated how micro-lending was traditionally organized.

Hybrid Ventures

Hybrid ventures are those that pursue social and economic goals equally—for instance, City Fresh Foods, a retail grocery store in Boston, prides itself on being a minority-owned business that employs minorities from the ethnic community. If you ask the founder, he will say that the social and economic missions are equally important. Therefore, the distinction between social/economic goals and social/economic outcomes is not often clear cut because missions and outcomes are more blended.

Ten Principles of the United Nations Global Compact

Human Rights

- Principle 1: Businesses should support and respect the protection of internationally proclaimed human rights; and

- Principle 2: make sure that they are not complicit in human rights abuses.

Labor

- Principle 3: Businesses should uphold the freedom of association and the effective recognition of the right to collective bargaining;

- Principle 4: the elimination of all forms of forced and compulsory labor;

- Principle 5: the effective abolition of child labor; and

- Principle 6: the elimination of discrimination in respect of employment and occupation.

Environment

- Principle 7: Businesses should support a precautionary approach to environmental challenges;

- Principle 8: undertake initiatives to promote greater environmental responsibility; and

- Principle 9: encourage the development and diffusion of environmentally friendly technologies.

Anti-Corruption

- Principle 10: Businesses should work against corruption in all its forms, including extortion and bribery.

It is also important to note that customers are increasingly demanding that companies consider human rights, social justice, and environmental issues in their operations. We have seen cases where problems at suppliers for companies like Walmart, Apple, or Nike have led to customer action and damage to their brands. As customers become more aware of companies' global operations through the Internet and social media, companies are increasingly being held accountable to a wider variety of stakeholders. This is a global phenomenon as illustrated by the fact that over 7,000 firms in 145 countries have joined the UN Global Compact since its founding in 2000. Joining the UN Global Compact represents a commitment by firms to align their operations and strategies to ten principles in the areas of human rights, labor, the environment and corruption.

Being a hybrid venture does not require signing onto the UN Global Compact, but it does involve balancing both the mission and the impacts between social and economic objectives. One example of this type of firm would be Stonyfield Farms, a yogurt company in New Hampshire. The venture was started by Samuel Kaymen and Gary Hirshberg in 1983 as a farming school that taught sustainable agricultural practices with the goal of helping family farms and protecting the environment, clearly a social mission. They made and sold yogurt in order to fund the school. As the yogurt business grew, they focused on building an economically successful and sustainable business that would not only provide profits, but would have social impact by supporting family farms that used organic practices. This not only gave small family farmers a market for their products, but also encouraged them to use practices that were less harmful to the environment. Stonyfield Farms extended this into its own operations and has clearly stated its economic and social goals in its mission statement:

Our mission: We're committed to healthy food, healthy people, a healthy planet, and healthy business.

- Healthy food. We will craft and offer the most delicious and nourishing organic yogurts and dairy products.

- Healthy people. We will enhance the health and well-being of our consumers and colleagues.

- Healthy planet. We will help protect and restore the planet and promote the viability of family farms.

- Healthy business. We will prove that healthy profits and a healthy planet are not in conflict and that, in fact, dedication to health and sustainability enhances shareholder value. We believe that business must lead the way to a more sustainable future.

The company also pursues social impact through the creation of their Profits for the Planet (PFP) fund, which to date has given over $15 million in support of organizations that care for the earth.[28]

Another example of a hybrid venture would be Preserve Products. Preserve Products was founded in 1996 by Eric Hudson who was concerned about the fact that recyclables were not being turned into new products. This meant that additional resources were being used to make products rather than using recycled materials. He was particularly concerned about plastic because roughly 9% of the world's petroleum usage goes into making plastic products. Preserve Products' mission is "to deliver consumer products that offer great looking design, high performance, and are better for the environment than alternative products."[29] The company uses recycled plastic to make consumer products such as toothbrushes, razors, cutting boards, tableware, and other products which it sells. As Eric puts it:

> *I saw an opportunity in that 45% percent of people recycled and I thought they would have an interest in products made from their efforts.*

While the company's mission is clearly focused on an environmental concern, it is still a for-profit firm that looks for the most profitable and attractive product markets as it develops new lines. At the same time, Preserve also considers environmental and social impacts. It supports the recycling industry through volunteer and community efforts and, in February 2012 it further signaled its commitment to economic and social impacts by joining over 600 other firms in becoming a Certified B Corporation™ (see box on benefit corporations).

The Rise of Benefit Corporations

While there is increasing interest on both the customer and venture side regarding social missions and social impact, firms in the United States have been limited in the extent to which they can pursue social outcomes due to existing legal frameworks. The Michigan Supreme Court ruled in 1919 that

"A business corporation is organized and carried on primarily for the profit of the stockholders. The powers of the directors are to be employed for that end. The discretion of directors is to be exercised in the choice of means to attain that end, and does not extend to a change in the end itself, to the reduction of profits, or to the non-distribution of profits among stockholders in order to devote them to other purposes."

While this ruling is over 100 years old, it has been reaffirmed in other court rulings as well. As a result, the pursuit of social impact can put its directors at risk of legal action for violation of their fiduciary responsibility if the actions cannot be shown to benefit shareholders. Without legal authority, directors may be hesitant to make decisions to pursue both economic and social impacts, even if this is part of the company's stated mission.

In response to this situation, an enterprising non-profit named B Lab was launched in 2007. B Lab created a third-party certification system that allowed companies to become Certified Benefit Corporations (or B Corporations). Becoming a Certified B Corporation requires meeting a minimum score on a B Impact Assessment, which looks at the firm's environmental and social impacts. Next, it may be necessary to amend the firm's governing documents to allow directors to consider the impact of its decisions on its employees, customers, suppliers, community, and the environment in addition to its shareholders. However, it is important to note that this may provide some legal protection to directors in states with constituency statutes, those in non-constituency states (including Delaware where the vast majority of U.S. companies are incorporated) are not permitted to consider the interests of stakeholders other than shareholders. Even still, as of 2013 over 600 firms in 60 countries have become Certified B Corporations.

The movement is gathering steam, and to date legislation creating a new legal entity, called a Benefit Corporation, has been passed in seven states and introduced in several others. This legislation generally addresses three major provisions: (1) a corporate purpose to create a material positive impact on society and the environment; (2) expanded fiduciary duties of directors that requires consideration of non-financial interests; and (3) an obligation to report on its overall social and environmental performance as assessed against a comprehensive, credible, independent, and transparent third-party standard.[30]

Choosing Your Venture Type

It should be clear that each of the different types of ventures requires different resources and strategies. Therefore, it might be helpful to look at how the same firm could choose to operate in the different sectors. Let's take the case of Aravind Eye Hospital in India. India has the highest rate of blindness in the world. The approximately 15 million blind people in India represent almost one-third of the total number of blind people worldwide, yet up to 80% of these cases are preventable or treatable with cataracts being a major cause of unnecessary blindness.[31] Upon reaching the government's mandatory retirement age, Dr. Govindappa Venkataswamy, or Dr. V. as he is often called, decided to start the Aravind Eye Hospital as a means of addressing this issue.

If we consider the ways in which Dr. V. could have positioned this business, it is easy to see how Dr. V., a highly renowned eye surgeon, recognized that the demand for cataract surgery far exceeded the supply. As such, he could have created a firm whose mission was to maximize profits by providing high-quality eye surgery to patients in India. In this situation, his primary mission would be economic, or profit maximization (quadrant1). For example, he might discover that the wealthier people in India are willing to pay the equivalent of $1000 for the surgery while those in the middle class can only afford $600. His costs per surgery would be $600, a large part of this being the cost of the lenses at $300. The middle class may be a larger market, but would generate less profit per surgery. Alternatively, the upper class is willing and able to pay more, but may represent a smaller number of customers. Each may have different needs or expectations that could further affect operating expenses, so in a purely traditional venture, he might determine which market is most profitably served and then acquire the resources to meet the needs of those customers. Since profitability is the main measure of success, he could look at ways to increase his profit margins through operational efficiencies, cost reductions or by offering higher margin services. While the business may have a social impact by improving eyesight for some individuals, the primary outcome from the businesses perspective would be economic and would be measured in net profits to the business, with minimal focus on social benefit.

If Dr. V. wanted to have a social mission, his mission statement might be revised to a primary purpose of "eliminating unnecessary blindness for the largest number of people in India" (quadrant 2). However, he would still be looking at economic impact. The difference would be that instead of simply maximizing profits, he is looking at how he can maximize profits given his social mission. In this case, rather than looking at the most profitable segment, he might consider which is the largest segment he could serve profitably. The largest markets are likely to be people with lower incomes, which makes accomplishing his mission more challenging. In this case he would focus on reducing costs, not to increase his profit margins, but to be able to serve a larger segment of the population at the same margins. By lowering his costs, for example, from $600 to $350, he would be able to charge less than $600, making him able to serve a larger portion of the population while maintaining the same margins. He may even decide that he can increase overall profitability further by decreasing his margins and reaching yet a larger group. He might decide that the best way to do this is to cut the cost of the lenses, so he could start a local lens factory that produces lenses for $50. But because he knows that the wealthy are still willing to pay $1000, he might institute a tiered pricing scale based on ability to pay. This would allow him to maximize profits for the customer segment that can afford to pay, and at the same time serve people in lower income brackets by providing the service at a lower cost. In this case, because Dr. V.'s social mission drives the cost/pricing equation for the business. He establishes a price to achieve acceptable profits while helping the largest number of people.

Alternatively, Dr. V. could decide that he is concerned about other causes of blindness in India, not just eyesight lost due to cataracts that his business is focused on. So while the firm maintains its economic mission, it looks to have greater social impact as well by taking a portion of the profits and donating these to charities that focus on nutritional issues for rural children, another source of blindness in India (quadrant 3). Operationally, the business would still be focused on maximizing profits, but the primary impact he is trying to have may be measured by considering the social outcome—the total number of individuals helped, so the business could be considered a social consequence venture in our typology.

If Dr. V. decided that he wanted to be an enterprising nonprofit (quadrant 4), then he would have a social mission and focus on social, rather than economic, impact. In some cases, such as in the United States, this may involve an entirely different legal structure for a venture if it is to be a nonprofit. As an enterprising nonprofit, Dr. V. would have a social mission, like the one stated above, but the outcome would be measured in maximum social impact, or people treated, rather than profits or economic returns. Dr. V. might first start by charging only $350 (the cost with the less expensive lenses) in order to be able to reach the largest number of people. As revenue sources to support his business, he might seek to attract donations or government grants that could pay for some of the operating expenses. In this way, he could lower price even further and reach a larger number of people.

But, what if the people most in need of eye care cannot afford to pay at all? This is a common situation for enterprising nonprofits. Often those that are not being served by society are those on the fringes, in extreme poverty. In this case, the potential to achieve revenues from the market you want most to serve is zero because the product or service needs to be provided for free. This means that the organization must raise money from government sources or philanthropists to pay for costs. Fundraising becomes a major focus of day-to-day activities because it is the source of operating funds. Reliance on volunteers keeps costs down, but this can make management of the venture more challenging. You will often see these types of companies create large boards of directors because a key function of the board becomes raising money for the venture. While the board still has responsibility for organizational oversight, members are more often chosen for their personal or corporate connections, personal wealth, and/or enthusiasm for the mission of the organization rather than for their management or industry expertise.

This was the situation facing Dr. V. in India. His mission was to eradicate unnecessary blindness across the entire country. While he had a primary social mission, Dr. V. took an unusual and creative approach, which is an example of a hybrid venture in our typology. He recognized that the poorest in the country could not afford even basic eye care. However, at the same time, he recognized that there was a large population with the ability to pay. As a result, he used a market-based approach similar to a traditional venture to serve the population that was able to pay. He created an assembly-line type process that enabled his doctors to perform 10 times the number of surgeries that doctors in the West performed in order to increase the revenues and profit from the business. However, because he had a social mission, he used these profits to pay for free surgeries for the poor. In other words, by charging $1000 with a cost of $600, his profits were $400. That meant that for every three paying customers he could use the profits to perform two surgeries for free. So you can see that while his primary mission is social, he also has an economic mission to the extent that it enables him to achieve his social mission. Profit maximization is still important because it allows him to achieve greater social impact. The difference for an enterprising nonprofit is that the increase in revenues is not translated into an increase in profits but rather in operating capital. Another way to think of this is that he is essentially turning his customers into philanthropists by providing a service that they value and are willing to pay for, rather than simply asking them for donations.

So you can see that it is possible to position a venture in different quadrants of Figure 14.1, but that this requires a considerable amount of thought as it will ultimately impact all aspects of the Timmons Model (referred to in chapter 2)—the nature of the opportunity, the resources required, and team needed to accomplish your mission. However, while you may start in one quadrant, circumstances, strategies, or values can change over time, and you may decide that you are interested in different outcomes or want to change the goals of the organization and a venture can move between quadrants or, as in the case of Dr. V., occupy a space in more than one quadrant. However, it is important to recognize that movement between quadrants is not simple. Each type of venture has unique characteristics that affect the strategies and resources that the firm needs to succeed.

Measuring Impact

One of the critical things for social entrepreneurs to consider is how they will measure their impact or outcomes. For some ventures it is straightforward. Preserve Products can tell you how much new petroleum was saved by using recycled plastic, BigBelly Solar can determine how many pounds of CO_2 emissions were saved by decreasing the pickup frequency of trash, Aravind Eye Hospital can determine the number of cataract surgeries they performed. Each of these represents measures of the social impact related to their mission. Other social issues are more difficult to quantify. You can provide clean water to children in rural Pakistan, but measuring the impact of this is more difficult. Social problems are often quite complex, and there are usually a number of social ventures and other organizations trying to address issues such as infant mortality or AIDS through education, health services, treatment, or other means. In these cases it is difficult to say which approaches are responsible for subsequent outcomes. While it would be nice to think that everyone would be happy if the problem is being diminished, many organizations and companies are fighting for the same resources and often believe very strongly in their particular approach. Further, sometimes reducing the consequences may not solve the problem. For instance, medical problems with dysentery or nutrition in a barrio can be treated with medicine, but it may be that clean water and nutrition education are the causes, therefore the solutions are multi-pronged. It is important for social ventures to determine performance measures that are related to their objectives and that can be directly tied to their particular activities. You remember that Stonyfield Farms' mission revolved around healthy food, healthy people, healthy planet, and a healthy business. Obviously, it would be difficult to measure the health of people who buy its product and tie that back to its yogurt. Similarly, how would one determine the impact of its business on the health of the planet? However, Stonyfield Farms does realize that any waste from its production has a negative impact on the environment and represents a cost to the business. As such, they measure waste water, plastic, packaging, and other byproducts of their production that do not contribute to the health of the food, people, planet, or business. By decreasing this waste, Stonyfield Farms can show that it is making progress toward social goals and it can be directly attributed to its business.

While it is difficult, more and more companies are realizing that measuring environmental and social impact is increasingly important for their business. As Jeffrey Immelt, CEO of General Electric, puts it,

> "It's up to us to use our platform to be a good citizen. Because not only is it a nice thing to do, it's a business imperative. . . . If this wasn't good for business, we probably wouldn't do it."[32]

The need to consider impacts beyond those of traditional measures of growth and profitability has led to interest in what is known as the Triple Bottom Line (TBL). The TBL is a way of measuring success that was originally proposed by John Elkington in his book, *Cannibals with Forks*.[33] Elkington argued that businesses need to look at not only the traditional financial bottom line, but also their impact on the environment and society. The key for succeeding is in finding ways to make "doing good" and "doing well" synonymous, thus avoiding the implied conflict between society and shareholders. For entrepreneurs, this will become increasingly important. As we have discussed in this chapter, companies are no longer able to divorce themselves from the communities with which their products and

Economic	Environmental	Social
Sales	Air quality	Labor practices
Profits, ROI	Water quality	Community impacts
Taxes paid	Energy usage	Human right
Jobs created	Waste produced	Product responsibility

Figure 14.2

Sample Impacts[34]

operations interact. And these communities are becoming increasingly informed and able to mobilize. We are also finally acknowledging that we live on a planet of finite resources and that using up or damaging those resources affects our business as well as our lives. Companies on the coasts are seeing higher insurance premiums as a result of the increasing volatility of weather events, which most scientists believe is related to global climate change and CO_2 emissions. Climate change may also result in a carbon tax or carbon cap and trade system, either of which will impact a new venture's costs, which means that even for ventures with a purely economic mission, the need to understand how they interact with society and the environment is important. And as the saying goes, you measure what you care about and you care about what you measure.

So how do you go about deciding what to measure? First, you need to think about the way in which your business touches society and the environment. What communities do your operations affect? In what way? What materials are used in your products? Where do they come from and where do they go? Does your business produce waste products or byproducts? Where do these go and how do they affect the environment? It is important to remember that these not only represent costs or potential areas for improvement, but also potential liabilities if not measured and addressed (just ask Walmart, Nike, or Apple). Figure 14.2 gives some general examples of social and environmental impacts that ventures might consider measuring, but because every venture interacts with the environment and society in a different way and has different objectives based on its mission, it is impossible for us to provide an exhaustive list. Ultimately, it is up to the entrepreneur to determine what measure of performance and impact she needs to keep track of in order to best achieve her mission in the long run.

CONCLUSION

It should be clear from this chapter that social entrepreneurs have the opportunity to enact enormous change in a variety of ways. In addition to having either a social or economic mission, entrepreneurs need to think about their impacts and how they will measure them. We presented a typology that included what we called "traditional ventures," but one might argue that this type of venture, once the most dominant in entrepreneurship, may become a thing of the past. As we illustrated, firms are increasingly being forced to consider, measure, and report their performance with regards to social impacts as well as economic returns and leading companies are increasingly taking on a hybrid forms, illustrating the ability to move between forms. However, the entrepreneur should take the time early on to consider the type of venture he wants to have as changing forms can be difficult and costly. It is important to recognize the cost and resource trade-offs that determine how your venture is positioned in the market.

Entrepreneurship is about doing different things or doing things differently. As Albert Einstein said,

We can't solve problems by using the same kind of thinking we used when we created them.

The world is looking for answers to a wide range of social and environmental issues that have resulted from our current thinking. We believe it is up to social entrepreneurs to find the new way of thinking that will be needed to solve these problems and create a better tomorrow.

YOUR OPPORTUNITY JOURNAL

Reflection Point	Your Thoughts...
1. What social problems are of particular interest to you?	
2. What are some of the root causes of these problems and in what ways might these be addressed?	
3. What type of venture would you want to create? Do you want to have primarily a social mission or an economic mission? Why?	
4. If you are considering a new venture, how does it interact with the social problems you are concerned with? What are the ways in which your venture could have impact on these problems?	
5. In what other ways does your venture impact society and the environment?	
6. Think about how you might measure your venture's social impact. What can you directly attribute to your business? How would you measure it and what does this measure mean?	
7. What resources would you need to have or acquire in order to have the type of venture you envision in terms of both mission and impact?	
8. Does it give you information you can act on to improve your impact?	

WEB EXERCISE

Think about companies you admire or aspire to be similar to. Go to two or three Web sites and look at their missions. Is their mission primarily economic, social, or both? Next, see if you can find how each one reports its performance. If it is a public company, this can often be found by going to the "Investor" link on the Web page and looking at the annual report. For nonprofits or other companies this can often be found under the "About" link. What is each one reporting? Are these consistent with the mission? If not, why not? What do you think each company should report? Use this information to make a list of possible ways in which you can measure performance for your own venture and describe how this information will tell you whether you are achieving your mission.

NOTES

[1] www.who.int/malaria/world_malaria_report_2011/WMR2011_factsheet.pdf

[2] www.dayoneresponse.com

[3] Ali, A., et al. 2010. *2010 Global Entrepreneurship Monitor 2010 United States Report*. Global Entrepreneurship Research Association.

[4] Buchanan, R. 1992. Wicked problems in design thinking, *MIT Press*, 8:2, 1–25.

[5] The Debate over Doing Good, *Business Week*, Aug. 15, 2005, p. 76.

[6] Schaper, M. 2002. The Essence of Ecopreneurship. In GMI, Greenleaf Publishing, pp. 26-38

[7] Dean, T. J., & McMullen, J. S., 2007. Toward a Theory of Sustainable Entrepreneurship: Reducing Environmental Degradation through Entrepreneurial Action. *Journal of Business Venturing*, 22: 50–76.

[8] Austin, J., Stevenson, H., & Wei-Skillern, J. 2006. Social and Commercial Entrepreneurship: Same, Different, or Both? *Entrepreneurship Theory & Practice*, January: 1–22.

[9] Zahra, S.A., Rawhouser, H.N., Bhawe, N., Neubaum, D.O. and Hayton, J.C. 2008. Globalization of Social Entrepreneurship Opportunities. *Strategic Entrepreneurship Journal* 2(2): 117–131.

[10] www.schwabfound.org/sf/SocialEntrepreneurs/Whatisasocialentrepreneur/index.htm

[11] www.skollfoundation.org/about/skoll-awards/skoll-award-for-social-entrepreneurship-glossary

[12] Dees, G. 1998. The Meaning of Social Entrepreneurship, p. 4. (www.caseatduke.org/documents/dees_SE.pdf)

[13] https://www.ashoka.org/social_entrepreneur

[14] Neck, H., Brush, C. & Allen, E. 2009. The Landscape of Social Entrepreneurship. *Business Horizons*, 52:13.

[15] Ibid., pp.13–19.

[16] Andrews, K. 1971. *The Concept of Strategy*. Homewood, IL: Irwin.

[17] www.cartrawler.com/about/cartrawler-goals.php

[18] www.waterforpeople.org/about/mission-and-vision

[19] www.benjerry.com/activism/mission-statement

[20] Mair, J., & Marti, I. 2006. Social Entrepreneurship Research: A Source of Explanation, Prediction, and Delight. *Journal of World Business*, 41: 36–44.

[21] C.A.F.E. Practices ensure that Starbucks is sourcing sustainably grown and processed coffee by evaluating the economic, social, and environmental aspects of coffee production. These aspects are measured against a defined set of criteria detailed in the C.A.F.E. Practices Evaluation Guidelines. According to an impact study performed by Conservation International, C.A.F.E. Practices has significantly benefited more than one million workers employed by participating farms. www.scsglobalservices.com/starbucks-cafe-practices

[22] Dees, G. 1998. The Meaning of Social Entrepreneurship, p. 4. (www.caseatduke.org/documents/dees_SE.pdf)Massarsky, Cynthia W. and Beinhecker, Samantha L. *Enterprising Nonprofits: Revenue Generation in the Nonprofit Sector*, Yale School of Management, The Goldman Sachs Foundation Partnership on Nonprofit Ventures, 2002

[23] Neck, H., Brush, C., & Allen, E. 2009. The Landscape of Social Entrepreneurship. *Business Horizons*, 52:13.

[24] www.gemvara.com/About-Us/pages/v/about

[25] www.thinklite.com/index.htm

[26] www.babson.edu/news-events/babson-news/Pages/10-28-11Babson-Startup-ThinkLite-Ranked-2-Among-Bloomberg-Businessweek%E2%80%99s-America%

27 E2%80%99s-Best-Young-Entrepreneurs-2011.aspx

27 www.kiva.org/about

28 www.stonyfield.com

29 www.preserveproducts.com/aboutus/index.html

30 Clark, W. H., Jr,. 2012. "*The Need and Rationale for the Benefit Corporation: Why It Is the Legal Form that Best Addresses the Needs of Social Entrepreneurs, Investors, and, Ultimately, the Public*". White paper available at http://benefitcorp.net/for-attorneys/benefit-corp-white-paper

31 www.blindfoundation.org/facts.html

32 Quoted in "Money and Morals at GE," by Marc Gunther, *Fortune*, Nov. 15, 2004, p. 176.

33 Elkington, J. *Cannibals with Forks*. Capstone Publishing Ltd. , 1997.

34 Savitz, A.W. & Weber, K. *The Triple Bottom Line*. Jossey-Bass, 2006.

35 Radha Roy Biswas, Case Study Our Success Is Our Graduates, Jobs for the Future, 2005.

36 According to Year Up, "Although *disconnected young adult* has become convenient shorthand to refer to this population, it can be perceived as pejorative and overly static, failing to honor the fact that many of these individuals strive to improve their lives through employment and education."

37 U.S. Department of Labor Statistics, www.bls.gov, June 2011.

38 Reprinted with permission from Year UP: Empowering Urban Talent to Reach Their Potential, *Prospectus for Philanthropic Investment*, Year Up, 2011.

39 *Losing Our Future: How Minority Youth Are Being Left Behind by the Graduation Rate Crisis*, Harvard Education Publishing Group, 2004, p. 6.

40 Labor market study, U.S. Census Board, 2009.

41 *Pathways to Prosperity*, Harvard Graduate School of Education, February 2011.

42 The weekly stipend amount varied by site and geographic location.

43 "According to the Bill and Melinda Gates Foundation, the United States is facing a shortage of 14 million college-educated workers over the next decade." Hillary Pennington, Director of U.S. Program Special Initiatives, Bill and Melinda Gates Foundation, Speech to the American Council on Education, March 8, 2009.

44 Sara Enright, Executive Director, Year Up, Providence, 2009.

45 Best NonProfits to Work For, *The Non-Profit Times*, May 18, 2011.

46 Registered as a not-for-profit corporation.

47 Year Up *Prospectus*, 2011.

48 *2009 Kids Count Data Book*, The Annie E. Casey Foundation, 2009.

49 Department of Labor Statistics, December 2011.

50 Year Up *Prospectus*, 2011.

51 David Bornstein, Training Youths in the Ways of the Workplace, *The New York Times*, January 24, 2011.

52 A two-year external study conducted by the Economic Mobility Corporation in 2010 found direct causality between Year Up and the wage rates of its graduates. The study showed that on average, Year Up graduates earned 30% more, or $3,500, compared to a control group. Few other comparable programs operating in the past 10 years could prove similar effectiveness.

53 *Pathways to Prosperity*, Harvard Graduate School of Education, February 2011.

54 American Association of Community Colleges, December 2011.

55 Richard Fry, College Enrollment Hits All-Time High, Fueled by Community College Surge, www.pewsocialtrends.org/2009/10/29/college-enrollment-hits-all-time-high-fueled-by-community-college-surge

CASE

Year Up: Workforce Training for Urban Youth

The greatest challenge our nation faces today is an under-utilization of human capital. Joseph Stiglitz, Nobel Prize-winning economist, April 2011

The year 2011 should have been a year of intense satisfaction for entrepreneur Gerald Chertavian. Year Up, the nonprofit workforce training program for urban young adults Chertavian founded in 2000 had met or surpassed all goals outlined in the first two phases of the company's original long-term strategy. It was now halfway through a second successful capital campaign. By spring 2011, Year Up was serving over 1,300 young adults a year at nine sites across the United States: Boston, New York, Atlanta, Providence, DC, Chicago, San Francisco, Seattle, and Baltimore. The program had seen unparalleled success in the workforce training arena: 84% of Year Up graduates were enrolled in college and/or working part-time, earning an average of $15/hour (over $30,000 a year).[35] Chertavian and his team had proven to investors and corporate partners that the organization could effectively scale to multiple sites while maintaining program quality. The company was being lauded nationwide as the new role model in workforce training, even drawing the attention of the Obama White House.

The summer of 2011, however, posed especially challenging circumstances for the population Year Up served: talented urban young adults who were "disconnected"[36] from the economic mainstream, meaning they were out of work, out of school, and lacked access to postsecondary education and meaningful career pathways. For the first time since the 1940s, fewer than 50% of Americans under 21 had secured summer jobs, and the unemployment rate for Americans ages 18–24 was at a 50-year high.[37] With 30% of American high school students failing to graduate from high school, 1.4 million total unemployed young adults ages 18–24, and an average 20% unemployment rate for 16- to 24-year-olds, Gerald Chertavian was beginning to think Year Up would never create enough of an impact. Since 2000, Chertavian and Year Up had worked with young adults from some of the toughest urban neighborhoods in the nation, individuals who experienced social and economic damage caused daily by epidemic unemployment. As the company poised to roll into Phase 3 of its long-term strategy, Chertavian was having second thoughts about its direction for the next five years.

Year Up leadership was moving forward with plans to expand the program to three new cities in the next five years, and one thought kept nagging the determined founder. "This problem, the skills gap, is huge, and it's getting worse. It's going in the wrong direction. We aren't doing enough. How are we going bring it to the next level? We serve 1,300 young adults a year, but we need to serve 100,000 to make any kind of real impact in this country. We need to reach a lot more young adults before it's too late."

The Opportunity Divide

Gerald Chertavian grew up in the old mill city of Lowell, Massachusetts. Gerald's father was a WWII veteran who, although he never graduated from college, was able to become a dentist through the GI Bill. Gerald grew up with a strong awareness of how the GI Bill had enabled his father to take a leap forward in his education and professional career. Gerald attended Lowell High School, where a teacher recognized his potential and helped him apply to Bowdoin

This case was prepared by Professors Edward Marram and Les Charm with casewriter Jesseca Timmons. Intended to serve as a basis for class discussion rather than to illustrate either effective or ineffective handling of an administrative situation. Funding for this case was provided by The Lewis Institute at Babson College.

College in Brunswick, Maine. At Bowdoin, Gerald volunteered for Big Brothers Big Sisters as a friend and mentor to children in need. He continued volunteering for the organization after graduating from Bowdoin and went to work on Wall Street in the Chemical Bank training program. In New York, Big Brothers Big Sisters matched Gerald with David Heredia, a 10-year-old boy growing up in the Rutgers housing development on the Lower East Side of Manhattan. Gerald grew close to David and his family. Moving between the two worlds of Wall Street and the Lower East Side, Gerald reflected on the difference between the opportunities he had received personally and the bleak situation faced by David Heredia and his siblings.

> One day I was talking to David's brother, Willie, and I said to myself, this man has out-argued me so well, he has out-thought me so well. He would be a great lawyer, and he has no idea how to get into the mainstream of this country. None. Nor did David, nor did any of his family, or any of his friends. So you have these really smart, talented people who lack the means necessary to get into the mainstream. It just struck me as a huge waste of human capital, in a country where we have no capital to waste.

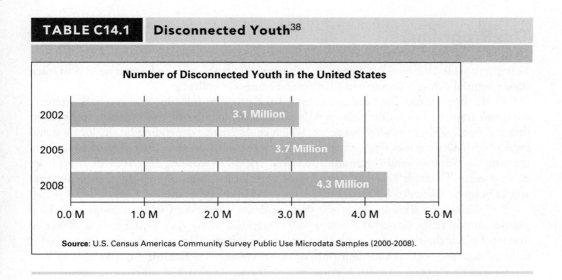

TABLE C14.1 **Disconnected Youth**[38]

Number of Disconnected Youth in the United States

2002	3.1 Million
2005	3.7 Million
2008	4.3 Million

Source: U.S. Census Americas Community Survey Public Use Microdata Samples (2000-2008).

The people he met through David were talented and intelligent, but they were unable to reach their potential because they lacked the opportunity to connect with the economic mainstream. They had been born on the wrong side of an *opportunity divide*. This gap struck Gerald as the key issue confronting the nation. He began to conceive of a program that could someday close the opportunity divide. He wrote his entrance essay to Harvard Business School on the concept, proposing, "Let me in, and this is what I'll do someday."

A Hand Up, Not a Hand-Out

After graduating from Harvard Business School with an MBA but $100,000 in debt, Gerald founded a software consulting firm in England, where he had moved with his British wife. Over the course of eight years, he and his two partners bootstrapped the firm to $19 million in revenue with no debt or outside financing. The company was ranked the 15th fastest-growing firm in England for five consecutive years. Gerald and his partners sold the business during the software boom of the early 1990s for $83 million, and they exited the business in 1999. In February 2000, Gerald started to develop his plan for closing the opportunity divide by creating a life-skills training program for urban young adults. He called the program Year Up.

It would serve disconnected urban young adults, ages 18–24, who had a high school diploma or GED but lacked the means to pursue a post-secondary education or enter the mainstream job market. Nationwide, high school graduation rates for Latino, African American, or Native American students hovered around 50%, with 17% of all 18- to 24-year-olds never obtaining a high school diploma or a GED, and 1.3 million new dropouts leaving school every year.[39] Despite the vast number of young people needing work, only 22% of all available jobs required a high school education or less.[40] Of Americans who graduated from high school, an average of 60% would not have an associate's degree or above by their mid-20s.[41] All of these statistics contributed to the growing opportunity divide, which Gerald believed a dangerous legacy to leave the next generation. He lamented to his staff, "If you want to pass down a lower standard of living to your children, this is how—create a structural imbalance in the labor market like the one we have."

The Program

Year Up provided talented young adults with the skills, experience, and access needed to reach their potential through professional careers and success in college.

In the first six months, students attended the program full-time and received extensive hands-on training in specific high-growth career areas (commonly information technology, financial operations, or quality assurance, which could change depending on site location and local needs). During this time, equal emphasis was placed on the *ABCs* of professionalism: the attitude, behavior, and communication skills critical to working effectively in a corporate environment. Through Year Up partnerships with local community colleges, students were able earn up to 18 credits for classes they completed in the program.

For the second six months of the year, students were placed in internships with local partner corporations, primarily Fortune 500 enterprises where they would have a chance to develop further their technical skills through on-the-job training, gain the experience needed to build a career, and expand their professional network. (See **Exhibit** 14.1: Sample of Year Up Corporate Partners.) In 2011, corporate partners provided 127 different internships for Year Up students across the country.

The program model was designed to facilitate a "high expectations, high support" culture. High expectations encouraged students to challenge themselves and take responsibility for their work and behavior while preparing for the high standards of the business world. For example, throughout the year, students earned a weekly educational stipend (up to $171 per week depending on the site[42]), which was tied to their performance in the program. At the beginning of the program, every student signed a contract that outlined typical standards and expectations of a professional working environment, such as arriving on time, turning in all assignments, dressing professionally, and treating colleagues respectfully. (See **Exhibit** 14.2: Year Up Student Contract 2010–2011.)

A student who did not meet one of the expectations laid out in the contract would be financially penalized for that week and would also lose a set number of points. A student who did meet all expectations would earn the full stipend amount and gain 15 points. When a student's point total fell below zero, he or she was considered to have "fired himself or herself from the program." Gerald believed real-life consequences held the key to program success. "Our young people earn their money. It is not handed out. They sign a contract

EXHIBIT 14.1 Sample of Year Up Corporate Partners

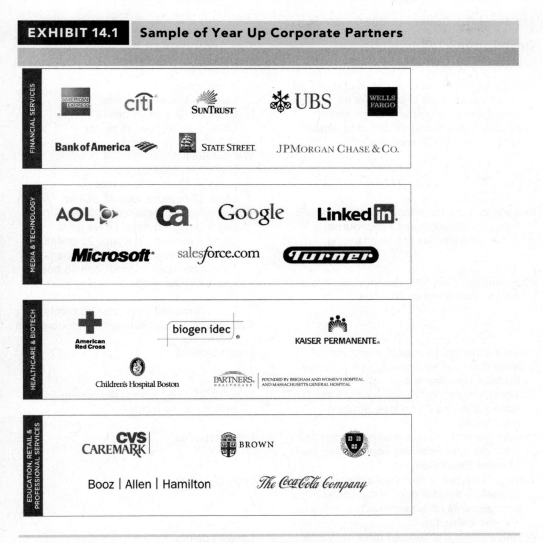

Source: Reprinted with permission from "Year UP: empowering urban talent to reach their potential," *Prospectus for Philanthropic Investment*, Year Up, 2011.

that is very specific about expectations, and those expectations simulate a professional working environment. If they are late to class, or don't turn in an assignment, or don't show up, they lose money out of their stipend, just like in the real world."

To help students rise to the challenge and navigate such a rigorous environment, Year Up provided "high support" both during and after the program. Students benefited from a multi-layered, integrated support system that included academic tutors, volunteer mentors, and staff advisors. They also regularly attended classes and guest-speaker presentations on career and life skills development and went on field trips to various business settings.

Year Up students lived with tremendous challenges outside the program such as lacking health insurance, coming from single-parent homes, growing up in the foster care system, or acting as primary caretaker for a household. On average, 29% of students were non-native English speakers and 20% had experienced temporary homelessness. The level of personal

EXHIBIT 14.2	Year Up Student Contract 2010–2011	
Expectation	**Description**	**Consequence of not meeting expectation**
Arriving and leaving on time and notification of lateness	You are expected to be on time and prepared to start each class or activity at its scheduled start time and at the end of breaks. You are also expected to remain until the scheduled end time.	With notification: Lates 1–4: lose 15 points Lates 5–10: lose 25 points Lates over 10: lose 35 points Without notification: Lates 1–4: lose 25 points Lates 5–10: lose 35 points Lates 10 or more: lose 45 points
Regular attendance and notification of absences	You are expected to attend Year Up regularly. Proper notification (see **Procedures**) is expected if you will not be attending. *Attending less than half the scheduled hours will be considered an absence.*	Absence with notification: no stipend, plus: Day 1-3 missed days: Leave days Day 4-6 missed days: lose 25 points Day 7-9 missed days: lose 30 points 10 or more days missed: lose 35 points Absence without notification: no stipend, plus: Day 1-3 missed days: lose 50 points 3 absences without notification: student fires him/herself
Business casual dress	You are expected to wear business casual attire during all activities at Year Up. (see **Student Handbook**.)	Lose 15 points
Appropriate use of Year Up computers	You are expected to follow the Computer Acceptable Use Policy (see **Student Handbook**).	Lose 15, 25 or 50 points, depending on the severity of the misuse
Appropriate use of electronic devices	You are expected to use your cell phone and other electronic devices appropriately (see **Student Handbook**).	Lose 15 points
Complete assignments on time	You are expected to turn in all assignments for classes by the due date, unless other arrangements have been made in **advance** with the instructor.	Lose 15 points
Attend all planned meetings	When you have a scheduled meeting, you are expected to honor the commitment. If unable, due to circumstances beyond your control, you should make alternate arrangements in advance with the other individual(s) involved.	Lose 15 points
Respect the law	At Year Up, you are expected to avoid engaging in theft, vandalism, sexual harassment (see **Student Handbook**), drug/alcohol possession or use, weapon possession, fighting, piracy, and other illegal activities.	At the discretion of the Year Up staff, penalties up to and including being fired from the program.
Respect the core values of Year Up	In addition to the expectations above, you are expected to behave in a manner consistent with the core values of Year Up.	At the discretion of the Year Up staff, loss of 15, 25, 50 or more points

Source: Year Up student contract provided by Michael Goldstein, Year Up, 2011.

and environmental difficulties made it necessary to hire at every Year Up site full-time social workers who could help students directly or connect them with the resources they needed.

Extensive data analysis of student outcomes and success rates indicated that young adults with more than four personal challenges were significantly less likely to graduate from the program. Gerald knew Year Up could not help every young adult in need, noting, "We are looking for students who will be the best fit for the program, for whom it is the next right step in their lives." The average graduation rate of 75% to 80% each year was considered an indicator that the program was taking on an appropriate amount of risk.

The program focused only on two positive outcomes by which to measure graduate success: working full-time and attending college part-time, or working part-time and attending college full-time. Even if a graduate achieved either outcome, and even with the skills and experience gained through Year Up, Gerald realized these young adults would continue to meet future challenges that could limit their long-term success. To ensure graduates crossed the opportunity divide, Year Up had to do more than provide a meaningful year-long experience. It had to empower students to succeed throughout their entire lives. Therefore, Year Up increased capacity in order to continue providing college and career services to all Year Up alumni.

Creating a Sustainable Non-Profit Business Model

As the program expanded to nine sites nationwide, Gerald and his executive team found high demand for the trained, entry-level talent Year Up students offered. A growing skills gap[43] in the United States meant that employers could not fill available positions because they could not find employees with the capabilities these jobs required. The nation's societal, educational, and workforce development systems were failing to produce workers ready to enter a 21st-century knowledge-based economy. The gap was causing large employers across the country to feel the pinch in filling entry-level jobs. More than one CEO lamented to the Year Up team, "Just *try* hiring a millennial and paying them $30K. They'll be gone in three months!" Potential corporate partners also deplored the severe lack of local talent offered by high school or college graduates from the communities in which their firms operated. (See **Exhibit** 14.3: Employer Rating of High School Graduates.) When pitching Year Up to prospective corporate partners, Gerald suggested his organization could offer employers a strategic business solution by providing skilled, reliable, local, entry-level talent at a lower cost than if the company were to hire full-time workers.

> I say to CEOs if we can show you a cost-effective source of human capital, would you be interested? If the answer is no, it took 10 seconds, and that's the end of it. Let's save your time and my time. If they say yes, then I ask them to give me a one-year pilot program, and we're going to prove we can provide a cost-effective source of human capital. It happens to be lower-income, and it happens to be 98% people of color, but that's not what we're selling. What we're selling is a cost-effective pipeline of talent. We would argue that diverse talent actually adds a lot to the company. What we're selling is a way to bring in talented, highly trained, highly accountable young people, so the partnership is equally valuable to the corporate partner and the young person.

Gerald had designed Year Up to provide tangible value to employers. He proposed that partners could realize savings and increased productivity by hosting Year Up interns, with the option to hire the student at the end of the internship. (See **Exhibit** 14.4: Internship Partner Agreement.) Employers routinely pointed to critical business needs addressed when they entered into or expanded a partnership with Year Up: access to a skilled, diverse, talent

| EXHIBIT 14.3 | Employer Rating of High School Graduates |

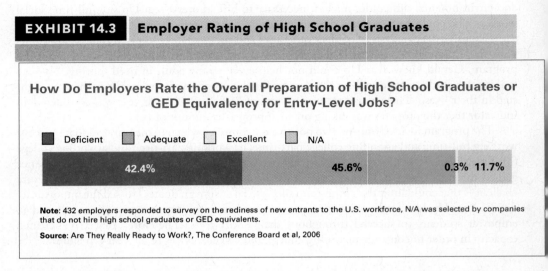

How Do Employers Rate the Overall Preparation of High School Graduates or GED Equivalency for Entry-Level Jobs?

■ Deficient ■ Adequate ☐ Excellent ☐ N/A

| 42.4% | 45.6% | 0.3% | 11.7% |

Note: 432 employers responded to survey on the rediness of new entrants to the U.S. workforce, N/A was selected by companies that do not hire high school graduates or GED equivalents.

Source: Are They Really Ready to Work?, The Conference Board et al, 2006

Figure 1 Since 1973, jobs that require at least some college have exploded while opportunities for those with just a high school education have shrunk dramatically

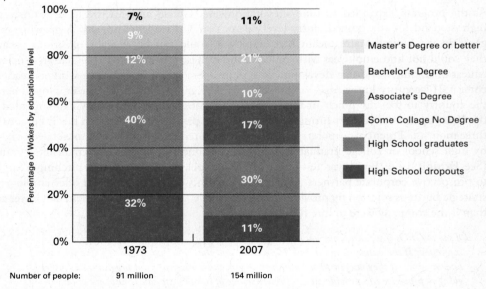

Number of people: 91 million   154 million

Source: March CPS data, various years: Center on Education and Workforce.

Source: Reprinted with permission from "Year UP: empowering urban talent to reach their potential," *Prospectus for Philanthropic Investment*, Year Up, 2011.

EXHIBIT 14.4	Internship Partner Agreement

1. <u>Key Internship Partner Information.</u>

   Internship partner name:
   Internship partner ID #:
   Primary work site:
   Key contacts:
   Purchase order:

2. <u>Internship Program:</u> As part of the training experience offered to student participants in the Year Up program, Year Up will place student Interns with the Internship Partner for the purpose of providing on-the-job training to the student Interns as part of their educational experience. The specific training opportunities afforded to the student Interns are described in *Exhibit A*: Role Description, provided by Internship Partner. Further details regarding the day-to-day logistics surrounding the Year Up Internship program can be found in *Exhibit B*: Year Up Internship Logistics.

   The purpose and intent of the Year Up Internship Program is to provide on-the-job training to students who are concurrently enrolled in the Year Up program, a nonprofit experiential training program, and in a local institution of higher education. Each student apprentice receives college credit for the Internship experience. Year Up and the Internship Partner agree and understand that the training offered the Interns is similar to that which would be given in a vocational school; that the training is for the benefit of the Interns; that the Interns will not displace regular employees, but will work under their close observation; that the Internship Partner derives no immediate advantage from the activities of the Interns; that the Interns are not necessarily entitled to a job with the Internship Partner at the conclusion of the training period; and that the Interns and the Internship Partner understand that the Interns are not entitled to wages for the time spent in training. As part of the Interns' training program, they attend a weekly educational seminar about their training at the Year Up site. No apprentice shall be expected or required to participate in training in excess of 40 total hours in any work week.

3. <u>Term.</u> The internship partner agrees to host _____ IT interns who will commence on _____. This agreement automatically renews for future internships, unless amended by mutual agreement. Upon mutual agreement, Year Up and the Internship Partner may terminate this agreement at any time.

4. <u>Fees.</u> The Internship Partner shall pay Year Up a fee of $___ per week per Intern for its participation in the Year Up Internship Partner program.

5. <u>Terms of payment.</u> Year Up will invoice the Internship Partner the first day of each month for the upcoming month. The Internship Partner shall make payment to Year Up upon receipt of the applicable invoice.

6. <u>Contact.</u> If the Internship Partner has any questions, concerns, or suggestions related to the Year Up Internship program, they should be directed to: ___, Senior Director of Internships, 93 Summer Street, Boston, MA 02110, (617) 542-1533

7. <u>Relationship.</u> The Intern is a full-time student in the Year Up program and in a local institution of higher education. Because the intern is participating in an educational training program, s/he is not considered an employee of Year Up or the Internship Partner. The Intern receives a weekly educational stipend, paid directly by Year Up. The Intern shall not be expected or entitled to participate in direct compensation, health or disability insurance, retirement benefits, or other company welfare or pension benefits (if any) to which employees of the Internship Partner may be entitled.

8. <u>Work Product.</u> All Work Product of the Intern shall be considered works made by the Internship Partner and shall belong exclusively to the Internship Partner and its designees.

9. <u>General.</u> This Agreement constitutes the entire agreement of the parties and there are no other agreements or understandings, either written or oral.

Source: Year Up internship partner agreement provided by Michael Goldstein, Year Up, 2011.

pipeline; reduced training and placement costs; and lower turnover rates among the interns they decided to hire.

Corporate partners agreed to sponsor learning and professional development by contributing about $21,000 to Year Up for every student hosted. Gerald knew the contribution was contingent on intern performance: showing up on time, producing satisfactory work, and adding value to the company.

> *When we place these students in internships, say, at JP Morgan, and you do the math, you realize Year Up is not a cheap resource. It is more cost-effective than if JP Morgan paid a full-time person scaled up with benefits, but it's not cheap. And if the student doesn't deliver, we don't get paid. Using our people eliminates a lot of risk for the employer because our young people are accountable. If the student is happy and performing well, then JP Morgan is happy.*

In addition, Gerald rejected the traditional nonprofit business model as unsustainable. "Year Up success depends on alignment of economic incentives between corporate partners and the nonprofit sector. In the traditional nonprofit business model, the nonprofit receives money from one party to render services to another, providing no economic incentive. We are unusual because our economic incentives are completely aligned."

In 2010, about 39% ($12.5 million) of Year Up's $32 million operating capital came from internship revenue. Underwriting the organizational cost of student stipends and college credits took up 100% of internship revenue. The rest came through local and national philanthropy with a small percentage from government grants. This mix made Year Up unusual in publicly funded workforce development because of its deep engagement with and heavy financial reliance on employer partners.

The Cost of Scaling

Year Up launched its first program site in Boston in January 2001 with a class of 22 students. The first growth phase sought to determine whether the program could scale to multiple sites nationwide while maintaining consistent graduation rates and successful student outcomes. In 2005, the second site opened in Providence, Rhode Island, followed by Washington, DC. The DC site grew rapidly with 72 students enrolled by 2007. The program expanded to New York City with 23 students entering in September 2006. By the end of 2007, Year Up was training 500 students a year with over 85% successfully completing the program. By spring 2011, the company had expanded to nine sites and was scouting for the next three locations.

Each site launch was a three- to four-year process from initial location scouting to breakeven, with average total cost about $6 million per site over that period. Initially, cost differences at each new site depended on factors such as local rent, which varied greatly from site to site, and the timing of key staff coming on board. Cost differences after the launch phase depended on local site growth plans. The executive team that oversaw expansion typically secured $300,000 to $500,000 from local funding sources the year before a launch. New sites would not open until this revenue was brought in. Each new site also received a $1 million startup subsidy of growth capital raised by the national office, to be used as needed. The subsidy helped support the first six months of operations, covering lag time before internship revenue began to flow from corporate partners in the second six months.

Of the five newest sites launched by 2011, only one needed to draw on the entire $1 million subsidy. After breakeven in year 3 or 4, each site was required to contribute 12% from revenue surplus toward the national operating budget. Due to the nature of nonprofit and education business cycles, Year Up cash inflows and outflows varied widely from quarter to quarter. The organization typically had negative net cash flow in the first quarter, neutral or negative net cash flow in the second and third quarters, and highly positive net cash flow in the fourth quarter. In Q1 2011, cash inflow was $7.96 million and cash outflow $9.6 million. (See **Exhibit** 14.5: Pro Forma Financials 2010–2011.)

EXHIBIT 14.5	Pro Forma Financials						
	2011B	**2012E**	**2013E**	**2014E**	**2015E**	**2016E**	**Total: 2012-2016**
STUDENTS SERVED	1,432	1,760	1,944	2,144	2,440	2,584	10,872
REVENUE:							
Internship Income	$20.5	$25.7	$29.1	$33.3	$37.1	$40.8	$166.1
Philanthropy	$24.7	$13.5	$18.0	$20.6	$22.4	$24.9	$99.4
Public Funds	$1.5	$2.5	$2.5	$2.5	$2.5	$2.5	$12.5
TOTAL REVENUE	**$46.7**	**$41.7**	**$49.7**	**$56.4**	**$62.0**	**$68.2**	**$278.0**
EXPENSES:							
Ongoing Operational Expenses							
Core Program	$25.8	$25.8	$25.8	$25.8	$25.8	$25.8	$128.8
National Infrastructure	$4.4	$4.4	$4.4	$4.4	$4.4	$4.4	$22.0
Total for Ongoing Operational Expenses	$30.2	$30.2	$30.2	$30.2	$30.2	$30.2	$150.8
Expenses for 2012-2016 Impact Strategies							
Grow and Strengthen Core	$7.8	$19.3	$26.0	$30.4	$38.1	$41.9	$155.9
Develop Million-Person Model	$0.9	$2.9	$2.5	$2.0	$1.9	$1.9	$11.2
Create Systems Change	$0.2	$1.0	$1.3	$1.9	$1.8	$2.2	$8.3
Total for 2012-2016 Impact Strategies	$8.9	$23.3	$29.9	$34.3	$41.8	$46.0	$175.4
TOTAL EXPENSES	**$39.0**	**$53.4**	**$60.0**	**$64.5**	**$72.0**	**$76.2**	**$326.1**
(Surplus)/Deficit	$(7.7)	$11.8	$10.4	$8.1	$10.0	$7.9	$48.1
Risk Reserve Requirement		$2.0	$2.7	$0.8	$1.3	$-	$6.9
DEPLOYMENT OF CAPITAL		$13.8	$13.1	$8.9	$11.3	$7.9	$55.0
GROWTH FUND BALANCES							
Beginning		$55.0	$41.2	$28.1	$19.2	$7.9	
Ending		$41.2	$28.1	$19.2	$7.9	$-	

Note: Any apparent addition errors within this table are the result of rounding error, due to presenting figures in millions with one decimal.

Source: Reprinted with permission from "Year UP: empowering urban talent to reach their potential," *Prospectus for Philanthropic Investment*, Year Up, 2011.

The Expansion Process

For every new site, the national expansion team reviewed and revised a short list of five or six potential cities, then evaluated and ranked them on several criteria. The first factor considered was the supply of young adults needing employment compared to local demand for entry-level white-collar workers. Other key factors included access to public transportation between employers and target population, connections to innovative community colleges eager to partner with Year Up, the local political climate, and depth of the local philanthropic base. The team also took into account the extent of existing or potential contacts and support networks in the new city. Gerald found that local political support, especially from the mayor, was key to launching a new site successfully. "If we tell one city, hey, the mayor over in this other city is interested, they're going to have Year Up, it is very effective. No one just waltzes into a new town and says we're going to help your young people. You have to be very respectful and very humble."

Selection of each new site focused on risk-reduction measures to eliminate factors that had created obstacles at previous sites. Corporate partners with a national presence were asked to play anchor-tenant roles at new sites. Gerald and the executive team met with local CEOs to develop new internship partners. Before hiring a local executive director, the team identified support networks and initiated contracts with corporate partners. Upon receiving partner commitments, the team began seeking an executive director, which Gerald found the most challenging part of launching a new site.

> *Finding the executive director, that's the longest timeframe to put in place. The first thing we look for is complete commitment to the mission. They have to believe in the young adults we serve. We need people who believe in our mission. If you're not a zealot or fanatic for our mission, you can't work here! We also need people with cultural competency, which makes it a lot tougher. Really we're looking for some pretty unique people. They should be entrepreneurial, someone who is a leader, not a follower, who has a high desire to build relationships. They should be pretty impatient by nature, and they should have a level of attention to detail which is sufficient but not overly attentive, because they are going to have a lot of trouble scaling the business if their attention to detail is too high, which tends to correspond to lack of delegation.*

After expansion to New York—when Gerald hired Lisette Nieves, a native New Yorker with long-time experience in New York City social services and education bureaucracy—the expansion team made finding locally based executive directors a priority. Nieves, who had strong experience in city government and higher education, was able to leverage both her local support network and her knowledge of the business and political atmosphere.

She put an effective team in place quickly and accelerated the New York launch. Previous executive directors had found launching a new program in an unfamiliar city inefficient, noting "two things working against us: We were new to management roles and new to cities we were moving into."[44]

In 2011, as the expansion team began planning three new sites, they found it increasingly challenging to identify cities offering characteristics that could assure Year Up success, such as a robust job market in growing professional industries, a deep philanthropic base, innovative community college partners, and comprehensive public transportation. Year Up did best in large cities such as New York, Chicago, and San Francisco, but had difficulty operating in "second-tier" cities (Albany) or those with less established urban centers (Phoenix). The national leadership team wondered how to overcome these issues and make Year Up's model more versatile without compromising program quality.

Nonprofit Sector Issue: Attracting and Retaining Talent

After running a lucrative and successful software consulting firm, Gerald found that nonprofit business posed challenges. Chief among them was finding and keeping a first-class team. Attracting the best and brightest to nonprofit was a constant struggle. Although the *NonProfit Times* had named Year Up "Best Nonprofit to Work For" more than once,[45] few nonprofits were able to compensate leadership as well as for-profit entities. Leadership and staff had to be willing to work at Year Up because of their commitment to the mission; losing key people to the for-profit sector was a constant threat. Gerald knew such losses were inevitable. "My current head of development took a 92% pay cut to join this company. I know this is not the only career choice. When I lose someone because they want to make a big capital gain, I understand. I have all the respect for that in the world. Go out and make a big capital gain, then come do this work."

Not only did Gerald face the challenge of attracting the best and brightest to a nonprofit, he was also competing to hire high-achieving young people of color. Getting Year Up students into the professional workforce was a first step addressing widespread under-representation of people of color in leadership positions nationwide. Gerald believed corporate America needed to change drastically, and he was determined that Year Up reflect the changing population.

> If you look at who is in charge in this country, it does not reflect the population. Of all people born in this country, 50% are now black or brown. So roll the clock forward 50 years. Who is going to lead this diverse population? Right now, leadership at our Fortune 500 companies is still almost all white male! At Year Up, we want to look ahead, we want to be at the forefront of this change, we want to get our young people out there where they need to be.

In Boston, Gerald personally recruited "top-drawer" young people of color by developing relationships with students and alumni at Harvard and other graduate schools near his home in Cambridge. Although convincing these young people, who had many options, to work for less at a nonprofit was difficult, Gerald was encouraged to observe a sea change in the 20 years since he had left business school. In the late 1980s and early 1990s, going to work for a nonprofit was considered fringe or even laughable. Gerald recalled, "When I started at HBS, the nonprofit club had six students in it. But in 2011, the Social Enterprise Club was the largest student organization on campus. We need to inspire young people to welcome this as a valid career choice."

The Role of National and Local Boards

As a 501 (c) (3),[46] Year Up was governed by a national board of directors that assisted the national executive team in areas such as strategic direction, fundraising, financial control, and overall corporate governance.[47] Each program site also had a local advisory board that worked with the executive director to develop internships and relationships with local investors and philanthropists. Local boards were non-fiduciary and were recruited by the executive directors. Foremost among Gerald's goals was that the board push the organization to the highest level of achievement. "My feeling with my board is push as hard as you want! The board is supposed to push me into thinking hard and will let me know if my thinking is shallow or poor."

For the first 10 years, Gerald had personally been involved in raising most of Year Up operating revenue. He had also led the first capital campaign for $20 million to grow the business. In the second decade, the national board limited Gerald's responsibility for raising operating revenue from philanthropists and business partners to 15% of the total in order to create a sustainable model. As he was gradually phased out of this responsibility, Gerald remained pragmatic about his future role in the business. "We are trying to set up a sustainable revenue model that does not depend on me or on any one person. There is a real incentive that I become redundant. I want the board to decide whether they still want me, because founders can get old and start to smell. It's very dangerous if the founder thinks he is going to be there forever."

However, he was spearheading the second major capital campaign, which aimed to bring in $55 million for the next five to seven years. (See **Exhibit** 14.6: Expected Use of Growth Capital.)

EXHIBIT 14.6	Expected Use of Growth Capital (in $M)					
		2012	2013	2014	2015	2016	Total

GROW AND STRENGTHEN CORE	2012	2013	2014	2015	2016	Total
Scale Direct Service Model	$5.4	$3.9	$2.2	$3.7	$1.7	$17.8
Ensure Long-Term Graduate Success	$0.5	$0.6	$0.6	$0.7	$0.7	$3.1
Subtotal	$6.4	$5.0	$2.8	$4.3	$2.4	$20.9
Growth in National Infrastructure	$0.9	$1.0	$0.9	$1.3	$0.9	$4.9
Capital Expenditures / Depreciation	$0.6	$0.6	$0.5	$0.7	$0.5	$2.9
TOTAL-Grow and Strengthen the Core	$7.8	$6.5	$4.2	$6.3	$3.9	$28.7
DEVELOP THE MILLION-PERSON MODEL						
Research and Design Alternative Models	$0.9	$0.6	$-	$-	$-	$1.5
Pilot Model(s) (e.g. Community College Professional Training Corps, "PTC")	$1.4	$1.3	$1.3	$1.3	$1.2	$6.5
Subtotal	$2.4	$1.9	$1.3	$1.3	$1.2	$8.1
Growth in National Infrastructure	$0.3	$0.4	$0.4	$0.4	$0.4	$1.9
Capital Expenditures/Depreciation	$0.2	$0.2	$0.3	$0.2	$0.3	$1.2
TOTAL-Develop Million-Person Model	$2.9	$2.5	$2.0	$1.9	$1.9	$11.2
CREATE SYSTEMS CHANGE						
National Influence	$0.5	$0.5	$0.6	$0.6	$0.6	$2.7
Metropolitan Area-Level Systems Change	$0.4	$0.5	$0.7	$0.7	$0.8	$3.1
Subtotal	$0.8	$1.0	$1.3	$1.3	$1.4	$5.7
Growth in National Infrastructure	$0.1	$0.2	$0.4	$0.4	$0.5	$1.6
Capital Expenditures/ Depreciation	$0.1	$0.1	$0.2	$0.2	$0.3	$0.9
TOTAL-Create Systems Change	$1.0	$1.3	$1.9	$1.8	$2.2	$8.3
Total Funding for 2012-2016 Impact Strategies	$11.8	$10.4	$8.1	$10.0	$7.9	$48.1
Risk Reserve Expansion	$2.0	$2.7	$0.8	$1.3	$-	$6.9
TOTAL GROWTH CAPITAL REQUIRED	$13.8	$13.1	$8.9	$11.3	$7.9	$55.0

Note: Any apparent addition errors within this table are the result of rounding error, due to presenting figures in millions with one decimal.

Source: Reprinted with permission from "Year UP: empowering urban talent to reach their potential," *Prospectus for Philanthropic Investment*, Year Up, 2011.

In winter 2010, the Year Up national board suffered a loss when a long-serving, deeply committed member retired. Both the national board of directors and the organization felt the loss keenly, because this individual had been a pivotal support in Year Up's first decade. In 2011, Gerald's focus switched to seeking board members with national reach combined with influence in media, policy, and higher education, rather than only those with access to or expertise in obtaining capital. Gerald strongly felt that both board and employees would need to represent the cultural competency that defined Year Up's mission. Finding people to serve on the national board was a greater challenge than finding people for local boards around the country. Gerald knew exactly what type of expertise he needed. "We are broadening the board to be a little more political, to have more pragmatic and evaluation expertise, a board that is diverse, and that truly understands the mission. We don't want people who stand on ceremony. It's a working board."

In 2011, one of Gerald's long-term goals was realized when the first two Year Up alumni were voted onto the national board. Both had graduated from Year Up in the previous five years, one in Boston and one in the D.C. area. The first alum was now employed full-time at MIT and attending community college, while the second was a junior systems engineer at Affiliated Computer Services and enrolled with the University of Phoenix. Elevating alumni to the board validated Gerald's hope that they could one day take on leadership roles within the organization.

In spring 2011, the national board of directors decided that in the next three to five years, they would need to expand to 20 members and diversify their collective expertise in order to tackle challenges of a fast-growing organization with a much larger reach.

Re-evaluating the Mission

By early 2010, each of Year Up's original goals had been successfully realized: The program had expanded from three to six sites in just six years, with plans under way to open sites in three new cities, and they expected to serve 2,500 students per year by 2016. When the executive team revisited goals and strategy for the next growth phase (2012–2016), they assessed how Year Up was taking on the true mission of the company, which was not necessarily to expand the existing program, but to close the nation's widening opportunity gap. Discussions focused on the fact that despite program success, Year Up's 3,600 graduates represented only a drop in the bucket compared to five million disconnected young adults in the United States.[48] Gerald expressed frustration to the national board and the executive team. "This number of disconnected young adults is huge, and we're not getting there fast enough. Are we going to have a different strategy for 2012–2016, other than maintaining the status quo? We have a very specific model, and it works, but the question is, is it OK for us to serve just a few thousand young people a year when there are over a million who need help?"

Gerald, his team, and the national board realized that even if Year Up grew to 25 cities, it would only reach a fraction of the target population, far from achieving its mission of closing the opportunity divide in the United States. Gerald reasoned that Year Up had created one of the most successful workforce training programs in the country. The company had a responsibility to fulfill its mission and to leverage its unique track record, experience, and leadership to help the largest possible number of disconnected urban young adults enter "living wage career pathways" and quality post-secondary education.

Gerald believed the recession was creating an opportunity for Year Up. While both the skills gap and the population of disconnected youth had been growing for decades, the problem had historically received little attention from mainstream media. After years of a bubble economy, the nearly 10% unemployment rate[49] and the lack of opportunity for many Americans were suddenly in the national consciousness. Daniel Adler, a member of the team that designed the new long-term strategy, saw a "dichotomy between opportunity and responsibility" that the company needed to breach. "The economic and political climate is all about international competitiveness and restarting this economy. The political climate is very harsh, and politicians are looking for bipartisan solutions that promote jobs without taking a whole lot of funding, and we're perfect for that. We have this opportunity to do something really meaningful."

Demand remained high among U.S.-based companies for qualified, entry-level talent whose skills matched available jobs. In 2009, 80% of employers nationwide who participated in any type of apprenticeship program felt the program helped meet their need for skilled, productive workers, and 86% would "strongly recommend" an apprenticeship program to other employers.[50] Yet many workforce training programs were losing government support and shutting down due to a lack of proven results.[51] Year Up was meeting a vital need and could prove its approach was effective.[52] It was decided: Year Up had to do more to close the opportunity divide.

Going Back to the Drawing Board

As they started planning Year Up's 2012–2016 strategy, the executive team and the national board of directors faced an important question. Could Year Up realistically go from serving thousands to serving hundreds of thousands without sacrificing program quality? Nearly all company resources for the past four years had gone to the previous goal of expanding to serve 2,500 students a year. To achieve its mission, Year Up needed to scale its social impact. First, Gerald and his team needed to evaluate scalability of the existing program model. It relied heavily on private philanthropic funds, limiting where and how much the program could grow. Reducing program cost could help overcome these limitations, but what parts of the budget could be cut? Consistent, transformative outcomes relied on key components that could not be eliminated without risk of compromising results: the stipend, which enabled students to attend school while working only part-time; the college credits, which positioned graduates to continue post-secondary education; the large support staff and the student services department; and the internship team, which managed relationships with corporate partners.

When analyzing the program cost structure, the national board of directors and the executive team saw that paying Year Up's highly qualified staff absorbed the largest part of the operating budget, but reducing staff could undermine program success. Gerald reflected on the high-cost staffing needs.

> *It* is *highly supported. We make sure each student has an adult actually looking into his or her eyes on a regular basis. This is what we're all about. It is hopefully a caring and supportive program, yet in a way unemotional. It empowers young people rather than treating them as they may have been treated in the past, which is not in an empowering way. Our young adults come from very challenging backgrounds. The intense support we give is what enables them to succeed.*

After repeatedly running the numbers and debating, the leadership team and the national board concluded that lowering costs to increase scalability would require altering program components that were key to success. Daniel Adler felt strongly that to alter substantially the core model was too risky. "When you think about all the work we did to get our core models to the outcomes where they are now, when you think about all the systems we put in place, there is only so much you can change before there is a cultural problem. There is only so much you can tweak without disrupting the systems that led to program success."

Gerald conceded the core model was not feasible at a super scale. "Like any service organization, we have to be very specific about what services we provide. That is how you replicate fidelity across sites. We have to look at this current model and say to ourselves, we're never going to get to where we can train 100,000 young adults a year with this model. It's too much capital, it's too expensive, and it's not going to take us there."

Developing the 2012–2016 strategy, Gerald and his team realized they needed to explore alternative options for scaling Year Up's impact. They also had another hard decision to make. If the core model could never impact more than 1% of the target population, was it worth keeping? Should the program stop growing after adding the next three cities? Should Year Up continue to allocate resources to a model that lacked scalability but offered results?

Effecting Systemic Change

Since founding Year Up, Gerald had known that growing the program regardless of scale could only be part of the solution for closing the opportunity divide. "We need to ramp up the systems change piece at both the local and the federal level. We help young people get over a divide, but systemically, why does that divide exist? There are systems around it, like the legal system, that perpetuate a divide between who has access to opportunity and who doesn't."

Given the serious issues in public education and workforce development that left students without the skills to enter the workforce or matriculate at the community college level,[53] the second key element in Year Up strategy had always been to affect systems change externally. Time and again, Year Up staff had seen hard-working students sidetracked by profound personal challenges, despite the best efforts of the program's extensive social work staff. The company began to put more resources toward addressing systemic barriers that prevented urban youth from accessing quality post-secondary careers and meaningful career pathways.

The executive team identified four strategies through which they could influence broad systemic change: advocacy for local and national legislative change, catalyzing a social movement, engaging corporate partners in achieving change, and grassroots organizing of the program's 4,000 alumni and network of supporters. In the 2008 election cycle, Year Up advocated for creation of an office of social innovation and a social innovation fund (SIF), a federal funding mechanism intended to leverage private dollars and support growth of organizations addressing urgent social issues. In 2010, two SIF intermediaries, New Profit Inc. and Venture Philanthropy Partners, awarded two grants to Year Up. On the legislative front, the company began working with a loose policy coalition, including both Corporate Voices for Working Families and also Jobs for the Future, which participated in many conversations resulting in creation of a disconnected youth tax credit, the Department of Labor innovation fund, and the Community College and Career Training Grant Program.

Other successful initiatives included organizing an annual *Walk for Opportunity* event in each Year Up city. Another systemic change initiative encouraged corporate partners to invest in creating their own future workforce. The executive team proposed a customized internship model for which partner corporations would design programs for their own potential employees and take a greater role bringing local young people into the company. Similar to the historic apprenticeship model on a large scale, employers could use the new model to develop their future workforce from within the local community.

Creating a Million-Person Model

With wide-reaching change initiatives in the works, Gerald's imagination turned to what he thought of as Year Up's *million-person model*. Once they had agreed to take on the challenge of closing the opportunity gap nationwide, Gerald and the leadership team considered whether they could incorporate Year Up's core elements into existing systems or institutions that worked with young adults, thereby sharing resources, reducing costs, and potentially reaching more disconnected youth at a faster rate. They wondered whether they could leverage Year Up experience to design a new kind of program capable of serving 100,000 young people every year for at least 10 years. Gerald saw enormous change ahead. "The question for us now is, where do we innovate the model, how do we innovate it, and why do we innovate around what we've decided to do? Creating this new model means experimentation, a lot of fast failing, and failure is not something this company has had a lot of experience with in the past 10 years!"

Managing the innovation required proposing, vetting, and developing new models for a much larger scale; running pilots and assessing outcomes; and building an R&D capability. Although the company had a strong internship engine to manage corporate partnerships and a cohesive process for expanding the program, it did not yet have staff dedicated to innovation and creative development, unlike most for-profit companies, especially in technology or pharmaceuticals. The national board and the leadership team now had to consider whether to bring in management and staff for this purpose, and how to determine which ideas would ultimately meet company goals.

No matter which way he examined the issue, Gerald's thoughts returned to the community college system, already an integral part of the core program. All sites were already partnered with a local community college. Year Up and community colleges worked with a similar population of young adults: 45% of community college students were members of a minority group, and 42% were first-generation college students.[54] However, community colleges served a much larger population: more than three million 18- to 24-year-olds (about 12%)[55] were enrolled in community college at any given time. Gerald wondered how to utilize the nation's 1,167-site community college system to educate Year Up students. "Here is a system already in place that knows and already excels at educating this population. The problem is, they don't have a huge incentive for students to stay in school. The incentive system is poorly aligned, and there is no labor market attachment."

As Year Up prepared for the next growth phase, the same questions kept running through Gerald's mind. What were the pitfalls ahead as he attempted to build Year Up to a level 20 times larger? As the organization contemplated a massive new effort, the risks were real. Gerald needed the national board to guide him. "Our real risk is structuring this innovative effort as we take the organization to a much higher level. How do you share knowledge, how do you set that up, how do you structure it? The biggest single challenge we face right now is not pulling this off right! What mistakes lurk in the next shift? How do I get this innovative effort right?"

Case Questions

1. Should Gerald grow Year Up to serve more students?

2. How would you advise Gerald to put in place such a growth plan? What are the potential risks of your plan?

3. Examine Year Up's revenue plan. Can they continue to grow income from sponsoring companies? Is there a saturation point?

Glossary

Accredited Investor: Under the Securities Act of 1933, a company that offers or sells its securities must register the securities with the SEC or find an exemption from the registration requirements. The Act provides companies with a number of exemptions. For some of the exemptions, such as rules 505 and 506 of Regulation D, a company may sell its securities to what are known as "accredited investors." The federal securities laws define the term **accredited investor** in Rule 501 of Regulation D as:

1. a bank, insurance company, registered investment company, business development company, or small business investment company; an employee benefit plan, within the meaning of the Employee Retirement Income Security Act, if a bank, insurance company, or registered investment adviser makes the investment decisions, or if the plan has total assets in excess of $5 million.

2. a charitable organization, corporation, or partnership with assets exceeding $5 million.

3. a director, executive officer, or general partner of the company selling the securities.

4. a business in which all the equity owners are accredited investors.

5. a natural person who has individual net worth, or joint net worth with the person's spouse, that exceeds $1 million at the time of the purchase.

6. a natural person with income exceeding $200,000 in each of the two most recent years or joint income with a spouse exceeding $300,000 for those years and a reasonable expectation of the same income level in the current year; or

7. a trust with assets in excess of $5 million, not formed to acquire the securities offered, whose purchases a sophisticated person makes.

Acquisition: Acquiring control of a corporation, called a target, by stock purchase or exchange, either hostile or friendly; also called **takeover.**

Agency theory: A branch of economics dealing with the behavior of principals (for example, owners) and their agents (for example, managers).

All-hands meeting: A meeting of managers, lawyers, accountants, and investment bankers that sets the timetable and tasks to be accomplished prior to an initial public offering.

American Stock Exchange (Amex): Stock exchange located in New York, listing companies that are generally smaller and younger than those on the much larger New York Stock Exchange.

Angel: An individual who invests in private companies. The term business angel is sometimes reserved for sophisticated angel investors who invest sizeable sums in private companies. *(See informal investor.)*

Anglo-Saxon capitalism: So-called Anglo-Saxon capitalism (also Anglo-Saxon finance) is largely practiced in English speaking countries such as the United Kingdom and the United States. It is a capitalist macroeconomic model in which levels of regulation and taxes are low. In addition, Anglo-Saxon economies generally are more "liberal" and free-market oriented than other capitalist economies in the world. Another major difference between Anglo-Saxon and non-Anglo-Saxon countries is the legal system, which is based on case-law rather than civil code law.

Antidilution (of ownership): The right of an investor to maintain the same percentage of ownership of a company's common stock in the event that the company issues more stock. *(See dilution.)*

Asked: The price level at which sellers offer securities to buyers.

ASP (Application Service Provider): An ASP deploys, hosts, and manages access to a packaged software application for multiple parties from a centrally managed facility. The applications are delivered over networks on a subscription basis.

Asset acquisition: Means of affecting a buyout by purchase of certain desired assets rather than shares of the target company.

Asset-based valuation: This method considers the fair market value of fixed assets and equipment, and inventory. It is most appropriate for asset intensive businesses such as retail and manufacturing companies.

Audited financial statements: A company's financial statements prepared and certified by a certified public accounting firm that is totally independent of the company.

Babson College: Babson College, located in Wellesley, Massachusetts, is recognized internationally for its entrepreneurial leadership in a changing global environment. Babson grants BS, MBA, and custom MS and MBA degrees, and has a school of executive education. The Arthur M. Blank Center for Entrepreneurship was dedicated in 1998, and provides a dynamic home for Babson's world-famous entrepreneurship program.

Backlog: The sales that have been made but not fulfilled due to lack of inventory to finalize the sale.

Bake-off: When a private company compares offers from different investment banks to take it public.

Balance sheet: Summary statement of a company's financial position at a given point in time. It summarizes the accounting value of the assets, liabilities, preferred stock, common stock, and retained earnings. Assets = Liabilities + Preferred stock + Common stock + Retained earnings. *(See pro forma statements.)*

Basis point: One-hundredth of a percent (0.01%), typically used in expressing yield differentials (1.50% - 1.15% = 0.35%, or 35 basis points). *(See yield.)*

Bear: A person who expects prices to fall.

Bear market: A period of generally falling prices and pessimistic attitudes.

Best efforts offering: The underwriter makes its best efforts to sell as much as it can of the shares at the offering price. Hence, unlike a firm commitment offering the company offering its shares is not guaranteed a definite amount of money by the underwriter.

Beauty contest: When investment banks make their best offers to take a company public.

Bid: The price level at which buyers offer to acquire securities from sellers.

Big Board: *See New York Stock Exchange.*

Blue sky: Refers to laws that safeguard investors from being misled by unscrupulous promoters of companies with little or no substance.

Book value (of an asset): The accounting value of an asset as shown on a balance sheet is the cost of the asset minus its accumulated depreciation. It is not necessarily identical to its market value.

Book value (of a company): The common stock equity shown on the balance sheet. It is equal to total assets minus liabilities and preferred stock (synonymous with net worth and owners' equity).

Bootstrap: To build a business out of nothing, with minimal outside capital.

Bottom-up forecasting: Forecasting your income sheet revenue and expenses based upon a typical day and then multiplying those forecasts by the number of days in the period (i.e., month, quarter, or year).

Brain-writing: Similar to brainstorming, but the process is done with written versus oral communication. Ideas are presented and participants add their thoughts in writing. The key is to build on the idea rather than argue why the idea can't work.

Break-even point: The sales volume at which a company's net sales revenue just equals its costs. A commonly used approximate formula for the break-even point is Sales revenue = Total fixed costs/Gross margin.

Bridge financing: Short-term finance that is expected to be repaid relatively quickly. It usually bridges a short-term financing need. For example, it provides cash needed before an expected stock flotation.

Burn rate: The negative, real-time cash flow from a company's operations, usually computed monthly.

Business Angel: *See angel.*

Business model: The way in which a business makes a profit. As an example, here is IBM's definition of its business model: "IBM sells services, hardware and software. These offerings are bolstered by IBM's research and development capabilities. If a customer requires financing, IBM can provide that too." Southwest Airlines' business model is to provide inexpensive fares by keeping costs low through being more efficient than its major competitors.

Business plan: Document prepared by entrepreneurs, possibly in conjunction with their professional advisors, detailing the past, present, and intended future of the company. It contains a thorough analysis of the managerial, physical, labor, product, and financial resources of the company, plus the background of the company, its previous trading record, and its market position. The business plan contains detailed profit, balance sheet, and cash flow projections for two years ahead, and less detailed information for the following three years. The business plan crystallizes and focuses the management team's ideas. It explains their strategies, sets objectives, and is used to monitor their subsequent performance.

Buyback: A corporation's repurchase of stock that it has previously issued; for example, a company buys its stock back from a venture

capital firm that has previously been issued stock in return for money invested in the company.

Call: A contract allowing the issuer of a security to buy back that security from the purchaser at an agreed-upon price during a specific period of time.

Capital gain: The amount by which the selling price of an asset (for example, common stock) exceeds the seller's initial purchase price.

Capitalization rate: The discount rate, K, used to determine the present value of a stream of future earnings. PV = (Normalized earnings after taxes)/$(K/100)$, where PV is the present value of the firm and K is the firm's cost of capital.

Carbon tax: A tax on emissions caused by the burning of coal, gas, and oil, aimed at reducing the production of gases that contribute to the warming of the Earth's atmosphere by reflecting radiation from the Earth's surface, e.g., carbon dioxide and ozone.

Carried interest: A venture capital firm's share of the profit earned by a fund. In the United States, the carried interest (carry) is typically 20% of the profit after investors' principal has been repaid.

Cash flow: The difference between the company's cash receipts and its cash payments in a given period.

Cash-flow statement: A summary of a company's cash flow over a period of time. *(See pro forma statements.)*

Channel coverage: The product distribution strategy in regards to how many channels to use. It can be intensive (multiple channels), selective (a subset of channels), or exclusive (one channel).

Chattel (or property) mortgage: A loan secured by specific assets.

Classic venture capital: Money invested privately in seed-, startup-, expansion-, and late-stage companies by venture capital firms. The term "classic" is used to distinguish from money invested privately in acquisitions, buyouts, mergers, and reorganizations.

Collateral: An asset pledged as security for a loan.

Common stock: Shares of ownership, or equity, in a corporation.

Common-sized income statement: Converting the income statement into percentages with total revenue equaling 100% and all other lines a percentage of total revenue.

Comparable: Using existing industry or company financials to forecast your own venture's financials.

Compensating balance: A bank requires a customer to maintain a certain level of demand deposits that do not bear interest. The interest

forgone by the customer on the compensating balance recompenses the bank for services provided, credit lines, and loans.

Conversion ratio: The number of shares of common stock that may be received in exchange for each share of a convertible security.

Convertible debt: A loan that can be exchanged for equity.

Convertible security: Preferred stock that is convertible into common stock according to a specified ratio at the security holder's option.

Cooperative (co-op): an autonomous association of persons united voluntarily to meet their common economic, social, and cultural needs and aspirations through a jointly-owned and democratically-controlled enterprise.

Corporation: A business form that is an entity legally separate from its owners. Its important features include limited liability, easy transfer of ownership, and unlimited life.

Cost of capital: The required rate of return of various types of financing. The overall cost of capital is a weighted average of the individual required rates of returns (costs).

Cost of debt capital: The interest rate charged by a company's lenders.

Cost of equity capital: The rate of return on investment required by the company's common shareholders (colloquially called the hurdle rate).

Cost of goods sold: The direct cost of the product sold. For a retail business, the cost of all goods sold in a given period equals the inventory at the beginning of the period plus the cost of goods purchased during that period minus the inventory at the end of the period.

Cost of preferred stock: The rate of return on investment required by the company's preferred shareholders.

Covenant: A restriction on a borrower imposed by a lender. For example, it could be a requirement placed on a company to achieve and maintain specified targets such as levels of cash flow, balance sheet ratios, or specified capital expenditure levels in order to retain financing facilities.

Crowdfunding: Using social media to raise small amounts of capital from a large number of individuals to finance a business venture.

Cumulative dividend provision: A requirement that unpaid dividends on preferred stock accumulate and have to be paid before a dividend is paid on common stock.

Current ratio: Current Assets/Current Liabilities. This ratio indicates a company's ability to cover its current liabilities with its current assets.

Customer relationship management (CRM): Systems designed to compile and manage data about customers.

Customer value proposition (CVP): The difference between total customer benefits and total customer costs, which are both monetary and non-monetary.

Deal flow: The rate at which new investment propositions come to funding institutions.

Debenture: A document containing an acknowledgment of indebtedness on the part of a company, usually secured by a charge on the company's assets.

Debt service: Payments of principal and interest required on a debt over a given period.

Deep pockets: Refers to an investor who has substantial financial resources.

Default: The nonperformance of a stated obligation. The nonpayment by the issuer of interest or principal on a bond or the nonperformance of a covenant.

Deferred payment: A debt that has been incurred and will be repaid at some future date.

Depreciation: The systematic allocation of the cost of an asset over a period of time for financial reporting and tax purposes.

Dilution (of ownership): When a new stock issue results in a decrease in the preissue owners' percentage of the common stock.

Discounted cash flow (DCF): Method of evaluating investments by adjusting the cash flows for the time value of money. In the decision to invest in a project, all future cash flows expected from that investment are discounted back to their present value at the time the investment is made. The discount rate is whatever rate of return the investor requires. In theory, if the present value of the future cash flows is greater than the money being invested, the investment should be made. *(See discount rate, internal rate of return, net present value, and present value.)*

Discount rate (capitalization rate): Rate of return used to convert future values to present values. *(See capitalization rate, internal rate of return, and rate of return.)*

DJIA: Dow Jones Industrial Average. The Dow Jones Industrial Average is a price-weighted average of 30 significant stocks traded on the New York Stock Exchange and the NASDAQ. The DJIA was invented by Charles Dow back in 1896. Often referred to as "the Dow," the DJIA is the oldest and single most watched index in the world. The DJIA includes companies like General Electric, Disney, Exxon, and Microsoft.

Doriot, General Georges: Founder of the modern venture capital industry, Harvard Business School professor, and one of the creators of INSEAD.

Double bottom line: captures both the financial profit the organization earns and also the social benefit it provides society; associated with social entrepreneurship.

Double jeopardy: The case where an entrepreneur's main source of income and most of her/his net worth depend on her/his business.

Due diligence: The process of investigation by investors into a potential investee's management team, resources, and trading performance. This includes rigorous testing of the business plan assumptions and the verification of material facts (such as existing accounts).

Dun & Bradstreet (D&B): The biggest credit-reporting agency in the United States.

Early-stage financing: This category includes seed-stage, startup-stage, and first-stage financing.

Earnings: This is synonymous with income and profit.

Earnings before interest and taxes (EBIT): *See operating income.*

Earnings before interest, taxes, depreciation, and amortization (EBITDA): Often referred to as cash flow. It removes non-cash charges, such as depreciation and amortization, to get a clearer view of the cash-flow-generating ability of a company.

Earning-capitalization valuation: This values a company by capitalizing its earnings. Company value = Net income/ Capitalization rate.

Earnings per share (EPS): A company's net income divided by the number of common shares issued and outstanding.

Earn-out: A common contract provision when a company is sold or acquired. The founders will earn a portion of the sales price over time based upon continuing performance of the new venture.

Elasticity of demand: The percentage change in the quantity of a good demanded divided by the percentage change in the price of that good. When the elasticity is greater than 1, the demand is said to be elastic, and when it is less than 1, it is inelastic. In the short term, the demand for nonessential goods (for example, airline travel) is usually elastic, and the demand for essentials (for example, electricity) is usually inelastic.

Employee stock ownership plan (ESOP): A trust established to acquire shares in a company for subsequent allocation to employees over a period of time. Several possibilities are available for structuring the operation of an ESOP. Essentially, either the company makes payments to the trust, which the trust uses to purchase shares; or the trust, having previously borrowed to acquire shares, may use the payments from the company to repay loans. The latter form is referred to as a leveraged ESOP and may be used as a means of providing part of the funding required to affect a buyout. A particular advantage of an ESOP is the possibility of tax relief for the contributions made by the company to the trust and on the cost of borrowing in those cases where the trust purchases shares in advance.

Employment agreement: An agreement whereby senior managers contract to remain with the company for a specified period. For the investing institutions, such an agreement provides some measure of security that the company's performance will not be adversely affected by the unexpected departure of key managers.

Equity: *See owners' equity.*

Equity kicker (or warrant): An option or instrument linked to the provision of other types of funding, particularly mezzanine finance, which enables the provider to obtain an equity stake and hence a share in capital gains. In this way, providers of subordinated debt can be compensated for the higher risk they incur.

EU: The European Union, originally included the following countries: the Netherlands, Sweden, Finland, Denmark, Germany, Belgium, Luxembourg, the United Kingdom, Ireland, France, Austria, Portugal, Spain, Italy, and Greece. Since May 1, 2004, the following countries also belong to the EU: Cyprus, Estonia, Hungary, Latvia, Lithuania, Malta, Poland, Slovakia, Slovenia, and the Czech Republic.

Exit: The means by which investors in a company realize all or part of their investment. *(See harvest.)*

Expansion financing: Working capital for the initial expansion of a company that is producing and shipping products and has growing accounts receivable and inventories.

Factoring: A means of enhancing the cash flow of a business. A factoring company pays to the firm a certain proportion of the value of the firm's trade debts and then receives the cash as the trade debtors settle their accounts. Invoice discounting is a similar procedure.

FAQ: Frequently asked questions—a computer text file that contains answers to common questions about a topic.

FASB (Financial Accounting Standards Board): A private sector board (industry) that establishes financial accounting and reporting standards.

Filing: Documents, including the prospectus, filed with the SEC for approval before an IPO.

Financing flows: Cash flows generated by debt and equity financing.

Finder: A person or firm that attempts to raise funding for a private company.

Firm commitment offering: The underwriter guarantees to raise a certain amount of money for the company and other selling stockholders at the IPO.

First-round financing: The first investment made by external investors.

First-stage financing: Financing to initiate full manufacturing and sales.

Five Cs of credit: The five crucial elements for obtaining credit are character (borrower's integrity), capacity (sufficient cash flow to service the debt), capital (borrower's net worth), collateral (assets to secure the debt), and conditions (of the borrowing company, its industry, and the general economy).

Fixed and floating charges: Claims on assets pledged as security for debt. Fixed charges cover specific fixed assets, and floating charges relate to all or part of a company's assets.

Floating lien: A general lien against a group of assets, such as accounts receivable or inventory, without the assets being specifically identified.

Flotation: A method of raising equity financing by selling shares on a stock market, and often allowing management and institutions to realize some of their investment at the same time. (See initial public offering.)

Follow-on financing: A second or subsequent round of funding for a company.

Founder shares: Shares that the founders issue to themselves in exchange for their "sweat equity;" meaning that the founders buy their shares for a nominal amount of cash. Founder shares are typically issued prior to the first round of financing.

Four Fs: Founders, family, friends, and foolhardy person who invest in a person's private business, generally a startup. (See informal investor and angel.)

Franchising: An organizational form in which a firm (the franchisor) with a market-tested business package centered on a product or service enters into a continuing contractual relationship with franchisees operating under the franchisor's trade name to produce or market goods or services according to a format specified by the franchisor.

Free cash flow: Cash flow in excess of that required to fund all projects that have a positive net present value when discounted at the relevant cost of capital. Conflicts of interest between shareholders and managers may arise when the organization generates free cash flow. Shareholders may desire higher dividends, but managers may wish to invest in projects providing a return below the cost of capital. (See cost of capital and net present value.)

Future value: The value at a future date of a present amount of money. $FV_t = PV \times (1 + K/100)^t$ where FV, is the future value, PV is the present value, K is the percentage annual rate of return, and t is the number of years. For example, an investment of $100,000 must have a future value of $384,160 after four years to produce a rate of return of 40%, which is the kind of return that an investor in an early-stage company expects to earn. (See net present value, present value, and rate of return.)

Gatekeeper: Colloquial term for a person or firm that advises clients on investments in venture capital funds; formally called an investment advisor.

G7: Group of Seven Countries—Canada, France, Germany, Italy, Japan, United Kingdom and USA—that meet to discuss issues covering macroeconomic management, international trade, international finances, relations with developing countries, and other global issues. They are sometimes joined by Russia, making the co-called G8.

GDP (Gross Domestic Product): The total market value of goods and services produced by workers and capital within a country's borders during a specific period, which is generally a calendar year.

Gearing: British term of leverage. (See leverage.)

GEM (Global Entrepreneurship Monitor): An annual study of entrepreneurial activity within different countries.

General partner: A partner with unlimited legal responsibility for the debts and liabilities of a partnership.

Going concern: This assumes that the company will continue as an operating business as opposed to going out of business and liquidating its assets.

Golden handcuffs: A combination of rewards and penalties given to key managers to dissuade them from leaving the company. Examples are high salaries, paid on a deferred basis while employment is maintained, and stock options.

Goodwill: The difference between the purchase price of a company and the net value of its assets purchased.

Gross margin: Gross profit as a percentage of net sales revenue.

Gross profit (gross income, gross earnings): Net sales revenue minus the direct cost of the products sold.

Guarantee: An undertaking to prove that a debt or obligation of another will be paid or performed. It may relate either to a specific debt or to a series of transactions such as a guarantee of a bank overdraft. For example, entrepreneurs are often required to provide personal guarantees for loans borrowed by their companies.

Guerilla marketing: Unique, low cost marketing methods to capture attention in a crowded marketplace.

Harvest: The realization of the value of an investment. (See exit.)

Headcount: The number of employees within a company at a particular point in time.

High-potential venture: A company started with the intent of growing quickly to annual sales of at least $30-50 million in five years. It has the potential to have a firm-commitment IPO.

Hurdle rate: The minimum rate of return that is acceptable to investors. (See return on investment.)

Hybrid organization: Nonprofit with an earned income component dedicated to achieving social value at a level significantly higher (say, two-thirds or more) than economic value.

Income statement: A summary of a company's revenues, expenses, and profits over a specified period of time. (See pro forma statements.)

Informal investor: An individual who puts money into a private company—usually a startup or a small business. Informal investments range from micro loans from family members to sizable equity purchases by sophisticated business angels.

Initial public offering (IPO): Process by which a company raises money, and gets listed on a stock market. (See flotation.)

Intellectual property (IP): Knowledge that a company possesses and considers proprietary. IP can be protected through patents, trademarks, etc.

Interest cover: The extent to which periodic interest commitments on borrowings are exceeded by periodic profits. It is the ratio of profits before the deduction of interest and taxes to interest payments. The ratio may also be expressed as the cash flow from operations divided by the amount of interest payable.

Internal locus of control: Persons with an internal locus of control see themselves as responsible for the outcomes of their own actions. These individuals often believe that they control their destiny.

Internal rate of return (IRR): The discount rate that equates the present value of the future net cash flows from an investment with the project's cash out-flows. It is a means of expressing the percentage rate of return projected on a proposed investment. For an investment in a company, the calculation takes account of cash invested, cash receipts from dividend payments and redemptions, percentage of equity held, expected date of payments, realization of the investment and capitalization at that point, and possible further financing requirements. The calculation will frequently be quoted in a range depending on sensitivity analysis. *(See discount rate, present value, future value, and rate of return.)*

Inventory: Finished goods, work in process of manufacture, and raw materials owned by a company.

Investment bank: A financial institution engaged in the issue of new securities, including management and underwriting of issues as well as securities trading and distribution.

Investment flows: Cash flows associated with purchase and sales of both fixed assets and business interests.

IPO: *See initial public offering.*

IRR: *See internal rate of return.*

ISP: Internet Service Provider—a company that provides direct connections to the Internet for computer users.

Junior debt: Loan ranking after senior debt or secured debt for payment in the event of a default.

Junk bonds: A variety of high-yield, unsecured bonds tradable on a secondary market and not considered to be of investment quality by credit-rating agencies. High yield normally indicates higher risk.

Key person insurance: Additional security provided to financial backers of a company through the purchase of insurance on the lives of key managers who are seen as crucial to the future of the company. Should one or more of those key executives die prematurely, the financial backers would receive the insurance payment.

Key success factors (KSFs):   The attributes that customers use to distinguish between competing products or services. KSFs go beyond just product attributes, and may include brand and other intangibles.

Lead investor: In syndicated deals, normally the investor who originates, structures, and subsequently plays the major monitoring role.

Lead underwriter: The head of a syndicate of financial firms that are sponsoring an initial public offering of securities or a secondary offering of securities.

Lead venture capital firm: The head of a syndicate of venture capital firms that is investing privately in a company.

Lemons and plums: Bad deals and good deals, respectively.

Leverage: The amount of debt in a company's financing structure, which may be expressed as a percentage of the total financing or as a ratio of debt to equity. The various quasi-equity (preference-type shares) and quasi-debt (mezzanine debt) instruments used

to fund later-stage companies means that great care is required in calculating and interpreting leverage or gearing ratios.

Leveraged buyout (LBO):   Acquisition of a company by an investor group, an investor, or an investment/LBO partnership, with a significant amount of debt (usually at least 70% of the total capitalization) and with plans to repay the debt with funds generated from the acquired company's operations or from asset sales. LBOs are frequently financed in part with junk bonds.

Lien: A legal claim on certain assets that are used to secure a loan.

Limited liability company: A company owned by "members," who either manage the business themselves or appoint "managers" to run it for them. All members and managers have the benefit of limited liability, and, in most cases, are taxed in the same way as a subchapter S corporation without having to conform to the S corporation restrictions.

Limited partnership: A business organization with one or more **general partners**, who manage the business and assume legal debts and obligations, and one or more **limited partners**, who are liable only to the extent of their investments. Limited partners also enjoy rights to the partnership's cash flow, but are not liable for company obligations.

Line of credit (with a bank):   An arrangement between a bank and a customer specifying the maximum amount of unsecured debt the customer can owe the bank at a given point in time.

Line of credit (with a vendor):   A limit set by the seller on the amount that a purchaser can buy on credit.

Liquidation value (of an asset):   The amount of money that can be realized from the sale of an asset sold separately from its operating organization.

Liquidation value (of a company):   The market value of the assets minus the liabilities that must be paid of a company that is liquidating.

Liquidity: The ability of an asset to be converted to cash as quickly as possible and without any price discount.

Listing: Acceptance of a security for trading on an organized stock exchange. Hence, a stock traded on the New York Stock Exchange is said to be listed on the NYSE.

Living dead: Venture capital jargon for a company that has no prospect of being harvested with a public offering or an acquisition; hence, the venture capital firm cannot realize its investment in the company.

Liquidation value: The total amount that could be realized from selling the business'

individual assets, after satisfying all of the business' liabilities.

Loan note: A form of vendor finance or deferred payment. The purchaser (borrower) may agree to make payments to the holder of the loan note at specified future dates. The holder may be able to obtain cash at an earlier date by selling at a discount to a financing institution that will collect on maturity.

Lock-up period: An interval during which an investment may not be sold. In the case of an IPO, employees may not sell their shares for a period of time determined by the underwriter and usually lasting 180 days.

Locus of control: The perception of the factors responsible for the outcome of an event. Individuals with an internal locus of control believe their actions caused the outcome. Conversely, individuals with an external locus of control believe the outcome was determined by outside forces.

Management buy in (MBI):   The transfer of ownership of an entity to a new set of owners in which new managers coming into the entity are a significant element.

Management buyout (MBO):   The transfer of ownership of an entity to a new set of owners in which the existing management and employees are a significant element.

Market capitalization: The total value at market prices of the securities in issue for a company, a stock market, or a sector of a stock market, calculated by multiplying the number of shares issued by the market price per share.

Market-comparable valuation: The value of a private company based of the valuation of similar public companies.

Marketing: An organizational function and a set of processes for creating, communicating, and delivering value to customers and for managing customer relationships in ways that benefit the organization and its stakeholders. [1]

Merger: The combining of two or more entities into one, through a purchase acquisition or a pooling of interests.

Mezzanine financing: Strictly, any form of financing instrument between ordinary shares and senior debt. The forms range from senior mezzanine debt, which may simply carry an interest rate above that for senior secured debt, to junior mezzanine debt, which may carry rights to subscribe for equity but no regular interest payment.

Microcredit: Tiny loans to entrepreneurs too poor to qualify for traditional bank loans.

[1] American Marketing Association, 2004; http://www.marketingpower.com/content21257.php

In developing countries especially, microcredit enables very poor people to engage in self-employment projects that generate income.

Microfinancing: Same as microcredit.

Modified book value: Valuation of a business in which all assets and liabilities (including off-balance sheet, intangible, and contingent) are adjusted to their fair market values.

Money left on the table: The difference between the price at the end of the first day's trading and the initial offering price, multiplied by the number of shares in the offering.

Multiple: The amount of money realized from the sale of an investment divided by the amount of money originally invested.

Murphy's Law: What can go wrong, will go wrong. An unexpected setback will happen at the most inconvenient moment.

National Association of Securities Dealers Automated Quotation (NASDAQ): An electronic system for trading stocks. It is owned and operated by The Nasdaq Stock Market, Inc.

Necessity entrepreneurship: A business started out of necessity by an entrepreneur who cannot find a better source of income through employment.

NGO: Non-Governmental Organization.

Net Assets: Assets less liabilities.

Net income (net earnings, net profit): A company's final income after all expenses and taxes have been deducted from all revenues. It is also known as the bottom line.

Net income margin: Net income as a percentage of net sales revenue. In a typical year an average US company has a net income margin of about 5%.

Net liquid value: Liquid financial assets minus callable liabilities.

Net present value: The present value of an investment's future net cash flows minus the initial investment. In theory, if the net present value is greater than 0, an investment should be made. For example, an investor is asked to invest $100,000 in a company that is expanding. He expects a rate of return of 30%. The company offers to pay him back $300,000 after four years. The present value of $300,000 at a rate of return of 30% is $105,038. Thus, the net present value of the investment is $5,038, so the investment should be made. (*See free cash flow, future value, present value, and rate of return.*)

Net profit: *See net income.*

Net surplus: Total revenue minus total cost and expenses in a non-profit organization; equivalent to net income in a for-profit enterprise.

Net worth: *See book value.*

New York Stock Exchange (NYSE): The largest stock exchange in the world, located in New York. Also known as the Big Board.

Nonprofit organization: Organizations that are considered public charities are owned by the public and, as such, cannot accrue privately owned profits. These organization have applied and been granted nonprofit status and thus do not have to pay taxes.

NPO: Non-Profit Organization; also Not-for-profit Organization.

OECD: The Organization for Economic Cooperation and Development comprises Australia, Austria, Belgium, Canada, Czech Republic, Denmark, Finland, France, Germany, Greece, Hungary, Iceland, Ireland, Italy, Republic of Korea, Japan, Luxembourg, Mexico, the Netherlands, New Zealand, Norway, Poland, Portugal, Spain, Sweden, Switzerland, Turkey, UK, and United States.

Offering circular: *See prospectus.*

Olin College: Starting in the late 1980's, the National Science Foundation and the engineering community at-large started calling for reform in engineering education. In order to serve the needs of the growing global economy, it was clear that engineers needed to have business and entrepreneurship skills, creativity, and an understanding of the social, political, and economic contexts of engineering. The F.W. Olin Foundation decided the best way to maximize its impact was to help create a college that could address these emerging needs. Olin College was chartered in 1997 and took its first freshman class in 2002. It is located adjacent to Babson College.

Operating cash flows: Cash flows directly generated by a company's operations. The cash flow from operating activity equals net income plus depreciation minus increase in accounts receivable minus increase in inventories plus increase in accounts payable plus increase in accruals. (*See financing flows and investment flows.*)

Operating income: Earnings (profit) before deduction of interest payments and income taxes, abbreviated to EBIT. It measures a company's earning power from its ongoing operations. It is of particular concern to a company's lenders, such as banks, because operating income demonstrates the ability of a company to earn sufficient income to pay the interest on its debt. (*See times interest earned.*)

Opportunity: An idea that has commercial viability and that provides the entrepreneur and company the potential to earn attractive margins and a return on their investment.

Opportunity entrepreneurship: The pursuit of a new venture because it is deemed as better than remaining in one's current job or other jobs that might be available.

Options: See stock option plan.

Out of cash (OOC): A common problem with entrepreneurial companies. The OOC time period is cash on hand divided by the burn rate.

Over the counter (OTC): The purchase and sale of financial instruments not conducted on a stock exchange such as the New York Stock Exchange or the American Stock Exchange. The largest OTC market is the NASDAQ.

Owners' equity: Common stock plus retained earnings. (*See book value of a company.*)

Pain point: A potential customer's problem that a business can relieve with its product or service.

Paid-in capital: Par value per share times the number of shares issued. Additional paid-in capital is the price paid in excess of par value times the number of shares issued.

Partnership: Legal form of a business in which two or more persons are co-owners, sharing profits and losses.

Par value: Nominal price placed on a share of common stock.

Patent: Granted by the government, patents protect unique devices (or combinations of components integrated into a device) and processes.

Penetration pricing: Pricing your product at a relatively lower price to gain high market share, but with lower margins.

Piggy-back registration rights: The right to register unregistered stock in the event of a company having a public stock offering.

Pledging: The use of a company's accounts receivable as security (collateral) for a short-term loan.

Pop (first day): Percentage increase in the price of a stock at the end of the first day's trading over the initial offering price.

Positioning: A company's offering on certain product attributes—the ones customers care about most—relative to competitive offerings.

Portfolio: Collection of investments. For example, the portfolio of a venture capital fund comprises all its investments.

Post-money valuation: The value of a company immediately after a round of additional money is invested.

Pratt's Guide to Private Equity Sources: Annual sourcebook for private equity, especially venture capital.

Preemptive rights: The rights of shareholders to maintain their percentage ownership of a company by purchasing a proportionate number of shares of any new issue of common stock. (*See antidilution, dilution, and pro rata interest.*)

Preferred stock (Preference shares): A class of shares that incorporate the right to a fixed dividend and usually a prior claim on assets, in preference to ordinary shares, in the event of a liquidation. Cumulative preference shares provide an entitlement to a cumulative dividend if, in any year, the preference dividend is unpaid due to insufficient profits being earned. Preference shares are usually redeemable at specific dates.

Pre-money valuation: The value of a company's equity before additional money is invested.

Preliminary prospectus: The initial document published by an underwriter of a new issue of stock to be given to prospective investors. It is understood that the document will be modified significantly before the final prospectus is published; also called a red herring.

Prepayment: A payment on a loan made prior to the original due date.

Present value (PV): The current value of a given future cash flow stream, FV_t after t years, discounted at a rate of return of K% is $PV = FV_t/(1 + K/100)^t$. For example, if an investor expects a rate of return of 60% on an investment in a seed-stage company, and she believes that her investment will be worth $750,000 after five years, then the present value of her investment is $71,526. *(See discount rate, future value, net present value, and rate of return.)*

Present value of future cash flows (valuation): Present value is today's value of a future payment, or stream of payments, discounted at some appropriate compound interest, or discount rate; also called time value of money.

The present value of company is the present value of the future free cash flows plus the residual (terminal) value of the firm:

$$PV = \sum_{t=1}^{N}(FCF_t)/(1 + K)^t + (RV_N)/(1 + K)^N$$

Where K is the cost of capital; FCF_t is the free cash flow in year t; N is the number of years; and RV_N is the residual value in year N.
Free Cash Flow

= Operating Income
− Interest
− Taxes on Operating Income
+ Depreciation & Other Non-Cash Charges
− Increase in Net Working Capital
− Capital Expenditures (Replacement & Growth)
− Principal Repayments

Prevalence rate: The percentage of a population participating in a particular activity.

Price discrimination: A strategy where different customer segments are charged different prices.

Price-earnings ratio (P/E ratio): The ratio of the market value of a firm's equity to its after-tax profits (may be calculated from price per share and earnings per share).

Price points: Product pricing in standardized or fixed points.

Price promotion: Discounts from the base price for a short period to attain specific goals such as introducing a product to new customers.

Price skimming: The strategy of pricing your product high to generate high margins, but recognizing that you'll gain limited market share because prices are relatively high.

Primary data: Market research collected specifically for a particular purpose through focus groups, surveys, or experiments.

Primary target audience (PTA): A group of potential customers identified by demographic and psychographic data that will be the focus of the company's early marketing and sales efforts.

Prime rate: Short-term interest rate charged by a bank to its largest, most credit-worthy customers.

Private placement: The direct sales of securities to a small number of investors *(See Regulation D.)*

Product life cycle: A stage model of a product's life, including introduction, growth, maturity, and decline; a similar concept to the S-curve lifecycle for an industry.

Profit: Synonymous with income and earnings.

Pro forma statements: Projected financial statements: income and cash-flow statements and balance sheets. For a startup company, it is usual to make pro forma statements monthly for the first two years and annually for the next three years.

Pro rata interest: The right granted the investor to maintain the same percentage ownership in the event of future financings. *(See antidilution and dilution.)*

Prospectus: A document giving a description of a securities issue, including a complete statement of the terms of the issue and a description of the issuer, as well as its historical financial statements. Also referred to as an offering circular. *(See red herring.)*

Psychographics: Information that categorizes customers based upon their personality, psychological traits, lifestyles, values, and social group membership. It helps to understand what motivates customers to act in the ways they do, and is important because members of a specific demographic category can have dramatically different psychographic profiles. Marketing strictly based on demographic information will be ineffective because it ignores these differences.

Purchasing Power Parity (PPP): A method of measuring the relative purchasing power of different countries' currencies over the same types of goods and services. Because goods and services may cost more in one country than in another, PPP allows us to make more accurate comparisons of standards of living across countries. PPP estimates use price comparisons of comparable items, but, since not all items can be matched exactly across countries and time, the estimates are not always "robust."

Put: A contract allowing the holder to sell a given number of securities back to the issuer of the contract at a fixed price for a given period of time.

Quiet period: The period starting when an issuer hires an underwriter and ending 25 days after the security begins trading, during which the issuer cannot comment publicly on the offering, due to SEC rules.

R^2 (R-Square): The fraction of variation in the dependent variable that is explained by variation in the independent variable. A high value indicates a strong relationship between the two variables.

Rate of return: The annual return on an investment. If a sum of money, PV, is invested and after t years that investment is worth FV_t the return on investment $K = [(FV/PV)^{1/t} — 1] \times 100\%$. For example, if $100 is invested originally, and one year later $108 is paid back to the investor, the annual rate of return is 8%.

Realization: *See exit and harvest.*

Redeemable shares: Shares that may be redeemable at the option of the company, or the shareholder, or both.

Red herring: Preliminary prospectus circulated by underwriters to gauge investor interest in a planned offering. A legend in red ink on its cover indicates that the registration has not yet become effective and is still being reviewed by the SEC.

Registration statement: A carefully worded and organized document, including a prospectus, filed with the SEC before an IPO.

Regulation D: An SEC regulation that governs private placement exemption.

Reserve(s): Non-profit organization's equivalent of owners' equity in a for-profit company.

Residual value: Market capitalization of a company at a specific time.

Revenue drivers: Elements within a business model that can be influenced to increase revenue, such as price, quantity purchased, awareness of product, availability, and so forth.

Retained earnings: The part of net income retained in the company and not distributed to stockholders.

Return on investment (ROI): The annual income that an investment earns.

Roll-up: A strategy to consolidate a fragmented industry.

Running returns: Periodic returns, such as interest and dividends, from an investment (in contrast to a one-time capital gain).

Road show: A series of meetings with potential investors and brokers, conducted by a company and its underwriter, prior to a securities offering, especially an IPO.

SBA: Small Business Administration.

SBDC: Small Business Development Centers (supported by the SBA).

SBI: Small Business Institutes, run by universities and colleges with SBA support.

SBIC: Small Business Investments Companies.

SBIR: Small Business Innovation Research Program.

S-curve: A model of new market product adoption. It illustrates market emergence, rapid growth, stability, and decline.

Schumpeter, Joseph A.: Moravian-born economist whose book *The Theory of Economic Development*, written in Vienna in 1912, introduced the modern theory of entrepreneurship, in which the entrepreneur plays the central role in economic development by destroying the static equilibrium of the existing economy. Excellent modern examples are the roles played by Steve Jobs, Bill Gates, and Dan Bricklin in creating the microcomputer industry in the late 1970s. By the beginning of the 1990s, microcomputers (personal computers) were the principal force shaping the computer industry, and the old companies manufacturing mainframe and minicomputers, which dominated the computer industry until the mid-1980s, were in distress, ranging from outright bankruptcy to record-breaking losses.

SCORE: Service Core of Retired Executives, sponsored by the SBA to provide consulting to small businesses.

Secondary data: Market research that is gathered from already published sources, like an industry association study or census report.

Second-round financing: The introduction of further funding by the original investors or new investors to enable the company to grow or deal with unexpected problems. Each round of financing tends to cover the next period of growth.

Second-stage financing: Financing to fuel the growth of an early stage company.

Secondary offering: The sale of stock by an issuer or underwriter after a company's securities have already begun trading publicly.

Secondary target market (STA): See primary target audience. A group of potential customers identified by demographic and psychographic data that will be a secondary or alternative focus of the company's early marketing and sales efforts.

Securities and Exchange Commission (SEC): Regulatory body for investor protection in the United States, created by the Securities Exchange Act of 1934. The supervision of dealers is delegated to the self-regulatory bodies of the stock exchanges and NASD under the provisions of the Maloney Act of 1938.

Seed financing: A relatively small amount of money provided to prove a concept; it may involve product development and market research but rarely involves the initial marketing of a product.

Seed-stage company: A company that doesn't have much more than a concept.

Sensitivity analysis: Examination of how the projected performance of the business varies with changes in the key assumptions on which the forecasts are based.

Short-term security: Generally, an obligation maturing in less than one year.

Slotting fees: The fees that a product manufacturer pays a retail outlet to place products in its warehouse and then ultimately in the retail store.

Small business: The SBA defines most small businesses as ones with 500 or fewer employees; but there are exceptions. Details can be found at http://web.sba.gov/faqs/faqindex.cfm?areaID=15

Social capital: Networks, norms, and trust that facilitates coordination and cooperation between people for mutual benefit.

Social entrepreneur: Someone who develops social innovation through entrepreneurial solutions. A social entrepreneur recognizes a social problem or need, comes up with a solution, and creates an organization to pursue it. Business entrepreneurs typically measure performance by profit and financial return, whereas social entrepreneurs also take into account a positive return to society.

Social media: Web sites and other online means of communication that are used by large groups of people to share information and to develop social and professional contacts.

Social model: This term is often applied to the economic systems of nations where there is high welfare protection including restrictions on employer's rights to hire and fire employees,

generous unemployment benefits, and mandated work weeks (e.g., 35 hour maximum in France). The social models are especially strong in France and Germany.

Sole proprietorship: A business form with one owner who is responsible for all the firm's liabilities.

Startup company: A company that is already in business and is developing a prototype but has not sold it in significant commercial quantities.

Startup financing: Funding provided to companies for use in product development and initial marketing. Companies may be in the process of being organized or may have been in business a short time (one year or less), but have not sold their product commercially. Generally, such firms have assembled the key management, prepared a business plan, made market studies, and completed other preliminary tasks.

Stock option plan: A plan designed to motivate employees, especially key ones, by placing a portion of the common stock of the company under option at a fixed price to defined employees. The option may then be exercised by the employees at a future date. Stock options are often introduced as part of the remuneration package of senior executives.

Stock-out: Demand for a product exceeds the inventory that a company has on hand. Stock-outs may lead to lost sales as customers seek other options.

Strategic acquisition: When a company buys another company to get access to a product or service that complements its existing business.

Subchapter S corporation: A small business corporation in which the owners personally pay the corporation's income taxes.

Subordinated debt: Loans that may be unsecured or, more commonly, secured by secondary charges that rank after senior debt for repayment in the event of default. Also referred to as junior debt or mezzanine debt.

Sustainability: *Environmental Science.* The quality of not being harmful to the environment or depleting natural resources, and thereby supporting long-term ecological balance.

Sweat equity: Equity acquired by the management team at favorable terms reflecting the value to the business of the managers' past and future efforts.

Syndicate: A group of investors that act together when investing in a company.

TEA Indices (Total Entrepreneurial Activity Indices): The percent of the adult population that is participating in a specific type of entrepreneurship. For example, the TEA (Overall) Index is the percent of the adult population that is in the process of starting a new business or has a business less than 42 months old.

Tertiary Target Audience (TTA): See primary target audience. A group of potential customers identified by demographic and psychographic data that will **not** be the focus of the company's early marketing and sales efforts.

Term loan: Debt originally scheduled to be repaid in more than one year, but usually in 10 years or less.

Term sheet: Summary of the principal conditions for a proposed investment in a company by a venture capital firm.

Third-stage financing: Funding to fuel the growth of an early stage company.

Times interest earned: Earnings before interest and taxes, divided by interest (**EBIT/I**). The higher this ratio, the more secure the loan on which interest is paid. It is a basic measure of the creditworthiness of a company.

Top-down forecasting: Determining projected revenues by estimating what a certain percentage of market share translates into in terms of revenues. This method is highly suspect and bottom-up and comparable projections tend to be better.

Trade promotion: Price promotions offered to retailers to induce them to carry your product.

Trade sale: This is the sale of a business to another company, often, but not always, in a similar line of business.

Trade secret: Knowledge that is kept secret for the purpose of gaining an advantage in business over one's competitors.

Trademarks: Protection obtainable for any word, symbol, or combination thereof that is used on goods to indicate their source.

Triggering event: An incident that prompts a person to take steps to start a new venture.

Triple bottom line: Captures the financial profit the organization earns and also the social and environmental benefit it provides society; associated with social entrepreneurship.

Underpricing: The difference between the closing price on the first day of trading and the initial offering price of a stock.

Underwater stock options: When the price of a stock is lower than the exercise price of a stock option. *(See stock option.)*

Underwrite: An arrangement under which investment banks each agree to buy a certain amount of securities of a new issue on a given date and at a given price, thereby assuring the issuer of the full proceeds of the financing.

Underwriter: An institution engaged in the business of underwriting securities issues.

Underwriting fee: The share of the gross spread of a new issue accruing to members of the underwriting group after the expenses of the issue have been paid.

Unsecured loans: Debt that is not backed by a pledge of specific assets.

Valuation (of a company): The market value of a company. *(See market capitalization.)*

Value-added (by investors): Many venture capital firms claim that they add more than money to investee companies. They call it value-added, which includes strategic advice on such matters as hiring key employees, marketing, production, control, and financing.

Venture philanthropy: Applying the concepts of venture capital to achieving philanthropic goals.

Value proposition: The value of a business' products and services to its customers.

Venture capitalist: A financial institution specializing in the provision of equity and other forms of long-term capital to enterprises, usually to firms with a limited track record but with the expectation of substantial growth. The venture capitalist may provide both funding and varying degrees of managerial and technical expertise. Venture capital has traditionally been associated with startups; however, venture capitalists have increasingly participated in later-stage projects.

Vesting period: The time period before shares are owned unconditionally by an employee who is sold stock with the stipulation that he must continue to work for the company selling him the shares. If his employment terminates before the end of that period, the company has the right to buy back the shares at the same price at which it originally sold them to him.

Visible venture capital (formal venture capital): The organized venture capital industry consisting of formal firms, in contrast to invisible venture capital or informal venture capital.

Vulture capital: A derogatory term for venture capital.

Waiver: Consent granted by an investor or lender to permit an investor or borrower to be in default on a covenant.

Walking wounded: Venture capital jargon for a company that is not successful enough to be harvested with an IPO or acquisition, but might be worth another round of investment to try to get it into harvestable condition.

Warrant: An option to purchase common stock at a specified price. *(See equity kicker.)*

Warranty: A statement of fact or opinion concerning the condition of a company. The inclusion of warranties in an investment agreement gives the investor a claim against the company if it subsequently becomes apparent that the company's condition was not as stated at the time of the investment.

Yield: Annualized rate of return on a security.

INDEX